MARK:
God on the Move

Student Workbook

A Young Fisherman Bible Studyguide Series

by Carolyn Nystrom

HAROLD SHAW PUBLISHERS
WHEATON, ILLINOIS

Wording of questions is based
on *Revised Standard Version*
of the Bible

Commentary Notes are from:
The New Bible Commentary: Revised
edited by D. Guthrie, J. A. Motyer, A. M. Stibbs, D. J. Wiseman
Wm. B. Eerdmans Publishing Co.
1970

ISBN 87788-311-4
Second Printing, November 1979
Printed in the United States of America

What's in it?

A Letter to Group Members

Dear Group Member,

Some people say that kids aren't old enough to understand the Bible, that they should be told stories from the Bible and someone should teach them how to live. Others say kids should read the Bible, but it has to be explained to them. I disagree! If you can read the Bible, God can speak to you through it.

This guide book has some questions that will help you know what to look for as you study the book of *Mark*. Ask God to help you become what the Scripture says his followers should be. Then be ready to share your discoveries with others in your group. You will probably find that they discovered different ideas than you did. You will certainly find that God is changing them in different ways, because God works with all of us in ways that are special to us alone.

Don't *read* your answers to each other. That's dull! Instead, *talk* about them. Study *Mark* together and share from your head what you learned.

Disagree with others in your group if you need to, but try to do it kindly. God can teach you through each other's discoveries too.

Each question has lots of possibilities, so see how many answers you can find.

Be sure to speak up about what you see. It will help you remember your ideas if you talk about them. If you notice someone in the group being particularly quiet, see if you can help draw him into the discussion. You might ask what he thinks about a particular question. That will help him know that what he thinks is important to you.

Help your group to stay on track. It may be fun to talk about yesterday's ball game, but it will take valuable time away from what God could teach you through *Mark*.

As you begin to see how God is helping you and the others live as he expects, pray for them even when you are not together. God wants us to care about each other, and he answers these prayers. It will be exciting to see how he works.

Now enjoy your study of *Mark*. It's an exciting book. Discover your way through it.

Because of Jesus, Carolyn

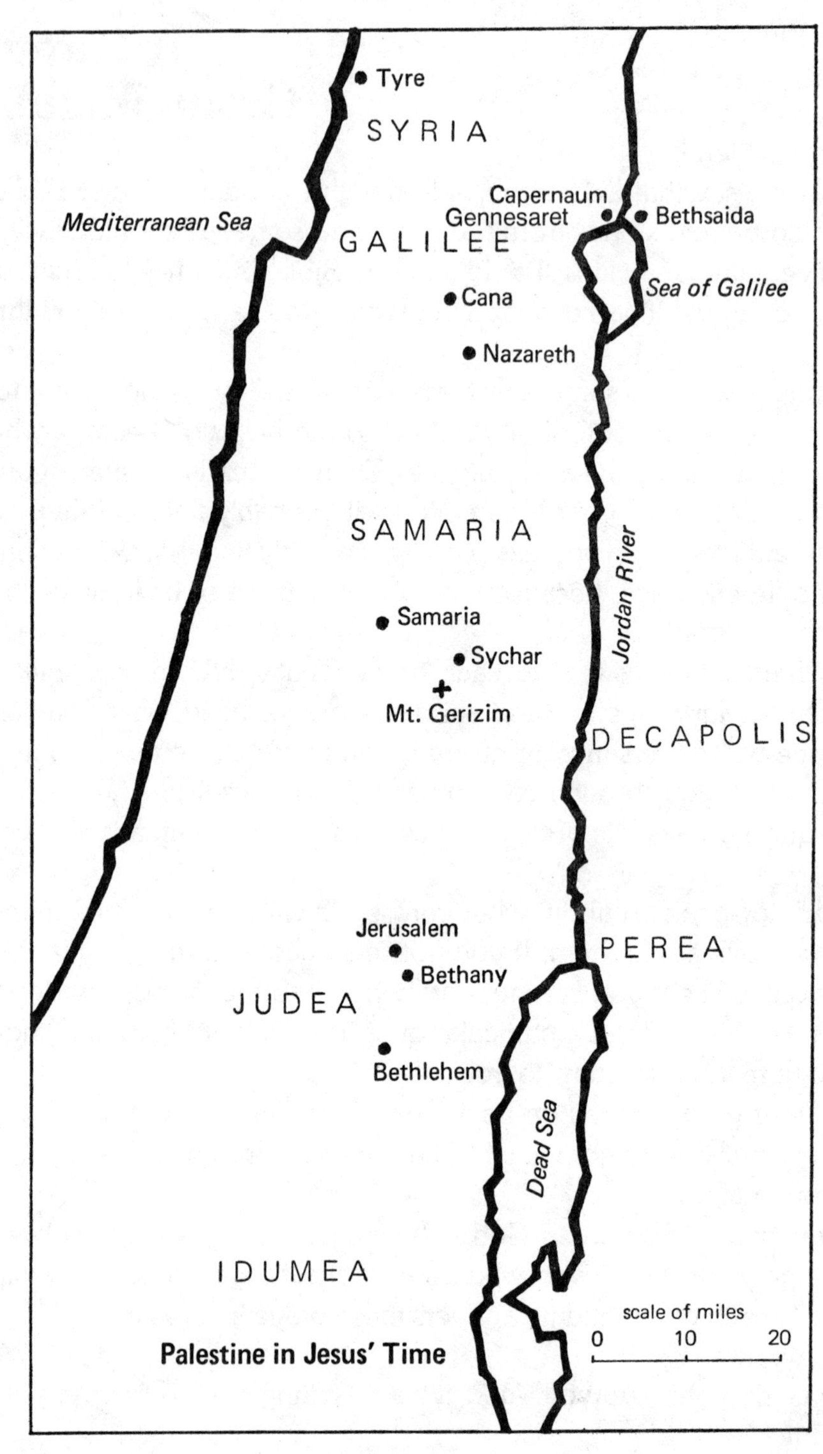
Tyre
SYRIA
Capernaum
Gennesaret
Bethsaida
Mediterranean Sea
GALILEE
Cana
Sea of Galilee
Nazareth
SAMARIA
Jordan River
Samaria
Sychar
Mt. Gerizim
DECAPOLIS
Jerusalem
PEREA
Bethany
JUDEA
Bethlehem
Dead Sea
IDUMEA
scale of miles
0
10
20
Palestine in Jesus' Time

The book of Mark: Who wrote it?

If you are looking for a dull book to help you go to sleep, don't try the book of *Mark*. *Mark* opens when Jesus starts his public ministry. It plunges into a breath-taking series of miracles, teaching and argument, and it ends when he is seen alive again after having been killed. Throughout the book, Jesus is shown as a servant to both God and man even though his power reveals him to be no less than God the Son.

Who wrote this stirring account of Jesus' life? Its author was a young man named John Mark, a cousin of the Barnabas who was Paul's early missionary partner. While still young, John Mark was active in the early church and, for reasons not entirely explained, was the source of a disagreement between Paul and Barnabas serious enough to split that missionary team.[1] Barnabas went his way with Mark while Paul continued his work with a new partner, Silas. Later Mark and Paul were reconciled, and Mark was with Paul when Paul wrote some of the letters that are now in the New Testament. When Paul was near death, he asked that Mark be sent to be with him.[2]

Mark was probably a teenager during Christ's lifetime. Perhaps he hung around near the fringes of the crowd that followed Jesus. He may have been the young man who, collared by a soldier during Jesus' arrest, wriggled out of his robe and dashed naked into the darkness to escape.[3] But when he started to write his book, he needed more than these memories; he needed inside information. It was probably aggressive Peter, Jesus' companion and follower during much of his ministry, who gave Mark most of the information for his book. Like Peter, the account is one of action and strong, blunt words. You can almost see the brawny fisherman sitting by a campfire telling what he saw and heard to John Mark.

Mark is the shortest of the four gospels, but it records more miracles than any of the others. Christ's ceaseless activity among needy people continues without stopping as he willingly chooses to go to Jerusalem and certain execution. The last third of the book tells of this final week in his life.

Mark ends with a mystery. The oldest records stop abruptly at Mark 16:8 —right in the middle of a thought, as though an ancient scroll had been torn and the last piece lost. What else did Mark have to say? We can only guess. But we do have fifteen and a half chapters of rapid-fire narrative; so, take a deep breath and get ready for action. Here comes the book of *Mark*!

1. Acts 15:37-38
2. 2 Timothy 4:11
3. Mark 14:51-52

Should I follow Jesus?

Mark 1

A new teacher has appeared on the scene in Palestine. He comes from Nazareth (no place important), and though he's thirty, nobody has heard of him until now. But strange things are happening. His words are like magnets. Crowds form around him. There are reports of miracles, new teachings and strange powers. What keeps those crowds clustered in his presence? Am I missing something? Should I follow Jesus too?

***1.** What kind of power impresses *you*?

____

____

Read aloud Mark 1:1-13.

2. If you were painting a picture of John, how would you paint him?

____

____

____

3. How did John prepare the way for Jesus?

***4.** How might John have felt when he experienced what happened in verses 9-11?

5. What do you know about the Holy Spirit from verses 8-12?

Read Mark 1:14-20.

***6.** How might Jesus have been different after his forty days in the wilderness?

7. Why might it have been hard for these four men to follow Jesus?

8. What reasons might they have had for following him?

Read Mark 1:21-34.

9. What caused the people to be amazed?

10. What power did the evil spirits have?

***11.** How is Jesus' love and understanding for people shown in these verses?

Read Mark 1:35-45.

12. What does verse 35 tell about the source of Jesus' power?

***13.** Leprosy was thought to be a contagious and hopeless disease. Because of this, people who had it were isolated. If one of them said he was cured, the law said he had to show himself to the priest to prove that it was safe for him to be with people again. What were the results of the leper's disobedience to Jesus?

14. Name as many things as you can from this chapter that show the power of Jesus. Give the verse where you find each answer.

15. Jesus, who had all of that power when he was here on earth, is now alive in heaven. Name one problem you can expect him to help you with.

16. What does this chapter tell you about Jesus that makes you want to follow him?

**Questions with asterisks may be omitted of you're short of time.*

Who is Jesus?

Mark 2

You live in Palestine about 30 A.D. Your church is strict. There are hundreds of laws to obey, and if you forget one or decide it's too much bother, you have to take an animal to the temple and have it killed for this sin. There is a rumor around that some new religious teacher forgives sin by just *saying* it is forgiven. Though his followers have been breaking some of the religious laws, he doesn't even criticize them. Your own church teachers are mad. But you wonder, "Who is Jesus?"

***1.** Pretend you live in Christ's time. What would it take to convince you that Jesus is God?

____

____

____

Read aloud Mark 2:1-12.

2. If you had been in the crowd, what would you have seen, heard, and felt?

____

3. What reasons did the scribes have to be surprised? Angry?

4. How does knowing that Jesus sees your thoughts make you feel?

5. What proof did Jesus give them that he had power to forgive sins?

Read Mark 2:13-17

***6.** Nobody likes tax collectors now, but they were even more hated in Jesus' time. They collected as much money as they could from the people, paid the government what they had to, and kept the rest for themselves. Why might it have been hard for Jesus to have a man like Levi following him?

7. If Levi had answered *No*, when Jesus said *Follow me*, what reasons could he have given?

8. Why was it even harder for the scribes and Pharisees to come to Jesus than it was for Levi?

____

____

9. What do you know about Jesus from the way he treated Levi?

____

____

____

Read Mark 2:18-22.

***10.** What reasons do the followers of Jesus have to celebrate?

____

____

____

***11.** What reasons will they have for being sorry and fasting later?

____

____

12. How are Jesus and his teachings like unshrunk cloth or new wine?

____

____

____

Read Mark 2:23-28.

***13.** The Pharisees had very strict laws about the Sabbath. People were not allowed to cook food, walk more than 1000 yards, or work in the fields. Why are the Pharisees angry this time?

____

How did Jesus make them even more angry?

---

14. Jesus caused disagreement with the religious leaders of his time. What was the fight about in each of the four paragraphs?

---

15. Who is Jesus? Give a name to Jesus for each paragraph.

---

16. When Jesus says that he has authority, that means that he has power, control or charge over something. What authority does Jesus claim in Mark 2:1-17? In 2:18-28?

---

17. The paralyzed man and Levi both wanted Jesus to change their lives. And Jesus did. Think of one thing you *do* that you would like Jesus to help you change. Share this with the group. Listen to what the others say.

Now pray for the person on your right.

**Optional question*

Am I in Christ's Family?

Mark 3

Nobody said *ho-hum* when Jesus was around. Some were so angry they would go to their worst enemy to ask for help in killing this man who said he was God. Some were afraid he had evil supernatural powers. Some came to him in desperation, wanting to be made well. But a few believed, and loved and followed him. They became his family. Try to discover which of the people in Mark 3 you are most like. Jesus is still taking people into his family. Are you a part of it?

Read aloud Mark 3:1-6.

1. Pretend that you are the man with the crippled hand. What kind of problems have you had because of your hand?

____

____

____

____

____

***2.** How do each of the characters in this paragraph feel? The Pharisees? Jesus? How do you think the man felt at the beginning? At the end?

Read Mark 3:7-12.

Find all of the places mentioned in these verses on the map at the front of this book.

3. What does this tell you about Jesus' effect on the people?

4. What do the people seem most concerned about?

5. What do the unclean spirits know that no one else seems to have guessed?

***6.** How do you think they knew that Jesus was the Son of God?

Read Mark 3:13-19.

7. How did these twelve people get to be disciples of Jesus?

8. What three things did Jesus expect of them?

9. If we are disciples of Jesus, we will have some of these same characteristics. How do you stay with Jesus? How do you preach? What power does he give you over evil?

Read Mark 3:20-30.

10. Jesus said that he could not be possessed by Satan. What four reasons did he give?

11. Look at verse 27. If Satan is like a strong man, what is Jesus saying about himself?

***12.** What spirit did the scribes say that Jesus had? What Spirit *did* he have?

***13.** Jesus gave the doubters a strong warning before they went too far. What was his warning?

14. What is the eternal sin?

Read Mark 3:31-35.

***15.** Considering the mood of the crowd around Jesus, why do you think that Jesus' mother and brothers came to him?

16. According to Mark 3, how can you tell if you are a member of Christ's family? Give examples of how each one of these qualities affects what you do?

For more information on becoming and living as a child of God see these related passages.
John 1:9-13, John 3:16-18, 1 John 1:9.

**Optional question*

What happens when I talk about Jesus?

Mark 4

Jesus told his followers stories. Many who stood in the distance heard the stories and went away puzzled, shaking their heads. But to those who stayed with him, Jesus told the meaning of his stories. They nodded their heads thoughtfully as the mysteries of his teachings unfolded before them. Mark has given us a place to sit in that inner circle. We too can hear the stories and Jesus' gentle explanation. Lean forward and listen.

Read aloud all of Mark 4.

1. A writer sometimes repeats words because they are important. What words or groups of words are repeated in this chapter? Give the verses where you find them.

____

____

____

2. Review the first story (verses 3-8). What stays the same in each of the four situations?

____

What is different?

3. List the kinds of soil.

4. A parable is a story that places two things side by side for comparison. In verses 14-20, Jesus explains the first parable.

Who is the sower?

What is the seed?

Who is the soil?

5. Describe a person for each kind of soil.

6. What kind of soil are you becoming?

How do you know?

7. The three parables in the second half of the chapter further explain the parable of the sower. Verses 21-25 speak in more detail about the sower (one who shares the gospel). What happens to us if we do not share our knowledge of Jesus?

____

What happens to us if we do share it?

____

***8.** When has telling someone else about Jesus increased your own understanding and faith?

____

____

____

Review verses 26-29.

9. What does this parable add to our knowledge of the seed (Word of God)?

____

____

What does it add to our knowledge of soil (the people who hear God's Word)?

____

____

Read verses 30-32.

10. What are the characteristics of the seed?

____

____

***11.** How did Jesus treat his twelve disciples differently than the others? (See verses 11-12 and 33-34.)

____

____

Why?

______

______

______

***12.** Why might Jesus deliberately keep information away from some of the people?

______

______

______

What kind of soil would a casual listener become?

______

How might he later react to the gospel?

______

______

Review verses 35-41.

***13.** List some of the qualities of Jesus that the disciples have discovered this far.

______

______

______

What are they now beginning to suspect?

______

14. In chapter 3, Jesus stated that one of the characteristics of his disciples is that they preach (talk) about him (Mark 3:14). How do you feel when you talk about Jesus to someone who does not know him?

______

What holds you back?

What makes you want to share?

***15.** What makes the difference in whether or not the seed of God's Word grows?

What encouragement is this when you talk to unbelievers about your faith?

16. What would you ask God for in praying for someone who has just heard the gospel?

17. What can you expect to happen when you talk to others about Jesus?

What will happen to them?

To you?

To God's Kingdom?

**Optional question*

Will God help me believe?

Mark 5

Did you ever glance in a brightly lighted living room window and, just for an instant, wish that you could be on the other side of that window and really know the people there?

Mark 5 gives us that kind of picture of three different characters. He paints them clearly, shows us their surroundings, then gives us a quick peek inside at what makes them tick. We see each one at the point when that person meets Jesus. For an instant we seem to know him as if we'd been friends forever.

Come and see.

Read aloud Mark 5:1-20.

***1.** Make a pencil sketch of the man described in verses 1-5.

2. What powers did the unclean spirits have?

____

____

What fears?

____

____

3. What might Jesus have intended to teach by allowing the pigs to be destroyed?

____

____

____

4. What are the indications that the demon possessed man was made completely well?

*__5.__ What are the reactions to this miracle?
Reactions of the herdsman?

The former demoniac?

The townspeople?

Why did the townspeople react this way?

6. Would it have been easier for the healed man to go with Jesus or to stay in his home town?

Why do you think that Jesus would not let this man follow him?

7. For a time, Satan had complete control of the man. How does Satan demonstrate this kind of power today?

What can you do to protect yourself from his power?

Read Mark 5:21-43.

8. Who was Jairus and what was his problem?

***9.** How would Jairus feel toward the woman who touched Jesus?

10. Was the woman's illness as serious as the problem of Jairus?

Why or why not?

11. The woman touched Jesus secretly, because she was ceremonially unclean and, according to Jewish law, not allowed to be in public. Anyone she touched would also be unclean. In view of this, why did Jesus stop and call attention to her?

12. Describe the scene that greeted Jesus at Jairus' house?

***13.** What changes are likely to take place because of this miracle?
Changes in the girl's parents?

____

____

The people waiting outside?

____

____

The girl?

____

____

Peter, James and John?

____

____

***14.** Jesus healed three people in this chapter. What power did he demonstrate in each?
Demoniac?

____

Woman?

____

Jairus' daughter?

____

15. How was faith a part of each miracle?
Demoniac?

____

____

Woman?

Jairus' daughter?

16. How did Jesus aid their faith?
Demoniac?

Woman?

Jairus?

17. What has God done that has helped you to believe in him?

Pray, thanking God for one way that he has helped you believe.

**Optional question*

When is belief not belief?

Mark 6

Belief—a funny word. It can be used to mean everything from, "Yes, I believe in my friend, Doug. He exists. I can see him." To "I believe in my friend, Doug. I'd let him hold the rope if I climbed down a cliff."

Lots of people believed in Jesus. But they believed in different ways. For some the belief was so shallow that it was unbelief. For others the belief was limited by lack of understanding and immaturity. Many based belief on what Jesus could do for them.

Were all these kinds of belief adequate? No, but some later grew to be the all-encompassing faith that Jesus is Lord. Let's watch these people as they encounter Jesus and begin to question—or believe.

Read aloud Mark 6.

1. What questions did the people of Jesus' home town have about him? (See verses 1-5.)

___

___

___

2. How did their attitude limit what they could know about him?

***3.** Mark 6:7-13 records a "trial run" for the time when the disciples would become missionaries.
What were their instructions?

What power was given them?

What was their work?

4. What might the disciples learn from this experience?

5. Close your Bibles and describe, in as much detail as you can, how John the Baptist died.

Now check verses 14-29 and add what you missed.

6. What mixed feelings did Herod have about John?

***7.** Why might he have wanted John raised?

Why might he have feared this?

8. Herod had John killed because he didn't want to be embarrassed in front of his family and friends. When does pressure from other people keep you from doing the right thing?

***9.** What reasons did Jesus have for taking his disciples to a lonely place? (See verses 30-44).

***10.** How was their plan changed?

11. What power of Jesus' was shown by this miracle?

Review verses 45-56.

12. What is the relationship between the two miracles in verses 51b-52?

13. What do the disciples believe about Jesus?

What do they not yet know?

***14.** What explanation can you give for their work of 6:7-13 when they are so lacking in understanding?

15. What type of belief is demonstrated in each of this chapter's six paragraphs on the part of:
The people of Nazareth?

The disciples on foot?

John the Baptist?

Herod?

The five thousand?

The disciples in a storm?

The people of Gennesaret?

16. What do you have trouble believing about Jesus?

How can others help you with these questions?

**Optional question*

What makes me "dirty?"

Mark 7

"Cleanliness is next to godliness," grandmothers used to say. They weren't the only ones. The Jews in Christ's time had a real thing about washing. And they didn't even know about germs yet! In their case, cleanliness was *not* next to godliness. In fact, it had just the opposite effect. It made them feel guilty and worried a lot of the time.

Jesus used their wrong ideas as an occasion to talk about dirt—"uncleanness"—not the kind you get from working in the soil, but the kind that makes you sin. And it was all linked with the Law. The problem was—whose law was most important?

Jesus left these religious Jews, as they reconsidered the question of dirt and washing, and turned again to Gentile country. These Gentiles made no pretense of obeying those carefully kept Jewish laws. But Christ helped them anyway—just as though they were little pets in his Father's house! For that is exactly what he called them.

***1.** What laws do you resent?

____

____

____

Read Mark 7:1-23.

2. How were the disciples' eating habits different from other Jews?

***3.** Jesus talked about being "unclean" to three groups of people in this passage. Who were they, and which verses are addressed to each?

4. Read verse 8 again. Which traditions of men did the Pharisees keep?

Which law of God did they disobey?

5. How did the Jews get around God's law about taking care of their parents?

What did the custom of Corban say about the Pharisee's attitude toward the Law?

6. How might *you* offer something to God to avoid being thoughtful of your parents?

7. What makes people unclean in God's sight? (Verses 14-23.)

***8.** How is Jesus' teaching even more strict than the law of the Pharisees?

9. Read the list of thirteen sins in verses 21-22. Which ones are frequent sins of even "good" people?

10. Why was it useless for the Pharisees to try to wash away their uncleanness with water?

Read verses 24-30.

11. Trace Jesus' movements on the map on page 6. Begin at Gennesaret (6:53). The last two paragraphs are set in Gentile territory.

Jesus sometimes spoke in symbolic language. The "children" of verse 27 are God's chosen people, the Jews. "Dogs" (household pets) are Gentiles. What did Jesus mean by his statement of verse 27?

*12. What did Jesus demonstrate by this miracle?

Read verses 31-37.

13. What change in attitude do you see in the people of Decapolis? (See Mark 5:17ff.)

Why this change?

14. In what ways did Jesus show his personal interest in the deaf-mute?

*15. What does this chapter teach of the importance of God's Law?

What does it teach of its limitations?

16. When you see yourself in the description of verses 21-22, what does God's love mean to you?

*Optional question

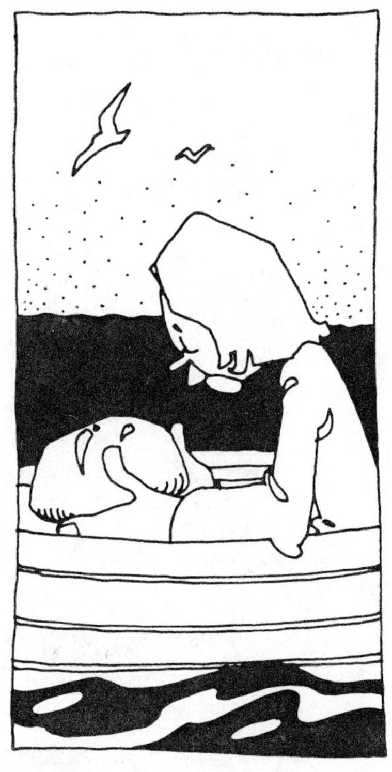

What does it cost to follow Jesus?

Mark 8

Sometimes Jesus' disciples seemed incredibly dumb. If you want an example of that, take a look at verse 4 of today's chapter. But Jesus didn't give up on them—or us.

Then there were the Pharisees. No sign from God was good enough for them, unless it came straight from heaven and zapped them on the head. We wonder if they would have accepted Jesus even then.

But occasionally a flash of truth zoomed into the dull human minds of those around Jesus. One of those flashes came to Peter. Peter had hardly comprehended the whole meaning of this truth when Jesus began to build on his new insight. He wanted his followers to know the cost of continuing to be his disciples. Jesus gives us the same valuable teaching about discipleship, and its cost.

***1.** How do you decide whether or not to buy something?

____

____

____

Read aloud Mark 8.

2. In what ways was the miracle of 8:1-10 the same as the miracle of 6:30-44?

How was it different?

3. Why did the Pharisees want a sign?

***4.** How was Jesus' response different to the questions of the Pharisees and to those of his disciples?

Why?

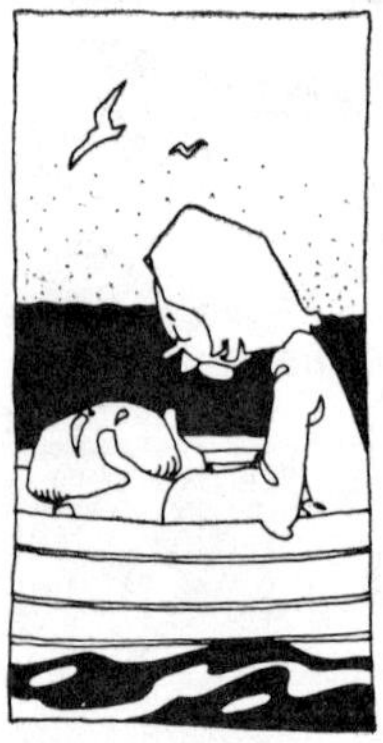

5. Jesus used the one loaf of bread in the boat as an object lesson for his disciples. What is the meaning of his warning?

6. Yeast or leaven is the symbol of a contagious kind of sin. What sinful situation do you need to avoid so that you don't "catch it" too?

7. What are the similarities between Christ's healing the blind man of 8:22-26 and the deaf-mute of 7:31-37?

***8.** What do these miracles tell you about what Jesus was like?

9. What were some of the current theories about who Jesus was?

What reasons could people have for believing each of these?

10. What did Peter mean by "the Christ?" (See also Isaiah 11:10, Micah 5:2, Isaiah 9:6-7.) From these passages, list some of the things that people expected the Christ to be.

11. What four things did Jesus predict would happen to him? (Verses 31-38.)

The Old Testament had also prophecied this about the Christ. Read Isaiah 53:3; 8-9.

***12.** Why did Jesus speak so harshly to Peter?

13. What are the five costs of being Christ's disciple? (Verses 34-38.)

What does each mean to you?

14. When Satan tempts you by saying that the cost of following Jesus is too high, what does he suggest as too high a price to pay?

15. What promises of God help you battle that temptation?

____

____

____

____

**Optional question*

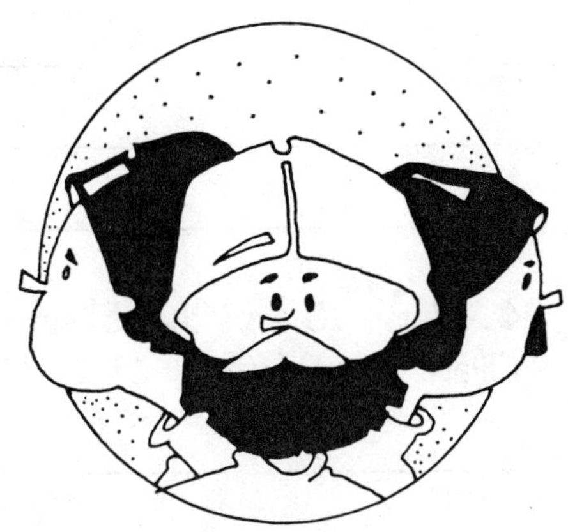

Jesus teaches. Am I tuned in?

Mark 9

You've passed the half-way point in *Mark*. With Peter's confession in the last chapter, Jesus begins the final part of his ministry. Rarely in the last half of *Mark* will we see Jesus performing miracles in large crowds. Instead he begins to teach his own disciples. He tells them how to work with each other, how to please God, how to draw on God's power. He prepares them for his death.

Mark lets us in on these private instruction sessions. Perhaps he knew that we, too, would want to be disciples and would need the lessons Jesus taught.

***1.** Who is the best teacher you have ever had?

____

What made that person the best?

____

____

____

Read aloud Mark 9.

2. How was Christ's glory displayed at the transfiguration? (Verses 1-8.)

3. What might Peter, James and John have learned from this experience?

***4.** Verse 13 says that Elijah had already come again. Who was this new Elijah? (See Matthew 11:11-14 if necessary.)

5. Find four references to Christ's death in this chapter.

***6.** Make a list of what the disciples could know about Christ's death so far. (See also Mark 8:31.)

7. If you had been a disciple hearing these hints, what would you have wanted to know but been afraid to ask?

8. What powers did the dumb spirit have over the boy? (Verses 14-29.)

9. Read in dialogue the conversation between Jesus and the boy's father (verses 21-24).

Under what circumstances has your faith been a mixture of belief and unbelief?

*What are you likely to believe and doubt at the same time?

***10.** Why couldn't the disciples cast out this demon? (Review Mark 6:13.)

What effect might this failure have on them?

11. Summarize in one sentence the teaching of verses 33-37.

What contacts do you have with little children that ought to be affected by this teaching?

12. Summarize in one sentence the teaching of verses 38-41.

What should your attitude be toward a person who is working for God, but doesn't believe all the same things you believe?

What cautions should you exercise?

13. Summarize in one sentence the teachings of verses 42-50.

Jesus does not mean to get rid of a physical hand, foot or eye. He is again using symbolic language. Describe a situation where it would be best to get rid of something very close to you in order to avoid sin.

***14.** Quickly list as many things as you can that the disciples have been taught in this chapter.

15. Which of these teachings do you most need to work on?

Why?

16. What is one step you can take to put this teaching into practice?

**Optional question*

How are God's values different from mine?

Mark 10:1-31

"Everybody's doing it—even the most religious people. It can't be wrong." Heard it? Thought it? Said it? It's an old song. People in Jesus' time were singing it too. And he taught them about values—God's and theirs. At times his teachings were hard. At other times, they were loving and gentle. But no one could mistake his point: God has high standards for his people. The excuse that everybody's doing it doesn't swing much weight.

***1.** If I said, "It can't be wrong, because everybody's doing it," what might I be talking about?

Read Mark 10:1-12.

2. How were the Pharisees' standards of divorce different from God's standards?

3. The Pharisees referred here to Moses' law in Deuteronomy 24:1-4. Read it. Why was this law given?

In what ways was God's original law of marriage more fair than his law to Moses?

***4.** According to this paragraph, what value does God place on families?

5. In view of Christ's standards for marriage, what kind of person should you look for when you are ready to get married?

6. What questions should you ask yourself before you decide to marry that person?

Read Mark 10:13-16.

7. Contrast the disciples' behavior with the teachings of Mark 9:35-37, 42.

How would they have acted differently if they valued children the way God does?

8. What do you think Jesus might have had in mind when he told them to receive the kingdom of God like a child?

Read Mark 10:17-31.

9. What difference is there between the value that the rich man put on being good and Christ's value of it?

10. How does their evaluation of riches differ?

11. In view of the rich man's actions, which of the Ten Commandments was he breaking?

12. In what way did Peter feel that he was better than the rich man?

*__13.__ What results does Jesus promise when we give up something in order to follow him?

How does he keep Peter (and us) from too much pride in this?

14. What contrasts do you see in each section between the values of most of the people you know and the values that Christ teaches?
Verse 1-12?

Verses 13-16?

Verses 17-31?

15. Are some of these wrong ideas of what is important already becoming a part of your thinking?

In what ways?

16. How can you keep yourself from picking up these commonly held false values?

**Optional question*

Am I pushing ahead in line?

Mark 10:32-52

Have you ever watched a primary class of children on a field trip? The kids walk in a long line, sometimes hand in hand, to be sure no one gets lost. The teacher is at the head of the line explaining the sights to all who listen. But somewhere along that line are a few children busily trying to shove their way further toward the front. If you watch their faces, you'll see that they have missed every word that the teacher said in order to gain what they think is a good position.

Jesus had some line-pushers among his followers. He still does. What they seek to gain in position, they risk losing in understanding. As you study this part of *Mark*, ask yourself, "Am I pushing ahead of line?"

***1.** What do you do when you are waiting in line?

____

____

Read Mark 10:32-52.

2. Trace Jesus' movements on your map. Begin at Galilee (Mark 9:30). See also 9:33, 10:1, 10:32, 10:46. Jesus had consistently avoided confrontation with the Jewish religious leaders. Why do you think that he was now deliberately headed for their capital city Jerusalem?

3. What did Jesus do about the disciples' fears? (Verses 32-34.)

What can you now add to the list of what the disciples should know about Christ's death? (See your answer to question 6 of page 52.)

4. When does knowing what will happen help you to be less afraid?

5. What kept James and John from understanding what Jesus had been saying? (Verses 35-45.)

6. If these two disciples had been listening, what might they have understood from Jesus' words of verses 38-39?

See Acts 12:1-2 and Revelation 1:9 to find out what Jesus knew would happen.

7. What errors were all twelve disciples making?

***8.** What did Jesus mean when he said, "It shall not be so among you?" (Verse 43.)

9. How was Jesus an example of the way his disciples ought to relate to each other?

10. How can we avoid wrong ways of ruling over each other in our church, Christian clubs and other groups?

11. What words and phrases does Mark use to paint the picture in verses 46-52?

12. What reasons might the crowd have had for telling Bartimaeus to be quiet?

***13.** What does this reveal of how they felt about Bartimaeus?

About themselves?

About Jesus?

14. What kind of people are you likely to overlook?

***15.** What examples of "pushing into line" have you found in this chapter?

16. Is position more important to you than it ought to be? Give examples.

17. What should you do to be more of a "servant" in these situations?

**Optional question*

How can I pray with power?

Mark 11

How many times have you asked God for something and waited in vain for his answer? A dozen times? Even more? Did you feel that God hadn't heard you? Had turned away from you? Or that he didn't have the power to grant your request? Maybe you felt there was something wrong with your prayer —or with you.

Jesus was preparing to leave his disciples and return to his Father in heaven. But first these disciples needed to learn a few things about prayer —and about God's power. So Jesus allowed them a glimpse of the honor that was due him. He illustrated a sliver of God's power. Then he taught them how to tap this power through prayer. They needed to be ready to communicate with God, for Jesus would no longer be with them.

***1.** Share with the group a time when God gave something you asked for or a time when he *did not* give what you asked.

____

____

____

Read aloud Mark 11.

2. This chapter covers parts of three days. Name the days and tell briefly what happened on each.

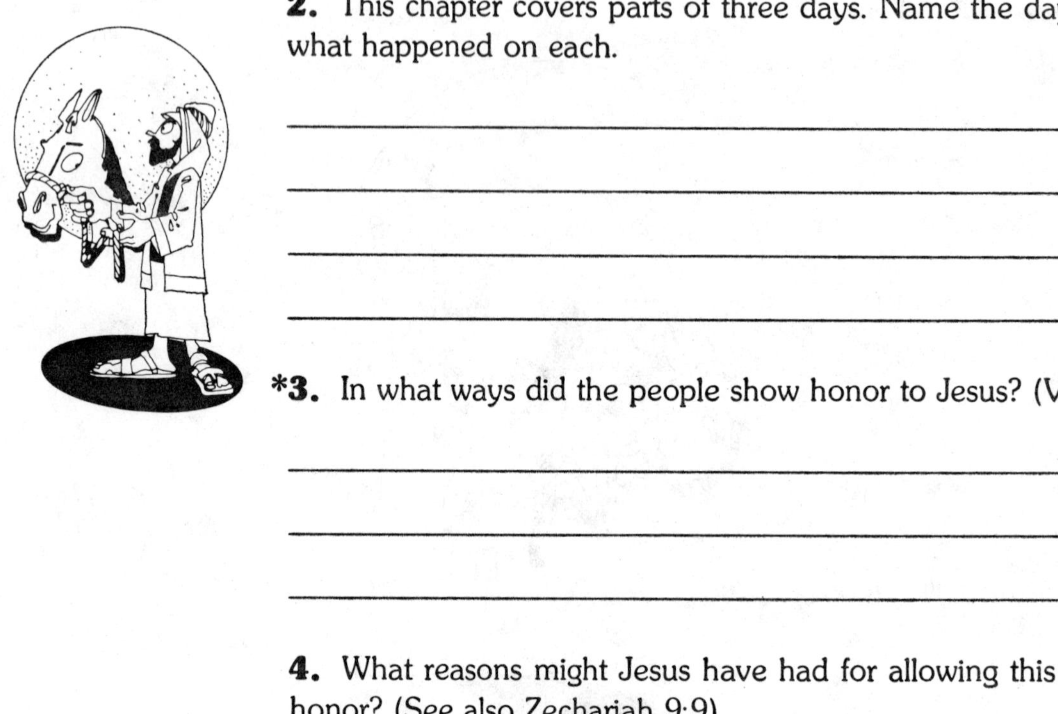

***3.** In what ways did the people show honor to Jesus? (Verses 1-11.)

4. What reasons might Jesus have had for allowing this public display of honor? (See also Zechariah 9:9).

5. If the fig tree is a symbol of the Jewish nation, what was Christ's teaching about the wrongs of this nation? (Verses 12-14, 20-21.)

About what will happen to the Jewish nation?

6. What could the disciples learn about the character of God from this happening?

7. Part of the Jewish temple was set aside for Gentiles who wanted to worship the true God. It was in this area that the activities of verses 15-19 took place. What was wrong with the way the temple was being used?

***8.** What authority was Jesus assuming in this action? (See also Malachi 3:1-4.)

9. What are the ingredients of successful prayer according to verses 20-25?

***10.** If God doesn't answer your prayer, what might be wrong?

11. How can your faith be increased?

12. Why is it essential to your prayer relationship with God that you forgive other people?

13. Review verses 27-33. How was the question Jesus asked the temple leaders also an answer to their question to him? (Read again Mark 1:1-8 if necessary.)

***14.** What reasons are given in this chapter for these religious leaders to be afraid?

15. In what ways are Christ's power and authority shown in this chapter?

16. It is this power that we connect with when we pray. What changes need to be made in your praying?

*Optional question

What happens when I question God?

Mark 12

It is three days before Christ's death. He is still in the temple of Jerusalem observing, listening and teaching.

As if to give the people one last chance to clear up misunderstanding, he allows himself to be questioned. Some of the questions are hostile with obvious intent to trap him. But at least one question is an honest one that brings the inquirer close to salvation. And then Jesus has a question of his own.

Draw near and listen as these questions fly—and discover the answers.

***1.** If you could ask Jesus one question, what would you ask him?

Read aloud Mark 12.

2. The Tuesday before Christ's death was a day of questions. Find five questions beginning with Mark 11:27.

Who asked each question?

Review verses 1-12.

3. A parable is a short symbolic story that teaches a lesson. In Christ's parables, what does each of the following parts mean?
landlord?

tenants?

servants?

beloved son?

vineyard?

stone?

builders?

4. What does this parable tell about the past?

The present?

The future?
a)
b)
c)

***5.** How was this parable an answer to the question of 11:27-28?

6. How did the coin demonstrate the good things that Caesar had done for the questioners? (Verses 13-14.)

7. What does a believer owe to this country?

What does he owe to God?

8. What was wrong with the Sadducees' question? (Verses 18-27.)

9. How did Jesus help them re-think their ideas about resurrection?

10. Why do you think that love is a part of each of the two great commandments? (Verses 28-34.)

***11.** Why was the scribe's agreement with these laws not enough to get him into the kingdom?

12. In what way was Jesus both the son of David and also David's Lord? (Verses 35-37.)

***13.** What was wrong with the scribes' activities? (Verses 38-40.)

14. What do the happenings of verses 41-44 tell about the nature of true giving?

About the nature of God?

15. Look again at your answer to Question 2. Give a one sentence answer to each of the five questions.

***16.** What does this chapter teach about the way God deals with questions?

17. When has God answered one of your questions?

What questions still need answers from him?

**Optional question*

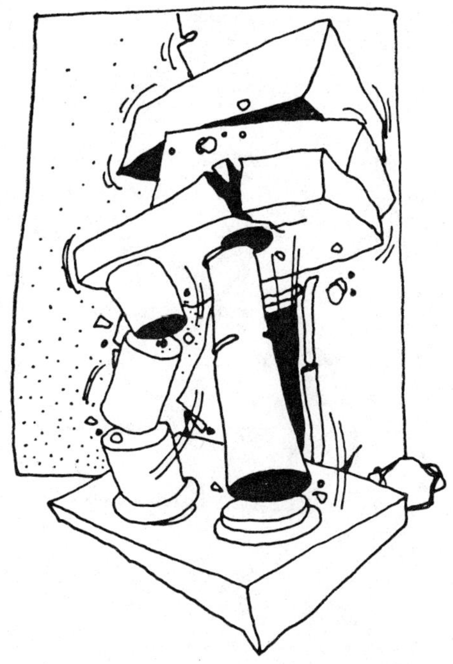

What can I expect at the end of the world?

Mark 13

What does the future hold? That's a question asked by thousands. They seek out fortune tellers, try to talk with the dead, join witches' covens, ask Ouija boards—all dangerous ways of getting involved with Satan's powers.

Other more right-minded people try to find the answer to this question in careful study of a financial prospectus, in the analysis of history and current events, in the genetics of their family tree.

God doesn't answer all of our questions about the future, but he does devote a whole chapter of the book of Mark to telling us what to expect in the end times. It's a future we need to know about.

***1.** If you could have an answer to one question about the future, what would you ask?

____

____

Read Mark 13.

2. What did Jesus prophesy would happen to the temple?

____

____

3. What two questions did the disciples ask when they reached the Mount of Olives?

4. What will happen at the beginning of the end times? (Verses 5-8.)

5. What will happen to the followers of Christ? (Verses 9-13.)

***6.** What are the dangers in thinking the end is sooner than it really is? (Verse 7.)

7. Review verses 14-23.
A part of this paragraph was fulfilled in 70 A.D. when the temple was destroyed by the Romans. The final sentences of the paragraph seem to show that an even greater time of destruction is yet to come. What steps of self-protection did Jesus tell his followers to take?

***8.** What kind of deception will Christ's followers need to be aware of?

9. What signs will occur just prior to Christ's return? (Verse 24-27.)

10. Find the warnings in this chapter against following false Christs.

What powers will these false Christs have?

What will be different about Christ's appearance and the appearance of these false Christs?

11. How can we keep from being deceived by these false Christs?

12. How are the leaves on the fig tree like the signs in this chapter? (Verses 28-31.)

*__13.__ In what ways did Christ answer the two questions of his disciples? (Verses 32-37.)

In what ways are their questions still unanswered?

14. What comforts does this chapter offer the believer in Christ?

15. How can you prepare for the kind of world crisis this chapter describes?

16. What kind of work do you feel that God wants you to be doing while you watch for Christ's return?

____

____

____

____

**Optional question*

Would I claim Jesus in a tight spot?

Mark 14

How well do you know yourself? You look in the mirror in the morning and quip, "Yep, that's me." But as the day progresses, could you have predicted your actions? Would you have guessed that when your friend Bob caught you at a bad moment and asked you to go divvies on sandwiches, you'd snarl, "Go eat your own lunch"? Or that when Sue stumbled in gym and lost the volleyball game for the whole team, that you'd find enough kindness inside you to sit next to her in the locker room and reassure her with, "It's all right," while everyone else gave her the silent treatment?

You check out the same mirror in the evening and notice, "It's still me." But you surprise yourself sometimes. So did Peter and Judas and the other disciples.

***1.** When have you discovered something about yourself that surprised you?

____

____

____

Read aloud Mark 14.

***2.** Find as many predictions as you can of Jesus' coming death.

3. In verse 6 Jesus said, "She has done a beautiful thing to me." What was beautiful about this woman's actions? (Verses 1-9.)

4. Christ and his disciples celebrated the Passover one day early. What added importance did Christ give to this new Passover, the Lord's supper?

***5.** When Jesus announced that he would be betrayed, what did the response of the disciples show?

6. What does this last meal together reveal of the relationship between Jesus and his disciples?

7. What aspects of this relationship do you now enjoy?

8. What had Peter known about himself before the events of that night?

What did he learn about himself?

9. What help to Jesus might Peter, James and John have been if they had stayed awake in Gethsemane?

How might the disciples themselves have benefited?

10. Of what crime was Jesus convicted?

What was the evidence?

Who were his accusers?

Who was the judge?

What was fair about the trial?

What was unfair?

*11. What is the difference between what Judas did and what Peter did?

In what ways were their actions similar?

12. How might Peter have prevented this denial?

13. If you had been Peter, what comfort might you remember from this chapter?

***14.** Under what circumstances would it be hard for you to admit that you belong to Christ?

15. In what day-to-day situations is it hard for you to admit that you are a follower of Jesus?

16. How can you keep from letting Jesus down in these tight spots?

**Optional question*

What did I cost God?

Mark 15:1-16:8

George Stimpson once said that the average human body is worth $1.00 in isolated chemicals.* At today's values that converts to about $1.76. Pretty cheap, yes? But we will spend thousands of dollars on medical treatment that just might preserve one $1.76 person a little longer. Families may pay a million dollars for a kidnap victim. Ask a parent to put a price tag on his child; the parent will just smile and walk away.

But God paid for us in full. Since no amount of money would be sufficient, God paid with something even more valuable than money—his son Jesus. We can be forever freed from that $1.76 price tag. We are worth much more than that to God.

*George Stimpson, *The Book About a Thousand Things* (Harper and Brothers, 1946).

1. What experiences have showed you that God cares for you?

____

____

____

____

Read aloud Mark 15:1-16:8.

2. What do you think Pilate's feelings were during the trial? (Verses 1-15.)

3. How did the religious leaders pressure Pilate?

4. What torture was Jesus subjected to apart from routine execution?

5. Why might taunting Jesus to come down from the cross have been particularly cutting?

***6.** Why do you think Mark mentions the temple veil?

7. What do you think caused the centurion to comment as he did? (Verse 39.)

8. What evidence is there that Jesus' suffering was real?

***9.** How do you feel when you read these details?

***10.** Why might Joseph have needed courage to go to Pilate?

11. In what ways did Christ's followers demonstrate their love?

***12.** Why was Peter singled out in 16:7?

13. If you had been one of the women of chapter 16:1-8, what thoughts and feelings would have gone through your mind?

***14.** The oldest copies of *Mark* end at chapter 16, verse 8. What questions might have been answered if we had the rest of the book?

15. What qualities of God do you see and appreciate from this study?

16. How can you express your thanks to him?

**Optional question*

DOING PROJECTS

Jamal Khan
Wayne Soverall

University Press of America,® Inc.
Lanham • New York • Oxford

4720 Boston Way
Lanham, Maryland 20706

12 Hid's Copse Rd.
Cumnor Hill, Oxford OX2 9JJ

Printed in the United States of America
British Library Cataloging in Publication Information Available

Library of Congress Cataloging-in-Publication Data

Khan, Jamal.
Doing projects / Jamal Khan, Wayne Soverall.
p. cm.
Includes bibliographical references and index.
1. Industrial project management. I. Soverall, Wayne. II. Title.
HD69.P75K516 2000 658.4'04—dc21 99-085977 CIP

ISBN 0-7618-1626-7 (cloth: alk. ppr.)

The paper used in this publication meets the minimum requirements of American National Standard for Information Sciences—Permanence of Paper for Printed Library Materials, ANSI Z39.48—1984

Contents

To the people of the Caribbean

Preface

The volume is intended for policy-makers, planners, analysts, evaluators, consultants, technical specialists, funding and technical agency personnel, academics, researchers, students, media personnel, and public and private sector employees. Working on the volume 'Doing Projects' stirred up an escalatory project of its own in terms of data-collection, information-gathering, fieldwork, accessing, writing, collaboration, time, finance, resources and publication, not to mention numerous, major as well as niggling obstacles, impediments, misfortunes, exigencies, diversions, and job pressures.

It is a pleasure to express our gratitude to the many people kind enough to help us. In the preparation and publication of this study, we received assistance, support and fellowship from many individuals and organizations. However, we are especially indebted to Abeda Khan, Ansar Juman, Anthony Bryan, Basil Scott, Bentley Norville, Bradley Niles, Colin Alert, Delisle Bradshaw, Dermot Blackett, Elsworth Young, Fred Webster, Glynn Pooler, Ian Storey, Ismail Adam, Janice Bourne, Louis Moore, Marcel Daher, Neville Duncan, Om Prakash, Prakash Vensimal, Ram Mirchandani, Ramesh Thani, Therold Fields and Tyrone Estwick. We are thankful to numerous authors, researchers, respondents, interviewers, interviewees, and service providers. For making part of research material available for this volume, we acknowledge most appreciatively the valuable, timely and collegial contributions of Alvin Burgess, Carlston Trotman, Rudolph Hinkson, and Sylvester Welch.

Mentionable too for cooperation during the various stages of briefing, fact-finding, backstopping, data-building and verification are Allan Jones, Alvah Hunte, Arthur Archer, Bertram Corbin, Carlyle Brathwaite, Christopher Griffith, Frank Watson, John Vaughan, Jerry Thomas, Leon Knight, Luther Jordan, Michael Thompson, Ralph Carvalho, Sam Headley, Stanton Alleyne, Steven Lindo, Wilton Conliff, and Wismore Butcher. We owe enormous debt to our family members - Asif, Joan, Katrina, Natasha, Shirley and Wilson - who endured a great deal directly attributed to this enterprise. The errors and omissions in this study are our sole responsibility.

Jamal Khan
Wayne Soverll
Barbados

1
INTRODUCTION

Development projects have tended to receive less than their due share of attention from empirical social science. While social scientists from various specialties have dealt with many aspects of social, political and economic reality, the project process has been largely neglected until recently. In project research the emphasis is usually on considering the economic and technical appraisal and project planning/control rather than on examining the multifaceted project process. The focus is placed mostly on conventional economic analysis and selective disaggregation (Abelson, 1996; Austin, 1992; Behren and Hawranek, 1991; Bussey, 1978; Curry and Weiss, 1993; Department of Environment, 1991; Food and Agriculture Organization, 1977; Hanson, 1966; Harvey, 1983, 1986; Hirschman,1958; Horton, 1994; Kirkpatrick and Weiss, 1996; Levy and Sarnat, 1986; Lewis, 1966; Little and Mirrlees, 1991; MacArthur, 1988; Maddock and Wilson, 1994; Overseas Development Administration, 1995; Pearce, 1994; Roemer and Stern, 1975; Schneider, 1975; Tinbergen, 1967; United Nations, 1958; van Pelt, 1993; Ward, 1991; Waterston, 1965; Weiss, 1994; Yaffey, 1992).

Attention continues to be paid to similar analyses (Angelson, 1994; Austin, 1992; Brent, 1990; Clifton and Fyffe, 1977; Coombs and Jenkins, 1991; Dinwiddy and Teal, 1995; Department of Treasury, 1984; FitzGerald, 1978; Hanley and Spash, 1993; Inter-American Development Bank, 1977; International Labor Organization, 1979; Jenkins and Herberger, 1994; Lumby, 1994; Ministry of Overseas Development, 1977; Organization of American States, 1978; Overseas Development Administration, 1988; Perkins, 1994; Project Planning Center for Developing Countries, 1982; Randolph and Posner, 1988; Sell, 1989; United Nations Development Program, 1988; Walsh and Daffern, 1990; Williams and Giardina, 1993; World Bank, 1979).

Diverse thematic and analytical trends are discernible from a host of research (Asian Development Bank, 1984; Attwood, 1988; Baum and Tolbert, 1985; Birgegard, 1975; Bridger and Winpenny, 1991, 1991; Brinkerhoff, 1986, 1991; Bryant and White, 1980; Caribbean Development Bank, 1986; Cusworth and Franks, 1993; de Vries, 1971; Dupriez, 1979; European Community, 1978; FitzGerald, 1978; Goodman and Love, 1979, 1980; Gross, 1966; Hirschman, 1963, 1967, 1984; Hulme, 1995; Kirkpatrick, 1991; Krutilla and Eckstein, 1958; MacArthur, 1988, 1993; Morris and Hough, 1987; Morss, 1976; Murphy, 1983; O'Connor and Reinsborough, 1992; Rondinelli, 1976, 1977, 1977, 1978, 1978, 1979, 1979; Thimm, 1979; Waterston, 1965; White, 1991; Wilson, 1997; Wynia, 1972). To identify some directions, for instance, King (1967) summarizes project experience gained by the World Bank of project appraisal. Hirschman (1967) examines behaviors as well as misbehaviors of a sample of development projects. The essential unity of systems analysis and project management is demonstrated by Cleland and King (1968). The appraisal component of development projects commands scholarly attention, e.g. Little and Mirrlees (1968, 1974), UNITAR (1969), Solomon (1970), Dasgupta et al. (1972), Gittinger (1972), Herberger (1972), UNDP (1974), Roemer and Stern (1975), Squire and van der Tak (1975), and USAID (1976). More works continue to appear, namely, Clifton and Fyffe (1977), FAO (1977), IDB (1977), MOD (1977), FitzGerald (1978), OAS (1978), World Bank (1979), ILO (1981), Project Planning Center (1982), and Harvey (1983).

Other researchers, such as Lock (1968), Harrison (1981), Awani (1983), Ahuja (1984) and Meredith and Mantel (1985) put stress on project planning and control. While the project cycle receives adequate attention from Goodman and Love (1979, 1980) and Stallworthy and Kharbanda (1983), Rondinelli (1977) highlights both political and technical needs and explores the social, behavioral and organizational aspects of project implementation. Some project-oriented approaches, aiming at improving the design of implementable strategies, are presented by Honadle and Klauss (1979). Kelley (1982) provides a broad overview of the project-management environment of the 1980s. A great deal of project research has concentrated on the economic, financial and technical aspects of the project cycle. Less attention has been given to the institutional, behavioral, social and cultural aspects, political constraints or realities, implementation process, management capability or the context in which projects unfold.

In addition, research on project management points to various emphases and directions (Adams, 1979; Ahuja, 1984; Analoui, 1989, 1994; Anderson, 1984; Anderson, 1987; Archibald, 1976; Augustine, 1989; Austin, 1984; Austin and Neale, 1984; Avots, 1969, 1975; Awani, 1983; Bainbridge and Sapire, 1974; Baumgartner, 1963, 1979; Benningson, 1977; Bergen, 1986; Berger, 1974, 1979; Biggs, 1980; Burbridge, 1992; Cleland, 1968, 1988; Davis, 1983; Dinsmore, 1990; Duncan 1993; Frame, 1987; Gaddis, 1959; Gemmill and Wilemon, 1970; Goodman, 1988; Goodman and Love, 1979; Gray, 1981; Grool, 1986; Gross, 1966,; Hackney, 1977; Hajek, 1984; Hayes, 1959; Hoare, 1973; Kelley, 1982; Kerzner, 1979, 1982; Kezsbom, 1989; Khan, 1982, 1992; Kleim, 1986; Knutson, 1991; Lock, 1968, 1987; Martin, 1976; Martino, 1968; Martyn, 1975). Just so, more works continue to appear (Nichols, 1990; Obeng, 1996; Obradovitch and Stephanou, 1990; Paul, 1983; Pessimer, 1977; Randolph, 1988; Reiss, 1992; Roman, 1986; Rosenau, 1981; Sayles, 1971; Shaheen, 1987; Shotub, 1994; Silverman, 1973; Smith, 1984; Solomon and Rizo, 1976; Spinner, 1992; Steiner and Ryan, 1968; Taylor and Watling, 1970, 1973; Thomsett, 1990; United Nations, 1969, 1993; United States Agency for International Development, 1975, 1976; United States Department of Agriculture, 1976; United States Office of Personnel Management, 1982).

Several rationales lie at the basis of this study. Few activities are more crucial to accelerating the pace of economic and social progress in poor countries than effective planning and implementation of development projects. A project represents a rational basis for the decision to set varied dynamics in motion and, hence, it deserves to be studied as *thoroughly* as possible. In fact, for over half of a century, projects have been the primary instruments for grant, credit, loan and technical aid to developing countries by international assistance agencies. The volume of lending and the number of funded projects have increased sharply during the past several decades.

Projects can be, and sometimes are, one of the most tangible, explicit and visible expressions of large-scale, multilateral, goal-specific, concerted and fast-moving activities. They often represent human achievements most vividly. Development projects in many developing countries now provide the bulk of capital formation and have tended to change the view of such activity from one of 'infrastructural support' to one of 'socioeconomic leadership' (FitzGerald, 1978:xi). In a world of painful nonperformance, elusive accountability, nasty surprises, frantic confusion and recurrent distractions, development projects - their accomplishments and fruition, disappointments notwithstanding - can be heartening and refreshing.

While the empirical context is provided by Barbados, the basic approach and techniques are broadly applicable elsewhere, but, of course, differences need to be noted. This study grew out of an interest in project behavior. In this volume, development projects are considered the *units of analysis*. The underlying hypothesis advances on the premise that development projects in Barbados, embedded in the social setting, proceed in an evolutionary, incremental and collaborative mode.

It is a retrospective study, carried out on the basis of a sample of seven projects, owing its existence to years of fact-finding, documentation, evidence-building, information-processing, and surveying. The data were collected in parts of the 1980s and the 1990s. Part of the study was conducted in Bridgetown and various parishes of Barbados where the sample projects had been initiated and completed. While the analytic aspect of the study is based on the project-setting model, project tool, appraisal process, implementation process and management capability, the empirical aspect is focused on the institutional development, project behavior and survey data. Empirical research provided a variety of documentary and corroborative evidence.

The collection and analysis of empirical data is an important objective in this management research. It has been attempted via advancing a number of assumptions and producing evidence in support of or against the assumptions. We set out several research problems in this study: laying down a project-setting model; examining projects as a tool of development activity/management; examining appraisal, implementation and management capability functions/processes; highlighting the institutionalization of development projects; comparing and illustrating the project cycle of a sample of projects; and generating and analyzing survey data concerning projects. Further, an effort has been made to reduce apriorism, and the project cycle has been documented at a disaggregated empirical level.

A number of specifications and caveats are in order now. Several types of projects are excluded from the study, e.g., private-sector, nongovernmental, regional, joint-venture, ongoing and preindependence projects. It was not feasible to include projects from other sectors like energy, culture, family planning, social security, law enforcement, etc. The project-making or project-building process refers to the entire gamut of projects ranging from conception to evaluation. Project-makers, a generic aggregative term used for convenience, refer to policy-makers, decision-makers, planners, analysts, implementors, and operators. The executing agencies are the same as implementing agencies. A comprehensive umbrella term, executive organizations embrace operating ministries, departments, field offices, and public enterprises. The titles of the projects under study are used uniformly in the interest of consistency, e.g. Greenland, Handicraft, Cave, Pulverization, Polytechnic, Sewerage, and Ferneihurst.

We use development project and investment project, project decision and investment decision, and project analysis and project appraisal interchangeably. So it is in respect of project, undertaking, investment, exercise, enterprise, venture, scheme, and endeavor. It is mentionable too that 'appraisal' and 'evaluation' are often employed synonymously elsewhere. In this volume, we treat them separately, and are concerned with ex ante appraisal as well as ex post evaluation. While evaluation is indicative of an assessment of a consequence of a project after or during its lifetime, appraisal refers to the same exercise ex ante. We distinguish between project authority or agency and operating agency. The former concerns a unit that implements a project, and the latter runs a project on its completion. Likewise, reference is made to in-project period and postproject period. The former refers to the project status, i.e. when it was underway, and the latter to the postproject situation, i.e. its postcompletion and current operational standing.

We use 'management' and 'administration' synonymously, although some make a distinction between the two in that the former refers to the execution of policies or decisions, while the latter implies the setting of policies or decisions. We employ them synonymously in the modern sense of the process of getting results through organizational action (Gross, 1969:226). For ease of presentation, respondents and beneficiaries are referred to in the male gender throughout the volume. The label 'beneficiary' is to be understood in a nonspecific way in the sense that all members of the public are potential users of all public service and, therefore, its clientele.

There is a false distinction and a sham battle between the 'economic' or 'productive' and 'social' or 'service' sectors. The separation of economic from social sectors, often an artifact of academic analysis and organizational compartmentalism, is in a sense arbitrary and ambiguous since each impinges on and affects the other. Practically, all social projects have an economic content of finance and allocation of scarce resources, while economic projects cannot be detached from their social effects. To analyze economic projects without regard to social realities is to lose sense of purpose; to analyze social projects without regard to economic conditions and constraints is to lose contact with reality. Besides, one should not make the mistake of using the term social in the sense of noneconomic.

It is neither feasible nor desirable, on the basis of research on a sample of projects in one country, to set out precise judgements on the conditions and factors which make for success or setback in development activities. The very complexity and interaction of the sectors, the multidimensionality of projects and the limited resources available for research mean that findings shown here are not offered in the belief that they provide *final* answers to the formidable problems of development (Baum and Tolbert, 1985). The findings should, accordingly, be regarded as being more in the nature of working hypotheses, which have been formulated on the basis of cumulative experience with a view to informing future project action and increasing the efficacy of resources used to promote socioeconomic development. The research results should be further extended and verified in the future by means of more wide-ranging studies and intensive research on specific sectors, projects and phases.

REFERENCES

Abelson, Peter (1996) *Project Appraisal and Valuation Method*. London: Macmillan.

Adams, John et al. (1979) *Managing by Project Management*. Dayton: Universal Technology.

Ahuja, Hira N. (1984) *Project Management*. New York: John Wiley.

Analoui, Farhad (1989) "Project Manager's Role: Towards a Descriptive Approach", *Project Appraisal* 4(1).

Analoui, Farhad (ed.) (1994) *The Realities of Managing Development Projects*. Aldershot: Avebury.

Anderson, E.S. et al. (1984) *Goal Directed Project Management*. London: Kogan Page.

Anderson, Stuart D. (1987) *Project Manpower Management*. New York: Wiley.

Angelson, Arild et al. (1994) *Project Appraisal and Sustainability in Less Developed Countries*. Bergen: Michelson Institute.

Archibald, Russell D. (1976) *Managing High-Technology Programs and Projects*. New York: John Wiley.

Asian Development Bank (1984) *Rural Development in Asia and the Pacific*. Manila: Asian Development Bank.

Attwood, D.W. et al. (eds.) (1988) *Power and Poverty: Development and Development Projects in the Third World*. Boulder: Westview Press.

Augustine, Norman R. (ed.) (1989) *Managing Projects and Programs*. Cambridge:

Harvard Business School Press.

Austin, A.D. and R.H. Neale (1984) *Managing Construction Projects*. Geneva: International Labor Organization.

Austin, James E. (1992) *Agricultural Project Analysis*. Baltimore: Johns Hopkins University Press.

Austin, Jane E. (1992) *Agroindustrial Project Analysis: Critical Design Factors*. Baltimore: Johns Hopkins University Press.

Austin, V. (1984) *Rural Project Management*. London: Batsford.

Avots , Ivor (1969) "Why Does Project Management Fail", *California Management Review* 12 (Fall).

___ (1975) "Managing Project Management Work", *Advanced Management Journal* 40(4).

Awani Alfred O. (1983) *Project Management Techniques*. New York: Petrocelli Books.

Bainbridge, J. and S. Sapire (1974) *Health Project Management*. Geneva: World Health Organization.

Baum, Warren C. and Stokes M. Tolbert (1985) *Investing in Development: Lessons of World Bank Experience*. Washington, D.C.: World Bank.

Baumgartner, John S. (1963) *Project Management*. Homewood: Irwin.

___ (1979) *Systems Management*. Washington, D.C.: Bureau of National Affairs.

Behren, W. and P.M. Hawranek (1991) *Industrial Feasibility Studies*. Geneva: United Nations Industrial Development Organization.

Benningson, L.A. (1977) *Project Management*. Stockholm: Scandinavian Institute of Administrative Research.

Bergen, S.A. (1986) *Project Management*. Oxford: Basil Blackwell.

Berger, M.J. (1974) *Project Management*. Nashville: Graduate School of Management, Vanderbilt University.

___ et al. (1979) *Developing Organization Systems*. Nashville: Graduate School of Management, Vanderbilt University.

Biggs, Charles L, (1980) *Managing the Systems Development Process*. Englewood Cliffs: Prentice-Hall.

Birgegard, Lars-Erik (1975) *The Project Selection Process in Developing Countries*. Stockholm: Economic Research Institute.

Brent, R.J. (1990) *Project Appraisal for Developing Countries*. New York: New York University Press.

Bridger, G.A. and J.P. Winpenny (1991) *Planning Development Projects*. London: Overseas Development Administration.

Brinkerhoff, D.W. and J.C. Garcia-Zamor (eds.) (1986) *Politics, Projects and People*. New York: Praeger.

___ (1991) *Improving Development Program Performance*. Boulder: Lynne Rienner.

Bryant, Coralie and L.G. White (1980) *Managing Rural Development*. Hartford: Kumarian Press.

Burbridge, R.N.G. (1992) *Perspectives on Project Management*. Hartfordshire:

Peregrimus.

Bussey, Lynn E. (1978) *The Economic Analysis of Industrial Projects*. Englewood Cliffs: Prentice-Hall.

Carribean Development Bank (1986) *Public Sector Investment Program*. St Michael, Barbados: Caribbean Development Bank.

Cleland, David I. and William R. King (1968) *Systems Analysis and Project Management*. New York: McGraw-Hill.

___ et al. (eds.) (1988) *Project Management Handbook*. New York: Van Nostrand Reinhold.

Clifton, David S. and David E. Fyffe (1977) *Project Feasibility Analysis*. New York: John Wiley.

Coombs, H.M. and D.E. Jenkins (1991) *Public Sector Financial Management*. London: Chapman & Hall.

Curry, Steve S. and John J. Weiss (1993) *Project Analysis in Developing Countries*. London: Macmillan.

Cusworth, J.W. and T. Franks (1993) *The Planning and Management of Projects in Developing Countries*. London: Longman.

Dasgupta, Partha S. et al. (1972) *Guidelines for Project Evaluation*. Vienna: United Nations Industrial Development Organization.

Davis, E.W. (1983) *Project Management: Techniques, Applications and Managerial Issues*. Norcross, Georgia: Institute of Industrial Engineers.

Dean, B.V. (ed.) (1985) *Project Management: Methods and Studies*. Amsterdam: Elsevier.

Department of Environment (1991) *Policy Appraisal and the Environment*. London: Her Majesty's Stationery Office.

Department of Treasury (1984) *Investment Appraisal in the Public Sector*. London: Her Majesty's Stationery Office.

De Vries, Egbert (1971) *Administration of Development Programs and Projects: Some Major Issues*. New York: United Nations.

Dinsmore, Paul C. (1990) *Human Factors in Project Management*. New York: American Management Association.

Dinwiddy, C. and F. Teal (1995) *Principles of Cost-Benefit Analysis for Developing Countries*. Cambridge: Cambridge University Press.

Duncan, William (1993) *Project Management*. Lexington: Duncan Nevison.

Dupriez, Hughes (1979) *Integrated Rural Development Projects in Africa*. Brussels: European Community.

European Community (1978) *Integrated Rural Development Projects in Black Africa*. Brussels: European Community.

Fitzgerald, E.V.K. (1978) *Public Sector Investment Planning for Developing Countries*. London: Macmillan.

Food and Agriculture Organization (1977) *Guidelines for the Preparation of Agricultural Investment Projects*. Rome: Food and Agriculture Organization.

Frame, J. Davidson (1987) *Managing Projects in Organizations*. San Francisco: Jossey-Bass.

Gaddis, Paul O. (1959) "The Project Manager", *Harvard Business Review* 37 (May-June).

Gemmill, Gary and David L. Wilemon (1970) "Power Spectrum in Project Management", *Sloan Management Review* (Fall).

Gittinger, J.P. (1972) *Economic Analysis of Agricultural Projects*. Baltimore: Johns Hopkins University Press.

Goodman, J. L. (1988) *Project Planning and Management: An Integrated System for Improving Productivity*. New York: Van Nostrand Rein.

Goodman, Louis J. and Ralph N. Love (eds.) (1979) *Management of Development Projects: An International Case Study Approach*. New York: Pergamon Press.

___ (eds.) (1980) *Project Planning and Management: An Integrated Approach*. New York: Pergamon Press.

Gray, Clifford F. (1981) *Essentials of Project Management*. New York: Petrocelli Books.

Grool, Marjolijn C. et al. (1986) *Project Management in Progress*. Amsterdam: North-Holland.

Gross, Bertram M. (1966) *The Administration of Economic Development Planning: Principles and Fallacies*. New York: United Nations.

___ (1969) "Some Factors Involved in Appraising Administrative Performance in Development Planning", in United Nations, *Administrative Aspects of Planning*. New York: United Nations.

Hackney, J.W. (1977) *Control and Management of Capital Projects*. New York: McGraw-Hill.

Hajek, V.G. (1984) *Management of Engineering Projects*. New York: McGraw-Hill.

Hanley, N. and C.L. Spash (1993) *Cost-Benefit Analysis and the Environment*. Aldershot: Edward Elgar.

Hanson, A.H. (1966) *The Process of Planning*. London: Oxford University Press.

Harrison, F.L. (1981) *Advanced Project Management*. Aldershot: Gower.

Harvey, Charles (1983) *Analysis of Project Finance in Developing Countries*. London: Heinemann.

Hayes, Samuel P. (1959) *Measuring the Results of Development Projects*. Paris: United Nations Educational, Scientific and Cultural Organization.

Herberger, Arnold C. (1972) *Project Evaluation*. London: Macmillan.

Hirschman, Albert O. (1958) *The Strategy of Economic Development*. New Haven: Yale University Press.

___ (1963) *Journeys Toward Progress*. New York: Twentieth-Century Fund.

___ (1967) *Development Projects Observed*. Washington, D.C.: Brookings Institution.

___ (1984) *Getting Ahead Collectively*. New York: Pergamon Press.

Hoare, H.R. (1973) *Project Management*. New York: McGraw-Hill.

Honadle, George and Rudi Klauss (eds.) (1979) *International Development Administration*. New York: Praeger.

Horton, Forest W. (1994) *Analyzing Benefits and Costs*. Ottawa: International

Development Research Center.

Hulme, David (1995) "Projects, Politics and Professionals: Alternative Approaches for Project Identification and Project Planning", *Agricultural Systems* (47).

Inter-American Development Bank (1997) *Social and Economic Dimensions of Project Evaluation*. Washington, D.C.: Inter-American Development Bank.

International Labor Organization (1981) *Project Preparation and Appraisal*. Geneva: International Labor Organization.

Jenkins, Glenn P. and Arnold C. Herberger (1994) *Program on Investment Appraisal and Management*. Cambridge: Harvard Institute for International Development.

Kelley, Albert J. (ed.) (1982) *New Dimensions of Project Management*. Lexington: Lexington Books.

Kerzner, Harold (1979) *Project Management: A Systems Approach to Planning, Scheduling and Controlling*. New York: Van Nostrand Reinhold.

___ (1982) *Project Management for Executives*. New York: Van Nostrand.

Kezsbom, Deborah S. et al. (1989) *Dynamic Project Management*. New York: John Wiley.

King, John A. (1967) *Economic Development Projects and their Appraisal*. Baltimore: Johns Hopkins University Press.

Kirkpatrick, Colin (ed.)(1991) *Project Rehabilitation in Developing Countries*. London: Routledge.

Kirkpatrick, Colin and John Weiss (eds.) (1996) *Cost-Benefit Analysis and Project Appraisal in Developing Countries*. Cheltenham: Edward Elgar.

Khan, Jamal (1982) Public Management: The Eastern Caribbean Experience. Leiden, Holland: KITLV Press.

___ (1992) "Project Management: The Bridgetown Fisheries Project", *Public Administration Review* 30 (January-June).

Kleim, R.L. (1986) *The Secret of Successful Project Management*. Chicester: John Wiley.

Knutson, Joan and Ira Bitz (1981) *Project Management*. New York: AMACOM.

Krutilla, John V. and Otto Eckstein (1958) *Multiple Purpose River Basin Development*. Baltimore: John Hopkins University Press.

Lewis, W.A. (1966) *Development Planning*. New York: Harper & Row.

Levy, H. and M. Sarnat (1986) *Capital Investment and Financial Decisions*. Englewood Cliffs.: Prentice-Hall.

Little, I.M.D. and J.A. Mirrlees (1968) *Manual of Industrial Project Analysis in Developing Countries*. Paris: OECD Development Center.

___ (1974) *Project Appraisal and Planning for Developing Countries*. London: Heinemann.

___ (1991) "Project Appraisal and Planning Twenty Years On", Paper presented at the *World Bank Annual Conference on Development Economics*. Washington D.C.: World Bank.

Lock, Dennis (1968) *Project Management*. London: Gower.

Lock, Dennis (ed.) (1987) *Project Management Handbook*. Aldershot: Gower.

Lumby, S.C. (1994) *Investment Appraisal and Related Decision*. London: Clapham and Hall.

MacArthur, J.D. (1988) *Appraisal of Projects in Developing Countries*. London: Overseas Development Administration.

MacArthur, J.D. and J. Weiss (eds.) (1993) *Agriculture, Projects and Development*. Aldershot: Avebury.

Maddock, N. and F. A. Wilson (eds.) (1994) *Project Design for Agricultural Development*. Oxford: Avebury.

Martin, Charles C. (1976) *Project Management*. New York: AMACOM.

Martino, R.L. (1968) *Project Management*. Webster, N.C.: Management Development Institute.

Martyn, A.S. (1975) "Some Problems in Managing Complex Development Projects", *Long Range Planning* (April).

Meredith, Jack R. and Samuel J. Mantel (1985) *Project Management: A Managerial Approach*. New York: John Wiley.

Ministry of Overseas Development (1977) *A Guide to the Economic Appraisal of Projects in Developing Countries*. London: Her Majesty's Stationery Office.

Morris, P.W.G. and George H. Hough (1987) *The Anatomy of Major Projects*. Chicester: John Wiley.

Morss, Elliott et al. (eds.) (1976) *Strategies for Small Farmer Development: An Empirical Study of Rural Development Projects*. Boulder: Westview Press.

Murphy, K.J. (1983) *Macroproject Development in Third World*. Boulder: Westview Press.

Nichols, John M. (1990) *Managing Business and Engineering Projects*. Englewood Cliffs: Prentice-Hall.

Obradovitch, M.M. and S.E. Stephanou (1990) *Project Management: Risks and Productivity*. Bend, Oregon: Daniel Spencer Publishers.

Obeng, Eddie (1996) *Putting Strategy to Work*. London: Pitman.

O'Connor, M.M. and L.H. Reinsborough (1992) "Quality Projects in the 1990s: A Review of Past Projects and Future Trends", *International Journal of Project Management* 10(2).

Organization of American States (1978) *Development Projects Program*. Washington, D.C.: Organization of American States.

Overseas Development Administration (1988) *Appraisal of Projects in Developing Countries*. London: Her Majesty's Stationery Office.

___ (1995) *A Guide to Social Analysis for Projects in Developing Countries*. London: Her Majesty's Stationery Office.

Paul, Samuel (1983) *Strategic Management of Development Programs*. Geneva: International Labor Organization.

Pearce, David et al. (1994) *Projects and Policy Appraisal*. Paris: Organization for Economic Cooperation and Development.

Perkins, F. (1994) *Practical Cost Benefit Analysis*. Melbourne: Macmillan.

Pessimer, Elgar (1977) *Project Management Strategy and Organizations*. Santa Barbara: John Wiley.

Project Planning Center for Developing Countries (1982) *A Manual on Project*

Planning for Small Economies. London: Commonwealth Secretariat.
Radosevich, Raymond and Dennis Rondinelli (1974) *An Integrated Approach to Development Project Management*. Washington, D.C.: United States Agency for International Development.
Randolph, W.A. and Barry Z. Posner (1988) *Effective Project Planning and Management: Getting the Job Done*. Englewood Cliffs: Prentice-Hall.
Reiss, G. (1992) *Project Management Demystified*. London: E. FN Spon.
Roemer, Michael and Joseph S. Stern (1975) *The Appraisal of Development Projects*. New York: Praeger.
Roman, Daniel D. (1986) *Managing Projects: A System Approach*. New York: Elsevier.
Rosenau, M. D. (1981) *Successful Project Management*. Belmont, Calif.: Lifetime Learning.
Rondinelli, Dennis A. (1976) "Why Development Projects Fail: Problems of Project Management in Developing Countries", *Project Management Quarterly* (7).
___ (ed.) (1977) *Planning Development Projects*. Stroudsburg: Dowden, Hutchinson & Ross.
___ (1978) "Implementing Developing Projects: The Problem of Management", *International Development Review* (20).
___ (1979) "Planning Developing Projects: Lessons from Developing Countries", *Long Range Planning* (June).
___ (1979) "Designing International Development Projects for Implementation", in George Honadle and Rudi Klauss (eds.) (1979) *International Development Administration*. New York: Praeger.
___ (1979) "Administration of Integrated Rural Development Policy: The Politics of Agrarian Reform in Developing Countries", *World Politics* 31 (April).
Sayles, Leonard R, (1971) *Managing Large Systems*. New York: Harper & Row.
Schneider, Hartmut (1975) *National Objectives and Project Appraisal in Developing Countries*. Paris: Organization for Economic Cooperation and Development.
Sell, Axel (1989) *Investment Projects in Developing Countries: Financial and Economic Analysis*. Hamburg: Hamburg Institute of Economic Research.
Shaheen, S.K. (1987) *Practical Project Management*. Chicester: John Wiley.
Shotub, Avraham et al. (1994) *Project Management*. Englewood Cliffs: Prentice-Hall.
Silverman, S. (1973) *Project Management*. New York: John Wiley.
Smith, Peter (1984) *Agricultural Project Management: Monitoring and Control of Implementation*. London: Elsevier.
Solomon, Morris J. (1970) *Analysis of Projects for Economic Growth*. New York: Praeger.
Solomon, Morris J. and E.E. Rizo (1976) *Elements of Project Management*. Washington, D.C.: United States Department of Agriculture.
Spinner, M.P. (1992) *Elements of Project Management*. Englewood Cliffs: Prentice-Hall.

Squire, Lyn and Herman G. van der Tak (1975) *Economic Analysis of Projects*. Baltimore: Johns Hopkins University Press.

Stallworthy, E.A. and O.P. Kharbanda (1983) *Total Project Management: From Conception to Completion*. Aldershot: Gower.

Steiner, George A. and William G. Ryan (1968) *Industrial Project Management*. New York: Macmillan.

Taylor, W.J. and T.F. Watling (1970) *Successful Project Management*. London: Business Books.

___ (1973) *Practical Project Management*. London: Business Books.

Thimn, Heinz-Ulrich (1979) *Development Projects in the Sudan*. Tokyo: United Nations University Press.

Thomsett, Michael C. (1990) *The Little Black Book of Project Management*. New York: AMACOM.

Tinbergen, Jan (1967) *Development Planning*. London: Weidenfeld & Nicolson.

United Nations (1958) *Manual on Economic Development Projects*. New York: United Nations.

United Nations (1969) *Administrative Aspects of Planning*. New York: United Nations.

United Nations (1993) *Managing the Development Projects*. New York: United Nations.

United Nations Development Program (1974) *UNDP Operational and Financial Manual*. New York: United Nations Development Program.

___ (1988) *Cost-Benefit Analysis of Industrial Projects*. New York: United Nations Industrial Development Organization.

United Nations Institute of Training and Research (1969) *Criteria and Methods of Evaluation*. New York: United Nations Institute of Training and Research.

United States Agency for International Development (1975) *Project Assistance Handbook*. Washington, D.C.: United States Agency for International Development.

___ (1975) *Strategies for Small Farmer Development: An Empirical Study of Rural Development Projects*. Washington, D.C.: United States Agency for International Development.

___ (1976) *Evaluation Handbook*. Washington, D.C.: United States Agency for International Development.

___ (1976) *Elements of Project Management*. Washington, D.C.: United States Agency for International Development.

United States Department of Agriculture (1976) *Elements of Project Management*. Washington, D.C.: Development Project Center.

United States Office of Personnel Management (1982) *Project Management*. Washington, D.C.: Science Training Center.

Van Pelt, M.J.F. et al. (1993) *Ecological Sustainability and Project Appraisal*. Aldershot: Avebury.

Walsh, Graham and Peter Daffern (1990) *Managing Cost Benefit Analysis*. London: Macmillan.

Ward, William A. et al. (1991) *The Economics of Project Analysis*. Washington, D.C.: Economic Development Institute.

Waterston, Albert (1965) *Development Planning: The Lessons of Experience*. Baltimore: Johns Hopkins University Press.

Weiss, John (ed.) (1994) *The Economics of Project Appraisal and the Environment*. Cheltenham: Edward Elgar.

White, L.G. (1991) *Creating Opportunities for Change: Approaches to Managing Development Programs*. Boulder: Lynne Rienner.

Williams, Alan and Emilio Giardina (eds.) (1993) *Efficiency in the Public Sector: The Theory and Practice of Cost Benefit Analysis*. Cheltenham: Edward Elgar.

Wilson, F. (ed.) (1997) *Towards Sustainable Project Development*. Cheltenham: Edward Elgar.

World Bank (1979) *Operations Evaluation*. Washington, D.C.: World Bank.

Wynia, Gary W. (1972) *Politics and Planners: Economic Development Planning in Central America*. Madison: University of Wisconsin Press.

Yaffey, Michael (1992) *Financial Analysis for Development*. London: Routledge.

2
METHODOLOGY

Several research techniques have been used in this volume: secondary analysis, comparative analysis, observational method, and survey method. We have sought to avoid strict operationalism after the natural sciences and to break the single-method mold, and have opted for a strategy of multioperationalism. We believe that the multiple research techniques hedge against the limitation of a single strategy and provide flexibility, thoroughness, realism, variety and richness of data not feasible with a single approach. We have attempted different ways of examining the research object on the ground that pursuing the same object in different ways may lead to greater confidence in its validity.

Secondary Analysis

The first research technique, secondary analysis, involved an intensive research and use of data and evidence from previous studies and documents with a view to studying, regrouping, refining, recombining and analyzing relevant and available materials. The tool provided the researcher with important sources of data in acquiring basic know-how about particular organizations and in examining how projects evolved. Secondary analysis was employed because it allowed for considerable savings in time, money, and personnel.

The search for locating relevant material was instituted, and clearance to study these had to be obtained. Attention had to be paid to the collection, selection, coding, classification, analysis, indexing, retrieval, comparability, accuracy and reporting of secondary data and published works. Access was gained over time to several data sources, each of which yielded different data: university organizations, public and private sector organizations, and funding/technical-assistance agencies.

This technique made use of secondary data, which extended to literature review, archival data, official records, statistical data, and media reports. The literature review included bibliographies, books, journals, monographs, papers, periodicals, reference materials, and published works. Archival data embraced directories, handbooks, parliamentary debates, and yearbooks.

Official records were myriad: blueprints, budgetary estimates, contracts, correspondence, development plans, discussion papers, economic surveys, enterprise accounts, financial statements, forms, legislation, manuals, material and equipment records, memoranda, ministerial surveys, minutes, organization charts, payment certificates, photographs, production census, reports, sketches, staff lists, test results, workflow charts, and work schedules. Of the reports, there were many, e.g. annual reports, consultant reports, commission/committee reports, country reports, inspection reports, progress reports, and project reports.

Statistical data included aggregate census and sample data. Also available for research purposes were media reports comprising editorials, editorial letters, newsreports, notifications, and press releases. A total of 181 items representing the coverage period - late 1960s through late 1990s - was collected. Secondary analysis has used such data essentially in two ways. First, secondary data have been utilized as partial data - data complementing other information and facts assembled in the study. Second, secondary data have been used to validate and check data gathered by the researcher.

Comparative Analysis

In our choice of comparative analysis we have been guided by the observation that management research needs to be based on and tested by systematic comparison. Comparison was carried out in an attempt to make research results additive, to attain greater comparability and generalizability, and to observe some regularities, uniformities and variations in project behavior.

We chose to study a set of development projects financed by the Government of Barbados and external funding agencies and implemented by national executing agencies. We avoided self-selected samples of projects and, instead, put together a small sample of projects on the basis of several criteria. The sampling process involved the compilation of a sampling frame comprising 33 completed public-sector projects with some postcompletion operational experience and visibility, which were developed mainly during the 1970s and represented the seven sectors of agriculture, industry, tourism, infrastructure, education, health and housing. A 21% sample of the 33 projects was obtained, which yielded 7 projects - one project from each of the seven sectors.

We have focused on single-country but intersectoral and interproject comparison. To avoid ethnocentrism, limited crossnational comparisons were attempted, i.e. we employed a *comparative systems* approach as well as a *within-system* approach. To illustrate, we undertook comparison both within and across projects, e.g. comparisons within the sample projects, between sample and other Caribbean projects, and between sample and other overseas projects. We became attentive to not only synchronic but also, to the extent it was feasible, diachronic comparison.

We have employed a set of categories by means of which projects were compared in an effort to underline their uniformities and variations. Projects, for instance, were compared in relation to objectives, budget size, lead time, gestation period, target group, implementation techniques, etc. The cyclicity of projects was examined comparatively, laying stress on the eight distinct phases of the project cycle. Instead of typically treating individual projects seriatim or producing essentially 'parallel' descriptions of project phases, we crosscompared the phases.

Observational Method

To study organizational milieu and behavior in their natural settings over time without controlling them, observational method became desirable as a data-gathering tool, which simultaneously combined various forms, such as perusing published data from the past, finding facts from respondents and informants, and observing directly ongoing processes and behaviors. We used this research strategy because it enabled us to study methodically those aspects and practices of the sample organizations that were not easily available or were part of oral tradition, and to obtain certain data from the field which yielded data with high operational content. An effort was made to be longitudinal in that observations were conducted at several points in time.

We opted for structured, direct and nonparticipant observation in the fieldwork. The research-site personnel were told of the researchers' observational interest and access was sought and gained on that basis. Data were obtained by watching what was happening and by checking what conditions existed at the research sites. We did not go for sampling in this respect; instead, we observed and collected data in relation to organizational milieu and operation. We compiled observational repertoires that directed attention to significant milieu and operational data. What essentially followed was the observation of layout and physical conditions, general flow of work, staff movement, and materials and equipment use. Partly, observation related to whatever behavior was being exhibited by the subjects at the scheduled observation periods. While the milieu data comprised materials on specific features, characteristics and ambience of the study organizations, the operational data were collected on the forms of activities and practices throughout the workdays. Two records were used to register these data, containing numerous entries, the milieu record and the operation record described organizational features and noted activities respectively. Fieldwork embraced site visits, visual checks, coding, categorizing, indexing, counting, recording and informant contacts. Observations were compiled over a period of time during the late 1980s and the early 1990s. Insofar as it was possible, observation was done under conditions that permitted satisfactory results.

With mechanical methods being ruled out, fieldnote was adopted as a form of recording data obtained from observations. The basic tools for recording the data included observationnnaire and the fieldwork log. For observation and recording purposes, checklists were followed, observationnaires were used and fieldnotes were taken. Mnemonic devices were used and recollections were employed. To ensure accuracy, reliability and completeness of observational data, fieldwork was repeated.

Survey Method

Another source of data was probed in the early 1990s by applying the survey method with a view to generating some primary data directly and obtaining useful information that was not available from other sources. Involving four sets of survey, the survey method used the crossectional approach, probability as well as nonprobability sampling and the standardized and scheduled approach incorporating open-ended questions. First, the project-maker survey sought to identify the roles of development projects and to underscore respondent perception of the project process. Secondly, the general-beneficiary survey was an attempt to capture beneficiary reactions to development projects and related concerns. While the operating-agency survey was concerned with personnel of the project-operating agencies, the target-group survey related to specific target groups associated with the sample projects.

We opted for the open-ended question approach because the research content was considered fairly complete, relevant dimensions were deemed less known in the context of Barbados, closed-ended categories are potentially more reactive, exhaustive and mutually exclusive response categories could not be fully anticipated, and concern over exciting pseudoattitudes and imposing falsely structured alternatives was real. The open-ended questions allowed the widest possible exploration of respondent perceptions, enabling each respondent to reveal as much of his experience and inclination as he was willing.

A pretesting phase was initiated to help in the design and layout - especially the flow, structure and length - of the study questionnaire and interview schedules. One mail questionnaire and three interview schedules were drafted, which were based on the objectives to be satisfied for the four groups of respondents. We found it useful to try out those on a small scale. Several pretests were held and pretest responses were examined. The mail questionnaire was pretested in terms of wording, length, clarity, readability, etc. The interview schedules were pretested in relation to the sequence of questions, the avoidance of ambiguity of terms and words, and the identity of questions that did not elicit the intended information. Question wording, phasing and sequencing were carried out gradually through the process of trial and error. For instance, questions were worded keeping in mind such concerns as meaning, ambiguity, leading questions, generalization, unidimensionality, and cushion statements. Sampling design occurred on the basis of what was desirable given the nature of the four surveys and what was possible in view of financial and other resource limitations.

Project-maker Survey

The questionnaire survey, designed to produce a representative crosssection of the project-related policy makers and decision-makers in Barbados, was used on ground of reduced costs, wider accessibility, and greater response time. The survey presented a uniform stimulus to all subjects. The anonymity that accompanied the mail survey could persuade subjects to be open, especially on sensitive matters. The approach to the questionnaire survey was the transmission of a questionnaire, accompanied by a cover letter. The respondent completed the questionnaire and returned it to the researcher through the mail.

We pursued with some combination of different approaches those who did not return the questionnaires after three weeks since mailing. We visited some respondents at their workplaces, reminded them of the questionnaires, and sent a follow-up letter. Callbacks were made on several respondents. Occasionally, the drop-off approach was involved, entailing the hand delivery of a questionnaire to sampling points. There was, however, the time factor, for callbacks prolonged the survey process. Although initially the response level was low, persistence played a major role in the overall response rate of 75% eventually. The reaction of the target population to the survey was generally favorable.

The sampling frame was compiled from multiple sources: pretest material, official records, Barbados Staff List, telephone directory, media reports, and telephone survey. The sampling frame comprised respondents from the following eight specialty areas: policy-makers, project analysts, project managers, civil servants, funding-agency personnel, consulting-agency personnel, contracting-agency personnel, and trade unionists. We drew a sample frame with a population of 120 project-makers. A 50% sample of the project-makers was obtained, which yielded a sample size of 60 project-makers, and of these 45 or 75% responded. We opted for the more common practice in social research, i.e., sampling without replacement.

The sampling frame was drawn with a certain rationale. For instance, policy-makers were those political executives and senior civil servants who enjoy membership of a key national policy-making body, entrusted with coordinating, selecting, prioritizing and monitoring development projects. Project analysts were identified on the basis of the specialized roles they played in the project appraisal process at the organizational levels. Project managers were those who had carried out managerial functions in respect of projects. The identification of civil servants was based on seniority in and leadership of various development-oriented public service organizations.

The funding-agency personnel, representing several regional and international agencies with their missions in Barbados, were the key participants in deciding feasibility and fundability of projects. The consulting-agency personnel were those who worked for organizations specializing in engineering and architectural consultancy, city and town planning and surveying. The contracting-agency personnel enjoyed membership of those organizations which were either specialist contractors or materials suppliers, or both. Trade unionists, being affiliated to Barbados' two larger worker organizations, were those who held senior executive positions.

General-beneficiary, Operating-agency and Target-group Surveys

As an economic rationale, a small and manageable sample was chosen for the three surveys. The sampling type adopted was quota sampling. The relatively small sample size justified the use of quota sampling. As researchers with limited resources, it was not possible to utilize samples that were representative of the population under study. Also, a high-cost probability sample did not suit our purpose, since the aim was to compare various subgroups within the population and to identify and aggregate various responses of the survey groups, and not to describe the distribution of some characteristics among the population. However, an attempt was made to combine the need for accessibility and convenience with consciously avoiding sampling biases, including an effort to build into the sample the type of diversity that would be reasonably representative of the Barbadian respondents.

Having completed the task of drawing a definite number of sampling units from the target population, the interview quota was set up with a view to securing certain information from the sampling units. The type of survey adopted was the interview survey. A motivating reason underlying the three interview surveys was the intention to gain greater rapport with the respondent by first asking nonthreatening questions and then leading to more substantive issues. The three interview surveys enabled the researchers to assist the survey population in grasping the intended meaning of the questions and to probe or inquire about the meaning of the respondents' answers.

For the general-beneficiary survey, the sampling frame was based on the noninstitutional, resident, civilian, adult and male-female population of Barbados according to the population census 1980 (Department of Statistical Services, 1984). The adult population of 161,741 comprised all persons aged 15 years of age and over. It was decided that no more that a 0.1 percent national sample of Barbados could be covered as this would overextend the available resources. Of the adult population of 161, 741, a quota sample of 220 persons was taken, giving a ratio of 1:735 - one interviewee to every 735 persons of adult age. The sample covered all the eleven parishes of the country, with adequate quota controls being established and exercised on residence, sex, age, education, and employment. Of these, 220 or 100% responded.

The spread of the survey participants over all the eleven parishes enabled us to obtain as wide a coverage as possible of both the urban and rural parishes. The sample was selected in this way, because we wanted to ensure reasonable representation in terms of geographical location, age, and sex. We wanted to ensure that the specified characteristics were reflected in the sample. The sample was also crosssectional because it comprised respondents from various occupational backgrounds - homemakers, students, farmers, laborers, artisans, technicians, artists, nurses, teachers, sales representatives, secretaries, clerical personnel, security personnel, civil servants, private-sector employees, clerics, professionals/specialists, the self-employeds, and the unemployeds.

For the operating-agency survey, the elements of the sampling frame were obtained from official contacts, telephone directories, and media reports. Having drawn the sampling frame, we arrived at the population size of 285 operating-agency personnel, representing seven sample agencies, namely, Greenland Agricultural Station, Handicraft Center, Harrison's Cave, Pulverization Plant, Samuel Jackman Prescod Polytechnic, Bridgetown Sewerage Plant, and Housing Maintenance Division. Quota controls were established on sex, age, and work specialization. A sample of 35 was taken, and of these 35 or 100% responded.

For the target-group survey, the elements of the sampling frame were obtained from official contacts, telephone directories, and media reports. Having drawn the sampling frame, we arrived at the population size of 179,823 target-group beneficiaries, representing seven target groups, namely, sheep farmers, craft producers, cave visitors, householders, technical-vocational students, Bridgetown residents/users, and housing tenants. Quota controls were exercised on residence, sex, and age. A sample of 35 was taken, and of these 35 or 100% responded.

Process

The interview process involved dealing with each individual respondent separately. The purpose of the interview was explained to each respondent verbally. Effort was made to make respondents feel free to express views or feelings without sensing any kind of pressure, coercion, threat, reaction, or preference from the interviewer. All information given to the interviewers was held in strictest confidence and was handled in such a way as to prevent recognition of any individual.

The interview could clarify questions the respondents did not understand. When questions were asked, some respondents tended to reply with unclear, incomplete, or irrelevant answers. When that occurred, probing was used by the interviewer to provide stimulus to respondents in an attempt to elicit fuller and clearer responses from them. In each interview questions were posed in the same sequence to minimize the risk of halo effect and interitem contamination. During each interview notes of the responses were taken in as much detail as possible, including key words or phrases.

While the majority of the interviewees demonstrated openness, some were guarded in their response. Occasionally, a respondent talked freely and extensively after an open-ended question, supplying a good deal of information. Certain monitorial and follow-up measures were taken in some cases with regard to abruptly-cancelled or postponed interviews, sudden appointments, interim absence of respondents, sudden illness, the need for official clearance, and the need to curtail the overall survey period. Interviews were held in workplaces as well as residences. The interviews usually lasted between twenty-five and thirty-five minutes. The responses of respondents to the interview situation were generally cooperative, resulting in a high response rate, and a low refusal rate. Interviews were conducted by the researchers and several volunteers.

Supplementary Techniques

A study based on these research techniques could not be considered fully satisfactory, for problems arose and needs remained unmet. Consequently, use had to be made of several supplementary research strategies. Used varyingly during the search process, the tools were routine correspondence, telephone calls, field checks, periodic visits, occasional meetings, extended discussions, technical briefings, direct contacts, brief queries, and focused interviews. The focused interviews, involving several respondents, were carried out during the early 1990s. From time to time, field checks, i.e. direct contacts were made with the sample organizations in order to verify and preserve the factuality of reported material. A series of site visits were initiated and completed. Site visits enabled the researchers to assess the status of the completed projects and to examine their operations at first hand, resulting in two types of data, viz. project and postproject data.

We conducted, in addition, a project organization survey, embracing all the seven Projects under study. Given the nature of this particular survey, a purposive sampling was used in this exercise to obtain caches of data with a view to building and providing database for the Projects. At times, we were forced to employ convenience sampling for the reason that as organizational researchers we found ourselves in a position of using a convenience sample - collecting data from the Projects because they were available at the time - or doing no research whatsoever. We, further, undertook the collection of data via unobtrusive measures, helping us to obtain information without requiring the cooperation or participation of an organization member, retaining the naturalness of the research setting, avoiding any structuring of the situation from which data were being collected and avoiding any intrusion into the social setting being inventoried.

Data-collection and information-gathering took numerous field studies, telephone inquiries, secondary materials search, personal contacts and persuasions and routine correspondence precisely because a great deal of the data and information presented here are not available anywhere in a written form and systematic manner, and whatever is available is dispersed across myriad organizations and jurisdictions. Sometimes, entirely new data were generated, in other cases existing data were collected and used.

The reliability, representativeness and accuracy of data and information were established by repeated checks, rechecks, and counterchecks. Data and information collected relate, for instance, to the Projects' location, physical size, catchment area, target group, customer base, revenue base, sales volume, and so forth. A group of personnel was contacted and consulted, internal documents and published materials were searched, project sites were visited and studied, and other useful sources were tapped.

One of the payoffs of the survey is that the Project-relevant data and information are presented in a capsule, convenient and economical form in one place, facilitating a deeper and wider appreciation of development projects in Barbados, especially what it takes to build, sustain, and transform projects.

Far too frequently, difficulty as well as resistance was experienced in locating, accessing, verifying and acquiring data and information. For reasons of noncooperation and evasion, certain kinds of data were not available. In other instances, confidentiality forestalled the sharing and release of useful information.

General Observations

The collection of data occurred during the 1980s and the 1990s. Time lags have occurred between the collection of data and the subsequent analysis and presentation of the study. The research design features some attributes. The research questions dealt with were derived from a general theoretical context, the data were collected with the strategy of multioperationalism and sampling was utilized to obtain data. It is noteworthy that identifying, locating, accessing, collecting, generating and verifying secondary, comparative, observational and survey data were, to a varying extent, rewarding, challenging, exciting, exhausting, uncertain, problematic, demanding, and frustrating.

The dross rate was not allowed to go high. Throughout the research process, efforts were made to keep the proportion of collected irrelevant data to a total reported data as low as possible. The sociodemographic data, viz. sex, age, education, employment and residence were collected because our review of the research literature and first-hand information suggested that the way in which the survey participants responded could be influenced by the above demographics. Some judgement went into compiling the sampling frames. We recognize that there is possibly a gap between the frame and the population. With the population being highly specialized, no frame was available. We cannot guarantee that the frame is complete in that every element in the population is represented in the frame. However, we are reasonably confident that the frame includes a sufficient portion of the population to provide adequate information about the population.

Development projects belong to a class of organizational activities that is not easy to approach and enter for research purposes. Involvement in the data-collection process taught us that no piece of scientific research is without flaws of one or another kind. We confirm that compromise, adjustment and modification are inherent in the research process. Research enterprises tend to generate a dynamic of their own which can rarely be foreseen in the planning phase. The research process is much more muddled and dialectic than textbooks typically reflect. An operational accommodation between the ideal and the practical emerges forcefully.

Fieldwork Problems

This study, like any other, has its limitations and its share of fieldwork and technical problems. Many and varied challenges, difficulties and uncertainties were encountered in the fieldwork process. These are due partly to constraints in the research setting within which the fieldwork was conducted, partly to limited resources and divided time, and partly to limitations in the research techniques themselves. Our surveys were affected by such factors as the time a respondent had available, his disposition to tell what he knew, the sensitivity of certain issues, sociopolitical conditions in the country at the time, etc. Respondents were willing to cooperate largely to the extent that they felt the research might be useful to the country or that they found the survey enjoyable.

There is very little centralized and easily accessible information about development projects in Barbados. Varied and detailed information and documentation in some instances were not available. Due to the lack of proper records and because of failure to keep records in some order, it was difficult, and sometimes quite impossible, to obtain satisfactory and reliable data and information. We returned repeatedly to field notes to check, test, revise, and extend our analytical framework. Several problems were encountered in conducting research, namely, where to carry out interviews, what type of ambience to create, introduction of the questionnaire, inquisitive onlookers, and anonymity. The statistical material on the sample projects was insufficient. Statistics that were available had gaps which added to the difficulties of measurement.

An achieved sample almost always falls short of the selected one: at a general level, some members of the sample are away from home or work, some refuse to take part, some give runarounds, some evade, some remain suspicious, and some are indifferent. Due to these reasons, it was not possible in our study to obtain a response from all those approached for surveys. Since nonresponse can be a source of bias, we tried to reduce it to a minimum. Some respondents did not fill in questionnaires or grant interviews. In those cases where the respondents stated that they were unwilling to participate in the surveys, reasons were given for nonparticipation, viz., no certainty could be placed in the guarantee of anonymity and confidentiality, official clearance could not be obtained in some instances, and lack of time to take part in the surveys.

Methodological Issues

Secondary analysis became a useful source of information for the reconstruction of the sample projects, yielded a considerable amount of information, aided in the exploration and initial classification of data, resulted in cost and time savings, enhanced the verification process, and served to provide information of a longitudinal nature. The research method moved through several problems, namely, the paucity of project documents, a disjointed picture of the project process, available project information being fragmentary and variable in quality and completeness, and nonrelease and nondisclosure of data. The projects were neither documented and stored at one central location nor indexed and catalogued. The search process was sometimes impeded by dilatory and elusive behavior of some officials. In the absence of complete indexation, crossreferencing, classification and cataloguing, we had to muddle through. Prior official clearance for accessing files was slow and uncertain.

Comparative analysis allowed for comparability, facilitated isomorphism, yielded comparable categories via interproject comparisons, and helped avoid ethnocentrism and parochialism. Problems experienced included locating information and obtaining clearance, project data not presented in a standardized fashion, and lack and paucity of documented reliable data. Having noted that the quest of equivalence cannot be completely solved, we settled for functional equivalence. It is recognized that any comparisons are at best only approximations. We note that every unit of analysis - development projects or whatever - is only selectively comparable to others. We further hope that our sample of development projects is not too small to be reasonably representative of the aggregate project investments in Barbados.

Observational method had the advantage of recording what people did, not just what they said. Observations were made of actual conditions as they really existed at the research sites. It captured part of the natural contexts and real-life situations in which behavior occurred. Some complications were experienced with respect to the difficulties of collecting certain kinds of data - unanticipated consequences due to the presence of an observer, difficulties due to the varied nature of the work, and the difficulty of coding. Other limitations were experienced, i.e. reactivity problems.

For all the four surveys, we opted for open-ended questions. Despite this approach being somewhat time-consuming and variable and having difficulties of codability, comparability and quantification, we found it useful in our research. For the project-maker survey, we selected the questionnaire technique because of the associated advantages of being less expensive, having easier accessibility, and greater response time. A number of survey participants proved to be prompt, helpful, and responsive. For the general-beneficiary, operating-agency and target-group surveys, quota sampling was chosen on the grounds of economy, cost, time, practicality, substitutability, convenience, and speed. It had the additional advantages of higher response rate, greater flexibility, low cost of data collection, ready accessibility, and quick results. Besides, with quota sampling we could largely avoid the problem of refusals, evasions, callbacks, or unavailability. The intended sample was covered; the sampling form ensured that respondents could easily be replaced.

With the use of nonprobability sampling, we are aware that the results of the three surveys do not allow us to generalize beyond the sample. We remain convinced, nonetheless, that the results offer some insights into the perceptions and belief systems of the surveyed groups. The findings also present a basis on which trends and patterns among the projects in Barbados may be compared with those of the projects elsewhere. Such an exercise may generate tentatively a number of hypotheses which serve as a basis for further research.

As to the project-maker survey, cost consideration determined the limitations of the sample size. Doubts were raised about the difficulty in maintaining confidentiality in a small society. Some appeared cooperative, but questionnaires were not returned; others did return but failed to answer one or more of the questions. Nonresponse occurred despite repeated contacts and communication. Some expressed reluctance to take part in the survey, some refused claiming lack of expertise, some denied on account of being busy, and some seemed to indicate that the questionnaire was a threat to anonymity and an intrusion into set schedules.

As for the general-beneficiary, operating-agency and target-group surveys, interviews had to be limited in duration, politically nonsensitive, and personally nonthreatening. Certain limitations were experienced, i.e. courtesy bias and evaluation apprehension. Another snag encountered in the field was the semantic problem of meaning. It turned out, somewhat to our surprise, that there were words, which some respondents had some difficulty in interpreting, in spite of the fact that we carried out a pretest of the instrument. Concepts, such as 'cost' , for example, appeared to be unclear. Some respondents seemed to consider certain questions as somewhat touchy and, consequently, preferred not to respond to those queries.

Summary

The study questionnaire and the interview schedules are produced in their entirety in the appendix. The primary as well as the secondary data collected for this study with the aid of several research techniques were subsequently processed, analyzed, and presented. Research, as we find, is a process of progressive focusing and funneling. As data and information were collected, we could see more and more clearly the factors that brought the events into a meaningful pattern. We make no claim, therefore, to be presenting a decisive work on development projects in Barbados. Rather, we view this study as an incremental step toward linking the project setting with the analysis of individual project behavior, and toward the utilization of systematic data collection and analysis in the contemporary Caribbean.

REFERENCE

Department of Statistical Services (1984) *Population Census 1980*. St. Michael, Barbados: Department of Statistical Services.

3
PROJECT SETTING

Some discussions of development projects have tended to take place in a theoretical vacuum. Development projects are discussed as if they were autonomous sets of organizational responses unrelated to the ongoing social, political, economic and technological realities. Some model-building efforts, however, are in evidence, e.g. the United Nations (1969), Baum (1970), Rondinelli (1977) and Goodman and Love (1979). Others include Bunker (1972), Pressman and Wildavsky (1973), Smith (1973), van Meter and van Horn (1975), Williams (1975), Bardach (1977), Dunsire (1978), Honadle and Klauss (1979), Grindle (1980), Bridger (1986), Honadle (1991), Kirkpatrick (1991), Austin (1992), European Community (1992), MacArthur (1993), and van Pelt (1993). These works, nevertheless, are limited by their preoccupation with either the project cycle or the implementation process. The earlier research had not focused on the entire project process.

Project-setting Model

We prefer to approach projects with the aid of a theoretical context and a model. Our theoretical context views the project as an open sociotechnical entity composed of a number of components in constant interaction with its overall societal framework. We lay out an eight-element schematic model of development project called a project-setting model, which is a composite of elements, processes and interactions. The model provides a conceptual and analytical framework around which a set of relationships are developed. It illustrates the value of an orderly, explicit and systematic approach, its logic follows the deductive-inductive sequence, and it implies a progression of interdependent decisions. Characterized by a conversion process, the model is an adaptive one in that it attempts to adjust to contingencies. Also a learning model, it endows the framework with sufficient flexibility and capacity to react to new and unpredictable conditions.

The project setting is defined as a specific matrix of interrelated elements and activities. As an open system, it interacts with its environment; in turn, the manifold elements within the internal and external environment make an impact on the setting. The setting as a whole is made up of several interacting elements, transacting with its environment, receiving inputs and giving out outputs to the environment in order to ensure maintenance and unfolding. Without inputs the setting ceases to function; without outputs one cannot identify the work done within the setting. This dynamism seeks a congruence between the project setting and the environment and between the environment and the interacting elements. Development projects are examined within an interactive setting so that they can be appreciated holistically.

The project setting is not only complex, interactive, interdependent and constrained by time but also involves different functional groups, manifold resources and various technologies, with a set of principles and practices for gearing up, meeting goals and winding down. An appreciation of the setting allows for planning projects as integrated sets of activities so that projects are implemented purposefully and can remain effective operationally. Project success rests in many ways on the overall project setting within which the project takes place. A project is driven by its setting-the larger environment - from which it draws its resource and support.

Included in the model are such elements as development projects, the project cycle, the appraisal process, the implementation process, management capability, output, feedback, and environment. Development projects introduce ideas, innovations, goals or intentions into the setting. A conversion process, the project cycle transforms ideas or assumptions into reality. The appraisal process ensures the examination of alternatives. The implementation process manages the actual delivery of intentions. Management capability undergirds the general as well as specific capacity of the delivery system, including executing agencies. Output is the end-product of transforming inputs into goods and services. It is what is actually delivered to clients. Produced by project and its ancillary activities, output would have not been produced in the absence of project. Output from a project creates an impact on society, groups and individuals (Asian Development Bank, 1984; Attwood, 1988; Baum and Tolbert, 1985; Bridger and Winpenny, 1983; Brinkerhoff and Garcia-Zamor, 1986;

Bryant and White, 1980; Caribbean Development Bank, 1986; Chambers, 1974; Chenery, 1974; Cleland and King, 1968; Dupriez, 1979; FitzGerald, 1978; Gittinger, 1972; Goodman and Love, 1979; Harrison, 1981; Hirschman, 1967; Honadle and Klauss, 1979; Howe and Richards, 1984; Irvin, 1975; Kelly, 1982; Khan, 1982, 1997; Lock, 1968; Londero, 1996; MacArthur and Weiss, 1993; Meredith and Mantel, 1985; Morss and Gow, 1985; Project Planning Center for Developing Countries, 1982; Roman, 1986; Rondinelli, 1977; Stallworthy and Kharbanda, 1983; Taylor and Watling, 1973; United Nations, 1993; Waterston, 1965).

Through the feedback process, output influences input, permitting the adjustment of input and output to accomplish project objectives. It provides the flow of information and ensures remedial or corrective action. The function of feedback is to act on an identifier. It identifies the extent to which output deviates from some present standard or performance measure (Asian Development Bank, 1984; Birgegard, 1975; Brinkerhoff and Garcia-Zamor, 1986; Bryant and White, 1980; Cernea, 1991; Chambers and Belshaw, 1973, 1974; Dupriez, 1979; Gitelson, 1972; Goodman and Love, 1979; Graham, 1989; Gran, 1983; Hirschman, 1984; Irvin, 1975; Khan, 1974; Londero, 1996; Murphy, 1974; Oakley, 1991; Organization for Economic Cooperation and Development, 1989; Paul, 1982; Rondinelli, 1976, 1978, 1979, 1979; Salmen, 1987; Stallworthy and Kharbanda, 1983; United States Agency for International Development, 1975; Waterston, 1965; World Bank, 1983).

A development project operates in an environment (Asian Development Bank, 1984; Attwood, 1988; Baum and Tolbert, 1985; Brigegard, 1975; Bridger and Winpenny, 1983; Bryant and White, 1980; Chenery, 1974; Dupriez, 1979; FitzGerald, 1978; Garcia-Zamor, 1977; Goodman and Love, 1979, 1980; Hirschman, 1963, 1984; Honadle and Klauss, 1979; Howe and Richards, 1984; Kelley, 1982; Khan, 1976, 1978, 1982, 1987, 1994, 1996; Kirkpatrick, 1991; Mills, 1973; Morss, 1976; Murphy, 1983; Radosevich and Taylor, 1974; Riggs, 1961; Rondinelli, , 1976, 1976, 1976, 1976, 1977, 1978, 1979, 1979; Schmidt, 1990; United States Agency for International Development, 1975; Waterston, 1965; Wynia, 1972; Zeldman, 1980). Environment is both a task environment - immediate and operational - and a contextual environment - remote and general. A project is neither conceived and developed in a vacuum nor does it operate in isolation. Projects should not be considered in seclusion, as FitzGerald notes (1978: xii), but as part of an overall sectoral program. It represents a milieu, an interaction of interests, and a mix of resources. A vital part of its rationale involves obtaining resources from the environment, providing services and functions and responding to influences. Its output must be acceptable to the environment. It is essential to consider the environment or context in which project action is pursued.

To illustrate, the project process is significantly influenced by some of the dominant ideas and orientations, viz. state system, political type, regime type, production relations, power/authority type, institutional orientation, cultural practice, and legal-judicial system. The same is true of economy type, civic culture, management system, interest-aggregating mode, conflict-resolving mode, market-operation type, proprietary relations, resource-distribution type, and others.

Figure I
Schematic Model of the Project Setting

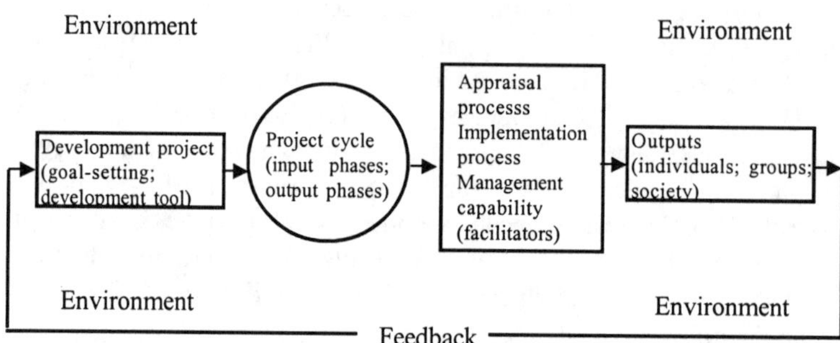

We are aware that models are nearly always tentative; they cannot claim finality. We are also mindful that models involve a process of abstraction, selection, simplification, and generality. One must not lose sight of the fact that a model is only a model. Perfection, even if it could be achieved, would be so complex as to be useless. It is recognized in our model that virtually all aspects of the real world are subject to various degrees of instability and uncertainty. The environment, in which a project becomes and remains operational, is dynamic, and it is this fact - that the environment in which one has to live and plan is ever changing - that creates uncertainty.

Development Project

Project management is old in history, i.e. the Egyptian pyramids, the Tower of Babel, the Roman aqueducts, the Great Wall of China, and so forth. They are current evidence that projects of tremendous scope -

employing thousands of people - were undertaken much before modern times. In recent years, project characterized work which took place in water resource development in the United States in the 1930s. The Manhattan project during the Second World War was another example. In the 1950s and 1960s research on the theory of public investment decisions grew rapidly. With the use of project being intensified in public and private sectors, service and product-based organizations and bilateral as well as multilateral funding agencies, the adoption of the project approach, as evidenced, inter alia, by the Apollo, Hubble and Eurotunnel projects, has been influenced by rapid technological advancements, changing industrial complexes, and critical lead times.

The development of the project concept owes to the fact that the traditional forms of organization and management do not ordinarily carry out project operations effectively. To be able to respond to the special characteristics of projects and the problems caused by them, lateral coordination and a central technical and managerial interface become necessary. The conceptual basis of development projects is laid down by researchers spanning several decades (Abouchar, 1985; Ahmed, 1975; Attwood, 1988; Baumgartner, 1963, 1979; Bridger and Winpenny, 1983; Chambers, 1978; Choldin, 1969; Cleland, 1967; Cleland and King, 1968; de Vries, 1971; Esman, 1972; Garegziabher, 1975; Gemmil and Wileman, 1970; Goodman and Love, 1979, 1980; Harrison, 1981; Hirschman, 1963,1967; Honadle and Klauss, 1979; Kast and Rosenszwig, 1963; Kelley, 1982; Khan, 1976, 1977, 1978, 1982, 1990, 1997; Kirkpatrick, 1991; Lewis, 1968; Lock, 1968, 1977; Lowi, 1972; MacArthur, 1988; Meredith and Mantel, 1985; Montgomery, 1974; Radosevich and Rondinelli, 1974; Reeser, 1979; Roman, 1986; Rondinelli, 1976, 1976, 1976, 1976, 1976, 1977, 1977, 1977, 1977, 1978, 1978, 1979, 1979, 1981, 1981, 1982, 1983, 1983; Schmidt, 1990; Silverman, 1973; Spulber and Horowitz, 1976; Stallworthy and Kharbanda, 1983; Taylor and Watling, 1970, 1973; Tinbergen, 1964, 1966, 1967; United Nations, 1958, 1971; Weiss et al., 1976, 1977; White, 1991; Wynia, 1972).

The objectives of projects are to attain certain parameters, such as growth, efficacy, and equity. Concomitant objects are to generate employment, achieve self-reliance, satisfy merit wants, generate foreign exchange, and increase trade efficiency. Few activities are more crucial to accelerating the pace of economic and social progress in poor countries than effective planning and implementation of development projects. The importance of projects in development activity differs from country to country (United Nations, 1969: 385; 1971: 71-72). In many countries, projects are used for the purpose of obtaining external funding. In most countries, a large part of the development efforts is handled by existing organizations as part of their normal work, while only special development efforts are put on a project basis. Certain major activities are put on a project basis to achieve greater impact, better results, quicker action and faster pace. The project approach is useful in meeting the demands of complexity, size, interdependence, targetgroup, technological change, regulation, and development.

Definitions

Development projects have been defined and delineated in a variety of ways. A project is a tool for the production of specific goods or services (United Nations, 1958); the heart of development planning consists of projects (Waterston, 1965: 88); a project is an input of production factors with the consequence of obtaining products (Tinbergen, 1966:2); a project is a special kind of investment, connoting purposefulness, size, location, etc. (Hirschman, 1967: 1); it is a confirmation of human and nonhuman resources pulled together to achieve a purpose (Cleland and King, 1968: 184); and the task of a project is to provide the best possible solutions to the problems confronted (Lewis, 1968: 13).

The United Nations (1969:205) identified a project as the most concrete step in the planning process; a project is the smallest unit of activity that can be separately planned, analyzed, and managed (Solomon, 1970:496); projects are the 'cutting edge' of development (Gittinger, 1972:1); it is a group of activities with a starting point, a completion point and a need for central expertise (Taylor and Watling, 1973:3); it is a design for investing resources which can be analyzed and evaluated as an independent unit (Little and Mirrlees, 1974:3); and projects, as crucial components of development activity, translate plans into action (Rondinelli, 1977:1).

Still other definitional exercises are in currency. Lock (1977: xi) points out that a project is a single, nonrepetitive and risky enterprise, undertaken to achieve results; every development project contains an implicit or explicit statement about social change (Cochrane, 1979:73); a project can be seen as a sequence of intended changes (Honadle and Klauss 1979:13-16); projects are the 'building blocks' of development (Goodman and Love, 1980:7); a project is a nonroutine, nonrepetitive and one-off activity (Harrison, 1981:1); and a project is an interaction that addresses a problem (Bryant and White, 1982:110). What emerges from all these delineations is that a project is an entity which produces outputs from inputs within a time limit and a cost schedule. It is an identifiable development initiative, the effects of which can be distinguished from other ongoing activities. It consists of several elements: managerial action, analytical method, advocacy role, communication pattern, deliberative and determinate action, perceived course, and linkage pattern.

Types

Hirschman (1967:87-88) makes a distinction between site-bound and footloose projects. Site-bound investments consist most typically of the exploitation of some natural resource, such as harbors. Footloose projects are those whose location is not improved by some natural forces but determined in general terms by the community need for the service that is to be provided, such as schools. One may classify types of projects as being distributive, redistributive and regulative (Lowi, 1972). Different kinds of projects tend to evoke different sets of participants and level of intensity according to the stakes presented by the project. Redistributive projects are harder to implement than distributive ones. The success of regulative projects may often rest on the extent to which they have redistributive consequences. Montgomery (1974) refers to three types of projects, namely, pilot, demonstration, and diffusion projects.

A sequence of project types, with each kind of project servicing an important function, includes experimental, pilot, demonstration, and production projects (Radosevich and Rondinelli, 1974; Weiss, Waterston and Wilson, 1976; Rondinelli, 1979). Experimental projects have the purpose of defining problems in new ways and of assessing alternative solutions. Pilot projects build on the lessons gained from experimental projects. Demonstration projects are intended to exhibit new techniques and approaches and to diffuse practices which promise wider applicability. Finally, production projects require entrepreneurship and need to work with multiple organizations to achieve production-oriented goals. Spulber and Horowitz (1976:188) distinguish between shiftable and nonshiftable projects. The former can be undertaken in several different areas, the latter must be sited in a particular area. One other typology of project involves service-delivery or input-delivery project and problem-solving project (Weiss, Waterston and Wilson, 1977:144).

Features

Certain features are known to characterize development projects.

Projects may be regarded as segments of an integrated plan of socioeconomic development or as individually conceived exercises for the achievement of specific purposes (United Nations, 1969:383-85; 1971:71-72). A project may be large or small, limited or comprehensive, capital or labor-intensive, production or problem-oriented. It may be limited to a specific sector or it may cut across a number of sectors. A project emphasizes more immediate rather than very remote goals. A sense of urgency is a major impetus for a project. A project is action-oriented in that it marshals resources and designs methods to achieve specific goals. To similar effect, Smith postulates (1973:197-209) that projects induce deliberate action in a society to establish new transaction patterns or change established patterns.

The substance of a project is nonrepetitive. Projects frequently entail a certain degree of uncertainty about what is likely to happen, e.g. an increased implementation cost, a stretchout in implementation time, a fall in price, or an error in output estimates. Uncertainty subsumes the estimates of cost, demand, shadow prices, consumer surplus, and externalities. Other project decisions too - investment size, implementation time, operating cost, discount rate, project lifespan, etc. - are subject to an uncertain future.

Usually, a project requires a special management mode for the achievement of its specific objective. The special modality may involve the creation of a new organizational structure, a new combination of existing agencies and substantial reform of existing organizations and management. Project activities are characterized by strong interdependencies among them (Cleland and King, 1968:199). Separate but interrelated and interdependent activities must be completed to achieve the objectives for which the project was instituted.

A development project has a clear beginning, a finite task, a definite work schedule, considerable procedural latitude and an orderly specified end, which is in contrast to the all-purpose continuous-process operation. Once the objective has been achieved and the work is accomplished, the project is disbanded. Projects are also complex organizationally, technically and financially. Due to this complexity, a central technical and managerial interface is in place.

Projects, when aimed at bringing about changes in client behavior, involve risks. Gebregziabher (1975:65) observes that building a project is never a self-executing or self-fulfilling process. The risks can stem from several factors: adoption of priorities or practices which differ from those of the environment, technical approaches which are too alien to the environment, excessive pressure from funding or technical-assistance agencies which do not know enough about the constraints of the environment, and inadequate communication between project-makers and beneficiary groups. Taylor and Watling (1973:11, 35-36) note that almost anything that leads to complexity in a project also leads to risk. Development projects are time-critical as well as time-bound. The rigor and specificity of deadlines, timetables and schedules are conspicuous in project activities (Hirschman, 1967: 95-101).

There is evidence that the use of project concept has helped to advance innovation within organizations. Innovation comes about because an idea is born in which the relevant resource groups have faith and are committed to it. The openness, the advocacy, the autonomy, the freedom of expression and the need to demonstrate effectiveness all seem to be conducive to the creativity necessary to innovate. As Rondinelli notes (1976:216), projects diffuse the benefits of entrepreneurship and innovative change. Organizationally, projects are highly distinctive. They are intensely goal-oriented, temporary, in constant change, and cut across the traditional functional structures. They follow a life cycle of change segments that involve progressing through markedly different phases of work.

All this notwithstanding and despite all the novelty, glamor and speed, projects are work systems. In each phase of the project process a group of people collaborate to form a work organization which - like any other - has characteristic problems of planning, structure, leadership, motivation and control in the pursuit of goal management.

Development Tool

Project is a tool of development activity, making a significant contribution to the development process. The increasing participation of the public sector in socioeconomic activities - involving the allocation and distribution of public resources - is meant to provide goods and services which are not supplied by the market, or to attempt to alleviate inefficiencies and inequalities which are caused by market failures. This participation has resulted in an increase in the number of public sector operations.

It is the project that translates plans into action - converting overall planning into tangible action programs. In the absence of projects, as noted by the United Nations (1971:74), planning tends to remain too general and aggregative. The gains and experiences of projects, the new capabilities, expertise and accents these introduce and the interorganizational communications these sometimes engender make a substantial impact on the development process. The process of project definition, project selection, priority-setting and target-setting through country programming, mission reconnaissance, sector studies and preinvestment analysis have exerted some beneficial pressure on the entire range of project activities.

By direct investment in the public sector, governments use projects as a tool of development action. If a government is unable to secure a desired distribution of income through taxation, it can use the allocation of investment resources as an alternative method of redistributing income. Likewise, a government may wish to use development projects as a means of increasing savings, raising consumption and standard of living, expanding employment, reducing dependence and developing self-reliance, and satisfying merit wants.

Projects are at the crux of the development process; projects are a critical means of achieving development (Rondinelli, 1976:215-16). Squire and van der Tak (1975:19) confirm that projects increase the supply of outputs. Without projects, the supply of outputs to the rest of the country would have been different. Some projects are aimed at bringing about changes in the level or quality of output or in the pattern of input use. Projects contribute to the integration of markets by linking productive activities, providing the organization and technology for transferring raw materials into socially and economically useful goods and services, and establishing the sociophysical infrastructure necessary to increase exchange among organizations and areas. Projects can increase the factor endowments through mobilization, acquisition, transformation, and utilization of resources.

As vehicles for internal development assistance and investment, projects channel the flow of external capital, mobilize scarce national resources and allocate them among competing needs and opportunities. Projects are a vehicle of prioritizing, identifying, selecting and mobilizing resources of a country; they channel resources in directions that may activate desirable goals. They are essential links between strategic planning and task-level management. Projects emphasize substantial management capability - the capability to mobilize and use a wider variety of physical, human and financial inputs, to establish and manage executing agencies, and to design and maintain operational systems for controlling and evaluating project results (Rondinelli, 1977: vii).

In a broader context, projects have become in many developing countries vehicles for social change. As part of larger programs, they can create the capacity for ameliorating serious problems that obstruct growth and delay progress. The outputs of completed projects - institutionalized in permanent organizations - expand productive capacity, increase problem-solving and management capabilities, and add to the critically low stock of management talent available to developing societies. Hirschman (1967:160) observes that projects have a variety of subtle and powerful effects from the acquisition of new skills to greater readiness to produce for the market or serve the community. The project approach has been and can be used to deal with organizational resistance to change. A development project presents organizations with a potential source of new resources. Organization is an important task in the project-building process (Goodman and Love, 1980:125). For instance, new organizations are established and strengthened, operating procedures are developed and standardized, executive capacity is enhanced and consolidated, resources are mobilized and deployed, and ongoing and critical support is enlisted.

Project efficacy, however, need not cause anyone to forget multiple nonoutput and negative effects. Injection of resources via a project alone is insufficient and unpredictable in its ultimate development impact. Few appreciate a project as an interrelated set of purposeful activities and few plan and implement projects within an integrated management framework. Among the negative effects cited are the incidence of the unknown, uncertain and hazardous, the ignorance of ignorance, uncertainties and difficulties, new or heightened social tension, fresh opportunities for spread of corruption (Hirschman, 1967:15,35,160), loss of resources, unsolved socioeconomic problems, dissipation of opportunities for accelerated development, dashing of beneficiary hopes (Rondinelli, 1977:21), the nonrepetitive short-term nature of projects presenting special difficulties in decision-making (Goodman and Love, 1979:20), the arousal of interpersonal problems and conflicts (Harrison, 1981:10), varied attendant costs (Taylor and Watling, 1973:20-21), and duplication, corner-cutting, we-they divisiveness and projectitis (Meredith and Mantle, 1985:100-101).

Project Cycle

Several accounts of the project process are available, e.g. pyramidal, reticular, cyclical and linear. The accounts contain assumptions about the number and ordering of the phases, their characteristics and their interrelations. Some accounts assume linearity - movement begins at the first phase and develops to the last. Other accounts speak of cycles, so that movement through the process is not linear but circular and cyclical. Still others conceive of episodic movement, each exercise beginning at operating levels, working its way up to top levels and then back down again. Alternatively, the project begins with decision and moves to implementation, but then back through reappraisal to decision again, presumably on a succeeding cycle.

Current practice and research lay stress on a multiple-phase sequential project cycle (Awani, 1983; Barndt, 1977; Baum, 1970, 1978, 1982; Burch, 1979; Birgegard, 1975; de Vries, 1971; Eggers, 1992; European Community, 1992; Goodman and Love, 1977, 1979, 1980; Harrison, 1981; Hirschman, 1967; Hogwood and Gunn, 1984; Honadle and Klauss, 1979; Kelley, 1982; Kelman, 1984; Khan, 1976, 1978, 1989, 1991, 1994; Kirkpatrick, 1991; Meridith and Mantel, 1985; Morris, 1982; Noorbaksh, 1989; Olivares, 1979; Roman, 1986; Rondinelli, 1976, 1976, 1976, 1977, 1977, 1978; Rosenthal, 1982; Thamhain and Wilemon, 1975; United Nations Industrial Development Organization, 1971; Waterston, 1965). The project cycle is common to all projects. Baum (1970:3) notes that a project involves a continuous and self-sustaining cycle of activity, which runs through several phases. There is an underlying unity of process that is the same in all projects, even though each one is different (Goodman and Love, 1979: 2,7). Projects have a characteristic evolutionary pattern and a distinct life cycle (Harrison, 1981:48). The work of the cycle follows an institutional-strategic-tactical sequence (Morris, 1982: 156-57). Like organic entities, projects have a life cycle (Meredith and Mantel, 1985: 4). The project cycle is a flexible model or a conceptual tool/framework. Projects follow a process which can be construed as a cycle because one phase normally leads to the next, the terminal point of one phase is often the initial part of a new one, and feedback to an earlier phase is not only possible but necessary. The reason this is considered a cycle, Baum suggests (1970: 3), is due to the fact that each phase not only grows out of the preceding ones, but leads to the subsequent ones.

Features

The cycle, comprising several phases which interlock with each other, is a continuing, reiterative process, not a discrete event. The project cycle has a number of distinctive features. It suggests interdependence, integratedness, regularity, continuity, orderliness, self-sustenance, and repeatability. The phases are distinct; they are not separate per se but integral parts of the project cycle. The phases are overlapping and interdependent rather than discrete. Phasing in and phasing out of resources is a process that occurs throughout the project cycle. Several parallel activities can take place within each phase and overlap into the succeeding phase. Each phase is dependent on and influenced by the others. The phases are related from back to front as well as from front to back (Pressman and Wildavsky, 1973: xxi). A continual feedback and dependency relation exists among the phases. The strength and integrity of the earlier phases largely determines the ultimate performance of the subsequent phases. Dynamic interfaces between phases are real and important.

The phases of the cycle are different as well; the interphases between the phases act as checkpoints in the project process (Morris, 1982: 156-57). Each phase tends to be somewhat different from the others in mission, size, technology, scale and rate of change. These differences create distinctive characteristics of work, behavior, direction, and control.

Usefulness/Caution

It is useful to have a framework like the project cycle within which development project may be viewed. The cycle is useful in analyzing how well the various phases and tasks are done, outline what is expected in the project, assess actual performance, highlight weaknesses in the phases, remove snags and avoid unnecessary delay. An analysis of performance can indicate whether or not a weakness during one phase can cause difficulties in the other phases. The project cycle is helpful for several other reasons (United Nations, 1969: 384-402; 1971: 88; Rondinelli, 1977: 5-6). First, the cycle provides an overview of tasks performed by a diversity of organizations, each considered essential to a project's success. A second reason for using the cycle as an ordering framework is the potential value of seeing the complexity of the entire process in its integrated totality. Third, it is useful to visualize the phases of the cycle in terms of links in a chain and to think of project management as a means for making these links of equal strength. Finally, the cycle as an organizing framework helps one to quickly identify and remedy some common and recurring problems and some unique ones at each phase of the cycle.

There are, however, certain caveats. Project cycle is not unique; there are cycles to life, season, ecology, policy, program, business activity, etc. Unlike many cycles observed in nature, project cycles are not uniform in frequency, dimension, or duration. The entire project process seldom takes place within a single institution. A participant or organization may be involved in one or several phases. The project cycle is an ideal model; not every project conforms exactly to it nor all projects go through all phases. Some projects may not proceed beyond the first phase. The project cycle should not be viewed as something mechanical and rigid. The application of the cycle stresses the need for judgement, selection and flexibility.

The phases are not necessarily sequential, i.e. the sequence in which the phases are activated varies, and several, if not all, phases may be activated simultaneously. Some of these may take place at the same time in parallel or in a different order, nor are all of these necessarily required. A smooth sequence is rarely observed, for things move less tidily in the typical course of a project. Nor does a phase go through such a cycle only once. Constant reviewing, monitoring and checking are required, with appropriate reassessment and modification.

The practical project process does not follow the neat and tidy logic of the project cycle model. It is not usually possible to draw a neat line between one phase and the next. The phases are not completely self-contained. The project process frequently loops between phases - for example, conception and formulation - as the project progresses. Crosswalks to other phases are noteworthy. Some phases - for example, appraisal, implementation and evaluation - are potentially relevant to more than one phase. The phases are not exclusively conceptual, formulative, analytical or implementational by nature. Decomposing the project phases under actual field conditions is difficult.

The project cycle seldom proceeds smoothly. Objectives may be obscure, in conflict, or difficult to clarify and quantify. None of the implementation measures may be adequate to reach the objective. A particular design may be unattainable, or the policy-makers may shift their emphasis. One pass through the cycle is usually not enough and it is necessary to recycle, i.e. go through the various phases until an alternative is chosen.

Project Phases

A multiple-phase project cycle is commonly accepted. As identified by various analysts, the number of phases of the cycle varies, e.g. 4 phases (Baum, 1970: 3) 12 phases (Rondinelli, 1977: 5), 4 phases (Goodman and Love, 1979: 1-4; 1980:7-9), 6 phases (Harrison, 1981: 48), 4 phases

(Morris, 1982: 155-57), and 7 phases (Stallworthy and Kharbanda, 1983: 26). For our purposes (United Nations, 1969: 386: 1971: 73), a project comprises eight phases, namely, conception, formulation, appraisal, approval, implementation, reporting, termination and evaluation. It is possible to place these eight phases in two overriding phases: the input phase - conception, formulation, appraisal and approval - and output phases - implementation, reporting, termination and evaluation.

Conception is the phase where a need has been identified and an idea has been recognized (King, 1967: 4; Baum, 1970: 3-5; United Nations, 1971: 73; Weiss et al., 1976, 1977; Rondinelli, 1977: 9-10; Goodman and Love, 1980: 58; UNIDO, 1980:10). It is meant to demonstrate that worthwhile ideas or a profitable investment potential exists and that it can be realized within the general development framework of the country. The impetus for project ideas may come from multiple sources, e.g., annual plan, executive organizations, legislative bodies, political parties, political leaders, specialized institutions, private enterprises, bilateral multilateral agencies, nongovernmental organizations, and civic groups. Project ideas may also arise from country experience, market and special studies, needs surveys, sectoral analyses, export possibilities, import schedules, internal resources, demand patterns, technology studies, development literature, reconnaissance missions, and external pressures. Rondinelli (1977:9) confirms that international assistance agencies have assumed a role in project identification, viz. the UNDP through country programing and preinvestment studies, the IBRD through economic analysis, sectoral studies, reconnaissance missions and needs surveys, and the USAID through development assistance programs and sector analyses. Most projects originate in existing organizations, including the central planning agency. Normally, an existing agency adopts and processes the idea to bring the life-cycle of a project. In exceptional cases, a special committee, task force or working party may be formed to consider an idea.

Formulation (Baum, 1970: 6; United Nations, 1971: 76-77; Rondinelli, 1977: 11; Weiss et al., 1977: 13, 114-16; Goodman and Love, 1980: 11, 61-74) means developing a plan, method or prescription. The activities in this phase are by nature research, review, projection and selection types of task. Formulation can be integrative or sequential, comprehensive or segmented, systematic or unsystematic, and projective or reactive. The styles of formulation can be either routine or analogous, or creative. The project idea has to be spelled out in greater detail and specific terms, e.g. conducting feasibility studies, including preliminary design, technical description and preliminary assessment of socioeconomic and financial worth. Formulation embraces establishing goals, linking with other plans and sectors, determining the preconditions for project success, identifying potential funding sources, tentatively approaching potential beneficiaries, and working out information on cost, location, inputs, etc. As regards the design task, improving design involves exploring alternatives, identifying strategies for maximizing objectives, and tapping alternative measures.

Appraisal is an ex ante analysis of the effect of a determined course of action (Baum, 1970: 10-12; United Nations, 1971: 80; Rondinelli, 1977: 13; Weiss et al., 1977: 104; Goodman and Love, 1980: 14). It is concerned with the allocation of resources to achieve the best, the maximum, or the most effective production of goods and services. The core of appraisal is identifying the quality, quantity and timing of physical inputs and outputs to compute the value of costs and benefits, and measuring costs and benefits of the project to facilitate its comparison with alternative projects. Appraisal involves the use of selection criteria. Selection is based on a comprehensive examination of a project, e.g. technical, economic, financial, social, organizational and political aspects. The test is that a project emerges from the process of choice among alternatives as offering the best claim on scarce resources.

To illustrate, technical appraisal encompasses physical-planning, architectural, engineering and other investigative inputs. While economic appraisal is used to determine the desirability of carrying out the project from the standpoint of economic efficiency, financial appraisal is concerned with estimating the return on investment, ascertaining financial viability, and verifying costs, returns and timing of returns. Social appraisal examines a project's likely social impact and social factors in the environment bolstering or hindering goal-achievement. Organizational appraisal is concerned with the adequacy of the management to implement and run a project on completion and with the sufficiency of staffing at all levels of the organization. Finally, political appraisal relates to assessing political support for project at various levels, assessing a project's likely political impact and identifying the political factors in the environment. In addition, negotiations are made during this phase to secure formal agreement from various project participants as to the projects' objectives, content, scope, activities, outputs, terms of lending, loan provisions, tendering, etc.

Approval (United Nations, 1971: 80-81; Goodman and Love, 1980: 111-12) is secured from competent authorities at different times and at different levels. At this phase, a project may be approved, delayed, changed, modified, or scaled down. The phase involves obtaining approval for loan agreements, funding authorization, counterpart financing, legal endorsement, legislative authorization, and institutional support. Approval depends on the comparative merits of the venture in competition with other possible alternatives. The major test of the soundness of approval is the extent to which it provides for a rational choice between sound alternatives.

The purpose of implementation is to ensure that a project is executed as planned, or modified in the light of changing conditions (Baum, 1970: 12; United Nations, 1971: 81-84; Rondinelli, 1977: 14-16; Goodman and Love, 1980: 117-121). Implementation may be viewed as a process of interaction between goal-setting and goal-achieving actions. Speedy and effective implementation being a basic criterion, the phase involves site preparation, goods and services procurement, building construction, facility installation, ancillary-service construction and equipment creation and installation in accordance with schedules. The early designation or appointment of a project manager is useful for organization-building and implementation. An important task is to develop a full organization and management plan, including scheduling, budgeting, staffing, continuous assessment, reporting, contingency planning and termination.

Reporting (Baum, 1970: 12; United Nations, 1971:85; Rondinelli, 1977:15; Weiss et al., 1977: 121; Harrison, 1981: 227) embraces information-gathering, documentation, review, and status-reporting. The purposes are to ensure control, take necessary action, and communicate relevant information to contact points. Periodic and timely reporting is essential for the successful realization of a project. Reports are needed to ensure remedial and corrective action, ensure communication flow to facilitate decisions and operations, enforce accountability for resources and performance, enforce sound financial management by ensuring permissible expenditure rate and spending limits, and provide data to assist in control, analyses and planning.

Termination (United Nations, 1971: 86-87; Rondinelli, 1977:16; Goodman and Love, 1980: 6-17, 204-206; Harrison, 1981: 58-59; Meredith and Mantel, 1985:407) is a brief but technically critical span in project development. It links the preceding phases and the succeeding operational stage. The success achieved here demonstrates the effectiveness of phasing and execution and is an indicator of a project's future performance. The transition, however, from the project status to that of normal operation cannot take place spontaneously. The transition has to be planned early and systematically, related activities must be anticipated and careful preparation has to be made with a view to protecting the investment and assuring a proper return on it. Once a project has been completed, it is tested and debugged, trial runs are made, and the executing agency is either dismantled or integrated into the normal management stream. Some tasks in this phase include organizational and procedural modification, personnel reallocation, surplus-asset disposal, removal of operational snags, provision of maintenance services, and prompt handling of contingencies.

Evaluation (Baum, 1970:13; United Nations, 1971: 87-88; Rondinelli, 1977: 17; Weiss et al., 1977: 128-134; Honadle and Klauss, 1979: 6; Olivares, 1979: 243-245; Goodman and Love, 1980: 17, 134, 213, 230; Cracknell, 1984: 13; Meredith and Mantel, 1985:368) relates to ex post facto or postcompletion assessment. The phase provides information which allows the project cycle to close. This stage examines if what was planned was in fact achieved. Sometimes, there is in-house ex post evaluation, and at other times it is carried out by outside agencies. The purpose of evaluation is to incorporate the learning dimensions, i.e. fact-finding, documenting, learning and improving so far as investment decision-making is concerned. An important role is played by it in modifying organizational behavior, facilitating the replication of successful projects, providing feedback to planning and management, and enabling an assessment of performance. A degree of concreteness is required in the absence of which evaluation may turn out to be a futile exercise.

Operation is not a project phase, but it is included in the study for the purpose of interfacing and action continuity. It relates to the period subsequent to project completion and the commencement of service or production. It embraces a set of components whose function is to transform resource inputs into goods and services. Planning, organizing, follow-up and control are the tasks of operation and maintenance. Operation ensures continuity, maintainability and usability, with provision for subsequent expansion. Competent operation and maintenance can make the difference between revenue and loss. All the four types of maintenance - routine or corrective, emergency, predictive and preventive - result in cost and manpower saving, increased production and equipment life, longer and uninterrupted work and higher overall maintainability.

Problem Areas

Certain common and recurring problems at each phase of the project cycle can be pointed out. As regards conception, numerous organizations are currently not geared to generate or process project ideas. Projects, moreover, may be initiated impulsively or without much careful analysis, resulting thus in the misapplication of effort and resources. In some cases, projects appear to serve the interests of particular pressure groups and politicians. Considerable time taken in formulation is a common complaint.

Appraisal runs into trouble because of specification inadequacy. The economic, financial and technical criteria tend to be overplayed to the neglect of social, cultural and organizational variables. Biased, improper or incomplete appraisal is not infrequent. There are also difficulties of estimating the true costs of capital, comparing sets of alternative projects and estimating returns on investment. The approval process gets complicated by the fact that policy-makers are called on to choose one project over another, not simply for the present but for five, six or more years' time. Approval of project not only takes a long time but also an unpredictably long time.

If not planned, scheduled and enforced properly, implementation may overextend itself to endanger the potential worth or profitability of the project. A set of recurring problems include excessive fragmentation of responsibility, inability to obtain trained and competent project staff, corrupt practices, interorganizational rivalries and conflicts, lack of cooperation, interference, inadequate leadership and direction, etc. The reporting system can be abused by insisting on numerous reports at frequent intervals. Too many agencies may call for separate periodic reports, which may overlap and fail to provide some of the information needed. Maintaining numerous and conflicting reports is uneconomical and could lead to misunderstanding among participant groups. False or misleading impressions can be created by the omission of data in reporting or by outdated and ineffective reporting.

Advance planning and action for a smooth changeover is neglected in practice. Failure or deficiency in this respect may result in rapid depreciation and deterioration of surplus resources and assets, unanticipated developments, and protraction. It is possible to point to recurring difficulties like failure to prepare completion reports/exception checklists, failure to plan for operative and user training, maintaining pace and momentum, loss of interest in remaining tasks, fear of no future work, and loss of team identity.

As with implementation, evaluation may run into trouble because of specification failure. All too often, evaluation is passed over, valuable experience is lost or not communicated, and the personnel involved rationalize their experience, make the same mistakes elsewhere and do not improve their systems. Reasons for evaluation's low priority seem to be the lack of appreciation for evaluation and follow-up, the tendency not to seek accountability for spent funds, and the loss of interest in completed projects. Varied problems arise, viz. lack of readily available data, measurement, difficulty, questionable transferability of lessons, and limited applicability of findings. All too often, much of the excessive cost of development has resulted from waste, negligence and indifference to operation and maintenance. Among the outcome of inadequate operation and management are poor running of postproject organizations, indifference to equipment/facilities/resources, low utilization of installed capacity and work interruption.

Appraisal Process

Starting in 1844 with Jules Dupuit's discussion of investment methodology via cost-benefit analysis, the application of investment appraisal took off with water resource development in the United States in the 1930s. Sharing an underlying common process and a heritage in welfare economics and systems analysis, investment appraisal has gradually evolved away from a narrow concern for special types of enterprises toward a more fully articulated set of concepts and tools applicable in principle to all investment decisions. Project appraisal, an active field of research and application since the early 1960s, is critical to the project cycle because it provides a comprehensive review of all aspects of the project, and lays the foundation for implementing the project and evaluating it when completed.

A spate of research continues with Abelson, 1996; Angelson, 1994; Austin, 1992; Austin, 1992; Behren and Hawranek, 1991; Brent, 1990; Bridger, 1986; Bridger and Winpenny, 1983; Caribbean Development Bank, 1986; Clifton, 1986; Coombs and Jenkins, 1991; Cracknell and Rendall, 1986; Curry and Weiss, 1993; Department of Environment, 1991; Dinwiddy and Teal, 1995; Gardiner, 1991; Geoghagen, 1985; Hanley and Spash, 1993; Harvey, 1986; Her Majesty's Stationery Office, 1988; Horton, 1994; Jenkins and Herberger, 1991, 1994; Kirpatrick and Weiss, 1996; Levy and Sarnat, 1986; Little and Mirrlees, 1991; Lumby, 1994; MacArthur, 1988; Maddock and Wilson, 1994; Overseas Development Administration, 1988, 1995; Pearce, 1994; Perkins, 1994; Randolph and Posner, 1988; Sell 1989, 1991; United Nations Development Program, 1988; van Pelt, 1990, 1993; Walsh and Daffern, 1990; Ward, 1991; Weiss, 1994; Williams and Gardina, 1993; Yaffey, 1992.

During 1980-85 the appraisal process was researched from different perspectives (Asian Development Bank, 1983; Becker, 1985; Benjamin, 1981; Bridger and Winpenny, 1983; Clarke, 1981; Department of Treasury, 1984; Dickey and Miller, 1984; Duffy and Thomas, 1984; Gramlich, 1981; Harvey, 1983; Inter-American Development Bank, 1981; International Labor Organization, 1981; Kujvenhaven and Mennes, 1985; Levin, 1983; Organization for Economic Cooperation and Development, 1981; O'Riordan and Sewell, 1981; Pearce and Nash, 1981; Powers, 1981; Project Planning Center for Developing Countries, 1982; Ray, 1984; Souder, 1984; United Nations Industrial Development Organization, 1980; Weiss, 1980).[1]

The essential purpose of appraisal is that of allocating inherently limited resources rationally to a variety of different uses in such a way that the net benefit to society is as large as possible. Appraisal involves an examination of objectives and alternative means of achieving them. It clarifies the nature of the alternatives, examines viability and efficiency, identifies the quality, quantity and timing of physical inputs and outputs, determines effective demand for the output, and estimates costs and benefits.

The exercise assesses benefits and costs and reduces them to a common standard, identifies and quantifies incremental benefits, aggregates the cost of operationalizing a project and compares this with the value of expected benefits, encourages comparison with alternative projects, and makes the final selection. Estimating may embrace identifying and measuring direct as well as indirect costs and benefits to aggregate consumption, assessing the shadow prices of labor and investment, calculating the social rate of discount, and estimating net benefits accruing to various groups.

The rationale for appraisal lies in finding out what difference a project would make if it were not chosen. Reasons for doing appraisal are to develop criteria by which projects competing for relatively limited resources would be rationally sifted and to subject project choice to a consistent and appropriate set of objectives. An important reason for concentrating on appraisal is the extent of externalities.

The basis for appraisal of projects is the maximization of net present value. The acceptability of a project can be ascertained by comparing it with lending capital at a certain rate of interest per annum, by comparing it with variants or alternatives of the same project, and by comparing it with competing projects. If, as Squire and van der Tak affirm (1975: 16), benefits exceed costs, the project is acceptable; if not, the project should be rejected. Where mutually exclusive projects are being considered, projects with largest net present value should be selected. The basic criterion is to accept all projects with positive present social value. Justification lies in a variety of issues - trade efficiency, consumer demand, technology selection, employment, income distribution and redistribution, and growth.

Project decisions often result from a series of general long-standing principles. Each project proposal should take account of possible alternatives of achieving the same task. The essential purpose of appraisal is to sort out the best of the feasible alternatives. The basic purpose is that of allocating inherently limited resources rationally to a variety of different uses in such a way that the net benefit to society is as large as possible. Sound appraisal requires an authority structure with a uniform and strong sense of purpose. Sound appraisal needs to integrate efficiency and equity. New issues and questions evolve in the appraisal process in response to related developments in technology, economics, finance, etc.

While the Little-Mirrlees method stresses investment, the UNIDO guidelines consider the raising of aggregate consumption - maximizing the present value of net aggregate consumption benefits - to be a fundamental objective in project appraisal. Other objectives, the redistribution of income or the net contribution to equity, may be taken into account. Other specific objectives include, as the UNIDO observes (1980: 16-17, 85-88), employment and net-value addition. All appraisal techniques embody certain assumptions, and identifying and dealing with these assumptions during appraisal increase the chances for project success.

Selection Criteria and Concomitants

There are several well-known selection criteria based on a comparison of cost incurred and benefit to be derived in the future. For example, cost-effectiveness analysis is concerned with an assessment of the least cost per unit of physical output. Net present value appraises present net benefits by comparing different time streams of benefits and costs. Under benefit-cost ratio, the present value of both cost and benefit is stated as a ratio. Internal rate of return is a measure of the earning capacity, value or profitability of a project. There are several other criteria in use, e.g. payback period method, simple rate of return method, output-capital ratio, accounting rate of return method, annual value method, and terminal value method. There is, on the whole, no one best criterion for estimating project worth, although some are better than others and some are especially deficient. The NPV, BCR and IRR being discounted, dynamic and time-adjusted criteria, they take into consideration the entire life of a project and the time factor by discounting the future inflows and outflows to their present values.

Central to a system of project appraisal, shadow prices are meant to be measures of value. Shadow prices are chosen so as to reflect better the real costs of inputs to society and the real benefits of the outputs than do actual prices (Little and Mirrlees, 1974:36). Accounting ratio is the ratio of the shadow price of a good to its market price. It is a shortened method of converting actual price of a good or service into its shadow price. Essential to project appraisal is discounting, which is the process of finding the present worth of a future income. It enables costs and benefits of a project occurring at different points in time to be expressed in terms of present values.

To quantify cost and benefit and to maintain a basis of comparison, numéraire is used as a common unit of account or standard of value. Once it has been chosen, the numéraire must be used consistently. The Little-Mirrlees numéraire, for instance, is present uncommitted social income measured in terms of convertible foreign exchange of constant purchasing power (OECD, 1968; Little and Mirrlees, 1974: 151). Aggregate consumption is used as the UNIDO numéraire, i.e. the present value of domestic consumption in the hands of the average individual (UNIDO, 1972: 41-42). The Squire-van der Tak numéraire (1975: 28) is freely available public sector income or constant purchasing power measured in units of local currency. Finally, mentionable are externalities when cost and benefits do not accrue directly to a project but occur outside it to other sectors. While negative externalities bring about negative effects, positive externalities occur with further input acquisition or output exchange on more favorable terms.

Appraisal Types

There are a number of types of project appraisal, e.g. technical, economic, financial, social, political and organizational. Technical appraisal, for example, relates to the following concerns: geographical data (boundaries, natural factors, etc.); cartographic data (contoured small-scale maps, topographic/alignment maps, etc); topographic data (maximum elevation, relative relief, gradients, settlement density, road network, housing, aerial surveys, etc.); geological data (terrain type, soil sampling, soil quality, load-bearing capacity, etc.); hydrogeological, hydrographic, hydrological and climatological data (groundwater level, groundwater isochloride curves, drainage structure, water quality, water loss, streamflow, river crossings, flood frequencies, flood level, bank scour, chemical shifting, rainfall, temperature, humidity, evapotranspiration, thunderstorm, wind, wind speed, runoff, drought, frost, etc.); demographic data (population, distribution, growth rate, migration movement, birth/mortality ratio, age/sex structure, etc.); site planning (site selection, ground/site survey, location, access, physical layout, scale, environs, threshold analysis, etc.); cost estimating (estimated building, furnishing and equipping cost, etc.); site construction (construction schedule, access-road construction, site development, utility installation, site construction, drainage, landscaping, sanitation, etc.); equipment planning and installation (technology choice, machine utilization, capacity, location, layout, process flow, etc.). There is a natural overlap between technical and environmental appraisals. An environmental appraisal is concerned with the accountability of the environment to the success of the project, the impact of the project on the environment, the project's capacity of a country's ecosystem to support a project over the long term, and the collection of baseline data (Goodman and Love, 1980: 90-92).

Economic appraisal has several purposes, namely, to see whether in general the project makes economic sense, to identify sensitive areas which have a critical importance for success or failure, and to identify ways of improving project by making it less risky, more cost-effective, or both. Then again, financial appraisal concerns itself with whether a project can secure finance it needs, repay loans, secure return on the invested capital, become financially viable, maintain liquidity position, earn new income, and afford expansion cost. Noteworthy is a distinction between economic and financial appraisal. While financial appraisal is concerned with the return on investment at market prices, economic appraisal is concerned with the determination of a set of prices which best reflects net efficiency benefits to the nation.

Social appraisal is sensitive to the issues of productivity and development with close attention to income redistribution and self-reliant growth (FitzGerald, 1978: xi-xii). The significance of social appraisal lies in incorporating the distribution objectives into project planning and examining the social soundness of projects - the identity of beneficiaries, their social origin, the identity of payers, the social commitment to ensure the project's success, the mobilization of the social leadership and civic participation, etc. Organizational appraisal is concerned with the adequacy of staffing at all levels, the adequacy of the management to direct implementation and manage a project on completion and the structure of the executing agency - operational autonomy, freedom from interference and rigidity, internal structure, chain of command, task organization and location, decision flow, and functional allocation and assignment (Baum, 1970: 10). This type of appraisal (Rondinelli, 1977: 13) relates to an assessment of organizational modes and forms for implementation, competence of the project workforce, and adequacy of accounting, scheduling, production, control and evaluation systems. Political appraisal indicates the probability that a project idea will be acceptable to the various resource groups - interest groups, citizens, project personnel - who must translate it into action. Several aspects of political feasibility are pertinent, namely, political impact, legislative impact, legislative sanction, political support, employment impact, constituency impact, etc. (Government of Turkey, 1974: 10; Weiss, Waterston and Wilson, 1977: 108; Goodman and Love, 1980: 92-93).

Techniques

Several appraisal methods have been expounded. The essence of the Bruno method, for instance, concerns dividing annual and capital costs into foreign exchange and labor. Essentially a shortcut tool, the Bruno method is limited in its application since it deals only with projects which produce tradable outputs (Bruno, 1967, 1972). The Balassa-Schydlowsky method selects those projects with the lower rate of effective protection. Also a shortcut tool, it deals only with trade distribution and takes no account of distortions in the domestic factor markets (Balassa and Schydlowsky, 1968, 1972).

The core of the OECD manual or the Little-Mirrless method, subsequently adopted by Squire and van der Tak, is that world prices be taken as shadow prices for all goods and services, valuing all traded commodities at border prices, decomposing all nontraded components into traded equivalents, and pricing every input and output in terms of foreign exchange or a foreign exchange-based shadow price. The UNIDO guidelines, having established a numéraire in terms of aggregate consumption measured at domestic market prices, are taxonomic in nature and do not offer any rigid operational rule. The approach measures benefits and costs in terms of consumption, takes into account national parameters like the discount rate, the shadow wage rate and the social value of investment, and lays stress on the distribution of project benefits and costs. The Squire and van der Tak method produces an orientation in investment decisions favoring projects that benefit the poor rather than the rich and that results in higher savings and increased growth rather than higher current consumption.

The benefits (Joshi, 1972: 31; Stern, 1972: 120; Stewart and Streeten, 1972: 90) of the Little-Mirrlees method are that it takes account of how the project costs and benefits are distributed and its emphasis on the importance of trade efficiency for project selection. In the UNIDO approach, the importance of income distribution makes it imperative that financing of the projects be carefully studied (Yotopoulas, 1976: 391). Skepticism voiced about the Little-Mirrlees method has centered around its complexity, ambiguity and applicability, whether the method leads to better investment decisions (Gittinger, 1972: 45-46), the tool seems unfair to the industrialization efforts of developing countries (Gutowski and Hammel,1972: 129), the appraisal of the nontrading sectors poses a problem (Joshi, 1972: 64), the casual use of world prices in project appraisals may cause developing countries to compete damagingly against each other (Stern, 1972: 120), it leads to the neglect of local efforts (Stewart and Streeten, 1972: 90,349-366), the lack of attention to nontraded outputs (Toye, 1976: 293-295), and its questionable assertion that all goods that can be traded should be treated as such (FitzGerald, 1978:43). As to the UNIDO guidelines, it does not deal explicitly with externalities. The numéraire used by the guidelines has been challenged on the basis of lack of specification . For various projects the application of the UNIDO method is either redundant or unclear (Irvin, 1978: 87). The Squire and van der Tak method has been contended with respect to its appearance of spurious accuracy and dependence on dubious assumptions. Seen over a period of time, it is likely that certain appraisal techniques are used more than others. The fact that the funding agencies tend to get standards for techniques to be used in project appraisal makes it likely that the exertion of influence is strong.

Review

Project appraisal can do considerably better than the ad hoc rules commonly used to select from among investment options and can thus yield greater gains. It can point out unrealistic or questionable assumptions and indicate ways in which a project can improve its income-producing capacity or increase its unmeasurable or unpriceable values. Appraisal of a project can show several incremental income flows and effects, e.g. project surplus, incremental income, domestic price change, incremental effects, net benefit accrual, and welfare increment.

A project carefully appraised has a much improved chance of being implemented on time and within budget and of yielding the desired benefits. Another merit is that appraisal may be used to test what happens to the earning capacity if and when something goes wrong. Proper and sound appraisal sharpens and informs the focus of decision-makers' intervention in choice-making, offers an alternative to 'muddling through', and contributes to allocative efficiency. Lack of attention to appraisal (FitzGerald, 1978: xi) can lead to incompetent investment planning and its consequent failure.

The choice of an appropriate discount rate is a common problem. A complaint is that appraisal tends to give too much importance to shadow pricing. Another complaint is that appraisal collapses a large and intricate process into a single number, such as the BCR, IRR, or NPV. Some techniques tend to overstress allocative efficiency at the expense of distributional equity. Appraisal has not yet succeeded in incorporating into analysis effects created by individual projects but felt elsewhere in the community. The tendency not to fully concentrate on the existence, identification, enumeration and qualification of externalities is perceptible. There are conceptual difficulties as well in appraisal, such as lack of consensus on choosing appropriate investment-related selection criteria, the cost of capital and the treatment of risk. The three appraisal criteria - BCR, IRR, or NPV - rank projects in the same way as if no constraints - budgetary or implementation - exist in project funding or implementation. Certain prescriptions like ascertaining a project's net contribution to growth and equity objectives and determining all feasible alternative use of resources are not always observed in practice.

Caution

In practice, decisions about projects are seldom clearcut. Techniques of project appraisal are at best approximations. Many calculations and estimates used, for instance, in economic appraisal are approximations, subject to various range of error. The estimation of social prices is normally subject to a considerable range of error and variance. Results of other types of appraisal which are necessary may conflict with economic appraisal. Undue reliance should not be placed on any one criterion. In many numéraires, for example, one deals in equivalent and not absolute values.

While social appraisal of projects and the use of social prices in certain situations can help in improving resource allocation, these cannot, in the final analysis, substitute for sound financial and economic appraisal. An aspect of appraisal that causes much concern is uncertainty about the future. Complete predictability in appraisal seems infeasible. It is clear (Project Planning Center for Developing Countries, 1982: 42) that project appraisal can be daunting, even though more work may not necessarily produce a better answer. Measurement of social prices can be a challenging task, involving considerable investigative and analytical talent. Any attempt to apply multifaceted appraisal in their entirety is illusive. There is also danger implicit in the direct transfer of appraisal techniques from developed to developing countries.

Many seem to believe that appraisal techniques are value-neutral. In fact, the value sets and assumptions of the analysts tacitly guide appraisal. The very choice of a particular appraisal technique over another is value-laden, often implicitly. It is remarkable that social and political choice can be analytical but never resolved by applied techniques alone. It is naive to think that appraisal techniques can insulate projects from social and political dynamics. There are limits to what appraisal can achieve at present. It is useless to pretend that appraisal techniques are able to quantify meaningfully all important aspects of investment planning. It is also easy to become so involved in the theoretical niceties of appraisal that it is carried to the point where it produces only superfluous information instead of better investment decision. One must warn against 'quantificationism' which holds that a quantitative solution to a project problem is *a prioi* better than a qualitative one. Judgement will necessarily remain the key in determining priorities and allocating resources among alternative uses.

There is no one best technique for appraising projects, although some are better than others and some are especially deficient. No appraisal method is a panacea, a solution to all or most problems of choice. Any appraisal technique can be easily discredited and its usefulness negated if there is not the will to apply it properly. Techniques do not solve problems spontaneously or easily. It is essential to season the quantitative aspects of appraisal with a large measure of commonsense.

Summation

Generally, the big need in project appraisal has not been for overpowering techniques but rather for reasonableness, sensitivity and the ability to order and synthesize diverse series of information that often are fragmentary and conflicting. Project decision-making is likely to involve for a long time to come, in addition to analytical rationality, the elements of compromise, bargaining, and interaction. It is the whole system of appraisal, implementation, management, monitoring and evaluation which justifies the time, money and effort devoted to project development and from which comes the payoffs in terms of better projects.

Implementation Process

Implementation has begun recently to receive greater attention than ever before all over the world. The importance of implementation is undeniable because it is a struggle over the realization of ideas. Great intentions are dashed, and it is important to understand why this happens and what to do to prevent it. Project experience shows gaps between intention and achievement, promise and performance and plan and reality, thus underscoring the importance of implementation. Implementation may be the most critical phase in determining project success or failure (Hirschman, 1967; Ingle, 1979).

The tendency to push implementation capability into a residual category is common. There is a mystifying neglect of implementation issues by specialists at several levels. Several reasons can be cited why neglect has persisted. Neglect is due in part to the naive assumption that once a project has been approved, the project will be implemented and the desired results will be near those expected. Second, the well-known analytical techniques may have encouraged project-makers to ignore the problems of implementation. Third, the difficulty and enormity of the task has discouraged detailed study of the process of implementation. Fourth, many of the variable needs to complete an implementation study are difficult, if not impossible, to measure. Finally, a comprehensive analysis of implementation requires that attention be given to multiple actors over an extended period of time, thus involving a considerable outlay of time and resources.

It was during the 1960s, the 1970s and the 1980s that a series of studies appeared dealing explicitly with implementation (Allison, 1975; Badach, 1977, 1980; Berman, 1978; Brinkerhoff, 1991; Bunker, 1972; Carvallo, 1996; Clayton and Petry, 1983; Cleland, 1990; Development Alternative, 1978; Dufty and Taylor, 1962; Duncer, 1978; Edwards, 1980; Elmore, 1980; Frame, 1987; Grindle, 1980; Gross et al., 1971; Gunn, 1978; Hanf and Toonen,

1985; Hargrove, 1975; Hjern and Hull, 1982; Hjern and Porter, 1981; Honadle and Klauss, 1979; Honadle and van Sant, 1991; Iglesias, 1976; Ingle, 1979; Israel, 1978; Kemps, 1992; Khan, 1989, 1989, 1992; Kilman, 1976; King, 1967; Knight, 1980; Lang and Drechsler, 1989; Larson, 1980; Lewis, 1976; Lippet, 1985; Mazmanian and Sabatier, 1981, 1983; Migdal, 1977; Montgomery, 1974; Morss and Gow, 1985; Mountjoy and O'Toole, 1979; Nakamura and Smallwood, 1980; Norweigian Agency for Development, 1991; Palumbo and Harder, 1981; Porter and Hjern, 1978; Pressman and Wildavsky, 1073; Rein and Rabinowitz, 1977; Ripley and Franklin, 1982; Rondinelli, 1976, 1977, 1978, 1979; Sabatier and Mazmanian, 1979; Smith, 1984; Smith, 1973; Stuckenbruck, 1988; United Nations, 1970; United Nations Industrial Development Organization, 1970, 1975, 1977; van Horn and van Meter, 1976, 1979; van Mete and van Horn, 1975; Vepa, 1974; Waterston, 1965; Williams, 1975, 1980; Williams and Elmore, 1976; Wolf, 1979).

Some of these studies indicate that project designs are now beginning to pay particular attention to 'capacity to implement'. The studies also show that implementation was the least regarded of the major tasks confronting the low-income countries. There are, perhaps, essentially two strands, as Dunsire reports (1978: xi, 14, 76), in the implementation research. One is concerned with evaluating performance, measuring outcome and accounting for variation between intentions and results. The other describes the operationalization process whereby ideas or plans become reality. Some studies set out typologies of implementation and others are taken up with the pathology of the execution process. The deviations and detours of implementation have attracted some analysts. While a few studies document a variety of pressures on field-level implementation, other analyses demonstrate that the ultimate action of executing agencies often tends to vary from original intentions. Looking explicitly at implementation, some studies seek to map the execution process in order to identify and weigh contingencies that affect the achievement of project goals. Some analysts attempt to develop models of the variables that may be important for understanding implementation. However, little attention so far has been paid to how project decisions are turned into goods and services, the link between decision and performance, the importance of a theoretical framework, the need to design or improve implementation, and investment-related policies.

Conceptual Development

Implementation has been defined, described and conceptualized in several ways. It tends to be a long voyage of discovery in the most varied domains (Hirschman, 1967: 35); it embraces periodic reporting, interim measurement, analysis, fact-finding and troubleshooting, periodic adjustment and schedule design (United Nations, 1972: 28); it is a proses of interaction between goal-setting and action-putting (Pressman and Wildavsky, 1973: xxi-xxii). Further, implementation relates to criteria and resources, policy-level support, socioeconomic conditions, executing-agency features and implementation dispositions (van Meter and van Horn, 1975: 445-488); it involves a series of games involving the efforts of numerous actors to protect their interests and gain access to project elements not under their control (Bardach, 1977: 51-57); implementation begins with an understanding of the degree to which the misperformance of implementation is actually rooted in the decision process (Hargrove, 1977: 4); it represents a set of objectives directed toward putting a program into effect (Jones, 1977, 1399); it involves the realization of the legal interest, institutional rationality and general goal consensus (Rein and Radinovitz, 1977).

Seen as a progression from the general to the particular, implementation embraces a sequence of operations to produce a range of output from a variety of inputs (Dunsire, 1978: 143-149, 223). Honadle (1979: 6, 103, 208) finds it as an essentially reactive process of converting resources into goods and services which support behavior changes in beneficiary groups. To Bardach (1977: 9, 36, 38-51, 57-58; 1980: 139), it is an assembly process of strategic interaction and a social activity that follows on and is stimulated by a mandate. Pressman and Wildavsky call (1979: 180) it a unitary process and not a tandem operation of setting a goal and enforcing a plan. Implementation involves a process of moving toward a project objective by means of managerial and political steps (Cleaves, 1980: 281). Grindle declares (1980: 20) it is neither entirely predictable nor always manageable.

Further, implementation may be placed in a continuum in which interaction takes place between those who seek objective and those on whom action depends (Barrett and Fudge, 1981). It comprises the ability to achieve specified ends by chosen means (Killick, 1981: 50). Mazmanian and Sabatier (1981: xii) point to executing-agency decision, target-group compliance, induced impacts, etc. To Jones (1984: 165), the interactive and dynamic elements are vital to implementation. Implementation is a process in which are involved operational flexibility, objective realization, and objective-action continuum (Ham and Hill, 1984: 106).

Of special significance is the fact that contingencies characterize implementation in several ways. Particular contingencies identified in implementation research include the number of actors/the clarity of objectives (Pressman and Wildavsky, 1973), the personal and institutional dispositions of actors (Bardach, 1977), the support of leaders (Migdal, 1977), the extent of power diffusion (Grindle, 1980), and the adequacy of implementation resources/the effects of institutional routines on the project process (Edwards, 1980). Pressman and Wildavsky (1973: xxi-xxii) see implementation as involving a capacity to forge links in the causal chain connecting actions to objectives. The longer the chain of causality, the more numerous the reciprocal relations among the links and the more complex implementation gets. The logic of implementation is not unilinear but multilinear, requiring divergences and convergences at strategic points and coordination of activities as multiple levels.

Model-building

A number of theoretical and methodological approaches are on stream. Implementation planning, Allison notes (1975:375), involves an assessment of the decision-makers' prospects to obtain alternatives to pursue preferred alternatives through successive stages of decision and implementation. Implementation analysis, Williams corroborates (1975: 532 - 539, 558-560), involves the scrutiny of design specifications and management capability. Honadle (1979: 6, 206) lends support that implementation analysis can affect the implementation process and can alter project impact.

Closely related to the same analytical cluster are implementation assistance, implementation estimate and implementation assessment. Implementation assistance involves assistance in negotiating technical know-how. Implementation estimate involves a forecast of the capabilities, interest and motivations of organizations in implementing each alternative. Finally, implementation assessment is a mid-stream examination of what is actually happening (Honadle, 1979: 6).

Model-building in implementation has gained some currency. Smith (1973: 197-209) incorporates four components in his implementation model, viz. interaction patterns, target groups, executing agency, and environmental factors. Dunsire (1978: 120-131, 226) differentiates two main models of implementation - the developmental and the aggregative model. The development model holds that the original decision or idea contains the blueprint for the many different activities in the course of implementing the idea. In the aggregative model, getting something done is seen as a matter of putting together a number of discrete units.

Majone and Wildavsky (1979: 178-182, 190-194) speak to three models of implementation. First, in the control or planning model, implementation is logically implied by planning and the task is the realization of the initial plan. Second, the interaction model posits that the control task of implementation is whether it results in consensus on goals, individual autonomy and commitment to project on the part of implementers. Finally, the evaluation model suggests that it involves changing or modifying intentions, varying the amount or type of resource inputs, altering outputs, learning from experience and correcting errors.

Alternatively, Hogwood and Gunn (1984: 209-218) set out a number of approaches to implementation. In structural approaches, emphasis is laid on different structures as being appropriate to different types of tasks and environments. As regards managerial approaches, the concern is to employ a repertoire of management techniques and procedures, involving those of scheduling, planning and control. As for behavioral approaches, the task begins by recognizing that there is often resistance to, fear of and resentment toward change. As to political approaches, the reasoning is that if implementation takes insufficient account of the realities of power, then the project is unlikely to succeed.

Executing Agency

The degree, quality, frequency and level of implementational success rests considerably on the executing agency (United Nations, 1969: 16, 221; Archibald, 1970: 73-86). Several features of executing agencies are noteworthy. First, the structural location of an agency in the entire network is significant. Another feature concerns interdependence and cooperation. As most projects are linked by relations of interdependence, the agencies must enter into horizontal relations of cooperation. Also, the need for vertical control within the agency for task fulfillment and effective implementation is still strong, notwithstanding a project's horizontal orientation.

Other characteristics include the competence and size of an agency staff, the degree of hierarchical control of interagency decisions and processes, an agency's political resources, the vitality of an agency, the degree of open communication within an agency, and the agency's formal-informal linkages with the policy-making system. The quality of the agency personnel influences implementation. The nature of the communication network and the leadership style can either facilitate or hinder effective implementation.

Techniques

Several approaches seem helpful in designing and executing implementation techniques. First, force-field analysis (Lewin, 1947: 5-41) assumes that in any situation there are both driving and restraining forces. Driving forces help push a situation in a particular direction. Restraining forces constrain or curb the driving forces. Second, the participative change cycle (Hersey and Blanchard, 1982: 272-273) involves a gradual move away from directive change - where change is imposed and forced - to participative change - where group participation in problem-solving is possible. Third, three phases of the change process are identified: unfreezing, changing and refreezing. Unfreezing motivates and makes the individual or group ready to change. Changing is adopting and imbibing new patterns of behavior. The process by which the newly acquired behavior comes to be integrated is referred to as refreezing. Fourth, as regards intragroup and intergroup conflict, discord may be approached on the assumption that although there is conflict, agreement is possible and desirable. Finally, in pursuing organization development, either collaborative or interpersonal approaches may be utilized.

Waterston (1965: 350-365) offer a number of broad-based approaches. The first concerns improving implementation conditions. Every effort needs to be made in facilitating and accelerating implementation. Second, the project gap, which frustrates most implementation, needs to be closed. Third, project progress in relation to events must be continuously reviewed and assessed because changing conditions result in deviations from original design. Last but not least, the prior analysis of projects is another approach to improving implementation. Williams (1975: 561-5640 suggests demonstration and monitoring as two techniques to carry out and facilitate implementation. Other appropriate techniques - a set of dynamic questions, a common scaling system or a sampling frame - may facilitate implementation - related work.

Some well-known operational techniques are employable, viz. Gantt chart, time-line chart, milestone chart, flow process chart, precedence diagram, work breakdown structure, line of balance method, critical path method, performance evaluation and review technique, work study, and work planning and review. A number of behavioral techniques are on stream as well, which include transactional analysis, motivational research, conflict management, leadership research, change management, stress management, and creativity management. Several other techniques are employable from an expanding field of creativity management, viz. attribute list technique, checklist technique, brainstorming, synectics, morphology, nature analysis, Delphi method and nominal group techniques.

Needs

The availability of suitable personnel and the presence of management capability often decide the success or failure of a project. Early implementation analysis and assessment can be critical. Designing alternative implementation strategies and motivating the executing agencies are worthwhile. The attitude of management is an important factor in improving implementation. Wanting better implementation goes a long way towards achieving it (Williams, 1975: 551). It is also desirable to observe the time, logic and organization sequence in the interest of competent implementation (Dunsire, 1978: 133). Effective implementation hinges on such factors as the availability and skill of personnel, the complementary activities and supportive roles of participating agencies and related organizations, the receptivity of intended beneficiaries, and the persistence of organized effort.

Implementation requires understanding and observance of the sequence of activities which depend on the complex chain of reciprocal interactions. The United Nations (1983: 14, 16) observes that the improved synchronization of the input and output phases is critical. Van Meter and van Horn (1975: 482) lay stress on the absence or reduction of dispositional conflicts.

Basic questions about the viability of the executing agency need to be asked. Archibald (1970: 73-86), for instance, intimates that the executing agency needs a closer look in terms of its internal acceptability of project decisions, objective and means, potential effectiveness, political feasibility, internal structural qualities and needs, individual needs and organizational needs. Quade suggests (1975: 262) designing alternative implementative strategies, providing incentives to the executing agencies, and including more social scientists in project development.

The United Nations (1969: 5, 76-77; 1983: 15-16) maintains that implementation needs to be dynamic, flexible and adaptable to changing situations. Pressman and Wildavsky (1973: xxii-xxiii) prescribe that attention needs to be paid to the structural position of policy-makers and implementors. Ham and Hill (1984: 99) point to the need for ensuring the unambiguous nature of project, keeping links in the chain to a minimum and preventing undue outside interference.

Evaluation

Implementation is a control task in contemporary societies. The success of a project is related to the execution of decisions inherent in a project. Yet, the attention given to implementation appears to be more verbal than real. Breakdowns of implementation represent a fundamental failure of societies to translate meaningful ideas into effective action.

It is useful to distinguish between nonimplementation and unsuccessful implementation (Hogwood and Gunn, 1984: 197). In the former case, a project is not put into effect as intended. Unsuccessful implementation, on the other hand, occurs when a project is carried out, but the project fails to produce the intended results.

Implementational snags not only hold back implementation, but remain very much at work once implementation has started. These snags then turn into forces making for sluggish or abortive implementation. Implementation seems vulnerable to the domino effect in that when the initial phase is troubled the implementation failure tends to be transmitted to the other phases. Once projects begin to operate, Bardach notes (1977), they become vulnerable to forces called drift or mutation which pull them away from their original design.

Implementation problems are essential control problems. Not only the unusual, the dramatic or the conflictual problems, but also the prosaic, everyday and ordinary ones can inhibit implementation (Pressman and Wildavsky, 1973: viii). Experience shows that implementation is far from a harmonious and socially rational process for the attainment of present goals. Actually, it contains substantial elements of conflict, inefficiency, misallocation, time overruns and bureaucratization (Ellman, 1979: 43-50). Implementation problems are widespread (Quade, 1975: 259) and serious and pervasive (Rondinelli, 1976: 10-15). Waterston (1965), Hirschman (1967), Myrdal (1968), Dean (1977), Faber and Seers (1972), Caiden and Wildavsky (1974), Shen (1975, 1977) and Killick (1976), among others, point to a rather widespread disillusionment with implementation. The fundamental causes of implementation failure and inadequacy are theoretical (Ellman, 1979: 65-79). The actual problems of implementation, as Hargrove notes (1979: 6), have their origins in the design process.

There is a tension between the normative assumptions - what should be done and how it should happen - and the struggle and conflict between interests (Ham and Hill, 1984: 112). Difficulty is likely to follow whenever a completely packaged external solution is imposed on a target group (Quade, 1975: 262). The 'infinite regress' that has plagued all other planners has also beset the implementation process (Majone and Wildavsky, 1977: 180).

Some of the effects of unsuccessful or inadequate implementation are noteworthy. Dilatory effects (Waterston, 1965: 299-309; Seidman, 1979: 3-27; Bardach, 1977: 180) are commonplace. Evidence discloses that the completion time often results in a stretchout (United Nations, 1969: 385; 1971: 71) over several years. Damage is done in the form of deviation, distortion, underachievement of planned targets, shortfall and implementation gap. Other manifestations include underutilization, unused capacity, overemphasis on financial targets, underspending, inferior work, low yields (Waterston, 1965: 299-309), and underestimation of cost and completion time (Caiden and Wildavsky, 1974: 17).

Poor relation between what was envisaged and what was realized and low project-plan linkage are not uncommon. Poor conception (Caiden and Wildavsky, 1974: 17) results in disappointment or failure. Frequent adjustments, schedule slippage, insufficient compliance and objective dilution are known to occur. Intentions undergo major revisions (Seidman, 1979: 3-27) during the course of implementation. Investment cost overruns (Waterston, 1965: 299-309; United Nations, 1969: 385, 1971: 71) are familiar. Other effects extend to resource misallocation, effort and opportunity loss, resource loss, resource diversion, goal deflection, long gestation period, high incidence of project underperformance, uneven growth, resistant behavior and high cost of organizational change (Quade, 1975: 260; Rondinelli, 1976: 10-15; Bardach, 1977: 66-177). Hirschman reports (1967: 46-55) that even successful projects can have unintended effects, namely, unduly disturbing the political/social/organizational environment, antagonizing established agencies, and the growth of a project as a power base.

It is unsurprising that in numerous instances intentions remain symbolic (Seidman, 1979: 3-27), failure to have a substantial impact is experienced (van Meter and van Horn, 1975: 449), the relevance for project efficacy diminishes, related developments are impeded, uncertainty and anxiety are generated, and aspirations are ruined. Further, projects are abandoned, socioeconomic problems remain unsolved, beneficiary hope is dashed, confusion appears, waste occurs, corruption spreads and frustration rises (Caiden and Wildavsky, 1974: 17; Rondinelli, 1976: 10-15; Seidman, 1979: 3-27).

There are many limiting or constraining factors which are likely to restrain implementation. These include lack of clarity of objective, lack of understanding of objectives (Kaufman, 1973), project based on wrong theories or mistaken assumptions, poor initial assessment and planning, failure to consider the feasibility of implementing project alternatives (Williams, 1975: 531-534, 546-553), inadequate preplanning and postplanning (Stigler, 1961: 224: Chambers, 1969: 43-136), objectionable targets, overambitious targets (United Nations, 1969: 39), vague and unrealistic goals (Larson, 1980: 2-7), internal inconsistencies, erroneous estimates, faulty forecasts, lack of proper implementation planning, planner/analyst naivete about operationalization, perfunctory implementation analysis and assessment (Williams, 1975: 531-534, 546-553), imperfect knowledge (Fesler, 1980: 256-274), insufficient information (van Meter and van Horn, 1975: 482; Hadden, 1980: 190), incomplete and imperfect information (Stigler, 1961: 224; Chambers, 1969: 43-136), questionable and incomplete data and little use of available information (Archibald, 1970: 73-86), poor or inappropriate design and specification (Williams, 1975: 531-534, 546-553), lack of harmony between design and objectives/inputs, mismatch between goals and operational measures (Hadden, 1980: 190), inadequate integration of organizational and individual objectives (United Nations, 1969: 299-300), and internal rigidities and communication failure (Fesler, 1980: 256-274).

At the organizational and operational level, one comes across overworked and poorly trained staff (van Meter and van Horn, 1975: 482; Hadden, 1980: 190), underutilized personnel (Archibald, 1970: 73-86), shortage of competent staff and skilled labor, incomplete and unbalanced monitoring (Horst et al., 1973: 303), lack of technical supervision (Waterston, 1965: 314-332, 340), few inspection, inappropriateness of inherited and traditional management structure and methods, inadequate executive capacity (Dean, 1977), management incapacity of executing agencies, unstable or incompetent management (Hirschman, 1967: 46-55), inefficient management structure and decision-making/planning tools, lack of appropriate interagency coordination (Kurz, 1973: 183-184, 189-191), and poor overall coordination (United Nations, 1969: 299-300).

Other factors of organizational-operational nature include bad scheduling, technical/analytical insufficiency, multiplicity of layers and actors (Williams, 1975: 531-553), poor procedures (Larson, 1980: 2-7), irregular accountability, insufficient financial control (van Meter and van Horn, 1975: 482), departmentalism, compartmentalism, fragmentation, functional duplication/dispersal/overlap, fund withholding and diversion

(Hirschman, 1967: 56-57), and poor or inadequate groundwork and deviations (Tinbergen, 1964: 62-63). Similarly striking are incorrect agency location, low productivity, industrial relations problems, site accidents, faulty material/equipment/work, excessive paperwork, implementation rigidity (Kenessey, 1978: 331), unclear direction, large number of decision points, lack of flexibility (Hadden, 1980: 190), limited access and lack of sanction for goal nonfulfillment. Still other factors embrace leadership problems (Fesler, 1980: 256-274), excessive caution, low morale, uncompliant behavior, role obfuscation, noncooperation, outside interference (Hirschman, 1967: 46-55) and organizational attitudes and behavior (Rondinelli and Ingle, 1981: 11-18).

At the conflictual level, one is faced with difficulty in securing agreement and cooperation, disagreement with objectives (Kaufman, 1973), goal conflict, incompatible needs (Hadden, 1980: 190), dispositional conflicts (van Meter and van Horn, 1975: 482), jurisdictional conflicts (Williams 1975: 531-553), and interagency rivalry and conflict and debilitating conflicts (Hirschman, 1967: 46-55). At another level, the passage of time causes deviations from the planned project focus. Mentionable are timing problems (Williams, 1975: 531-533) and procedural/process delays (Waterston, 1965: 314-340; Bardach, 1979: 5, 125; Fesler, 1980: 256-274). Added to these are impossible time constraints (van Meter and van Horn, 1975: 482; Hadden, 1980: 190), timing of implementation schedule (Kurz, 1973: 183-191), improper time-sequencing, and time-lapse in adapting and using modern management techniques.

One may take into account at the social level cultural traditions and practices (Rondinelli and Ingle, 1981: 11-18), short attention syndrome, insufficient discipline (Waterston, 1965: 314-340) and social entropy raising the problems of incompetence, variability and coordination (Bardach, 1979: 5, 125). Again, some problems are spawned by political factors (Killick, 1981: 64-66), such as the political traits of a regime, questionable political criteria and priorities, change in political leadership and program priority, policy-makers' fickleness and second thoughts (Hirschman, 1967: 56-57), feeble political will (Rondinelli and Ingle, 1981: 11-18) and ideological shift. As regards environmental factors, implementation is faced with a high level of uncertainty and overwhelming complexity (Williams, 1995: 531-553). This is compounded (Larson, 1980: 2-7) by uncertainty in the economic environment and varied disruptive contingencies and conjunctural factors.

Caution

Nothing comes across more strongly than the great naivete about implementation. Implementation is not a brief interlude between a bright idea and opening the door for service (Williams, 1975: 531). Some seem to think of implementation as a subordinate function, lacking in social consequence or intellectual distinction (Montgomery, 1979: 56). There is further assumption that once a decision has been made or a project formulated by an agency, the results that subsequently follow are those originally intended. Loasby (1976: 89) cautions that it is dangerous to assume that what has been decided would be achieved, or what happens is what was intended. Quade intimates (1975: 259) that there is difficulty in implementing certain kinds of projects, particularly those of a new nonincremental nature.

More precisely, implementation capability must not be considered as a residual category in the designing of development projects and the achievement of self-sustaining development. Implementation is not self-executing; it is not a process that follows automatically once a project has been formulated. It requires the presence of an action-forcing mechanism. Williams warns (1975: 535, 553) that implementation carries us into social science's one weak area, i.e., dynamics.

Management Capability

The experience in socioeconomic development of many countries in the recent past has underwritten the fact that management capability at all levels is a scarce resource and a limiting factor in the achievement of overall or project goals. The involvement of the public sector in the socioeconomic realm places a heavy demand on management capability. Successful project development requires high levels of management capability (Alderfer, 1967; Anderson, 1987, 1987; Barratt, 1976; Braibanti, 1969; Brinkerhoff, 1991; Bryant and White, 1980, 1982; Caiden, 1969, 1973; Chapel, 1977; de Vries, 1971; Dinsmore, 1990; Eaton, 1972; Esman, 1963; Esman and Montgomery, 1980; Grant, 1979; Gran, 1983; Green and Slyfield, 1982, Gross, 1966, 1969; Honadle and Klauss, 1979; Honey, 1968; Hope, 1984; Hope and Armstrong, 1980; Israel, 1987; Katz, 1969; Khan, 1975, 1982, 1989, 1989, 1990, 1993, 1995, 1995; Lewis, 1967; Luikart, 1966; Lynn, 1984; Ministry of Overseas Development, 1977; Montgomery and Siffin, 1970; Packard, 1974; Paul, 1982, 1983; Riggs, 1970; Rondinelli, 1976, 1977, 1978, 1979, 1981, 1981, 1981, 1982; Rothwell, 1972; Schaffer, 1972; Scott, 1981; Shull, 1965; Stone and Stone, 1976; Swerdlow, 1963, 1974, 1975; Swerdlow and Ingle, 1974; United Nations, 1969, 1969, 1975, 1978, 1978, 1983; Waterston, 1965; Weiss, 1966). The usefulness of management capability for the success or failure of development efforts is revealed in the ability to formulate and execute projects, the capacity for capital investment and absorption, the strength to implement new ideas and initiatives, the capability to accelerate and sustain transformative change, and the proficiency to elevate the quality and outcome of project activities.

A country has a fundamental stake in the realization and preservation of management capability in aiding the process of development and in harnessing various productive forces that generate output. Raising management capability is important because an increase in workload and involvement in new activity area without corresponding change in personnel competence and skill types may lead to organizational overload. Yet, one of the conspicuous features of new and developing countries is inadequate management capability. In the research output on project development that has appeared in recent years little attention is paid to management capability (United Nations, 1960: 67; Powelson, 1972: 202; Reid, 1973: 74; United Nations, 1983: 32).

Ongoing research reveals a number of definitions of management capability. Gross (1969: 227-228), Katz (1969: 99-100), the United Nations (1969: 8, 67, 112; 1978: 73-91; 1983:1) and Swerdlow (1975: 356) concur that management capability is the capacity to obtain desirable or intended results through organizations, and that it involves the ability to mobilize, allocate and combine the actions that are needed to achieve objectives. The United Nations (1975: 32) defines it as being the ability to mobilize inputs and increase productivity or efficiency.

Management capability means (Stone and Stone, 1976: 204) the institutional capacity to formulate and carry out activities to fulfil purposes. It consists of the methods, systems and activities (Gant, 1979: 9) by which policies, programs and projects are carried out to accomplish specific goals of development. Goodman and Love (1980: 21) report that capability relates to the exercise of decision-making skills, the existence of proper information systems and the dissemination of information to target groups. It concerns (United Nations, 1983: 27, 32) the ability of organizations to mobilize resources, convert them into goods or services and achieve complementaries with its external environment. Management capability is the combination of organizations, skills, resources, leadership and supports (United Nations, 1984: 32) required for specific projects or general activities.

Nature

Management capability can be considered a resource factor (King,

1967: 10-11; Swerdlow, 1975: 357-365; Israel, 1978: 28). This resource has to be consciously allocated to yield a return on the investment. It is not a mobile resource capable of flowing spontaneously to the point where it can yield the greatest return. It has to be viewed in all its dimensions, including its role as a generalizing and synthesizing activity, an instrument and mobilization system, and as supporting structure for growth and development.

It can be either specific or diffuse. When it is diffuse throughout a large organization, it tends to be overlooked and may be erroneously considered almost costless. An important distinction exists between management capability and other resource factors (Kindleberger, 1965: 118). Capital can be substituted for labor, or labor for land, or technology for land, and vice versa. But management capability is complementary rather than substitutable. The United Nations (1969: 95, 100) states that capability consists in identifying and securing the resources that the organization requires, including tools, services, facilities, methods and procedures. It involves (Gross, 1969: 227-228, 409) an ability to understand rapid and baffling environmental changes and to develop an organizational capacity to adapt creatively to these changes.

Stone and Stone (1976: 204-205) observe that capability involves identifying elements, understanding the process and planning the responses. Rondinelli (1977: 90-91) reports that capability entails improvement in analytical, operational and evaluative skills. Furthermore, management capability is measurable at both macro and micro levels. Its measurement includes input indicators, activity indicators, output/impact indicators and social impact indicators.

Management capability of a country is related to its history, culture, social structure and value system (Swerdlow, 1975: 358-365). It is desirable to make a distinction between actual and potential capability. The former is the capability demonstrated in the past or the present, and the latter is one which would be either required or would be available in the future. Also, the overall management capability of the public sector is distinguishable from the capacity in a specific agency. The former is a macro capability, a large aggregate capability, and the latter localized in a particular organization. The public sector's facilitation function - providing and promoting basic infrastructure, technical assistance, investment promotion, productive involvement - is strategic. The extent to which this facilitative role is dominant has been an important factor in determining management capability. Depending on the nature of policy/political leadership and institutional capacity, the facilitative role has developed more rapidly in some countries than in others. It is remarkable that there is a widespread tendency to see management capability in terms of a fixed quantum. It is pertinent to question this tendency (United Nations, 1983: 4)

The needs in building, expanding and improving management capability are multiple. To start with, the need for capability growth is high. A country may invest in it and plan such investments like any other. Planning for management capabilities deserves the same degree of attention as that given to other public sector activities. The organization structure needs to be redesigned to make it more compatible with the task of organizational management. A primary need should be to focus the attention of practitioners on achievable goals. Management capability must be renewed, recreated and revitalized. Dysfunctional and unsuitable structures and practices must be replaced.

Further, management capability requires strong political, legislative and executive support and widespread institutionalization. It requires a sense of direction, a resolve to overcome many snags, a high standard of leadership, a high level of commitment, sustained and cautious attention and a regular allocation of resources. A fairly high level of consistent work from different functional areas - programming, research, formulation, service/production operation and promotion - and a proper balance between and among them are essential. Fundamentally, the strength of management capability rests on the people, i.e. trained and motivated human resources.

Strategies

Several strategies and operational measures are available for realizing management capability. It may be attained either by the overall systemic approach or the incremental approach. While prescribing the introduction of programming units, Waterston doubts (1965: 291-292, 320-322) the usefulness of rather uncertain and slow overall reforms, and suggests instead a piecemeal approach, which involves focusing on a few important projects and structuring management initiatives around them in the hope that these 'nuclei' would later become springboards for wider reform. Similarly, the United Nations reports its skepticism about an overall approach (1969: 42), but is supportive of management reform/revitalization and institution-building. Katz finds (1969: 112) management capability a complex task and long-term process involving a strategy of successive approximations.

Swerdlow stresses (1975: 362-364) management training. Stone and Stone suggest (1976: 209) management planning and organization/ management development. Management by objectives and reward-system design are counselled by Iversen (1979: 92-93). Esman and Montgomery advocate (1980: 183-234) building management capability by involving a large number of organizations and by decentralizing authority and responsibility.

Evaluation

Seen as a major constraint on development activity, management incapacity and low levels of capability represent a pressing problem and turn out to be persistent factors of underdevelopment. Management inadequacies are known to obstruct development and become particularly prejudicial at the phase of implementation. Management capability is impaired by dysfunctional, wasteful and dilatory practices which suppress initiatives and erode motivation. It is widely held that management weaknesses cause project failure or shortfall, occasion project vulnerability, heighten the risk of drift or fiasco, and hurt or delay the effective use of resources and opportunities.

The United Nations (1969: 67) as well as Rondinelli and Ruddle 1977) speak to the growing concern over management incapacity in the public sector. Many countries and their management systems generally lack the capacity to turn ideas into reality, do not have adequate skill in designing and installing workable organizations and procedures, and cannot produce sound and productive projects. Mintzberg reasons (1973) that managers are constantly badgered with small problems that divide their attention among numerous short-term minutiae and make it difficult for them to engage in sustained planning of management capability. Lack of effective capacity (United Nations, 1984: 8) contributes to inability to discover when and how projects stray from their designed course during implementation or operation.

It seems fallacious to assume that centrally controlled management can accomplish objectives finally. Experience shows that the most valuable managerial capability is the ability to innovate, inform and lead - talents that tend to be discouraged by central control. Indigenizing management capability does not seem to be a direct concern to many as well. The casual adoption of inappropriate or unworkable management techniques tends to work against organizational capability.

Caution

Management capability is a difficult element of a project to appraise (King, 1967: 10 -11). Both individual organizations and the large system in developing countries have the opportunity to expand management capability. But neither the necessary analytical skill nor the required attitudinal change comes spontaneously. Even the most capable managers tend to become overextended. They have too little time to spend on organization-building, the development of junior personnel and the maintenance of morale. Building a capable management is a slow, difficult and painful task. One should not expect quick results or give up too easily (World Bank, 1980: 81) Situations of unused or surplus management capability may exist alongside acute shortage. An organization may maintain an ambience of false urgency and keep turning out at a brisk pace on subordinate or procedural questions, while the substantive ones are not properly examined. Lombard's warning (1974: 470-471) is timely when he observes that capability planning, if not geared to the main shaft of management decision-making, soon becomes a burden on the system. If, however, it is properly geared to current decision-making, its effectiveness is increased at an exponential, but almost costless, rate.

NOTE

1. Research continued to surge during 1975-80 (Anderson and Settle, 1977; Bruce, 1976; Bussey, 1978; Carley, 1980; Carnemark, 1976; Cochrane, 1979; Clifton and Fyffe, 1977; Finsterbush and Wolf, 1977; FitzGerald, 1977, 1978; Food and Agriculture Organization, 1977, 1979; Giersig, 1978; Gruff, 1975, Hansen, 1975, 1978; Helmers, 1979; Herberger, 1977; Irvin, 1978; Jansen, 1977; Kendrick, 1978; Lal, 1975; Lele, 1975; Lesourne, 1975; Little and Scott, 1976; Ministry of Overseas Development, 1977; National Economic Development Authority, 1978; Organization of American States, 1978; Overseas Development Administration, 1977; Peskin and Seskin, 1975; Roemer and Stern, 1975; Rondinelli, 1979, 1979; Sassone and Schaffer, 1978; Scheider, 1975; Schwartz and Berney, 1977; Scitovsky and Herman, 1975; Scott, 1976; Shaner, 1979; Soumelis, 1977; Squire and van der Tak, 1975; Sugden and Williams, 1978; Toye, 1976; United Nations Industrial Development Organization, 1978; United States Department of Agriculture, 1976; Weiss, 1976; Weiss, 1980; Whang, 1978; World Bank, 1976; Yatopoulos, 1976; Zeekhauser, 1975).

This was preceded by a wave of research on appraisal before 1975 (Alfred and Evans, 1967; Bainbridge and Sapirie, 1974; Balassa and Schydlowsky, 1968,

1972; Bergman, 1973; Bierman and Schmidt, 1971; Bruno, 1967, 1972; Chase, 1968; Dasgupta, 1972; Dasgupta and Pearce, 1972; Dasgupta et al., 1972; Davey, 1974; Dewhurst, 1972; Eckstein, 1958; Feldstein, 1964; Food and Agriculture Organization, 1969, 1971; Frederickson, 1965; Gittinger, 1972; Goldman, 1967; Goodman, 1970; Government of Turkey, 1974; Gutowski and Hammel, 1972; Hammel and Hemmer, 1971; Hayes, 1966; Hawkins and Pearce, 1971; Helfert, 1973; Henderson, 1970; Herberger, 1972, 1972; Hinrichs and Taylor, 1969; Holtz, 1969; Joshi, 1972; Joshi, 1972; Kendall, 1971; King, 1967; Krutilla and Eckstein, 1958; Lal, 1973, 1974; Layard, 1972; Little and Mirrlees, 1968, 1974; Maass, 1966; Marglin, 1967; Mears, 1969; Melnick, 1958; Merrett and Skyes, 1969, 1973; Ministry of Overseas Development, 1972; Mishan, 1972; Musgrave, 1969; Newton, 1972; Novick, 1967; Organization for Economic Cooperation and Development, 1972, 1973; Packard, 1974; Pearce, 1971; Pearce and Hawkins, 1971; Phillips, 1970; Pilcher, 1973, Porterfield, 1965; Pouliquen, 1970; Prest and Turvey, 1965; Quirin, 1967; Reutlinger, 1970; Sewell, 1969; Solomon, 1970; Stern, 1972; Streeten, 1972; Stewart and Streeten, 1972; United Nations, 1951, 1958, 1973; United Nations Industrial Development Organization, 1972; United States Agency for International Development, 1974; can der Tak, 1971; Walsh and Williams, 1969; Watt, 1973; Wolfe, 1973; World Bank, 1972).

REFERENCES

Abelson, Peter (1996) *Project Appraisal and Valuation Method*. London: Macmillan.

Abouchar, Alan (1985) *Project Decision-making in the Public Sector*. Lexington: Lexington Books.

Ahmed, Yusuf J. (1975) "Project Identification, Analysis and Preparation in Developing Countries", *Development and Change* 6 (July).

Aitken, N.C. and L.G. Salmon (eds.) (1983) *The Costs of Evaluation*. Beverley Hills: Sage.

Alfred, A.M. and J.B. Evans (1967) *Appraisal of Investment Projects*. London: Chapman & Hall.

Alderfer, Harold F. (1967) *Public Administration in Newer Nations*. New York: Praeger.

Allison, Graham T. (1975) "Implementation Analysis" in Richard Zeekhauser (ed.) *Benefit-Cost and Policy Analysis*. Chicago: Aldine.

Anderson, Lee G. and Russell F. Settle (1977) *Benefit-Cost Analysis*. Lexington: Lexington Books.

Anderson, Stuart D. (1987) *Project Manpower Management*. New York: Wiley.

Angleson, Aried et al. (1994) *Project Appraisal and Sustainability in Less Developed Countries*. Bergen: Michelson Institute.

Archibald, K.A. (1970) "Three Views of the Expert's Role in Policy-Making: Systems Analysis, Incrementalism and Clinical Approach", *Policy Sciences* 1 (1).

Asian Development Bank (1983) *General Guidelines for Economic Analysis of*

Projects. Manila: Asian Development Bank.

___ 1984) *Rural Development in Asia and the Pacific*. Manila: Asian Development Bank.

Attwood, D.W. et al. (eds.) (1988) *Power and Poverty: Development and Development Projects in the Third World*. Boulder: Westview Press.

Austin, James E. (1992) *Agricultural Project Analysis*. Baltimore: Johns Hopkins University Press.

Austin, Jane E. (1992) *Agroindustrial Project Analysis: Critical Design Factors*. Baltimore: John Hopkins University Press.

Awani, Alfred O. (1983) *Project Management Techniques*. New York: Petrocelli Books.

Bailey, S.K. and E.K. Mosher (1968) *ESEA: The Office of Education Administers a Law*. Syracuse: Syracuse University Press.

Bainbridge, J. and S. Sapirie (1974) *Health Project Management*. Geneva: World Health Organization.

Balassa, Bela and D.M. Schydlowsky (1968) "Effective Tarriffs, Domestic Cost of Foreign Exchange and the Equilibrium Exchange Rate", *Journal of Political Economy* 76 (May-June).

___ (1972) "Domestic Resource Costs and Effective Protection Once Again", *Journal of Political Economy* 80 (January-February).

Bardach, Eugene (1977) *The Implementation Game*. Cambridge, Mass.: MIT Press.

___ (1980) "On Designing Implementable Program", in G. Majone and E. Quade (eds.) *Pitfalls of Analysis*. New York: John Wiley.

Barndt, S.E. et al. (1977) "Organizational Climate Changes in the Project Life Cycle", *International Journal of Research Management* 20(5).

Barratt, John et al. (1976) *Strategy for Development*. London: Macmillan.

Barrett, S. and C. Fudge (1981) *Policy and Action*. London: Methuen.

Baum, Warren C. (1970) "The Project Cycle", *Finance and Development* 7(2).

___ (1978) "The World Bank Project Cycle", *Finance and Development* (December).

___ (1982) *The Project Cycle*. Washington, D.C.: World Bank.

___ and Stokes M. Tulbert (1985) *Investing in Development: Lessons of World Bank Experience*. Washington, D.C.: World Bank.

Baumgartner, John S. (1963) *Project Management*. Homewood: Irwin.

___ (1979) *Systems Management*. Washington, D.C.: Bureau of National Affairs.

Becker, H.A. et al. (1985) *Management of Water Projects*. Paris: Organization for Economic Cooperation and Development.

Behren, W. and P.M. Hawranek (1991) *Industrial Feasibility Studies*. Geneva: United Nations Industrial Development Organization.

Bell, C. et al. (1982) *Project Evaluation in Regional Perspectives*. Baltimore: John Hopkins University Press.

Benjamin, M.P. (1981) *Investment Projects in Agriculture*. London: Longman.

Bergman, H. (1973) *Guide to the Economic Evaluation of Irrigation Projects*.

Paris: Organization for Economic Cooperation and Development.

Berke, J.S. and M. W. Kirst (1972) *Federal Aid to Education: Who Benefits? Who Governs?* Lexington, Mass.: Lexington Books.

Berman, Paul (1978) "The Study of Macro and Micro-Implementation", *Public Policy* 26(Spring).

Bierman H. and Seymour Smidt (1971) *The Capital Budgeting Decision: Economic Analysis and Financing of Investment Projects*. New York: Macmillan.

Birgegard, Lars-Erik (1975) *The Project Selection Process in Developing Countries*. Stockholm: Economic Research Institute.

Brainbanti, Ralph (ed.) (1969) *Political and Administrative Development*. Durham: Duke University Press.

Braybrooke, D. and C.E. Lindblom (1963) *A Strategy of Decision*. New York: Free Press.

Brent, R.J. (1990) *Project Appraisal for Developing Countries*. New York: New York University Press.

Bridger, G. A. and J.T. Winpenny (1983) *Planning Development Projects*. London: Overseas Development Administration.

____ (1986) "Rapid Project Appraisal", *Project Appraisal* 1(14).

Bruce, Colin (1976) *Social Cost-Benefit Analysis*. Washington, D. C.: World Bank.

Bruno, M. (1967) "The Optimal Selection of Export-Promoting and Import-Substituting Project", in United Nations (ed.) *Planning the External Sector: Techniques, Problems and Policies*. New York: United Nations.

___ (1972) "Domestic Resource Costs and Effective Protection: Clarification and Synthesis", *Journal of Political Economy* (January-February).

Brinkerhoff, D.W. and J.C. Garcia-Zamor (eds.) (1986) *Politics, Projects and People*. New York: Praeger.

___ (1991) *Improving Development Program Performance*. Boulder: Lynne Rienner.

Byrant, Coralie and Louise G. White (1980) *Managing Rural Development*. West Hartford: Kumarian Press.

___ (1982) *Managing Development in the Third World*. Boulder: Westview Press.

Bunker, Douglas R. (1972) "Policy Sciences Perspectives on Implementation Process", *Policy Sciences* 3(March).

Burch, John G. et al. (1979) *Information Systems: Theory and Practice*. New York: John Wiley.

Bussey, Lynn E. (1978) *The Economic Analysis of Industrial Projects*. Englewood Cliffs: Prentice-Hall.

Caiden, Gerald E. (1969) "Development Administration and Administrative Reform", *International Review of Administrative Sciences* 39(4).

Caiden, Naomi and Aaron Wildavsky (1974) *Planning and Budgeting in Poor Countries*. New York: John Wiley.

Canadian International Development Agency (1991) *A Study of the Quality of CIDA Bilateral Evaluation*. Ottawa: Canadian International Development

Agency.

Caribbean Development Bank (1986) *Public Sector Investment Program.* St. Michael, Barbados: Caribbean Development Bank.

Carley, Michael (1980) *Rational Techniques in Policy Analysis.* London: Heinemann.

Carnemark, Curt et al. (1976) *The Economic Analysis of Rural Road Projects.* Washington, D.C.: World Bank.

Carvallo, Soniya et al. (1996) *Implementing Projects for the Poor.* Washington, D.C.: World Bank.

Casley, Dennis J. and D.A. Lury (1982) *Monitoring and Evaluation of Agricultural and Rural Development Projects.* Washington, D.C.: World Bank.

___ (1987) *Project Monitoring and Evaluation in Agriculture.* Baltimore: John Hopkins University Press.

Cernea, Michael (ed.) (1991) *Putting People First.* New York: Oxford University Press.

Chambers, Robert (1969) *Settlement Schemes in Tropical Africa.* New York: Praeger.

___ and Deryke Belshaw (1973) *Managing Rural Development: Lessons and Methods from Eastern Africa.* Brighton: Institute of Development Studies.

___ (1974) *Managing Rural Development: Ideas and Experience from East Africa.* Upsala: Scandinavian Institute of African Studies.

___ (1978) "Project Selection for Poverty-Focused Research Development", *World Development* (6).

Chapel, Yves (ed.) (1977) *Administrative Management for Development.* Brussels: International Institute of Administrative Sciences.

Chase, S.B. (ed.) (1968) *Problems in Public Expenditure Analysis.* Washington, E.C.: Brookings Institution.

Chenery, Holis (1974) *Redistribution with Growth.* London: Oxford University Press.

Choldin, Harvey M. (1969) "The Development Project as a Natural Experiment", *Economic Development and Cultural Change* 17(July).

Clayton, E. and F. Petry (eds.) (1983) *Monitoring Systems for Agricultural and Rural Development Projects.* Rome: Food and Agriculture Organization.

Clarke, B.D. et al. (1981) *A Manual for the Assessment of Major Development Proposals.* London: Her Majesty's Stationery Office.

Cleaves, Peter S. (1980) "Implementation Amidst Scarcity and Apathy: Political Power and Policy Design", in Merilee S. Grindle (ed.) *Politics and Policy Implementation in the Third World.* Princeton: Princeton University Press.

Cleland, David I. (1967) "Understanding Project Authorities", *Business Horizons* (Spring).

___ and William R. King (1968) *Systems Analysis and Project* Management. New York: McGraw-Hill.

___ (1990) *Project Management: Strategic Design and Implementation.* Blue Ridge Summit, Penn.: TAB Books.

Clifton, David S, and David E. Fyffe (1977) *Project Feasibility Analysis*. New York: John Wiley.

___ et al. (1986) *Manual for Project Economic Analysis*. Atlanta: Georgia Institute of Technology.

Cochrane, Glynn (1979) *The Cultural Appraisal of Development Projects*. New York: Praeger.

Coomes, H.M. and D.E. Jenkins (1991) *Public Sector Financial Management*. London: Chapman & Hall.

Cracknell, B.E.O. (ed.) (1984) *The Evaluation of Aid Projects and Programs*. London: Her Majesty's Stationery Office.

___ and J. E. Rednall (1986) *Defining Objectives and Measuring Performance in Aid Projects and Programs*. London: Overseas Development Administration.

Curry, Steve S. and John Weiss (1993) *Project Analysis in Developing Countries*. London: Macmillan.

Dasgupta, Ajit K. and David W. Pearce (1972) *Cost-Benefit Analysis: Theory and Practice*. New York: Harper & Row.

Dasgupta, Partha et al. (1972) *Guidelines for Project Evaluation*. New York: United Nations Industrial Development Organization.

___ (1972) "A Comparative Analysis of the UNIDO Guidelines and the OECD Manual", *Bulletin of the Oxford University Institute of Economics and Statistics* (February).

Datta, L.E. and R. Perloff (eds.) (1979) *Improving Evaluation*. Beverley Hills: Sage.

Davey, Patrick J. (1974) *Capital Investments: Appraisals and Limits*. New York: Conference Board.

Dean, Edwin (1977) *Plan Implementation in Nigeria: 1962-66*. Ibadan: Oxford University Press.

Department of Environment (1991) *Policy Appraisal and the Environment*. London: Her Majesty's Stationery Office.

Department of Treasury (1984) *Investment Appraisal in the Public Sector*. London: Her Majesty's Stationery Office.

Derthick, Martha (1970) *The Influence of Federal Grants*. Cambridge, Mass.: Harvard University Press.

___ (1972) *New Towns In-Town*. Washington, D.C.: Urban Institute.

Development Alternatives (1978) *Studies in Project Design: Approval and Implementation*. Washington, D.C.: Development Alternatives.

De Vries, Egbert (1971) *Administration of Development Programs and Projects: Some Major Issues*. New York: United Nations.

Dewhurst, R.F.J. (1972) *Business Cost-Benefit Analysis*. London: George Allen & Unwin.

Dickey, J.W. and L.H. Miller (1984) *Road Project Appraisal for Developing Countries*. Chicester: John Wiley.

Dinsmore, Paul C. (1990) *Human Factors in Project Management*. New York: American Management Association.

Dinwiddy, C. and F. Teal (1995) *Principles of Cost-Benefit Analysis for Developing Countries*. Cambridge University Press.

Dolbeare, K. M. and P. E. Hammond (1971) *The School Prayer Decisions*. Chicago: University of Chicago Press.

Duffy, P. J. and R.D. Thomas (1984) *Project Planning and Management: An Integrated Approach*. New York: Pergamon Press.

Dufty, N. F. and P.M. Taylor (1962) "The Implementation of a Decision", *Administrative Science Quarterly* (June).

Dunsire, Andrew (1978) *Control in a Bureaucracy*. Oxford: Martin Robertson.

___ (1978) *Implementation in a Bureaucracy*. Oxford: Martin Robertson.

Dupriez, Hughes (1979) *Integrated Rural Development Projects in Africa: Evaluation and Outlook for the Future*. Brussels: European Community.

Eaton, Joseph W. (ed.) (1972) *Institution Building and Development*. Beverley Hills: Sage.

Eckstein, Otto (1958) *Water Resource Development: The Economics of Project Evaluation*. Cambridge: Harvard University Press.

Edwards, George C. (1980) *Implementing Public Policy*. Washington, D.C.: Congressional Quarterly Press.

Eggers, Helmut (1992) "The Integrated Approach to Project Cycle Management", *Project Appraisal* 7(1).

Ellman, Michael (1979) *Socialist Planning*. Cambridge: Cambridge University Press.

Elmore, R. (1980) "Backward Mapping: Implementation Research and Policy Decisions", *Political Science Quarterly* (1).

Esman, Milton J. (1963) *The Politics of Development Administration*. Pittsburgh: University of Pittsburgh Press.

___ (1972) *Administration of Development in Malaysia*. Ithaca: Cornell University Press.

___ and John D. Montgomery (1980) "The Administration of Human Development", in Peter Knight (ed.) *Implementation Programs of Human Development*. Washington, D.C: World Bank.

European Community (1991) *Review of Effectiveness of Feedback Mechanisms*. Brussels: European Community.

___ (1992) *Manual on Project Cycle Management*. Brussels: European Community.

Faber, Michael and Dudley Seers (eds.) (1972) *The Crisis in Planning*. London: Chatto & Windus.

Feldstein, M. (1964) "Cost-Benefit Analysis and Investment in the Public Sector", *Public Administration* (42).

Fesler, James W. (1980) *Public Administration: Theory and Practice*. Englewood Cliffs, N.J.: Prentice-Hall.

Finsterbusch, Kurt and C.P. Wolf (1977) *Methodology of Social Impact* Assessment. Stroudsburg: Hutchinson & Ross.

Fitzgerald, E.V.K. (1977) "The Public Investment Criterion and the Role of the

State", *Journal of Development Studies* 13 (July).

___ (1978) *Public Sector Investment Planning for Developing Countries.* London: Macmillan.

Food and Agriculture Organization (1969) *Agricultural Project Analysis.* Romc: Food and Agriculture Organization.

___ (1971) *General Guidelines to the Analysis of Agricultural Production Projects.* Rome: Food and Agriculture Organization.

___ (1977) *Guidelines for the Preparation of Agricultural Investment Projects.* Rome: Food and Agriculture Organization.

___ (1979) *Near East Readings on Agricultural Investment Projects.* Rome: Food and Agriculture Organization.

___ (1990) *The Design of Agricultural Investment Projects: Lessons from Experience.* Rome: Food and Agriculture Organization Investment Centre.

Frame, J. Davidson (1987) *Managing Projects in Organizations.* San Francisco: Jossey-Bass.

Fredrickson, E.B. (1965) *Frontiers of Investment Analysis.* Scranton: International Textbook.

Gant, George F. (1979) *Development Administration: Concepts, Goals, Methods.* Madison: University of Wisconsin Press.

Garcia-Zamor, Jean-Claude (1977) *The Ecology of Development Administration in Jamaica, Trinidad-Tobago and Barbados.* Washington, D.C.: Organization of American States.

Gardiner, J.L. (1991) *River Projects and Conservation: A Manual for Holistic Appraisal.* Chicester: Edward Elgar.

Gebregziabher, Betru (1975) *Integrated Development in Rural Ethiopia.* Bloomington, Indiana: International Development Research Center, Indiana University.

Geoghegan, Tighe (ed.) (1985) *The Caribbean Seminar on Environmental Impact Assessment.* St. Michael, Barbados: Centre for Resource Management and Environmental Studies, University of the West Indies.

Gemmill, Gary and David L. Wilemon (1970) "Power Spectrum in Project management", *Sloan Management Review* (Fall).

Giersig, G. et al. (1978) *Manual for the Preparation of Industrial Feasibility Study.* New York: United Nations.

Gitelson, Susan A. (1972) "How Are Development Projects Selected?", *African Review* 2(2).

Gittinger, J.P. (1972) *Economic Analysis of Agricultural Projects.* Baltimore: Johns Hopkins University Press.

Goldman, Thomas A. (ed.) (1967) *Cost-Effectiveness Analysis.* New York: Praeger.

Goodman, Louis J. (1977) *The Integrated Project Planning and Management Cycle.* Honolulu: East-West Center.

___ and Ralph N. Love (eds.) (1979) *Management of Development Projects: An International Case Study Approach.* New York: Pergamon Press.

___ and Ralph N. Love (1980) *Project Planning and Management: An Integrated*

Approach. New York: Pergamon Press.
Goodman, Sam R. (1970) *Techniques of Financial Analysis*. New York: John Wiley.
Government of Turkey (1974) *Guidelines for Review and Evaluation: Agricultural Development Projects*. Ankara: Government of Turkey.
___ (1974) *Manual for Preparation and Analysis of Agricultural Projects*. Ankara: Government of Turkey.
Graaff, J. De V. (1975) "Cost-Benefit Analysis: A Critical View", *South African Journal of Economics* 43(June).
Graham, Robert (1989) *Project Management as if People Mattered*. Bala Cynwyd, Penn.: Primavera Press.
Gramlich, E.M. (1981) *Benefit-Cost Analysis of Government Programs*. Englewood Cliffs: Prentice-Hall.
Gran, Guy (1983) *Development by People*. New York: Praeger.
Green, Phyllis A. and Marie L. Slyfield (1982) *Problems in Strengthening the Administrative Capability of Small States*. Kingston, Jamaica: Administrative Staff College.
Grindle, Merilee S. (ed.) (1980) *Politics and Policy Implementation in the Third World*. Princeton: Princeton University Press.
Gross, Bertram (1966) *The Administration of Economic Development Planning: Principles and Fallacies*. New York: United Nations.
___ (1969) "Some Factors in Appraising Administrative Performance in Development Planning", in United Nations (ed.) *Administrative Aspects of Planning*. New York: United Nations.
Gross, Neal et al. (1971) *Implementing Organizational Innovations*. New York: Basic Books.
Gunn, Lewis A. (1978) "Why Is Implementation So Difficult?" *Management Services in Government* 33 (November).
Gutowski, Armin and Werner Hammel (1972) "An Aid Agency's Experience With the Little-Mirrless Method", *Bulletin of Oxford University Institute of Economics and Statistics* 34(February).
Hadden, Susan G. (1980) "Controlled Decentralization and Policy Implementation", in Mirrlees S. Grindle (ed.) *Politics and Policy Implementation in the Third World*. Princeton: Princeton University Press.
Ham, Christopher and Michael Hill (1984) *The Policy Process in the Modern Capitalist State*. Brighton, England: Wheatsheaf Press.
Hammel, Werner and Hans-Rimbert Hemmer (1971) *Basic Principles of Cost-Benefit Analysis of Projects in Developing Countries*. Frankfurt: Kreditanstalt fur Wiederaufbau.
Hanf, Kenneth and A.J. Toonen (eds.) (1985) *Policy Implementation in Federal and Unitary Systems*. Dordrecht: Martinus Nijhoff.
Hanley, N. and C. L. Spash (1993) *Cost-Benefit Analysis and the Environment*. Aldershot: Edward Elgar.
Hansen, J.R. (1975) *A Guide to the UNIDO Guidelines*. Washington, D.C.: World

Bank.

___ (1978) *Guide to Practical Project Appraisal: Social Benefit-Cost Analysis in Developing Countries.* Vienna: United Nations Industrial Development Organization.

Hargrove, Erwin C. (1975) *The Missing Link: The Study of the Implementation of Social Policy.* Washington, D. C.: Urban Institute.

___ (1977) "Implementation", in H. George Frederickson and Charles R. Wise (eds.) *Public Administration and Public Policy.* Lexington, Mass.: Lexington Books.

Harrison, F.L. (1981) *Advanced Project Management.* Aldershot: Gower.

Harvey, Charles (1986) *Analysis of Project Finance in Developing Countries.* Aldershot: Gower.

Hawkins, C.J. and D.W. Pearce (1971) *Capital Investment Appraisal.* London: Macmillan Press.

Hayes, Samuel P. (1966) *Evaluating Development Projects.* Paris: United Nations Educational, Scientific and Culture Organization.

Helfert, Erich A. (1973) *Techniques of Financial Analysis.* Homewood: Irwin.

Helmers, F.L.C.H. (1979) *Project Planning and Income Distribution.* Boston: Martinus Nijhoff.

Henderson, P.D. (1970) "Some Unsettled Issues in Cost-Benefit Analysis", in Paul Streeten (ed.) *Unfashionable Economics.* London: Wiedenfeld and Nicolson.

Herberger, Arnold C. et al. (1972) *Benefit-Cost Analysis.* New York: Aldine Atherton.

___ (1972) *Project Evaluation.* Chicago: University of Chicago Press.

___ (1977) "On the UNIDO Guidelines for Social Project Evaluation", in Hugh Schwartz and Richard Berney (eds.) *Social and Economic Dimensions of Project Evaluation.* Washington, D.C.: Inter-American Development Bank.

Her Majesty's Stationery Office (1988) *Appraisal of Projects in Developing Countries.* London: Her Majesty's Stationery Office.

___ (1989) *Appraisal of Projects in Developing Countries.* London: Her Majesty's Stationery Office.

Hersey, Paul and Kenneth Blanchard (1982) *Management of Organizational Behavior: Utilizing Human Resources.* Englewood Cliffs: Prentice-Hall.

Hinrichs, Harley H. and Graeme M. Taylor (eds.) (1969) *Program Budgeting and Benefit-Cost Analysis.* Pasadena: Goodyear.

Hirschman, Albert O. (1963) *Journeys Toward Progress.* New York: Twentieth-Century Fund.

___ (1967) *Development Projects Observed.* Washington, D.C.: Brookings Institution.

___ (1984) *Getting Ahead Collectively.* New York: Pergamon Press.

Hjern, Benny and David O. Porter (1981) "Implementation Structures: A New Unit of Administrative Analysis", *Organizational Studies* 2(3).

___ and Chris Hull (1982) "Implementation Beyond Hierarchy", *European*

Journal of Political Science (2).

Hogwood, Brian W. and Lewis A. Gunn (1984) *Policy Analysis for the Real World*. London: Oxford University Press.

Holtz, J. N. (ed.) (1969) *Project Planning and Evaluation*. New York: Praeger.

Honadle, George and Rudi Klauss (eds.) (1979) *International Development Administration: Implementation Analysis for Development Projects*. New York: Praeger.

___ and J. van Sant (1991) *Implementation for Sustainability*. Hartford: Kumarian Press.

Honey, John C. (1968) *Toward Strategies for Public Administration Development in Latin America*. Syracuse: Syracuse University Press.

Hood, Christopher (1976) *The Limits of Administration*. London: John Wiley.

Hope, Kempe R. and Aubrey Armstrong (1980) "Toward the Development of Administrative and Management Capability in Developing Countries", *International Review of Administrative Sciences* 46(4).

___ (1984) *The Dynamics of Development and Development Administration*. Westport: Greenwood Press.

Horst, Pamela et al. (1973) "Program Management and the Federal Evaluator", *Public Administration Review* (August).

Horton, Forest W. (1994) *Analyzing Benefits and Costs*. Ottawa: International Development Research Center.

Howe, John and Peter Richards (eds.) (1984) *Rural Roads and Poverty Alleviation*. London: Intermediate Technology Publication.

Iglesias, Gabriel U. (eds.) (1976) *Implementation: The Problem of Achieving Results*. Manila: Eastern Regional Organization for Public Administration.

Imboden, N. (1978) *A Management Approach to Project Appraisal and Evaluation*. Paris: Organization for Economic Cooperation and Development.

Ingle, Marcus D. (1979) *Implementing Development Programs*. Washington, D.C.: United States Agency for International Development.

Inter-American Development Bank (1981) *Estimating Accounting Prices for Project Appraisal*. Washington, D.C.: Inter-American Development Bank.

International Labor Organization (1981) *Project Preparation and Appraisal*. Geneva: International Labor Organization.

Irvin, George W. (1975) *Roads and Redistribution*. Geneva: International Labor Organization.

___ (1978) *Modern Cost-Benefit Methods*. London: Macmillan.

Israel, Arturo (1978) "Toward Better Project Implementation", *Finance and Development* 15 (March).

___ (1987) *Institutional Development*. Baltimore: Johns Hopkins University Press.

Iversen, Robert W. (1979) "Personnel for Implementation: A Contextual Perspective", in George Honadle and Rudi Klauss (eds.) *International Development Administration: Implementation Analysis for Development Projects*. New York: Praeger.

Jansen, H.P.J. Heukensfeldt (1977) *Evaluation and Discounting Cash Flow*. Amsterdam: North-Holland.

Jenkins, Glenn P, and Arnold C. Herberger (1991) *Cost-Benefit Analysis of Investment Decisions*. Cambridge: Harvard Institute for International Development.

___ (1994) *Program on Investment Appraisal and Management*. Cambridge: Harvard Institute for International Development.

Jones, Charles O. (1977, 1984) *An Introduction to the Study of Public Policy*. North Scituate, Mass.: Duxbury Press.

Joshi, Heather (1972) "World Prices as Shadow Prices: A Critique", *Bulletin of Oxford University Institute of Economics and Statistics* 34 (February).

Joshi, Vijay (1972) "The Rationale and Relevance of the Little-Mirrless Criterion", *Bulletin of Oxford University Institute of Economics and Statistics* 34 (February).

Kast, Fremont E. and James E. Rosenzweig (1963) *Science, Technology and Management: An Overview*. New York: McGraw-Hill.

Katz, Saul M. (1969) "A Methodological Note on Appraising Administrative Capacity for Development", in United Nations (ed.) *Appraising Administrative Capacity for Development*. New York: United Nations.

Kaufman, Herbert (1960) *The Forest Ranger*. Baltimore: Johns Hopkins University Press.

___ (1971) *The Limits of Organizational Change*. University: University of Alabama Press.

___ (1973) *Administrative Feedback: Monitoring Subordinates' Behavior*. Washington, D.C.: Brookings Institution.

Kelley, Albert J. (1982) *New Dimensions of Project Management*. Lexington: Lexington Books.

Kelman, Steven (1984) "Using Implementation Research to Solve Implementation Problem", *Journal of Policy Analysis and Management* 4 (Fall).

Kemps, Robert R. (1992) *Fundamentals of Project Performance Measurement*. San Diego: San Diego Publishing.

Kendall, M.G. (1971) *Cost-Benefit Analysis*. New York: Elsevier.

Kendrick, D.A. (1978) *The Planning of Industrial Investment Programs*. Baltimore: Johns Hopkins University Press.

Kenessey, Zoltan (1978) *The Process of Economic Planning*. New York: Columbia University Press.

Khan, Akhter Hameed (1974) *Reflections on the Comilla Rural Development Projects*. Washington D.C.: American Council on Education.

Khan, Jamal (1975) Administrative Change and Development in Barbados", *International Review of Administrative Sciences* 41(2).

___ (1976) *Development Administration: Field Research in Barbados*. St. Michael, Barbados: Yoruba Press.

___ (1977) "Development Project and Development Administration: A Study of the International Seafoods Limited", *Caribbean Quarterly* 23 (December).

___ (1978) *Managing Development: Theory and Practice*. St. Michael, Barbados:

Crown Caribbean.

___(1982, 1987) *Public Management: The Eastern Caribbean Experience*. Leiden, Holland: KITLV Press.

___(1989) "The Project Cycle: Lessons from the Caribbean", *Journal of Local Government* 18(1).

___(1989) "Management Capability: A Study in Public Sector Application", *Bangladesh Journal of Public Administration* 3(January)

___(1989) "The Implementation Process: Programs and Projects", Management Development 18 (July - September).

___(1989) "The Implementation Process", *Indian Journal of Public Administration* 35 (October - December).

___(1989) "Development Projects and the Barbadian Evidence", *Development Review* 2 (July).

___(1990) "The Commonwealth Caribbean: Management Capability Development in the Public Sector", *Bulletin of Eastern Caribbean Affairs* 16(July - August).

___(1991) "The Development Project Cycle and a Barbadian Project", *Project Management Quarterly* 22(June).

___(1992) "The Implementation Process: A Rural Development Project", *Journal of Rural Development and Administration* 24(October - December).

___(1993) "Examining Management Capability in Barbados", *Caribbean Labor Journal* 3(December).

___(1994) "The Bridgetown Sewerage Project: A Project Cycle Study", *Journal of Administrative Processes* 21 (July - December).

___(1994) "Probing Barbados' Management Environment", *Pakistan Administration* 31 (July-December).

___(1995) "Management Capability in Barbados", in Noel M. Cowell and Ian Boxill (eds.) *Human Resource Management: A Caribbean Perspective*. Kingston, Jamaica: Canoe Press/ University of the West Indies Press.

___(1995) "Organization-Building and Capacity-Building in a Developing Country", *Journal of Social Studies* 69(July).

___(1996) "Development Management in the Commonwealth Caribbean", *Pakistan Journal of Public Administration* 23(July - December).

___(1997) "The Project Approach to Development: Some Evidence from Barbados", *Journal of Social Studies* 76(April).

Killick, Tony (ed.) (1976) *The Kenyan Economy*. London: Heinemann.

___(1981) *Policy Economics*. London: Heinemann.

Killman, Ralph H. et al. (eds.) (1976) *The Management of Organization Design: Strategies and Implementation*. New York: North-Holland.

Kindleberger, Charles P. (1965) *Economic Development*. New York: McGraw-Hill.

King, John A. (1967) *Economic Development Projects and their Appraisal*. Baltimore: Johns Hopkins University Press.

Kirkpatrick, Colin (ed.) (1991) *Project Rehabilitation in Developing Countries*.

London: Routledge.

___ and John Weiss (eds.) (1996) *Cost-Benefit Analysis and Project Appraisal in Developing Countries*. Cheltenham: Edward Elgar.

Knight, Peter (ed.) (1980) *Implementing Programs of Human Development*. Washington, D.C.: World Bank.

Koppel, Bruce (1976) *The Evaluation Factor*. Honolulu: East-West Center.

Korten, David C. and Felipe B. Alfonso (eds.) (1981) *Bureaucracy and the Poor: Closing the Gap*. Singapore: McGraw-Hill.

Krutilla, John V. and Otto Eckstein (1958) *Multiple Purpose River Basin Development*. Baltimore: Johns Hopkins University Press.

Kurz, Johannes W. (1973) "Transformation of Plans into Action", *Journal of Urban Planning and Development* (September).

Kuyvenhaven, A. and L.B.M. Mennes (1985) *Guidelines for Project Appraisal*. Hague: Government Printery.

Lal, Deepak (1973) *Alternative Project Selection Procedures for Developing Countries*. Washington, D.C.: World Bank.

___ (1974) *Methods of Project Analysis*. Baltimore: Johns Hopkins University Press.

___ (1975) *Appraising Foreign Investment in Developing Countries*. London: Heinemann.

Lang, H. and H.D. Drechsler (1989) *Making On-Site Project Implementation*. Eschborn, Germany: GTZ Sonderpub.

Larson, James S. (1980) *Why Government Programs Fail: Improving Policy Implementation*. New York: Praeger.

Layard, Richard (ed.) (1972) *Cost-Benefit Analysis*. Harmondsworth: Penguin.

Lele, Uma (1975) *The Design of Rural Development*. Baltimore: Johns Hopkins University Press.

Lembke, H.H. (1984) *Evaluating Development Assistance Projects*. Berlin: German Development Institute.

Lesourne, Jacques (1975) *Cost-Benefit Analysis and Economic Theory*. New York: Elsevier.

Levin, Henry M.(1983) *Cost-Effectiveness*. Beverly Hills: Sage.

Levy, H. and M. Sarnat (1986) *Capital Investment and Financial Decisions*. Englewood Cliffs: Prentice-Hall.

Lewin, Kurt (1947) "Frontiers in Group Dynamics: Concept, Method and Reality in Social Science: Social Equilibrium and Social Change", *Human Relations* 1(June).

Lewis, David H. (1976) *Project Implementation: Organization and Staffing*. Washington, D.C.: Economic Development Institute.

Lewis, W.A. (1967) "Planning Public Expenditure", in M.F. Millikan (ed.) *National Economic Planning*. New York: Columbia University Press.

___ (1968) "The Shifting Fortunes of Agriculture", in A.M. Kushro (ed.) *Readings in Agricultural Development*. Bombay: Allied Publishers.

Lindblom, C.E. (1965) *The Intelligence of Democracy*. New York: Free Press.

Lippert, Longstretch (1985) *Implementing Organizational Change*. San Francisco: Jossey-Bass.

Little, I.M.D. and J.A. Mirrlees (1968) *Manual of Industrial Project Analysis in Developing Countries*. Paris: Organization for Economic Cooperation and Development.

___ (1974) *Project Appraisal and Planning for Developing Countries*. London: Heinemann.

___ and M.F. Scott (eds.) (1976) *Using Shadow Prices*. London: Heinemann.

___ (1991) "Project Appraisal and Planning Twenty Years On", *Paper presented at the World Bank Annual Conference on Development Economics*. Washington, D.C.: World Bank.

Loasby, B.J. (1976) *Choice, Complexity and Ignorance*. Cambridge: Cambridge University Press.

Lock, Dennis (1968) *Project Management*. London: Gower.

___ (1977) *Project Management*. Aldershot, England: Gower.

Lombard, Jan A. "The Development of Bantu Homelands", in John Barrett et al. (eds.) *Accelerated Development in Southern Africa*. London: Macmillan.

Londero, Elio (1996) *Benefits and Beneficiaries*. Baltimore: Johns Hopkins University Press.

Lowi, T. A. (1972) "Four Systems of Policy, Politics and Choice", *Public Administration Review* (September).

Lumby, S.C. (1994) *Investment Appraisal and Related Decision*. London: Clapham and Hall.

Luikart, Fordyce (ed.) (1966) *The Development of Administrative Capabilities in Emerging Countries*. Washington, D.C.: Brookings Institution.

Lynn, L.E. (1984) "Improving Public Sector Management", *California Management Review* 26(2).

Maass, A. (1966) "Benefit Cost Analysis: Its Relevance to Public Investment Decisions", *Quarterly Journal of Economics* (80).

MacArthur, J.D. (1988) *Approach of Projects in Developing Countries*. London: Her Majesty's Stationery Office.

___ and J. Weiss (eds.) (1993) *Agriculture, Projects and Development*. Aldershot: Avebury.

Maddock, N. and F. A. Wilson (eds.) (1994) *Project Design for Agricultural Development*. Oxford: Avebury.

Majone, Giandomenico and Aaron Wildavsky (1979) "Implementation as Evolution", in Jeffrey L. Pressman and Aaron Wildavsky (eds.) *Implementation*. Berkeley: University of California Press.

Marglin, Steven A. (1967) *Public Investment Criteria*. London: George Allen & Unwin.

Mazmanian, Daniel A. and Paul A. Sabatier (1981) *Effective Policy Implementation*. Lexington, Mass. : Lexington Books.

___ (1983) *Implementation and Public Policy*. Glenview, Illinois: Scott, Foresman.

Mears, Leon A. (1969) *Economic Project Evaluation*. Manila: University of the

Phillippines Press.

Melnick, Julio (1958) *Manual on Economic Development Projects.* New York: United Nations.

Meredith, Jack R. and Samuel J. Mantel (1985) *Project Management: A Managerial Approach.* New York: John Wiley.

Merreth, A.J. and Allen Sykes (1969) *Capital Budgeting and Company Finance.* London: Longman.

___(1973) *The Finance and Analysis of Capital Projects.* New York: John Wiley.

Migdal, Joel S. (1977) "Policy and Power: A Framework for the Study of Comparative Policy Contexts in Third World Countries", *Public Policy* 25 (Spring).

Mills, G.E. (1973) "The Environment of Commonwealth Caribbean Bureaucracies", *International Review of Administrative Sciences* 39 (1).

Ministry of Economic Cooperation (1986) *Learning from Mistakes: Nine Years of Evaluating Project Reality, Findings and Conclusions.* Bonn: Ministry of Economic Cooperation.

Ministry of Foreign Affairs (1990) *Efficiency and Evaluation in Development Assistance.* Stockholm: Ministry of Foreign Affairs.

Ministry of Overseas Development (1972) *A Guide to Project Appraisal in Developing Countries.* London: Her Majesty's Stationery Office.

___(1977) *A Guide to the Economic Appraisal of Projects in Developing Countries.* London: Her Majesty's Stationery Office.

Mintzberg, Henry (1973) *The Nature of Managerial Work.* New York: Harper & Row.

Mishan, Ezra J. (1972) *Elements of Cost-Benefit Analysis.* London: George Allen & Unwin.

Montgomery, John D. and William J. Siffin (eds.) (1970) *Approach to Development: Politics, Administration and Change.* New York: McGraw-Hill.

___(1974) *Technology and Civic Life: Making and Implementing Development Decisions.* Cambridge, Mass.: MIT Press.

___(1979) "Decisions, Nondecisions and Other Phenomena", in George Honadle ad Rudi Klauss (eds.) *International Development Administration.* New York: Praeger.

Morris, Peter W.G. (1982) "Project Organizations: Structure for Managing Change", in Albert J. Kelley (ed.) *New Dimensions of Project Management.* Lexington, Mass.: Lexington Books.

Morss, Elliott et al. (eds.) (1976) *Strategies for Small Farmer Development: An Empirical Study of Rural Development Projects.* Boulder: Westview Press.

___ and David D. Gow (eds.) (1985) *Implementing Rural Development Projects.* Boulder: Westview Press.

Mountoy, R.S. and L.J. O'Toole (1979) "Towards a Theory of Policy Implementation: An Organizational Review", *Public Administration Review* (September).

Myrdal, Gunnar (1968) *Asian Drama.* New York: Twentieth-Century Fund.

Murphy, D.C. et al., (1974) *Determinants of Project Success.* Chestnut Hills, Mass.: Boston College Institute of Management.

Murphy, K.J. (1983) *Macroproject Development in Third World.* Boulder: Westview Press.

Musgrave, R.A. (1969) "Cost-Benefit Analysis and the Theory of Public Finance", *Journal of Economic Literature* (September).

Nakamura, Robert T. and Frank Smallwood (1980) *The Politics of Policy Implementation.* New York: St. Martin's Press.

National Economic and Development Authority (1978) *A Guide to Project Development.* Manila: National Economic and Development Authority.

Nelson, Richard R. and Douglas T. Yates (1967) *Innovation and Implementation in Public Organizations.* Farnborough: Lexington Books.

Newton, Trevor (1972) *Cost-Benefit Analysis in Administration.* London: George Allen & Unwin.

Noorbaksh, Noor (1989) *Project Cycle Revisited.* Tokyo: Sophia University.

Norweigian Agency for Development (1991) *Strategies for Development Cooperation.* Oslo: Norweigian Agency for Development.

Novick, David (ed.) (1967) *Program Budgeting.* Cambridge: Harvard University Press.

Oakley, P. et al. (eds.) (1991) *Project with People.* Geneva: International Labor Organization.

Olivares, J. (1979) "Retrospective Evaluation of Agricultural Projects", in Food and Agriculture Organization (ed.) *Near East Readings on Agricultural Investment Projects.* Rome: Food and Agriculture Organization.

Organization of American States (1978) *Development Projects Program.* Washington, D.C.: Organization of American States.

Organization for Economic Cooperation and Development (1968) *Manual of Industrial Project Analysis in Developing Countries.* Paris: OECD Development Center.

___(1972) *Investing in Developing Countries.* Paris: Organization for Economic Cooperation and Development.

___ (1973) *Methods of Project Appraisal in Developing Countries.* Paris: Organization for Economic Cooperation and Development.

___(1981) *An Institutional Approach to Project Analysis in Developing Countries.* Paris: Organization for Economic Cooperation and Development.

___(1986) *Methods and Procedures in Aid Evaluation.* Paris: Organization for Economic Cooperation and Development.

___(1989) *A Review of Donor System for Feedback from Aid Evaluation.* Paris: Organization for Economic Cooperation and Development.

O'Riordan, T. and W.R.D. Sewell (eds.) (1981) *Project Appraisal and Policy Review.* Chicester: John Wiley.

Overseas Development Administration (1977) *A Guide to the Economic Appraisal of Projects in Developing Countries.* London: Hear Majesty's Stationery Office.

___(1988) *Appraisal of Projects in Developing Countries.* London: Her Majesty's Stationery Office.

___ (1995) *A Guide to Social Analysis for Projects in Developing Countries.* London: Her Majesty's Stationery Office.

Packard, Phillip C. (1974) *Project Appraisal for Development Administration.* Hague: Mouton.

Pajestka, Joseph (1969) "Plan Formulation and Implementation Machinery", in United Nations (ed.) *Administrative Aspects of Planning.* New York: United Nations.

Palumbo, Dennis J. and Marvin A. Harder (eds.) (1981) *Implementing Public Policy.* Lexington, Mass.: Lexington Books.

Paul, Samuel (1982) *Managing Development Programs: The Lessons of Success.* Boulder: Westview Press.

___ (1983) *Strategic Management of Development Programs.* Geneva: International Labor Organization.

Pearce, David W. (1971) *Cost-Benefit Analysis.* London: Macmillan.

___ and Christopher J. Hawkins (1971) *Capital Investment Appraisal.* London: Macmillan.

___ and C.A. Nash (1981) *The Social Appraisal of Projects.* London: Macmillan.

___ et al. (1994) *Projects and Policy Appraisal.* Paris: Organization for Economic Cooperation and Development.

Perkins, F. (1994) *Practical Cost Benefit Analysis.* Melbourne: Macmillan.

Peskin, H.M. and E.P. Seskin (eds.) (1975) *Cost-Benefit Analysis and Water Pollution Policy.* Washington, D.C.: Urban Institute.

Phillips, Richard (1970) *Feasibility Analysis for Agricultural Projects.* Seoul: Ministry of Agriculture.

Plicher, Roy (1973) *Appraisal and Control of Project Costs.* London: McGraw-Hill.

Porter, David O. and Benny Hjern (1978) "Implementation Structures: A New Unit of Analysis", *Paper presented to American Political Science Association Annual Meeting*, New York.

Porterfield, James T.S. (1965) *Investment Decisions and Capital Costs.* Englewood Cliffs: Prentice-Hall.

Pouliquen, Louis Y. (1970) *Risk Analysis in Project Appraisal.* Baltimore: Johns Hopkins University Press.

Powelson, John P. (1972) *Institutions of Economic Growth.* Princeton: Princeton University Press.

Powers, Terry A (ed.) (1981) *Estimating Accounting Prices for Project Appraisal.* Washington, D.C.: Inter-American Development Bank.

Pressman, Jeffrey L. and Aaron Wildavsky (1973) *Implementation.* Berkeley: University of California Press.

Prest, A.R. and R. Turvey (1965) "Cost-Benefit Analysis: A Survey", *Economic Journal* (75).

Project Planning Center for Developing Countries (1982) *A Manual on Project*

Planning for Small Economies. London: Commonwealth Secretariat.

Quade, E.S,. (1975) *Analysis for Public Decisions*. New York: Elsevier.

Quirin, G.D. (1967) *Capital Expenditure Decision*. Homewood: Irwin.

Rodosevich, Raymond and Denis a. Rondinelli (1974) *Integrated Approach to Development Project Management*. Washington, D.C: United States Agency for International Development.

___ and Charles Taylor (1974) *Management of the Project Environment*. Vanderbilt: Graduate School of Management.

Randolph W.A. and Barry Z. Posner (1988) *Effective Project Planing and Management: Getting the Job Done*. Englewood Cliffs: Printice-Hall.

Ray, A. (1984) *Cost-Benefit Analysis*. Baltimore: Johns Hopkins University Press.

Reeser, Clayton (1979) "Some Potential Human Problems of the Project Form of Organization", *Academy of Management Journal* (December).

Reid, Escott (1973) *Strengthening the World Bank*. Chicago: Adlai Stevenson Institute of International Affairs.

Rein, Martin and Francine Rabinovitz (1974) *Toward a Theory of Implementation*. Unpublished paper. Cambridge, Mass.: Harvard University.

___ (1977) *Implementation: A Theoretical Framework*. Cambridge: Joint Centre for Urban Studies.

Reutlinger, Shlomo (1970) *Techniques for Project Appraisal Under Uncertainty*. Baltimore: Johns Hopkins University Press.

Riggs, Fred W. (1961) *The Ecology of Public Administration*. New York: Asia Publishing House.

___ (1970) *Frontiers of Development Administration*. Durham: Duke University Press.

Ripley, Randall B. and Grace Franklin (1982) *Bureaucracy and Political Implementation*. Homewood, Illinois: Dorsey Press.

Roemer, Michael and Joseph S. Stern (1975) *The Appraisal of Development Projects*. New York: Praeger.

Roman, Daniel D. (1986) *Managing Projects: A Systems Approach*. New York: Elsevier.

Rondinelli, Dennis A. (1976) "Why Development Projects Fail: Problems of Project Management in Developing Countries", *Project Management Quarterly* (7).

___ and H.R. Radosevich (1976) "Administrative Changes in International Assistance", *Asian Economic and Social Review* (1).

___ (1976) "International Requirements for Project Preparation: Aids or Obstacles to Development Planning", *Journal of the American Institute of Planners* 42(July).

___ (1976) "Project Identification in Economic Development", *Journal of World Trade Law* 10 (May-June).

___ (1976) "International Assistance Policy and Development Project Administration: The Impact of Imperious Rationality", *International*

Organization 39(Fall).

___ (ed.) (1977) *Planning Development Projects.* Stroudsburg: Dowden, Hutchinson & Ross.

___ and Kenneth Ruddle (1977) "Local Organization for Integrated Rural Development: Implementing Equity Policy in Developing Countries", *International Review of Administrative Sciences* (43).

___ (1977) "Planning and Implementing Development Projects", in Dennis A. Rondenelli (ed.) *Planning Development Projects.* Stroudsburg, Penn.: Dowden, Hutchinson & Ross.

___ (1978) "Coping with Poverty in International Assistance Policy", *World Development* 6(April).

___ (1978) "Implementing Development Projects: The Problem of Management", *International Development Review* (20).

___ (1979) "Designing International Development Projects for Implementation", in George Honadle and Rudi Klauss (eds.) *International Development Administration.* New York: Praeger.

___ (1979) "Planning Development Projects: Lessons from Developing Countries", *Long Range Planning* (June).

___ and Marcus D. Ingle (1981) "Improving the Implementation of Development Programs: Beyond Administrative Reform", in G.S. Cheema (ed.) *Institutional Dimensions of Regional Development.* Singapore: Maruzen Asia.

___ (1981) "Government Decentralization in Comparative Perspective: Theory and Practice in Developing Countries", *International Review of Administrative Sciences* 47(2).

___ (1982) "The Dilemma of Development Administration", *World Politics* 35(October).

___ (1983) *Development Projects as Policy Experiments: An Adaptive Approach to Development Administration.* New York: Methuen.

___ (1983) "Project as Instruments of Development Administration", *Public Administration and Development* 3(4)

Rosenthal, Stephen R. (1982) *Managing Government Operations.* Glenview, Illinois: Scott, Foresman.

Rothwell, Kenneth J. (ed.) (1972) *Administrative Issues in Developing Countries.* Lexington: Lexington Books.

Sabatier, Paul and Daniel Mazmanian (1979) *Conditions of Successful Implementation: A Conceptual Framework and Empirical Studies.* Lexington, Mass.: D.C. Health.

___ (1980) "The Implementation of Public Policy: A Framework of Analysis", *Policy Studies Journal* (8).

Salmen, Lawrence F. (1987) *Listen to the People.* New York: Oxford University Press.

Samset, K.S. et al. (1993) *Internal Learning from Evaluation and Reviews.* Oslo: Ministry of Foreign Affairs.

Sassone, Peter G. and William A. Schaffer (1978) *Cost Benefit Analysis.* New

York: Academic Press.

Schaffer, Bernard (1972) *The Administrative Factor*. London: Frank Cass.

Schmidt, Gregory D. (1990) "Balancing Structure and Flexibility in Development Projects", *American Review of Public Administration* 20 (December).

Schneider, Hartmut (1975) *National Objectives and Project Appraisal in Developing Countries*. Paris: Organization for Economic Cooperation and Development.

Schwartz, Hugh and Richard Berney (eds.) (1977) *Social and Economic Dimensions of Project Evaluation*. Washington, D.C.: Inter-American Development Bank.

Scitovsky, Lyn and G.V.T. Herman (1975) *Economic Analysis of Projects*. Baltimore: Johns Hopkins University Press.

Scott, E.N. (ed.) (1981) *International Perspectives in Public Administration*. Canberra: College of Advanced Education.

Scott, M. F. G. et al. (1976) *Project Appraisal in Practice*. London: Heinemann.

Seidman, Robert B. (1979) "Development Planning and the Legal Order in Black Anglophonic Africa", *Studies in Comparative International* Development 14 (Summer).

Sell, Akel (1989) *Investment Projects in Developing Countries: Financial and Economic Analysis*. Hamburg: Hamurg Institute of Economic Research.

___ (1991) *Project Evaluation: An Integrated Financial and Economic Analysis*. Aldershot: Avebury.

Seng, Heng-Kang (1995) *Project Evaluation: Techniques and Practices for Developing Countries*. Aldershot: Avebury.

Sewell, W.R.D. et al. (1969) *Guide to Benefit-Cost Analysis*. Ottawa: Queen's Printer.

Shaner, W.W. (1979) *Project Planning for Developing Economies*. New York: Praeger.

Shen, T.Y. (1975) "Sectoral Development Planning in Tropical Africa", *Eastern Africa Economic Review* (June).

___ (1977) "More Development Planning in Tropical Africa", *Journal of Development Studies* (July).

Shull, Fremont A. (1965) *Matrix Structure and Project Authority for Optimizing Organizational Capability*. Carbondale: Southern Illinois University.

Silverman, S. (1973) *Project Management*. New York: John Wiley.

Simon, Herbert A. (1947) *Administrative Behavior*. London: Macmillan.

Smith, Peter (1984) *Agricultural Project Management: Monitoring and Control of Implementation*. London: Elsevier.

Smith, Thomas B. (1973) "The Policy Implementation Process", *Policy Sciences* 4(June).

___ (1973) "Policy Roles: An Analysis of Policy Formulators and Policy Implementors", *Policy Sciences* (4).

Solomon, Morris J. (1970) *Analysis of Projects for Economic Growth*. New York: Praeger.

Souder, W.E. (1984) *Project Selection and Economic Appraisal*. New York: Van Nostrand Reinhold.

Soumelis, Constantin G. (1977) *Project Evaluation Methodologies and Techniques.* Paris: United Nations Educational, Scientific and Cultural Organization.

Spulber, Nicolas and Ira Horowitz (1976) *Quantitative Economic Policy and Planning: Theory and Models of Economic Control.* New York: Pergamon Press.

Squire, Lyn and Herman G. van der Tak (1975) *Economic Analysis of Projects.* Baltimore: Johns Hopkins University Press.

Stallworthy, Ernest A. and O.P. Kharbanda (1983) *Total Project Management.* Aldershot: Gower.

___ (1983) *How to Learn from Project Disasters.* Aldershot: Gower.

Stern, N.H. (1972) "Experience with the Use of the Little-Mirrlees Method for an Appraisal of Small-Holder Tea in Kenya", *Bulletin of Oxford University Institute of Economics and Statistics* 34 (February).

Stewart, Frances and Paul Streeten (1972) "Little-Mirrlees Methods and Project Appraisal", *Bulletin of Oxford University Institute of Economics and Statistics* 34 (June).

Stigler, George J. (1961) "The Economics of Information", *Journal of Political Economy* 69 (June).

Stokke, Olav and L. Berlage (eds.) (1992) *Evaluating Development Assistance.* London: Frank Cass.

Stone, Donald C. and Alice B. Stone (1976) "Creation of Administrative Capability: The Missing Ingredients in Development Strategy" in John Barrett et al.(eds.) *Strategy for Development.* London: Macmillan.

Streeten, Paul (1972) *The Frontiers of Development Studies.* London: Macmillan.

Stuckenbruck, Linn C. (ed.) (1988) *The Implementation of Project Management.* Reading: Addison-Wesley.

Sundquist, J. L, (1969) *Making Federalism Work.* Washington, D.C.: Brookings Institution.

Sugden, Robert and Alan Williams (1978) *The Principles of Practical Cost Benefit Analysis.* Oxford: Oxford University Press.

Swerdlow, Irving (ed.) (1963) *Development Administration: Concepts and Problems.* Syracuse: Syracuse University Press.

___ and Marcus Ingle (eds.) (1974) *Public Administration Training for the Less Developed Countries.* Syracuse: Maxwell School, Syracuse University.

___ (1975) *The Public Administration of Economic Development.* New York: Praeger.

Taylor, W.J. and T.F. Watling (1970) *Successful Project Management.* London; Business Books.

___ (1973) *Practical Project Management.* London: Business Books.

Thamhain, Hans J. and David L. Wilemon (1975) "Conflict Management in Project Life Cycles", *Sloan Management Review* (Spring).

Tinbergen, Jan (1964) *Central Planning.* New Haven: Yale University Press.

___ (1966) "Development Planning", In Shimon Daniel (ed.) *Organization for Sectoral Planning.* Santiago: Economic Commission for Latin America.

___ (1967) *Development Planning*. London: Weidenfeld & Nicolson.

Toye, J. (1976) "Review of Little and Mirrless (1974)", *Journal of Development Studies* 12 (April).

United Nations (1951) *Formulation and Economic Appraisal of Development Projects*. New York: United Nations.

___ (1958) *Manual on Economic Development Projects*. New York: United Nations.

___ (1969) *Appraising Administrative Capability for Development*. New York: United Nations.

___ (1969) *Administrative Aspects of Planning*. New York: United Nations.

___ (1969) *Appraising Administrative Capability for Development*. New York: United Nations.

___ (1970) *Programming and Control of Implementation of Industrial Projects in Developing Countries*. New York: United Nations.

___ (1970)*Project Selection and Evaluation*. New York: United Nations.

___ (1971) *Administration of Development Programs and Projects: Some Major Issues*. New York: United Nations.

___ (1972) "Planning Process and Programming Techniques", *Economic Bulletin for Asia and the Far East* 23 (September).

___ (1973) *Cost Estimation of Water Resource Projects*. New York: United Nations.

___ (1975) *Development Administration: Current Approaches and Trends in Public Administration for National Development*. New York: United Nations.

___ (1978) *Survey of Changes and Trends in Public Administration and Finance for Development 1975-1977*. New York: United Nations.

___ (1983) *Enhancing Capabilities for Administrative Reforms in Developing Countries*. New York: United Nations.

___ (1984) *Issues and Priorities in Public Administration and Finance in the Third United Nations Development Decade*. New York: United Nations.

___ (1993) *Managing the Development Projects*. New York: United Nations.

United Nations Development Program (1974) *UNDP Operational and Financial Manual*. New York: United Nations Development Program.

___ (1983) *Cost-Benefit Analysis of Industrial Projects*. New York: United Nations Industrial Development Organization.

United Nations Educational, Scientific and Cultural Organization (1984) *Project Evaluation*. New York: United Nations Educational, Scientific and Cultural Organization.

United Nations Environmental Program (1988) *Evaluating Implementation Impact: Basic Procedures for Developing Countries*. Bangkok: United Nations Environmental Program.

United Nations Institute of Training and Research (1969) *Criteria and Methods of Evaluation: Problems and Approaches*. New York: United Nations Institute of Training and Research.

United Nations Industrial Development Organization (1970) *Programming and*

Control of Implementation of Industrial Projects in Developing Countries. New York: United Nations Industrial Development Organization.

___(1971) *Maintenance and Repair in Developing Countries.* Vienna: United Nations Industrial Development Organization.

___(1972) *Guidelines for Project Evaluation.* Vienna: United Nations Industrial Development Organization.

___(1975) *The Initiation and Implementation of Industrial Projects in Developing Countries.* New York: United Nations.

___(1977) *Technical Assistance and Training in the Implementation and Follow-up of Industrial Projects.* Vienna: United Nations Industrial Development Organization.

___(1978) *Guide to Practical Project Appraisal: Social Benefit-Cost Analysis in Developing Countries.* Vienna: United Nations Industrial Development Organization.

___(1978) *Manual for the Preparation of Industrial Feasibility Studies.* New York: United Nations.

___(1980) *Manual for Evaluation of Industrial Projects.* Vienna: United Nations Industrial Development Organization.

___(1980) *Manual for Evaluation of Industrial Projects.* New York: United Nations.

United States Agency for International Development (1974) *Guidelines for Capital Project Appraisal.* Washington, D.C.: United States Agency for International Development.

___(1975) *Strategies for Small Farmer Development: An Empirical Study of Rural Development Projects.* Washington, D.C.: United States Agency for International Development.

___(1975) *Project Assistance Handbook.* Washington, D.C.: United States Agency for International Development.

___(1976) *Evaluation Handbook.* Washington, D.C: United States Agency for International Development.

___(1990) *The AID Evaluation System.* Washington, D.C.: United States Agency for International Development.

United States Congress (1971) *Deficiencies in the Management and Delivery of United Nations Technical Assistance, 92nd Congress, 1st Session.* Washington, D.C.: Government Printing Office.

United States Department of Agriculture (1976) *Elements of Project Management.* Washington, D.C: Development Project Center.

Van Horn, Carl E. and Donald S. van Meter (1976) "The Implementation of Intergovernmental Policy", Sage Publications (ed.) *Public Policy Making in a Federal System.* Beverly Hills: Sage Publications.

___(1979) *Policy Implementation in the Federal System.* Lexington: Lexington Books.

Van Meter, Donald S. and Carl E. van Horn (1975) "The Policy Implementation Process: A Conceptual Framework", *Administration and Society* 6(4).

Van Pelt, M.J.F. et al. (1990) "Project Appraisal and Sustainability", *Project*

Appraisal 5(3).

——. (1993) *Ecological Sustainability and Project Appraisal.* Aldershot: Avebury.

Van der Tak, Herman G. et al. (1971) *The Economic Benefits of Road Transport Projects.* Baltimore: Johns Hopkins University Press.

Vepa, Ram K. (1974) "Implementation: The Problem of Achieving Results", *Indian Journal of Public Administration* 20 (April-June).

Walsh, Graham and Alan Williams (1969) *Current Issues in Cost-Benefit Analysis. London*; Her Majesty's Stationery Office.

___ and Peter Daffern (1990) *Managing Cost Benefit Analysis.* London: Macmillan.

Ward, William A. et al. (1991) *The Economics of Project Analysis.* Washington, D.C.: Economic Development Institute.

Waterston, Albert (1965) *Development Planning: The Lessons of Experience.* Baltimore: Johns Hopkins University Press.

Watt, G.R. (1973) *The Planning and Evaluation of Forestry Projects.* Oxford: Commonwealth Forestry Institute, University of Oxford.

Weiss, Carol H. (1972) *Evaluation Research.* Englewood Cliffs: Prentice-Hall.

Weiss, Dieter (1976) *Economic Evaluation of Projects.* Berlin: German Development Institute.

Weiss, John (1980) *Practical Appraisal of Industrial Projects.* New York: United Nations.

___ (ed.) (1994) *The Economics of Project Appraisal and the Environment.* Cheltenham: Edward Elgar.

Weiss, Moshe (1966) "Some Suggestions for Improving Development Administration", *International Review of Administrative Sciences* 32 (3).

Weiss, Wayne, Albert Waterston and John Wilson (1976) *Managing Planned Agricultural Development.* Washington, D.C.: Government Affairs Institute.

___ (1977) "The Design of Agricultural and Rural Development Projects", in Dennis A. Rondinelli (ed.) *Planning Development Projects.* Stroudsburg, Penn.: Dowden, Hutchinson & Ross.

Wenner, I (1978) "Pollution Control: Implementation Alternatives", *Policy Alternatives* 4 (Winter).

White, L.G. (1991) *Creating Opportunities for Change: Approach to Managing Development Programs.* Boulder: Lynne Rienner.

Whang, In-Joung (1978) *Administrative Feasibility Analysis for Development Projects: Concept and Application.* Kuala Lumpur: Asia and Pacific Development Administration Center.

Wildavsky, Aaron (1974) *The Politics of the Budgetary Process.* Boston: Little, Brown.

Williams, Alan and Emilio Giardina (eds.) (1993) *Efficiency in the Public Sector: The Theory and Practice of Cost Benefit Analysis.* Cheltenham: Edward Elgar.

Williams, Walter (1975) "Implementation Analysis and Assessment", *Policy Analysis* 1 (Summer).

___ and Richard Elmore (eds.) (1976) *Social Program Implementation.* New York: Academic Press.

___ (1980) *The Implementation Perspective.* Berkeley: University of California Press.

Wolf, Charles H. (1979) "A Theory of Non-Market Failure: Framework for Implementation Analysis", *Journal of Law and Economics* (22).

Wolfe, J.N. (ed.) (1973) *Cost-Benefit and Cost-Effectiveness.* New York: George Allen & Unwin.

World Bank (1972) *Instructions on Project Analysis.* Washington, D.C.: World Bank.

___ (1976) *Economic Analysis of Rural Road Projects.* Washington D.C. :World Bank.

___ (1979) *Operations Evaluation: World Bank Standards and Procedures.* Washington, D.C.: World Bank.

___ *(1980) World Development Report 1980.* Washington D.C.: World Bank.

___ (1983) *Learning by Doing.* Washington D.C. : World Bank.

World Health Organization (1983) *Minimum Evaluation Procedure for Water and Sanitation Projects.* Geneva: World Health Organization.

Wynia, Gary W. (1972) *Politics and Planners: Economic Development in Central America.* Madison: University of Wisconsin Press.

Yaffey, Michael (1992) *Financial Analysis for Development.* London: Routledge.

Yotopoulos, Pan A. (1976) *Economics of Development.* New York: Harper & Row.

Zeekhauser, Richard et al. (eds.) (1975) *Benefit Cost and Policy Analysis.* Chicago: Aldine.

Zeldman, M.E. (1980) "How Management can Develop and Sustain a Creative Environment", *S.A.M. Advanced Management Journal* (Winter).

4
INSTITUTIONAL MATRIX

Here we examine the evolution of project development in Barbados. Planning in Barbados had its origin in the Colonial Development and Welfare Act of 1940 and the Moyne Commission Report of 1945. As a result of the grave socioeconomic conditions which the Moyne Commission revealed and the need that was recognized for increasing the volume of productive activity (Government of the United Kingdom, 1945: 247), the British Government undertook to provide development assistance for the dependencies. To this end, an agency was established in the West Indies to help governments identify and prepare proposals for assistance. Following requests for the submission of a development plan to form the basis for the allocation of British Government assistance, a plan document "A Ten Year Development Plan for Barbados: Sketch Plan of Development 1946-56" was published - essentially a number of projects which seemed likely to qualify for assistance (Emtage, 1969: 205-206). The first plan has been followed by a series of medium-term plans (Government of Barbados, 1979: ix).

Since independence in 1966, long-term planning has been further recognized as a tool for ensuring maximum efficiency in the implementation of a development strategy or policy and as a deliberate ongoing strategy designed to promote change. It is an organized, conscious and continual attempt to select the best available alternatives to achieve specific goals. It involves an attempt to allocate human, financial and material resources in a rational manner and with optimum results. As Barbados has moved through the various plan periods, the planning process and techniques have become more institutionalized and advanced, and efforts are being made to make the planning process more integrative.

The project activities in the 1940s and the 1950s assumed the form of capital works programs, which were outlined in annual budget documents. Explicit reference to development or investment projects, project management, executing agencies, project authority, funding agency, etc. was rare or absent. There occurred in those early years from sector to sector and from parish to parish a variety of capital and nonrecurrent expenditures. The sectors included agriculture, education, health, public works and waterworks. References to development projects and related activities begin to appear in the 1960s and the 1970s in the Barbados Estimates, Development Plans, Economic Survey and Economic Report.[1]

Planning Institutionalization

The successive development plans point to the gradual institutionalization of the planning process in Barbados. First, the Development Plan 1946-56 sought to provide a framework for Barbados' welfare and indicated the broad lines of development. The plan was an 'indicative' or 'directive' one, setting out the general objective of programs and scheduling the approximate order of priority. Involving a total cost of $3.4m. in project outlay (Government of Barbados, 1946: 17-40), the plan dealt with eleven sectors and addressed the priority of investment decision and allocation. The Development Plan 1952-57, entailing a total cost of $16m. in project outlay, mounted projects in agriculture and infrastructure (Government of Barbados, 1952: 20-24).

A leading project envisaged in the plan period 1955-60, involving a total cost of $50m. in project outlay, was the construction of a deep water harbor for the port of Bridgetown. This project, estimated to cost $19.56 m. (Government of Barbados, 1955: 3) overshadowed all other developments and was given the first priority. Involving a total cost of $53.4m. in project spending, the Development Plan 1960-65 underscored several policy measures, e.g. reduction of unemployment, provision of new jobs, reduction of poverty, etc. (Government of Barbados, 1960: 68).

The Development Plan 1962-65 with a total cost of $50.1m. committed resources to the customary social and economic sectors (Government of Barbados, 1962: 17-20). Next was the Development Plan 1965-68 with a total cost of $41.3m., which represented a phase in the government's long-term plan in guiding the country along a socially desirable path (Government of Barbados, 1965: 66).

The first postindependence development plan (Government of Barbados, 1969: 88-89), covering the years 1969-72 and more wide-ranging than previous plans with a total cost of $45.9 m. in project outlay, marked another stage in the evolution of Barbados' planning process. Subsequently, the Development Plan 1973-77 (Government of Barbados, 1973: 77-124) with a total cost of $175.6m. designed numerous projects in an attempt to build on developments initiated by the earlier plans.

With a total cost of $561.7m. in project outlay, the Development Plan 1979-83 (Government of Barbados, 1979:77) represented another phase of a process of long-term planning, aimed at effecting the transformation of Barbados into an industrialized society. Involving some $722.7m. in project outlay (Government of Barbados, 1983: 54-56), the Development Plan 1983-88 unfolded a number of initiatives in resource allocation and management, including the financing of projects in housing and transportation.

The Development Plan 1988-93, with capital expenditure estimated at BDS $989.9m., aimed to improve the quality of life, reduce the pockets of poverty that existed, increase the output of goods and services, provide jobs through productive activity, improve income distribution and demonstrate commitment to create a more just process of social and economic transformation that would take Barbados into the twenty-first century (Government of Barbados, 1988: 5). The Plan identified an export-led strategy as the one that was required for economic growth and the realization of the medium and long-term targets.

Capital spending being estimated at BDS $1,088.6m., the Development Plan 1993-2000 was developed within a policy parameter that emphasized the importance of the private sector in the sustained growth and development of the economy. The main thrust of the Plan was to improve the country's international competitiveness, provide jobs through productive activity, carry out a series of structural adjustment measures, provide the conditions for continued transformation and accelerated growth, boost export competitiveness, restore real growth in the economy through higher levels of domestic and foreign investment, and provide an environment conducive to the growth and development of private sector activities (Government of Barbados, 1993: 3).

Project Institutionalization

The institutionalization of the project process in Barbados took various forms over time. With the advent of the cabinet system of government in 1954, the representatives of the people became involved in development planning and project processes. The institutional structure comprises a high-level political and policy-making body (Central Planning Committee), a central planning agency (Ministry of Finance and Economic Affairs) and a planning and coordinating unit for sectors and areas (Public Investment Unit). Established in 1962 to coordinate socioeconomic activities and investment strategies, the Central Planning Committee (CPC) played a key role in Barbados' planning process. It brought together all the ministers and their principal executives responsible for program and project implementation, coordinated the implementation of development plans, programs and projects, monitored their periodic reviews, considered the intersectoral linkages, checked progress, and recommended action. The Planning Unit of the Ministry of Finance and Planning provided secretariat services to the Committee. The Committee was replaced by a similar body established in February 1978 called the Planning and Priorities Committee (PPC) which became a standing committee of the Cabinet with executive authority for plan formulation and project selection/monitoring. With the Prime Minister as the chairman, the PPC is composed of certain cabinet ministers, permanent secretaries and professionals. The PPC monitors the project cycle and plan/project implementation, coordinates approaches to implementation and advises the Cabinet on various matters. The Public Investment Unit (PIU) acts as the Committee's secretariat. The organization of the planning structure is charted here.

Figure 2
Organization of the Planning Structure

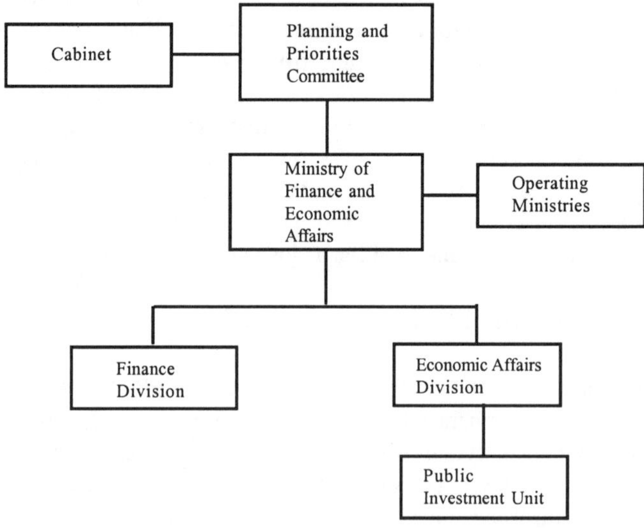

Noteworthy in this regard is the Ministry of Finance and Planning, which became operational on June 1, 1973 after the merger of the former Ministry of Finance and the Economic Planning Unit established earlier in 1966. It is an important agency responsible for formulating, coordinating, supervising, negotiating and financing development plans and projects.

The origin of the Public Investment Unit is traceable to a high-level policy decision and subsequent technical and financial assistance in 1974 and 1975 from the Inter-American Development Bank (The Advocate News, 1978: April 12). The Unit, operating within the planning division of the Ministry of Finance and Planning, has been functional since 1978. The Ministry of Finance and Planning is currently called the Ministry of Finance and Economic Affairs. Concerned with identification, planning, coordination, monitoring, reporting and follow-up, the Unit's overall objective is to increase the efficiency and effectiveness of decision-making in public sector capital resource allocations. To fulfill this role, the Unit coordinates project activities, undertakes appraisals, negotiates with funding agencies, maintains a database on project matters, assists in the selection of consultants, etc. Headed by a manager, the PIU is maintained by professional and support staff. The staffers, who are program/project analysts, become involved with the assigned projects, assist in the negotiation of finance and technical contracts, and assist the operating ministries in varied tasks and monitor disbursements.

The institutionalization of project-making at the operating or departmental level was carried out with a view to strengthening management capability and accelerating implementation. There was a felt need to establish separate programming units in some instances, e.g. ministries of agriculture and education, while in others it called for staff development. Greater emphasis on the expansion of planning capacity at the operational level was laid around 1973-74 in that the Ministry of Finance and Planning began to service smaller ministries directly and assist the programming units in the larger ministries.

The operating agencies carry out certain functions in relation to project development. For instance, the process of identifying and sponsoring a project takes place at the ministry level. The sponsoring agency prepares a project profile for submission to the Public Investment Unit when a project is being identified. As a project's beneficiary, the sponsoring ministry has ultimate responsibility for nurturing projects from identification to implementation. Operating ministries must obtain necessary approval and clearance from and must report to the PPC through the PIU during the various phases of the project cycle.[2]

The Ministry of Agriculture, for instance, established a Special Assignment Division in November 1978, which is staffed by managerial, accounting and secretarial personnel. The Division was associated with several projects, e.g. Oistins Fisheries Terminal Project (1979), Scotland District Development Project (1982), and Bridgetown Fishing Harbor Project (1984). The Barbados Agricultural Development and Marketing Corporation put on board in 1985 a Project Development Service in order to assist the local entrepreneurs in setting up manufacturing operations.

Having become operational during 1978-79, the Ministry of Education's Project Execution Unit is staffed by managerial and specialist personnel and is responsible for the development of primary, secondary and tertiary institutions. The Ministry of Health's Project Design and Implementation Unit became operational in April 1978, is staffed by various specialists, and is charged with the construction of polyclinics in the country. Responsible for developing projects, the Ministry of Transport's Project Division came on stream in 1979. The Division is associated with the Spring Garden Highway Project and the Industrial Access Road Project. The National Housing Corporation's Technical Division came into being in 1973, is staffed by technical personnel and other operatives, and is accountable for project development.

Sectoral Background

Here we discuss the seven sectors taken up in our study - agriculture, industry, tourism, infrastructure, education, health and housing. There are many factors and forces which influence these sectors. The overall development strategy relates to securing a sustainable growth rate, stressing the export-oriented path, stressing industry/tourism/agriculture services as the main generators of foreign exchange and employment, improving and expanding the delivery of basic services, and securing the foundation of a technologically dynamic society. Some of the sectoral problems include weak intersectoral linkages, low incidence of indigenous raw materials-based industrialization, high import content of domestic spending for both investment and consumption, the limited supportive role of agriculture in the industrialization process and the lack of high-quality local entrepreneurship and technical dynamism.

Agriculture

The development of an efficient and dynamic agriculture is considered crucial in the overall development strategy. Barbados' agricultural economy based on sugar started over 300 years ago when sugarcane farming was introduced in the island in the 1640s.[3] The objectives of the sector consist in raising income and productivity, reducing dependence on food imports, generating new sources of export revenue and improving domestic food imports, and nutritional levels. The strategies embrace foreign-exchange generation, import substitution, agricultural employment, income distribution, food and nutrition, industrial development, land/water use and resource conservation.[4] Program development extends to nonsugar agriculture and fishery.

Several problems constraining the sector are inadequate storage and processing facility, reducing available land area, a weak extension service, inadequate irrigation and local marketing, labor shortage, depressed price, unfavorable recovery rate, fluctuating export price, and rising production costs.

Around 65% of land resources is in agriculture. The output of agriculture stood at BDS$ 152.7m. in 1992, $161.5m. in 1993, $149.6m. in 1994, and $203.1m. in 1995. The GDP value of sugar was $57.5m. in 1993, $49.6m. in 1994, $52.8m. in 1995, and $73.4m. in 1996. In 1975 agriculture employed 21,900 persons or 27% of the total workforce. The number of workers decreased to 6,600 (1990), 6,100 (1991), 6,600 (1992), 5,700 (1993), 5,600 (1994), 5,100 (1995), and 6,500 (1996). The employment share is expected to decline to 2,000 by the year 2000. The sector's employment share stands around 8%.

Agriculture accounts for 6.0% avg. of the GDP, viz. 5.4% (1990), 5.6% (1991), 5.3% (1992), 5.3% (1993), and 5.1% (1994). Sugar's contribution to GDP has ranged from 35% (1953) and 20.3% (1960) to 2.5% (1990), 1.7% (1993), 1.7% (1994), 1.1% (1995), and 1.5% (1996). Sugar output grew at an average rate of 7.7% per annum in the 1980s. Total sugar output was 135,000 tonnes (1980), 54,000 tones (1992), 38,800 tonnes (1995), and 59,100 tonnes (1996). Sugar's foreign exchange contribution was around 10% in the 1980s. Export earnings moved from $115.5m. in 1980 to $66.7m.(1992), $56.8m.(1993), $59.5m.(1994), $52.5m.(1995), and $73.1m.(1996). Barbados' rum exports have been on the increase over the years, earning $18.7m.(1993), $19.7m.(1995), and $22.0m.(1996).

Industry

The industrial sector plays a critical role in contributing towards growth, employment, output generation, local income and foreign exchange revenue, improved balance of payments, intersectoral linkages and export expansion. The sector is largely characterized by foreign-owned, enclave-type and export-oriented enterprises. A set of investment stimuli, institutional/promotional initiatives and lending policies are on stream to sustain a favorable investment climate and boost production.

Early industrial activity was confined to light manufacturing, masonry, carpentry, sugar, molasses, rum, ice-making, bread, biscuits, clothing, and so forth.[5] The various objectives of the sector are increasing output and its share of the GDP, generating employment, promoting export, expanding production through capacity utilization, encouraging new investment, encouraging utilization of indigenous raw materials, fostering skills, and addressing structural problems.[6] Program development embraces diversification, promotion, substitution, and skill development. The outstanding problems are several: the intersectoral linkages and multiplier effects of investment have been weak, shortage of entrepreneurship and technological dynamism, high levels of attrition in employment, relatively high ratio of foreign investment, slow growth in domestic savings and investment, limited access to extraregional markets, small size of domestic market, dependence on imported raw materials, and high import content of local manufacturing output.

The sector's contribution to GDP has been 9.9% (1989), 8.0% (1990), 8.0% (1991), 7.5% (1992), 7.5% (1993), and 7.1% (1994). Real output of the sector grew at a rate of 7.3% (1994), 7.5% (1995), and 1.8% (1996). The GDP value of industry was BDS $206.6m. (1993), $208.0m.(1994), and $216.5m. (1995). In 1994, exports were valued at $270.2 m. In 1995, the value increased to $338.8m. The total number of persons employed in the sector was 11,300 (1986) and 12,400 (1987) and then declined to 11,800 (1990), 10,800 (1991), 10,400 (1992), 10,700 (1993), 10,800 (1994), 11,700 (1995), and 10,000 (1996). Between 1994 and 1995, 1,147 jobs were created, with the largest increase being 501 in information services. The ten industrial parks - with some 98.9 acres of land and a total of about 1.7 m.square feet of factory space with an insurable value in excess of $132m. and serviced with road, electricity, water and sanitation - are located at the Grantley Adams International Airport, Six Roads, Newton, Pine, Wildey, Harbor, Pelican, Spring Garden, Grazettes, and St. Lucy. There are between 6,000 to 12,000 small businesses in Barbados and about 35,000 to 40,000 persons employed in the small business subsector.

Tourism

The country's beaches, climate and landscape, including overall stability, general amiability and locational advantage, represent the sector's key resources. It has a relatively high labor content, is a generator of foreign exchange and domestic revenue, contributes to GDP, provides direct as well as indirect employment, stimulates infrastructural spread, secures linkages and spurs changes.[7] The sector's objectives include increased employment, foreign exchange generation, domestic income growth, enhancing attractions, enforcing necessary controls, protecting environmental heritage, improving tourism product/service delivery, and integrating tourism into sociocultural lifestyle. Of the strategies, increasing tourism demand, ensuring higher visitor arrivals, analyzing domestic value-added, increasing local ownership and participation and plugging external leakages are mentionable.[8] Program initiatives include infrastructural support, recreational attractions, duty-free operation, ancillary-service expansion, heritage preservation, cultural programming, crime containment, and conference-facility creation. Problems confronting the sector are multiple: the seasonal nature of its operations, high cost of stay, social cost, beach harassment, limited spread effects of benefits, unplanned expansion, reduced net benefits, and high import content. Tourism has established itself as the mainstay of the Barbadian economy, accounting in 1997 for 70% of foreign exchange revenue, netting 15% of GDP, employing some 20,000 persons, and registering arrivals of 990,178 visitors.

Tourism's contribution to GDP rose from 2.0% (1953) to 13% (1993), 14.0% (1994), 14.8% (1995), 15.4% (1996), and 20.0% (1997). The sector's contribution toward real GDP in 1996 exceeded BDS$139.0m. The sector employed 7.5% of the workforce in 1977, but the employment share dropped to 4.0% in 1978. Tourism employed 10,400 persons (1990), 9,500 (1991), 9,800 (1992), 9,600 (1993), 11,100 (1994), 11,900 (1995), and 12,300 (1996). The average length of stay by visitors was 6.9 nights (1992), 7.0 (1993), 7.1 (1994), 7.4 (1995), and 7.9 (1996). The hotel bed capacity has moved from 13,726 (1989) to 13,767 (1990), 11,674 (1991), 11,803 (1992), and 11,554 (1993). The hotel bed occupancy rate showed the following trends: 49.1% (1992), 51.3% (1993), 56.4% (1994), 56.7% (1995), and 69.2% (1996).

The hotel room occupancy rate was 56.3% (1990), 48.2% (1991), 49.1% (1992), 51.3% (1993), 56.4% (1994), 56.7% (1995), and 69.5% (1996). Tourist spending ranged from BDS$987.0m. (1990), $919.5m. (1991), $925.0m. (1992) to $1,055.9m. (1993), $1,196.0m. (1994), $1,359.0m. (1995), and $1,369.9m. (1996). The import content of total tourist spending stands at about 30-40% in a given fiscal year. Visitor arrivals numbered 432,092 (1990), 394,222

(1991), 385,472 (1992), 395,979 (1993), 425,630 (1994), 442,107 (1995), and 447,083 (1996).

Infrastructure

The existence of an adequate infrastructural base is essential to development. Infrastructure is a booster for continued improvement and expansion, development acceleration, and product/service expansion, contributes to the predictability of resource flows and the mobility and convertability of resources, strengthens productive linkages, provides a means of getting products to markets and services to consumers, and facilitates attempts to satisfy basic human needs. The sector embraces several operational areas, e.g. roads, bridges, culverts, drainage system, buildings, transport, water system, power network, harbor, airport, surface transportation, traffic management, environmental services, parking system, mail communication and telecommunications.[9]

Sectoral objectives cover a broad spectrum: facilitating the movement of goods, services and persons, maintaining the building stock, improving traffic flow, regulating water resources, modernizing the port and broadening its revenue base, and improving overall environmental quality. The strategies are varied, e.g. diversifying and strengthening the infrastructural base, strengthening the institutional capability, and improving the operational capacity.[10] The sector faces congestion, overwork and waste in some respects in addition to the deterioration and contamination of the environment, slower pace of replacement of facilities, lack of continuity in providing a regular service to commuters, increasing traffic volume and density, and improper environmental practices.

The road network, with ten major highways and many subsidiary roads, totals over 1,100 miles of road, approximately 900 miles of which are paved and all-weather. There are over 68,000 vehicles. Over 300 Transport Board omnibuses, 200 minibuses and 300 route taxis produce almost 24,000 daily trips for 53,000 school students of which 20,000 are on omnibuses. Some 178,000 passenger transactions - 31% by omnibuses, 38% by minibuses and 31% by route taxis - occur on a typical school weekday. In passenger miles, omnibuses carry 41%, minibuses 38%, and route taxis 21%. 145,000 people use the mass commuter vehicles daily, equivalent to over 57m. annual transactions. Providing 1,700 feet of quay space, offering 2,700 feet of protective breakwater, outfitting berths for eight ocean-going vessels and having containerization facilities, the Bridgetown Port is a major transhipment point in the Caribbean. The 11,000 feet long, 150 feet wide and asphalt runway-equipped Grantley Adams International Airport enjoys high reputation. The Post Office Department, with a general post office in Bridgetown and 16 district post offices, provides mail communication services.

Water consumption amounted to 50.3m. cubic meters (1992), 53.3m. (1993), 53.3m. (1994), 53.6m. (1995), and 58.8m. (1996). The number of consumers rose from 83,792 (1991) and 87,273 (1992) to 91,338 (1993) and 94,618 (1994). Electricity generating capacity moved from 511.9m. kwh (1993) to 602.7m.kwh (1994), 664.3m. kwh (1995), and 675.2m. kwh (1996). The number of service connections stood at 89,400 (1993), 91,500 (1994), 92, 800 (1995), and 94,192 (1996). The number of telephone lines has risen from 47,419 (1977) to 80,142 (1993), 86,205 (1995), and 94,196 (1996). In 1995, business lines increased by 2,251 to 20,663. Telecommunications provide over 1,500 voice channels, many thousands of telegraph and data transmission circuits, over four million international telephone calls and over 300,000 minutes of telex services. Natural gas consumption amounted to 30.6m. cubic meters (1992), 27.9m. (1993), 28.9m. (1994), 29.3m. (1995), and 28.9m.(1996).

Education

High priority is attached to the continuous modernization and expansion of the educational sector. Education is considered an important vehicle for individual self-realization, universal literacy and training, life opportunity, social change and progress, cultural vibrancy, attitudinal change, and productive growth and development.[11] Sectoral objectives include providing a sound basic education to every citizen, promoting the equality of educational opportunity, offering a wide range of educational programs including training in technical skills, modernizing technical and vocational education, promoting internal and external efficiency and quality, developing human capital, and providing special educational facilities for the disadvantaged.

Strategies range from promoting a unified approach to curriculum planning and development, reviewing existing institutional capacity, promoting complementarity among training institutions, and providing needed skills. Among program initiatives, the improvement and expansion of institutions, the development of staff and the modernization of curricula are mentionable.[12] A plethora of problems stands out. With education and training being long-gestating, labor-intensive and costly activities, it is not easy to match the supply of skill with the demand for it. Then, there are high upkeep and maintenance costs, the outputs are not readily absorbed into the employment process, high cost of creating net capacity of school places, and shortage or absence of guidance and counselling services. Education faces challenges not so much to reduce resource costs but to make the sectoral activities more relevant to a changing society.

From 1973 onward, almost one-fifth of the total budget is being allocated to education. The per capita spending on education in Barbados - approximately one dollar per person per day - outstrips that of most countries. The salience of education is reflected in 98% literacy rate in the country. There are between 7,000 and 8,000 pupils who attend public and private nursery schools. The 1,000 plus students who secure under 30% in the Secondary School Entrance Examination fail to attain the basic skills. On average, less than 20% of the students taking the Caribbean Examinations Council examinations pass four or more subjects at any one sitting. 68% of secondary school students leave school without certification. About BDS$249.2m. was spent on education during 1996-97. The sector received about 16.6% of total resources in 1996-97 compared to 16.9% in 1995-96. Expansion of student intake occurs at almost all tertiary institutions. For example, the Samuel Jackman Prescod Polytechnic increased its intake from 1,400 to 2,000 and finally to 2,500 students. Enrollment has increased rising from 2,102 in 1988-89 to 2,362 in 1992-93, and over 2,600 in 1996. Student enrollment reached 3,233 and graduation attainment numbered 729 during 1996-97 at the University of the West Indies, Barbados. 70% of the University's enrollment comprises women. School enrollment for primary and secondary schools was 29,285 (1992) and 29,500 (1993) and 23,830 (1992) and 23,279 (1993) respectively. Student-faculty ratio for primary and secondary schools was 18.3 (1989) and 19.1 (1990) and 21.3 (1989) and 16.9 (1990) respectively.

Health

The proper organization and delivery of health services is basic to the achievement of socioeconomic objectives. Health is a fundamental human right and a healthy population is essential to a productive nation. The improvement of the health of human inputs in the development process is seen as adding significantly to the achievement of goals. The attainment of the highest possible level of health is a most important social goal and health services need to be targeted to protect and improve the health of every individual as well as the entire community. Health indicators continue to show progress in the health sector. An established preventive and curative network of healthcare facilities provides service to Barbados' population.[13]

Objectives relate to providing primary/secondary/tertiary/emergency/ psychiatric/geriatric/ rehabilitative healthcare, ensuring a healthy and productive population, promoting and maintaining health, ensuring service delivery, integrating preventive and curative services, maintaining continuous supply of drugs to healthcare institutions and general public, decentralizing authority in health institutions, and increasing community participation. The strategies embrace increased community responsibility for health and welfare, greater access to varied services, various types of health services and popularizing the drug service.[14]

Among various program developments, the Barbados Drug Service, family planning, food and nutrition services, etc. continue to receive attention. Polyclinics, providing primary and healthcare on a five-day week basis, undertake prenatal care, child healthcare, environmental sanitation, immunization, home visiting, notifiable disease investigation and venereal disease control. There are areas of the sector which give cause for concern, i.e. the misuse of the emergency service of the general hospital, unequal coverage of different population groups, existing morbidity and mortality rates, disparity in care provision and service delivery, high cost of drugs and patient overload at polyclinics. Measured as a percentage of public spending, the cost of health service is among the highest in the world.

The health sector spent a total of BDS$240.8m. during 1996-97, which was 15.7% of the total public sector spending. Recurrent spending in 1996-97 amounted to $182.3.m., while capital spending was $58.5m. About 23% of the recurrent budget is allocated to primary healthcare programs.

Utilizing about 36.6% of the health budget, the Queen Elizabeth Hospital - with a budget of $81.3m., an annual intake of 2,506 patients and an average patient stay of eight days - has 593 active beds or 8% per 1,000 of the population and contains over 90.0% of all the acute care beds in the country. The Hospital accounted for the largest share - over 68.6% - of the hospital services budget during 1996-97. The number of admissions per year at the Hospital exceeds 18,000. The bed turnover rate increased to 32.7% in 1996 from 31.5% in 1995, the bed occupancy rate moved to 66.1% in 1996 from 65.6% in 1995, the average length of patient stay fell to 7.3% in 1996 from 7.5% in 1995, and the men bed complement was 547 for 1995 as well as 1996. In-patient discharges numbered 17,254 (1995) and 17,885 (1996), death rate per 100 discharges registered 6.3 (1996), out-patient visits totaled 106,068 (1995) and 104,373 (1994), emergency attendance tallied 52,036 (1995) and 53,030 (1996) and the number of x-rays taken was 41,857 (1995) and 44,940 (1996). The island's overall hospital services, in-patient as well as out-patient, are estimated at over 100,000 visits per year. While the Psychiatric Hospital has 630 beds, the Geriatric Hospital is equipped with 428 beds. Other district hospitals operate with a total of 459 beds, and private hospitals in the island maintain 88 beds. The polyclinics' comprehensive primary healthcare, such as preventive and curative care as well as referral services, are in demand.

In 1990, the population per physician was 1,120, while the population per nurse was 220. From 1990 to 1992, the number of dentists per 1,000 population was 0.1. Life expectancy was 75.3 years in 1992. The death rate is 1.1% per 1,000 of the population. In the 1950s, 132 infants died in every 1,000 births. From there, the infant mortality rate moved to 13.8 (1992), 9.8 (1993), 8.5 (1994), and 13.2 (1995). The contraceptive prevalence rate is about 67%. The fertility rate in 1996 was 52.5% as compared with 65.2% in 1992. Of the various illness types, the incidence of chronic and degenerative diseases is high. Cardiovascular diseases are widespread, and cancer is the fourth highest cause of hospitalization. Hypertension has a prevalence rate between 20 and 25%. Diabetes has a prevalence rate of 6.5% of the total population. About 34% of Barbados' hospital beds are currently occupied by the chronically ill.

Housing

Housing is one of the basic human needs. It is recognized as being essential for life chances, living standards, welfare, security, freedom, and identity. Housing is one of the principal means through which overall human development may be diversified and achieved. One recognizes the importance of housing in both economic and social terms. The social benefits, such as protection from elements, improved sanitation and access to health and education generally conduce to improved productivity and higher returns. Housing has grown in terms of home ownership, project activity, residential mortgage, joint venture, home improvement, and site development. The sector is influenced by such activities as house construction, house renovation, house relocations, house moving, rental unit refurbishing, housing losses, conveyancing, and ownership changes.[15]

The objectives are related to effecting a general improvement in living conditions, eliminating unhealthy and overcrowded housing, building rental units, providing serviced lots for sale to potential home-owners, facilitating tenancy and home-ownership, upgrading housing infrastructure, and strengthening the sector's institutional capacity. Of the strategies, citable are maintaining and expanding low-income housing fund, stimulating additional finance, establishing a mortgage bank and a secondary mortgage market, utilizing existing institutions fully and involving the private sector in low-income housing finance. Program developments, in part, are geared toward remedying housing shortage. The quality of housing, measured in terms of the number of units with water supply and waterborne systems, has been improving and expanding.[16]

There are some concerns in the sector: dilapidation, overcrowding, insufficiency of tenurial security, lack of slum clearance, deficiency in rental unit construction, rising cost of construction, high cost of transportation, increases in property tax, mortgage finance scarcity, shortage of bridging loans, variable quality of housing stock, overcautious mortgage lending and depressed supply of loanable funds, heavy dependence on direct imports of building materials with the import content being about 80%, inadequacies in building technology and housing standards, the unavailability of residential land, and the increasing cost of acquiring and developing land.

In the 1970s, there were 59,000 units to house 235,229 people, with the average household size being 4.01 persons. The 1980s showed 67,166 units for 248,783 people, with the average household size being 3.06 persons. About 6,200 units, or 10% of the total housing stock, are accommodated on tenantry lands.

The public sector's contribution to housing has continued throughout the 1970s, 1980s, and 1990s. The National Housing Corporation built an average of 350 units between 1977 and 1979. The Corporation's output declined in the 1980s and 1990s. The Corporation operates 6,000 rental units for low-income tenants. The low-income units are provided through loan finance, are built for rent, or are put up for sale. Built for sale, middle-income and low-middle income units account for 6% and 7% of sectoral output respectively. The Corporation, facing a backlog of 30,000 applications for renting housing units, has provided accommodation to over 11,000 families.

The sector is heavily dependent on direct imports of building materials with the import content being 80%. The proportion of materials to labor costs varies between 58:42 and 63:35, depending on the type of materials used. While the housing need is estimated to require 1,700 units per year to cope with newly-formed households, the losses to the housing stock and the replacement of aged units, the housing demand is estimated to be around 1,100 units per year. Estimates of effective housing demand indicate that about 35% of the population is unable to afford any form of new housing and some 25% is unable to afford the cheapest form of permanent housing.

Single units are built for sale and constructed by private developers under a contract agreement with the National Housing Corporation. Under this modality, the private developer builds and the Corporation markets the units. The starter homes program commenced in 1986 to provide a basic 2-bedroom house for sale to low and low-middle income families. The units are designed to facilitate further expansion. A total of 75 units was built - 54 at Oxnards Crescent, St. James and 21 at Parkinson Road, St. Michael. Besides, the joint-sector venture enables the Corporation to provide fully-serviced lots, the private developer to build in keeping with specifications agreed to by the Corporation, and the management to market the units.

Housing constitutes about 5% of GDP and accounts for about 11% of the country's total workforce. While the mortgage rate was 9% between 1986 and 1991, the current mortgage rate increased to 11%, which became effective in 1991. The mean occupancy rate is about 3 to 5 individuals per home, the average number of rooms per unit is two bedrooms in addition to bathrooms and dining areas, and about 85% of homes are owner-occupied. The public sector housing program has been filling social need for several decades. For example in 1992, the single units completed and in progress were 125 and 681 respectively, the rental units completed and in progress were 51 and 143 respectively, and the serviced sites developed and in progress were 172 and 1,976 respectively. The total long-term credit outstanding to the major financial institutions for housing, rising from BDS$203.7m. in 1983, has exceeded BDS$400 m.in the 1990s.

NOTES

1. For reference purpose, mentionable are some of the projects from the early times to mid-1970s, e.g. Peasants Loan Bank Extension Project/Agricultural Stations Project/Vocational Training Center Project (1946-56), Boat Building Project/Youth Employment Project/Tree Cultivation Project (1952-56), Water Resource Development Project/Tenantry Roads Project/Livestock Investment Project (1955-60), General Hospital Project/Tourism Promotion Project/Middle-income Housing Project (1960-65), Grammar Schools Project/Grasslands Development Project/Medical Staff Quarters Project (1962-65), East Coast Road

Project/ Varietal Improvement Project/Smallholders Irrigation Project (1965-68), Soil Conservation Project/Beach Control and Development Project/Feeder and Tenantry Roads Project (1969-72), and Comfith Project/Community Center Project/Peanuts Research Project (1973-77).

2. Project institutionalization has reached the operating agencies, i.e. ministries, departments and public enterprises. Some examples: Project Execution Unit (Barbados Agricultural Management Co. Ltd.), Research, Planning and Information Division (Barbados Investment and Development Corporation), Research and Planning Department (Barbados National Bank), Research and Information Department (Central Bank of Barbados), Agricultural Planning Units/Special Assignment Division (Ministry of Agriculture), Educational Project Implementation Unit (Ministry of Education), Project Design and Implementation Unit (Ministry of Health), Planning Unit (Ministry of Housing), Projects Division (Ministry of Transport), Technical Division (National Housing Corporation), Research and Planning Unit (Police Department), Research Section (Town and Country Planning Department), Research and Training Division (Customs Department), Project Implementation Unit (Ministry of Finance), Research Division (National Insurance Department), Research Division (Ministry of Tourism), Research Division (Ministry of International Transport), and Research Division (Ministry of Industry and Commerce).

3. Historically, sugarcane has been a suitable crop for the ecological conditions of Barbados, characterized by variable rainfall, high prevailing winds and shallow clay soils of good moisture retention. Before the emancipation in 1838, the majority of the black population worked on the 508 sugar plantations, which occupied nearly all the prime available land and rendered own-account farming practically impossible. Between 1861 and 1921 there occurred a transition from a situation where about half of the adult population was directly engaged in farming to one where one in three persons was connected with the land. The period between 1946 and 1980 witnessed its relative decline measured by its share of domestic output, employment and foreign exchange revenue.

4. The sector is serviced by the Barbados Agricultural Development and Marketing Corporation, Barbados Agricultural Society and its affiliates, Barbados Livestock Development Cooperative Society, Caribbean Agricultural Research and Development Institute, Food and Agriculture Organization, Ministry of Agriculture and its agencies and other private sector organizations.

5. Industrial impetus was provided in part by the Moyne Commission (1945), the Caribbean Commission (1945), and Lewis (1950: 1-61). The Lewis document provided a methodology of industrial development for small dependent countries faced with skewed resource base, inadequate marketing and financial system, little or no entrepreneurship, and high levels of employment. By 1951 Barbados

had adopted the policy of industrialization by external investment. Fiscal stimuli have been available since 1951. The legal framework consists of the Pioneer Industries (Encouragement) Act (1951), Barbados Development Act (1955), Pioneer Industries Act (1958), Industrial Development Act (1963), Industrial Incentive Act (1963), International Business Companies (Exempt from Income Tax) Act (1965), Industrial Incentives Act (1965), Industrial Incentives (Factory Construction) Act (1965), Industrial Development Act (1968), Industrial Development (Export Industries) Act (1969), Income Tax (Amendment/Export Allowance) Act (1974), Fiscal Incentives Act (1974), Income Tax Amendment Act (1974), Hotel Aids Act, Town Planning Act, Travel Services Act, Ministry of Health Regulations for Buildings, Hotels and Restaurants, Condominium Act, Barbados Tourism Investment Corporation, Hotel Registration Regulations (1982), Barbados Tourism Authority Act (1995), Special Development Areas Act (1996), and Value Added Tax Act (1996). Institutions linked with the sector were and are the Barbados Investment and Development Corporation (1965), Central Bank of Barbados (1972), Barbados Institute of Management and Productivity (1972), and Barbados National Standards Institution (1972).

6. The sector is serviced, among others, by the Barbados Investment Development Corporation, Barbados Institute of Management and Productivity, Barbados National Bank, Barbados National Standards Institution, Insurance Corporation of Barbados, Ministry of Trade and Industry, Samuel Jackman Prescod Polytechnic, Vocational Training Board, and private sector associational groups/financial institutions. Noteworthy is the Central Bank of Barbados which provides, inter alia, rediscounting facility, export credit insurance and credit guarantee, selective credit control, interest rate control, and exchange rate stabilization.

7. The history of the sector goes back to the 17th century, with Barbados playing host to overseas visitors. The Barbados Improvement Association, formed in November 1911, played a role in the early 20th century. The Barbados Publicity Committee was formed in July 1932, a promotional booklet was released, and a visitors information bureau was established. In the 1950s, the Tourist Development Association and the Hotel Association came into being. Emerging in the 1950s and early 1960s as a major activity, the early development was marked by a high degree of foreign ownership of tourist establishments. Mandated by the Hotel Aids Act (1956), the Barbados Development (Amendment) Act (1958) and the Tourist Board Act (1958), the sector benefitted from the establishment of the Barbados Tourist Board (1975) which was renamed the Barbados Board of Tourism (1975)/Barbados Tourism Authority (1995), Barbados Hotel Association (1957) and Barbados Hotel School (1964) / Hospitality Institute (1996).

8. The sector is serviced, among others, by the Barbados Tourism Authority,

Barbados Hotel Association, Barbados Licensing Authority, Barbados Port Authority, Barbados Transport Board, Barbados Tourism Investment Corporation, Customs Department, Immigration Department, International Transport Division, National Conservation Commission, Sanitation Service Authority and various other private sector organizations/tourism establishments. Programs are on stream to improve attractions/events/activities/accommodations/ services, encourage longer stay, host local festivals, continue with planning/ marketing/promotion and update airline routing. Promotional activities include marketplace presentations, audiovisual shows, strategic seminars, meetings, advertising/sales campaigns, special documentaries, cruise promotions, media reports, travel exhibition and trade fairs.

9. Road construction, mainly coastal sidewalks, started in 1657. The first major road was the link between Speightstown and the East Coast, St. Andrew. The roads were resurfaced in 1661 and extended in 1676 and 1681. The main basis of the highway system was constructed between 1662 and 1742. The first standpipe was erected at Trafalgar Square in 1857. The earliest mode of mechanical public transportation - the railways - was introduced in 1881. In 1911, there were 120 miles of main roads and about 300 miles of cross roads. While motor transportation was introduced in 1920, bus transportation started in 1938. Road maintenance was carried out by the parish authorities, the Central Road Board (1926), the Transport Board (1937, 1995), the Department of Highway and Transport (1945), and the Ministry of Communications and Works (1954). In 1955, the Transport Board ran between 116 and 130 buses plying 18 routes and carried 19,895 passengers a total distance of 3,665,100 miles at a cost of 1.2 cents per passenger. From 1955 to 1976 the Board ran over 100 omnibuses. By 1979 the Board carried 41.6m. passengers on 282 omnibuses. The fleet grew to 339 by 1984. Surface transportation became diversified with the introduction of over 200 minibuses and over 300 route taxis. There are about 900 taxis, 150 maxitaxis and 46 tour buses, almost exclusively used by tourists.

10. The sector is serviced by the Barbados External Telecommunications, Ltd., Barbados Light and Power Company Ltd., Barbados Licensing Authority, Barbados National Oils Company Ltd., Barbados Telephone Company Ltd., Barbados Port Authority, Barbados Transport Board, Barbados Water Authority, Electrical Engineering Department, Grantley Adams International Airport, International Transport Division, Ministry of Transport and Works, National Conservation Commission, National Petroleum Corporation, Post Office Department, Sanitation Service Authority, and many other organizations.

11. The introduction of formal education to Barbados goes back to 1686 when a country school was established. Among the earliest schools were Boys Foundation (1709), Harrison College (1733), Lodge (1745), and Alleyne (1785). Later, St. Mary's (1818), Combermere (1819), St. Mary's Girls' (1825), Queen's

(1883), Industrial School (1833), Alexandra (1894), St. Michael's Girls (1926), and Girls Foundation (1928). Following the recommendation of the Mitchinson Commission in 1878, an education legislation was enacted which signalled the advent of mass education in Barbados. By 1900 there were 169 recognized elementary schools with an enrollment of 24,145 students. More recently, St. Leonard's Boys and Girls (1952), Princess Margaret and West St. Joseph (1955), Parkinson (1960), Springer Memorial (1964), St. Elizabeth's and Ellerslie (1966), St. Lucy Secondary (1971), and St. George's Secondary (1972), among others, became operational. In 1962 education became free to all nationals attending public institutions. Tertiary, adult and continuing education, training and research was and is offered by Codrington College (1827), West Indies Central Sugar Cane Breeding Station (1932), Housecraft Center (1945), Erdiston College (1948), University of the West Indies - Cave Hill (1963), School of Continuing Studies (1963), Barbados Hotel School (1964)/Hospitality Institute (1996), Caribbean Institute for Meteorology and Hydrology (1967), Barbados Community College (1969), Samuel Jackman Prescod Polytechnic (1970), Barbados Institute of Management and Productivity (1972), Barbados School of Air Traffic Services (1973), and Labor College (1974). Special education has been targeted on a modest scale: School for the Deaf and Blind (1959, 1966, 1968, 1974), Challenor School (1964), Thelma Vaughn Memorial Home (1973), Learning Center (1977), Erdiston Primary Annex (1978), Children's Development Center (1981), Barbados Speech and Hearing Center (1981), St. Andrew Children's Center (1981), and Center for Prevocational Training (1982).

12. The sector is serviced by the Audiovisual Department, Archives Department, Barbados Public Library, Barbados Museum and Historical Society, Caribbean Examinations Council, National Cultural Foundation, National Library Service, School Meals Department and educational institutions. As regards research, training and consultancy, a large number of institutions are involved, e.g. Barbados Customs Institute, Barbados Museum and Historical Society, Barbados National Standards Institution, Barbados National Trust, Barbados Primate Research Center, Belairs Research Institute of Marine Biology, Caribbean Agricultural Research and Development Institute, Caribbean Conference of Churches, Caribbean Institute for Meteorology and Hydrology, Caribbean Tourism Research and Development Center, Government Training Center, Insurance Institute of Barbados, Institute of Social and Economic Research - Eastern Caribbean, National Council for Science and Technology, Barbados Vocational Training Board, and Regional Police Training Center. There are 126 public/private primary schools and 37 public/private secondary schools. There are over 45 fee-paying private nurseries, with another 15 operating under the Child Care Board. A number of theological, secretarial, language, trade, driving, cosmetological, modeling, music, dance, physical-education and martial-arts schools, tutorial centers, and professional/occupational associations are involved in diverse ways with the sector.

13. Initially, the church played a role in health management with a later shift of responsibility to local government and charitable organizations. During the colonial period, living and working conditions were poor, and mortality was high due to epidemics of infections diseases. The infant mortality rate, for example, fluctuated between 420 and 187 per 1,000 live births from 1902 to 1924. The Moyne Commission indicated the need for changing concepts of healthcare in the region and the need to establish proper medical and nursing care systems. The Department of Medical Services Act (1947) and the Public Health Act (1954) were repealed and replaced by the Health Services Act in 1969. This legislation made the Ministry of Health responsible for all matters relating to health of the community. Earlier in 1959 almshouses were changed to infirmaries. The first district hospital with twenty beds was opened at Oistins, Christ Church in 1960. The five district hospitals in Christ Church, St. Lucy, St. Michael, St. Philip and St. Thomas were absorbed into the Ministry of Health in 1969. In 1977, the St. Michael District Hospital was upgraded to a geriatric hospital. The Barbados Drug Service came on stream in 1980. The district medical office service, dating back to colonial times, was terminated with the introduction of polyclinic services in 1985. With the first polyclinic built in 1977, the polyclinic network - comprising a total of eight polyclinics located at Black Rock, Glebe, Ladymeade, Oistins, Six Cross Roads, Litchfield, Warrens, and Wildey - represents a move towards a comprehensive type of primary health care.

14. The sector is serviced by the Emergency Ambulance Service, Barbados Drug Service, Barbados Family Planning Association, dental clinics, district hospitals, dispensaries, Geriatric Hospital, Ministry of Health and its specialized programs, National Nutrition Center, Pan American Health Organization, Psychiatric Hospital, polyclinics, Queen Elizabeth Hospital, senior citizens homes, Sanitation Service Authority and others, such as private practitioners, private clinics, pharmaceutical organizations, drug/herbal stores, laboratory services, professional associations, etc.

15. Before emancipation in 1838, the majority of the population worked on the 508 sugar plantations, receiving in return communal subsistence-level shelter from the planters. Subsequently, people traded back their agricultural labor for a parcel of rented plantation land. The dispossession and subordination of the people was perpetuated, inter alia, by the Master and Servants Act (1891), the Encumbered Estates Act (1854) and the Landlord and Tenant Act (1897). With emigration occurring between 1891 and 1921, home remittances enabled many Barbadians to become small landowners. As recently as 1970, wooden houses accounted for 75.2% of the total stock. The passage of the Security of Tenure of Small Holdings Act (1955), the Tenantries Control and Development Act (1965), the Tenantries Freehold Purchase Act (1980) and the Tenantries Development

Act (1980) have increased the security of tenure, prevented unreasonable rent increases, facilitated the transfer of land ownership and promoted the improvement of the tenantry area. Recent initiatives have contributed toward securing housing finance and building materials.

16. A multifaceted sector, housing is serviced by the Barbados Mortgage Finance Company Ltd., Barbados Water Authority, Lands and Survey Department, Ministry of Housing, National Assistance Board, National Conservation Commission, National Housing Corporation, Sanitation Service Authority, Town and Country Planning Department, Environmental Engineering Division, Electrical Engineering Department, Valuation Division, Welfare Department, and other utility services and private sector organizations.

REFERENCES

Emtage, Steven E. (1969) *Growth, Development and Planning in a Small Dependent Economy: The Case of Barbados*. Sussex: Master's Thesis, University of Sussex.

Government of Barbados (1946) *A Ten Year Development Plan for Barbados: Sketch Plan of Development 1946-56*. St Michael, Barbados: Advocate Company Ltd.

___(1952) *Development Plan 1952-57*. St Michael, Barbados: Advocate Company Ltd.

___ (1955) *Development Plan 1955-60*. St Michael, Barbados: Advocate Company Ltd.

___ (1960) *Development Plan 1960-65*. St Michael, Barbados: Government Printery.

___ (1962) *Development Plan 1962-65*. St Michael, Barbados: Government Printery.

___ (1965) *Development Plan 1965-68*. St Michael, Barbados: Government Printery.

___ (1969) *Development Plan 1969-72*. St Michael, Barbados: Government Printery.

___ (1973) *Development Plan 1973-77*. St Michael, Barbados: Government Printery.

___ (1979) *Development Plan 1979-1983*. St Michael, Barbados: Government Printery.

___ (1983) *Development Plan 1983-1988*. St Michael, Barbados: Government Printery.

___ (1988) *Development Plan 1988-93*. St. Michael, Barbados: Government Printery.

___ (1993) *Development Plan 1997-2000*. St. Michael, Barbados: Government Printery.

Government of the United Kingdom (1945) *West India Royal Commission Report*.

London: Her Majesty's Stationery Office.
The Advocate News (1978) *News Report*. St Michael, Barbados: The Advocate News.

5
PROJECT BEHAVIOR

Background

Greenland

It is not possible to be certain of the original source of the Blackbelly sheep (Lydekker, 1912). Laurie (1971:22), however, reported that the sheep was originally domesticated in Persia. The sheep, believed to be of West African origin (Devendra, 1972:23-26; Patterson, 1976: 1; Rastogi, 1980:5-28), was brought to Barbados during the slave trade. At any rate, the sheep have been in Barbados for well over three hundred years. Ligon (1657:59)and Buttenshaw (1906:187) refer to their presence, especially in the drier parts and coastal areas. Due to the sheep's high prolificacy, they have enjoyed wide distribution. The sheep were sent to the British Museum of Natural History around 1900, St. Lucia in 1902, Tortola in 1903 , and the United States in 1904.

Established in 1944, the district agricultural stations dealt in livestock-raising, and the Central Livestock Station, formed in 1947, turned to livestock importation (Department of Science and Agriculture, 1944:11: 1945:9: 1947:62-63). In the 1950s, the Ministry of Agriculture imported the Wiltshire breed which were used in crossbreeding with the Blackbelly sheep. Sheep breeding continued at the Six Cross Roads Agricultural Station, St. Philip around 1974 with such objectives as producing and registering sheep, perfecting techniques and obtaining and evaluating data. The Barbados Sheep Farmers Association came into being in 1975.

To pursue research and experiments and to stop harmful practices, the Ministry of Agriculture established sheep farming at the Greenland Agricultural Station in St. Andrew in 1976. It was followed by setting up a Sheep Multiplication Unit at Sedgepond, St. Andrew. At about the same time, the extension services were upgraded, pastures were improved, acreage was extended, and increased sheep export was encouraged. The sheep are at present widely distributed throughout the world, including Aruba, Bahamas, British Virgin Islands, Canada, Curacao, Eastern Caribbean, Grenada, Guadeloupe, Guyana, Jamaica, Martinique, Mexico, Panama, Peru, Taiwan, Trinidad and Tobago and Venezuela.

Sheep farming was not a properly organized farming activity in Barbados until 1970s. It was normally a secondary interest and a background operation. Traditionally, sheep were raised by small farmers and low-income households as a means of income or for their own consumption. While some had reared sheep for over 20 years, keeping sheep was a lifelong experience for small farmers. The level of capital investment was low. Small farmers possibly owned more than 75% of the island's sheep. Some were also hobby-type breeders of the sheep. The tendency was to establish sheep flocks rather than sheep farms. Some farmers maintained sheep due to sentiment rather than economics. Flocks were established in conjunction with other farming pursuits. There were no specialist sheep farmers.

Systematic breeding was not widespread, selection and culling practices were unplanned and the selection pressure was not high. Sheep pastures were few and pasture rotation and parasite control were casual. Few farmers applied fertilizers on pastures as part of forage management. The animals were generally left to graze by the roadside or in empty areas. The majority of sheep were grass-fed, with occasional supplementary feed. Water was seldom offered ad libitum. The sheep were dewormed at 2-3 month intervals. All lambs intended for sale remained with their nursing mothers until they were weaned and sold at about eight weeks. Castration in young rams was almost never practiced. Disease and parasite control was not professionally done. There were few outlets for marketable sheep. Sheep were either slaughtered on the farm or sold or marketed through local butchers.

Handicraft

Barbados has a tradition of handicraft extending as far back as the time of the Arawaks (Boyce, 1976:3; Bynoe, 1978:1-2; BIDC, 1979:4). The Arawak influence is recognizable in traditional design. Subsequently, European and African cultures and craft skills spread their influence. Before emancipation, artisans fashioned useful and decorative household and market products. It was a part of the elementary-school curriculum in the 1930s. Basketry and shoe-making were well-known around this time. The fostering of handicrafts was bound up with the activities of Barbados Welfare Limited, a nonprofit organization formed in 1943 (Government of Barbados, 1946:5; Colonial Office, 1952). An attempt was launched in 1944 to improve pottery production by the erection of gas-filled kilns at Turner's Hall. Handicraft training was offered at the Housecraft Center, which opened in 1945 at Bay Street.

The Brannam Report (1948:3) noted, inter alia, that pottery-making had existed in Barbados longer than could be accurately recorded. Home-based work was identified as the cottage operation as far back as the 1950s and received government's attention as an area requiring assistance. Leighton commended (1951:1-7) the design and artisinal skills of William Bertalan's ceramic products under difficult and expensive conditions, dealt with production and export, looked into raw and accessory materials, and examined institution-building. Wiles et al.(1953) probed the methodology of developing the minor handicrafts in Barbados, worker training, production techniques, marketing and institution-building. The Jamaican influence became prominent around the early and middle 1950s.

Under the auspices of the Social Welfare Department, the Handicraft Development Center came into being in 1955. The Centre provided craft training, taught new skills, upgraded standards, developed programs, established a nucleus of handicraft production in the country, provided a marketing outlet, pioneered the use of some raw materials (BIDC, 1975:3,) and popularized handicrafts, (The Barbados Daily News, 1967: October 31). For instance, workshops for basketry and turtleshell work were held under the direction of Louis Gordon at Canefield, St. Thomas in 1956 and Danesbury, St. Michael in 1957 respectively.

A number of activities took place in rapid succession and close sequence. Allan Eaton, an International Corporation Administration consultant, recommended in 1958-59 craft skills for its high social value, studied new production techniques and explored marketing strategies. Paul Nicholas came to the island as an advisor in 1959. Edna Harrison was brought in from Jamaica to provide technical assistance. In 1961, following a request from the United States-based Baylis Brothers, smocking was introduced to the island. A marketing survey of handicraft products was carried out by Muriel Odle in the early 1960s. For years, Barbados found retail outlets in the Bridgetown-based Women's Self Help and West Indies Handicrafts Ltd. Besides Barbados Children's Wear, one of the earliest of the garment factories, exerted some positive influence.

Until the 1970s, however, handicraft production was fragmented, essentially a home-based small-scale activity, production and marketing were not conducted, individual producers were isolated, and progress as a whole was slow and uneven. To alleviate this, in accordance with Section 6(2) of the Barbados Industrial Development Corporation Act 1965 and following a Cabinet decision of October 25, 1973, the BIDC within the ambit of the Ministry of Trade, assumed responsibility for handicraft, and the Handicraft Development Center with effect from April 1, 1974, with a view to developing handicraft nationally and enhancing a commercially viable operation (BIDC, 1975:15). The former Handicraft Development Center, as a result of a reorganisation, became the Corporation's Handicraft Division.

Cave

The existence of Harrison's Cave has been known for hundreds of years. Ligon observers (1657:98) that "caves are very frequent in the island and of several dimensions, some small, others extremely large and capacious". Hughes noted (1750:56) the existence of many remarkable caves in Barbados. A document dated about 1760 in the possession of the Barbados National Trust contains a description of a visit to the Cave by a party of visitors from Great Britain (Barbados Caves Authority, 1977:3). The Cave was first chartered in the same year. Pinckard explored (1806:332) "one of the greatest natural curiosities of the island - a very extensive subterraneous cavern called Harrison's Cave". Schommburgk examined (1848:235-236) extensively Cole's Cave as well as Harrison's Cave. Clarke (1872) cited Harrison's Cave as providing springs which supplied water to the rural districts. Senn carried out (1946) the geological investigations of Barbados' groundwater resources and surveyed the uppermost and accessible part of Harrison's Cave.

The natural phenomenon lay buried and forgotten under the ground near the geographical center of Barbados for many years until 1970 when it was rediscovered by a Danish speleologist Ole Sorensen. Sorensen led an expedition of five researchers and rediscovered, explored and surveyed Harrison's Cave (Chandler, 1981:14; BCA, 1977:3; 1982:10). The Barbados Cave's Authority came into being in 1975 with the object of providing for the control, conservation, development and operation of caves in Barbados. With the Authority being terminated in 1982, the Cave's operation has been placed under the National Conservation

Commission.

Pulverization

Before 1834, during the preemancipation period, refuse disposal in Barbados was neglected resulting in repeated outbreaks of communicable diseases and consequently high mortality. The standard of environmental sanitation and general hygiene was poor, the provision of public services was meagre, the system of waste management was wasteful, and the collection and disposal of household and street refuse was primitive. Welch reports (1977:53-56) about open lorries or pushcarts collecting the refuse which the wind blew about and the indiscriminate dumping of refuse. There operated, under the provision of the Public Health Act 1908, separate public health authorities in each of the eleven parishes.

Created in 1928, the position of a sanitation officer remained unfilled for long (Chief Medical Officer, 1935:1). Until the middle of the 1940s refuse collection and disposal was put on contract by the local authorities and mainly involved the cleaning of streets and gutters. In 1945, the Scavenging Department was formed in St. Michael under the management of Beaumont Sharpe (Sanitation Department, 1947:15). The volume of refuse in Bridgetown was greater than in other areas, and some of the suburbs from where refuse was regularly collected included Belleville, Fontabelle, Hastings, Pine and Worthing (Clarke, 1979:3). In the rural areas where the collection service was inadequate at this time, refuse disposal was tackled by way of recycling.

Refuse containers were placed at various collection points. The most common means of disposal was the tipping method in which the refuse was dumped into open sites with earth covering and without any compaction. Some of the approved disposal sites were Hill Road, Jenkins, Lands End, Reef Ground, Welches Road, Carrington Village, Mason Hall Street, Belle Plantation, Codrington Hill and Military Road. In the Bridgetown area, collected refuse consisted of 40% organic and 60% inorganic matter and averaged around 65 tons daily. An average of 72 miles per day (Merritt, 1951:35) was covered by collection vehicles.

It was not until the early 1960s, when Barbados was reconstituted into northern, southern and St. Michael areas, that waste collection and rented services were reorganized and extended (Government of Barbados, 1962). The Zanten Report (1962) took a close look at workload, equipment, vehicles, staffing, standards, disposal sites and cover materials. Yet another change occurred in 1966 when the three areas were brought together and all services were placed under the direct control of the Ministry of Health. To manage waste disposal throughout the country, the Sanitation and Cemeteries Board - formed in 1969 - functioned until it was replaced by the Sanitation Service Authority in 1974.

Polytechnic

Some emphasis during the 1920s and 1930s was placed on skill development in elementary schools. Lovell reports (1980:26) on varied skills being taught at schools , e.g. gardening, carpentry, basketry, brush-making, fibrework, cookery, and needlework. In the 1920s , growing interest in technical training led to the establishment of the Board of Technical Training. The Board of Industrial Training, which came into being in 1928, provided technical training in various skill areas (Greaves, 1981:15). Besides, vocational courses became available at government industrial schools. The Moyne Commission (1945:21) wanted to see traditional education becoming expressly more prevocational . Opened in 1945, the Housecraft Center operated thirteen centers throughout the island and provided training in applied skills (Vaughan, 1970:19).

Technical education received a further boost when vocational courses were conducted in 1947 and 1948 as a program of the Barbados Evening Institute (Gittens, 1969:15). Efforts were put in by the Barbados Technologists Association to popularize technical education. The report of the Select Committee on Technical and Vocational Training was published in 1949 (Ministry of Education, 1963:30; Government of Barbados, 1963). A technical institute was recommended for the training of 500 students in various trades. Since 1950, the teaching of technical skills has been introduced in the grammar-school curriculum. On the recommendation of the Select Committee, the Barbados Technical Institute was established in 1953 (Browne, 1982:11). Training commenced in 1955 with an enrollment of 100 day-release trainees and 20 evening students.

In 1958, the functions of the Board of Industrial Training were taken over by the Apprenticeship Board (Ministry of Education, 1969:3-4). Industrial arts education was added in 1962 to the curriculum at ten secondary schools. The Barbados Hotel Training School opened in 1964. Since its outset in 1968, the Division of Technology of the Barbados Community College has been offering a wide range of technical courses (Waldron, 1982:22). Following the reports (Advisory Committee on the Trades Training Center, 1968:14) the Samuel Jackman Prescod Polytechnic - having grown out of the Barbados Technical Institute - was established in 1969 with a view to meeting the evolving needs of industrialization and skill development. Initially called the Trades Training Center (Price, 1983:10), the Polytechnic was located on three temporary campuses, with an annual enrollment of about 1,500 students.

Sewerage

Ligon described (1657:25) Bridgetown as an "unwholesome place" and observed that the "area should not have been chosen for the location of a city". Since then, of the numerous health-related developments, the Public Health Act 1908 sought to eliminate disease vectors and improve household sanitation. The UK-based consulting firm of Howard Humphreys & Sons was first engaged in 1921 to study sewage needs in Bridgetown (Town Planning Department, 1970:29). Archer (1983:1) intimated that the firm recommended the construction of a waterborne sewage system for the city, but no record of plans were available. Earlier, the Town Planning Department (1970:29) noted that the need for this type of system was not clearly established.

Throughout the 1930s, in any event, sanitation was managed on a parochial basis, giving rise to the fragmentation of service. The level of sanitation in urban and rural areas was generally low. In many schools, sanitation was deficient and poor and conditions were filthy (Chief Medical Officer, 1935:9). Lovell reports (1980:30) that poor sanitation resulted in the prevalence of a number of communicable diseases. Urban sanitation in Bridgetown was discussed in the Stanley Committee Report (1943:3-6), which noted sanitary deficiencies, health hazards, unsanitary toilet conditions, excreta disposal, beach pollution, fly-borne infection, and underground water-system pollution. Moyne et al. (1945:169) found sewage disposal often unsatisfactory in the urban areas. In 1945 Howard Humphreys & Sons in a second study indicated the need for a sewage system for Bridgetown and prepared preliminary designs and plans for a collector system with disposal of raw sewage into the sea off Cowell Street (Government of Barbados, 1946:31). In response to a health survey, financial assistance was given in 1954 for the installation of domestic latrines as part of health management (Colonial Office, 1954:71). Jackson found (1964:32) that of the 28,000 houses in the city area, only 20% had waterborne sewage.

A further study in 1965 by Howard Humphreys & Sons recommended the increased use of septic tanks in the city, a sludge collection system using tank trucks and treatment and disposal at Cave Hill (Howard

Humphreys & Sons, 1965:2). In the 1970s over 50% of the properties in Bridgetown used pit closets. Several interim sewage disposal methods were utilized, including absorption wells and septic tanks. Septic-tank effluent used to be flushed into storm drains and the sea. The pumping system was controlled at the Queen Elizabeth Hospital (1964), the Barbados Hilton (1966), and the Holiday Inn (1967). Small treatment units were set up at the St. Michael District Hospital (1976), and, subsequently, at the Barclays Bank and the Norman Center.

Ferneihurst

Housing conditions during the 1920s , 1930s and 1940s were deplorable and posed one of the most pressing problems (Colonial Office, 1935:10; Comptroller; 1945:1, Horn, 1957: 1-58; Rose, 1959:2-7; Clarke,1974:11-21; Husbands, 1979:1-51; Lovell, 1980:10-35;Greaves , 1981:4-5; Fraser and Hughes, 1982:49). Housing was characterized by squalor, deprivation, gloom, congestion, overcrowding and domestic insanitation. Overcrowding, poor ventilation, lack of light, leaking roofs and rotten flooring combined to cause sickness frequently. Inadequate sanitation, excessive overcrowding and dereliction resulted in slums. Poor sanitation, pit closets, fly-borne infection, polluted water and indiscriminate excreta disposal endangered the quality of life. The majority of homes contained not more than two rooms, in which a family of four or five persons lived. Pit toilets or pail closets were shared. The kitchen, if there was one, was separate. 68% of the population, for instance, lived in homes of less than two small rooms. Stanley et al. report (1943:5) that an area of 88,670 square feet was occupied by 76 houses and 16 businesses. Many rural homes consisted of one room only. Workers on plantations and in factories lived near the estates in small houses built on rented land. The houses, poorly designed and mostly built of timber with shingled roofs, were small, mobile and termite-ridden. The houses were not equipped with piped water supply, sewage disposal and rainwater clearance. On the contrary, the houses owned by the middle and high-income people were well-built mostly of stone. They were equipped with electricity, piped water-supply, waterborne sewage disposal system, kitchen and shower.

The occupants and owners of the low-cost houses comprised a miscellaneous group of artisans, smallholders, plantation workers, peddlars, domestics, industrial workers, porters, sailors, coopers, tailors, laundresses, fishermen and boatmen. The cost of house repair was not affordable mostly, since household income was extremely low. Slum clearance was infrequent due to initial and recurrent costs. In a housing survey in 1946 of 7,984 low-cost houses it was found that 3,022 were unfit for human habitation, 2,710 needed repairs and 1,617 were overcrowded (Housing Board, 1955:1). The number of houses was 46,282 in 1942, 47,987 in 1946, and 57,000 in 1955. The average household size for the island was 4.3 persons. In the 1950s, 70.0% of land was held in rented sites (Horn, 1957:12). The first self-help housing program was established at Clinketts, St. Lucy in 1953. There were 80 rental units in 1951 , 291 in 1956 and 855 in 1959. The housing agency had under its control 4,127 housing units in 1971 which had accommodated 4,585 families. It rose to 4,751 in 1977. Between 1970 and 1978, 7,185 units were constructed, of which the Corporation built 3,013 or 42%. Housing finance for private housing included only one small building society, with banks offering short-term loans, merchant credit being selectively available and credit unions advancing small repair loans. Rental applications were on the increase. As against 14,880 applications during 1956-69, only 3,983 were approved.

The history of indepth studies on housing is long, e.g. the 1933 Committee Report (1935), the Haslam Report (1935) the Stanley Committee Report (1943), the Desyllas Report (1944) the Moyne Commission Report (1945) the Lashley Report (1945), the MacPherson Report (1946), the Stockdale Report (1946), the Abrams Report (1963), the Judy Fisher Study (1965), the Burton Report (1975), the Hewitt Report (1975), the Organization and Management Study (1976), and the Hanschell Committee Report (1979). These reports dealt with housing conditions, urban and rural housing, land availability, low-cost housing, slum clearance, institution-building, policy capability, tenurial insecurity, cost escalation, urban congestion, town planning legislation, building materials, domestic sanitation, eviction control, housing design, accounting maintenance, materials control, operation, and malpractices.

Institutionally speaking, the Bridgetown Housing Board was established in 1939. In 1950, the labor welfare organizations, with particular mandate for housing loans, became operational which were followed in 1952 by the appointment of the Public Officers Housing Board. The Housing Authority came into being in 1956, having consolidated all the former agencies. The Urban Development Corporation was founded in 1965. Having merged the Housing Authority and the Urban Development Corporation, the National Housing Corporation was established in 1973.

Conception

Greenland

The Ministry of Agriculture's experiments between the Blackbelly and Wiltshire sheep started in the 1950s. Experimental work was planned to be carried out as early as 1958 and 1959 (Colonial Office, 1960:10). Young ewes and rams were given experimental feeding at the Animal Nutrition Unit. The current Project was the culmination of an earlier Ministry of Agriculture sheep operation first at the Six Cross Roads Agricultural Station in 1974 and later at the Greenland Agricultural Station in 1976 (Government of Barbados, 1969; Livestock Extension and Development Division, 1974; Agriculture Information Unit, 1978:16). Sheep registration was undertaken in 1974 with a view to identifying the serious sheep breeders and standardizing the characteristics of a particular breed. The Development Plan 1973-77 underscored the importance of livestock production and the commercialization of sheep-farming (Government of Barbados, 1973:102-103). A sheep (Patterson and Nurse, 1974:25) indicated that the Blackbelly sheep was the preferred breed and was the dominant stock on the estates and farms.

The Project was initiated following a mandate given by the Heads of Government to the CARICOM in 1975. It was consistent with the agreement of the CARICOM ministers of agriculture known as the 'Caribbean Food Plan'. The idea was provided in response to a request from the Barbados Ministry of Agriculture to assist in implementing the role identified as Barbados' commitment to the Caribbean Food Plan. Motta and Blades (1975:1-46) stressed the considerable potential for meat production from small ruminant animals -especially sheep - and identified the Blackbelly sheep as the base stock source and Barbados as the pivotal site for development of this resource. The insufficiency of livestock products caused food imports. In 1978, for instance, mutton imports totalled 1.1m. lbs. at a cost of BDS$1.6m. (Statistical Services Department, 1978:1).

The ongoing ministerial program entered a project phase in 1978 when the USAID as a funding agency and the United States-based Caribbeana Council as a technical assistance agency became involved with impetus being provided by the Inter-American Foundation, another United States-based private research and development institution. The Caribbeana Council insisted on projectization, arguing that a project basis had to be laid down to be eligible for obtaining funds. As the piloting agency the Ministry of Agriculture adopted the project idea after external financing was assured. The Ministry's personnel in livestock management and animal nutrition further probed the idea and checked technical accuracy.

The project objectives included:(a) establishing a flock of purebred and registered Blackbelly sheep as foundation stock for local farmers to meet Barbados' contribution to the Caribbean Food Plan; (b) providing some 500 sheep for export annually;(c) promoting selective breeding to increase productivity;(d) supplying mutton and lamb to the local market, commercializing the local products, and marketing the Blackbelly sheep as a source of protein food;(e) improving food self-sufficiency; (f) producing a new crossbred commercial mutton using the Blackbelly sheep as the base stock; (g) increasing the viability of farmers and profitability of sheep production; and (h) raising the flock-management skills of the small farmers.

Handicraft

A special six-member group named the Handicraft Development Committee - a Standing Committee of the BIDC's directorial board - was set up in 1974, which helped identify goals and objectives at an early stage and sought technical assistance from the UK-based Commonwealth Fund for Technical Cooperation (CFTC). In August 1974, the Ministry of Trade obtained technical assistance from the CFTC. Shyamadas Sengupta, a handicraft specialist, was assigned as a technical advisor to work with the Corporation's Handicraft Division (BIDC, 1975:1). A document (Sengupta, 1974), serving as an initial stimulus for the Project, provided data sources and historical background of the Handicraft Development Center, presented a survey of skill and raw material sourcing, highlighted possible linkages with the tourism sector, brought out the industry's positive factors and potentials, and suggested certain action plans.

The Project was taken up partly because the handicraft output contained a high local content and the development of this industry was considered important to the economy. The objectives included: (a) diversifying craft skills, intensifying training, and utilizing available human resources; (b) initiating product development, improving productivity, developing marketing, improving commercialization, and developing production and retailing skills; (c) tapping and expanding the sources of raw materials; (d) expanding the local industrial base and sustaining producer interest in local products; and (e) facilitating the development of craft cooperatives (BIDC, 1975: 1-3; 1978: 21-29).

Cave

The Project idea was born in 1973 after Sorensen had made survey of the Cave in 1970, realized the significance of the Cave formations and identified its potential. It was the Barbados National Trust which had sponsored the first comprehensive survey of the Cave. As a result of the survey findings and the advocacy of the Barbados National Trust, the Cabinet decided in principle at its meeting of March 8, 1973 and June 27, 1974 that the Cave should be developed as a tourist attraction and preserved as a natural asset (BCA, 1977:3).

A Steering Committee was set up on July 15, 1974 under the aegis of the Ministry of Tourism to work out proposals for the development of the Cave, e.g. exploring the Cave system, determining the more accessible and suitable areas for development, surveying and establishing coordinates, exploring the possibility of carrying out infrastructural work, and identifying the more inaccessible and difficult areas. In December 1974, Russell Gurnee and Jeanne Gurnee, two American speleologists, undertook an exploration of the Cave along with Sorensen and submitted a report on the Project's viability. The Gurnee Report, serving as an initial information base for the Project, spoke to the physical survey of the Cave, tunnel/trail construction, passageway/walkway development, stream movement, cave formation, cave lighting, surface development, budgeting and consultancy. In the light of he Gurnee Report, the Ministry of Tourism accepted in 1975 the proposals of the Steering Committee and recommend that the proposals for the design of the Cave be accepted.

The Project was conceived as part of response to increase the annual rate of growth of tourist expenditures, thereby stimulating an expansion in the GDP and in the number of job opportunities, and to exploit to the fullest potential for intersectoral linkages arising from tourist expenditures so as to ensure that the sector remains a powerful vehicle for promoting growth and development (BCA, 1975:81). The Cave's development was justified by comparing it with the development of show caves in other countries. It was expected that when the Cave would become open to the public, there would be sufficient and attractive cave features in place to please the most discerning visitor.

Pulverization

A number of specialist assessments influenced the Project's conception. The Zanten Report (1962), having looked at waste management in Barbados during the early 1960s, recommended that an incinerator be installed for Bridgetown. The insanitary conditions of refuse in and around urban areas caused problems, especially the traditional practice of tipping gave rise to complaints about fly nuisance in residential areas. It also became difficult to find suitable disposal sites owing to the increased volume of refuse and sprawling residential and industrial spread. The collection vehicles were obsolescent and insufficient in number. There was also the scarcity of material for adequate cover.

The Wason-Redman Report (1967:1) dealt with refuse collection/ storage/transportation/disposal, assessed existing practices and new developments of waste management, and made recommendations for its change. The Ministry of Health's Environmental Engineering Division highlighted around 1968-69 the danger of groundwater pollution by refuse disposal sites. The Town Planning Department pointed out (1970:62,103) that island-wide waste disposal needs and alternative disposal methods should be examined and recommended a central disposal plant. This was followed by the Ministry of Health's permanent secretary and public health engineer visiting a pulverization plant at St. Catherine, Canada in late 1970 and May 1971.

The Archer Report (1973:4-6) dealt with waste collection, disposal, landfilling, equipment, site selection and other development measures in relation to waste management. The Report also spoke to the pulverization method of refuse treatment. The Abrahams Report (1973), on the basis of a study in 1971 of the entire refuse collection and disposal service in Barbados, recommended pulverization as a disposal method. Following the Report, the Ministry of Health's Environmental Engineering Division recommended pulverization as the method of treatment before final disposal. Anderson (1973:4-9) endorsed the Abrahams Report with respect to a long-term refuse disposal method. Abrahams as well as Anderson recommended disposal by pulverization of the refuse and using the waste for landfills. At its biennial conference in June 1973, the Barbados Youth Council drew urgent attention of the government to the need for proper refuse disposal and to recognize the collection service.

Moreover, a report (Chief Medical Officer, 1974:24) described the system of a fleet of vehicles collecting refuse and hauling it to approved sites for disposal as inefficient and called for the pulverization of refuse as a disposal method. With the assistance of PAHO/WHO, the Ministry of Health carried out a survey of refuse collection and disposal techniques. The survey report (Government of Barbados, 1974:196) called for the use of new types of collection vehicles and disposal methods. In 1977, the Ministry of Health's Planning and Research Division indicated that government could build a pulverization plant at Workmans, St. George. Provisions were made in the 1978-79 budget document for the establishment of a plant.

The Project was conceived with a view to easing the solid waste disposal problem, putting an infrastructure in place to minimize environmental pollution and reprocess wastes and maximizing the capacity of landfills throughout the island, especially in view of the fact that landfills were very few. The objectives included providing a clear, healthy and litter-free environment, minimizing haulage costs due to the centrally-located site at Workmans, improving general efficiency of the Sanitation Service Authority due to the utilization of a weighbridge for refuse collection, reducing health hazards and nuisances utilizing the waste products as compost or as a source of refuse-derived fuel, and utilizing the recaimed quarry. The motivating factors for the Project lay in limited land space for waste disposal sites, and difficulty in collecting cover material for the operation of sanitary landfills.

Polytechnic

The conceptual phase of the Project was informed by a number of studies undertaken in the 1960s and the 1970s, e.g.Gailer (1965), Shurcliff et al. (1968), Emmerson et al. (1969), and Lavender(1970). Several specialist reports also influenced the conceptual process around the same time, namely, the Ministry of Education (1969), Sutter (1970), and Hercules (1970). The Project was based on a 1969 UNESCO study of Barbados' educational network which estimated the annual trainee output required to meet the projected skilled manpower needs of the country during a ten-year period. The UNESCO study was updated by another study in 1972. Two other studies (Oxtoby, 1974; McEvers, 1974) made impact on the initial phase, particularly in respect to establishing the demand for trainees, such as those trained at the Polytechnic. Initial support was drawn from yet another study (BIMAP, 1975:1) which related to probing the labor market, analyzing trends in technical manpower, making estimates and projections, and carrying out longitudinal-type tracer surveys for relevant cohorts.

The objectives included: (a) providing technical and vocational training; (b) developing a wider range of technical skills and occupational competencies; (c) preparing trainees for direct entry into paid employment and absorption into the workforce (Inter-American Development Bank 1977:51); (d) satisfying the growing needs of the industrial and service sectors; and (e) constructing a new self-containing complex to house the institution which was located in three temporary sites. The Project, conceived as one of the major investments of human resource development in the country, had also several academic and management objectives, e.g. developing a new pattern of courses, expanding teaching and operational capability, improving the Polytechnic management, expanding and upgrading faculty, creating a counselling and employment service, creating a vocational guidance and curricular development service, strengthening the capacity of the Ministry of Education in educational planning and manpower demand analysis, and improving organizational and financial management of the Polytechnic and the Ministry of Education.

Sewerage

It took several years of consulting and reporting before it was decided to sewer the city as a means of improving its sanitary and environmental conditions. The Ministry of Health's Environmental Engineering Division carried out in 1968 a study of sewage disposal in Carlisle Bay and the adjacent coastlines, aimed at determining the bacteriological quality of the water in these areas. Coliform counts were very high, e.g. 16,000 coliforms/100 mls in the surveyed areas, and floating solid faecal matter was a common sight (Archer, 1983:1). In 1969 (Moore, 1981:1-2) the city's parliamentary representative advised the government of the need to sewer Bridgetown. Government recognized after the Bridgetown fires of 1970 that the increase in building activity and sewage volume necessitated a modern sewage system.

The Archer Report (1970) recommended the installation of a sewage treatment plant to service the greater Bridgetown. A prefeasibility study of the Project was conducted in the same year by the Ministry of Health at the request of a Cabinet subcommittee. In December 1972, the IDB provided technical assistance in support of further studies. The Project was accorded high priority in the Development Plan 1973-77 (Government of Barbados, 1973:193) on the ground that health was the basis for wellbeing of individuals and their ability to participate in community life. Finally in 1974, the Ministry of Health made the declaration of intent in respect of the Project. In January 1975, the Ministry of Finance and Planning approached the IDB for a loan to finance the Project in part.

A number of reasons provided the impetus for the Project, e.g. the inability of the alluvial soil in the target area to absorb the large volume of sewage, the rapid expansion of office-blocks in the city center, the high population density and intensive land-use in the target area, the increasing pollution of the area, the environmental pollution and damage of the adjacent marine area, the practice of sewage, dumping and presence of a large number of pit toilets and pail closets in the city threatening health disorder and groundwater contamination, the outbreak of communicable diseases in the 1960s and 1970s, the overflow of absorption wells and septic tanks, the flooding of sidewalk sewers and the failure of the traditional method of subsoil disposal to cope with faecal waste.

The Project was aimed at (a) relieving the existing sewage problem in the Bridgetown area; (b) eliminating many sewage outlets which polluted the marine areas; (c) removing numerous earth and pail closets which perpetuated fly infestation; (d) eliminating the faecal points of environmental pollution; (e) reducing health risks, improving sanitation and environmental conditions in the target area and improving the quality of seawater in the adjacent area; (f) constructing a practical, economical and sanitary sewerage system to meet for the next 30 years projected demands of building development, urban renewal, aesthetic and health needs, tourism promotion, investment and employment (Bridgetown Sewerage Project, 1977-82); and (g) preparing institutional and rate-schedule studies, and creating a statutory authority to jointly manage water and sewerage services.

Ferneihurst

Two parcels of land at Ferneihurst in the Black Rock area were acquired in March 1972 by the Ministry of Education for the purpose of building a secondary school and a youth center (National Housing Corporation, 1978-81). After there was a change in the decision of constructing the school, the Ministry of Housing decided in 1978 to utilize the site for a housing project. The Project was conceived at the highest level in the Ministry of Housing, with inputs from its Housing Planning Unit, in recognition of the fact that there was a demand for low-cost housing to satisfy the needs of people in the lower income bracket. The Ministry chose to get involved in the Project since the private sector was not providing houses for the clientele in the low income category. Moreover, it was recognized that the public sector should take the lead in increasing the housing stock and at the same time creating employment and stimulating general productive activity.

The Project's main objective was to provide accommodation to low-income and low middle-income families in an urban residential area. Other goals extended to: (a) a more optimal utilization of limited residential space (National Housing Corporation, 1978-81); (b) the promotion of community activities; (c) moving out people living in depressed areas, putting them in adequate houses and uplifting their lifestyle and status; and (d) changing the concept and character of public housing and giving people reason to want to be proud of the places in which they live.

Formulation

Greenland

Formulation stressed that the Project's success rested on the cooperation of the small sheep farmers, involvement of the Barbados Sheep Farmers Association and the upgrading of the sheep. It was stressed that overseas buyers preferred to purchase registered sheep, which commanded a higher price.

Prepared by the Inter-American Foundation, the Project proposal, which appeared in February 1978, gave the Project's location, manpower needs, materials, financing, cost, time, benefits, objectives, justification and technical features. The reasons for the emphasis on the Blackbelly sheep were that mutton and lamb were dietetically popular, sheep required relatively less land for grazing , a relatively low internal capital outlay was required for sheep-raising, lamb and mutton were good sources of animal protein, and the breed was abundantly available in Barbados. Some budgerty estimates were included, the external resource personnel were named, the local counterpart staff needs were noted, and an estimated timetable of outputs was provided. The exercise was targeted to be completed by 1982. The proposal specified in detail both the human and material inputs required from several participating agencies.

The Caribbeana Council put in a request to the USAID for funds to assist the Barbados Ministry of Agriculture in the implementation of the Project (Caribbeana Council, 1978:1). It was formulated that the funds would be used to provide on-site technical assistance and equipment, and that a set of planned and coordinated activities would be launched. These included acquiring the best samples of the sheep, developing a flock through scientific breeding and husbandry, running a crossbreeding station commercializing local mutton and lamb, expanding lamb and mutton export, organizing sheep feeding trials, preparing the best feasible feed combination, running a sheep husbandry training center, providing high-quality stud service to local farmers, registering the Blackbelly sheep with the Barbados Agricultural Society, carrying out a promotional campaign, and distributing a number of crossbred sheep to farmers.

Handicraft

Sengupta (1974) highlighted the pressing need for craft skill development expansion in certain key areas, and immediate management action. The BIDC (1974-75; 1975:1-38) worked out several aspects of the Project, including the location, cost estimates, benefits, human resources, materials, financing, technical assistance, marketing, production diversification and development, and research and training. It was considered in 1975 that the Project would be partly developmental and in part commercial in its orientation. While training, research, design and product development and diversification were deemed developmental, the commercial role spoke to materials control, production, purchasing, marketing, promotion and exporting. The close cooperation of the private sector was highlighted to ensure success.

Some policies and priorities underlying the Project included the production of those crafts which utilized local raw materials, developing those products which generated higher employment, decentralizing production on an own-account craft-production basis, and facilitating private entrepreneurship in the sector. Other concerns were introducing better production techniques and tools, effecting design improvement, treating and processing raw materials, conducting marketing research, diversifying production, linking product with design development, adapting products to consumer preferences, developing quality control, learning modern production and business methods, seizing new opportunities, and improving work quality.

Training assumed some importance in this phase. To increase the number of skilled producers and upgrade skills, training was targeted to be provided to 150 enrollees during 1975 -76, 300 enrollees during 1976-77, and 660 enrollees during 1977-79. Research was aimed at improving existing standards, designing and producing new lines, and tapping new types of raw materials. Marketing was concerned with purchasing, quality-marking, wholeselling, retailing, promotion, and export marketing.

Cave

This phase embraced various moves to expand the range and number of attractions and services to improve the tourism product, encourage longer stay and sightseeing and increase tourist expenditure. A proposal for a visit by a specialist group from the UNESCO was considered. It related to examining the feasibility of some complementary development of a cultural and educational nature at the Cave (BCA, 1977:7; Greene, 1980). Dames and Moore, a Canada-based consulting firm, examined in December 1977 the work on excavation, tunnelling, safety and other underground operations, and reported on its assignment during January - February 1978 (BCA, 1978:3-4; 1980:2).

Further, an agreement was reached in February 1978 with the United States-based National Speleological Foundation to set up a study group, with a view to examining work and preparing a plan for the Cave's completion. Around February - March 1979, another round of negotiations was opened with the Foundation Study group. In October 1979, an agreement was finalized with the United States-based Barbados Cave Project Inc. (BCA, 1978:4; 1980:2). The American Explorers Association was contacted for a second-order consideration on the Project's work and feasibility.

Pulverization

A number of disposal methods, e.g. pulverization or shredding, incineration and composting were considered. All methods were examined in order to meet several criteria, namely, the method must have a low capital investment; being on an island, it must be a clean, environmentally-sound disposal method; a system of extracting reusable resource would be have to be a component; and the method must operate at a low cost. Among several basic criteria which emerged to influence the selection process were the shortage of cover material for sanitary landfills, the availability of quarries and other sites for disposal, the reduction of fire hazards, leaching, infestation, the size and geography of the island, the nature of the road systems and traffic conditions, the size of investment, and the type of support system involved in alternatives.

In February 1970, hydrolysis as a disposal method was considered and found to be infeasible. At the same time, incineration was examined and found to be costly with the disposal of ash posing problems. Composting was considered and was identified as being costly in capital and operation outlay. Other disposal methods, such s baling, recycling and pyrolysis were not considered feasible for Barbados at that time.

The Abrahams Report (1973) recommended the pulverization and sanitary landfilling methods and highlighted the storage, collection and disposal of refuse. The advantages cited for this method were that it resulted in fine shredding, resulted in uniform particle size, improved the appearance of shredded waste, provided a clear residue, allowed for ready and thorough compaction, resulted in volume reduction, required little covering material and less frequently, reduced the size of disposal sites, allowed for rapid stabilization, and facilitated the land reclamation. Of other advantages, attention was paid to restricting insect breeding, restricting communicable diseases, eliminating offensive odor, restricting blowing refuse, minimizing fire hazards/dust nuisance/spontaneous combustion, minimizing risk of underground water-supply contamination, minimizzng risk of trapped gas, minimising pollution, and allowing for recycling and reuse. It was further noted that the facility could be housed in a low-profile building with low capital cost and modest operating cost, did not require heat or chemicals in its operation, was more economical, and offered the best value for investment.

The Anderson Report (1973:4-9) endorsed the Abrahams Report with respect to accepting a long-term refuse disposal method. Anderson recommended that the selection disposal method should embody a number of features, e.g. shredding of all shreddable refuse, disposal in sanitary landfills, location of a shredding plant adjacent to a large-capacity sanitary landfill site, use of a two-shredder plant at a strategic location for service of the entire island with best hauling efficiency, use of route trucks for transport to disposal points, acquisition of additional high-capacity collection vehicles, and improvement of collection services in inaccessible areas.

The Ministry of Health's Environmental Engineering Division accepts pulverization as the disposal method on the ground that it was more economical than alternative methods and that it would meet the environmental protection needs of the country. Pulverized materials, as Greene notes (The Nation, 1980: November 28), emerged as a first stage to more advanced technology in the reuse of solid waste. The Project idea was transmitted to the Sanitary Service Authority for feedback.

Site selection and land acquisition were completed in 1974. Workmans, the Project site, was strategically located at a reasonable distance from St. Michael areas which produced about 73% of the waste. The Project was proposed to be built on quarry bed, with the site having adequate space for the disposal of refuse. The need to survey the Plant site, the disposal quarry area and the adjoining roadways was recognized. The residents of the target area and the district's parliamentarian brought up questions as to the Project's location, siting and impact. The Ministry of Health assured that the Project was environmentally safe and sound. It was observed (Welch, 1977:66) that the Plant would be out of the path of the winds blowing toward residential areas, that the residents would not be affected by its operation, and that the quarry did not pose a threat to the underground water-supply.

Polytechnic

The formulation phase was informed by a number of special studies, e.g. the Ministry of Education (1969), Sutter (1970), Hercules (1970) and Oxtoby Report (1974). The Oxtoby Report (1974), for instance, stressed that the Polytechnic should be relocated to a permanent central site and expanded to provide accommodation for 900-1,000 full-time and upwards of 1,500 part-time students. Five types of programs were considered, i.e. long-duration full-time, short-duration full-time, part-time, continuing, and pretechnical. The IDB programming mission pointed in 1975 to the need for compiling additional information, considered alternative project sites, and refined manpower demand estimates.

The site for the Project was selected in two stages. Selected in 1977, the first site was Delamere in Martindales Road, St. Michael. A feasibility study (Gillespie & Steel Associates Ltd., 1975) embraced several concerns, including the topographical survey of the site, the initial design of a building of about 10,000 square metres, technical specifications, tendering procedures, budget estimates, and time schedules. Some guidelines were established which related to the need for on-site information compilation, identifying restrictive land-use regulations, finding accommodation capacity and space utilization, identifying building accessories and equipment, recognizing future expansion, refining cost estimates and instituting contingencies. The study had shown that transportation of the Polytechnic students was 4% by cars, 25% walked or got rides, and 71% used public transport.

The decision to site the Polytechnic at Wildey, St. Michael in one large campus was taken in 1978. When the second site was chosen, alterations to the previous study were required (Gillespie & Steel Associates Ltd., 1977). Yet, much of the information compiled for the Delamere site was still valid for the Wildey site and became integrated into the second study. The Wildey site was supported by several considerations, e.g. airconditioning buildings was not needed as these could be laid out from north to south facing the prevailing winds, storage tanks for water would not be needed, and the housing located to the west would not suffer from downwind noise coming from the Polytechnic workshops because of the way the buildings would be laid out. With the new site, it was estimated that 85% of students would have to use public transport, but new and improved roads would enable some students to reach the Campus bypassing Bridgetown.

Sewerage

A study (Archer, 1970), carried out by the Ministry of Health's Environmental Engineering Division, initiated a request by the Ministry of Finance and Planning to the IDB for a loan to finance the Project. The Town Planning Department (1970:29-100) cited nine acres of Emmerton, which occupies low-lying and flood-prone urban land in downtown Bridgetown, as the country's worst depressed area with top priority for clearance. In October 1972, the IDB provided technical assistance worth BDS$420,000 to undertake necessary studies and designs of a sewerage system, including feasibility of forming an agency to manage water-supply and sewerage operations. The loan agreement between the GOB and the IDB was signed in 1976.

A demographic study conducted in early 1973 showed an initial population of 37,700 to be included in the sewerage system. The National Housing Corporation conducted a preparatory survey of the chattel houses in Emmerton. A social survey of the same neighborhood was carried out by the Town Planning Department. After considerable design development (Archer, 1981:4), five acres of Emmerton were earmarked in late 1973 as the site for the treatment plant, while an area east of Fairchild Street was selected for the associated pumping station.

Jordan reports (1984:11,27) that in an analysis of possible alternative sites for the treatment plant -south Emmerton, south Prescod Boulevard, south Constitution River, north Constitution River and north Bridgetown-Emmerton was chosen because it presented an optimum point for the sewage disposal system as it was the natural outlet of the area to be sewered. The location of the main sewage pumping station received some analysis in terms of sewage flow, concentration point, population density, and optimum site. The decision to locate the station in a relatively flat area between River Road and Constitution River was needed. On technical grounds, the Emmerton site was ideal in that the sewer lines would converge at the point where the minimum slopes of the city provided maximum gravity flow, thus restricting the use of pumping stations, It was also within short distance of a coastal location where the marine fallout could be located. Emmerton was chosen because of the relatively low cost of land acquisition and the opportunity to clean an area where urban decay was taking its toll.

Having decided to relocate 50% of the residents from downtown Emmerton to suburban Clapham, about 2.5. miles from the city center and to the southwest of Bridgetown, resettlement was formulated in such a way as to cover road-building, drainage system, house removal, house-building, utility services, and waste-disposal system. Several treatment processes were examined in relation to some guiding principles, e.g. energy conservation, simple operation, low sludge generation, and a low proportion of mechanical and foreign-supplied components. Besides, sewage treatment and disposal in a densely populated area like Bridgetown required that the target population be protected from adverse health and environmental effects. It was recognized that a sewer or collector system was not the only method available for sewage disposal. An alternative to the sewer system - an on-lot individual subsurface sewage disposal system designed to provide adequate soil filtration of the liquid fraction of the wastewater - was considered. However, the latter requires a large area for proper performance and the high cost of such a system limited its use in densely populated communities. The use of septic tanks represented only a rudimentary primary treatment and their construction was hazardous in Bridgetown, given the high level of underground water.

Ferneihurst

In a survey of 945 respondents and 195 households in the target area conducted in January 1978 by the Community Development Division , the needs identified related to a youth center, a daycare center for the elderly, a day nursery, and a children's playground. The provision of a community center, including vocational training facilities, was stressed. It was formulated initially (The Nation, 1978: November 29) that 120 terrace units would be built at Ferneihurst, St. Michael as a new low-income housing development to help meet the pressing demand for living in Barbados. Also highlighted were the majority of land being used for medium-density two-storey housing, a full-size playing-field including a pavilion with space for community facilities, a youth center, an estate warden's office and a day nursery (National Housing Corporation, 1978-81). Preliminary discussions were held with the Ministry of Housing, the Ministry of Health and the Town Planning Department for their inputs and to ensure that the Project followed the established regulations.

To expedite timing, the initial planning and design, carried out by the National Housing Corporation in collaboration with the Richard Gill Associates and Tyrone Mapp Architects, formed a continuous sequence. Attention was paid to (a) identifying the Project site in relation to the surrounding area; (b) surveying the location; (c) visualizing the layout of the houses; (d) identifying the major constraints on design including the physical nature of the site, vehicular and pedestrian movement and noise; and (e) preparing a plan providing for land-use including the tentative selection of house-type, subdivision of land, architectural and engineering designs, access-road and drainage design and budgetary estimates. Possible alternative forms of development were explored. In formulating the designs of housing-type, the Corporation adhered to the Health Services (Building) Regulations 1969 and the Ministry of Health's sewage disposal regulations. In the design of houses, some factors as cost, functionality, aesthetics and room-size were taken into consideration. When Brother Massiah's Church, located in the Project site faced possible relocation, it was reasoned that the Complex needed not only housing units but also social and cultural outlets, thereby recognizing the Church's contribution and ensuring its continued existence in the area. Having identified the land where houses were to be built, the availability of finance to get the Project off the ground was explored in a general way. The Ministry of Health and the National Housing Corporation examined the preliminary layout and the design plans and made certain modifications.

Appraisal

Greenland

Technical appraisal showed that Barbados' natural topographic and climatic conditions lent feasibility to the production of and increased productivity from the Blackbelly sheep. The sheep could survive on areas of sparse vegetation, lamb extraseasonally and produce several lambs per litter, besides producing high-quality mutton. The sheep's existing genetic traits- prolificity and potential productive capacity - further boosted feasibility.

The Project's output (Caribbeana Council, 1978:2-34) was estimated and targeted in relation to specific deadlines. For instance, 540 purebred Blackbelly sheep by June 1979 and 1,080 sheep by June 1980, 1981, and 1982 successively were targeted for export. The first cross varieties available to feeding trials were set for June 1979, and 1,000 high-grade crossbred sheep were slated for sale on the commercial market by June 1982. Other targets included, for example, 60 sheep completing 10 trials of feed and forage combinations by June 1981, 2,000 sheep farmers receiving 530 hours and 4,745 hours of direct training and technical assistance respectively, 12 purchased rams servicing 480 registered sheep, 35 crossbred rams and 200 crossbred ewes being available for breeding purposes, and 3,000 acres of land being earmarked for sheep production. It was estimated that by June 1982 there would be 1,080 purebred Blackbelly sheep, 3,300 high-grade crossbred sheep, 400 breeding rams, 900 culled and castrated rams and 1,000 ewes which would be cleared by CARICOM and extraregional exporting and commercial marketing. Feasibility was expected to be high as long as the infrastructure of breeding stock, stud service, extension assistance, farmer education, marketing and income generation continued to be in place.

Analysis showed that Barbados would move from being a net importer of BDS$1,613,743 in sheep products to a net exporter of BDS$3,478,257 in sheep products. The benefits appraised included meat packing and preservation, tanning and leather byproducts. Turning a net resource outflow for imported mutton into an 80-90% self-sufficiency position and generating income for the economy were considered basic productivity gains.

Financially, it appeared that an income of BDS$944,000 would accrue by June 1982 to Barbados, reaching over BDS$5m. by the mid 1980s. The domestic market would generate an income of BDS$3,760,000. Analysis recognized that the financial inflows could be influenced by changing domestic and export demand, price movements and internal sectoral changes. Financed by the USAID and the counterpart financing provided by the GOB, the Project budget went into expenditure breakdown and itemization for the first year of the exercise, with only estimates offered for the second and third year. Expenditures were earmarked for personnel compensation and benefits, equipment and materials outlay, livestock acquisition and maintenance, transportation, etc.

Organizational appraisal received some attention. Several task areas were identified, e.g. organization identification, equipment checklist, material needs, livestock needs, and personnel resources. Manhour budgeting was done in terms of percentage of time a staff member was required to spend on the Project, which ranged from 5% part-time to 100% full-time. The Ministry of Agriculture, the Project's piloting agency, was asked to appoint a project coordinator with necessary interpersonal and managerial skills. The role of a 12-member project advisory group as a communication and problem-solving structure was stressed. Importance was attached to on-job and on-site technical training for sheep farmers and extension officials. A strong link between the public and private sectors was envisaged, thereby facilitating information sharing, institutional support and activity timescaling.

Handicraft

Economic appraisal was informed by cost-benefit analysis. An investment of BDS$1,671,042 spread over 1975-79 was laid out in anticipation of deriving cumulative benefits worth BDS$2,207,877 (BIDC, 1975:30;1978:38). Benefit estimating relied on gains expected to be made by means of import substitution and demand generation. The benefit cost rate - 1.1:7-boosted the Project's justifiability. A number of assumptions underlay the analysis, e.g. the opportunity cost of raw materials and trainee labour was nil, the output from the trained craft producers would reduce handicraft import and satisfy import and satisfy increased demand in the ratio of 4:1, the output resulting from training one worker would be about BDS$40 per hour, and benefits from investments made in any given year would accrue at the end of the year. An interest rate of 8% and a 60% markup on local as well as imported handicraft were also assumed. Investments as well as benefits were discounted to determine their net present value.

Financially, a budgetary analysis was presented in which cost - split into capital and current outlay-spanned over 1975-79 while the development budget included the costs of training, research, equipment, vehicles, buildings and promotion, employee compensation and maintenance costs were charged to the operational budget. Utilizing the net present value tool, further analysis showed an investment and benefit value of BDS$1,352,216 and BDS$938,332 respectively.

Organizational appraisal (BIDC, 1975a, 1975b) examined the Project's staffing, training, production, marketing and viability. It proposed that implementation should be done in three stages of about one year each, starting from April 1, 1975, and highlighted several task areas, e.g. promotion, technical assistance, training work area expansion, tools and equipment, and raw materials. Analysis extended to several other concerns: producing for the tourist and other markets, training and strengthening craft producers, developing a register of producers, establishing research and design, initiating a wholesale outlet, emphasizing commercialization, developing an export market, assisting employment, and linking tourism , agriculture and handicraft. Some more analysis was made of organizational structure, staff needs and staffing pattern.

Cave

Technical appraisal started when the consulting firm National Speleological Foundation began work in May 1978 and completed its report in August 1978. In October the same year, the Barbados Caves Authority submitted to the GOB a comprehensive appraisal (BCA,1979:3). The agreement between the Barbados Caves Authority and the Barbados Cave Project, Inc. was signed in October , 1979. Under this agreement, consultancy commenced in the same month. There were resident consultants and engineers and other types of visiting consultants worked from time to time.

The Gurnee study (1980:11-24) related to reshaping and finishing the walls and floors, providing concrete walls, designing drainage systems, fashioning lakes, streams and waterfalls, installing special lighting, placing ventilation systems, designing underground features, building access roads, providing carpark, building a visitors center, providing external drainage and constructing a mechanical workshop.

A drainage map was prepared showing different sectors and points in the drainage system. Soil analysis was conducted and all necessary materials and equipment were tested. An underground lighting system was designed and a lighting overlay map was prepared. Equipment selection, cable routing and insulation, maintainability, circuitry, switching and control were planned. Interior trails were planned to be paved with concrete and aggregates. Underground modifications consisted of cave-entrance and cave-wall reshaping, viewing-platform construction, and dam construction. Cave transportation included analyzing the mode of visitor transportation, the type and cost of vehicle, visitor participation and safety, vehicle maintenance, boarding-deboarding area and tour timing.

Tests of the hazards of rockfall ceiling collapse within the Cave were carried out. Tunnels were examined and no evidence of significant spalling or ceiling collapse was found. The periodic inspection and scaling of the terminal areas was recommended. The safety of the visitor and the vehicle was examined. Conducted in May 1978, a series of tests of ventilation showed that the natural airflow in the Cave with multiple entrances was adequate to protect the health of the Cave personnel and visitors. In a series of tests conducted in May 1978, test data showed that the natural temperature in the Cave was 75°F. or lower, relative humidity values ranged from 97.5% to 100% and air movement at different Cave locations measured a maximum of 13,000, 4,500, 7,000 and 1,500 cubic feet of air per minute. Even so, reestablishing more natural air exchange in the Cave was recommended. Tests of groundwater pollution were run in October 1978 and January 1979. The tests failed to produce any conclusive evidence of sewage contamination. However, appraisal counselled some precautionary measures.

Financial appraisal underwrote the Project's financial viability. The Ministry of Finance and Planning analyzed the Project's financial projections. First, having assumed interest rates on loan capital of 8%, 10% and 13%, the investment budget presented three estimates of investment capital of over BDS$1.6m., 1.7m. and 1.8m. respectively. The amortization period was assumed to span 5,10, 15 and 20 years. With the capital investment to visitor ratio being high, the phasing of the capital investment was recommended. Second, the operations budget estimated annual cost of BDS$179,000, BDS$185,000 and BDS$188,000 at 25%, 40% and 50% visitor attendance respectively. On completion, the Project was recommended to be run on commercial lines.

Third, cashflow projections at 8%, 10%and 13% interest on loan capital were prepared. Cashflow was shown to be BDS$231,000, BDS$465,000 and BDS$622,000 at 25%, 40% and 50% visitor attendance respectively. The projected net cashflow was shown to depend on the interest rate, the attendance level, the repayment period, the admission rate, and other rental income. Analysis indicated that the Cave would have to generate a level of cashflow - approximately BDS$543,000 a year - so that the Project should be in a position to service its debt. Fourth, the revenue budget projected an annual revenue of BDS$410,000, BDS$650,000 and BDS$810,000 at 25%, 40% and 50% visitor attendance respectively. An admission price of BDS$5.00 per visitor and an annual return of BDS$10,000 from proposed rental were included. Analysis indicated that financial viability rested in large part on the number of visits the Cave could attract. Finally, a breakeven point was identified by breakeven analysis which showed that at the worst loan conditions with high interest rate and a low amortization period, it would be necessary to have a visitor attendance of 44%. On the other hand, at the best loan conditions with low interest rate and high amortization period a visitor attendance of 22% would be necessary. It was initially estimated that the Project would be completed at a cost of about BDS$1.7 m.

Organizational appraisal was brought into the process when the consulting firm submitted a plan and schedule of operation to the GOB in February 1979 (BCA, 1980:2). A two-year implementation timeframe was targeted. It was formulated that while the consultants would be concerned primarily with the Project's underground work, the project manager would be involved with the external work. The consultants, however, would advise on the overall coordination of the work, with the project manager acting as the Barbados Cave Authority's representative and reporting on the work. The consultants also assumed other roles, e.g. training guides, drivers and other personnel to maintain the Cave system and its installations, assisting in marketing and public relations, advising on underground transportation and storage in workshop area, consulting on vehicle servicing and maintenance, and supervising the construction of internal scenic features.

Pulverization

Technical appraisal showed that the Project would protect the island's water-supply since the Plant would be built in such a way as to prevent seepage, that the pulverized waste would minimize insect breeding, that the refuse would convert back to soil in 7-10 years and that it would be more adaptable to waste recycling. The Project would remove the need to look for scarce and costly disposal sites, mitigating against the leaching of chemicals which do not break down too easily. The Ministry of Health's Environmental Engineering Division carried out in early 1974 a study of leachate pollution at refuse sites. The same year in April, the Ministry of Health entered into an agreement with the UK-based Millbank Technical Services Ltd. for the purchase and supply of plant machinery and sanitation equipment and for providing consulting services. Brown Lennox & Co. provided technical assistance on the Plant equipment, supply, installation, and maintenance. The Brown Lennox equipment was chosen because of its ability to pulverize the refuse and shred it to small pieces. The twin units were each rated to pulverize 25 tons of domestic refuse per hour and were expected to handle the majority of refuse generated in Barbados.

Inspection of the Plant equipment was carried out in October and December 1975. Subsurface explorations were done at the Plant site in December 1975. Released in January 1976, the findings of technical appraisal related to field survey, laboratory test, site planning, Plant building, subsidiary building, external works, construction materials, sketches, drawings, maps and layouts. The load-bearing properties of the foundation materials were investigated in April 1976. Groundwater hydrological tests were conducted in 1977 (Ministry of Health, 1967-83). A topographic survey of the Plant site and the quarry was undertaken. Drawings were prepared, setting out necessary road improvements in the Plant's vicinity. The valuation of acquired land and properties on the Project site was done . Quantity survey was carried out .

Financial appraisal picked up with examining the investment and operational costs of various methods of waste control. The projected cost in 1972 was BDS$300,000 . A 1973 estimate indicated that the cost of Plant building, access roads and landscaping would be about BDS$1m. Prepared in April 1975, an operational budget - comprising staff compensations, utility payments, accessories, and maintenance - was put at BDS$328,212 annually. In January 1976, the consulting firm prepared an estimate of BDS$813,700 covering varied constructions and contingencies, followed by a revised estimate of BDS$1.2m. in February the same year. Another estimate of over BDS$1.1m. was prepared by the quantity surveyor in November 1977. The Ministry of Health's Planning and Research Division estimated that the Plant would be built in 1978 at a cost of about BDS$2.1m.

Polytechnic

Included in technical appraisal were site selection, ground-condition tests, design analysis, architectural planning, and material specifications (Gillespie & Steel Associates Ltd., 1975, 1977). Site selection involved considering locational alternatives, and finally selecting a site at Wildey offering reasonable vehicular and pedestrian access. A ground-condition test of the site showed soil depth, soil occurrence, and terrain features. As to design analysis, preliminary designs were developed taking into account the site's topographical, climatic and habitational features. As regards architectural planning, the preliminary drawings focused on defining a structure which reflected climatic and topographical conditions. The drawings attempted to provide for higher percentages of horizontal circulation and complied with international standards for the condition of educational complexes. Questionnaires circulated to the Polytechnic staff elicited responses on such matters as the shape, dimension and layout of new buildings, fittings, general services, expansion, security, workshops, laboratories, and classrooms. Some more design changes were subsequently included (Inter-American Development Bank , 1976:91).

Material specifications concerned the measurement of the construction area, costing and construction supplies.

Economic appraisal entailed a general cost-benefit analysis and some manpower-need and population growth projections. Several assumptions which were made included admitting more students to meet future demands for trained manpower, upgrading the skills and qualifications of the existing workforce, enhancing the employability of trainees and job-seekers and providing pretechnical programs as necessary. It was recognized that technical-vocational training needed to be related to manpower needs and job openings. A Ministry of Education study (1973) employed a set of projections and pointed to the strategic significance of technical training. Launched in April 1974 by the Barbados Institute of Management and Productivity and the Statistical Services Department, a manpower survey examined the size of the workforce, employment expansion and output projection. Two other studies (McEvers, 1974; UNESCO, 1974) further informed appraisal. McEvers (1974:i-ii), for instance, performed a macroeconomic forecasting of technical manpower projections for 1971-85, using as a criterion the manpower standard of incremental needs for a fifteen-year period, including allowance for replacement as well as demands emanating from the country's growth. He noted that the limited supply of skills and qualified manpower become outpaced by annual growth increases that even the maximum output might not meet more than 50% of demands for qualified personnel and that the manpower shortage posed a constraint on development activities. The demographic limitations and the structure and content of the education system were held as contributing to the shortfall in the supply of qualified manpower.

The repayment/payback period was fixed at 2% interest rate to be paid semiannually until 2012. Financial appraisal, particularly budgetary analysis, compared cost estimates in respect of studies and consultancies, fees, staffing, constructions, materials, equipment, furniture, books and unallocated changes. Financial planning was executed, taking into account factors like currency use, disbursement, exchange rate and pari passu. Further, pari passu was to be adhered to in all outlays, several financial conditions were stipulated, accounting documents were to be recorded on a cash basis, the GOB's ability to provide counterpart funds was examined, and loan servicing was addressed. Recurrent costs of the Polytechnic's operations were projected for a 10-year period from 1977-78 to 1986-87, which were expected to range from 2.8% to 3.9% of the total recurrent budget of the Ministry of Education (IDB, 1976:66-69).

Social appraisal justified the project outlay and disclosed that the exercise would widen and deepen educational access including apprenticeship, on-job training and advanced studies. The Project's benefits were examined in terms of the social costs or benefits foregone. In the absence of the Project, the existing Polytechnic, located at three temporary sites, was poorly equipped to deliver quality-level training, where programs had evolved without much regard to social beneficiaries or market demand and employer need. Appraisal highlighted expanding educational access, meeting social demands, identifying key target groups, considering enrollment from all income groups, and encouraging dropouts, youths and unemployed/underemployed adults.

In respect of organizational appraisal, a major element involved promoting the institutional strengthening of the Polytechnic and the Ministry of Education. Appraisal indicated that a board of management should be established, that the institution should be organized departmentally, that each department should be headed by a senior faculty member, that subcommittees should be established in respect of each academic department, that a registrar and bursar should be appointed, and that industrial liaison and course development should be put in place to provide a job placement service and assist in the development of new courses (Oxtoby, 1974:30-31). Organizational appraisal evinced the importance of and need for professional growth, staff training, institutional development, curriculum development, vocational educational planning, educational technology, career guidance and placement, equipment procurement and installation, educational economics, and organization and financial planning. Emphasis was placed on enhancing planning, management and academic capabilities, facilitating an audiovisual center and its effective utilization, updating available equipment, and liaising with the employment market continuously. Also included were foci on preparing an education and manpower plan and introducing a cost-accounting system. In order to avoid duplication and to coordinate work, critical path networks and bar charts were drawn up. Establishing an executing agency to nourish and manage the Project arose as a stipulation.

Sewerage

Technical appraisal went into several design criteria, viz. sewer-area size, target-population size, sewage flow, sewer length/breadth/materials, subsystems, treatment processes, sludge disposal, and marine outfall features/materials. Marine-biological studies (Ott,1973) were concerned with the effects of the impact of sewage effluent on the nearshore coral reefs. Ott drew biological data from records of earlier studies by Vezina (1972-73), who recorded the nutrient levels in the careenage. From oceanographic studies by Peck (n.d.), the most suitable site for the marine outfall and the most probable direction and destination of residual pollutants were determined. Lawler, Matusky and Skelly, Engineers completed (1974) in association with David Lashley & Partners a technical appraisal, i.e. the studies, reports, designs, plans and specifications for the construction of the sewerage system.

The studies executed included demography of the target area, population projections, topography, soil conditions, water consumption patterns, sewage volume and characteristics, marine-biological standards and oceanographic studies (Archer, 1985:189). Oceanographic surveys were done to establish the physical, chemical and biological characteristics of the receiving-water environment. Hydrographic and meteorological data were collected and used in the design and construction specifications of the marine outfall. Design and specifications were prepared with respect to the type of waste treatment method. The methods of sewage treatment and disposal were reviewed. The contact stabilization process of secondary treatment expected to produce an acceptable effluent for marine disposal was recommended. The design presented was in accordance with acceptable engineering standards and offered a feasibile technical alternative.

A second-level consultancy (Foxworthy, 1974:2-3) reviewed the adequacy of the oceanographic and hydrographic studies. Foxworthy confirmed the final design and siting for the marine outfall-diffuser system and concurred that the secondary biological treatment with continuous disinfection would produce a wastewater effluent of acceptable quality. The IDB technical staff verified the consultancy mission's appraisal.

As regard the disposal of sludge formed from the treatment process, solid disposal to the land was recommended. Another study of the marine environment around and off the marine outfall was effected. Material specifications selected ductile-iron, asbestos-cement and pvc pipes due to their toughness and resistance.

Economic appraisal identified the sanitation practices in Bridgetown as a threat to health, an obstacle to urban development and a public nuisance. It observed that the sewerage modernisation in the target area would have a wider impact as it would benefit not only the direct users, but also a large target population. By eliminating the focal points of environmental pollution from a critical location, there would be a positive effect on the marine environment, tourism growth, slum clearance, urban renewal and other externalities. Analysis indicated (Bradshaw, 1982; Bishop, 1990:13) that the recommended treatment method would save 20% in treatment costs over comparable alternatives.

Financial appraisal revealed that the Project would be financially feasible, that it would make a cost impact of 3.6% on public revenue, and that annual commitments could be met by the GOB. The timely establishment of a tariff structure was stressed (IDB, 1975: 42-43). The loan agreement, effected in April 1976, between the IDB and the GOB included the total cost, loan finance, counterpart finance, pari passu, payback period, interest rate and grace period (Bridgetown Sewerage Project, 1977-82). Stipulation covered an interest rate of 2% per annum, an amortization period ranging from 1984 to 2011 in 54 semiannual payments, and a grace period of 8 years. The loan agreement dwelt on cost breakdown, financing responsibility, annual budgetary appropriations by the GOB, fiscal schedules, disbursement preconditions, manual preparation and competitive public bidding.

Covering a ten-year period, budgetary analysis indicated generating operating revenue from sewage charges, connection fees and septage charges. The expenditures were earmarked for capital investment, depreciation, supplies, staff compensation and energy costs. Depreciation was determined by the straightline method assuming no salvage value. The useful life of the Plant equipment was estimated to range from15 to 50 years. Annual costs for capital investment were determined by the capital recovery method. Breakeven analysis pointed out that after three years since the Project's completion the revenue inflow would make up for the expenditure outflow and would yield a small return.

Social appraisal indicated that the initial beneficiaries represented 37,000 users, viz. low-income and low-middle income residents of the target area, employees and students working in the Bridgetown area, and people commuting daily to the city. The entire community was expected to benefit for the Project would have an effect on tourism and other productive activities. A Project with a large social content, the IDB drew attention to its improved social and environmental conditions, faster urbanization and greater well-being (IDB, 1975:43-44).

Organizational appraisal looked at time-scheduling , e.g. whether a single shift or multishift system should be put in place during construction. A multishift system was chosen for contracts 2 and 3. A study was undertaken to establish an authority to concurrently manage water and sewerage in Barbados, and to examine the authority's legal, management, financial, operational and rent-schedule aspects. Prequalification notices were first published in November 1977. Prequalification of the contracts through an international competitive bidding procedure took place in June 1978.

Ferneihurst

Following the preparation of the initial sketch designs in March 1978 by the Richard Gill Associates Ltd., the Ministry of Housing , in association with the National Housing Corporation, agreed in August 1978 to hire consultancy services. Prepared in November 1978 by the same firm, technical appraisal involved work in topographic survey, cartographic analysis, site planning and design objectives. Designing extended to landscaping, layout structure, house type, access road and drainage. Related work concerned compiling benchline data, consulting with other firms, preparing and submitting planning application, and doing follow-ups. This consultancy brought out some technical data (National Housing Corporation, 1978-81), which informed the decision on retaining on the site as many mature trees and smaller flowering trees and shrubs as possible.

Material specifications were undertaken in April 1979. In May of the same year, the implementation team and the Environmental Engineering Division personnel conducted site visits in order to examine sewage disposal options. Compliance with the provisions of the Health Services Act 1969 and the Health Services (Building) Regulations 1969/Section 14 (1) was sought. The layout plans for drainage/sewage disposal, a standard design for septic tanks , the level of amenity, the size of the bedrooms, the public-health aspects of housing, water connection, the cost of water connection and the feasibility of power connection were examined.

Architectural consultancy, done by the Gillespie & Andrew Associates Ltd. and Tyrone Mapp Architect, extended to design, plans and drawings, correspondence and meetings, and supervision. In keeping with the Corporation's specification - offering optimum living conditions compatible with budget - the consultancy was forced on designing houses and other features on the site. The sketch designs and original drawings were reviewed repeatedly before moving toward finalization. The Project's secondary objectives - medium density two-storey housing, youth center, estate warden's office and day nursery - were deemed feasible in appraisal except for a full-size playing field. A smaller sporting area on the lower and flatter ground was considered desirable, and two small tree-shaded areas were set aside as a sitting area for elderly persons and as a children's playground. With no other permanent site readily available, it was decided that the Church would remain in its present location.

Economic appraisal attempted to ensure that the Project serviced those most in need of housing, especially the low-income consumers. To reducc the need for transportation, it was proposed that the Complex be located not too far from the existing residential areas. Building standards were assumed to ensure basic safety and functional need. It was claimed that in the absence of such a design factor, the targeted low-income tenants would be forced to continue living in substandard conditions without any hope for assistance. The high housing need and the acute shortage of affordable shelter in the community were kept in focus. This was reflected in the housing mix, i.e. the percentage of space allocated to two or three-bedroom units.

Financial appraisal took account of the costs of land, construction, development, and incidentals. The question of supply in relation to demand came under scrutiny. A budgetary estimate examined the costs of site planning and development relocation, consultancy, materials, and labor. Higher rental income was expected. In determining the rental rate, consideration was given to the total cost, unit cost, and payback period. The payback period stipulated was 20 years from the Project's completion and the units' occupancy. Organizational appraisal was taken up as a team-building exercise, giving consideration to the number and expertise range of project personnel, suitability for project assignment, and ability to work under pressure.

Approval

Greenland

Project funding was authorized from 1978, with an incremental life of the Project for another three years. While the GOB sanctioned BDS$100,000 annually for four years from 1978 to 1982, the USAID disbursed BDS$550,000, BDS$290,000 and BDS$190,000 for 1978, 1979 and 1980 respectively (USAID, 1978-82).

The Project's approval was secured from the Cabinet in September 1978. The criteria used for approval were the Project's relative simplicity, low resource demand, the easy availability of the base stock and the ready financial as well as technical assistance. Approval took about seven months from the presentation of the draft proposal to the approval of the Cabinet. A BDS$600,000 agreement among the Ministry of

Agriculture, the USAID and the Caribbeana Council was reached in February 1981 (The Advocate News, 1981:February 10). In February of the same year, the Caribbeana Council and the Barbados Blackbelly Sheep Association signed an agreement concerning regulations of all Blackbelly sheep in the island.

Handicraft

The approval of the Project, spanning a period of two months, was secured in 1975 from the Ministry of Trade. It received Cabinet-level attention via the Central Planning Committee. Examined in considerable detail, approval was sought for the Project as a whole. The Venture secured necessary support and cooperation from the Ministry of Finance and Planning, Soil Conservation Section and Customs Department. During the same year, the BIDC's board of directors approved a multiyear development plan for the Project, including its outreach and expansion. Approval was given for establishing a sales area, teaching shellwork, woodwork, dyeing and pottery, and "Pride Craft" approved in September 1977.

Cave

A high-level steering committee, set up in 1974, lent approval periodically to the ongoing operations, procedural matters and policy questions. The Cabinet approved the Project in May 1975. Legislation was passed in early 1975 to provide for a Cave Authority in Barbados. The Cabinet approved a loan fund of BDS$1.7m. to the Barbados Caves Authority to finance the Cave development (Barbados Caves Authority, 1977:4;1979:3). It also approved that 286,008 sq. ft. of land should be acquired for the Cave's development. In October 1979, an agreement was signed between the Barbados Caves Authority and the National Speleological Foundation/Barbados Cave Project, Inc. Following the acceptance of the consultant report, the Ministry of Tourism asked the consulting firm to complete the Cave's development. The Cave's revised appraisal was approved for the second time by the PPC in February 1979. The executing agency obtained necessary endorsement from all the participating organizations having relation to the Project.

Pulverization

Around January 1967, the Cabinet discussed matters relating to consultancy for the Project (Ministry of Health, 1967-83). In May 1968, the Cabinet noted relevant technical measures concerning the Project. The Cabinet mandated in September 1973 the installation of a pulverization plant. While other forms of refuse disposal, such as incineration, pyrolosis and composting were considered, pulverization was found more suitable for Barbados. Further information on the Project in respect of technical assistance and equipment planning was submitted by the Ministry of Health to the Cabinet and the Central Planning Committee in July 1974. The Cabinet approval was granted in August 1974. The GOB signed a contract in April 1974 to acquire two shredders, with the total capacity of the Plant being 400 tons of domestic refuse daily. To acquire land for siting the Project, the Ministry of Health submitted a cabinet paper for approval in November 1974. An application for planning approval was made to the Town Planning Department in December 1976.

Polytechnic

With the Ministry of Education and the Public Investment Unit placing the necessary documents before the Planning and Priorities Committee for its scrutiny, the Project in its entirety was approved by the Committee in July 1977 when the loan agreement between the GOB and the IDB was signed in the same month, giving approval for the release of funds to start the Project's lifecycle.

The organizations contracted for the confirmation of statutory mandates included the Town Planning Department for permission to develop the site, the Environmental Engineering Division for briefing on the acceptable noise level and future expansion, the Barbados Water Authority on the supply and availability of water, and the Barbados Light and Power Co. Ltd. for the supply of power. Besides, the Barbados Telephone Co. Ltd., National Petroleum Corporation, Caribbean Institute of Meteorology and Hydrology, Barbados Transport Board and Caribbean Conservation Association were contacted for assistance in their respective fields.

Sewerage

Approval was granted by the Cabinet initially on condition that the prefeasibility studies showed promise. The signing of the loan agreement in April 1976 with the IDB was an affirmation of approval. The Planning and Priorities Committee rendered approval at various stages of the Project. The IDB loan agreement facilitated the financing of BDS$200,000 towards meeting the cost of a study related to the Project's organizational and management appraisal. Part of approval was rendered in July 1977 when the GOB opted to relocate and rehabilitate residents from downtown Emmerton to suburban Clapham.

The option to retain the consultancy and resident-engineering services of Lawler, Matusky & Skelly, Engineers doing the Project's construction was approved. The special tenders committee met in December 1978 and its recommendation were endorsed by the Cabinet.

Ferneihurst

A Cabinet decision was reached in April 1978 to proceed with the Project. It was fully endorsed by the National Housing Corporation and the Ministry of Housing's Planning Division. The Project was submitted in 1979 to the PPC. The PPC considered the Project's cost effectiveness, the timing of its implementation, the availability of funds, the priority of the Project, the availability of human resources and the completion time.

The planning applications in respect of location, layout , floor and elevation plans were submitted in March 1979 to the Town Planing Department. The specifications of septic tanks, drainage designs and road profiles were lodged in May 1979. Sanction from the Department came in November 1979. The Project's estimated cost was included in the NHC's capital budget of 1980-81. The estimates were endorsed by the Ministry of Housing and approved by the Ministry of Finance and Planning Estimates Committee and subsequently by the PPC. Parliamentary approval for the Project's funding was given when the annual budget was debated during 1980-81.

Implementation

Greenland

The Project, having been implemented in two stages through the Ministry of Agriculture, covered the period 1978-82. An implementation team was set up which comprised officials from the Ministry of Agriculture, Greenland Agricultural Station, Central Livestock Station, Animal Nutrition Unit, Veterinary Laboratory, Caribbeana Council, Barbados Marketing Corporation, Barbados Agricultural Development Corporation, Barbados Sheep Farmers Association, Barbados Agricultural Society and the United States Peace Corps. Also attached to the unit were technical specialists from the United States-based Lincoln University for the genetics and carcass evaluation studies. Gantt charts were prepared. The scheduling of activities started as early as May 1978. By May 1978, all infrastructure was in place for the receipt of the imported stock. The operating procedures for livestock management were agreed on, the training of animal husbandry personnel had started and the senior technical officials had met on several occasions to decide on resource allocation and records management. Sheep breeding trials were held with the Blackbelly sheep being used as foundation stock. The sheep were being crossed with Dorset and Suffolk breeds with a view to providing top-quality mutton. At difficult periods in 1980 and 1981 semen of the Blackbelly and imported rams was collected and studied at the Greenland Station to understand the important reproductive traits.

The purebred Blackbelly sheep were identified and registered in a central file by the Barbados Agricultural Society and the United States Peace Corps. The registration process itself - numbering and certification - was organized by the Caribbeana Council. The first registration drive got underway in 1978. Subsequently, 1,000 sheep were registered between February and July 1981. During 1981-83 another 3,500 sheep were registered. The four classifications used were three-quarters purebred, seven-eighths purebred, fifteen-sixteenth purebred, and purebred. Most of the technical work involved in pasture management was done with the aid of the Animal Nutrition Unit, Greenland Research Station and Soil Conservation Section. To promote marketing and to encourage local competition, seminars and workshops were held in 1981. Taste testing trials were conducted at several locations. Seminars and workshops were held on evaluation, grading and fabrication of lamb meat with special reference to carcass composition, quality, cutability, muscle-bone ratios and by-product production (USAID, 1978-82).

Handicraft

Located within the BIDC Handicraft Center, an implementation team took the responsibility for executing the Project. A project manager was appointed, and other personnel were hired and trained. For instance, 13 position were created on the staff in February 1975, namely, designers, craft supervisors, craft operatives, and support staff. Activities were scheduled to facilitate speedy and effective implementation. Timescales, work schedules , work breakdown structure, time and motion study , systems planning and analysis and bar charts were used. Building construction, roofing, painting, carpentry and equipment installation were done by the BIDC's Construction Department.

In January 1975, craft training was initiated in shellwork, woodwork, pottery, and batik (BIDC, 1975:16-17). Workshops were held at strategic points, particularly those rural areas in proximity to the raw-material suppliers. The first Craft Training Center was established at the Six Cross Roads Industrial Park, St. Philip in August 1977, and the second one was opened at St. Bernards, St. Joseph in September 1981. Later, similar centers were opened in other areas.

A handicraft emporium was set up in November 1975 to serve as a central marketing agency and as a display center for products. Products were taken on consignment, displayed, and sold either locally or overseas. A catalog was drawn up to include products for sale in large quantities. To expand marketing, retail outlets were established, decorated and displayed. A sales outlet was opened in January 1977 at Sam Lords Castle, St. Philip, and in the same year in September another outlet was started at the Dover Convention Center, Christ Church. Other sales outlets were opened subsequently. A manual was prepared with standard specifications for the main product lines. Sales promotion was pushed in CARIFESTA'76, CARICOM Awareness program and Buy Local Program. Wayside craft markets were introduced. The BIDC's trademark for its products -Pride Craft - became operational in September 1977.

Research and development was introduced in late 1975. Research on the production process was carried out and the findings were released to producers. Production methods were introduced to increase craft-maker productivity. Piece rates were revised to allow for maximum feasibile increase. A measure of production diversification was pursued. Research started in 1977 on designing with a view to developing continuously new designs for products, upgrading the design of local handicrafts, retaining competitiveness, capturing modernity and appeal, and linking products and local heritage. Research was carried out on the preservation of raw materials.

A rationalization of workflow was attempted with the preparation of an organization chart. A manual of standard operating procedures was prepared and made available to staff in 1976. In the same year, about 9,000 sq. ft. of additional storage space area was built. An improved stock record system came into existence in still the same year. A register of craft producers was developed. Discussions were held for establishing craft cooperatives. The implementation team collaborated with the BADC to plant pandamus. A system of raw-material procurement came on stream.

Cave

A project execution unit was set up by the Barbados Caves Authority when the project manager was appointed in October 1975 and other executive and support staff were hired. A technical committee, comprising representatives of ministries and the Barbados Board of Tourism, was put in place to supervise the work in relation to the Cave. Work involved coordination, supervision, procurement, direction, documentation, liaison and communication. For instance, decision was made on marketing promotion, and it embraced a wide-ranging area. Meetings were held with tour operators, design agencies, printers and the Barbados Board of Tourism in preparation for the printed material and sales promotion. Subcontracts were awarded in segments of implementation, e.g. roofing and woodwork, underground drainage and roadwork, surface electrical installation, underground electrical installation, and plumbing. Besides, Gantt charts and other workflow charts were used. Bar charts were employed showing the estimated completion of each of the various inputs. Activity was scheduled in terms of various tasks. Time estimates, cost estimates and operational budgets were utilized. Operational procedures were reviewed and updated. Extensive records and accounts were maintained.

Implementation, carried out in two stages, entailed tunnel excavation, land acquisition, plant installation and equipment procurement. Work was divided into two parts, e.g. surface and underground. The underground work concerned the upstream and downstream areas of the Cave. The surface work included land acquisition, access roads, carpark, cave building, drainage, trails lighting, transportation, maintenance, and health and safety. While the first stage lasted two years, the second stage spanned twenty months. The Visitors Center was built and surface drainage was completed with direct labor. The service area, having the mechanical workshop and the maintenance office, was built with technical assistance from the Ministry of Works. Consultations were held regarding the most suitable form of building required to house the Project's facilities, e.g. restaurants, boutique, offices, entrance area, visitors area and rest area.

Initial work on the execution of the Cave began in 1973 (Barbados Caves Authority, 1977-78:3;1978-79: 2; 1979-80:2-3;1980-81:2-3; 1982:10). Some more exploratory work continued in 1974. Preliminary excavations were underway in the same year. The Cave area was surveyed and mapped. A geological study of the area became necessary. The infiltration rate of rain water was calculated from observations and the maximum amount of water that could flow through the Cave was estimated. Between October 1975 and March 1976, work related to cleaning wooded areas, erecting site offices and providing a temporary access road. Between April 1976 and March 1977 other ancillary work included selecting a site for the scenic access road, building a culvert, and levelling of land to build a carpark. Work between January 1978 and January 1979 concerned cleaning the tunnel, repairing equipment and vehicles, and cleaning carpark.

Tunnelling started in March 1976. It entailed the blasting of a tunnel about 12ft. high and 12ft. wide, reshaping it where necessary, the digging of boreholes, the extension ventilation shafts and the construction of a sub-base. By 1978, the large tunnels giving access to natural cave rooms were complete. The tunnel had been excavated to a distance of about 3,000 ft. from the entrance and, at its deepest point, is about 150ft. below the surface. The more accessible 1,500ft. long southwesterly part of the Cave system was developed. Later, the less accessible northwesterly part was developed. In October 1979, the architectural service of the Athelston King Partnership Ltd. was engaged for the Visitors Center. In December of the same year, the firm presented preliminary designs. Later, the detailed planning and drawings were finalized.

The Unites States-based consulting firm, Barbados Cave Project, Inc., commenced the second and final stage of implementation in November 1979 and completed its work on the Cave's interior in October 1980. The water of the two subterranean streams was diverted from the center of the passageways to a course alongside the roadway. A dam was built to hold and measure the water that flowed into the Cave each day. The dam allowed part of the flow to run over waterfalls and through the stalagmites in the Cave's upper passage, while the rest was carried off down an underground drainage system. The drainage system was installed over the Cave passage to insure that water in all seasons could be accommodated (Gurnee, 1981: 11-12). Underground lighting was installed by the USA-based Cumberland Caverns, Inc. An electrical service building was constructed underground. All lighting, control lines and communication lines were installed in keeping with technical specifications. All lighting is kept indirect and unobstrusive. The trails were lit by bounce light from ceilings and walls. Special lighting effects and underwater lights were installed in a few locations. To retain naturalness, all cables, services and utilities were concealed from public view. An underground service center was covered with rock and painted to match the Cave. The dams were cement-colored and camouflaged. The floor of the Cave beyond the trail is a sandy nonsticky material . The pool's floor was colored black to give an illusion of depth.

Cave walls were reshaped so that they were less geometrical and more rounded, irregular and cavelike. Interior trails were built. Paving was four inches thick, laid on a crushed rock base. To prevent vehicular collision with the Cave wall, a six-inch high curb was built at the edge of the paving. A viewing platform, equipped with guard rails and provided with nonskid surface, was built to allow visitors to view a waterfall from all sides. The Cave entrance was reshaped to give as natural an appearance and contour as possible. It was agreed in March 1980 to purchase two electrically-driven jitney buses and trailers from the USA-based Boyertown Battronic Corporation. The carriers, each accommodating 38 passengers, arrived in Barbados in March 1981. Work on the mechanical workshop and additional access roads commenced in early 1981 and made adequate progress. Advice on health and safety measures was sought from the ILO to ensure that the showcave system was safe in all respects for all concerned. The training of tour guides and other personnel in running and maintaining the Cave system and its installations was put on stream.

Pulverization

An implementation team within the Ministry of Health directed the overall execution. Collection vehicles were acquired in a package agreement around 1973-74 to build a collection and disposal fleet. Following sales demonstration of the Plant equipment in the United Kingdom in November 1973, the GOB signed a contract in April 1974 to acquire two Brown Lennox shredders. Further sales demonstrations took place in the United States in 1974. The first set of equipment arrived from Britain in July 1975. The contracted company held responsibility for the manufacture, assembly and commissioning of the Plant.

Site clearance was undertaken to clear the area to the west of the quarry for building the approaches to the Plant and to plan the roads leading to the site. Eighteen portions of land totalling 12,414 sq. ft. were considered for purchase for siting the Plant. Six houses were resited. The Barbados Light & Power Co. Ltd. was contacted in February 1975 for the supply of electricity to the site. Tender documents were completed in February 1976 for the supply of steelwork, sheeting and rainwater materials. A tender committee invited tenders in October 1978 for the construction of the Plant. The PIU and the Project personnel met in June 1978 to consider contract allotment, projected costs and estimated completion time. The Ministry of Health initiated a media campaign to ease the anxiety of some residents worried about siting the Plant at Workmans, St. George and assured that there would be no health or odor problem. The Government Information Service had shown a film on refuse pulverization, which was followed by discussions.

Construction, having begun in March 1979, ended in April 1980. It involved site preparation, building construction, ancillary works and equipment installation. Durahome Construction Ltd. signed the main contract for construction. Structural Systems Ltd. delivered structural steel and cladding. Constructed on a quarry bed, the Plant and its premises were landscaped. In order to cope with an increased volume of traffic, the adjacent roads were widened.

A number of implementation techniques were employed. Gantt charts were prepared in relation to 32 weeks and 10 activities. Bar charts were used by the consultants, and the expenditure charts, drawn in monthly and cumulative terms, were followed through. Delivery schedules were prepared, site meetings were held among the participating organizations, daywork records were maintained, and completion schedules were prepared and revised.

Polytechnic

As a part of the Ministry of Education, a project execution unit came into being in 1978. Headed by a project manager, the unit was assisted by varied engineering, technical, management, accounting and support services. A resident engineer supervised construction. Brain F. Griffith & Co. audited the accounts. The unit, in association with the Ministry of Education, selected and contracted several consultants. Construction commenced in May 1979 with a projected completion time of 104 weeks. Initial work included checking site, ordering basic construction material and arranging with the utilities companies for essential services. Repairs were done on the Plant equipment. Sand blasting was used where rust had developed and welding was done on plate tacks. The Ministry's public health engineer visited England to observe the operation of a similar pulverization plant to ensure proper implementation.

The bidding procedures for public tendering were followed. While Gillespie & Steel Associates Ltd. was responsible for building design and related planning work, a two-year construction contract was awarded in May 1979 to Canada-based Wilmac Construction Co. Ltd.

Subcontracts related to numerous construction-related specialty areas. Books procured from overseas suppliers were delivered to the Institute. A committee handled tenders for furniture supply and equipment supply/installation.

The Project's organization and management development task was carried out by several consultants. Chiappetta (1982:1-6) focused on educational planning, management capabilities and institution-building. Moldstad (1982: 1-6) helped establish the introduction of audiovisual materials, audiovisual department and related training in the field. Hanitchak looked at establishing and conducting career guidance and counselling, placement service, staff advisory council, and tracer studies of past graduates (1982:1-19). Lewis (1982:1-6) dealt with equipment procurement and installation, including upgrading, replacement and maintenance. Urrejolas' work on financial planning and management resulted in the installation of a new cost accounting system (Project Execution Unit, 1977-83). Correa's work on educational economics and planning involved preparing plans, studies and reports, and stressing the need for quantification (1981:10-11).

A number of academic and nonacademic positions were approved between 1978 and 1981. In academic divisions, staffing was done at the level of instructors and demonstrators. Nonacademic positions included deputy principal, vocational guidance/liaison officer, librarian, maintenance technicians and other support staff. Staff training comprised overseas, regional and local training. In-house staff training entailed short courses, seminars and workshops. To demonstrate the schedule of physical as well as financial progress, Gantt charts were employed. The graphical method was also used, especially disbursement schedule graphs and progress schedule graphs. The tabular display technique was put to use. Timescales were put to use as necessary. Critical path analysis was also a part of the technical set.

Sewerage

A project execution unit was established in 1977 within the Ministry of Health. Headed by a project manager, the unit was assisted by management, engineering, technical, accounting and support services. A few committees were set up which functioned in an advisory capacity, e.g. project advisory committee, coordinating and public information committee and tenders committee. The unit was engaged in varied activities, namely, coordination, liaison, procurement, review/evaluation, selection, scheduling, monitoring, supervision, accounting documentation and compliance-seeking. Execution was aided by a number of management techniques. The Gantt chart was employed, which consisted of a timescale divided into 39 monthly units extending from April 1979 to June 1982, and four activities, e.g. contract 1, contract 2, contract 3, and institutional study. Work breakdown structure was put into use. Whenever possible, scheduling was done and plotted graphically to facilitate implementation and monitoring. Flow diagrams, bar charts, milestone charts, reference tables and monthly contractor payment claims further facilitated implementation.

During implementation the project manager, consultants, resident engineer, project engineers, contractors, construction inspectors and support staff played their part in maintaining the Project's progress. The contractors were responsible for the execution of the three contracts, while the project manager prepared an operational budget and schedules, ensured that all the facilities and supplies were available, scrutinized monthly reports submitted by consultants for validity, carried out various surveys, approved all the work done by the contractors, gave final authorization for payments and submitted progress reports to the GOB and the IDB. Each contract had a project engineer who supervised the work of the contractor according to specifications. The project engineer worked with the resident engineer to oversee the work done by the contractors. Just so, the project manager assisted in getting the necessary professionals, technicians, support staff, employees and various participating organizations together. Vehicles for transportation of personnel, materials, equipment and supplies were put in place. Supervision and control were put in place in that there was daily monitoring of what a contractor was doing and how the consultants were performing.

The Project provided for a treatment plant, pumping/lift stations, a marine outfall, a sewer network, an institutional study, and user conditions (Bridgetown Sewage Project, 1982:1). Construction started in April 1978 and was completed in July 1982. The areas to be sewered were identified and divided into three sections 12, 8, 6, and a central area. During construction, the United States-based Lawler, Matusky & Skelly Engineers provided consultancy and resident engineering services.

In 1976, a five-acre area at Emmerton was acquired and cleared to site the treatment plant. The removal of 143 houses and the relocation of nearly 500 resident at Clapham Park were effected between July 1977 and July 1978 (Archer, 1979: 6-7; 1981:4-12). Several committees and participating agencies contributed to relocation. Work by the Canada-based Fitzpatrick Construction Ltd. on the sewage treatment plant started in March 1979 and ended in June 1982. A reinforced concrete-structure raw wastewater pumping station at a depth of 23 feet below ground level and drawing over 500 sheet piles and expected to be adequate until 2002, the Plant comprises primary, secondary and tertiary processes with a flow capacity of 2.4m. gallons of sewage a day, which is divided between two process units of 1.2m. gallons a day. It has built-in safety factors. In an emergency, it can handle up to 5m. gallons of sewage per day. It has built-in safety factors. In an emergency, it can handle up to 5m. gallons of sewage per day for a short period. The treatment method is based on contact stabilization with the aerobic digestion of sludge. The sludge is put away by spreading it on farmlands. The treatment effluent is disinfected by hypochlorites derived from the electrolysis of seawater before disposal by outfall into the sea. Located at Lakes Folly, the Plant serves as a catchment center in which waste is delivered by underground sewers and is chemically treated before its disposal. The Plant is also equipped to treat and dispose of the waste material from earth closets and cesspool emptiers.

The pumping/lift stations pump sewage from the target area to the Plant. Made of reinforced concrete, the River Road complex is the main pumping station. The collection tank is located here and is connected to the Plant by a maze of pipes. The sewage flow of the station is 1.8m. US gallons a day. The other pumping /lift stations are located at Bay Street, White Park Road, Bridgetown Port, Prescod Boulevard and Harbour Road. The station at Prescod Boulevard is a seawater pumping station, the others are sewage pumping stations. Each of the five stations has a storage capacity of 4,500 imperial gallons of sewage/day and is equipped with a 10-foot diameter underground steel tank.

1,000 feet in total length, the marine outfall, located off Princess Alice Highway and serving as an underground effluent discharger for the Plant, was built by the United States-based Meisener Marine Construction, Inc. over the period April to December 1979 (IDB,1981:47). The work involved a 24-hour three-shift system. The outfall emerges from Lakes Folly, runs underneath Motor Services Road and Prescod Boulevard, and empties into Carlisle Bay. The outfall comprises a 30-inch diameter polyethylene pipeline which terminates 984 ft. from the shoreline in 39ft. of water. To blast the effluent through the sand and coral seabed, the outfall pipe is partly laid in a submarine trench with the last 10 ft. of the pipeline having 24 three-inch diameter diffusers projecting 39 inches from the seabed in 39ft. of water.

Work by the Canada-based Sintra Inc. on the sewer network commenced in February 1980 and ended in June 1982. Having used a 24-hour three-shift system, the task involved trench excavation, traffic diversion, sanitary-sewer laying, and manhole installation. The perimeter of the sewered area is defined by Bay Street, Jemmotts Lane, Martindale Road, Halls Road, Roebuck Street, Country Road, White Park Road, Light Foot Lane, Mason Hall Street, Lakes Folly, Fontabelle and Harbour Industrial Park. The network serves a target area of 0.3 sq. miles of the central Bridgetown area and comprises 13 miles of sanitary sewers ranging from 6 to 36 inches in diameter, with the total length of the sewer being 17 miles, and one mile of 6 to 30 inches force mains. Sewer materials used are ductile iron, epoxy-lined asbestos cement and polyvinyl chloride pipes. Lateral sewers are provided for about 3,000 connections to user premises. It is a collector system which takes sewage from an area of about 494 acres with 3,000 user connections and a population of 37,700 consumers. Though the expected flow is 2.4m. gallons a day, the sewers are designed to cope with an average flow of 3.6m. gallons a day. Hurley (1981) and Roach (1984:16) report that the sewers were laid underground at specific angles so as to allow the waste to flow by gravity to the Plant. Sewers were laid in trenches in such a way that they sloped in the direction of the Plant, with the slope permitting sewage to flow by gravity. Street sewers were laid as straight as practicable as waterborne waste must be allowed to flow freely without sharp turns or bends which could cause waste to become stuck in the pipelines and cause blockages. Manholes were installed wherever there was a change in direction of the sewer from a straight line, enabling operations to clear sewers of blockers and keep the sewage flowing freely.

After the sewers were laid, an inspection survey was carried out by the Ministry of Health engineers. An institutional study for the establishment of a water and sewer authority was executed between April 1979 and February 1981. Eleven studies including the legal, managerial, financial, operational and rate-schedule aspects of the new authority were coordinated by the PAHO. Finally, included in the phase was the construction of about 3,000 service connections and the adaptation of in-house installations so that all existing user premises in the sewered area could be linked with the sewage system.

Ferneihurst

To realize the Project, an implementation team was put together from the staff of the NHC's Technical Division. Moreover, the Project's special management needs were met by the NHC's financial, supplies, legal, and housing staff. The implementation time lasted from January 1979 to March 1981 (National Housing Corporation, 1978-81). The team's work ranged from resource mobilization, site clearance through utility service installation to construction start and construction completion. 3,030ft. of pipe were laid, together with control valves and fire hydrant. One hundred sq. ft. of road was reinstated, and sidewalks were built. The Barbados Light & Power Co. Ltd. supplied energy to the Complex and took over responsibility for installation, operation, and maintenance. The plans for drainage and sewage disposal were executed. Landscaping was carried out by the implementation team with assistance from the NCC. The materials for the Project were acquired by direct local purchase or through the tender process.

Several contracting firms involved in the work process included the Decorex Ltd. and Rudolph C. Walcott (trowel plastic application), Everson R. Elcock & Co. Ltd. (electrical installation), the Early Bird Exterminating Co. Ltd. (termite treatment), the Rayside Asphalt Paving Co. (access roads/carpark construction), the Bryden & Sons (Bds) Ltd. (supplies), and Trowel Plastics B'dos Ltd. (supplies).

Implementation techniques included time schedules which were utilized while doing foundation work and installing utility services. Bar charts were prepared in which the target dates for activity completion were set out. Completion notices were employed which served the purpose of time scheduling. For record-keeping and accountability, costing was implemented. A cost control system was maintained in the NHC's accounts division in addition to in situ cost control. Site visits were also carried out. Inventory of materials and supplies was made on a quarterly basis.

Reporting

Greenland

Record-keeping was an ongoing activity at the Project. Notes and statistics were placed on records in respect of the sheep's date of birth, parent history, breeding type, disease/problems pattern, treatment, breeding time, lambing rate, and genetic traits. Crossbreeding was reported to yield encouraging results. Preliminary work indicated that weight gains of the crossbred sheep were better than that of the Blackbelly sheep. There were indications that wholesale cuts from the carcasses of the crossbred sheep compared favorably with imported cuts as regards meat-bone fat ratios. A funding agency team visited the Ministry of Agriculture in 1981 to ascertain the Project's progress. The Project's local counterpart official put out a quarterly report.

Handicraft

Reporting was done weekly, monthly and quarterly. Weekly meetings generated oral reports on the Project's movement. The implementation team reported monthly to the Handicraft Development Committee, and the Committee in turn reported to the BIDC's board of directors. Three types of reports were in use, e.g. production reports, sales reports, and personnel reports. The first report had to do with inventorying production, cost of raw materials, number of operations, and problem areas. The second and third reports dealt with the volume of sales, best-selling products, sales comparison, and personnel attendance. Reporting was done not only as a tool of control but also as a management and planning tool. It embraced budgetary and accounting needs, maintained a flow of communication, and allowed for accountability.

Cave

It was reported that the Project was funded in its entirety by the GOB. Land had cost $56,023, fixed assets cost $261,225, development cost $3,832,329, and some expenses were incurred on incidentals (Barbados Caves Authority, 1979: 4; 1980:3;1981: 1-4; 1982:1-3). Reporting further intimated that the first part of implementation - land acquisition, tunnel excavation, equipment purchase, management services and employee compensation - cost about $1.8m., that the second part involved a capital outlay of $1.7m., that the Project's first 18 months were spent almost entirely on tunnelling , and the Cave underground vehicles had cost $282,628. Daily and weekly reporting followed at the Project. The daily work records covered the area of operation, number of operations, description of work, subcontractor identification, reporter observations and explanatory notes. The weekly reports related to a summary of work done during the week. Quarterly reports were also submitted within 15 days of the preceding month. Progress schedules were turned in by the implementation team to the Barbados Caves Authority.

Pulverization

Reports (Ministry of Health, 1967-83) indicated that the total cost amounted to BDS$4.2m., spanning consultancy, construction, materials, equipment, access roads, and incidentals. Reporting involved site meetings among consultants , contractors and executing agency personnel, and progress or status reports being written and circulated. Periodically, reports were sent to PIU. Reporting related to forecasting expenditures and completion, cost and expenditure summary, explanation of major delays, explanation of major cost variances and justification for new capital outlay requests. The project manager reported to the permanent secretary and the minister in the Ministry of Health who in turn reported to the Cabinet. Construction costs were recorded on preset forms on a monthly basis. Interim payments to contractors were also recorded on forms.

Progress reports submitted by the consultancy firm to the Ministry of Health included six reports spanning from February 1979 to March 1980. The reports contained periodic developments, data summary, actual progress, costs, expenditure chart, progress photographs, and equipment supply/installation/maintenance.

Polytechnic

Internal reporting took place among project staff and concerned participating organizations. Project meetings and site meetings were held, serving as tools of reporting. The executing agency was answerable to the Ministry of Education, reporting through the Educational Planning Unit. The agency transmitted status reports periodically to the PIU and the PPC. Periodic reports were also sent to the Accountant-General's Department, Auditor-General's Department, and the Ministry of Finance and Planning.

Periodic reports covered the period from the signing of the loan agreement in July 1977 until January 1984 when the final report was submitted. Eleven periodic reports were completed and submitted by the executing agency to the funding agency. The reports were filed mostly on June 30 and December 31 of each project year. Biannual reports flowed from the executing agency to the funding agency. Reporting concerned project management, tendering, contract-awarding, ground-breaking, construction commencement, expenditure, financial matters, progress schedule deadlines, equipment-handling, financing, labor availability, counterpart contribution, third-party coordination, weather conditions, and technical aspects.

The Project's organization and management development consultants presented their reports to the executing agency between May and

September 1982. Reporting revealed that the Project cost totalled $20.6m. of which construction accounted for 55.8%. It was reported that the cost of construction compared favorably with the going rate of $110 per sq.ft. for similar construction.

Sewerage

The executing agency, reporting to the PPC through the PIU and externally to the IDB, provided updated information on the status of the Project on a monthly, quarterly and biannual basis. Daily reports were prepared by the Fitzpatrick Consultants Ltd. Filed for 1979, 1980 and 1981, the reports included data on weather conditions, materials, construction, progress, and problems. Prepared by the consulting firm, monthly reports furnished data on site management, excavation, construction, electricals, work progress and work methods. Graphs were plotted to show monthly progress with respect to scheduled and actual progress and time consumption. Project reports were also prepared monthly by the PIU, with Gantt charts highlighting progress summary, problems, work schedules, cost breakdowns and updated expenditures. Quarterly reports were lodged by the project manager with the PIU on project progress, status and plans. Attached to each of these was a short-term cashflow plan.

Special committees - the Construction Coordinating Committee, the Technical Advisory Committee and the Public Information Committee - were set up and required to report on specific aspects. Reporting was conducted through the media to keep the target community informed of all activities causing inconvenience as well as the progress made in the Project.

Reports (Community Development Division, 1981: 14-16) from nearly 500 Emmerton residents resettled at Clapham expressed general satisfaction with their new environment and the improvement in their living standards. The relocation exercise's total cost reached BDS$1.6m., which was met from local funds (Archer, 1979: 6-7; 1981: 10-12). Reporting disclosed that the contracts 1,2 and 3 - the treatment plant, the marine outfall, and the sewer network - had cost $12.2m., $2.1m. and $18.0m. respectively.

Ferneihurst

Reports prepared periodically by the implementation team were submitted to the NHC directorial board, the Ministry of Housing, PIU, and the participating organizations. Internally, reports moved among the NHC's manager, assistant manager, financial controller, chief technical officer, chief estate officer, chief legal officer, and purchasing officer. The report data pertained to construction progress, time management , work schedules, material needs delatory factors, and explanatory notes.

Site meetings were held between the Project personnel and the contracting firms. There were periodic reports from the site engineer and other construction personnel. Continuous oral communications and confirmations were made at the site by works overseer, field supervisor, foreman, and site clerk. Completion notices, interim payment applications, payment certificates, pay vouchers and local purchase orders were used as tools of communication and confirmation. Notices were filled out with the required data and several copies were transmitted to the various contact points.

Termination

Greenland

The Project status ended in 1982 and the Project functions were absorbed into the Ministry of Agriculture's Central Livestock Station and the Greenland Agricultural Station. The Project personnel were transferred and assigned to the Ministry's other programs. There were surplus equipment in some cases which were reallocated or discarded because of obsolescence.

Handicraft

With the ending of the Project status in 1979, the handicraft operation was divisionalized and placed under the ambit of the BIDC. The Handicraft Division came to he headed by a manager who reported directly to the general manager. Some advance planning initiated for the transition from the Project stage to normal operation related to Project personnel, funds, equipment, designs, training center, trainees, official records, products, raw materials, sales outlets, and promotional materials. Nearly all the personnel who worked for the Project were absorbed into the Division. A number of gaps were closed, loose ends were put together, ad hoc operational measures were formulated, procedures were laid out, routines were built and installed, and interorganizational relations were consolidated.[1]

Cave

The Project was completed, officially inaugurated and opened to the public in November 1981, but tunnel-related work continued until April 1982. The Cave's management came under the Barbados Caves Authority. The phase involved checking and clearing outstanding payables, finalizing and preparing accounts for 1981-82, auditing accounts for 1980-91 and 1981-82, preparing annual report for 1980-81, preparing the final report on the Project, completing and closing filed correspondence/ minutes/other records, and disposing surplus assets (Barbados Caves Authority, 1981: 3;1982: 3-4).

The official records from October 1975 to March 1982, including furniture, equipment and supplies, were handed over to the Ministry of Housing. Other documents relating to the Project were shifted to the National Conservation Commission. Some inventories became integrated into the Cave's offices. Surplus assets like the traxcavator, air compressor and ancillary equipment were sold in early 1982 following management decision.

Positions at the Cave became available in October 1980, appointments were made in January 1981, and the manager as well as the maintenance supervisor assumed duty in March 1981 (Barbados Caves Authority, 1981:3). Management personnel were exposed to intensive training in the Cave operations. Guide training was carried out, stressing communication and interpretation skills. Some work involving drainage, water movement, natural formations, trails and electricals was wound up.[2]

Pulverization

The Plant commissioning took place in April 1980, which involved a running-in period after implementation before full-capacity operations began. The Plant's motors and drives were tested. Tests were carried out on the different types of refuse that could be pulverized. Tests were run to correct design deficiencies, adjust resource shortfalls, modify output, and ensure handover. The Project was completed in April 1980 and officially opened in June of the same year. The Ministry of Health's Sanitation Service Authority was charged with operational responsibility. Not a great deal of surplus materials or tools were left behind. A budget was prepared showing the annual recurrent costs of the Plant operation and maintenance. A complement of employees was recruited. A period of attachment began in early 1980. Some of the recruits underwent local and overseas training. Certain remedial work was undertaken, e.g. doing repairs to the second shredder's damage support system, retesting of the shredder, and replacing the first shredder's friction liner.[3]

Polytechnic

All activities earmarked for transfer to the Campus were completed. Some unfinished business was concluded, viz. fully staffing the Institution, setting up equipment and workshops, moving and installing machine tools and furniture, making payments for materials and services, remedying some structural flaws, and undertaking necessary repairs and servicing. Divisional/departmental headships were introduced and appointments were made in subject-areas like mechanics, electronics, carpentry, plumbing, masonry, engineering, commerce, human ecology, mathematics, natural science, social science, and language. The library became operational and was used by students and staff. The accessions were made, cataloged, and put into circulation. Local and overseas training was conducted for teaching, technical, and management staff.

The Project was mostly completed by May 1982, and it was officially opened in the same month. Classes, however, started earlier in September 1981. All classes were housed at the Campus by January 1982. The executing agency was merged with an ongoing World Bank education project agency in April 1982 to finish the Project's completion. Another project manager was appointed at this time, with the engineer, accountant and stenographer transferred to the merged agency. The remaining project personnel were reassigned to the various units of the public sector. Although it was opened in May 1982, it was not until January 1983 that completion was formally certified. On the Project's completion, the Polytechnic has become a unit of the Ministry of Education where the principal, assisted by two deputy principals and support staff, is the academic head of the Institution.

Sewerage

Advance action was taken for a transition from the Project stage to normal operation. The funding agency insisted that some technical staff of the Project be absorbed into the newly-created Barbados Water Authority. The executing agency was terminated, some support staff were transferred to another sewerage project, and some surplus materials were transferred to the Water Authority. A plant superintendent, technicians, operators and support staff were employed to run the system. Procedural manuals were prepared, staff training was initiated, operating systems were put in place, and maintenance services were activated. Some corrective work to the Plant was taken up.

Once construction was completed, the treatment plant became ready to accept sewage. The system went into operation from April 1982. The Ministry of Health officials made a final inspection of the Project's target and plant areas. The Project was completed in June 1982, the Plant was commissioned in August 1982, and it was officially opened in the same month. Test runs were conducted before the sewage operation started. Some consultancy services were accepted. Between June 24 and July 9, 1982, a two-week course sponsored by the PAHO-WHO and conducted by Ron Layton was held on the biological waste plant operations. Drawn from the Ministry of Health and the Barbados Water Authority, the 25 participants were addressed on odor and maintenance control of sewage plants, effluent and sludge control, wastewater treatment methods, pretreatment and industrial waste management, industrial waste and disinfectant, food and toxins, and nutrients. The system became the responsibility of the Barbados Water Authority which was established in October 1980 and commenced operation in April 1981 to manage the country's water and sewage system. The Authority assumed the responsibility of the Plant in November 1982.

Between September 1982 and March 1983, C.K. Abraham provided start-up, operation and technical training services to help familiarize the Plant personnel with the treatment process and the operating procedures. Technical assistance was provided in preparing operational and maintenance manuals for running the system. Supervision was provided for the start-up of the new system. Leonard Penner provided consultancy from September 1983 to March 1984 with respect to training Plant personnel in laboratory procedures and biological treatment process and advising the Authority on the best possible methods of septage-handling.

Ferneihurst

With the completion of the Project, the implementation team was not disbanded but was reorganized within the NHC's Technical Division. The Project personnel were reallocated to other projects and routine operations, supplemental staffing was trimmed, surplus materials and tools were taken back to the warehouse or utilized by ongoing projects, and other adjustments were put in place. The Project activity was absorbed by and integrated into the Corporation's normal operation. This obviated the need for any advance or special preparation for a bustling transition from the Project stage to regular management. The completed Estate was handed over to the Corporation's Housing Management Division.

Evaluation

Greenland

There was no formal in-house or external review or expost facto in situ evaluation of the Project. Any possible feedback from output users and beneficiaries was not obtained. Records did not show if the authority went through an evaluation of the results achieved and limitations faced during the project cycle. Yet, available information disclosed that basically the Project had met its objectives in that the breeding operation was generally successful, a flock of purebred Blackbelly sheep had been established, and some demand for lamb and mutton throughout the year had been generated. There were 1,100 sheep in stock, with an average supply of 2,000 lambs yearly. Crossbreeding had improved the meat production capacity of the local breed, but had done so at the expense of prolificacy.

Conclusive evidence had been difficult to build due to the long-term timescale characterizing, for example, the Project's genetic improvement aspect. The production level failed to match the domestic consumption demand and export need. Related to this was the insufficiency of penetration into the local meat market in respect of the mutton produced by the Station. A policy decision was awaited on whether to pursue the meat production objective or the breed development objective and whether to continue with the crossbreeding program.

Handicraft

A system for the review and evaluation of the Project's progress was considered and put in place. Periodic in situ reviews of activities and results were made and continued throughout the Project cycle in order that benefits could be drawn from the Project experience. Reviews revealed that the Project realized some objectives, production was adequate, the undertaking was on schedule at each phase, and that there were no significant errors of overestimation or underestimation. However, they also showed that commercial viability was not realized as soon as it was expected and that export sales were overestimated, having identified pricing as the contributing factor. It was anticipated that commercial viability might be achieved subsequently.

Later, the handicraft operation and the BIDC came under several ex post facto evaluations. The Peat Marwick study (1981:1) reviewed the

Corporation's organizational structure, goal-setting, human resources, programs and management techniques with a view to verifying whether or not the existing system could achieve its objectives and serve future needs. Included in the Booz, Allen & Hamilton study (1982:1) were a review of the industrial sector, a prescription for competitive strategies and analyses to assist the BIDC in developing an updated industrial development strategy for the 1980s with reference to organizational overview, key issues and program development/management. Finally, a task force (The Nation, 1983), evaluated the Handicraft Center's operations with a view to improving its overall efficiency and profitability. The study dwelt on organizational, management, production, purchasing, training, development, product development, pricing, promotion, and distribution.

Cave

There was no indication that an evaluation of the outcome was ever launched. No formal review - including an assessment of the permanence and desirability of results, the effectiveness of output, and continuing or unmet needs - was initiated with the Project's completion. All this notwithstanding, available information pointed to initial goal-setting and subsequent goal-attainment. The initiatives succeeded when the showcave was developed as a tourist attraction, contributing to the promotion of Barbados as a tourist destination. Just so, complementary to investment are the floral and vegetational beauty of the vicinity enhancing the external ambience of the Cave's site, the continuing and satisfactory operation of the Cave, and the carpark facilitating a smooth flow of visitor traffic. Internal assessments show an expectation for high revenue, not only to meet operational cost and to retain the Cave's self-financing status but also to enable its supervisory agency - the National Conservation Commission - to embark prudently on development programs. To this end, the Complex's tour-making capacity has been increased by adding a third cave vehicle, introducing night tours after 4:30 p.m. and putting on stream a scenic walk in the western side of the Cave featuring Barbados' plants.

Pulverization

A comprehensive postcompletion evaluation was not done to examine the Project's effectiveness in attaining its goals and its impact on aggregate development. No move was made to engage external evaluators or to assign internal staffers to attempt a formal review. However, in October 1980 the Ministry of Health commissioned vibrational tests on the shredders and reporting on the suitability of the support structural system (Pulverization Plant Project, 1967-83; Public Investment Unit, 1977). Prepared by William Aspinaee of the Trinidad-based Seismic Research Unit of the University of the West Indies and submitted in July 1981, the report indicated that the structure lacked appropriate stiffness and that the design of the existing steel support structure to the shredder was unsuitable, which had caused some cracking to one of the shredders. The consultant produced a design parameter for the replacement steelwork and prescribed that the shredders should be carefully inspected after daily operation and shut down if any cracking was detected.

Available information pointed out that the performance of the Plant since 1980 had been reasonable in the light of its given objectives. The Project had installed economical, volume-reducing and environmentally-sound waste management, made way for expanded landfill capacity, benefited refuse collection and landfill operation with the modern techniques of waste control and improved ergonomics. Yet, the high energy cost, frequent transfer of trained operatives from the Plant and inability or unwillingness to generate revenue constrained the Investment. The need for reprocessing, salvaging, recycling, composting, reclaiming or resource recovery remains unmet, with continuing inability to offset high operational cost and forge intersectoral linkages. Even though economic costs and benefits were largely known, social costs and benefits remained somewhat conjectural.

Polytechnic

The Project went thorough postcompletion reviews. While the first review was lodged in September 1982, the second and the third studies were submitted in June and December, 1983. The evaluations touched on the Project's background, basic objectives, and implementation. These further spoke to progress scheduled and attained, compliance with technical construction specifications and financial conditions, periodic modifications, cost/time schedules, technical problems, the adequacy of documentation, and performance of local participants. Also concerned were elements, such as predisbursement compliance, tendering, disbursements, and institutional capacity-building.

Still another review was done which contained data dealing with external and internal efficiency of the Polytechnic and permitted longitudinal comparisons during the life of the Project and for a prescribed period following the commencement of operation at the Wildey site. The review, based on the academic year 1982-83 (Samuel Jackman Prescod Polytechnic, 1980-83), consisted of an overview of the full-time student population at the Institution, analyses of surveys carried out on student guidance and counselling, socioeconomic status of the student population, and tracer studies of Polytechnic students and alumni.

Sewerage

Although a formal review of the functioning of the Barbados Water Authority, which was mandated by the loan agreement, was not done, but several other evaluations were run in relation to the Project. Meynell (1982) conducted baseline surveys at selected seabed sites around the marine outfall area. He reported on the chemical, biological and bacteriological characteristics of the area. It was found that water quality and the health of marine communities had been steadily deteriorating in the greater Bridgetown area since at least 1972.

A second-process evaluation was conducted by Toretta (1983:1-18). The study looked at process control and equipment, performance, operation, and management and laboratory. First, the equipment was found to be functioning satisfactorily, but process control was sometimes difficult which resulted in an unstable flow condition. Second, the Plant met all its discharge parameters and did not pollute the sea, the effluent appeared to be satisfactory, the biological oxygen demand and the suspended solids efficiency recorded 92%, the processing unit appeared to perform well, the effluent was visually clean, and the tests showed acceptable results. However, the dissolved oxygen tests revealed that generalizing about operational efficiency was not risk-free. Third, it was also revealed that sludge was treated at fifteen minutes per hour at a low rate, the return sludge rate could not be measured accurately due to hydraulic problems, operating the Plant at a return sludge rate lower than 40% was uneconomical, there was some concern over the inability to remove sludge at a 30% return rate, and that more tests were required. Finally, some needs and gaps were identified, such as the Plant personnel's full familiarity with the operation of such a Plant, training personnel in performance sampling and testing, running tests and analyzing results, maintaining records, and training in laboratory procedures. The procedures for sewage sampling, the use of the test results, the operating parameters and the minimum test procedures were highlighted and reviewed.

Having conducted surveys at selected seabed sites in the vicinity of the marine outfall, Hunte (1983:6-28) suggested that the environmental impact of the outfall was difficult to predict. The untreated discharge was supposed to be eliminated and the environmental condition in Carlisle Bay was expected to improve as a result of the Plant's operation. However, with the sewage being discharged through the outfall and chlorination being used in treatment which was partly stressful on marine life, conditions in the outfall vicinity might be expected to deteriorate. The survey data indicated that there had been a general deterioration in the health of the benthic communities in the surveyed sites. The conclusion was based on the decrease in the percentage of healthy corals and in the substratum covered by live coral. Decline in 1983 reflected a continuation of the deteriorating trend of the decade, and a single year of relief from the influx of raw sewage was not enough to arrest the trend. Finally, the Community Development Division, in an evaluation concerning the resettlement of the residents from Emmerton to Clapham, pointed out areas of achievement and shortfall.

Ferneihurst

During implementation an in situ evaluation was made to ensure that the construction was in accordance with the approved plans, the target dates were being met, the cost was within the budget, and the scheduled activities were properly conducted. Thereafter, an in-house evaluation was made in 1981 with the completion of the Project by the Corporation's Technical Division, which determined the reasons for cost overruns, ascertained performance of the site workforce and equipment, identified the main problems and verified the chief benefits. Evaluation identified exercising cost control and authority, the issuance of materials from stores as the critical elements in the project process, pointed to inadequacies in preparing material checklist and in carrying out quantity survey, and underwrote the effectiveness of cost control in keeping expenditure within budget. The review addressed the need for utilizing residential land optimally, appraising tenant perception and adjustment to a new living complex, and using additional space on the Estate prudently. Besides, the feasibility of the Corporation workforce building access roads and the suitability of large single holdings in high-density residential areas were looked at.

Available information disclosed that the need to integrate physical planning and housing design was neither always recognized nor appreciated. Running tenant surveys before housing projects were mounted was neglected, thus missing useful and usable information. The lack of follow-up with landscaping at Ferneihurst was a case in point. Among other concerns were improved estate management, regular postcompletion supervision, greater cost control, and more intensive monitoring of implementation.

Operation

Greenland

The Station focuses on introducing, selecting and breeding sheep. While introduction comprises bringing in the exotic breeds, selection is the choosing and increasing of certain desirable traits, i.e. appearance, fertility, growth rate, size, body capacity, meat quality, and disease resistance. Also on stream are various types of breeding, viz, inbreeding, outbreeding, and crossbreeding. Systematic castration of undesirable or scrub rams is done in keeping with sound husbandry practices. Careful attention is paid to feeding, mating, gestation, lambing, lactation and breeding. The Station becomes active during the lambing season, starting in either May or December and lasting for a month or two. The sheep for breeding are selected and grouped. The rams are marketed and placed among the ewes. Close to breeding time, ewes are kept on an increased level of nutrition as this increases the ovulation rate.

The small flock method of mating is practiced with an accurate pedigree, a shorter breeding time and a litter of lambs of uniform size at weaning. Mothering by the ewes of their young is regularly monitored. Lambing, lactation, weaning, culling, trimming, deworming, drenching, docking, and shearing are checked to ensure the quality of the livestock population. For nutritional purpose, the sheep receives a balanced ration of grasses, legumes, and concentrates. The lambs are weaned between 2-3 months of age. At weaning time, the lambs are removed to other pens where they are fed hay and concentrates for a short adjustment period. Sanitation measures include treating footrot, controlling and treating parasites, cleaning and disinfecting pens, draining pastures, isolating infected animals , safekeeping, watering and feeding , trials, rotating pastures, consulting veterinarian, and running diagnostic tests. The animal feet are examined, trimmed and pared. The sheep are dewormed at two to three months intervals. The drench is given while a sheep is on its four feet. Shearing of the imported breed is carried out twice a year. When the lambs are four weeks old, docking is done to keep them clean around the tail.

Animal health and sanitation measures include treating footrot, controlling and treating parasites, cleaning and disinfecting animals, draining pasture, isolating infected animals, safekeeping and watering feeding tools, rotating pasture, consulting veterinarian, and running diagnostic tests. The animal feet are examined, trimmed and pared. Sanitation also involves making certain that pens and sheds are disinfected, pastures are well-drained, lambs are fed in a special area, fresh and clean drinking water is provided, too many animals are not crowed into a small area, infected sheep are separated, and young animals and mature sheep are separated at all times. The sheep are dewormed at two to three months intervals. The drench is given while a sheep is on all its four feet. When the lambs are four weeks old, docking is done to keep them clean around the tail. Shearing of the imported breeds is carried out twice a year.

Paddocks and rotational grazing are in use at the Station. Overgrazing and undergrazing are avoided. With no water being available in the paddocks, it is given to the animals when they return to their pens in the afternoon. Once the animals are brought in, they are offered hay and dairy concentrates. Where possible, the nursing mothers and their lambs are grazed separately from the rest of the flock. Grazing young sheep ahead of older ones is the norm. Grass cultivation goes through several phases, e.g. preparation, planting, manuring, fertilizing, liming, weed control, pest control, and mowing. Alfalfa, a high-yielding legume of high nutritional value, is grown and is grazed or fed to the sheep. The pens are kept dry on a building with good cross ventilation in order to prevent footrot and the production of ammonia.

Lambs are sold at the Station. Two month-old lambs are sold directly to sheep farmers for the purpose of raising sheep. No sale takes place during breeding or lambing time. For the commercial market, 8-10 month-old sheep are sold every month to the Barbados Marketing Corporation for slaughtering. The sheep are slaughtered and the meat is wholesold. While slaughtering is carried out at the Corporation, the sale is supervised by the Station's personnel. While prime cuts are retailed to hotels and restaurants, other grades are sold to retail outlets. Residual byproducts are sometimes sold to make sausage and hide. Individuals can directly purchase sheep at the Station.

Job rotation is in use at the Station. Workers remain familiar with the rearing of cows, pigs and sheep. Some operations are carried out collectively to speed up work, e.g. hauling hay, mending pasture fences disinfecting and deworming ewes, and so on. The abattoir facility operational at the Corporation - having slaughtering, meat-cutting and meat-handling facilities and upholding hygienic and sanitation standards - ensures that the consumer is supplied with meat slaughtered under wholesome conditions. Health regulations are enforced and animals are inspected before and after slaughter by the health ministry personnel. Animals are slaughtered on a service charge. The carcasses are returned to their owners to be sold after health inspection and 24 hours in chill storage.

Handicraft

Raw materials are procured from various collection points across the country and brought to the workshop. The raw materials include acrylic, bamboo, bead, cardboard, clay, cloth cotton, fibre, glaze, grass, iron, leather, metal, nylon, palm, plastic, root, rug, seed, shell, stone, straw, wood, wool, and many such objects. Some materials go through drying, cleaning, bleaching, plaiting, marking, cutting, sticking, lining, assembling, and decorating. Other materials move from soaking, picking, trampling, kneading, pugging, throwing, modelling, coating, drying, cleaning, biscuiting/wedging, firing, baking, tempering, trimming, burnishing, decorating, and glazing. Still other materials entail some processes as shaving, staking, scudding and buffing.

Products are stored in the store area and are subsequently transferred to the various sales outlets. Inventory records are maintained to check the movement of products from the workshop through the store area to the sales outlets. The sales outlets are periodically checked to identify the slow-moving merchandise. Discounts are offered to accelerate disposal. Retail and bulk purchase is available. Cash as well as consignment sale is offered. The merchandise is labelled and displayed in the outlets. In the case of consignment sale, the outlet deducts a 15% service charge from the sale proceeds. The Corporation makes direct purchase from independent producers twice a week.

Routine and periodic maintenance is in force. While kiln and sewing machines are serviced periodically on contract, wheel and pug mill are checked by the Workshop personnel. As regards health and safety, gloves are used and respirators are recommended. For work-related injury, medical attention and compensation are available. Batch production is at work at the Workshop. Special orders are received, provided adequate specifications and supporting materials are made available in advance. Generally, trainees receive a three-month training program. Those who intend to work in pottery are trained for a longer period. Training sessions are held at the Corporation Workshop, training centers, community centers and the Industrial School.

Cave

The Cave is open daily except for some public holidays. The Cave operation spans from ticketing through waiting and tram-boarding to touring and returning. Cave visits are done by reservation system which allows for individual and group as well as advance and current booking. The tours continue throughout the day. Limited night tours are available. Group transportation is in operation. Normally, waiting time is involved between two tours.

Upon arrival at the Cave, visitors are accommodated at the Visitor's Center. After a short wide-screen video presentation, visitors board trams for the underground ride accompanied by a tour guide and an operator. The vehicles move slowly downward into the cavern, allowing the change from the typical sunlight to the Cave's dark environment to take its effect. The first view at the beginning of the Cave tour is the tunnel entrance, which is natural in appearance, contour, and vegetation. The vehicles leave the entrance area, complete the cavern tour, and return to the entrance area having made several assigned stops.

Basically, what the visitor sees in the mile-long Cave tour is enormous galleries filled with crystal-clear stalactites and stalagmites, tumbling waterfalls and deep pools, all appearing as nature created them. Indirect lights play around the shining and cascading waters. The assigned stops include the upper level of the Great Hall, Explorer Pool, Twin Falls, the lower level of the Great Hall, the two sites of unusual formations, complete vehicle and lights turnoff, Cascade Pool and Rotunda Room. The stops are each one minute in length except the ones at Cascade Pool, and Rotunda Room which last between 3-5 minutes. At the Cascade Pool, visitors become explorers as they are allowed to leave the tram and stroll to the pool. For the more adventurous, there is a walkway under the falls to be explored. At the lowest point in the Cave, visitors leave the tram and walk beside a forty-foot waterfall plunging downward into a deep blue pool. Within forty minutes, one is introduced with the assistance of guide services to an extensive cave landscape. The commentary is done mostly in English.

Maintenance includes periodically controlling unwanted underground and aquatic plant life. The Cave lighting system is monitored on a continuous basis. Attention is given to trash accumulation from visitors. Dirt or deposit accumulation on paved trails and rock/cave formation surfaces is cleaned. Speleothem growth in the upper passage is checked. A schedule of inspection and maintenance is in force for the Cave vehicles so that each vehicle is in prime running condition and looks clean. The vehicles, which require overnight changing of batteries, are housed in the service area where generator-charger recharge the batteries. To ensure safety, the Cave walls and ceiling are periodically checked.

Pulverization

The Plant not only pulverizes but also reduces refuse by crushing, grinding, shredding, or tearing it into small pieces. The Plant's operations spans from conveyor feed and pulverization sequence to ejection and refuse loading. Users put waste at a storage/transfer point for refuse pickup. The collection service is run by drivers and loaders. The collection vehicle operates on a prescribed collection route, makes the necessary stops, loaders fill the vehicles with waste, some of the collected waste is partially compressed, the route is completed, and the vehicles return to the Plant. The quantity of refuse brought to the Plant is weighed. The process of routing and assigning collection districts and manning collection vehicles are completed by the Sanitation Service Authority. The Plant can take four truckloads of refuse simultaneously.

Pulverization is a process in which refuse is fed into the system, shredded and ground through revolving hammers and a series of conveyor belts, and is converted into a finely ground powder, It can grind, shred or tear the refuse so that tough materials are torn into small pieces. The Plant, equipped with double-line shredders, takes only domestic refuse and has an installed capacity for providing 400 tons of waste per eight-hour day. It can operate in two sections which can be used alternately according to variations in the volume of refuse. For unloading, the vehicles reverse and from ground level tip the waste into the reception hopper. The conveyor-borne refuse goes into the shredder where the revolving hammers do the shredding. The refuse is pulverized and drops through the grids underneath the shredder. The shredded refuse drops on a conveyor and is carried to the reversing conveyor. The reduced end-product drops into the waiting discharge vehicles and is carried away to the adjacent Workman Landfill, where the disposal of raw refuse is prohibited and only the shredded waste is deposited. Four vehicles can be loaded with the pulverized refuse at the same time. Vehicles level off the shredded refuse on the surface of the Landfill, e.g. rolling, compacting, and covering the refuse. The shredded refuse is dumped into large holes or trenches, packed down, covered with earth and planted with grass.

Routine and preventive maintenance is in force. Repairs required on the collection vehicles are carried out by the SSA. Equipment maintenance follows through standard procedures, e.g. the level of oil in the conveyor's clutch system is checked every morning and shredders and conveyors are cleaned every day to prevent blockages. A welding unit repairs the worndown pulverization hammers. When a shredder gets stuck, workers get into the chute in a piece of protective clothing to clear it. In the event of mechanical breakdown, the repairs and testing are carried out. The Plant produces waste materials or emissions. The emissions are physical-noise, heat, vibrations - which are reduced to tolerable levels through the use of special equipment. The emissions, which are solid, are deposited at landfills. The Plant equipment has easy accessibility for operation and maintenance, large feed openings prevent jamming, has removable components, has easy adjustability, and can do both coarse and fine shredding. At times, a traxcavator is used to spread mold on the surface and sprays are applied to reduce odor.

Polytechnic

Application forms are available from April 1 each year and must be returned not later than April 30. Nonnationals apply through the Ministry of Education. The admission criteria include, depending on the applicant status, a minimum age of 16 years on August 31 in any particular year, a minimum of 9 years of school attendance, a school-leaving certificate in four subjects including English and Mathematics, an interview, an entrance examination, and an employer recommendation. Students are admitted full-time, part-time day, and part-time evening.

Students are required to pay certain fees. All books, supplies, basic tools and materials must also be acquired by the students. Standard norms, procedures and periodicity underlie routine matters, viz. academic term scheduling, contact hours, class-period duration, class timetabling, classroom intake capacity, training duration, training focus, course balancing, training orientation, type of education program, student enrollment, program duration, program phasing, curriculum design, training, practice, faculty development, student evaluation and examination timetabling. The level of training is pitched at ordinary and advanced levels. Teaching practices emphasize student involvement, teaching tools, audiovisual aids, handouts, and periodic visits. In the workshop, the demonstration method is on stream. Individual/group projects and problem-solving exercises are carried out . The underlying idea is to learn by doing. Term and annual progress reports are transmitted to students' parents/guardians. Disciplinary measures include suspension and expulsion. Term tests are held during the term. Final examinations are held during May-June each year. Supplementals are held only for the overseas examinations. Students who attain the necessary theoretical and practical skills can take external overseas examinations to enhance their qualifications. Following examinations, grading is done and results are notified. On successful completion of a program, students are awarded certificates or diplomas.

Guidance counselling is available to students who need assistance in certain concern areas. Students are provided with the necessary information on furthering their studies. Placement service is available which is instrumental in occupational development, and assists students in finding employment. On stream is also industrial attachment which places students in a particular work setting in order for students to acquire hands-on experience. The student council makes way for student involvement and potential actualization as well as recreation. Each faculty member is responsible for plan preparation, syllabus development and teaching. The Institution's senior personnel are responsible for organization management and operation, while the Board of Management is vested with policy matters. Routine as well as preventative maintenance is in stream.

Sewerage

The principal operations consist of the mechanical, primary/physical, secondary/biological, and tertiary/chemical processes. The mechanical process consists in sewage pumping. The sewage from user premises enters the sewer network. The influent flows by gravity or is pumped into the raw waste pump stations. From the station, sewage flows by gravity or is discharged into the gravity line which flows to the treatment plant. The influent is collected in a wet well. Concerned with pretreatment, this is where primary treatment occurs, which is a physical process. All large solids are shredded into fine particles by the communitor, and a bar screen traps all large particles. From the well the wastewater is pumped first into distribution chambers and secondly into four-compartment stabilization tanks. Secondary treatment consists of biological and chemical processes that accelerate the natural degradation process. The process takes place by adding dissolved oxygen to the sewage.

The sewage enters the first compartment known as the contact zone. The bacteria in the zone mixes with the sewage and absorbs it. After about four hours, the mixed sewage goes into another compartment called sedimentation unit or clarifier. Here the solid matter settles to the bottom of the clarifier, leaving clear water known as effluent. The effluent is directed to the effluent chambers when it is disinfected by adding a chlorine solution, which includes tertiary treatment involving a chemical process. Some of the solids settling at the bottom of the clarifier are airlifted to the third section known as the reaeration zone, and the rest goes into the fourth section called the sludge digester. The solids go thought another breakdown and this substance is known as sludge, which is stored in the digester until it is ready for disposal and use on farmland as fertilizer and soil conditioner. The disposal method involves spreading the sludge into land by a specially-equipped vehicle. The effluent is flushed through the marine outfall into the sea. The provisions are in place for underwater discharge to release the treated effluent and dilution of the effluent in the seawater. The action of the salt water destroys any remaining bacteria.

The Plant accepts and treats loads of septage daily. The septic and cesspool waste coming from public and private-sector consumers involves the use of special equipment and treatment. The Plant produces emissions some of which are physical, such as noise, heat and vibrations. Other emissions are liquid, which are discharged through pumps and remain at a distant and safe site. Other emissions, such as slurry, are specially treated for further use. Certain effluents that are unpleasant or noxious require special treatment. To control odor, chlorine is put when influent goes through the process. Routine and preventive maintenance is on stream. The pumps, blowers and sewers are checked periodically. The laboratory monitors the quality of influent and effluent. Specially-designed vehicles clear any blocks in the sewers.

Ferneihurst

The operational areas consist of tenancy agreement, rent collection, complaint service, and property maintenance. To obtain tenancy, one makes an application on the standard forms, attaches supporting documents, and indicates the form of payment. Fieldwork is done and need surveys are run by officials to verify and establish the applicant's statements, status and eligibility. The Tenants Committee examines applications for necessary decision before referring the matter to the Corporation's board for approval. The approved applicants sign tenancy agreements. Following the deposit of one month's rent in advance, the keys to the units are handed over to the tenants. Included in the tenancy agreement are several stipulations, viz. tenants should not sublet the premises, arrears must not accrue, the premises must be maintained satisfactorily, units must not be vacated without proper notice, and physical-planning and health regulations must not be breached.

Rent collection is done by deductions from wages/salaries or direct payment. Besides, rent collectors visit the Estate, collect rents, check general conditions of buildings and units, and report on unofficial tenants. Rent may also be paid at a nearby collection office. Each tenant is supplied with a rent book. A tenant pays for utilities and the use of refuse containers. As to rent default or arrears, an enquiry is made, the concerned tenant is notified , and he/she is given a time limit in which to clear accounts. Delinquent accounts are dealt with by means of reminder notifications, personal approach, legal action, levying of household furniture, collection-agency monitoring and eviction.

Tenant complaints about accommodation conditions and requests for service are made in person or on the telephone. Contact points have been established at the NHC head office as well as the maintenance depots where tenants can report problems which require attention. Complaints are noted in a complaint bok, problems are investigated, notes are written and workers are despatched to correct faults.

Routine and preventive maintenance is on stream (National Housing Corporation, 1980). Repairs and replacements through wear and tear, breakage and damage are made and minor repairs are carried out. While refuse collection and street cleaning are done by the SSA, routine chores like access-road maintenance, weeding, debushing, cleaning, landscaping, open-space grassing, and stormwater drainage system clearing are the responsibility of the NHC. Sewage control involves pumping and cleaning septic tanks/absorption wells and clearing chores. Attention is paid to maintenance of all natural vegetation.

Preventive maintenance mostly concerns plumbing, carpentry, masonry, electrical inspection, public-health inspection, interior/exterior painting, and termite/damp/leak control. A provision for emergency and urgent weekend services is on board. The maintenance depots keep various records, such as requisition orders, job cards, attendance rosters, and injury-sick lists. Safety measures are followed through. Materials are stored at the Pine Workshop, with other depots being used as service points. The Corporation head office transports personnel and materials among service points. Work is assigned by foremen on a daily basis.

NOTES

1. As a result of the Government of Barbados' privatization policy, a limited liability company known as Pelican Pride Cottage Industries Ltd. (PPCIL) took over in 1993 the BIDC's Handicraft Center. The Company - comprising the interested employees of the Handicraft Center as well as the management of the BIDC as shareholders - is directed by a board of directors - selected to provide a suitable mix of experience, knowledge and skill in both craft operations and business management - and operated by a manger, an assistant manager, a purchasing officer, a marketing officer and support staff. The PPCCIL took on several BIDC assets, namely, fixed assets, finished goods inventory, and raw materials inventory. The Company acquired the rights and concessions to operate outlets at Harrison's Cave, Grantley Adams International Airport, Pelican Village, and Pelican Industrial Park. The Company markets locally-produced crafts made with a wide range of raw materials. The goods are purchased primarily from shareholders. Where necessary, goods are bought from other craft producers to ensure a wide and varied assortment of products to maximize sales and secure a good share of the market. The PPCCIL continues to provide assistance in supply services, marketing, production, quality control, production design, raw materials procurement, equipment/accessories/tools/fittings supplies, craft producer training, and joint venture activity.
2. The Barbados Caves Authority, which managed Harrison's Cave until March 1982, was dissolved and the Cave management came under the aegis of the National Conservation Commission. A new management entity called Caves of Barbados has assumed responsibility for the management of the Cave.
3. The Workmans Landfill was officially closed when the Mangrove Landfill was opened.

RFERENCES

Abrahams, Michael (1973) *A Study on the Solid Waste Management Service in Barbados*. St. Michael, Barbados: Ministry of Health.

Abrams, Charles (1993) *Report on Housing Policy, Land Tenure and Home Finance*. St. Michael, Barbados: Housing Authority.

Advisory Committee on The Trades Training Center (1968) *Interim Report*. St. Michael, Barbados: Ministry of Education.

Agricultural Information Unit (1978) *Agricultural Newsletter Vol. 4, No. 3.* Christ Church, Barbados: Ministry of Agriculture.

Anderson, Robert L. (1973) *Report on Solid Waste Fires in Sanitary Landfills.* St Michael. Barbados: Ministry of Health.

Archer, Arthur B. (1970) *Sewage and Excreta Disposal in Barbados and a Sewerage System for the City of Bridgetown.* St. Michael, Barbados: Ministry of Health.

___ (1973) *Report on Refuse Collection and Disposal in Barbados.* St. Michael, Barbados : Ministry of Health.

___ (1973) *Report on Improvements in Sanitation Services.* St. Michael, Barbados: Ministry of Health.

___ (1979) "A Case Study of the Relocation of Residents from Emmerton, Bridgetown", *Paper presented at the Fifth Commonwealth Conference on Development and Human Ecology.* Georgetown, Guyana (April 2-6).

___ (1981) "A Case Study of the Resettlement of Residents from Emmerton, Bridgetown, Barbados", *Paper presented at the Sixth Commonwealth Conference on Development and Human Ecology*, University of Waterloo, Canada (May 24-29).

___ (1983) *Private Communication* (December 14).

___ (1985) "The Bridgetown Sewerage Project: Its Environmental Impact", in Tighe Geohegan (ed.) *The Caribbean Seminar on Environmental Impact Assessment.* St. Michael, Barbados: Center for Resource Management and Environmental Studies, University of the West Indies.

Barbados Caves Authority (1975-81) *Harrison's Cave Development Project Files 1975-81.* Christ Church, Barbados: Barbados Caves Authority.

___ (1977) *Annual Report 1975-77.* Christ Church, Barbados: Barbados Caves Authority.

___ (1978) *Annual Report 1977-78.* Christ Church, Barbados: Barbados Caves Authority.

___ (1979) *Annual Report 1978-79.* Christ Church, Barbados: Barbados Caves Authority.

___ (1980) *Annual Report 1979-80.* Christ Church, Barbados; Barbados Caves Authority.

___ (1981) *Annual Report 1980-81.* Christ Church, Barbados: Barbados Caves Authority.

___ (1981) *Financial Statements 1981.* Christ Church, Barbados: Barbados Cave Authority.

___ (1982) *Harrison's Cave: Barbados.* Christ Church, Barbados: Barbados Caves Authority.

___ (1982) *Final Report on the Harrison's Cave Department Project.* Christ Church, Barbados: Barbados Caves Authority.

___ (1982) *Harrison's Cave.* Christ Church, Barbados: Barbados Caves Authority.

Barbados Industrial Development Corporation (1974-75) *Annual Report 1974-75.* St. Michael, Barbados: Barbados Industrial Development Corporation.

___ (1975) *The Proposed Development Plan for the Barbados Handicraft Industry*

1975-79. St. Michael, Barbados: Barbados Industrial Development Corporation.

___(1975) *The Development of Local Handicraft*. St. Michael, Barbados: Barbados Industrial Development Corporation.

___ (1975) *Reorganization of the Handicraft Center*. St. Michael, Barbados: Barbados Industrial Development Corporation.

___(1975) *Annual Report 1974-75*. St. Michael, Barbados: Barbados Industrial Development Corporation.

___(1978) *Development Plan 1978-82*. St. Michael, Barbados: Barbados Industrial Development Corporation.

___(1979) *Handicrafts of Barbados*. St. Michael, Barbados. Barbados Industrial Development Corporation.

Barbados Institute of Management and Productivity (1975) *Report on the Determination of Actual and Projected Labor Market Requirements*. St. Michael, Barbados: Ministry of Education.

Bishop, Tony A. (1990) *The Bridgetown Sewerage Project*. St. Michael, Barbados: Unpublished undergraduate paper, University of the west Indies.

Booz, Allen & Hamilton, Inc. (1982) *Technical Proposal to Develop an Industrial Strategy: Barbados Industrial Development Corporation*. St. Michael, Barbados: Barbados Industrial Development Corporation.

Boyce, Dalton E. (1976) *A Survey of the Pottery Industry in Barbados*. St. Michael, Barbados: Unpublished undergraduate paper, University of the West Indies.

Bradshaw, Catherine (1982) *A Cost-Benefit Analysis of the Bridgetown Sewerage Project*. St. Michael, Barbados: Unpublished undergraduate paper, University of the West Indies.

Brannam, J.R. (1948) *Report on a Proposed Clayworking Industry in Barbados*. St. Michael, Barbados: The Colonial Secretary's Office.

Bridgetown Housing Board (1955) *Annual Report 1954-55*. St. Michael, Barbados: Bridgetown Housing Board.

Bridgetown Sewerage Project (1977-82) *Bridgetown Sewerage Project Files 1977-82*. St. Michael, Barbados: Ministry of Health.

___ (1982) *Official Opening of the Bridgetown Treatment Plant*. St. Michael, Barbados: Bridgetown Sewerage Project.

Browne, Marjorie L.(1982) *The Impact of Technical Education on Employment in Barbados*. St. Michael, Barbados: Unpublished undergraduate paper, University of the West Indies.

Burton, Carlisle A. et al. (1975) *Report on All Aspects of the Administration and Organization of the National Housing Corporation*. St. Michael, Barbados: National Housing Corporation.

Buttenshaw, W.R. (1906) "Barbados Woolless Sheep", *West India Bulletin* (6).

Bynoe, Marcia E. (1978) *A Study of Chalky Mount Potteries*. St. Michael, Barbados: Unpublished undergraduate paper, University of the West Indies.

Caribbeana Council (1978) *Project Design Summary*. Christ Church, Barbados: Ministry of Agriculture.

Chandler, M.J. (1981) "Early Explorations and Origin of the Cave's Name", *The*

Bajan and South Caribbean (May).

Chiapetta, Michael (1982) *Final Report for Consultancy in Educational Planning,* in Ministry of Education, Samuel Jackman Prescod Polytechnic Project Files 1977-83. St. Michael Barbados: Ministry of Education.

Chief Medical Officer (1935) *Annual Report 1933-34*. St. Michael, Barbados: Office of the Chief Medical Officer.

___(1974) *Annual Report 1972*. St. Michael, Barbados: Ministry of Health.

Clarke, Dennis (1974) *Some Aspects of the Government Housing Program*. St. Michael, Barbados: Unpublished undergraduate paper, University of the West Indies.

Clarke, J. W. (1872) "Water Supply of Island Considered", Government of Barbados, Official Gazette, No.555, August 5, in M.J. Chandler, "Early Explorations and Origin of the Cave's Name", *The Bajan and South Caribbean* (May 1981).

Clarke, Yvonne E. (1979) *The Garbage Problem in Barbados*. St. Michael Barbados: Unpublished undergraduate paper, University of the West Indies.

Colonial Office (1935) *Development and Welfare in the West Indies 1935*. St. Michael, Barbados: Advocate Company Ltd.

___(1952) *Development and Welfare in the West Indies 1952*. St. Michael, Barbados: Advocate Company Ltd.

Community Development Division (1981) "A Survey of the Clapham Community", in Arthur B. Archer et al., *Planning with People: A Case Study of the Resettlement of Residents from Emmerton, Bridgetown, Barbados*. St. Michael, Barbados: Community Development Division.

Comptroller for Development and Welfare in the West Indies (1945) *Housing in the West Indies*. Christ Church, Barbados: Office of the Comptroller for Development and Welfare in the West Indies.

Correa, Hector (1981) *Final Report*. St. Michael, Barbados: Ministry of Education.

___ (1981) *Notes on Quantitative Methods of Education Planning Applied to Barbados*. St. Michael, Barbados: Ministry of Education.

___(1981) *Preliminary Quantitative Results for an Educational Plan for Barbados*. St. Michael, Barbados: Ministry of Education.

___(1954) *Development and Welfare in the West Indies 1954*. St. Michael, Barbados: Advocate Company Ltd.

___(1960) *Barbados 1958,1959*. London: Her Majesty's Stationery Office.

Department of Science and Agriculture (1944,1945, 1947) *Annual Reports 1943-44, 1944-45, 1946-47*. St. Michael, Barbados: Advocate Company Ltd.

Desyllas, L.M. (1944) *Report on Preliminary Housing Survey of Two Blocks of Chapman Lane Tenantry*. Bridgetown, Barbados: Bridgetown Housing Board.

Devendra, C. (1972) " Barbados Blackbelly Sheep of the Caribbean", *Tropical Agriculture* 49 (January).

Emmerson, R.P.H. et al. (1969) *Barbados: Education and Priorities for its Development*. Paris: United Nations Educational, Scientific and Cultural Organization.

Fisher, Judy (1965) *Report on Chattel Housing.* St. Michael, Barbados: Town Planning Department.

Foxworthy, James E. (1974) *The Bridgetown Sewerage Project: Report on the Predesign Oceanographic Survey and the Design and Siting of the Outfall-Diffusion System.* Washington, D.C.: Pan American Health Organization.

Fraser, Henry and Ronnie Hughes (1982) *Historic Houses of Barbados.* St. Michael, Barbados: Barbados National Trust.

Gailer, J.W. (1965) *Proposals for the Development of Technical Education in the Leeward and Windward Islands and in Barbados.* London: Ministry of Overseas Development.

Gillespie & Steel Associates Limited (1975) *Feasibility Study for the Development of the Samuel Jackman Prescod Polytechnic on the Delamere Site, Bridgetown, Barbados.* St. Michael, Barbados: Ministry of Education.

___ (1977) *Samuel Jackman Prescod Polytechnic Feasibility Study for Wildey, St. Michael, Barbados.* St. Michael, Barbados: Ministry of Education.

Gittens, Timothy (1969) " Technical Education in Barbados", *Operation Beehive* 2 (December).

Government of Barbados (1946) *Development Plan 1946-56.* St. Michael, Barbados: Advocate Company Ltd.

___ (1962) *Report on Refuse Collection and Disposal.* St. Michael, Barbados: Advocate Company Ltd.

___ (1963) *Development Plan 1962-65.* St. Michael, Barbados: Advocate Company Ltd.

___ (1969) *Development Plan 1969-72.* St. Michael, Barbados Government Printery.

___ (1973) *Development Plan 1973-77.* St. Michael, Barbados: Government Printery.

Greaves, Betty Dawn (1981) *A Study of the Development of Social Services in Barbados between 1937-1945.* St. Michael, Barbados: Unpublished undergraduate paper, University of the West Indies.

Greene, Peter (1980) *News Report.* St. Michael, Barbados: The Nation.

Gurnee, Jeanne (ed.) (1980) *A Study of Harrison's Cave, Barbados, West Indies.* Closter, New Jersey: National Speleological Foundation.

___(1981) "Rediscovered After 200 years: The Development of Harrison's", *The Bajan and South Caribbean* (May).

Hanitchak, John J. (1982) *Final Report: Career Guidance and Placement in Ministry of Education*, in Ministry of Education, Samuel Jackman Prescod Polytechnic Project Files 1977-83. St. Michael, Barbados: Ministry of Education.

Hanschell, W.H.A. et al. (1979) *Report of the Commission of Enquiry into the Barbados Housing Authority and National Housing Corporation 1969-1976.* St. Michael, Barbados: Heritage Chambers.

Haslam, J.F.C. (1935) *Minority Report.* St. Michael, Barbados: Legislative Council Debates, Session 1934-35, Legislative Council.

Hercules, Dillon A. (1970) *The New Polytechnic*. St. Michael, Barbados: Samuel Jackman Prescod Polytechnic.

Hewitt, Ken (1975) *Report on the Operations of the National Housing Corporation*. St. Michael, Barbados: National Housing Corporation.

Horn, Edwin (1957) *Report of a Survey on Housing*. Christ Church, Barbados: Comptroller for Development and Welfare in the West Indies.

Howard Humphreys & Sons (1965) *Sewage Disposal of the City of Bridgetown*. London: Howard Humphreys & Sons.

Hughes, Griffith (1750) *The Natural History of Barbados*. London: Griffith Hughes.

Hunte, Wayne (1983) *The Monitoring Program for the Bridgetown Sewage Plant*. St. Michael, Barbados: Ministry of Health.

Hurley, Marcia (1981) *A Study of the Implementation Process of the Bridgetown Sewerage System*. St. Michael, Barbados: Unpublished undergraduate paper, University of the West Indies.

Husbands, Sandra (1979) *The Development of the Government's Low-income Housing Policy and its Achievements: 1937-1979*. St. Michael, Barbados: Unpublished undergraduate paper, University of the West Indies.

Inter-American Development Bank (1975) *Project Report, Barbados: Bridgetown Sanitary Sewerage System Project*. Christ Church, Barbados: Inter-American Development Bank.

___ (1976) *Project Report, Barbados: Samuel Jackman Prescod Polytechnic Institute*. Christ Church, Barbados: Inter-American Development Bank.

___(1977) *Annual Report 1976*. Washington, D.C.: Inter-American Development Bank.

___(1981) *Annual Report 1980*. Washington, D.C. : Inter-American Development Bank.

Jackson, Richard M. (1964) *Report on Local Government in Barbados*. St. Michael, Barbados: Government Printery.

Jordan, David D. (1984) *A Social and Economic Cost-Benefit Analysis of the Bridgetown Sewerage Project*. St. Michael, Barbados: Unpublished undergraduate paper, University of the West Indies.

Lashley, T.O. (1945) *Report on a Housing Survey of Eight Slum Tenantries in Bridgetown*. St. Michael, Barbados: Bridgetown Housing Board.

Laurie, Keith (1971) "The Barbados Blackbelly Sheep" , *The Bajan and South Caribbean* (June).

Lavender, J.G. (1970) *Technical and Vocational Education in the Commonwealth Leeward and Windward Islands: A Summary of Proposals*. St. Michael, Barbados: Institute of Social and Economic Research, University of the West Indies.

Lawler, Matusky & Skelly Engineers (1974) *Report on the Bridgetown Sewerage Study*. St. Michael, Barbados: Ministry of Health .

Leighton, Fred (1951) *Report on Handicrafts and Cottage Industries in the British West Indies*. Kingston, Jamaica: Government Printery.

Lewis, Delbert E. (1982) *Final Report*, in Ministry of Education, Samuel Jackman Prescod Polytechnic Project Files 1977-83. St. Michael, Barbados: Ministry of Education.

Ligon, Richard (1657) *A True and Exact History of the Island of Barbados*. London: H. Moseley.

Livestock Extension and Development Division (1974) *Annual Report 1974*. St. Michael, Barbados: Livestock Extension and Development Division.

Lovell, Antoinette P. (1980) *The Barbadian Economy between 1925 and 1946*. St. Michael, Barbados: Unpublished undergraduate paper, University of the West Indies.

Lydekker, R (1912) *The Sheep and its Cousins*. New York: E.P. Dutton.

Macpherson, John (1946) *Development and Welfare in the West Indies 1945-46*. St. Michael, Barbados: Advocate Company Ltd.

McEvers, Norman C. (1974) *Socioeconomic Evaluation and Manpower Assessment in Relation to the Proposed Samuel Jackman Prescod Polytechnic and Student Revolving Loan Fund Projects*. Christ Church, Barbados: Inter-AmericanDevelopment Bank.

Merritt, W.W. (1951) "Some Aspects of Refuse Disposal in Urban and Suburban Areas", in Sanitation Department, *Annual Report 1950*. St. Michael, Barbados: Sanitation Department.

Meynell, P.J. (1982) *Baseline Survey of the Marine Environment Around the New Bridgetown Sewage Outfall*. St. Michael, Barbados: Ministry of Health.

Ministry of Education (1963) *Annual Report 1960-63*. St. Michael, Barbados: Ministry of Education.

___ (1969) *Proposals for the Establishment of the Samuel Jackman Prescod Polytechnic*. St. Michael, Barbados: Government Printery.

___(1977-83) *Samuel Jackman Prescod Polytechnic Project Files 1977-83*. St. Michael, Barbados: Ministry of Education.

Ministry of Health (1967-83) *Pulverization Plant Project Files 1967-83*. St. Michael, Barbados: Ministry of Health.

___(1973) *Manpower Requirements and Educational Planning: An Exploratory Survey and Its Implication for the Development of Trades Training*. St. Michael, Barbados: Ministry of Education.

___(1980-82)*Pulverization Plant Project Files 1980-82*. St. Michael, Barbados: Sanitation Service Authority.

Moldstad, John (1982) *Final Reports of Work Activities and Recommendations*, in Ministry of Education, Samuel Jackman Prescod Polytechnic Project Files 1977-83. St. Michael, Barbados: Ministry of Education.

Moore, Merton C. (1981) *A Cost Benefit Analysis of the Bridgetown Sewerage Project*. St. Michael, Barbados: Unpublished undergraduate paper, University of the West Indies.

Motta, Sam and Hayden Blades (1975) *A Preliminary Design for a Regional Livestock Complex*. Georgetown, Guyana: Caribbean Community and Common Market Secretariat.

Moyne, W.E.G. et al. (1945) *West India Royal Commission Report 1938 -39.* London: Her Majesty's Stationery Office.

National Housing Corporation (1978-81) *Ferneihurst Housing Project Files 1978-81.* St. Michael, Barbados: National Housing Corporation.

___ (1980) *Annual Report 1979-80.* St. Michael, Barbados: National Housing Corporation.

Organization and Management Division (1976) *Organization and Management Study: The National Housing Corporation.* St. Michael, Barbados, National Housing Corporation.

Ott, Bruce (1973) *Report on Coral Reef Survey North of the Deep Water Harbor.* St. James, Barbados: Bellairs Research Institute.

Oxtoby, Robert (1974) *The Development of Technical and Vocational Education and Training in Barbados.* St. Michael, Barbados.

Patterson, Harold C. and James J. Nurse (1974) *A Survey on Sheep Productions in Barbados 1972.* St. Michael, Barbados: Ministry of Agriculture.

___ (1976) *The Barbados Blackbelly Sheep.* St. Michael, Barbados: Ministry of Agriculture.

Peat Marwick (1981) *Barbados Industrial Development Corporation Organization Study.* St. Michael, Barbados: Barbados Industrial Development Corporation.

Peck, G. S. (n.d.) *A Physical Oceanographic Study off the Southwestern Coast of Barbados.* St. James, Barbados: Bellairs Research Institute.

Pinckard, George (1806) *Notes on the West Indies.* London: Longman, Hurst, Rees and Orme.

Price, Sanka (1983) "Preparing for Future Technology as Emphases and Values Change", *The Bajan and South Caribbean* (February).

Public Investment Unit (1977) *Discussion Papers.* St. Michael, Barbados: Ministry of Finance and Planning.

Pulverization Plant Project (1967-83) *The Pulverization Plant Project Files 1967-83.* St. Michael, Barbados: Ministry of Health.

Rastogi, R.K. et al. (1980) "Barbados Blackbelly Sheep", in I.L. Mason (ed.) *Prolific Tropical Sheep.* Rome: Food and Agriculture Organization.

Roach, Roderick G. (1984) *The Implementation Process: An Examination of the Bridgetown Sewerage Treatment Project.* St. Michael, Barbados: Unpublished undergraduate paper, University of the West Indies.

Rose, J.C. (1959) *Planning and Housing in the West Indies.* Port-of-Spain, Trinidad: Federal Ministry of Labor and Social Affairs.

Samuel Jackman Prescod Polytechnic (1980-83) *Report Files 1980-83.* St. Michael, Barbados: Samuel Jackman Prescod Polytechnic.

Sanitation Department (1947) *Annual Report 1946.* St. Michael, Barbados: Sanitation Department.

Schomburgk, Robert H. (1848) *The History of Barbados.* London Longman, Brown, Green and Longmans.

Sengupta, Shyamadas (1974) *Handicrafts of Barbados.* St. Michael, Barbados; Barbados Industrial Development Corporation.

Senn, Alfred (1946) "Report to British Union Oil Company Ltd.", in M.J. Chandler, "Early Explorations and Origin of the Cave's Name", *The Bajan and South Caribbean* (May 1981).

Shurcliff, A.W. et al. (1968) *Development in the Eastern Caribbean Islands: Manpower Surveys in Barbados.* St. Michael, Barbados: Institute of Social and Economic Research, University of the West Indies.

Stanley, R.C.S. et al. (1943) *Housing in Barbados.* St. Michael, Barbados: Advocate Company Ltd.

Statistical Services Department (1978) *Annual Overseas Trade 1978.* St. Michael, Barbados: Government Printery.

Sutter, Otto L. (1970) *Schedule of Accommodation: The Permanent Structure of the Samuel Jackman Prescod Polytechnic.* St. Michael, Barbados: Ministry of Education.

The Advocate-News (1981) *News Report.* St. Michael, Barbados: The Advocate-News.

The Barbados Daily News (1967) *News Report.* St. Michael, Barbados: The Barbados Daily News (October 31).

The Nation (1978) *News Report.* St. Michael, Barbados: The Nation.

___ (1980) *News Report.* St. Michael, Barbados: The Nation.

___ (1983) *News Report.* St. Michael, Barbados: The Nation.

___ The 1933 Committee (1935) *The 1933 Committee Report.* St. Michael, Barbados: Legislative Council Debates, Session 1934-35, Legislative Council.

Town Planning Department (1970) *Physical Development Plan for Barbados.* St. Michael, Barbados: Government Printery.

Toretta, Paul (1983) *Bridgetown Sewage Treatment Plant, Contact Stabilization Unit: Performance Evaluation*, in Ministry of Health, in Ministry of Health, Bridgetown Sewerage Project Files 1977-83. St. Michael, Barbados: Ministry of Health.

United Nations Educational, Scientific and Cultural Organization (1974) *Barbados: Prospects for Educational Development.* Paris: United Nations Educational, Scientific and Cultural Organization.

United States Agency for International Development (1978-82) *Greenland Sheep Development Project Files 1978-82.* St. Michael, Barbados: United States Agency for International Development.

Urrejola, Herman (n.d.) *Project Report*, in Project Execution Unit, Samuel Jackman Prescod Polytechnic Project Files 1977-83. St. Michael, Barbados: Ministry of Education.

Vaughan, Jeanette P. (1970) *A History of the Progress Made Since 1960 in the Primary, Secondary and Tertiary Fields of Education in Barbados.* St. Michael, Barbados: Unpublished undergraduate paper, University of the West Indies.

Vezina, Robert R. (1972-73) *Sea Water Quality and Plytoplankton of Inshore Waters of Barbados: A Study of the Effect of Organic Pollution in a Tropical Environment.* St. James, Barbados: Bellairs Research Institute.

Waldron, Mary (1982) *The United States of America's Involvement in the Tourist and Manufacturing Industries of Barbados*. St. Michael, Barbados: Unpublished undergraduate paper, University of the West Indies.

Wason, Alwyn T. and Louis B. Redman (1967) *Report on Refuse Collection and Refuse Disposal*. St. Michael, Barbados: Ministry of Communications and Works.

Welch , Joseph N. (1977) *A Study of the Development of Solid Waste Disposal System in Barbados During the Period 1957-1977*. Mona Jamaica: Unpublished graduate thesis, University of the West Indies.

Wiles, D.A. et al. (1953) *Report of Minor Handicrafts Development Committee*. St. Michael, Barbados: Government Printery.

Zanten, W.A. (1962) *Refuse Collection and Disposal*. Washington, D.C.: Pan American Health Organization.

6
ANALYSIS

Our analysis, not assuming a singular process, has been dimensionalized so as to avoid disparateness, clarify the reference system, and promote analytical pluralism. We reiterate that analysis should attempt to be multifaceted, unicausal explanations are inadequate, social reality represents a complex of forces, dynamics and relations, analysis is not bias-free and cannot fully capture reality, analysis is complementary, and not substitutable, analysis is not to be equated with quantification, and that multilayered reality is not homogeneous.

We present results of analysis by means of a multidimensional construct, which is predicated on the premise that development project has to be viewed in the context of many parameters, such as history, political will, economic soundness, social structure, and organizational resources. The critique is ex post, a posteriori, disaggregated, quantitative, qualitative, and interproject. The dimensions interlock and interpenetrate. Analysis relates to the inproject as well as postproject periods of the sample Projects. Our position (Sabatier, 1986) is that analysis must take account of how project evolves, behaves, and adapts over a period of time. These dimensions are theoretical, institutional, formative, sectoral, policy, ethical, social, legal, political, economic, financial, organizational, environmental, technological, comparative, international, and measurement.

A range of caveats, cautions and explanations are in order now. The dimensions are analytically distinguishable, but they are not separable functionally nor do they exist in self-containing segments. They blend into and overlap with each other. Not only are problems in various dimensions linked but they are cumulative, with reality exhibiting continuum. We separate, as far as possible, facts from judgements, do not intend to miss the wood for the trees, and recognize that achievements tend to go wrong over time with no unmixed or continuous success and quick-fix solution.

We are aware that no analysis is complete and that analysis must be made in the face of incomplete information about project processes and behaviors that are dynamic, nonlinear, lagged, stochastic, interactive, and intricate. We are mindful of the pitchfork effect in which one or two weak aspects are allowed to color the whole evaluation of a project. Notwithstanding generality, no two projects are alike; each has its own particular history, features, dynamism, and trajectory.

Theoretical Dimension

The sample Projects and the phases of the project cycle relate varyingly to the theoretical strands that have emerged in recent times to address projects. Two projects - Greenland and Cave - corroborate Hirrschman's principle of the hiding hand (Hirschman, 1967), underscoring that project is so complex and intertwined that comprehensive planning is almost impossible, since implementation is fraught with uncertainty and unpredictability. In keeping with the principle, the Projects revealed a variety of complex side-effects in design and the limitations of comprehensive planning. A combination of factors and events - a hiding hand - compensated during execution for deficiencies in planning.

Rooted in the formal policies of international funding and technical assistance agencies, the second strand formulates that successful implementation rests on comprehensive planning, appraisal, activation, organization, and systematic management procedures. Gittinger (1972) notes that careful project preparation in advance of expenditure ensures that efficient use of resources and timely implementation. Substantial resources were invested in feasibility analysis and appraisal - Polytechnic and Bridgetown projects for instance - implying that the more elaborate the feasibility analysis, the greater the probability that the project would be successfully implemented and operated.

The third strand, based on quantitative analysis, applies appraisal methods for viable resource allocation, as was seen in nearly all our Projects. It reasons that projects must be planned in their entirety as complex sets of interrelated activities within an integrated management cycle. The approach, as Esman and Montegomery note (1969), is one which applies logic to organizational performance, identifies the interrelated factors of an action system, phases timing of related activities, and controls operations through the use of advanced tools.

Next, the blueprint approach, also known as the project cycle approach and the topdown approach, divides the project cycle into discrete stages - design, implementation and, evaluation. On the basis of replicability and prefeasibility, projects are identified and prepared in detail sufficient for assessing their economic, financial, technical and organizational feasibility by means of established techniques. The approach considers economic and environmental systems, establishes a methodological base, sees a project as a means to push the production possibility curve outwards (Coverdale and Healey, 1987), comes with a time-bound and mechanistic delivery system, emphasizes planning, and it is personnel-intensive (Roe, 1991). The approach works best with capital-intensive projects in which large resources are utilized in implementation, normally resulting in physical assets, i.e. roads, bridges, warehouses, plants, and so forth. This is in evidence with respect to the Cave, Pulverization, Polytechnic, Bridgetown and Ferneihurst projects.

The design approach is premised on the interaction of design, implementation and evaluation throughout the life of the project, in contrast to the compartmentalization of the blueprint approach, for example, initial design, implementation, redesign, implementation, rolling implementation, and so on. The design approach is iterative, participatory, and open-ended. Ferneihurst, more than any other Project in our sample group, evinces this approach, even if participation in the process was not entirely satisfactory. The inadequacies of the blueprint approach lead to the formulation of the adaptive approach (Rondinelli and Ruddle, 1977). It is more applicable to the rural and social sectors since the activities and reactions of the target-group members determine the success or failure of projects. The approach avoids imposed rationality from external (Handicraft and Ferneihurst) sources, utilizes existing local (Handicraft and Ferneihurst) support systems and seeks compatibility with the local conditions (Cave), ensuring that there is a measure of harmony with existing conditions.

The participatory or bottomup approach is sensitive to social and political issues, involves people in decision-making, stresses people's empowerment and self-reliance (Chambers, 1987; Paul, 1989; Oakley et al., 1991), highlights people as the ultimate purposes of development effort, emphasizes that well-being is fostered not only by production of goods and services but also security, self-esteem and natural environmental services, participation is seen as an essential factor for project success (Kottak, 1985), a flexible learning approach in projects actively emerges (Korten, 1980), is responsive to coevolutionary development (Norgaard, 1988), allows a more interactive data-gathering than expensive time-consuming data-collection (Kahn Kaen University, 1987), and development initiatives spring from within the local community (Lecombe, 1986). While other sample Projects played a marginal role in these processes, the Bridgetown Project actually sought and enlisted the participation of the target group. The habit of viewing the Projects as self-contained limited activities, rather than as a set of related functions designed to achieve larger development goals, is perceptible. Equally observable is the tendency to select projects on the basis of the total money available for investment rather than on the basis of productivity or potential development impact.

Formative Dimension

The Projects' management was more topheavy and hierarchical than participative and synergistic. The actual Project developments were not always consistent with the project cycle. The project cycle had to adapt to the needs of the Projects because sometimes the phases overlapped. The Projects did not always go through all the phases fully. In some cases, the project cycle was shortened. Besides, occasionally an unfinished conceptual or formulative task was taken up much later when the project cycle ran far into, for instance, the approval phase. Noteworthy too is that not all the eight phases of all the seven Projects were equally complete and developed. Within the same Project, not all the phases were uniform in coverage or depth. Some phases were, in fact, sketchy and information was unavailable, not shared, or did not exist. Within the same Project, not all components or elements were equally covered.

The initial phases were reasonably planned. They, however, experienced lapses and lags at the subsequent phases. Phasing a Project and timing its activities were not always in keeping with each other. Several Projects tended to move on in spurts rather than maintaining a steady continuity. Several phases were run almost concurrently. Even different parts of the same phase were done in several instances at different times.

Time was not properly managed in that delays occurred. Time was consumed by lengthy negotiations, protracted loan agreements, slow staff recruitment, and tardy materials procurement. The tasks were not performed in correct sequence and synchronization. Delay resulted in increased cost, reduced performance, stalled decisions, and cost overruns. The cost of delay manifested in the costs of capital, disruption, redeployment and idle resources, delayed service and income, foregone opportunities, resource tieups, frustration, and uncertainty.

Conceptually, the Projects were often not perceived in their totality within the development process. They were compartmentalized among organizations, agencies, and jurisdictions. With regards to formulation, all likely versions of the Projects were not developed by careful analysis. Only a few alternatives were examined in some instances.

The application of appraisal techniques tended to be influenced by the funding agencies. From Project to Project, we have seen the evidence of using cost-effectiveness analysis and breakeven analysis. Appraisals ensured that the output targets were reasonably specified. The growth objective as well as the equity objective influenced appraisal. Growth was more stressed on the assumption of the mobilized resources yielding the maximum possible increment in total national income. Project finance received an adequate share of attention. In the financing of the Projects, external finance played a prominent role. External finance was in the form of bilateral, multilateral, long-term and medium-term interest-carrying loans with fixed schedules of debt service, grace period, drawdown period, commitment fee and repayment period. The Projects were both high-geared and low-geared. Donor financing occasioned lengthy negotiations with clear costs, i.e. time loss, project choice-related spending, design and lending conditions, donor-imposed changes, donor preferences, lead time cost, delaying factor, tying cost, front-end fees, insurance fees, bank charges, management fees, and miscellaneous charges. Some of these costs tended to reduce the Projects' net benefits and offset the gains of concessionary finance, fixed interest rate, long repayment period and nontied assistance. Risk reduction was, however, attempted by increasing design flexibility, doing feasibility studies, permitting contingency allowance and mobilizing management skills.

The financing needs were broken down into foreign exchange and local currency outlay. Terms and conditions of external financing varied according to the source of finance. Most funding agencies placed conditionalities on the proportion of the Project's costs they were prepared to finance. There was in each case a residual of local currency cost and foreign costs that was financed internally. The agencies were reluctant to finance cost overruns except under special circumstances. Such overruns ultimately became the responsibility of GOB. The organizational, social and political appraisals received limited attention. There was not much certainty if shadow pricing was done - attaching values to specific commodities (mutton, handicrafts) and services (vocational-technical education, unskilled labor). The Projects did not entail much participation by beneficiaries in initial decision-making or designing in large part due to the Projects being topheavy. Approval involved basically seeking and obtaining endorsement for the Projects or their constituent segments from some high-level GOB policy or management units. Frequently, approval had to be obtained for the different tasks and needs of the Projects from multiple organizations.

In respect of implementation, some of the Projects tended to get work done in spurts rather than maintaining a continuity. Given the dash, muddle and tumult in executing the Projects, confusion and conflict appeared, site productivity became volatile and delay occurred. Especially, lack of cooperation and coordination arose when implementation cut across several specializations, organizations, and jurisdictions. As a result of schedule slippages, the throughput time, lead time and budgeted cost had increased. Procuring the necessary goods and works consumed a great deal of effort, planning, money, and time. Delays in procuring compounded into further delays and escalated costs for some of the Projects. Costly mistakes were made, schedule disruptions occurred, and adequate forward planning was not in place. The transfer of funds from the donor to the recipient was slow - taking an average of two years to get the loan fully approved. Some of the operational techniques used were Gantt chart, critical path analysis, performance evaluation review technique, logical framework analysis, procedure diagramming, and line of balance. Serious technical problems concerning architecture, engineering and soil analysis tended to be relatively infrequent. Useful implementation techniques - closing the project gap, evaluating project progress, reporting system, and prior analysis of projects - were not brought into sharp relief. Sound project scheduling - ensuring timeliness and resource availability, doing revision and updating, and identifying and resolving problems - was not well-established. The executing agencies - relying in some instances heavily on external organizations and contracting out work to consultants, contractors and subcontractors many of whom were foreign-based - tended to get into dependency relations, i.e. dependence on a long, and often uncontrollable, sequence of cause and effect relations which showed signs of distress and obscured the probability of quick and transparent action.

With regards to reporting, while there were attempts to improve communication and to match information flow to needs, it was not enough to counter anomalies and irregularities. The termination phase was not fully planned and properly carried out. The period between project completion and project operation was underestimated. Evaluation was a weak spot, especially indifference to ex post facto evaluation and nonutilization of ongoing periodic evaluations. Evaluation findings, even when and where they were available, were not put to use because they aroused fear of loss of prestige. The findings tended to produce resentment and defensiveness because they seemed to question managerial competence.

Greenland

The Project established a Blackbelly sheep breeding station and completed sheep feeding trials. It facilitated sheep breeding at home and abroad by means of husbandry, replacement, and multiplication. It restrained indiscriminate breeding and interbreeding. Pasture management was done by the Ministry of Agriculture's Animal Nutrition Unit, Grassland Research Station and Soil Conservation Section. The Caribbeana Council and the United States Peace Corps lent assistance to sheep registration. The logical framework analysis, relating inputs to outputs, was used.

Yet, it was a difficult venture with ambitious components built into it. The sense of direction was somewhat diluted. The initial attempt to produce top-quality mutton and multiple lamb births did not succeed. The Project's design may not have been based on a valid theory of cause and effect. It could not meet its commitments under the Caribbean Food Plan. The services of the geneticist and other specialists were produced perfunctorily. Work on assessing the breed's genetic and productive potential was not sustained. Crossbreeding was discontinued subsequently because of undesirable genetic traits and costly maintenance. Conducting on-site training on sheep husbandry was unsuccessful. Sheep registration eventually petered out. Unexpected delays, cost escalation and tardiness in decision-making produced long gestation in that the Project did not yield benefits readily. The sheep farmers' response was cursory and conditional. Many farmers seemed to perceive that the Project was shrouded in secrecy right from the outset and the Project's developments were not properly communicated to the target group.

Deadlines were not met and targets were not reached on several occasions. The Project's promotion was low-key and intermittent. The commercialization drive did not work adequately. Land and farmer identifications were not fully made. Production incentives were not fulfilled. The private sector's participation in the Project did not work out as planned. The executing agency did not demonstrate sufficient familiarity with standard management practices. No project coordinator was ever appointed formally. Working relations among the participating groups and pcrsonnel were strained. The financing was tied to accepting overseas consultants and to purchasing certain goods and services from the donor country. Budget failed to maintain parity with subsequent project developments. Reporting was superficial and episodic. No firm periodicity or reporting format was laid down. The Caribbeana Council was accused of fund misappropriation in the closing weeks of the first year (Interview, 1983: May 27). Not much advance planning was done as regards termination. With the closing of external financing in 1982, the Council disappeared quickly. The relations between the Council and the Ministry project staff deteriorated. The Council's performance in technical assistance, on-site training, workshop session, sheep registration, artificicial insemination, taste testing trail, fund management, and equipment/material control left much to be desired.

Handicraft

The industry was structurally and functionally reorganized and expanded, managerial and technical tasks were redefined, training of 1,150 people in different craft areas was completed, handicraft competitions and exhibitions were held, independent craft producers grew in number, a register of independent producers was developed, a product catalog was published, the trademark 'pride craft' was registered, a central marketing agency and retail outlets were opened, sales grew from BDS$102,157 in 1974-75 and BDS$83,000 in 1975-76 to BDS$389,000 in 1978-79 and subsequently BDS$1.1m., production-purchasing-marketing systems were redesigned, research and design capability was improved, standardization was ensured, product development was diversified, working space was expanded at the BIDC workshop and producer homes, the former Handicraft Development Center was reorganized and expanded, handicraft skills were developed, production was increased, product quality was improved and standardized, the raw material base was expanded and promotion and marketing strategies were developed. The number of producers grew from 40 in 1975 to 139 in 1979. During the same period, the use of the consignment system grew from five consignees to 120. Then again, failure to form craft cooperatives, the paucity of training and purchasing centers and the delay in personnel selection and appointment constrained the Project's formative stage.

Cave

The entrance area was reshaped to give as natural an appearance and contour as possible with pockets left in the limestone to encourage the growth of mosses, ferns and indigenous vegetation which commonly grow in and around limestone cliffs. The blasting was carefully done to avoid damaging the structural integrity of walls and ceilings. Cave walls were gouged, textured and roughened to simulate natural cave passageways. Interior trails were paved and underground modifications were carried out. Paved trails were widened and facilities were added to accommodate underground vehicles. Special lighting effects were put in place in several locations to enhance the Cave's beauty. Underground lighting was used to bring out the brilliant colors of the pools. The Visitors Center was built to blend into the natural limestone contour. The coordination of work between consultants and the executing agency was good. The transfer of personnel from the surface to underground work proceeded smoothly. Progress schedules were used which provided necessary data and benchmarks for setting out work.

Setbacks included ceiling collapse during tunnelling, subsoil problem in the upper passage, personnel problems in the executing agency during April-December 1977, instability in the management structure, and a cost overrun rate of 178%. As many as three project managers were hired between 1975 and 1981. The management did not have a complete set of architectural plans for surface development. Budgets were revised and material costs escalated. The investment budget relied on guesstimates. The cost of the Visitor Center was estimated without reference to square footage, furnishing, and equipping. Financial appraisal failed to take account of cave visits by residents.

Time was lost owing to temporary closure in the later part of 1977 and from January 1978 to July 1979. Downtime was experienced during the tunnelling operation in the upper passage and was discontinued in 1977 due to subsoil instability. Delays were caused by labor shortage, heavy unseasonal rains, flooding, power failure, temporary work stoppages, construction holdups, and equipment breakdown. Progress on surface development was not fast. Quick action on access road-building, land acquisition and zoning was lacking. Delay occurred during the construction of the Visitors Center between June 1980 and June 1981. Recurrent time overruns and schedule slippages occurred, e.g. December 1976, May 1977, October 1977, September 1978, October 1980, November 1980, December 1980, March 1981, June 1981, June 1981, and October 1981.

Pulverization

Alternative methods of refuse disposal and types of plant equipment were compared. Only few properties had to be acquired or resited due to the Plant's convenient location. Landscaping of the grounds enhanced the vicinity's aesthetic appearance. The Plant was built in an old low-lying quarry in such a way that noise became muffled. There was no delay in putting an implementation team in place, nor was any time lost in selecting project personnel. The Plant commissioning or startup was good. There was no industrial action. The progress reports were reasonably comprehensive. The Plant personnel received local and overseas training.

Setbacks included resiting, electrical and mechanical snags, corroded equipment, bent and twisted structural elements, damaged structural steel support system, and cracks on the physical structure. The Plant equipment lay idle since 1974 and deteriorated. The siting of the Plant at Workmans was not as ideal as it was thought initially. Concern for noise, odor, pollution and fly infestation was voiced by residents. The cost of tying to the external supplier for the future purchase of replacement equipment was high. The cost of long gestation showed up with the Plant not yielding benefits readily. Substantial foreign exchange was spent on acquiring factor services, retraining skilled and unskilled labor, and acquiring capital and replacement equipment.

Delay interfered with land acquisition, resiting, preparatory work, site clearance, the arrival of overseas technical personnel, fencing, cleanup, building access roads, tender documentation, equipment selection, fund release, running tests, electrical installation, safety provision, and final commissioning. Delay caused schedule slippages by a total of 11 weeks, extended the contract time from 30 to 55 weeks, and escalated costs. Time schedules were made and remade. Several schedule slippages occurred, e.g. completion was targeted for December 1979, March 1980, and April 1980. The lead time was drawn out to a point where as many as eight years had passed between conception and completion.

Implementation commenced without the appointment of a special execution unit. The delivered materials at the site lacked proper certification. Slow excavation work held up planned concrete work. Negotiations relating to the removal of houses from the site procrastinated. The Gantt charts were prepared insufficiently and tardily. The installation drawings for the weighbridge, the drawings for the access road and the electrical certification had not been prepared. Some raw materials were not unavailable, replacements were costly, translucent and aluminium sheets were in shortage, and transport vehicles were varyingly unavailable. The wrong indicator dial was ordered for the weighbridge. Raw materials were estimated correctly. An error in the height of the reversing discharge conveyors was detected. The four specially-supplied Bedford trucks were too tall to fit under the reversing conveyor. The original design of the two access doors was reviewed.

Problems arose concerning the unavailability of supervisory engineers needed to oversee the erection of the mechanical and electrical works. Coordination was made difficult when friction developed between the main contractors and subcontractors. The Project's staffing needs were inadequately prepared and the late negotiations for new staff resulted in delay. There was a lack of communication and cooperation between overseas suppliers and Barbados-based planners and counterparts. A fund shortage occurred because of the late submissions by the overseas engineers, and the estimates had to be upgraded to account for the deficit. Painful adjustments had to be made with respect to contracts, conditions, operations and construction to keep work in progress. There was a lack of involvement of the target group and those people who were affected by the Plant's construction.

Owing to delays experienced, many of the components of the Project during the last stages were rushed or omitted. The total running of the second line was about two days, while the Plant was planned to have been run for two weeks on a continuing basis. Both the shredders were only run together for a maximum of two hours when the Minister of Health visited the site on April 5, 1990. This was evident as the Barbados Light & Power Co. installed fuses on the same morning only, and the timers for the control panel only arrived two days previously.

Polytechnic

Carried out in 1975 and 1978, the Project's feasibility studies were informative. Appraisal was done in part by cost-effectiveness analysis. Appraisal, which took 4 months, was comprehensive and professional. Built into the appraisal were a 12.5% contingency for labor and a 10% provision for material. Extensive reporting was carried out, relating to as many as seven investment categories from engineering and management to unallocated cost. Quantity surveying, structural engineering and mechanical engineering were of acceptable standard. Construction was done in keeping with drawings and specifications. Subcontractor performance was fair in some instances. Many Barbados-based subcontractors used local materials and building components. Three units in the Complex - assembly hall, changing rooms, and kitchen/cafeteria - were built so that they could also serve as hurricane shelters.

Yet, no sound reason could be found why the Project was originally planned to be located at Delamere, an area prone to flooding. Shortcomings included lapses in security, supervision and monitoring on the site, some inadequacies in the quality of work, architectural designs lacked detail, i.e. over 600 verbal directives were issued during construction (Samuel Jackman Prescod Polytechnic, 1980-83), landscaping was not of satisfactory standard, difficulty in acquiring building materials, an inventory and identification of equipment was not made on time, and incomplete electrical installations.

No action was taken on installing the windmill at the Project site. Getting the workforce to produce reasonable output was hard. The building contractor claimed additional loss and expense. Time and cost estimates and design factors were revised several times. Physical progress lagged behind financial disbursement between June 1979 and December 1981. The cost of tying to external sources was conspicuous. Much foreign exchange was spent on acquiring factor services, retaining skilled and unskilled labor, and acquiring capital and replacement equipment. The cost of imported skills was high which comprised compensation the specialists received, remittances made by them, and compensation within the country. As many as three project managers took over and left. Subcontractor performance was not reliable in some cases.

Delay was caused by industrial action, labor shortage, bad weather, additional work, funding-agency conditionalities, building materials shortage, subcontractor runarounds, and site problems. The Project was nearly 18 working days behind schedule by December 1979, 10 weeks behind schedule by June 1980 and 14 weeks behind schedule by December 1980. It moved through a series of schedule slippages, e.g. March 1981, May 1981, August 1981, September 1981, December 1981, and February 1982. The Complex was opened in May 1982, but still far from completion. Work continued throughout 1982 and 1983. Even though the construction commenced on May 24, 1979 and the official opening took place on May 26, 1982, it was not until January 21, 1983 that the certification of completion was formally obtained. A time overrun of 138.5 working days occurred as a result.

Sewerage

The system's process was extensive, including mechanical, primary/

physical, secondary/biological, and tertiary/chemical processes. Action was taken fairly promptly in choosing a site for the treatment plant, clearing the site, selecting an alternative resettlement site and relocatingdisplaced Emmerton residents. For instance, 143 homes at Emmerton were cleared and nearly 500 people were resettled at Clapham Park. The average rate of house removal from the target area was 4 houses per week. Appraisal was done in part by means of cost-effectiveness analysis. The Gantt chart was used as a scheduling tool. The provisions in the loan agreement were complied with. By employing a 24-hour 3-shift system, several Project components were completed on schedule. Contract 2 and the institutional study were completed ahead of schedule.

To illustrate, the laying of the marine outfall by Meisener was expected to last 12 weeks, but it finished in 6 weeks. The contractor had preassembled 114 feet lengths of the pipe in Miami and brought them by barge to Barbados. Good weather condition and the preassembled pieces accounted for the shorter time period. On another note, the contractors were responsible to Lawler, Matusky and Skelly, Inc. which, apart from being consultants, acted as contract supervisor. The resident contract supervisors, acting as field engineers, were responsible to the project manager. The executing agency's technical personnel consulted with the resident field engineers and served as overall overseers. The contractors executed physical work in the field, managed labor and materials, and enforced construction schedules. Each schedule had a 600-day limit. Local construction labor was employed, viz. about 200 workers employed during construction, benefiting from income and consumption gains, and acquiring varied work experinces. Some local business-owners gained by providing support services, i.e. equipment rentals, material transportation, and car rentals.

An efficient system of reporting and feedback was utilized in respect of information generation and availability, management of the loan agreement, meeting of deadlines, and corrective action. Media reporting kept the target community informed about construction schedule, disruption, and traffic diversion.

The flip side is that all likely versions of the Project were not developed by careful analysis. Certain stipulations in the loan agreement - material procurement, competitive public bidding, committee-system operations, manual preparation - had put restrictions on the executing agency. Appraisal became questionable when the site for the River Road pumping station collapsed. Appraisal underestimated cost escalation. Extensive road repairs were not budgeted for. Errors of underestimation of the

Project costs were committed. While the marine outfall contract was within the budgeted cost and the treatment plant went over by 10%, the sewer network contract had 100% cost overrun. The Plant's capacity to service the target area was underestimated. No provision seemed to have been made to accommodate the expanding business sector and the increasing urban population. Appraisal overlooked to provide information on the system's operational and maintenance costs, amodal life expectancy, efficiency criteria, availability of skilled technical personnel to operate the Plant, and industrial waste generated in the target area. Cost-benefit analysis was not well-researched, thereby failing to identify or ascertain welfare gains, externalities, opportunity cost, shadow prices, sensitivity analysis and other social variables. PERT was not used during implementation, thereby missing the leverage of visualization, planning, time control, management information, flexibility, dynamism, critical path, scheduling, rescheduling, crashing/coordination and predictability. When delays occurred, the relationships between and among the activities were not known and there was no mechanism in place to facilitate reorganization of the work, as in the case of contract 1. If a critical path were known, management could have tried crashing as a means of speeding up the Project. There were lapses in monitoring and feedback, too.

The Project went through several schedule slippages, e.g. December 1979, September 1981, December 1981, and March 1982. The schedules were too static and too inflexible, too. Schedule slippages adversely affected contracts 1 and 3. Time loss was incurred in tendering, contract-awarding, site selection, unfavorable weather condition, work stoppage for ten months at the River Road pumping station site, resiting of resident from the target areas, soil testing, errors in laying pipelines, the redesign of the treatment plant's foundation, and unavailability of the right mix of cement. Originally scheduled for 18 months, the Project took approximately 36 months. Initially estimated at BDS$24m. and reestimated at BDS$42 m., the Project's cost had eventually climbed to BDS$43.5 m. due to inflation, accidents, redesigns, site preparation, rework, high contract prices, management inadequacy, machinery breakdown, industrial action, and additional transport cost. The cost of tying appeared in that capital equipment and periodic consultancy services had to be obtained from specified external sources. Most of the construction materials were imported as well.

Last but not least, a variety of problems, difficulties and complications arose, e.g. design error/defective work/structural collapse/shifting/ rebuilding of the River Road pumping station, vehicular damage, loss of life and serious injury at sites, traffic tie-ups and diversions, utility disruptions, road closures, inconvenience, hardship, anxiety, stress, flooding and slushing, road and sidewalk damage, incomplete and inadequate road resurfacing, lack of pedestrian and commuter safety, lack of control over excavated trenches, target-group disaffection and resistance, uncollected refuse, dust inconvenience, noise nuisance, stench discomfort, hazardous work conditions, unsuitability of soil at the Plant area, and redesign of the entire foundation of the Plant.

The consultants made cost-estimating errors, work stoppages occurred, there were construction-time cash shortfalls, prices continually rose, cement shortages caused delay, the allotted schedule of 600 days for construction could not be met, and putting down sewers on narrow roads in densely-populated areas created complications. During construction a number of pipelines were laid down erroneously and as a result lines had to be dug up and relaid, incurring higher costs and longer delays. Inadequate and inaccurate information on the underground location of utilities resulted in breakdowns, dislocations, supply interruptions, unnecessary rework, additional repairs, increased cost, time loss, and schedule slippages. The terms and conditions of the loan agreement acted in part to the detriment of materials procurement. Reports tended to be lengthy, repetitious, and time-consuming. The reporting process appeared to be rigid and did not cater for unexpected events. The French Canadians, who were working with the contractor in laying the sanitary sewers, were reported to be aggressive, did not speak or pretended not to understand English, and were reluctant to take instructions from the local construction engineers. When the system was handed over, the BWA found on checking that 1,850 laterals were left off and was forced to do a comprehensive street survey to locate the other 1,598 properties that existed within the target area. All in all, delays were caused by time loss in redesigning, site problems, errors and accidents, tendering, contract-awarding, relocation and resettlement of the target-area residents, industrial action, work stoppage, materials availability, rescheduling, and system-user connection.

Ferneihurst

Appraisal was done in part by cost-effectiveness analysis. Included as benefits were the alleviation of low-income household shelterlessness and vulnerability, family cohesiveness, cost-effective accommodation, and community awareness. The Project was executed reasonably effectively. It pushed back wastage, avoided a ragged look, saved space, and effected construction economies. There was no labor dispute. Work on access roads, site clearance and sewerage provided employment to unskilled workers. The Project offered an opportunity for the NHC personnel to utilize and improve their managerial and technical skills.

The debit was that a budget was not prepared prior to executing the Project, with the result that expenditures were recorded on an ongoing basis. The adequacy and availability of funds at the right time was impaired by time-consuming procedures. Cost economy could not be effected as much as desirable. Implementation was affected by inclement weather, materials shortage, delayed purchasing and delivery, cashflow problems, inadequate site supervision, centralized financial and purchasing procedures, absence of on-site purchasing and delivery, indifferent organizing and scheduling, and redtape. Materials estimate was not done in an orderly way. A systematic quantity survey was lacking. The quality of materials control was variable. Early scheduling of the required number of personnel to work on the site was not done. Appraisal suffered due to the public sector often being seen as an entity promoting higher employment. A time-lapse occurred between the construction's start - January 3, 1979 - and the Town Planning Department's approval - November 16, 1979. Record-keeping and reporting was neither timely nor comprehensive. A number of planned ancillary elements were not implemented, e.g. a day nursery, a community center/pavilion, and a warden's office. The sewage system that was built for the Estate proved to be insufficient. Although the housing mix was planned at a ratio of 3:1 - 90 two-bedroom and 30 three-bedroom units - it was built at 2.3:1 ratio 108 two-bedroom, and 46 three-bedroom units. A full-fledged review of postcompletion situation was lacking.

Legal Dimension

From the inception of a project to its termination, the law pervades its activities. The types of law that are germane to projects include constitutional law, legislation, institutional regulations, and judicial decisions. Also pertinent are such related aspects as registration, property rights, liability, warranty, copyrights, trademark, royalty payments, contract negotiation, materials procurement, and contract-awarding.

The sample Projects were established by organizations that were set up under the law and operated under the rules of law. It is expected that the Projects abide by and conform to the law and pay penalties for any infringement or violation of law. They are held accountable if their action violates the rights of others. Any conduct that violates the rights of others is subject to legal action, which may be in the form of civil suit or criminal prosecution. The Projects, for instance, involved zoning and regulations pertaining to licenses, permits, and rights of obstruction. There were numerous subcontractors and purchase orders for materials, equipment, and equipment rental. There were access rights and labor disputes with unions and the Ministry of Labor. There were subcontracting clauses, security provisions, safety provisions, coverage, bonding provisions, and environmental regulations. Project decisions and their implementation can cause an organization to commit acts that infringe on the rights of others or which adversely affect an entire community. A project manager needs to become familiar with the provisions of loan agreement and contracts. This is needed with a view to ascertaining performance, mobilizing required resources, avoiding breach of contract, and assessing goal advancement.

The contracts were bilateral and in writing. Some contracts were covered by the existing legislation. The contracts embodied the identity of the parties and their obligations. One party was required to perform and the other was required to provide the consideration. The contract documents were prepared in clear and unequivocal terms to avoid the problems of ambiguities, inconsistencies, and vagueness. Efforts were made to ensure that no contract was negotiated on erroneous premises and that no contract would be entertained that would be difficult to enforce. To illustrate, the Pulverization Project's negotiation and contract involved the definition of the legal obligations in respect of financing, technology acquisition, buildings, facilities, machinery, and equipment supply. It also entailed the signing of contract and agreement between the Ministry of Health as the client and the executing agency, on the one hand, and consultants, contractors, equipment suppliers and other participants on the other.

Legal and quasilegal inputs went into the loan agreement, e.g. loan, disbursement, commitment charge, interest rate, amortization schedule, repayment period, grace period, currency provision, withdrawal, additional finance, cancellation and suspension, acceleration of maturity, enforceability, arbitration, and termination. Laws related to safety, personnel, finance, pollution, land acquisition, taxes, imports, exports, foreign exchange, remittance, labor, industrial relations, building codes, zoning, supplies, compensation, tenancy, contract, sanitation, utilities, and vehicular traffic.

It was the Projects which established the performance requirements. The Project authorities intimated to the contracting organizations what they desired from the contractors/subcontractors as to the quality, quantity, delivery time, and delivery place. Attention was paid to examining the performance requirements of the contracts. Warning was issued to the contractors as to the performance deficiencies, which presented problems and grave consequences. The contract documents permitted the Project authorities to terminate contracts for default if a contractor failed to perform its contractual provisions. In the tendering process, the Projects adhered to certain long-standing procedures, such as open competitive bidding and the prevalence of the lowest bid. Under certain conditions, the authorities negotiated contracts with higher bids. The types of contracts included firm, fixed price with an escalation provision, cost reimbursement, cost plus incentive fee, and letter contract. To illustrate, the Polytechnic Project had accepted the lowest fixed price contract.

After the parties had entered into a contract, the phase of contract implementation had begun. In that phase the Project authorities attempted to ensure the provisions of the contracts and to assure that the contracting organizations complied with the provisions of the contracts. The Projects continued to closely monitor the functional activities to meet the targets and objectives. The contractors took care not to get into any breach of contract. The Projects maintained surveillance during this phase to assure that the objectives of the contract were fulfilled within the prescribed time. A system of reports and feedback operated between the executing agencies and the contractors.

Each Project authority exercised its right to inspect the perfomance before accepting and paying for it. As and when inspection was done, there were rejections of nonconformance. The Project authorities insisted on maintaining an acceptable inspection system by the contractors, giving the project managers a right to make inspections and testing while work was in process, checking the quality of work carried out, doing scheduling surveillance and requiring that records of inspection be kept complete and available to Project personnel. As the needs became more complex - such as the Cave, Pulverization, Polytechnic, and Sewerage Projects - a high and more frequent level of quality control was mandated.

Changes and modifications took place in the contractual documents. After the parties entered into contracts, it occurred that the executing agencies desired some modifications of their specifications and provisions. In those instances, the parties entered into supplemental agreements to modify the existing contracts. The changes provided flexibility in Project implementation. When the authorities exercised their right to direct the contractors to perform under changes in the specifications, the contractors were obligated to comply and subsequently claimed equitable adjustment in the contract prices.

The law of agency was in force through the project process. The ministries and cabinet subcommittees, as piloting/sponsoring agencies, had established and vetted project objectives, organization policies, and appointed implementation teams. So, the delegated authority flew down through policy-makers to project managers. But it was impossible for project managers to become personally involved with each transaction or activity. So, the authority flew down further under organizational procedures to focal points, e.g. accounting, personnel, purchasing, engineering, and so forth. For the most part, the type of authority that was recognized by law involved express authority. There was no apparent authority, while implied authority was very limited. There were instances of implied authority resulting from the conduct of the Projects in the course of implementation. There were also situations of apparent authority established by letting project personnel assume authority not originally stipulated. Project personnel were also delegated functional authority. Law and regulations had the full force and effect of the law.

Legal provisions like propriety, accountability and the due process restricted options and consumed time in building the Projects through a tangle of real-life situations. Although the contract documents had set up target time and delivery schedule, the contracting firms, more often than not, could not adhere to the scheduled time. From Project to Project, some of the contractors did not perform exactly as planned to the satisfaction of the executing agencies. This was partly due to misinterpretations which caused imperfect description of specifications. Besides, design errors, delays and cost escalations generated dispute between the GOB and the contractors and brought the parties to arbitration. Arbitration continued for about two years ending in favor of the GOB, which was awarded BDS$2m.

The Projects concerned with materials procurement and equipment selection/installation were careful about preparing need specifications. When the suppliers or the manufacturers' representatives supplied certain equipment and materials to the Project authorities, they did not always meet the required features and standards. In some instances, the equipment failed to function properly. In still other instances, subcontractor performance provided basis for liability and breach of warranty, and corrective action followed. To illustrate, in the case of the Pulverization Project when mechanical breakdown occurred at the Plant, extensive legal counsel was sought among other things. The situation was complicated by the lapse of warranties on the equipment due to the lengthy passage of time between the supply and erection of the Plant. A compromise agreement was reached when the repair costs were shared by the Ministry of Health as the piloting agency and the principal contracting agency.

Ethical Dimension

Moral and ethical values are at the core of organization management, including project management. Organization programs and responses are rooted in institutional values. Values guide, shape and exemplify organizational behavior. Management ethics influences the actions and desires that create the social impact of organizational performance. Management ethics is influenced by a number of forces present in the actual situation within which the manager must perform. While acquisitiveness, social decay, profiteering, unfair practices and corruption are known to cause declining standards and untenable compromises, professionalism, management education, media pressure, regulation and social response raise standards. The declining standards make it difficult for organization members to remain allegiant to high ethical standards.

A set of moral-ethical values lay implicitly in the unfolding of the Projects, e.g. achievement orientation, development drive, accountability, responsiveness, equity, and compassion. Project decisions were not made by project management techniques alone. From start to end in the project cycle, the critical choices included such matters as the accountability of decision-makers to the people's will, the discretion and prudence displayed in making choices among competing values, and the ethical principles that influenced the areas of operations, e.g. consultancy, contract, and procurement. These values, however, varied from project and dynamics to project and dynamics. The values continue to characterize the operation of the postproject organization to a varying extent, in the absence of which project dysfunctions are likely to escalate and even threaten the existence of organizations. For instance, the organizations are and should be accountable to a large public clientele for sustaining a set of objectives, and remain or should remain answerable to the people they serve for their actions and behavior.

A common thread running through virtually all ethical inquiries - and the sample Projects are no exception - is the need to bring together responsibility, accountability and managerial decisiveness around the critical issue of the public interest. Ethical standards assume that there are acceptable and unacceptable practices in organization management. The basis for judging such practices stems from constitutional-legal tradition, which suggests that the people are the ultimate authority and final arbiter of public activities, including regular operations and project developments. The public has a right, either directly or through representatives, to know, examine and evaluate how organizations perform their functions - for instance, whether the Sewerage Project is succeeding in making prompt in-property connections or whether the Handicraft Project is adding to industrial output expansion.

At issue here is not merely some purist idea of abstract morality. Ethics has profound practical consequences - the Projects have shown those time and time again - for member behavior and organization management, both in the effects and in the communications relayed. Frustration, dishonesty, burnout, indifference and jaded cynicism toward the job and the environment are all related to the absence of sincerity, honesty, openness, authenticity and candor among those who must work together for goal attainment. Unethical practices and behavior exist partly because of the belief that ethics and economics do not mix - which, eventually is a recipe for project dysfunction.

The opportunities for abuse of power by decision-makers are numerous and come in many sizes and shades from lawful to unlawful. For instance, project revenue from the Greenland, Handicraft, Cave, Sewerage or Ferneihurst Projects can be diverted or misused, if not carefully monitored. There is a collection of abuses which do not necessarily involve wrongful intent, i.e. gross inefficiency, neglect of duty, failure to show initiative, and unfair treatment of employees. There is also a collection of abuses sometimes within the law, but tinged with conscious intent to do wrong, e.g. unethical behavior, disregard for legislative intent, and conflicts of interest. There is, again, a collection of flatly illegal abuses, including some which are criminal, such as theft and graft, and others which are civil wrongs, such as acting beyond one's authority and violating due process of law.

Notwithstanding this fact, ethics is a neglected interest. The moral-ethical landscape is becoming cluttered. Expediency and opportunism seem to replace morality and ethics. Over the years, public trust in organizations seems to have declined - Fernehurst's supervisory agency National Housing Corporation comes to mind - especially as the organizations have become increasingly visible and involved in daily lives. Distrust and suspicion seem to have been fuelled by indiscretions, favoritism, and spoils system. The signs and signals are there - a steady decay and erosion of traditional moral values, moral ambiguity, relative morality, tangential ethical inquiry, etc.

The personal values of top managers have a strong effect on the behavior, practice and strategies the organizations demonstrate. Top management in the sample Projects has not entirely succeeded in establishing and enforcing clear policies that generally encourage ethical behavior across the board. Professionalism is at work, but professionalism rooted in moral reasoning and ethical choices is not evenly distributed at all levels. There is failure to assume responsibility for disciplining wrongdoers promptly and fairly. Inaction, delay and selective treatment set a poor example for organizations.

A high and abiding commitment to ethical behavior appears to be exceptional and low-key in the Projects. Though there are few reported irregularities, abuse, waste and carelessness, there is gnawing mistrust and suspicion among personnel. Recognition and reinforcement of and reward for certain behavioral traits - integrity, courtesy, responsiveness, fairness, fortitude - is from spotty and unclear to nonexistent. Personnel seem to face less sensational, but no less insidious, ethical problems, i.e. dissimulation, hegemonism, despotism, and authoritarianism. External controls in the form of openness, access, institutional reciprocity and public concern are nascent and uncommon.

Management education and training tends to gloss over such concerns as instilling desirable qualities, ethical values and moral principles, offering ethics education, and internalizing the values. Sensitizing personnel to ethical conduct, accountability, transparency and responsiveness to public trust are seldom widespread. Many of the unhelpful and self-serving values decision-makers and concerned participants demonstrate were internalized at early stages of the life cycle. Internal controls, in terms of personal responsibility for principled behavior, appear unevenly spread. For instance, some Project beneficiaries are reported to be careless with domestic refuse, sewage disposal, and apartment maintenance.

The relationship between client and service provider leaves room for improvement in our Projects. The relationship between employees and supervisors is far too often reduced to superficiality and caginess when it comes to setting objectives and evaluating performance. There is hardly any productive forum to air the feelings of the employees without any fear of sanction, reprisal, or victimization. Inability to maintain a level of professionalism and effectiveness stands out when suspicion, disbelief and fault-finding permeate nearly everything. It is hard to be cooperative or creative in that milieu; it is hard to seek excellence when one spends so much time and effort looking over his shoulder or covering his tracks. Cynicism and indifference result not only from dishonesty and suspicion but also grow from the perception that no one really cares.

Whistle-blowing is not yet in vogue in our reviewed Projects. There is scarcely any safe and reliable mechanism for whistle-blowing. Employees who observe or become aware of questionable/criminal practices or unethical behavior are not encouraged to report such incidents to higher-level management. There are, in effect, real constraints in small-size close-knit societies, such as Barbados in relation to reporting on discrimination, fraud, mismanagement, abuse, skulduggery, coverup, malfeasance, and deception. When confronted with specific ethical decisions, the Project management tends to adopt obstructive, defensive, or accommodative responses. Several factors militate against exposing unethical and questionable behaviors, e.g. fear of reprisal, strict chain of command, task-group cohesiveness, ambiguous priorities, wavering top-management support for high ethical standards, and lack of legislative protection to encourage whistle-blowing and public disclosure. The real challenge to bring out into the open ongoing ethical issues, which remain unreported and privatized for fear of retaliatory reaction, is yet to be met.

Policy Dimension

Policy occupies a central position in the entire project management process. An overall policy context is vital to the success or failure of development projects. Without adequate policy input, projects either become delinked from reality or get replicated uncritically without the benefit of networking. Projects succeed or fail only as they draw life from the policy environment. Poor policies leading to poor procedures can mean both routine avoidable delays and costly delays. The absence of well-conceived policies abort projects at every stage - the world is littered with the carcasses of projects that become the victims of poor planning, funding, or operational policies.

The success of project management is in many ways predetermined by the policy setting within which the project takes place. Many countries do not have a strongly-articulated and firmly-enforced policy framework to ensure effective projects. At every turn of the project cycle, such a policy - effective both through the basic fabric of the society and through specific public sector initiatives and responses - would set the framework that will encourage or allow effective management of projects.

It is noteworthy that the seven sample Projects are one of a package of several constituting major programs, which in turn articulates the implementation of even larger policies. The project activities link project objectives with program objectives, which in turn are linked with the policy objectives they support. The Projects are as good as the existing policies that guided their identification, selection, approval, and implementation. The cyclical relatinships within and between the Projects are linked together by policy. The responsibility for success or failure of the Projects spills over from the individual or the group traditionally identified as the project manager or the implementation unit and is shared by a number of participants and entities, including planners, evaluators, the central project authority, participating/collaborating organizations, and so on. Not only is the project manager a link in the chain, but the entire chain exists within a management and political environment defined, shaped and controlled by a number of explicit as well as implicit policies. Even a competent project manager is likely to be suboptimal, as we saw in the case of the Cave Project, if he operates within a policy context that renders him managerially ineffective.

The Projects are in keeping with some existing policies - policies which refer to goals made definitive by an adopted course of action, policies which correspond to goals made definitive by the adopted prescription of a course of action to guide present and future decision-making. In Barbados, there is the presence of an overall policy for executing reasonably effective initiatives, not so much to control and direct the entire range of project-specific organizations but to recognize, develop and direct interrelated activities to ensure effective projects. For the sample Projects, we now look at a number of policy issues and factors.

a. General project planning context: The overall planning infrastructure of the projects in Barbados is generally clearly delineated. To the extent that the GOB planned these Projects, provided the necessary management support and funding and rationalized the Projects in Barbados' overall scheme of operations, project management was facilitated.

b. The organizational setting: A number of organizations were included in these Projects, e.g. the planning agency, implementing agencies, funding agencies, supplying organizations, and participating/collaborating organizations. They were involved separately as well as collectively in one or several phases of the Projects either simultaneously or at different times.

c. The participation of beneficiaries: The intended beneficiaries of the Projects assumed variable roles. The beneficiaries played visible roles in the Sewerage Project. However, the value and usefulness of beneficiary participation as an opportunity to indigenize an aspect of the project cycle and adapting this to the sociocultural and management environment of Barbados, was not fully seized.

d. Evaluation status: Evaluation was not a prioritized part of the project framework right from the start, with the exception of the Sewerage and Polytechnic Projects. Much of the disappointment and shortfall of the Projects can be traced to the deficiency of evaluation. Ongoing evaluation on a regular basis, especially in all these multiyear ventures, should have been built into the project designs and carried out routinely. The timing of the postcompletion evaluation should have been more explicitly incorporated into the total project schedule. Enough attention was not paid to the fact that measuring the outcome or impact of the Projects could usually only be done after a few years had elapsed. It is a matter of policy issue that postcompletion evaluation requires not only time and effort but also finance, and managing evaluation must include acquiring and utilizing the needed resources.

e. Goal articulation: The Projects were embodiment of a set of goals. The goals for the Projects came from development plan documents, annual development reviews, executive organizations, and international agencies.

f. Role of socioeconomic institutions: Barbados used for the Projects a range of nongovernmental institutions and instruments, e.g. the family, the church, schools, nonprofit associations, voluntary organizations, business enterprises, and formal as well as informal networks.

g. A central review agency: Barbados' effort to ensure maximum utilization of its institutions and resources for effective projects lay in the designation and utilization of a central review agency - the Public Investment Unit - which, within the existing public sector framework, reviewed the Projects' development and implementation. The agency for this task has broad overarching interests covering society, the economy and the public sector authority, has access to toplevel policy units, and has a deliberate position on development.

h. Project generation within a planning framework: The Projects were generated within a planning framework. The central planning agency - the Ministry of Finance and Planning - had the responsibility for overall policy-making. A feasible number of project ideas from the operating agencies were identified and addressed in such a fashion that the most useful and attainable ones were considered, planned, implemented, and evaluated.

i. Policy monitoring: The actual success of project implementation and completion, in Barbados as elsewhere, depends on establishing an appropriate organizational structure and a set of procedures for acquiring and utilizing the needed resources. Because project demands varied and were often unique to particular situations, this led to a wide variety of organizational responses and several 'special' procedures not normally evident in ongoing activities. Examples included the Polytechnic and Sewerage Projects. Overall policy was rigid - in the case of the Ferneihurst Project - to the extent that the lack of flexibility delayed project implementation. Again, overall planning was pliant, in the case of the Cave Project, that a proliferation of structures and exception to standard policies and procedures caused unwanted entanglements. Again, with respect to the Polytechnic Project, waste in terms of nongraduation, dropout and voluntary as well as involuntary unemployment is undeniable. Remedying this situation by establishing an effective system of student selection, orientation provision, guidance, job placement and tracer services is not as focused and consistent as the situation warrants.

j. Financial resource policy: The overall policy ensuring the aggregate availability of funds in a timely fashion for efficient and effective implementation wavered. With the exception of the Polytechnic and Sewerage Projects, funding was not as regular as desirable. Funds were not properly budgeted in advance for reasonable design of such projects as Greenland and Ferneihurst. After the Projects were formulated and designed and their feasibility and claims to resources were established through the budget process, the distributions between the capital budget and the recurrent budget were not scrupulously maintained. Project management had to wait for budget approval before seeking funds for project needs and the budget was submitted on a line-item basis focusing only on inputs and costs. A separate transaction released the funds, there was preaudit of approved budget expenditures and set procedures were required to shift funds from one appropriate expenditure line to another and to shift funds from one budget period to the next - all these opened the door to costly uncertainty, interruptions, tangles, and delays for the Projects.

Fund disbursements showed that the procedures for the acquisition of equipment, supplies and contractual services tended to be complex, ponderous, and time-consuming. When disbursements became excessively legalistic, they reduced the capacity of participating/collaborating organizations to operate effectively, and caused delay and high costs, e.g. Pulverization and Ferneihurst Projects. Cash flows were not maintained to allow prompt payment when due.

The accounting systems set up for the Projects did not report spending as promptly as desirable and financial data did not become available routinely for reporting purposes. Audits were mechanically focused on detailed examination of adherence to budget categories, with disincentive to project management for exceeding detailed authorizations.

One of the weakest areas concerned project finance in relation to funds required to meet subsequent, recurrent needs. This is particularly important if project finance is provided by external organizations - especially the Polytechnic and Sewerage Projects - but subsequent operations must be funded locally. In several respects, policies were weak, e.g. budgeting an adequate flow of funds to the Projects on a multiyear project basis, providing approved funds with simple and well-defined procedures for budget modification, allowing prompt payment to suppliers without cash-flow problems, providing prompt and useful accounting data, facilitating an audit focused on outputs, and taking due account of subsequent operating needs.

k. Human resource policy: Project personnel policies did not reflect that the Projects - from Greenland through Ferneihurst - were priority activities under pressure to be started and completed as soon as possible. There were no noticeable differences between regular public sector personnel and project personnel in terms of recruitment, compensation, benefits, and employment conditions. There was no enabling mechanism in place which could attract and retain motivated, skilled and experienced personnel for the Projects, or a mechanism to acquire the best possible personnel immediately and maintain them in an environment that kept them reasonably productive. Ability to recruit quickly, ability to offer reasonable compensation and capacity to provide rewards were undermined by orthodox personnel policies.

l. Technological resource policy: All the Projects brought in and utilized a body of knowledge for project purposes. Some of this technology was based on biological services (Greenland, Sewerage), some on physical and energy services (Cave, Pulverization, Sewerage). All of the technology had to be adapted to the needs of the specific Projects and their specific environment in Barbados. The extent to which Barbados could obtain command over technology determined which and how many projects she could identify, formulate, and implement. The Projects provided technical personnel within organizations in which to work and outlets for them to utilize their knowledge and skills.

Institutional Dimension

A study of project development in Barbados cannot take a nonhistorical stance. Institutional development entails a lengthy process of experiment and adaptation that does not take place spontaneously. The institutions are like a mosaic of intentions and activities. Forging purposeful institutions is a primary means of ensuring the development of projects and the management of resources. Attention to the quality of institutional performance in projects can help to build up managerial capacity and development potential. The project organizations themselves have accumulated some experience, have tried out certain modes of action and have lived through some changes in the political, economic, and technological climate.

Colonial planning, to start with, was mainly indicative, epiphenomenal, short-term, disjointed, and descriptive. The plans resembled each other considerably, made little use of macrolevel planning and aggregative models, was mainly concerned with fiscal and economic housekeeping, and demonstrated incipient interest in production diversification. Some of the plans were little more than an accumulation of organizational statements and program breakdowns. Financed partly from metropolitan public revenues, the plans were not oriented toward production, but only infrastructure and certain social services. The priority given to each initiative was set by the metropolitan power structure according to its operational strategies. Development mainly meant growth and quantitative expansion was the route. There were neither annual reports of the plan's progress nor were the private sector investments taken into account. Individual operating agencies carried out their own program separately. The plans suffered from too much planning from above and from an overemphasis on general aggregate goals rather than specific development projects coordinated within an integrated framework. Donor preferences were accepted frequently. The link between aggregate data and specific investment choices was tenuous. The aggregation of organizational projects in various sectors lacked systemic rationale. The attempt at intersectoral coordination was inadequate.

Since independence, development planning in Barbados has been based on conventional planning theory and strategy. Reflecting conventional explanations of underdevelopment, planning tends to focus on allocating resources, not planning institutional, behavioral, and attitudinal change. Planning has virtually championed planning for growth and diversification, with it reliance on trickledown effects and catchup approaches. Consequently, planning has produced macro models, expenditure programs and policy measures, but only small and cautious adjustments to the range of choice of institutional actors and productive agents. It has not yet produced coordinated, specific and far-ranging plans for institutional change. The productive changes that have occurred have been gradual rather than structural. Planning is still hierarchical and compartmentalized, its operational mode being incremental and fragmented. Agency perceptions of reality, ideologies, values and power seem to militate against systems management. Planning is still, in some respects, intentional and projective because it does not incorporate the techniques essential to implementation. Barbados has not fully integrated project planning and overall planning. Project planning and management tend to suffer in the dearth of frequent feedback between the project planners and the central analysts.

The more recent plans, however, place stress on assessing resources and ordering priorities to assure attainable growth. Over the years, the targets have been more realistic, date are more available, and plans embrace more social, physical and managerial elements. Reid observes (1974) that development planning in Barbados is a learning process and that it has moved from microlevel organizational planning to integrated public sector investment planning. Of late, planning is being used as a strategy in promoting socioeconomic progress and structural change, as a tool of goal achievement and as a lever for securing balance and diversification in the growth process.

At the institutional level, the Central Planning Committee/Planning and Priorities Committee plays a key policy-making and decision-making role. Yet, the PPC tends to get involved in minutiae. The PIU's facilitative role in coordinating, executing and harmonizing projects of different operating ministries is noted. By virtue of its institutionalization, role, location and specialization, the Unit is in a strong position to influence project decisions. The number of development projects in Barbados at any given time is not large. It is not too difficult for the Unit to oversee, monitor, and guide the investment activities. Noteworthy also is the Unit's operational practice. There is usually a degree of task specialization in reviewing projects. The operating agencies, for instance, prepare and submit projects to the Unit. The Unit reviews the substantive merit of the submitted projects. Since both time and expertise normally are less than adequate, analysts use past reputation as an index of future performance. They tend to end up trusting and relying on some operating agencies and project personnel more that others.

It is equally noteworthy to recognize a link between management techniques and the institutional process. Such management and appraisal techniques as cost-effectiveness analysis, cost-benefit analysis, Gantt chart, logical framework analysis and critical path method - which were used during the Projects' implementation - cannot be divorced from the institutional setting. In fact, it was the latter which helped to determine whether and to what extent particular techniques or procedures could be employed. It is only where the institutional setting is clearly defined that it becomes possible to judge the worth of management techniques and operating procedures.

In any event, the Unit seems to be hindered by a shortage of qualified, skilled, and experienced personnel. The appraisal staff at the Unit as well as operating ministries is, by and large, small. They have trained personnel but can use a greater variety and spread of expertise. Project planning capacity has not yet reached many agencies. Even where it has, the degree of institutionalization is low. Institutional development - in the sense of increasing the ability of institutions to set clear development objectives and work effectively with their varied resources toward meeting them - has been difficult. Institutions in the various sectors seem to be held back by insufficient and untrained staff, overloaded services and facilities, inadequate compensation, and a counterproductive policy environment. Learning and coping take place but is overcautious, selective, and hierarchical. There is organization and management development, but it is limited and controlled. The experience gathered and the challenges faced outstrip institutional capacity. Barbados continues to be dependent on external finance and technical support for these projects. It is a case where the investment priorities seem to be influenced on the basis of which funding agency is thought to be lending for what purpose and conditionality. One comes across a situation in which the Public Investment Unit may function less for improving the allocation and management of resources than for attracting external finance.

Response from operating agencies is sometimes unsatisfactory. Some staff know little about project design and remain insecure about it. They plan projects when they have never before planned and seem to have only vague ideas as to what project planning means. Some proposals the Unit receives are in a very preliminary stage. The Unit at times has to make plans on the basis of sketchy reports and missing information. Sometimes, the officials ascribe failure to get projects approved to their inadequacies in presenting their case rather than their own inability to justify their project needs. The structure of the public sector itself is often not conducive to project planning. Resistance to project planning continues, though at a subdued level. While operating agencies may not pay needed attention to future planning, they do not want anyone else doing it for them. If there is a future, they want to control it. When the Unit gets involved as a facilitator, some agencies tend to get offended. The agencies long accustomed to deciding their own programs in conjunction with senior managers, seem to resist checks on their actions, particularly by having to relate to middle-level personnel of the Unit. Interaction between programming units in the operating agencies and the Unit at times lacks harmony. Working relations between the newer units as part of the economic affairs division and the older and more established finance division can be tense. Project planning experience has not yet permeated throughout the public sector. The operating ministries have remained in some cases somewhat aloof from the planning mainstream. The PIU's monitoring activity, having been limited to receiving and checking periodic reports from operating agencies, is not adequate. The need is high for supplementary visits to project sites to verify reports in situ and obtain a better appreciation of possible problems. Visits and in situ observations can help maintain alertness, boost morale and motivation, facilitate decision-making, and improve follow-up and reporting.

Sectoral Dimension

No sector functions in isolation from the rest of the country. Sector analysis helps resolve the questions of choice and priority, bridge the gap between macrolevel intentions and microlevel realities, determine the impact of a sector on the development of other sectors, ensure consistency in investment measures from one sector to another, and understand the relations between projects and the related sector, between one sector and another and between sector and the country as a whole.

The sample Projects represent a mix of typologies, e.g. footloose, site-bound, regulative, demonstration, experimental, diffusion, shiftable, nonshiftable, distributive, redistributive, production-oriented, and service-oriented. There are production sectors (Greenland, Handicraft, Cave), infrastructure sectors (Pulverization), social sectors (Polytechnic, Sewerage, Ferneihurst), primary sectors (Greenland), secondary sectors (Handicraft, Cave), and tertiary sectors (Pulverization, Polytechnic, Sewage, Ferneihurst). The Projects were of reasonable priority in meeting the objectives of the relevant sectors. While some Projects provide collective benefits and stimulate categorical demands, others offer divisible benefits and mobilize more particularistic kinds of demands. The Projects have varied costs, consequences and returns, benefitting users directly as well as indirectly. Successful planning and management required translating aggregate objectives into specific sectoral programs as well as specific individual projects. Too often, this process of translation is not done properly, competently, and continuously.

Greenland

The Blackbelly sheep - a small ruminant suitable for Barbados' small land mass, described sometimes as the 'national pest' and representing a hobby-type small-scale production - is estimated to be about 30,000, is an ideal crossing breed, is in great demand in many parts of the world, is favored for raising by local farmers, and is unique among tropical sheep in its prolificacy. The traditional rearing of this curious but gifted animal in small flocks by small farmers in close association with humans has rendered them intelligent and gentle. Demonstrating a unique local asset and a valuable genetic quality, the Project is involved with Barbados' natural resources with the Blackbelly sheep showing worthy traits, e.g. prolificacy, hardiness, mothering ability, extraseasonal breeding, high-quality mutton, low incidence of disease, low reactor rate, good constitution, excellent conformation, reproduction growth rate, carcass quality, and favorable weaning rate. Other notable features include the upgrading of stock by controlled breeding with superior animals, increasing productivity by feeding improved forages, controlling internal and external parasites, easy and compatible combination with other types of farming such as dairy and sheep or vegetable and sheep, withstanding high tropical temperature, showing activity and liveliness, surviving in areas of sparse vegetation, providing stud service to local farmers, and supplying food to numerous smallholders. Greenland has registered modest success in improved selection, breeding and crossbreeding, retaining breed homogeneity, pasture management, livestock research, disease resistence, useful experimental data, trying different production system, upgrading stock by artificial insemination, and embryo transplantation. 50-56% of the sheep in the island are reared by landless farmers and about 35-40% are owned by smallholding farmers. It is largely the latter group that continues to try to commercialize sheep production. The meat of the sheep is well-known for its delightful flavor. The meat is almost totally lacking in subcutaneous fat. Whatever fat there is has lower percentage of saturated fats than that of typical temperate-country mutton sheep.

In any event, the Venture's potential production capacity has not been fully realized. As a result, the genetic, nutritive and agronomic aspects have suffered. Prior to the mid 1970s, sheep production was a neglected area of the livestock production. Despite sheep-rearing in Barbados being traditionally in the hands of small farmers, this group's maximum participation has not been achieved yet. Drawbacks include indiscriminate crossbreeding, inadequate flesh on legs and loin, difficult pasture management, lean carcasses, high lamb mortality, limited milk yield, lower conformation and growth rate. Besides, pasture-grown lambs not only grow slowly than full-fed lambs but also take longer to reach market weight, and their carcasses are less tender and generally of a poorer quality. The Project is marked by uncertainty and ignorance, weak intersectoral linkages, weak extension services, lack of integration between sheep development and forage production/marketing, inability to get into semiintensive production system, weak sheep farmer organization, absence of a concentrate feed, high feed cost, defective sheep registration system, lack of silage facilities, and inadequate data base. Enhancing the value of the animal by proper selection and husbandry seems to have been scaled down. Sheep management faces problems in the scarcity of grazing land, the nutrients of the grass, the rainfall cycle, and the soil type. The long-term objective of increasing use of sheep to 35% of consumption needs and supplying 25,000 lamb carcasses of about 25kgs/yr. has been realized only partly and tardily.

Handicraft

Sectorally, the industry has contributed toward an expanded industrial base, indigenous craft entrepreneurship, creativity and cultural awareness, small-scale employment and cash income, retail marketing, decentralized production, diversified materials, designs, products, entrepreneur training, and export potential. The Project points to handicraft development in a diversifying sector where, for instance, handicraft-tourism linkage has been formed, e.g. an estimated 90% of products is sold to visitors. Unlike some foreign-owned enclave-type industry, handicraft remains indigenous, employment-generating, and local value-added. Located in urban as well as rural areas, the own-account craft producers own their tools and accessories, organize supplies, and service local/export markets. Numerous and varied products are produced by producers independently in their homes. A product-line industry, handicraft is stimulated by the twin combination of young skilled people and the availability of raw materials and industrial scrap. Handicraft skills are transferrable from producer to producer in a variety of formal as well as informal ways. Inexpensive utility crafts as well as high-quality articrafts have benefitted.

However, the industry is characterized by low productivity and low gross revenue per product. The development and commercial roles do not easily blend into each other. Relatively long training period is required during which trainees earn only modestly. The link between handicraft and other sectors is not robust. It has failed to move into waste and residue recycling. The research and development area lacks creative vigor.

Cave

The Project, featuring a scenic limestone cave of unusual and unique beauty and high amenity value with sightseeing, educational cultural and scientific interest, has enhanced Barbados as a major, attractive and popular tourist destination and provides an experience unlike anything else in nature. Situated near the geological center of Barbados, the Cave, having preserved resources in their natural conditions, contains features which compare favorably with the best of other showcaves in the world. Especially noteworthy are one of the numerous stalactites which has a diameter of over four feet and is numbered among the largest in the world, a 40-foot waterfall plunging into a pool at the lowest point in the Cave, and an underground tunnel which is 3,000 feet in length, 200 feet in depth at some points and 12 feed high and 12 feet wide. The Cave's structural features and visitor attractions stand out: thousands of gleaming and actively-growing crystal-clear stalactites and stalagmites, rushing and thundering water, bubbling stream, tumbling cascades, glistening reflection on the falling water, pure white and cream-colored formations, erratic formations, chambers, passages, halls, corridors, walls, floors and ceilings, glistening water cascades plunging downward, colored flowstones, mud-flowers, deep reflecting pools, dripping water, sparkling crystals, water-worn walls, sparkling waterfalls, rushing cataracts, breathtakingly high ceiling, snow-white walls and floor, and large cavern. Other features include viewing platforms, deboarding and strolling areas, paved graded trails, guided routes, extensive drainage, strategic indirect lighting, reshaped walls, pedestrian walk, and manmade tunnels. A number of achievements are noteworthy, e.g. tunnelling, diverting water, building dams, channeling water, installing drainage, building passageways and trails, reshaping walls, mounting underground lighting, and a scenic access road. The Cave site features several tourist attractions, e.g. ornamental plants and trees, lush tropical vegetation and an open-air flowery scenic walk with a series of citrus and fruit trees. In the lounge a boutique displays local products, and an exhibit of Arawak artifacts found in Barbados can be viewed. The downswing is that the Project operates in a foreign-dominated tourism sector with restricted local entrepreneurship and limited linkages with the rest of the sectors.

Pulverization

The Plant, along with a large-capacity sanitary landfill, is sited at a strategic location for service of the entire island, addresses high-volume waste generated by urban areas and fills a serious gap in the island's waste management. Pulverization seems to offer the best value for the investment because it is less expensive and, unlike incineration, involves no heat or chemicals. The sanitary landfill maximizes the advantages of combined collection, low capital investment, moderate operational cost, bacteria destroying the organic matter in the refuse, land reclamation and usability, and adaptability to small community. The pulverized waste is much denser than crude waste, is more compactable and homogenous, is less flammable, is less attractive to rodents and insects, breaks down rapidly, is converted back to soil in 7-10 years, is more adaptable to waste recycling, is space-saving, is less offensive, extends the life of a disposal site, is nuisance-free, and fills void.

The Project manages waste stream, maintains sanitation standards, ensures safe and reliable infrastructure, and is supportive of community well-being, service and product development, population movement, urbanization, industrialization, traffic growth, housing development, utilities expansion, and so forth. It improves the traditional method of refuse disposal, protects the infrastructure, environment and water-supply, and alleviatcs problcms of traditional disposal, viz. littering, fly-mosquito breeding, rat harborage, unsightliness, flying debris, offensive odor, inconvenience, spontaneous combustion, fire/smoke hazard, property damage and undervaluation, health risk, and pollution. The Plant services households, workplaces, open space, leisure areas, recreational facilities, utility facilities, streets, sidewalks, and neighborhoods.

At any rate, the landfill requires selected soil and cover and standby fire control as a safety measure. Leaching adds pollutants to groundwater and surface-water sources. Land space is limited in Barbados and the SSA is near the end of its tether relative to landfill sites for waste disposal. Various options for waste management - source reduction, multimaterial recycling, and waste/energy incineration - are not being pursued. The volume of residential and commercial waste continues to increase annually, viz. over 218 tonnes of waste/day. Waste stream is getting varied each year, consisting of paper, paperboard, yard wastes, metals, glass, food wastes, plastics, inorganic wastes, rubber, leather, textiles, and wood. The facilities for adequate disposal of hazardous and industrial waste are lacking. Weak enforcement and regulation with little or no deterrence to offenders continue to cause improper collection and handling, roadside dumping, refuse trails on highways, airblown refuse, and roadside litter. The regulations relating to landfill siting, closure and postclosure have not been updated.

Polytechnic

The Project responds to labor market needs and an increased intake capacity, cuts out overlap and duplication and mobilizes technical skills at one setting, enhances technical-vocatinal and artisinal training, produces outputs ranging from semiskilled/skilled operatives to technical personnel, prepares full-time and part-time trainees for direct entry into paid employment, own-account activity and further studies, plugs the gap between the number of school-leavers and the inadequate level of opportunities in education, training, employment, experience and skill-building, builds and equips a new educational complex, expands and improves teaching and management capability of staff, and strengthens human resource development and management capability of the Ministry of Education and the Polytechnic. The existing program stresses marketable skills and on-job training needs, broadens program and course base, offers courses for secondary school students and school-leavers, emphasizes short-term courses at both basic and special levels, stresses industrial attachment, liaison and apprenticeship, and supports the learning process by dealing with student health and safety, sports and clubs, financial assistance and student council.

The Polytechnic features spacious facilities, improved physical conditions, modern equipment, equipped workshops and laboratories, proper offices and layout, workable classrooms, efficient laboratory and audiovisual services, increased visibility, greater variety, improved institutional capacity, and a museum comprising relics of past technology. Six 2-storied and fourteen 1-storied building blocks built at Wildey house 22 classrooms, a visual aids room, a library, 28 workshops/laboratories, offices, assembly hall, central store, bath-toilet blocks, and support-service units. Available also are placement service, vocational guidance and counseling and staff advisory council. Financial assistance in the form of scholarship is available to eligible trainees. Faculty development is on stream, which includes overseas training, refresher training, short-course participation, workshop experience, and trainee faculty program. Teaching approach and evaluation focus on student competence in performing a specific task. Curriculum updating and development is a prior concern. Some faculty, staff and library professionals have gained from training relating to pedagogy, student enrolment, record-keeping, financial management, and accounting.

The downside is that the development of the Polytechnic as a practically and locally-oriented, adaptative, innovative and decentralized institution has not occurred as yet. Technical-vocational training is not as yet respectable as an educational attainment. Lack of flexibility in curriculum, lack of local adaptability and limited sensitivity to local conditions create a mismatch between expectations and resources. The dropout rate is high in certain skill areas, such as carpentry, joinery, masonry, and plumbing. It is common for students to leave the programs before competing to start work. The orientation to certification and wage employment, rather than self-employment and job creation, is deeply entrenched. Faculty development is restricted because of constraints. The Institution has tended to develop a rigid course structure - opportunities for course accessing, subject sampling and transferring between courses are limited, traditional pedagogy dominates, and mostly full-time courses persist. Other weaknesses in the Venture include overdependence on overseas examining bodies and curricula, lack of local input and conditions in technical education, lack of regularity in faculty development, and lack of steady contacts between faculty members and employers.

Sewerage

The Project replaces the archaic sewage disposal system - polluting water supplies, overflowing septic tanks and absorption wells, causing faecal pollution, and inducing outbreak of diseases. The first comprehensive sewage system in Barbados - showing merit good features, providing cost-effective waste disposal, and pushing modern management of community waste - the Project provides Bridgetown with a collection-disposal system, serves a target area of 0.8 sq. mile of the central Bridgetown area, addresses a target population of 37,700 consumers, and serves a port, commercial districts and residential areas of 494 acres including 3,000 user connections. The sewer system was not designed to serve the entire watershed of the Constitution River but was developed as a 'limited system' to serve Bridgetown and its immediate environs, allowing for a modest expansion of the initial service area to adjacent districts. The system has provided a conduit to convey a mix of waste materials and flushing water from the point of origin to the point of disposal. The secondary-treated effluent with chlorination is usable in irrigating crops, cooling water for turbines and airconditioning, and reclaiming. The sludge can be transported as a slurry to farmlands for use as fertilizers. The Project objectives have been attained, viz. sanitary conditions in the central part of Bridgetown have improved, the discharge of hazardous and offensive sewage effluents into open storm drains and the careenage has ceased, and hydrogen sulphide and other gases now rarely emanate from the careenage and the lower areas of the Constitution River.

The sewering of Bridgetown town promotes and protects general health and well-being, reduces health risks and hazards, maintains healthy living and working areas, produces healthy neighborhoods, improves the quality of life, facilitates slum clearance and urban renewal, improves the value of health and life in the target area, preserves the health of future generations, raises public health standards, improves personal hygiene, alleviates insanitary conditions, reduces sanitation hazards, generates civic cleanliness, improves aesthetic and functional aspects of the target area, enhances tourism, decreases infection rate, reduces sickness and absenteeism, maintains better human waste treatment and disposal, destroys excreted pathogens, contains communicable diseases, provides pollution-free drinking water, alleviates inadequate sewage disposal, averts epidemic risks, provides improved housing conditions for relocated Clapham residents, modernizes sanitation, upgrades faecal waste and domestic wastewater disposal, and promotes fitness and productivity of workforce. The flip side is that the delay in service connections exacerbates the health risk. As to the likely impact on the reduction of communicable diseases in the target area, no hard data are available as yet. The Plant operates on large quantities of water thus involving considerable outlay. The setting up of a fish farm and the recycling of water have not got underway, and so there is little or no reuse.

Ferneihurst

Ferneihurst represents a relatively new housing concept in Barbados - terrace or row housing - which has certain advantages over barrack-range, detached, or semidetached housing. Terrace housing links together under one roof independent family units and is accepted as a desirable option for comparatively dense developments in urban areas. It has a visual character and coherent architectural feature, expressing naturally the close-knit community life of the country. It represents affordable housing as a basis for long-term development and an improvement on previous housing approaches and low-cost accommodation lacking space, ventilation, and sunlight. Furneihurst promotes multiple housing, which continues to expand in Barbados in response to the demand for it and the need to make the most of the limited land space available for house-building. The Complex - although not entirely completed until 1981 but tenants moving in as early as December 1979 - reflects the shortage of low-rental accommodation in the country. Of about 5,000 residential units in 31 rental housing estates, Ferneihurst serves a part of Barbados' tenant population. It prudently uses scarce housing land in a high-density urban area like Black Rock. Ferneihurst - located in the midst of a largely urban residential area and being part of metropolitan Bridgetown - is served by available utilities, surface transportation, bus routes, highway communication, shopping centers, retail outlets, general businesses, medical centers, schools, clinics, hospital, church, other urban amenities, and housing estates.

The Project provides medium-density housing by use of two-storied terraces, wall structures with corrugated asbestos roofs, a statement about existing values, resources and orientation, a quiet and relaxing ambience in the Estate, well-designed family units linked together under one roof, a more economical than comparable type of housing, 154 terrace units, basic shelter, and safe and sanitary housing for families of modest or low income. In addition, the Project alleviates poor housing and living conditions causing disease conditions and accidents, houses low-income consumers and minimizes their living and transport costs, responds to the private sector's failure to produce and distribute a socially acceptable supply of housing, caters to consumers who cannot afford or do not want to move into home-ownership, produces a safety net for those who cannot or do not make out, provides a bundle of services in relation to shelter, family life support, recreation and community living, charges rent which are relatively low and remain at the same level for a longer time, and shows the public sector's participation in housing and land/property market and commitment to provide the low-income households with affordable accommodation.

Each unit features a front patio for relaxation, a compact internal layout, an attractive and new elevational appearance, adequate insulation, greater degree of privacy, cleanliness, openness, functionality and variety, garden space, better health and sanitation standards; every room is directly or indirectly crossventilated, improves safety, the roof is placed to provide permanent protection and continuous ventilation, and waterborne toilet facility. Improved housing at the Complex has reduced the hazards of poor living, viz. overcrowding, higher incidence of fire, higher rate of home accidents, rat bites, poor lighting, inadequate locks, poor ventilation, insanitary conditions, and inadequate kitchen equipment.

Yet, the prejudice against terrace or row housing continues, with multiple-type housing associated with the fear of loss of privacy. The concern is real that the Ferneihurst housing does not decline into residualization, moving toward a position in which it provides a safety net only for those who, for reasons of low income and other disabilities, cannot or do not wish to obtain suitable accommodation elsewhere. Residualization almost certainly tends to involve the lowering of status and increasing the stigma attached to public housing. Housing has long delivery schedules, and Ferneihurst is no exception. The final cost of low-cost housing such as the Ferneihurst Project tends not to be as one may think (Pandor, 1980). The factors which push cost per unit are insufficient use of prefabrication, rising construction cost, inflexible building system, high-cost capital, land scarcity, rising development costs and institutional weaknesses, high transport cost, lengthy period of construction, limited use of advanced building techniques, and absence of appropriate building and planning codes. Various sectoral initiatives, following Ferneihurst and similar low-cost housing projects, have not been worked through, including housing subsidy policy and rate, building and planning codes, building regulations, rental policy, multiple rental and land/property market involvement, low-cost building technique development and materials research, and new structural materials.

Social Dimension

Some social values and social priorities implicit in the Projects point to distributive justice, opportunity creation, poverty alleviation, and dependency reversal. Demonstrating social significance and soundness, the Projects represent attempts at improving condition of various income groups by distributing income and benefits, increasing the efficiency of human productive capacities, promoting indigenous resources, pushing human resource development, and serving a clientele group. The Projects, rooted in the Barbadian society with a history of colonialism, domination and class division, exhibit certain operating culture. A mix of values, beliefs, norms, attitudes and behaviors drove the project-building process. The power and person culture, more so than the role and task culture, became prominent. Each of the Ventures has made an impact on people. New opportunities for work, income, leisure, or training - which ultimately affect bevavior - have been created.

The use of concepts and tools, such as consumer surplus, willingness to pay, consumption weights, beneficiary identification and savings premium illuminates the Projects' social significance, meaning, and issues. The Projects have extended social development in Barbados, which is equal to the difference between the social value of the benefits generated and that of the resources used. The Projects' net contribution to social development is multiple. The social value of some of the Projects, for instance Polytechnic and Ferneihurst, is considered more than their efficiency value. But resources tended to be misdirected in some respects. For example, too many resources were oriented toward input cost rather than output value. Some social costs were also ignored. Certain outputs are deliberately undercharged or sold for less than their socioeconomic value. The Pulverization Project supplies output on a no-charge basis, and the Sewerage Project supplies output for less than its worth. As yet, efforts in supplying these outputs at prices which equal the marginal social cost are in wanting.

The Projects in our sample, which are too top-down and do not involve much participation by beneficiaries, not only benefit people but also inflict pain, perhaps unintentionally. Project choice can create conflict, stress and dissonance, and undermines consensus. When one project is chosen and implemented, the other alternatives are turned down. Noteworthy is that a project has little chance of sustainable success if it runs counter to or ignores the basic traditions, values and social organization of the intended beneficiaries, or if its objectives are too abstract to be understood by them or too remote from their everyday experience. Despite the Projects' logic and rationality, the concerns, cleavages, schisms, anxieties and tensions of the real social situation appear repeatedly. Despite varied benefits, some of the Projects tend to make for differentiation, polarization, social tension and income inequality.

The Projects, not using much user participation and facing special problems in obtaining the acceptance and cooperation of the target groups involved consultant participation - consultants going into the Project entities, conducting or initiating studies, making observations, compiling information, analyzing, designing, and making recommendations. The approach was essentially consultant-centered, those most involved in using the organizations were peripheral to the project-making process. The Projects could not make use of either representative participation - allowing for a working group which included both consultants, analysts, and users - or consensus participation - users being involved in the analysis, design, and implementation processes. In the aggregate, the ability of the participating organizations to coordinate and control activities, responses and resources was not as strong and was complicated by personal differences, sectoral factionalism, and organizational rivalry.

Greenland

The Project, based on demonstrating sheep-raising skills, served to spread its potential within a crosssection of Barbadian farmers with varying degrees of aptitude, interest, land resources, and financial ability. For many, sheep-raising is a hobby-type social and recreational activity who own small numbers of high-quality sheep in preference to large numbers of poor sheep. Yet, farmers perceived that the Project was all along shrouded in secrecy and that developments were not fully shared with the target group. Livestock production is a demanding occupation with long working hours and constant vigilance. Farmers' cooperatives, the broadening of participation, and greater ministry-farmer understanding were in shortage.

Handicraft

The Project underscored indigenous entrepreneurship, boosted small business, created public awareness, improved social attitude, preserved traditional practices and cultural heritage, improved the cultural flavor of the local crafts, and improved handicraft's uncharitable image and unfavorable stereotype. Moreover, it facilitated the acceptance of handicraft production as an acceptable means of earning a living or supplementing household income. However, social rejection is fueled by the belief that handicraft is an activity that people get into when everything else is out of reach. Stereotyping trainees and producers as people with marginal learning abilities exacerbates the poor image and low social acceptance of the industry. The Venture lacks continuous effort to build and sustain an awareness among domestic consumers of the quality and reliability of products.

Cave

The amenity value of the Cave is high, providing a joy of unique underground experience, releasing tension and producing sound and light effects in a subterranean location which is a thrilling experience for the visitor. At each turn of the tour a new view is seen and with each step a different scene is sighted. The experience of visiting the Cave arouses curiosity and a sense of exploration. It is an adventure of benefit to young and old alike. The Cave experience creates and sustains interest in people, lifestyle, history, culture, contacts, understandings, goodwill, and enables visitors to learn about local culture and foods. The visitor leaves the Cave landscape untouched so that posterity may also have exploratory fun. The visitors represent a broad crosssection of the target population, i.e. residents, regional and extraregional tourists, upscale and mass-market tourists as well as long-stay and short-stay visitors. Nontheless, the Cave may suffer in the event of careless visitors removing a cave formation and causing atrophy in the process. The dominance of metropolitan tourism interests continues, and superficialities of contacts between visitors and residents holds out. Sudden tour cancellations, forced by tram breakdown, cause embarrassment to tour operators and customer inconvenience and disappointment.

Pulverization

The social value of the Investment exceeds the social value of consumption. There is greater appreciation of the roles played by the

SSA, households, organizations and community groups in maintaining infrastructural viability. Especially, user role in placing refuse at the right place and time for proper collection and disposal is more readily recognized than before. The downside is that the poor image of waste management of the past still persists. The litany of the woes is long: the improper disposal of refuse by the users, wayside littering, illegal dumping, indiscriminate disposal, insensitivity and carelessness toward waste disposal, user treatment of waste disposal on a casual ad hoc basis, unauthorized disposal in improper container, offensive material, and improper disposal point. Widespread resistance was shown to the location of waste processing and disposal site in the vicinity of residential areas. The outputs are sold for much less than their social value for policy reasons.

Polytechnic

The Project's social objective is to democratize Barbados' educational system in the sense of providing an opportunity for education/training to Barbadians of all socioeconomic groups, with particular reference to the pattern of student flows through the educational system and to the stages at which various cohorts leave formal education. In planning and execution terms, this means identifying and working with such diverse target groups as 2,000+ youths who drop out abruptly from school each year, students who are less successful academically for varied reasons, the existing stock of dropouts especially unemployed, and workers who seek occupational upgrading.

The Project's forte includes positive interactive effects of schooling on family size, health, nutrition, social awareness, and civic culture. It reinforces equity, democratization, social access, mobility, and opportunity diversification. Indeed, higher social acceptance of vocational training is facilitated by taking part in annual careers showcases. Certain outcomes attributable to the Polytechnic include skill development and acquisition, learning ability, student achievement, dropout reduction, program completion, improved attitudes, greater employability, faculty-skill improvement, personal development, self-reliance, attitudinal change, and occupational competence. The Institution enjoys positive support from the community in that several private sector organizations have made donations of equipment, money and prizes and sponsored training seminars for faculty members. It must be reported, however, that an uncharitable social image of the Polytechnic persists. Some people seem to have an image of the Polytechnic as a school for students who are dropouts. There seems to be a grudging acceptance of technical-vocational education in the community, which is reflected in the traditional prestige structure downgrading vocational work. The Institute's sporting and recreational activity suffers because a playground is not available.

Sewerage

Landscaping, general beautification and eliminating one of the worst downtown slums and serious pollution sources improves the social quality of life in the target area. The Project's social significance and soundness increases by enhancing user convenience by discharging human waste and household wastewater and serving 3,000 user connections and a target population of 37,700 consumers. The clearing of 143 houses and resettling nearly 500 people in more spacious and healthier ambience, the availability of waterborne toilet facilities and the building of the Luther Thorne Memorial School for the resited residents have high social returns. A great deal of planned social and communitywide communication was done for disseminating information and seeking acceptance from the target group.

But the Venture is constrained by disruption and stress caused to the cohesive community of Emmerton, loss of life and injury at work sites, reluctance of the low-income users in the target area in making in-house connections with the system due to high connection costs, residents in the target area complaining of strong stench coming from the Plant, and users disposing improper objects into the system causing clog and congestion. Although sludge produced by the Plant is used by farmers as fertilizer, thereby cutting down on import costs for overseas fertilizers, there is a stigma in Barbados attached to sludge-type fertilizer, no matter how chemically treated it may be.

Ferneihurst

The Complex at Ferneihurst - providing housing not only for the low-income households but also the elderly and the disadvantaged groups - represents a fundamental human and social need. Ferneihurst improves the quality of life, benefits low-income families, provides a better ambience to raise families, satisfies the social need for housing at low cost, improves living conditions, provides spacious accommodation, provides tenants with a sense of community and cohesiveness, curbs the tendency for delinquency, improves tenants' general health, well-being and sanitation standards, makes for healthier and responsible citizens, provides recreational facilities, and contributes through greater rest and relaxation to making alert students, productive workers and contented homemakers. The tenants like living in well-designed units gardened with plants which cost them far less than alternative accommodations. Improved housing has reduced housing-related pathologies, i.e. juvenile delinquency, inadequate school performance, questionable work record, promiscuity, drug addition, and family disorganization. A system of feedback maintains link between housing management staff and tenants. An NHC Tenants' Association continues to establish communication with the management and facilitate discussions on the estates' maintenance. The annual Ferneihurst Street Fair promotes community cohesiveness, participation, and social vibrancy.

Ferneihurst faces negativity, e.g. uneasiness about spitefulness among certain tenants, disorderly and inconsiderate behavior by some tenants, prejudice against terrace housing, lack of privacy in some units, the image of public housing as poverty enclave persists - the clientele is poor, problem families, indigent people, the elderly, etc., and residualization seems to be at work - the concentration of low-income tenants and increase in stereotyping and uncharitable labelling. Tenants are concerned about the lack of sufficient and prompt repair to the units. Slackness in estate management perpetuates a culture of accusation, distrust, and apathy. While some tenants disapprove of the closeness of toilets to kitchens, other residents feel the need for a playground in the Estate. Some tenants do not pay their rents or clear their arrears regularly. Some middle-income tenants continue to occupy units meant for low-income and low middle-income consumers. Other tenant misbehavior includes failure to hand in keys before moving out, failure to notify NHC before vacating or going abroad on a trip, squatters moving into empty units and tenants subletting units and violating tenancy agreement.

Political Dimension

The political-ideological setting in and around which investments operate in the public sector has often been downplayed. Politics, inter alia, is an instrument of goal-setting, resource allocation, value generation, and alternatives creation. It is a means of injecting values into rational choices and assimilating and accommodating group inputs and interest. The essential political traits - decisions and commands, compliance and enforcement, support, opposition or resistence, power and authority, advocacy, value allocation, concession, accommodation, bargaining, persuasion, alliance, consensus-building, etc. - are far too fundamental to miss. Power resources, such as wealth, status, position, leadership skills, information, expertise, alliance, and authority continue to be employed. Political support for projects, which cannot be taken for granted, is critical to their success. Its absence or laxity helps explain partly some of the failure and disappointments. The trade-off of costs and benefits and conflict and coordination is extensive. Ideologies and values are at the core of project development, even if often implicit.

The relation between investment and politics is often subtle and tangential. Investment management done in ignorance of political reality may be ineffectual. Taking insufficient account of the realities of power and interest may cause the risk of nonsupport or sabotage. The investments are not to be isolated from the power and interest complex, enmeshed in domestic class relations, demands, pressures, expectations and conflicts in relation to external actors and power centers. The investments are operational in Barbados which is small, highly penetrated, and structurally dependent. The island shows dependence on metropolitan power centers in diverse forms and degrees. Implicit in this process is Barbados' dependence on external funding, her sensitivity to donors and her need to avoid antagonizing the donors for ensuring a continuing flow of assistance.

Barbados' dependence on foreign capital and technology, external stimuli, expertise, communications and markets has deepened over time. For instance, 40% of investment capital comes from foreign sources. Her incorporation into the international community continues, the dominance by the center grows more and more subtle and certain features restrict the drive for autonomy and self-reliance. Dependency undergirds the power structure in Barbados which demonstrates through these and similar investments its subscription to accommodation, incrementalism, and gradualism.

The donor-recipient relation, neither uniform nor well-defined, is often based on unclear premises and shifting assumptions. Some of the donor agencies, having their own priorities, deadlines, accounting rules and operating procedures, impose their own priorities and preferences on recipient organizations (Ahmad, 1977). The investment criteria are not always uniform, differing from country to country, and even regime to regime. Although the donors go through a learning and adaptive process, nearly all donor agencies tend to prefer larger, technically-complex projects precisely because they can exercise greater and longer control over large projects (Harvey, 1983).

Donors tend to utilize the leverage capacity afforded by their financing to influence and shape development policy and project decision to their own preference. Some of the recipient countries tend to follow, in search of new and continuing assistance, a policy of appeasement and a course of least resistance and comply superficially with funding-agency criteria without fundamentally changing indigenous management culture or behavior (Birgegird, 1975). Besides, policy-maker disposition toward an investment can be strategic to its success. The policy leadership makes decision and provides direction. Identification with the investments seems to strengthen the credibility, legitimacy and competence of a regime, with the political sector becoming gradually more capable of performing certain governance/management roles, i.e. review, monitoring, advocacy, and direction.

Development is certainly not apolitical. The investments do not occur in a vacuum. Numerous resource and interest groups take part in the influence-exerting process, short-term or partisan factors are recognizable (Little and Mirrlees, 1974), and clientelism is visible (Stone, 1983). The Projects were initiated for a variety of reasons - attracting resources, gaining status, fulfilling needs, and maintaining legitimacy and support. A redistributive strategy via the Projects can be seen at work. All in all, the Projects' political feasibility - the probability that within a given time a particular alternative tends to receive sufficient political push and support - was reasonably clear. The Projects, in part, point to egalitarianism and developmentalism, i.e. a kind of developmentalist ideology initiating and pursuing growth-providing, future-facing and deliberate action, and using the public sector as a purposeful vehicle (Jones, 1970) for fruitful initiatives. A notable feature of the Projects is that limited and carefully-structured beneficiary participation had diminished project effectiveness, acceptance and success. The current topheavy topdown approach has failed to secure firm beneficiary commitment to the Projects. Overall capacity-building has so far been somewhat unclear. The Projects seem to reinforce the disproportionate absorptive capacity of the more affluent and organized client groups with respect to benefits, access, and influence.

We now turn to a brief assessment of some of the Projects. The Handicraft Project enhances the scope of ownership and participation by small-scale indigenous craft producers throughout the country. But problems of political and partisan nature militate, from tome to time, against commercial operation. The Sewerage Project faced political cost in terms of hostility and disaffection displayed by Project-affected residents who were eventually relocated. Finally, the Ferneihurst Project, underscoring political success and performance, is a visible symbol of public sector achievement. Social welfare function continues to be carried out in the form of affordable rents provided for low-income tenants. A community orientation has influenced housing design, favoring functional, multilevel rental units. On the other hand, as housing is a divisible rather than a collective good, competition for housing is usually individualistic, with the competitors keenly aware that the supply of units is limited. The profit motive residualizes low-income housing and the provision of habitational units for low-income aggregates becomes a low-priority option. Some tenants, who earn higher income, continue to occupy the units, receive low-rent benefits and deprive more deserving applicants of occupancy. Partisan factors - tenant selection, preferential treatment, patronage dispensation, etc. - militate against rationality and effectiveness in organizational decision-making. The misplaced political criteria, too, obscure efficiency, cost-consciousness, profitability and time-criticality in Ferneihurst and similar housing.

Economic Dimension

The Projects fall under various categories of public or collective goods, with a mix of social, merit, traded, and nontraded goods. Some of the Projects are nonrival and nonexludable. Some Project outputs are tradables, such as Greenland and Handicraft. For the Project with nontraded outputs, such as Sewerage, factor services are the leading inputs. Some Projects, such as Cave, evince their locational or sitebound feature. Some of the Project outputs, which are not allocated via markets (Polytechnic, Sewerage) are instead provided by the budget (Pulverization).

The Projects provide collective benefits (livestock development, refuse disposal, technical-vocational training, sewage disposal) as well as divisible benefits (handicraft development, cave development, housing development). The Projects' siting has not induced rural-urban migration or exacerbated regional inequality by concentrating investments in a particular area of Barbados.

There are time horizon aspects. The costs and the benefits are not realized immediately, nor do they occur simultaneously. Certain aspects are deliberately undercharged or sold for less than their socioeconomic value. The Pulverization Project is one which supplies output on a no-charge basis, or the Sewerage Project which supplies output for less than its worth.

We see the contributions of the Investments as accruing to the entire society, both costs and benefits being distributed within the population. The Projects reveal that the choice has consequences for employment, output, resource utilization, foreign exchange earning, and income distribution. The value of an investment depends not only on the benefits produced by it but also on its distribution and efficiency. Through these Investments, the public sector sends the signal that it would not sacrifice future consumption in favor of immediate consumption.

Broadly, benefits relate to creating economic infrastructure, creating externalities, securing intersectoral linkages, utilizing skills, securing diversification, inducing scale economies, creating and sustaining market, and increasing capital assets. We look at the Investments not as ends in themselves but as creating present as well as future streams of consumption, expanding the net national value added, raising the standard of living of population, allocating investment to achieve growth, and providing positive externalities. The Projects can be seen as instruments of transferring income to the poor and redressing certain imbalances. The Ventures aim at welfare enhancement, e.g. consumer surplus, scarcity values of goods and services, externalities, the distribution of income between contemporaries as well as between generations, obtaining self-sufficiency in products and services, allocative gains, and redistributive gains. Several effects have occurred and are underway, e.g. user benefits (output expansion, net welfare improvement), second-round multiplier effects (consumer spending), international effects (export promotion), linkage effects (labor market expansion), substitution effects (local mutton vs. imported mutton), complementary effects (refuse disposal and land reclamation), value-added effects (increase in output value), and demonstration effects (sheep-raising, handicraft production, technical-vocational training). Also, the Project shows subtle far-reaching effects from the stimulation of entrepreneurship, the acquisition of new skills, greater readiness to produce for the market or serve the community, greater sensitization to the values of cooperation and discipline, greater propensity to engage in sociopolitical intervention, resource mobilization, and popular participation.

The effects, on the balance, relate to employment, income, output, consumption, savings, mobility, work/life satisfaction, foreign exchange earning, income distribution, skill development, local value addition, employment creation, output expansion, resource utilization, consumption spending, export promotion, welfare achievement, option demand generation, common demand satisfaction, regulation, market creation, capacity-building, opportunity generation, technology selection and transfer, diversification, local ownership, equity provision, income generation, and linkage formation.

Insofar as investment decisions are concerned, the risk element is spread fairly widely in the Projects and among the population groups. Investment decisions were made reasonably carefully because the grave consequences of failure, disappointment or resource misdirection cautioned decision-makers. Attempts were made, although not always consistently, to broaden and widen the Project base so that large target population could share in the Projects, thereby minimizing the risk element. The social value and the social rates of return of these Projects - especially Pulverization, Polytechnic and Sewerage Projects - is high. Social value is discernible when one recognizes that the public sector through these Investments deals with inadequate investment and income inequalities by including explicit distributional objectives, such as Polytechnic and Ferneihurst.

The Project users are willing to pay for the services of the Ventures. The continued operation of the Projects shows the demand for the Projects' outputs. The various transactions that take place between and among the participating actors/organizations underscore that consumers are willing to pay for a quantity of the Project output. Even in the case of nontraded outputs, the value of technical-vocational training as provided through the Polytechnic, for instance, lies not in what consumers are willing to pay but in its net socioeconomic contribution to increased employment, such as placement, job creation, and self-esteem.

The Projects have contributed to increase in capital values, augmented the future stream of earnings accruing to individuals or property, and increased benefits of urban renewal and downtown redevelopment. The Ventures reduce costs for certain purposes, diminishing, for instance, the need for importing mutton and handicrafts and reducing the import costs of the two products. The Sewerage Project has cut down the spendings incurred by users for constructing septic tanks. There is some psychic income to be derived from the Projects in terms of pleasure, satisfaction, accomplishment, prestige, status, and well-being. The very act of weekend homely family lunch at a Ferneihurst apartment or a weekend leisurely family drive to the Cave has an amenity value in itself. Even though some impacts of the Projects cannot be monetized or measured, they can be clearly identified and thoroughly appreciated, viz. cleanliness, beauty, peace, quiet, dignity, and discretion.

As to costs, the Projects point to project outlays (planning, preparation and investment costs, sunk costs, contingencies), OMR costs (operation, maintenance and repair costs), indirect and external costs (losses in output, productivity and increase, delays, waste, pilferage, leakage), opportunity costs (value of lost or missed opportunities), and transfer payments (transfer of purchasing power, transfer of control over resource allocation, taxes, subsidies, interest payments). A host of related costs sprung up. There were, for example, transaction costs - high cost of lengthy negotiation and design costs. Some Projects, for instance Pulverization, facing a slow and lengthy process, sustained life cycle costs - the costs of long gestation, uncertainty, and ambiguity. Dilatory costs sprang from time losses and holdups, deferring, postponing and prolonging the accrual and flow of benefits and reducing the new present value.

The Projects from Greenland to Ferneihurst showed varying degrees of cost-effectiveness. Two situations arose in this regard. One was maximizing output for a given amount of money - for example, mutton, handicraft, cave attendance - and the second was minimizing costs for a given set of objectives - for example, disposing solid waste, offering technical-vocational education and providing family accommodation. In all these Ventures, the project organizations were allotted a fixed sum of money and asked to maximize the returns they could get on their investments. In the second situation, the organizations were given specific goals and told to minimize the costs of achieving those objectives. The objectives were established and the organizations' tasks were to achieve their goals with the minimum spending of funds.

Inspite of Barbados using the social opportunity cost of capital as a discount rate, certain problems have not been altogether avoided. The identification of a single rate of return for a particular sector or project tends to be debatable. It is equally difficult to apply the discount rate as a practical working tool. Intergenerational time preference continues to pose difficulty in that nearly all the Investments weigh heavily in favor of current generations and tend to diminish the values of future generations. This is especially the case in investments with a long operating life and a need for capital equipment installation, active maintenance program, and replacement cost management.

At any rate, the positive effects need not cause anyone to forget the Projects' negative results, nonoutput effects and disamenity effects, i.e. noise nuisance, inconvenience, discomfort, pain, disruption, dislocation, relocation, delays, stench, site injury, accidental deaths, home and neighbor loss, and property depreciation. Some disutilities occurred, viz. some dissatisfaction, unhappiness, risks, losses and uncertainties were generated by the Projects.

Greenland

The Project helps improve rural production and grow local sales, meets local consumption needs, utilizes indigenous animals, generates gainful occupation and cash income in rural areas among the low-income groups, provides year-round employment and reduces unemployment, saves foreign exchange, enhances small and large-scale business, and attempts to attain self-sufficiency and contain meat import cost estimated at about BDS$8m.annually. The sheep, like goats, is successfully reared as backyard animals by many small farmers, helping with their income or in producing meat. Diversification occurs by providing work to people who reap roughage for the animals and by plantations undertaking livestock operation based on pasturage and sugercane-based feeds. The sheep's high prolificacy is of sound economic importance. The Venture has links with agriculture, rural economy, rural development, small-farm promotion, nutrition, employment, import substitution, and export marketing. Through this Project and supporting activities, employment has expanded in slaughtering, selling, tanning, handicrafts, and exporting. Incremental incomes accrue to sheep farmers, farm workers, input suppliers, output consumers, and the public sector. An economic network has come on stream, i.e. farmers, families, butchers, supermarkets, public markets, retail outlets, minimarts, and consumers. As a result of the meat's tenderness, juiciness and delicious flavor, it is promotable as a unique entrée in local hotels and restaurants.

Export market boosting export revenue includes CARICOM as well as non-CARICOM markets. Internationally, the sheep has been exported to Central America, South America, United States, Taiwan, Malaysia, and other countries. As to regional market, the sheep has been exported to Antigua, Dominica, Grenada, Montserrat, St. Kitts-Nevis, St. Lucia and St. Vincent in order to improve their stocks. Exports are likely to continue. Many small farmers depend on the revenue from the sale of live sheep for exports. The price for exporting sheep is BDS$5 per pound live wight, which is more than double what is offered for slaughtered mutton. Exports help develop sheep-farming, earn foreign exchange, create employent and help subsidize the local lamb industry.

The constraints are not to be overlooked. Commercialization has been adversely affected by high feed cost and large lamb imports. Sheep-farming for mutton alone is not profitable under existing conditions (Patterson and Nurse, 1974), mutton production needs much land for pasturing (Phillips, 1979), the externalities and sheep-farming - animal waste recycling, hides, biogas, sludge, leather goods, and other by-products - have not been explored much (Rice, 1986), slim profit from sheep-farming, limited mutton production because of imported mutton's cheapness and availability, insufficient flesh on the sheep's leg and loin keep down its commercial value, processing mutton products and moving toward specialized breeder/meat-producing farms have not been explored, slow commercialization drive, high cost of production and animal feeds, longer and uncertain production time, unsteady supply, variable quality, inadequate marketing system, and insufficient price support system. A farmer, for instance, fetches BDS$500 for an exported ram and gets around BDS$250 for the carcass of the sheep locally after slaughter and transport fees. The fact is that nearly all sheep farmers are in a position to produce more animals if they have a reliable market for them.

The export market has its share of problems, such as the limitations of the CARICOM's Agricultural Marketing Protocol, the animal's proneness to certain diseases, high freight and insurance cost, foreign exchange restriction, import restriction, and confusion and delay over sheep export. Export policy geared toward strategic conservation and export promotion has not been updated. Export also tends to suffer because some farmers do not bother to register their animals with the Barbados Agricultural Society, maintain proper records of the sheep, and preserve proper identification ear tags.

The Project's long-term goal is being hurt by imported lamb. As much as 75% of mutton and lamb - the equivalent of 125,000 lamb carcasses - is imported from the overseas. Sheep producers cannot compete at the lower end of the market with the majority of the lamb imported from New Zealand as it is subsidized. As yet, no levy has been placed on imported lamb to protect lamb production. In spite of various efforts, the sheep production in Barbados has remained at about 30,000 heads for the past 30 years. In contrast, lamb imports have grown remarkably along with foreign exchange outflows. Such imports rose to 2.4m.kgs. or over 5m.pounds in 1988, for example, valued at BDS$7.8m.

Underfeeding diminishes lamb production, cuts down the growth rate, and lengthens the time to market sheep. For successful market for commercial lamb production, a continuous supply of lamb is essential.

The lambs must be full-fed in order to get rapid growth, proper fattening and tender meat. For a quality market, it is essential that only those lambs, which have been full-fed so that they attain market weight in 6-7 months, be used. Smaller or slow-growing lambs may be acceptable for home consumption or occasional sale but fail to meet commercial standards.

Handicraft

The Project is an indigenous, labor-intensive and local value-added activity, making a successful transition from a noncommercial welfare-oriented initiative to a visible and recognized commercial operation. It utilizes indigenous resources, materials and skills, expands output, promotes exports, substitutes imports, generates and distributes income, absorbs labor, satisfies domestic consumption and tourist demand, upgrades jobs and skills, expands local ownership and participation, diversifies the production base, promotes urban as well as rural and female employment, engages family labor and helps low-income families, offers work on a seasonal or part-time basis, employs traditional as well as modernizing means of production, helps decentralize development, helps diffuse artisinal skills, unfolds entrepreneurial orientation and spurs home-based entrepreneurship, and creates market and diversifies skills.

Regional as well as extraregional export marketing is done, involving varied promotional measures. A Design Center is in place, which is seen as a key to the extraregional export thrust. Maintaining a strong link with tourism and selling an estimated 90% of products to visitors, its development partly ensures the retention in the economy of a growing portion of tourist spending. The domestic base, strengthened by tourist/resident demand, has extended into export market. It earns considerable foreign exchange, employs many producers and entrepreneurs, generates over BDS$2m. in business annually, and uses over 90% of local raw materials during the production process. The industry, on this basis, is a net producer, not a net user, of foreign exchange. Handicraft will make its greatest possible contribution to the economy if it utilizes a high percentage of local raw materials and adds a high local value-added.

Then again, handicraft's share in the total industrial sector is modest in terms of value added, output, investment, and employment. It is small-scale with relatively small value-added to gross outputs. Small-scale producers are limited in production capacity, fail to introduce time-saving equipment and fail to get into a cooperative. The Project's constraints are varied and plentiful: high freight cost affecting export volume, difficulty in packing and shipping of fragile pottery and delicate wares, difficulty in maintaining high-volume and cost-competitive export production, tenuous transport and communication links with extraregional markets, inability to intensify exports trade, inability to fill large orders for export markets, wage sensitivity of the industry making export market somewhat uncompetitive, inability to initiate active product development, getting retailers to sell local handicrafts, inability to satisfy the demands of tourists, inability to integrate the production and sale of handicrafts in tourism facilities, unfair extraregional competition, high price level of products spawned by high labor input and high wage levels, low productivity of labor, high price level of products and uncompetitiveness in certain products, insufficiency of policy and institutional support, lack of initiative in recycling available raw materials, adverse foreign competition, high cost of inputs, and lack of greater intersectoral linkages.

Encapsulation is in evidence, i.e. the more powerful and organized imported craft business surrounds and dominates a less powerful indigenous market. Local handicraft accounts for 30% of all handicrafts sold in the island with the remaining 70% being imported. The size of the handicraft market in Barbados (Browne, 1980) stands at about BDS$12m., of which the local industry accounts for about BDS$4m. Conflict of interest continues between craft producers and retailers of imported products. The local population is not a significant buyer of handicrafts. With the annual import value standing at about BDS$7m., the pressure to stop importing souvenirs and protecting local products is put, but the issue is complex in that imported products are more price-competitive than the local wares and that the purchase of souvenirs represents discretionary spending by tourists.

Cave

The Project raises the value of output, creates backward linkages by stimulating surface transportation in the island, promotes exports, utilizes indigenous resources, and substitutes imports. As a tourism product, the Cave can be seen as a service export activity. The Venture contributes to the balance of payments, earns foreign exchange, generates and distributes income, and enlarges tourism by-products, e.g. hotel-building, infrastructural services, tourism products/facilities, food supply, and the service sector. Recreation values are conspicuous. The primary value is the visitors' willingness to pay for recreation services. The impact values relate to spending on travel, transport, equipment, accommodation, refreshment, souvenirs, and shopping.

The Cave uses resources that are indigenous as well as plentiful in the country and in its absence might have been unutilized, e.g. natural beauty, scenic amenity, environmental serenity, and land-based resources. A link with the local, regional and extraregional markets has been forged - the flow of goods and services, capital, information, technology, and foreign exchange revenue. Some externalities result via training in the showcave operation and maintenance, the demonstration effects of a showcave on local tourism, and the product of tourist souvenirs and food. Direct employment in various occupational categories has been generated. Indirect employment has been created in ancillary services, viz. tour services, transport services, physical-input supplies, and on-plant business activities. Work has been generated for tour operators, activity/event directors, travel agents, taxi drivers, and coach concessionaires. It helps create multiplier effects through forging links with other sectors. The effects come into play as visitor spending circulates, recirculates and results in employment, income, transaction, and capital multipliers. It serves decentralization and results in the dispersion of development and growth by moving from the urban southern and western parts to the rural central part of the country.

Nonetheless, the Venture is constrained by insufficient intersectoral linkages, limited local participation, infrequent repeat visits, limited investment capital, seasonal fluctuation of visitor attendance and operating revenue, limited night-tour clientele, limited penetration of the tourist market and share of the package tours, and difficulty of replacement cost planning. Penetration as a displacement process continues to occur whereby external actors, such as the tour operators, are able to exert general influence over the sector and use specific leverage over visitor arrival at the Cave. Sudden tour cancellations cause business loss.

Pulverization

Although the service is free or the output is a social nontraded good at this time, the Plant's yield is a potential money-earner. The Project provides basic-need satisfaction whose output is valuable in terms of its marginal social benefit to consumers, where complementary efforts have occurred, namely, refuse disposal and land reclamation/development, and domestic resources and skills are the source of refuse disposal as a producer service. The Project's impact includes increasing and diversifying employment, spurring infrastructural and traffic growth, pushing public utility services, assisting with the movement of people and business, facilitating the increase of service and production activities, and enhancing the safety and reliability of resources. Using the Workmans landfill as a development or recreation site in future, resource recovery - such as composting or energy development - and reduced disposal cost/ decreased disposal disamenities can be cited as externalities.

The downturn is that some externalities - landfill stench, plant noise, leachate, land or neighborhood depreciation, health anxiety, resident inconvenience - may be overlooked. Waste disposal is subject to external diseconomies. Many users abuse available land, ambient air and available water, thus imposing costs on others to whom their high quality is valuble. There is also the failure to get into resource-recovery and revenue-generating programs. Reuse and recycling have not been taken up, i.e. mixing pulverized refuse with bagasse, turning it into fertilizer or soil conditioner, using organic waste as fuel in electricity generation, using shredded refuse in soil conservation, and converting shredded waste into compost material and fuel. The possibilities of reducing landfill costs by selecting low-quality sites, using them for development or recreation after their use as landfills and offsetting some landfill costs by capital gains made on the sites' resale are not being seized. Besides, while estimating demand, the value placed on disease prevention or reduction, pollution control, inconvenience alleviation or cost savings can be contentious. There is difficulty as well in measuring reduction in user costs resulting from refuse disposal and neighborhood improvement.

Polytechnic

The Venture serves the country's expanding production and service sectors, adds to a pool of skilled personnel and trained workforce serves the island by advancing technical/vocational education and training, meets the needs of the labor market, helps raise employability, labor productivity, worker income, occupational competence and problem-solving ability, increases the school-leavers' chances for wage employment and gainful own-account activity, counters unemployment and underemployment among school-leavers, youths, first-time job-seekers and women, encourages entrepreneurship, and creates forward linkages by absorbing the successful trainees in the labor market.

A significantly high proportion of the Polytechnic graduates are employed, more so than the nongraduates. The Polytechnic's more successful students tend to stay on the island to work rather than emigrate. There is a rapid turnover in jobs, especially among the younger graduates, moving upward in the job market as reflected by compensation. An increasing number of graduates return to the Polytechnic for advanced studies to increase their skills, enhance their credentials, and improve their marketability.

The willingness to pay criterion of the Project's nontraded outputs is met by assessing thc output's end-use in terms of its balance-of-payment impact on production. Returns on the investment in education/training extend to the present value of the additional stream of earnings a Polytechnic graduate may expect to receive as a result of skill acquisition, including increased earning capacity, a flow of benefits to the better-skilled and trained individual continuing over his working career, suitable employment, and self-employment. The level of compensation tends to be higher than comparable support-level workers, store personnel, and clerical-secretarial staff. There are net economic, productivity and employment benefits, viz. additional production in the future, training the future workforce, acquiring productivity-boosting skills, varied secondary effects on the present and future output, placement, job creation, skill intensification, market diversification, self-employment, work expansion, and capacity expansion. The Institution creates international effects by making admission and training available to students from the neighboring Eastern Caribbean countries. Complementary effects take place as well, e.g. technical-vocational training and own-account activity.

Still, it is difficult, and sometimes contentious, to establish 'willingness to pay' for the nontraded outputs. Size is a constraint on the expansion of technical-vocational training. This is partly so because the job market is small and only limited job openings become available periodically. Employment creation, over time in the aggregate, has tended to be slow, cautious, and uneven. The pace of growth has been too modest to create a steady market for maintenance, repair, and expansion work. Some private enterprises are stagnant, saddled with low productivity, and uncertain future. Besides, a penchant for paid employment in the modern sector tends to inhibit the development of local skills, business growth, and self-employment. Moreover, for some Polytechnic leavers, employment tends to be irregular and income modest. They also tend to be particularly disadvantaged in the market by their youth, inexperience, shortage of capital and credit, shortage of tools, materials and premises, and negligible business skills.

Sewerage

A potential income-earner, the Project's nontraded services are verifiable in terms of discounting the willingness to pay on the part of the rich, revaluing that of the poor and utilizing consumption weights. It shows merit good features, i.e. urban renewal, business development, residential growth, tourist arrival, and revenue generation. Complementary effects take place, e.g. sewage disposal and sludge use. The Venture has important economic value and consequences. Its output benefits users directly and widely, including contributing to Bridgetown metropolitan development in respect of urban renewal, business promotion, tourism promotion, visitor arrival, housing development, and revenue generation. The Project's reversal of beach pollution and the beaches' declining regenerative capacity saves tourism, retains tourism revenue and raises the living standards of the residents in the urban target areas. A useful soil conditioner and high-quality fertilizer, the sludge is used at Fairy Valley and Spencer where fodder crops are grown and is further usable as a fertilizer for lawns, trees and plants. The flammable gas may be bottled off and used as a source of energy. Sewered Bridgetown has helped increase property value and development. Connection to the sewage system is a means of preserving the economic heritage of the current as well as future generation. The Project provided over 200 jobs for local workers, served to bring down unemployment, and injected money into the local economy.

The debit is that significant costs were incurred, viz. foreign exchange spent on acquiring factor services, retaining skilled and unskilled labor, and acquiring capital and replacement equipment. The cost of imported skills was high which comprised compensations the specialists received, remittances they made, and consumption within the country. Additional costs incurred included unscheduled transportation costs ran by users in the target area, vehicular damage caused by excavations, and impaired road surfaces. The relocation of homes from the target area to Clapham eventually necessitated the building of a new school to accommodate the transplanted community. The school cost about BDS$1.8m. To determine whether the fund spent on the Project would have some returns, cost-benefit analysis was done which showed that the Investment was considered community-friendly, but that it was difficult to break even on costs. The cost of constructing a sewerage system was high, but high service charge could not be passed on to users.

The high capital, operating and replacement costs with the need to import all or much of the inputs and the consequent high foreign exchange cost put additional strain. Providing sewerage services to a depressed urban area and to low-income urban residents tends to show low and unsteady returns. The Plant consumes much water, and water rates are relatively high in the country. The recycling and reuse of the treated effluent has not been pursued. The reuse of the effluent for stock and garden watering and the fertilization and irrigation of edible crops is ignored. Aquacultural reuse, including freshwater fish farming, mariculture, algal production and aquatic macrophyte production (Mara, 1982) is missed. The anaerobic digestion of organic wastes yielding biogas - 60 to 70% methane, carbon dioxide and other gases - that can be used as energy for cooking and lighting is disregarded.

Ferneihurst

Ferniehurst is the result of such demand factors as demographic forces, housing market conditions, sectoral policy, and household demand. The economic payoffs are multiple: the outputs benefit users directly, the cost of shelter to the poor and low-income households is curbed, indigenous building materials are used, the local value-added is raised, employment is created, seasonal slack is picked up, the basic-need imbalance is partly redressed, tenant hardship is alleviated by low rent, steady and long-tem tenancy, complementary effects such as low-income housing and household saving are created, more cost-effective accommodation than private-sector housing, and functional layout. The multiplier effects were seen in building and construction supplies, utility services, transport and communications, financial institutions, and merchandising. A set of external costs, associated with substandard housing, have been saved or curbed, i.e. poor health, fire risk, crime, vandalism, and overcrowding.

As a package of shelter and services, Ferneihurst offers substitution and complementarity by increasing economic participation, saving scarce urban space, minimizing the cost of urban infrastructure, improving the location of dwellings in relation to jobs and services, reducing commuting costs, and improving mobility. Low rental protects the low-income tenants from the high-market rents and housing shortages. The Project shields tenants in situations where supply inelasticity tends to cause rents to rise sharply in the face of increased demand. Ferneihurst includes an investment element as well as an income transfer element. The latter is justified because the incomes of the poor are below base-level income, and a subsidy on the rent is an accepted income transfer. The annual benefit stream consists of rent paid by the tenants and the subsidy received from the public sector, thus maximizing welfare and improving the rate of return.

Even so, traditional analysis does not seem to justify the investment because the willingness of the low-income tenants to pay is often fragile, with the Project's inability to pay for its way and to have an acceptable rate of return on outlay. The prevailing market system tends to act against most tenants' interest in that low rent makes investment in rented housing less profitable, reduces the supply of such housing, and decreases the replacement of substandard housing. The utility of the housing stock drops if and when maintenance and repairs are postponed, or even, slowed down. Then again, single tenants - causing apartment deterioration or holding noisy parties - can cause disamenity in the neighborhood.

Financial Dimension

As a result of the Projects, the net worth of the public sector, which uses its fund both for investment and consumption, has increased. Capital budgeting is demonstrated in the Projects, creating identifiable and visible outputs. These capital investments are relatively long-term commitments for GOB, and they are compatible with the overall growth strategies and development initiatives of the country. Capital investments are the driving forces of an organization, public as well as private. Such investments in resources, facilities, working capital, research, promotion and other areas make possible the provision of goods and services to the customers of the organizations. Underlying the Projects is the management decision to deploy resources for financial gain. Viewed in this sense, the decisions involve three areas, e.g. the investment of these resources, the operation of the project entities through the use of these resources, and the proper mix of financing with which to provide the resources. Despite variety of the Projects in terms of size, function and structure, common to all, however, is the fundamental focus of management - planned commitment of resources for the purpose of generating, over time and by choice, financial value/worth sufficient to recover the resources employed and to earn a return. Over the long run, the result of resource deployment is aimed at net improvement in the financial position of the community, including the ability to make further resource commitment.

The task and challenge of management is involved in managing the Project entities and concomitant investments that promise to give the desired level of reward within the constraint of the degree of nonachievement and risk that is acceptable. The analysis of decisions about capital investment is part of a complex set of issues and choices that must be resolved continuously by management, and it is in this respect that we come across management inadequacy. All the investments are not performing equally well in breaking even, recovering cost or generating revenue. Some of the Projects are the recipients of budgetary support each year and they incur some losses. One of the recurrent constraints includes requiring the organizations to sell their outputs for less than consumers are willing to pay, delivering free services, and overlooking overstaffing. The public sector seems reluctant to take initiative to reverse the situation, i.e. permitting price increases or cost reduction, improving revenue-earning position, and seriously considering efficiency pricing. As to cost recovery, the collection mechanisms are frequently inefficient, arrears are substantial, and resistance to paying is high. With cost recovery being a contentious issue, the introduction of new charges or an increase in existing charges is often unpopular. But the principle of equity posits that the users of a project should pay its costs. Cost recovery entails economic efficiency, income distribution, and revenue generation. Failure or unwillingness to recover costs from the users creates imbalance, encourages indulgence, erodes resources, and threatens financial viability and soundness.

Other aspects of financial performance are not in strong and clear position. For instance, the revenue standards (the ratio of return on invested capital, cash generation criterion, operating ratio test, breakeven test), which are central to an organization's satisfactory financial performance, are not clear yet. Besides, capital structure standards (debt-service coverage, debt-equity ratio, absolute debt limit) and liquidity standards (current ratio, quick ratio) are underutilized. Financial analysis remains underutilized for insufficiency of updating in respect of the balance sheet, the income statement, and financial statements. The absence of an integrated system of management information, including budgeting, accounting, internal control and financial reporting, impedes progress toward achieving financial objectives. As a result, such objectives as covering operating costs, servicing debts and contributing to investment from internally-generated funds remain largely unmet.

The long-standing cash-basis accounting, annual accounting, vote accounting and expenditure-line itemization, vast paperwork, persistence of fragmented fund accounting, excessive and time-consuming controls and mandatory compliance with elaborate statutory provisions militate against the production of useful cost data. A capacity for management accounting, output measures and cost control is lacking. Relative inattention to breakeven analysis, pricing decision, capital investment decision, capital planning, budgetary planning, unit costing, standard costing and variance planning, economy and efficiency auditing and program-result auditing continue. Record-keeping, billing procedure, credit control, payment procedure, basic-accounts maintenance, asset management and estimation procedure are constrained by proceduralism and, even in some instance, tardiness. The Projects' operating leverage is not robust in that resources are deployed and assets are employed by organizations, but sufficient revenue is not generated to cover all fixed and variable costs. The inability is attributable, inter alia, to public sector financial management culture. With management often missing the totality of the organization, the Projects tend to be weak in raising funds, managing cash position, facing competition, confronting inflation, dealing with technological advances and grappling with international operations. To the extent objectives are mismanaged and funds are misallocated, the productivity of the Projects is undermined.

Greenland

Sheep-raising, an income generator and a profitable operation, is based on the controlled export of registered purebred Blackbelly sheep. The fact is that farmers appreciate the gains of export marketing. For example, young rams can fetch a price of EC$250 in parts of the Eastern Caribbean. But the Greenland Station cannot produce much reliable data on production cost because most of the information is scattered throughout the Ministry of Agriculture with no organized way to record it. Revenue generation through the sale of by-products, such as sheep manure, offal and hides is yet to be realized. Income is variable because of shifting weather, fluctuating prices, unpredictable exports, and animal diseases. The reasons for low productivity are high prices of concentrate feed, the relative scarcity of grass and the low price paid by butchers. No sizable increase in sheep production is likely to occur unless the farmer can see that he can make a reasonable profit. Cost is a major constraint. One can amortize fixed costs, but there are some significant variable costs, namely, feed cost and weaning cost.

The Station's increased financial and commercial success hinges on extending size, reducing feed and other costs, dovetailing experiment and commercialization, sustaining weight gains relative to feed intake, and improving the feedlot system. Higher success also depends on managing the spinoffs, i.e. recycling skins and pelts into leather, utilizing gut in animal feed, and using sheep manure as fertilizer.

Handicraft

The Project produces goods and services for which demand is reasonably high and persistent and income, as result, is generated. Sales are aimed at ensuring reasonable return on investment and financial viability for the producers, many of whom are small-scale, home-based entrepreneurs. But the downside is that several products have low retail value, thus not always covering cost sufficiently and regularly. The inability to operate on a cost recovery basis renders the industry somewhat uncompetitive in certain respects in the labor market. Financing the needed inputs for the industry is slow and somewhat unpredictable. No proper accounting system seems to be in place in many enterprises, especially the smaller ones.

Cave

The rate of growth of net increase over the next 15 years or so in the Cave is considerable. Benefits are locally retained variously, e.g. package tours, group tours, use of local travel agents, use of national regional carriers and charter flights. Income from admission fees, transportation cost, value-added taxes and office rental accrues to the Cave management. Group/summertime tours and concessional trips partly complement the declining revenue during the lean season. The Cave is a successful, self-supporting and income-earning enterprise that has over the last few years brought in revenue of over BDS$2m. and has recorded increased visitor attendance over the last few years. The revenue is directly attributable to patronizing by Cave visitors. A number of programs are in place to maximize the intake of revenue. Certainly, operating revenue of the Cave could be higher. However, Cave attendance competes with airfare, accommodation, food and drink, transportation, purchases, sightseeing, and incidentals. The Cave also competes with the Animal Flower Cave, Andromeda Gardens, Flower Forest, Farley Hill, historic sites, seabathing, watersports, tennis, golfing, horseriding, and nightlife.

Pulverization

The discounted value of future, residential benefits and productivity gains from upgrading the disposal site is noteworthy. The spinoff gains arise out of land reclamation and availability, residential development, business expansion and facilities creation, both in the short and long term. But the downswing is that sanitary landfills like Workmans are more costly to operate and maintain than ordinary disposal sites. The cost of collection, treatment and disposal rises periodically. Narrow financial base cannot ensure Plant modernization and maintenance. There is little cost analysis at the Plant, for instance, marginal cost pricing. Unwillingness to charge service fees for the collection and disposal services points to lack of policy initiative, militates against the delivery of an adequate service and perpetuates inability to raise revenue to defray and recover operational costs.

Polytechnic

A maximum of quality results at lowest possible unit-cost is being stressed. Financial returns for technical-vocational training tend to outstrip those of their counterparts in the other occupational areas. The Polytechnic, whose graduates enjoy improved earning capacity, generates revenue from varied sources, e.g. tuition fee from nonnationals, registration fee, student affairs fee and examination fee. Then again, the average cost per student per year has increased over the years and so has the Institution's operating cost.

Sewerage

In-house connection with the system saves money which is otherwise spent periodically on emptying earth toilets. Property value is raised in the seaward area, connection fees are collected from users, and increased property taxes are accumulated from property-owners. The Plant raises revenue by putting service fee on the sewer connections it makes with the user premises. In view of a smaller target area with limited operating revenue, a relatively high fixed service charge, as reflected by total water use, was prescribed. All customers, residences as well as organizations, were considered as chargeable customers of the system. Finance reflected the policy that some service charges are basically utility charges and that the cost of the service should be defrayed to the greatest possible extent by those who benefit from its availability.

The rate schedule employed by the Barbados Water Authority has met one of the conditions of the loan agreement which was that the Authority should be able to finance its capital development as well as operation and maintenance. With the rate structure in place, the Authority was expected to break even within the first five years of operation. The Authority has been able to do it. The Project's financing has somewhat eased the current financial situation. For instance, the IDB supplied 70.6% and the GOB 29.4% of the Project cost. The loan was disbursed at the rate of 10% during the first two years, 50% in the third year, and 30% in the fourth year. The loan agreement stipulated that repayment by the GOB to the IDB would begin after an 8-year grace period during which the interest rate on the outstanding balance would be 1%. Once repayment started, the interest rate would be 2% for the remaining 27 years. The loan would carry a credit commission of 5% per year on the undisbursed part of the loan and an inspection/supervision fee of 1% on the loan amount.

In any event, the rate of turn on high capital investment has been so far low and slow. Moreover, the costs of connection, collection, treatment, operation and maintenance have gone up. The costing of sewage disposal is not clear as yet. One is not sure if, for instance, the average incremental cost - on a per capita household basis or a volumetric basis - has been established by the management. The ability of the Plant to recover its initial investment outlay and remain profitable has been weakened as a result of its inability to initiate necessary management action and realize some financial benefits.

The Project's financial appraisal revealed interesting information. When net present values were established for the Project, it was realized that even a discount rate of 0% would yield no financial gain from the level of investment in the Project. The internal rate of return for the Project yielded a negative value, too, but analysts decided that the benefits outweighed the costs. Also, the lack of financial feasibility reinforced the need for economic appraisal to ascertain the true benefits which would render the Project viable. Continuing weaknesses include failure to put an effluent fee on environmental discharges, neglecting to introduce market incentives into pollution control, failure to set the prices at which environmental discharges are permitted, and slackness in firming up the connection rate.

In some cases, rates are disproportionate to users of the system. While some use a large amount of water but release only a smaller amount of wastewater, others release large amount of wastewater into the system but pay less for the service as a result of reduced water consumption. The Barbados Water Authority has been unable so far to stand depreciation and capital cost. This is because the customer base and the revenue base are not broad as yet, nor has the countrywide 5% increase in water rates to fund part of the Project's operational costs been implemented. The reasoning that, since a cleaner Bridgetown would be of benefit to all Barbadians and residents all should help bear the cost of sewering the city, has so far failed to translate into actual revenue increase. The rate increase became a political issue and was eventually dropped, which undermined the Project's desired revenue.

Ferneihurst

The Estate, offering affordable housing, is a capital asset with regular income. It produces goods and services for which demand is high, especially among low-income households, and income is generated. Savings in transport cost and commuting time accrue to tenants because of proximity to shopping centers, schools, bus stops, service stations, and other urban facilities. The benefits Ferneihurst produces are considerably above the rent which the tenants pay currently. Although tenants do not pay the full cost of their housing, they gain the benefits without paying for it fully. The flip side is that the cost of maintaining Ferneihurst and similar estates is relatively high partly because cost savings, when and where is possible, are not effected. Thus, the advantage of cost-effectiveness is lost and the cost per unit continues to be high. The problems of lost and delayed revenue, heavy arrears, poor and irregular payments, bad debts and delinquent tenants continue to cause financial stress. The NHC is unable to overcome some of the most serious problems and disincentives at Ferneihurst. For example, some tenants not only do not pay their rent regularly, but also refuse to pay and do not seem to care. Again, it cannot, owing to policy constrains, periodically revise rent level, based on tenant affordability, designed to ensure a reasonable return.

Organizational Dimension

Barbados, like many developing countries, has inherited from the former colonial power a pattern of public sector management which has become, in certain respects, outmoded and vestigial. The organizations, including programs and projects, operate within the overall context of extensive compartmentalism, proceduralism and adverserialism. The organizations are tools of control with the top management having the major share of power, authority, influence, and initiative. Decisions basically involve adjustments to decisions, adaptations to the existing organizational culture, and piecemeal tinkering rather than much-needed and systemic changes. Few tasks or positions are ever worked out once and for all. Decision-making continues to be, in general, serial, satisficing, and incremental. The presence of conflict and divisiveness, in various forms and fashion, in the organizational milieu is nearly constant. The inability or unwillingness to resolve or curtail organizational problems can push sound investments into continuing losses. Many investments leave room for higher efficiency and greater capacity utilization, i.e. the rate of actual to potential output. Once completed - after so much feasibility analysis, technical assistance, and project team-building - the resulting 'operation' tends to be undermined by weaknesses, inadequacies, obsoleteness and rigidity of the public sector environment, the work systems continue to be inadequate and performance-insensitive, and the projects tend to be become yet another indifferent or casual player. Once completed, organizations and facilities tend to deteriorate rapidly for want of routine and periodic maintenance. The organizations tend to be stymied by an extraordinary concentration of authority at the top echelons and consequential loss of operational latitude. They continue to be characterized by traditions that delay rather than expedite output generation, service/product delivery, and goal management. Many personnel are not inclined toward or trained in open, participative, cooperation-inducing, and problem-solving approaches. Management capability development is relatively low, isolated, and intermittent. Decisions are delayed, focusing falters, synergy suffers, initiative peters out, programs get obstructed, and losses are not contained due to a low level of management capability.

Performance or program auditing is spotty to nonexistent in the sample Projects. Nor are the organizations particularly strong in asset creation and management, cost control, forecasting, simulation, delivery system capability, product/service improvement and price-volume relationship. Time series analysis, debt servicing, operation analysis and performance appraisal remain superficial, sporadic, and nonstandardized. Annual reporting is not always regular and is less management-oriented. Noteworthy too are the absence of or deficiency in strategic management - changing patterns of global and cosmetic competition, organizational size adjustment, changing product/service mix, altering market scope, unhelpful or unfocused human resource analysis, high ratios of capital to value added, and high ratios of capital to labor. There is little or no application of risk analysis, decision tree analysis, queuing theory, marginal analysis and work sampling. Not enough is done by way of organizational image-building and promotion - market survey, segmentation, mix, positioning, and customer satisfaction. Progress, regularity, reliability, success, achievement-orientation, evaluation, follow-through, accountability and transparency are limited, even spotty, in several functional areas, e.g. operation, finance, personnel, procurement, and information-processing.

Greenland

The Station, where after-hour emergency services are available, is manageable with comparatively low labor content and low capital outlay. The Station employees have experience, know-how, and love for animals. The Station is attentive to the adequate supply of water for the healthy growth of sheep and the provision of adequate feed at all times and the improved pasture system during mating or breeding time, pregnancy time, lactation time, and growth time. The Facility pays attention to such factors as equipment, working area, slaughtering time and capacity, and sanitary conditions. The production cost has been brought under control by using local feed and inexpensive shelters. The Station has developed an export system to handle regional and extraregional shipment of live animals and products. The Project markets its livestock through the Barbados Agricultural Development and Marketing Corporation. The sheep farmers do their own marketing and use supermarkets, retail outlets, public markets and butchers. The abattoir facility has improved its slaughtering services to livestock producers. Lamb producers aim for the high end of the market, supplying consumers with some 25,000 lamb carcasses of about 25kg. each a year.

The downside is that work on animal selection, homegeneity retention and export-driven production have been scaled down. Farmers tend to overgraze pastures during the dry season. Adequate land allowing for pasture rotation is not available. The demand of sheep-farming as an occupation, such as constant vigilance and long working hours, remains unmet in many cases. The provision of stud service to local farmers is not regular. The disposal rate, especially to small farms, is slow. The life cycle of the parasites has not been broken. High lamb mortality and high incidence of respiratory complication persists. Some farmers fail to observe sound practices, viz. controlling mutton quality in terms of tenderness and flavor, feeding adult sheep with high-quality ration with molasses, avoiding rough handling of animal, hanging the hot carcass after slaughtering by the tenderstretch method, etc.

Certain needs are ignored, such as the continuation of sheep registration, undertaking periodic surveys, updating the Ministry of Agriculture's policy directives, providing feed credit, guaranteed market and price, export promotion, etc. The levels of productivity in terms of output of mutton and lamb per head per acre are low. Commercialization is weak because the clientele has not been fully developed. Marketing suffers from deficiencies, viz. it has not been proactive. Supermarkets' business practices adversely affect local lamb marketing. Business promotions, such as trade missions and export fairs are not frequent. Production and accounting record-keeping are not thorough. The current materials control system causes the loss of time and diminishes initiative. There are gaps in the Station's farmer relations, professional networking, and program coordination. Cost saving by way of bulk ordering and handling of physical input is not reliable. Ministerial redtape causes delay in fulfilling export orders. The supply of drugs, tools and other inputs in the local market is unsteady. There are deficiencies in slaughtering, i.e. proper fabrication, grading, and storing.

Handicraft

Both job-order and batch production are in existence. At workshops, the process layout is in evidence. Product planning and control is in force, viz. planning, routing, loading, scheduling, dispatching, and expediting. Skill upgrading and on-job learning are on stream. Record-keeping is extensive, embracing production, costing, personnel, inventory, and sales records. Organizational aspects are evident in a set of activities, e.g. product design, catalog development and publication, entrepreneurship training and assistance, raw material location and sourcing, shipment, customs clearance, materials delivery, marketing and accounting training, marketing tests, and loan securing. To develop and diversify handicraft, marketing strategies are in place to assist producers in promoting and marketing their products. The consignment as well as the direct purchase system boosts effective marketing. Sales are monitored with a view to enlarging marketing share.

The main promotional event - the handicraft competition/exhibition - is held annually, incorporates hundreds of entries and offers adequate display space to craft producers. Other promotional activities include the annual industry week and an occasional series of wayside crafts markets. Annual handicraft exports help improve product quality, increase consumer awareness, earn producer respectability, and ease product acceptance. The Project's relative flexibility, small turnaround time and adaptability to differentiating demands become increasingly important with rising income.

The constraints are numerous, viz. inadequate production planning and control, underutilization of strategic planning, low level of product standardization and diversification, uneven quality control, unsteady supply of raw materials, occasional unavailability of tools, accessories and chemicals, inability to use value analysis, inability to get into new design development, inability to analyze cost behavior, paucity of modern production techniques, short production runs, long setup time, unstable product specification, infrequent maintenance, insufficient safety measures, and frequent downtime. Other snags include insufficient research and development, inaccurate and irregular record-keeping, variable quality of product, limited orders, limited reordering, limited retailer support, missing delivery dates, high mark-ups, small market size, limited promotion, inadequate materials control, scale seasonality, lack of feasible mechanization, shortage of competent and marketable design, and inadequate pool of design skills.

Marketing decisions remain somewhat uninformed by strategic criteria. Overemphasis on production and selling of crafts is accompanied by neglect of research, design, training, product development, quality control, marketing, financing, export marketing, stock control, craft cooperative, machine service workshop operation, craft manual publication, and tracer studies of craft producers. Adverse retailer perception and judgement persists, i.e. local skills are inadequate and uneven, finishing is inferior, supplies are not organized, designs are repetitive and monotonous, and local products cannot compete with imported wares in quality, cost and variety. Small producers do not have access to export subsidies, tax exemptions on capital goods and raw materials favor the large producers over the small ones, import licensing creates bias against small entrepreneurs, credit policies and institutional criteria tend to operate against small producers, and small producers find it difficult to meet product specifications and standards. The Project is hamstrung in capturing a greater share of the local handicraft market, i.e. in a market share of BDS$12m. it has only 1.1m. or 9.1% of the market share.. Getting local products into the retail outlets is daunting. Local handicrafts, except in a few outlets, makes up only about 10-15% of the total stock carried.

Cave

The Visitors Center - comprising an information desk, a restaurant, a boutique, and a lounge/gallery - accommodates the visitors. The guide service provides in forty minutes an interesting and factual presentation to the visitor on the extensive Cave landscape. What the visitor sees, as he rides along the mile of underground visitor route aboard electric-powered tram-trailers, are the enormous galleries filled with crystal-clear stalactites and stalagmites, tumbling waterfalls and deep pools, all appearing as nature created them. A sense of viewer participation is achieved by having the passengers exit the vehicle at several viewing points during the tour of the fragile landscape.

A comprehensive maintenance schedule is in force, embracing underground plants, lighting, refuse, trail, speleothems, vehicle, safety, access road, carpark, directional signs, visitor reception area, and staff monitoring. There has been a steady increase of visitors from year to year. The bulk of the visitors is from North America, enhanced by cruise ships visiting Barbados. There is good support from European market and locals. The local visitors include summer camp groups, vacationing Barbadians, and church groups. Group tours, summertime tours and concessional trips partly complement the reduced revenue during the lean season. To accommodate and attract more visitors, underground night tours, special effects creation, sound/light presentation, a new workshop, a restaurant, a shopping arcade, bigger offices, better health and safety regulation, and a natural trail/scenic walk in the Cave vicinity are on the card.

The flip side is that the passenger concourse is small for the flow of visitors. A speedier ticketing and boarding procedure - easing congestion at the facility - is not in place. Periodically, the visitors have to queue in the sun and rain. There is difficulty in serving the heavy influx of cruise ship passengers. Due to time loss at the Cave, visitors are late getting back to cruise ships and miss dinner. Tight schedule reduces equipment lifespan and causes vehicle breakdown, resulting in delay, tour cancellation, trip reduction, and revenue loss. Paucity of multifaceted, professional and yearlong marketing and promotion persists, with external marketing being dominated by foreign interests and the tourist market having limited penetration. Liaising with tour agents, tour operators, media, schools, service clubs, civic associations and community groups leaves room for improvement. There are occasional lapses in preventive maintenance and high recurrent costs of vehicle maintenance. The breakdown of the trams and the delay in procuring replacement parts slow down operation. The local modifications to the imported trams, which call for advance planning and periodic analysis, are not in place.

Pulverization

The collection service follows an established process, i.e. vehicles operating on prescribed routes, making necessary stops, loading, returning, and unloading. The collection vehicles are equipped with attachment for self-loading. Using only route trucks for transport to disposal points and no auxiliary transfer system, hauling efficiency has been increased. With the current fleet, over 90% of households and institutions are directly accessible to the SSA vehicles. The Plant operations and the Landfill activities are monitored to ensure clean, competent, and hazard-free waste management. Deodorizers are used to combat the stench at the Plant and the Landfill. Landfill operations follow through a standard procedure. Vehicles collect shredded waste from the Plant and take it to the adjacent Workmans Landfill. Other vehicles roll, compact and cover the refuse. Equipment and vehicle maintenance follows a regular sequence to ensure service reliability. The SSA carries out maintenance in reasonably-equipped and updated mechanical workshops. Customers can call the SSA with queries and complaints. Callers query about collection dates, lodge complaint, report lapses, request for details, and ask for additional services.

A plethora of constraints stands out: lapses in collection, lack of suitable vehicles for waste collection in narrow streets, shortage of roadworthy vehicles, delay in getting replacement parts, poor or infrequent liaison with other organizations, wet and lumpy refuse causing mechanical problems, late arrival of some employees at the workplace, gaps in in-plant training, surface drainage insufficiency, occasional power failure, increasing overtime and payment, plastic materials causing disposal and drainage problems, and improper routing of collection vehicles periodically. There is more by way of downswing: waste dumping in unauthorized places, littering and pollution, uneven arrival of collection vehicles at the Plant causing queuing and handling problems, capacity underutilization, occasional landfill-generated stench in the neighboring areas, difficulty in getting suitable disposal sties, limited life of disposal sites, increased operational outlay due to higher input costs, difficulty in cleaning vehicles due to unavailability of proper power hose, facing occupational hazards such as skin disorder, and hauling refuse from a large catchment area.

The poor image of waste management of the past persists and delays the application of improved practices. Barbados is unable to keep pace with its growing waste generation. The volume of waste - 600 tons of waste a day - produced increases, the type and composition of waste vary, the demand for improved practices increases, and resistance to the location of processing or disposal sites is widespread. The entire process is not yet integrated, i.e. storage, collection, treatment, conversion, reuse, and disposal. There is failure, so far, to convert shredded refuse into compost, into recovered, reused and recycled resources, and into recovered energy. The careful planning of the collection service, such as routing and vehicle-emptying is not addressed properly. Maintaining on the road a fleet of mechanically-sound collection vehicles is not always efficient, thus affecting the Plant's operational efficiency and capacity utilization.

Modern personnel practices are lacking, resulting in undesirable employee behavior, lax supervisory control, ad hocism, dispositional conflict, and inadequate communication. Plant personnel work under conditions which are often difficult, demanding, and unpleasant. The Plant has suffered downtime with the shredders going through mechanical breakdowns, cracks appearing in the shredder support structure, service vibration appearing, shutdown occurring for repairs and testing, and other faults occurring. Equipment and vehicle maintenance lack clarity and consistency, affecting preventive maintenance, equipment amortization, replacement servicing schedules, and parts supply. The Landfill puts up with inefficiency in regulation enforcement, standard-setting, and inspection. Its operation is sometimes affected adversely by traxcavator downtime. It lacks water-supply to fight fires, fencing, gates, warning signs, and cautionary notes. It lacks watch service to check fires, illegal dumping and trespassing.

Polytechnic

The Polytechnic has helped mobilize institutional capability to service the country's technical-vocational training needs. Students and Campus personnel alike enjoy attractive features, e.g. offices, classrooms, workshops, laboratories, office aids, staff rooms, rest rooms, spacious premises, increased facilities, greater variety, and increased visibility. The Project has facilitated greater departmentalization, programme decentralization and personnel enrichment, e.g. institutional outreach, faculty development, program and option diversification and intensification, higher intake and service capacity, intensive training, skill marketing, technical and artisinal skill advancement, enrolment expansion, facility expansion, teaching-material acquisition, and production and equipment modernization. Collaboration with overseas institutions facilitates technical assistance, staff training, management development, organization-building, professionalism, work system development, modernization and computerization. The Polytechnic is a department of the Ministry of Education. It is headed by a principal who is responsible for supervision of the teaching program and kindred activities and management of the Institution's physical facilities. He is assisted by a deputy principal. Financial management of the Complex is the responsibility of support staff in the area of accounting. The Polytechnic utilizes the same operational procedures established for budgeting, accounting, purchasing and payments as prescribed by public sector management. The Polytechnic has on stream several useful operations. Its guidance counselling service provides student with concern and problem alleviation, assistance and study-related information. While placement service assists students in finding employment, attachment service places students in a particular work setting for a stated period for acquiring hands-on experience. Student council offers outlets for recreation, athletics, and human development. Campus security has been upgraded by hiring four security personnel.

Nonetheless, some of the deficiencies are noticeable: high dropout rate, tight budget and small revenue base, gaps in the current training and skill development programs, lack of a proactive role in program development, highlighting work-study programs and introducing new courses not fully addressed, inability to offer more marketable and relevant training, shortage of trained personnel to liaise continuously with employee organizations and emerging trends, inability to engage in developing an updated curriculum, failure to institutionalize aptitude test on a wider scale, declining enrolment in certain programs and courses, inflation and rising operational cost, and absence of a playground.

The Institution finds it difficult to accommodate the number of students who apply each year for full-time programs. Consequently, many students apply, but only some gain entry. The large volume of applications and supporting documents results in lengthy processing time and high staff-time consumption. The intake capacity is still small both in relation to the needs of the population and the total demand for school places. With limited communication between management and faculty, the practice of employing too many part-time and temporary faculty continues. It is also difficult to identify and recruit faculty at short notice. Little or no training is available in raising competencies and skills, viz. interpersonal relations skill, diagnostic competence, resource creation and mobilization competence, motivation skill, classroom management skill, program planning skill, and assessment competence. Employees are not well-informed of the objectives and activities of the Polytechnic. There are gaps in the counselling service, career guidance, and industrial liaison service and placement service. For example, placement service suffers from lack of follow-up and insufficiency of record-keeping, and failure to carry out tracer studies of graduates and dropouts persists.

Absence of an active maintenance program persists in relation to landscaping, building, equipment, services, facilities, and resources. The Campus lacks locker rooms for service and maintenance personnel. The Campus employees' and students' health and safety needs are not fully attended. Security in and around the Campus is not entirely satisfactory. Lack of safety tools and first-aid kits in the mechanical and technical divisions persists.

Sewerage

The merging of water-supply and sewage functions into the Barbados Water Authority resulted in institution-building. The collection system has been functioning satisfactorily, with a minimum of blockages. The Plant accepts and treats loads of septage daily. Effluent treatment is in keeping with the set standards. The Plant's physical emissions, such as noise, heat and vibrations, are reduced to tolerable levels through special equipment. Certain effluents that are unpleasant or noxious go through special treatment. For in-house connection, financial and other assistance from the Barbados Water Authority are available. The Plant personnel have benefitted from training in wastewater operation and maintenance. Training included hands-on training in laboratory methods and wastewater analysis. Operational and maintenance manuals are on steam, providing routine and preventive maintenance. Pumps, blowers and sewers, for instance, are checked. The Plant laboratory monitors the quality of the sewage as it comes into and leaves the Complex. Specially-designed vehicles clear away any blocks in the sewers.

The debit site is that only substance and industrial waste cannot be treated and its disposal poses problems, sludge disposal is odorous and hazardous, the number of user connections is low and delay in service connection represents revenue loss, improper disposal of objects into the system causes clog and congestion, the cost of treatment, operation and maintenance is high, the cost of connection is high and procedures are lengthy, high-pitch whining sound from the Plant creates noise disamenity in a residential area, and the strong stench from the Plant caused by septage overload and the movement of septic trucks is pervasive. Also in evidence is tardiness to sensitize the target market to the usefulness of connecting with the system. Moreover, the old unsafe practice of clandestine sewage dumping at varius points persists, sewage spillage occurs while cleaning septic trucks or cesspool emptiers, the effluent sometimes runs into sidewalks, difficulty to recruit and retain technically skilled and competent personnel, lack of timing and regular maintenance, unavailability of an adequate supply of chemicals, materials, accessories and replacement parts, in-service on-job operator training is insufficient and slow, occupational health and industrial safety measures for the Plant personnel are inadequate, absence of resource recovery, reclamation and reuse initiatives, and lack of binding legislative provision to ensure user compliance. Equipment breakdown at the Plant is not infrequent. The installed equipment is neither the newest nor the most uptodate. For instance, the comminutor or barscreen - which shreds debris coming in via the sewer lines - has not worked properly for several years. It is also not uncommon for the Plant to face periodically the problem of suboptimal operation due to inoperable equipment, repair delays, and occasional breakdowns.

The problem at the pretreatment stage is the insufficient removal of inorganic material, causing the clogging of pumps and diffusers. The Plant's capacity to treat sewage is way below its collection. The system's designed capacity has not been attained, operating at only 25% capacity. It treats about 25% of its designed volume level of 500,000 gallons. Designed to take in from 2.4m. to 8m. gallons of sewage a day, the Plant currently treats 0.3m. gallons a day. The total system may break down and pose hazards unless the waste treatment process is adequately controlled and balanced and critical situation is managed, e.g. pathogens may not be destroyed, effluent may remain unsuitable for direct reuse and unsuitable for direct reuse and discharge into water, and the safety of water-supply may be threatened. No laboratory technician is currently employed to test and determine the amounts of chemical solutions which should be added to the sewage, causing improper treatment of sewage and production of stench.

Besides, inadequate technical background on the part of some personnel is responsible for the inappropriate treatment of effluent and hazardous discharge into the sea with harmful effects on the seabed. Increasing the sewage flow to the Plant by getting all the users in the sewered area to tie into the Plant immediately has not been a priority.

Septage overload causes stress. There is a hydraulic overload problem. Built to take in 8-10 loads or 5,000 gallons of septage a day, as many as 26-28 loads or 30,000 gallons are trucked into the Plant some days. The detention time for breakdown of organisms by bacteria is lessened considerably. A heavy buildup of sludge is caused by infrequent disposal of sludge from the Plant. The septic-truck drivers sometimes transport all types of unauthorized waste, including oily substance, and fail to wash their tanks thoroughly. Pipes are subject to rapid deterioration due to sulphuric acid corrosion. The cost of operation is high, i.e. the cost of power generation required in the electrolytic method of disinfection, the aerobic treatment of the sewage sludge, and the cost of high water consumption. For instance, the sewage system with high-volume flush toilets increases domestic water consumption by around 50 to 70%. Trucks come to the Plant to draw off the grease accumulation, and this is an additional cost to the operation.

Ferneihurst

The Estate enjoys steady and long-term tenancy, with the NHC maintaining computerized tenancy and accounting records. The practice of appointing resident wardens at the Estate helps identify and communicate concerns. Community vibrancy, for example, is fostered by holding street fairs and garden competitions annually. The operating procedures employed by the Corporation in respect of rent arrears, arrears liquidation and court orders have been tightened. Rent collection has improved by decentralizing rent payment and collection, opening a collection office at Rosemont, retrieving arrears, monitoring defaulters and problem tenants, and drawing up new housing contracts.

The failings can hardly be exaggerated: difficult tenant selection in terms of tenants' ability and willingness to pay rent, large backlog of unprocessed applications, inability to respond favorably to approved applicants, difficulty in evicting delinquent tenants, defaulting tenants creating negative demonstration effect, breach of tenancy agreement, nonpayment of rent and accumulation of arrears, protracted nature of rent and arrears collection, financial shortfall causing lapse in the level of maintenance service, rent nonpayment, defaulting and arrears creating problems, absence of firm action against delinquent tenants, lack of advance forward planning, failure to review rental rate and level periodically for improving the revenue position, slackness in handling and storage practices causing wastage and pilferage, evidence of defects in building regulation, absence of housing code, slackness in tenancy records system, and absence of in-service on-job training program for the NHC personnel.

Likewise, other lapses command attention. The waiting line for prospective tenants to secure occupancy is indeterminate. Some tenants fail to honor their tenancy agreement and end up in heavy arrears. Some tenants consistently fail to pay rent or settle outstanding arrears. Some of those in arrears hold steady jobs, yet they fail to make their payments. The payroll deduction system with the employers to ensure regular payments by tenant is not yet in place. There are gaps in direct communication between the NHC and the tenants with regard to accommodation-related issues , viz. recreational and social facilities, refuse disposal, garden maintenance, and noise level. Desultory practice pervades activities, viz. monitoring tenant status, investigating rent nonpayment, identifying welfare or needy cases, settling tenant complaints, and checking upkeep and landscaping. Deficiencies in standard operating procedures are glaring in respect of accounting, regulation, safety, sanitation, fire prevention, tenancy agreement, rent collection, reporting, and communication. There is room for improvement in refuse collection, sewage disposal, security operation, and weekend watch service. Some of the units leak, and the toilets are too close to the kitchen and neighbors. Paint drift from a temporary unauthorized workshop on the Estate's eastern boundary affects vegetation and the units' furniture, poses health hazards, and disrupts general quiet, comfort convenience. Several planned ancillary elements have not been put in place yet, e.g. a day nursery, a community center/pavillion, and a warden's office.

The maintenance cost at the Estate is variable and tends to rise annually. For instance, some vandalism and carelessness have given rise to expensive maintenance. Servicing time as well as the length of servicing time is variable as well unpredictable. No maintenance manual is in existence. Maintenance is not regular. Despite numerous complaints from the tenants, toilets take long to fix. A few blocks are in need of facelifts. Mildew-covered walls and faded/pealing paint are not uncommon. Doors facing the east in a number of units have been changed, toilets and cisterns have been changed in several units, kitchen wastewater has caused clogs due to insufficiency of manholes in the sewage network, indiscriminate growth of plant or tree interferes with sewage lines, and inadequate maintenance of sewage system causes service disruption. Tardy materials control affects maintenance adversely. A maintenance chore is done sometimes hastily and under pressure only for the problem to reoccur shortly. Gaps in the level and range of maintenance personnel skills persist.

Technological Dimension

Technology is, as evidence shows increasingly, one of the prime movers in project development. The application of appropriate technology is a source of saving and utilizing scarce resources, attaining objectives and accelerating the pace of concerted action. Technology involves modernizing the production/service process, selecting appropriate technology, solving technical problems, improving output and service quality, learning new skills and methods, and introducing better machines. It also entails disseminating technical information, advising on industrial technology, and establishing know-how agreements. Technology further involves increasing the number of skilled producers, upgrading existing skills, and tapping and maintaining new kinds and sources of raw materials. Technology extends, for instance, to a project's physical planning inputs (topography, geology, climatology, hydrology, environment, etc.), architectural inputs (sketch design, site plan, specification, etc.), engineering inputs (site development, access road-building, utilities installation, construction, sanitation, equipment planning/installation, plant layout, plant capacity, etc.).

Technology underlying the Projects manifests itself variously, e.g. exploring and utilizing natural resources, venturing into new areas, introducing new and local technologies, improving adaptability and substitution, sustaining creativity, strengthening problem-solving capacity, improving absorptive capacity, generating confidence in Barbados' own forces and resources, creating a social awareness of technology, and expanding opportunities. Three categories of technology are seen at work. Consumption technology - the set of all possible consumption activities - pervades Greenland, Handicraft, Cave, and Ferneihurst. Process technology - know-how relating to the physical and chemical processes needed to transform raw materials into end products - extends to Handicraft, Pulverization, and Sewerage. Plant technology - the instrument of production such as machinery and equipment - touches on Cave, Pulverization, Polytechnic, and Sewerage.

In our Project, the modes of technology acquisition varied, e.g. technology chosen and supplied through or by foreign organizations, technology chosen by foreign consultants and supplied by foreign organizations, technology chosen by national/regional consultants but supplied by foreign organizations, and technology chosen by national/ regional consultants and supplied/assembled by national organizations. The level of mechanization involves hand labor, semimechanical, mechanical, semiautomatic, and fully automatic. The skill demands for technology utilization involve semiskilled as well as skilled. The output generation scale ranges from large scale, intermediate scale to small scale and craft scale. In terms of technology assimilation, one encounters such categories as local adoption and adaptation, repairs, replacement, accessorization, maintenance, and troubleshooting.

The Projects show technological dependence, viz. nonselective use of foreign and imported technology, low utilization of installed capacity, narrow scope, low linkage with the domestic economy, high import content, limited responsiveness to the factor endowments and limited control over technology impact. Local technological capability - a more integrated, appropriate, responsive and need-specific technology that enhances capacity, employs local labor, utilizes local goods and services, and energizes the local environment - is as yet limited. More effective assimilation of imported technology and stimulation of local technological development are not occurring. The links between science/technology institutions and user organizations tend to be tenuous. The appropriateness of technology was inhibited partly by the presence of tied external assistance and packaged overseas technology. The Projects' technological system remains weak and lacks the capacity to assimilate foreign technology, and workforce is not fully integrated with alleviating technological tasks. Barbados, like numerous developing countries, lacks adequate options in selecting technology in international technology markets. Technology-driven new options tend to be infrequent, new products and services are limited, reversing or reducing external technological dependence is not seen as important, and technology choices often evade local control.

Greenland

The Project, most particularly marked by technological challenge, provided, on a limited scale, a flock of purebred Blackbelly sheep, promoted selective breeding, assessed and followed up on the sheep's genetic features and reproductive traits, produced purebred Blackbelly sheep as foundation stock, demonstrated sheep-farming techniques, selected sheep for prolificacy, evaluated performance by rams, obtained growth data, conducted carcass evaluation, ran crossbreeding program, standardized purebred characteristics, improved the mutton-producing potential of the sheep, provided on-site technical assistance and extension services, practiced scientific husbandry, designed and conducted feeding trials, provided high-quality stud service, and upgraded flocks by breeding with purebred rams.

At the Station, the small flock method of mating is practiced, various lambing techniques are followed, and artificial insemination and embryo transplant capabilities are developed in order to quickly spread the genetic material. The Veterinary Diagnostic Laboratory provides technological support to sheep farmers by providing clinical diagnoses of diseases, implementing disease control and prevention, conducting disease surveys, and monitoring the incidence and levels of specific diseases. Pasturing extends to planting grass and legumes, manuring, fertilizing, liming, weed control, pest control, mowing, fencing, subdividing and rotating, and preserving trees. Health and sanitation measures include treating footrot, controlling and treating parasites, deworming the sheep, drenching the animal, docking the breed, shearing the animal, cleaning and disinfecting pens, draining pasture, isolating infected animals, safekeeping watering and feeding tools, rotating pasture, consulting veterinarian, and running diagnostic tests. Work was also done on the evaluation, grading, and fabrication of lamb meat. The taste testing trials were held at several locations. Work concerned evaluating carcasses for quality and cutability with a view to collecting data, and determining carcass composition and muscle-bone ratios in carcasses.

Handicraft

Handicraft is a hand tool-oriented, semimechanical, craft-based production activity, with the workshop tools being hand-powered, simple, durable, maintainable and inexpensive, and producing time-saving substitutes. Technology is inherent in raw materials and accessory acquisition, production, artisinal skill acquisition, and research and design. Technology is integrated, for example, in the production process, e.g. mold-making, glazing, firing, heat generation and control, fabrication and maintenance of tools, quality control, and complete vs. batch production. Technology has assimilated in all areas of pottery, i.e. throwing, casting, firing, decorating, and glazing. Technology is inherent in soil analysis, e.g, selection, identification, and preservation of clay deposits. Technology steps in while treating and processing some raw materials, such as leaching, dyeing, and splitting. Product standardization also relates to technology in respect of quality, size, finish, and presentation of the wares/products. Product designs incorporate such technological aspects as variety, originality, novelty, indigenousness, modernity, and appeal. The labelling system, product packing and presentation point to technological capability development. However, technological support for work relating to the improvement, treatment and discovery of suitable local material is not strong.

Cave

The application of science and technology involved geological surveys of the Cave area to establish, among other things, the thickness of the limestone. Soil analysis was made to ensure compliance with construction specifications. Tests of groundwater pollution were conducted at several points in the Cave system. Tests of Cave ventilation were made, including a series of temperature, relative humidity, and air movement measurements. Tests of the probability of rockfall, Cave wall and roof collapse and spalling were run. The rate of infiltration of rain water and the maximum amount of water that could flow through the Cave were estimated. The Cave walls were gouged, textured and roughened to simulate natural Cave passageway. Pockets were left in the limestone to encourage the growth of mosses, ferns, and indigenous vegetation. Various rails were constructed to facilitate access and viewing. Interior trails were constructed. Underground area modifications were carried out. The areas were paved even, accommodating a two-trailer vehicle, providing extra width around curves and turnaround zones, constructing high curb to ensure safe driving, and flattening curb to allow excess water entering and leaving. The water of two streams was diverted from the center of the passageways to a course alongside the roadway. A dam was built to hold and channel water and to facilitate the flow to advance over waterfalls and through Cave formations. The drainage system was installed for over a mile of the Cave passages to ensure that water in all seasons could be accommodated. Underground lighting was put in place to bring out the natural blue green color of the pools, highlight the crystal clearness of a forty-foot waterfall, and illuminate the glistening white formations of the rocks.

Pulverization

In terms of the Plant's siting, subsurface explorations were carried out. Soil analysis was conducted, especially when and where the sole source of potable water flowed from underground in a limestone formation. To ensure the environmental safety and to eliminate the possibility of groundwater pollution, hydrological tests were carried out. A study of lechate from refuse sites and the possible effect such lechate might have on underground water was undertaken. A topographic survey was conducted in relation to the contours of the Plant site, the disposal area, and adjacent access roads. The load-bearing properties of the foundation materials were checked. Technical designing made it possible to locate the Plant out of the path of the winds blowing toward residential areas, build the Plant in an old low-lying quarry in a way that muffles the in-plant noise, and set up the Plant in such a way as to prevent leaching into underground water supplies. Trial runs showed that the Plant equipment and electrical installations were correctly installed. Vibrational tests were run on the Plant equipment to check the suitability of the support structure system. Various disposal methods were examined in relation to the whole gamut of waste management. But the downturn shows that training for the SSA personnel in waste management - which is technical - lacks continuity and technological currency. Especially, training for the supervisory staff in learning how to collect and dispose of different types of waste material lacks continuity.

Polytechnic

The Polytechnic responds to, enhances and retains technological capability in the local environment. Such capability is sustained via technical training in classrooms, workshops and practicals, apprenticeship programs, faculty training, and audiovisual training material production. Extensive equipment management extends to maintaining machine tools, hand tools, ancillary accessories, classrooms, laboratories, workshops, offices, and other functional areas. A study of the site's soil characteristics and ground conditions was carried out, including testing soil depth, soil occurrence, and terrain features. Project design was attentive to the site offering the optimum advantages of accessibility, transport and location, the site's topographical, climatic and habitational features, the site's soil and drainage characteristics, a physical structure reflecting climatic and topographic conditions, and the provision for higher percentages of horizontal circulation for climatic reasons and noise levels.

Sewerage

The design chosen seems adequate to cope with the environmental health and urban problems that were being experienced in the design areas. Project design shows sensitivity to appropriate technology by identifying conservation need, simple operation, low sludge generation, low mechanization, and low dependence on foreign-supplied components. Technological soundness and safety is built into the system in that the Plant's process-based operation includes materials, primary/physical processes, secondary/biological processes, and tertiary/chemical processes. The analysis of waste treatment method involved whether electrolysis or chlorination should be used. Several technical criteria went into selecting sites for the treatment plant, the marine outfall, and the pumping stations. For instance, the Emmerton site was chosen for the treatment plant because it was optimally located in that the sewer lines would emerge at the point where the minimum slopes of the target area provide maximum gravity flow, thus minimizing the use of pumping stations.

To illustrate, to accommodate the gravity flow required of a sanitary sewer system such as Bridgetown and to make it economical, the sewer pattern follows the natural drainage pattern of the service area closely. Bridgetown's major sewers follow stream lines and other sewers are laid to follow the slope of the land. The site was also within short distance of a coastal location where the marine outfall could be so located as to reach deep water at a relatively short distance offshore.

Oceanographic and hydrographic studies established the physical, chemical and biological characteristics of the receiving-water environment. Hydrographic and meteorological data appraised the marine outfall's siting, design and constructability. Oceanographic studies determined the strength and direction of currents, temperature and salinity with a view to assisting in the siting and design of the marine outfall, and determined the direction and destination of residential pollutants. Marine biological studies were concerned with the effects of sewage effluent on the nearshore coral reefs, balancing the coastal and marine ecosystems, eliminating discharge of raw sewage into the sea, reducing nutrients and toxins in reefs, reducing coliform levels in bathing and offshore areas, improving the quality of inshore coastal waters, and providing beach protection. Several other studies were executed, e.g. topography with reference to ground levels and contours within the larger target area, soil studies to determine soil types, bearing pressure and groundwater levels, water consumption patterns to eliminate sewage flow, and analyses of volume and characteristics of sewage and other wastes to determine parameter values with respect to biological oxygen demand, suspended solids, total solids, nutrients and metals. Technical training was held at the Plant which involved odor control, effluent and sludge control, wastewater treatment, pretreatment, industrial waste management, disinfectants, toxins and nutrients.

Still, there is room for improvement in relation to personnel training in wastewater control and sustenance of technological awareness at the Plant. The Plant was not designed to treat grease in sewage - grease coming primarily from restaurants, industries and septic tanks in the target area - preventing air from going through the water in the sewage and causing solids to become septic too quickly. Then again, the equipment installed at the Plant was made to United States standards whereas Barbados uses British standards, which resulted in a frequency problem causing equipment breakdowns and posed problems for maintenance personnel who were not skilled to fix equipment.

Ferneihurst

Tests were run to determine the soil type and the site depth. Technical activities included perimeter survey, topographic survey including field survey and census of buildings and trees, physical planning and development designs, utilities planning and execution, architectural services, and infrastructural work. For example, 3,030 ft. of mains were laid within the Estate's sidewalks to supply water, together with seven control valves and six fire hydrants. One hundred square feet of access road was reinstated.

Environmental Dimension

The environment provides resources and constitutes 'natural capital'. Its wide range of services - water flow, soil protection, pollutant breakdown, waste recycling, climate regulation - support and enhance development. Environmental concerns embrace a range of issues, including waste management, slum clearance, occupational health, environmental safety and quality, sanitation, pollution control, erosion control, resource management, resource recovery, habitat/wildlife conservation, resource conservation, cultural preservation, noise abatement, accident prevention, and critical-system protection, e.g. mangroves, wetlands, coral reefs, seagrass beds, beach processes, rangelands, wild lands, watersheds, fisheries, and water resources.

The GOB's objectives are to avoid environmental damage or reducing it to an acceptable minimum, to achieve a balance between human demands on the natural resource base and the environment's ability to meet these demands, and to manage the country's renewable resources without diminishing the environment's carrying capacity. As a result of these Projects, the enjoyment and quality of life for many people in the target group has risen. Large as well as small communities have become more secure and viable. Preventive action is more preferred and taken up in Barbados and is nearly always less costly than remedial action. Environmental monitoring, for instance beach erosion control overseen by the Environmental Division, provides an early warning of potential or actual damage. Data on the environment, for instance water conservation overseen by the Water Authority, is used as regular input into planning.

Pollution control or abatement in Barbados remains limited. Public sector resource allocation in this area is limited, and the private sector's response to maintaining environmental quality appears uneven. Some of the main environmental problems extend to soil erosion, deforestation, fishing damage, crop damage, and wildlife extinction. Environmental degradation manifests itself in the depletion of topsoil, fuelwood and clean water and beach erosion, congestion, noise, and lack of open space and recreational areas. Lack of trained personnel and lack of firm policy initiative are some of the major constraints on environmental monitoring. Having a small and limited resource base and being ecologically fragile and vulnerable to developmental pressures, Barbados as a small-size country has a reduced carrying capacity to absorb and recover from the harmful effects of careless growth. Nearly all the discharges, for instance, have more or less adverse effects on the environment. The environmental aspects are frequently overlooked or their value underestimated because they are almost always public goods, not provided in the marketplace. Customarily, a project's ecological effects are less analyzed because they appear to be considered marginal or remote and are of the slowly accruing type. The community also poorly understands the nature of environmental degradation - spreading pollution through indiscriminate disposal of refuse and discharge of effluent, industrial/fluoride/effluent/vehicle emissions and toxic effects causing damage to health and resources, dust disfiguring the landscape, structures offending landscape aesthetics, noise causing stress, and activities diminishing sensory quality, such as appearance and odor.

Several strategies are in train to deal with environmental degradation, e.g. preventive action being more results-oriented and cost-effective and environmental monitoring providing an early warning of damage. Data on the environment is usable as a regular input into planning. While designing a project, safe, appropriate, minimum and environmentally-acceptable standards must be identified. The safeguards require relatively simple design changes relating to such matters as standards for health, sanitation, safety, open space, and plant/animal protection. For maximum effectiveness, environmental concerns merit inclusion in design at the earliest possible stage, when they can be accommodated at least cost. Environmental impact needs to be closely monitored during implementation. Among the most common measures needed are control on air and water pollution to reduce emissions and effluents to acceptable levels. The polluters who impose costs on the environment and its users must be charged the full costs of environmental safeguards. They may be required to pay service charges based on the amount of pollutant discharged. Pollution control may also be addressed through regulatory mechanism like licenses or permits.

Greenland

Some of the constraints include stray sheep scavenging in refuse containers, scattering domestic refuse, damaging gardens and parks, soiling paved areas, presenting a hazard to vehicular traffic, carrying parasitic diseases, occasional herbage contamination, inadequate slaughtering facilities, and disposal of organic wastes.

Handicraft

The Handicraft operation is environmentally-intensive in that it draws heavily on, relates to and is linked with the local environment, viz. raw materials, local plants, industrial byproducts, accessory materials, indigenous entrepreneurship and skills, local heritage, and tradition-based design.

Cave

The surface area is enriched by lush tropical vegetation. The Cave site, a ravine of ornamental plants and outstanding floral and vegetal beauty, provides high visual and scenic amenity value, is one of the most restful places in the island and offers an opportunity for communing with nature. The Scenic Walk, about 750 ft. in length and 75 ft. in width to the west of the Cave entrance, presents a series of citrus and fruit trees and indigenous plant communities. The Cave, a giant conduit and definitely fire-proof (Gurnee, 1981), is preserved in its natural condition with, for instance, interior trails and cave walls simulating naturalness. It is stable and rockfall/ceiling collapse does not constitute a significant danger. The chance of cave formations falling from ceilings and walls is extremely remote. With multiple entrances, the Cave enjoys natural airflow. Its drainage systems are the supply routes for underground food chains and help form and maintain its structural features. Unusual communities develop in the dark underground habitat which are of ecological interest, e.g. crustaceans, fish, bats, wall-fungus, and bacterial/fungal elements. Powered by electric batteries, the underground cave vehicles reduce odor and other pollutions as well as chance of spills of dangerous or toxic materials and eliminate haze and fogging.

In any event, the formations and processes in the Cave - stalactites, stalagmites, waterfalls, streams, pools, stalagtites rising from the floor beneath the dipping calcite-laden water which actively form them - are delicate and fragile. The Cave presents an environment where the temperature is almost constant, it has taken many years to create formations from small mineral-laden drops of water, and its seemingly static condition sustains unusual biological life-forms. The formations are alive, crystalline, growing and integral part of the total underground landscape. Gurnee and Gurnee warn (1980) that a cave's interior is possibly one of the nature's most fragile environments. It is a world in delicate balance. The intrusion of humans can tip this balance, causing massive changes in the cave biota, in the growth of formations, and in the very nature of the cave structure. Removing a cave formation amounts to destroying a form of nature's handiwork forever. At one point, water contaminated with human waste was entering the underground system. Spills of certain hazardous materials on the surface could threaten safety. The exhalation of the human breath is likely to affect the rock formation in perhaps a thousand years.

Pulverization

The Plant operates to ensure a hazard-free, clean, pleasant, safe, viable, healthy, and efficient environment. The Project, which meets the environmental protection needs of the country - especially water protection - impacts favorably on water, air, soil, plants, animals and landscape, and helps maintain hygenic conditions, safe countryside, lush vegetation, clean urban streets, unpolluted water, clean air, and underground water system. In-plant noise is low because the Plant is built in an old low-lying quarry where noise gets muffled. Noise and dust are further contained by the buildings' side walls. With the filling of the Workman's site, the land would be available for use. The danger in the Plant areas of the deep open quarry to children has been reduced. The pulverized refuse once disposed and covered periodically with a layer of soil, is processible over a period of 6-8 weeks to form compost, a soil conditioner capable of retaining moisture in the soil and preserving the nutrients which may be added in the form of manures. The pulverization method accelerates land reclamation, saves land, facilitates landfilling, reduces the size of disposal sites, minmizes refuse pollution, improves sanitation, lessens the risk of trapped gas, results in fine shredding, improves the appearance of shredded waste, cuts down the risk of disease spread, and provides an odor-free residue. The Plant's construction prevents the seepage of harmful chemicals and bacteria from refuse into underground water supplies. The Plant does not create disamenities, pathogens and parasites, e.g. odors, dust, flies and rodents. The shredded refuse is less pungent in odor than raw open refuse.

The downside is that with pulverized refuse tending to leach impurities in Barbados' fissured soil, groundwater pollution and other pollution threats to natural habitats cannot be ruled out. Some adverse impacts might be made in the long haul on water, air, soil, plants, animals, and landscape. Raw refuse can burn or smoulder and cause air pollution. Small accumulation of water in cans and containers in the landfill may serve as mosquito-breeding site. Plastic materials, even when finely shredded, do not dissolve and create drainage problems. Landfills are subject to subsidence for many years. Illegal and indiscriminate littering and dumping of wastes in gullies, ravines, water courses, vacant lands and other open areas, and clandestine disposal of hazardous materials and dangerous chemicals are known to cause groundwater pollution, chemical contamination, and leachate pollution. Disbenefits appear in varied ways, namely, occasional odor, plant noise, uncontrolled waste volume and type, littering, dumping, casual and improper disposal, inconvenience, and health hazards. Environmental and health risks stem from noise, odor, debris, dust, increased traffic, and air pollution. Household refuse, including toxic materials, are not collected and placed properly in many instances. A substantial volume of toxic, corrosive, reactive and flammable waste is generated by households each year. The unregulated household hazardous waste and its haphazard handling by an uniformed public produces disbenefits.

Polytechnic

The landscape, trees, shrubs and grass provide comfort and relaxation to the users of the Campus. Thc structurc of thc buildings is made of locally-made reinforced concrete frames and precast hollow pot floors which are structurally sound and inexpensive and eliminate the need for shutters. The exterior finish is natural, while the interior is painted. With the aim of making appropriate use of the prevailing winds in Barbados, the quiet teaching blocks have been located upward facing the prevailing breeze, while the noise-producing and recreation -providing blocks have been put up downwind with the noise being kept to a minimum.

Sewerage

The Plant is landscaped and lined with tropical vegetation. Former Emmerton residents, relocated to Clapham Park, enjoy the benefits of spacious environment. The upgrading of the faecal waste disposal improves the environmental quality of the target area and augments its reputation as a clean urban settlement. The system produces an effluent that meets strict aesthetic and sanitary standards and is dischargeable into the sea without harmful environmental effects. The system, replacing a poor and antiquated sewage disposal system destroying the coasts and reefs with waterborne pollutants, eliminated the need for pumping septic tank or cesspool emptiers. The Plant's physical emission, such as noise, heat and vibrations, are reduced to tolerable levels through the use of special equipment. The liquid emissions are discharged at a safe site. Some emissions are specially treated for reuse. Those effluents which are unpleasant or noxious go through special treatments.

The Project checks untreated sewage disposal and sewage effluent into sea, checks marine and beach pollution, improves the quality of marine life, checks damages to coral reefs and reef fisheries, regulates coral life, increases fish catch, protects the coastal/ nearshore/inshore ecosystem, lessens environmental eutrophication in the discharge area, checks beach erosion, improves the quality of seawater at Carlisle Bay, preserves the island's coastal and marine resources and the environmental heritage of the current as well as future generations, reduces pollutants like coliforms and toxins (Archer, 1985), improves coastal and benthic conditions, protects beach and reef, improves the sanitation and health of target urban and coastal areas, recolonizes the reef in Carlisle Bay, improves the clarity of water, restores the return of more and larger fish to the waters, removes sewage discharge by numerous users along Bay Street, reduces environmental hazards, protects and revives the south coast marine life by halting heavy pollution, and protects beaches, reefs and coastal properties from erosion. Besides, the Project also cleans the sea, regulates the coral reefs, prevents beach pollution, rebuilds inshore fisheries, minimizes environmental despoliation, contains faecal pollution and contamination, contains communicable diseases, stops exposed excreta, septic-tank effluents and fly infestation, eliminates pit privies, stops overflowing septic tanks and sewage wells, arrests the infiltration of faecal wastes into coastal and marine ecosystems, ensures environmental sanitation, enhances the quality of life, augments Bridgetown's reputation as a clean city, eliminates and reduces environmental pollution in an area where waste and sewage had reached critical levels, makes way for urban renewal, modern sanitation, clean streets, additional sidewalks, large and new buildings, greater recreation, better eating convenience and high shopping comfort, makes for reduced flooding, and provides pollution-free drinking water.

The Plant operates with minimum adverse environmental impact. For Barbados, the ocean is a precious biological, economic, and recreational resource. The chemical treatment method - the contact stabilization process useful for relatively small flow rate of domestic waste - is an improvement on the traditional subsurface disposal method. Under the latter method, active effluent could seep into and contaminate the underground water resources. The former method produces a treated effluent that can be discharged into water (Archer, 1985). The treatment of human waste and domestic wastewater includes the oxidation of organic matters, which prevents pollution of the seawater receiving the effluent. Waste treatment produces a clear, highly oxidized and disinfected wastewater effluent which meets aesthetic and sanitary standards, can be easily discharged into the sea without any harmful effects, and can prevent environmental pollution in the discharge area. The marine outfall discharges chlorinated effluent far and deep enough to preclude bacterial pollution of the inshore waters. The treatment processes eliminating pathogens, chemicals, organisms and other harmful materials, and ensuring sullage disposal by way of neutralizing pathogen-containing domestic wastewater - based on biological characteristics of the sewage flows - are capable of biological oxygen demand removals of 85% suspended solids removals in incoming wastewater of 90% and dissolved oxygen content of 7-8 mg/1 (Archer, 1985). Sewage treatment and disposal into the marine environment is designed to prevent pollution of the beaches, coastal waters and marine recreation areas, and minimize beach erosion which is caused by an indirect adverse impact from wastes discharged into the sea. An underwater discharge to release the treated effluent and dilution of the effluent in the sea are safety measures to prevent environmental pollution. The sludge disposal method chosen was the most environmentally sound for Barbados.

Then again, the constraints are numerous. With disinfectant being provided, the impact of free chlorine and chloramines on the ecology of the marine environment tends to be harmful. If the treatment processes are not adequately controlled and the critical situations competently tackled, the total system may break down threatening health and polluting the environment. The malfunctioning system may contribute to the destruction of coral reefs off Rockley Beach, beach erosion, alteration in the character of the seabed where lobster, conch, sea-eggs and other shell fish breed, and sharp decrease of these species. Reduced water quality, which kills the reefs, causes beach erosion. The shoreline ecosystem is complex and interactive in that the reefs, the shoreline vegetation, the quality of the ground and surface water and the health of marine life have a productive and regulative value. If this balance is upset by the slackness in discharge regulation, the tourism sector and other productive processes in the country would be severely damaged and would not survive without them. Some pathogens can survive for weeks in effluent-added water, representing a health hazard. During processing at the Plant, water in the reservoir can support growth of algae which are difficult to remove. The system places additional demand on water-supply and distribution. The heavy seas can damage the submerged sections of the marine outfall. If this occurs and is left unrepaired, discharge of sewage takes place close to the land and the beach pollution worsens.

Dust inconvenience and noise nuisance are suffered in the target areas. High-pitch whining sound from the Plant creates noise disamenity in a residential area. The aerobic digestion of the sewage sludge, the presence of industrial waste containing oil, the raw sewage brought in by the septic trucks and the release of sulphur dioxide, cause odor. Odor is also caused by the spillage made by the septic tanks as they enter the Plant, the excessive amount of septage taken in by the Plant, the reaeration zone not having enough wastewater to dilute whatever sewage comes into the Plant, incoming sewage containing an above-normal degree of solids, and solids becoming septic too quickly. Residents living around the Plant - which is located in a densely populated area - complain of strong stench coming from it. In fact, even when the system became first operational, the downstream community complained regularly of the odor. Pit toilets and septic tanks are still in use in the target area and the untidy conditions of the septic tanks or cesspool emptiers present hazards of contamination. The sewers can deteriorate over time and sewage can overflow through manholes after heavy rains. The dumping of some waste which cannot be treated because it is too oily poses problems. As a reaction to the rejection of industrial waste by the Plant, some industries have resorted to clandestine dumping of their waste near Cowell Street in Bridgetown. This risky practice damages and destroys coral reefs with their colorful variety of fish and other marine species and their ability to dissipate the force of waves and protect beaches and beachfront property. Some consumers tend to be casual about environmental discharges. There is slackness in controlling illegal sewage dumping and sludge dumping. The slow in-house connection to the Project causes spillage of sewage while cleaning septic tanks or cesspool emptiers.

Ferneihurst

The units, where mature shade trees enrich and diversify the environment, have attractive front gardens, trees lining the entrance and the roads. To illustrate, as many mature trees, smaller flowering trees and shrubs as possible have been retained on the Project site. Two small tree-shaded areas are set aside as a sitting area for the Estate's elderly residents and as a children's playground. The layout is aesthetically functional, standing in harmony with natural and social environment. By preserving natural vegetation, beautifying and landscaping the ambient area and putting in place safety measures, accidental risks for children playing in the Estate have been minimized. The downside is that a temporary unauthorized workshop adjoining the Estate's eastern boundary carries on spray painting. Paint drift, a health hazard, has affected trees, general undergrowth and some units' exterior and furniture.

International Dimension

This dimension is based on the premise that domestic and international subsystems are intertwined and that the Projects underpin interaction and interdependence in a global system. There are several interlocking relations and patterns between Barbados as a host country and the international domain. The patterns of international relations result primarily from the changing nature of the political, economic and technological linkages of Caribbean countries within the region and between Barbados and the metropoles or dominant powers. The various transactions and interactions via the Projects mean increased incorporation into the global structure. The Projects are influenced not only by domestic conditions but also external ones. The Project operations are driven by domestic conditions, and domestic conditions are in turn driven by external conditions.

The externalization of the Projects was necessitated as well as manifested by cooperation, transaction, linkage, interdependence, collaboration, and exchange. Internationalism results from and arises out of Barbados' openness of economy, traditional links with the metropoles, high international trade coefficient, narrow resource base, small size and population, limited negotiating power, forces of foreign penetration and influence, dependence on foreign capital, vulnerability to international pressure and powerplay, peripherality, frequent foreign commercial interest, the high import content of tradables, and the relatively high import propensity of consumption.

Throughout the project process, internationalism featured in nearly all the phases. Work was initiated and completed in the various phases by the domestic institutions and their personnel in association with strategic inputs from the international community, including financing feasibility studies, extended negotiations, technical assistance provisions, loan agreements, consultancies, in-project operative training, procurement, equipment/accessory planning and installation, supplier-client relations, technical skills, and marketing.

The expansion of the public sector via the Projects has helped form a policy/managerial group, within the wider context of its relationship to the metropolitan powers and its top organizational actors and overriding interests. At various levels and loci, there occurred interplay of domestic and international concerns, issues and interests. The interplay and interaction occur in terms of policy formulation and continuity, decision-making, materials and supplies, strategic support, technical expertise, resource flows, communication, transport, insurance, markets, and networks.

As with economic or social reality, organizational and managerial reality today is not primarily intelligible within the confines of a single country. The projects are influenced not only by the domestic dynamics but also by global cultural diffusion and social-structural processes, spurred by transcultural technology, capital, communication, transportation, enterprise, differentiation, integration, and so forth. What is more, there are structural relations at play between underdevelopment and development, i.e. project operation/behavior as part of underdevelopment in Barbados and external stimuli as part of development in the metropoles. The structural relations are historical as well as contemporary. The Projects reflect varyingly both structural and functional dependence. Structural dependence reflects the degree to which the project processes were exogenously propelled, i.e. idea, finance, technology, personnel and supplies, to some extent, externally directed. Functional dependence represented policy decisions which underpinned certain relationships between particular socioeconomic groups in Barbados and their counterparts in the metropolitan centers. What is noteworthy, too, is that through the Projects and similar investments, Barbados attempts to ensure continued access to export markets, obtain access to new markets, expand domestic markets, secure financial and technical assistance from public as well as private sources for the development of economic and social sectors, and gain increased benefits from diversification. The external objectives are both derived from and conducive to a domestic development policy based on the concept and practice of mixed economy.

Driving forces

Barbados' policy leadership has shown via the Projects its affinity with the international community. Bilateral as well as multilateral relations assumed various forms, such as technical, economic, financial, material, personal, organizational, legal, and so forth. International cooperation, which underlies international interdependence, has been enhanced through the Investments. For instance, technical cooperation, backstopping, collaboration and counterparting took place in respect of architecture, engineering, physical planning, environmental science, livestock management, equipment planning and installation, and management consulting. The organizations engaged in international cooperation embraced the Inter-American Development Bank, United States Agency for International Development, Canadian International Developement Agency, Caribbean Development Bank, Commonwealth Fund for Technical Cooperation, Caribbeana Council, and so forth. Especially, implementation entailed a noticeable range of participants from the international community. The participation involved contractors, subcontractors, suppliers, international public agencies, educational institutions, scientific organizations, and so forth. The interactions further involved survey missions, study tours, correspondence, information/ data exchange, understudy, technical exchange, international purchasing, technology transfer, resource flow, goods and services exchange, international movement of factors of production, capital mobility, labor mobility, debt servicing, negotiation, financing, contract, procurement, consultancy, implementation, and evaluation.

The Projects widen development options both through greater selectivity and greater geographical diversification in the trade and other economic relationships between Barbados and industrialized countries. By participating in international transactions, Barbados has used its resources and development potential more effectively - to focus on those activities it is best suited to control and to gain economies of scale. By taking part in international capital markets, Barbados, has, in certain respects, grown faster. By borrowing on those markets to supplement domestic savings, Barbados has been able to raise its rates of capital formation, increase its revenue base, diversify service and production network, expand consumer choice, and build assets. Some of the Projects - Greenland, Handicraft, and Cave - show specialization, factor endowments and factor movements. The Projects provided opportunities for consolidating existing relationships as well. Traditional ties with metropolitan powers have formed the core of national interest and remain a preeminent concern. This is not surprising, given the long history and the multiplicity of links between Barbados and the North Atlantic countries. Virtually, no area of socioeconomic activity is left untouched, though certain prominent interests can be identified, such as investment, trade, tourism, technology transfer, education/training, migration, and development assistance. All these areas are of particular concern to Barbados in its search for overall development.

Constraining forces

Although internationalism has contributed toward such aggregates as financial flows, capital/output ratios and growth rates, it has succeeded less in the painful task of transforming social institutions and human attitudes. The Projects reflected dependent development and peripheralism and mirrored some disbenefits, viz. dependent nonreciprocal linkages, dependency on foreign capital, technology, trade, market, expertise, institutional rationality and skill, historical trading ties, transferring large shares of income, ties, conditionalities and strings of external assistance, high cost of external assistance, asymmetrical interdependence and dependence on a high inflow of foreign direct investment.

The metropoles used varied methods of control, containment, and influence. The metropolitan domination and penetration limited the range of options open before the domestic decision-makers. Donor control and influence is seen increasing in Barbados at both covert and overt levels. Barbados' resource limitation, small size, perception and reality of vulnerability and limited production capacity serve to heighten donor influence, restrict discretionary decision-making, and curb project variety. Unequal relations existing between Barbados and the funding agencies - and the latter commanding resources far superior to those of Barbados in terms of finance, personnel, technology, and resource access - place strain on donor-recipient relations. The policy-making institutions in Barbados are relatively young, in contrast to those in the international domain, and the former's analytical and management capabilities are in the process put to an unequal test.

Comparative Dimension

Making comparison is an integral part of life. To move away from ethnocentrism and to press toward generality, the comparison of the Projects, where possible with similar projects in the identical sector, has been initiated at three foci, namely, local, regional, and international. Comparison has been done in relation to project features, benefits, and costs. Mindful of inherent difficulty of comparison, the objective is to examine selectively significant similarities and dissimilarities in project experience across culture and region, and to contribute to comparative behavior.

Local

Completed in 1983 at an estimated cost of BDS$5.4m., the Oistins Fisheries Terminal Project (Evans, 1986) intends to advance the development of the fishing activity in Barbados by making more fish available and generating increased employment. Jointly financed by national and external organizations, the Project has helped enhance the quality of life in Oistins through better traffic flows, improved roads, updated safety and reclaimed land. The payoffs include better public health condition, higher employment, increased fish catch, more nutritional protein to consumers, reduced fish importation, convenient retail shopping, greater cash income for fishers and fish vendors. Yet, cost and time overruns occurred, staff training failed to be thorough, and problems arose in acquiring materials and maintaining the premises, exacerbated by occasional pilferage, destruction of tools, vandalism and harassment.

Constructed in 1984 at a cost of BDS$198.9m.and jointly financed by the Caribbean and external sources, the Arawak Cement Plant Project is a venture for the production of cement to supply local and regional markets. The Plant, with a lifespan of some 50 years (Sealy, 1983), has helped create employment, generate skills and expertise, decentralize development, cause road improvement, and create an export market. The costs include resiting of households from the target area, pollution, dependence on expatriate personnel, and unstable industrial relations.

Built at a cost of BDS$61.8m.in 1983 and jointly financed by a consortium, the Heywoods Holiday Village Project has as its objective the aim of increasing local ownership in the country's tourism sector. Of the benefits (St. John, 1981), the most outstanding are increased jobs, growth impact on Speightstown and the ambient areas, improved beach and parking facilities, and increased foreign exchange and tax revenue. The costs are a shift away from agriculture in the neighboring rural areas, declining competitiveness of agriculture, and overbuilding along the west coast.

The Spring Garden Highway Project, built in 1984 at a cost of about BDS$12m., is intended to alleviate traffic volume and congestion, provide access into and through Bridgetown and offer an alternative route from Bridgetown to the northern parishes. Funded partly by IDB (Chase, 1983), the benefits comprise enhanced employment, improved rolling surface, reduced fuel consumption, reduced congestion, commuter time saving, and increased driving pleasure. Then again, failure to complete on the target date, extensive redesigning, relocation of houses, tardiness in coordinating the siting of utility services and the demand for higher compensation resulted in cost overruns.

Implemented in 1979, the Caribbean Examinations Council Secondary Education Certificate Project (Simmons, 1980) is aimed at secondary school-leavers, testing their subject-area attainment and providing them with certificates. The undertaking involved training, attachments, visits, workshops, examination organization, and evaluation and measurement. The payoffs point to initiating Caribbean-controlled secondary examination system and building educational management capability. The problems encountered related to difficulties in staff training and computerization, generic delays, and lags in time schedules.

Executed in 1980, the Barbados Drug Service Project (Seal, 1983) represents a new kind of drug management to meet the community's drug needs through a reduction in the cost of drugs. The Service ensures a continuous supply of quality drugs at bulk prices, realizing cost savings, making a favorable impact on beneficiary groups, improving drug availability and affordability and reducing the cost of prescribed drugs to consumers. However, complaints are made of excessive paperwork, low dispensing fee, and insufficient markup to cover the overheads.

Targeted for low-income and low middle-income families, the St. Cecilia Housing Project was completed in 1985. The benefits (The Nation, 1984) include affordable rent, ready transportation and low-cost accommodation. The Venture had its share of problems, e.g. schedule slippages, time and cost overruns, site problems, design changes, and contractual anomalies. Besides, money ran out, progress was slow, materials were inferior, planning was improper, and all the buildings were started simultaneously.

Regional

In his study of the Demerara Harbor Bridge Project in Guyana, Joseph (1984) found that the GUY$37.8m. enterprise was completed in less than two years, despite political interference and donor dominations. The Project, having shown in-house management/technical capability, has resulted in revenue generation, faster means of travel, quicker transportation of commodity, additional market for produce and products, additional employment, and greater access to services. Some of the costs comprise urban congestion and high crime rate in the Bridge area.

Next, the Cooperative Rural Settlement Project in Jamaica, reported by Gayle and Drori (1984) and implemented in 1979, was stymied by the lack of control mechanisms, weak discipline, inadequate information flow, the gap between the plan from above and the daily complexities of rural reality, and the overlooking of the need to involve the target communities in planning and implementation.

Benjamin (1987) studied nine development projects in the energy-based sector of Trinidad and Tobago in relation to timing, sequencing, scheduling, and other resource allocation tasks. The two findings relate to scheduling, i.e. first, the Projects could have been ordered in a more rigorous sequence using appropriate priority rules, and second, a project schedule could be generated to minimize project duration. The need for establishing an information system to allow for storage, retrieval and analysis of data was established.

The main objective of the Roseau Dam Development Project in St. Lucia (Stanley Associates, 1986; Frederick, 1991), initiated in 1983 with a net present value of EC$34.1m., was to increase water supply and to provide the residents of the area with piped water. The reservoir site lies within the rugged interior of St. Lucia, an area with extreme topography, heavy forest cover, and high rainfall. The Project, addressing a target group of about 18,000 customers, develops water storage in the Roseau river basin, increases water supply, helps irrigate banana farms, alleviates periodic water shortages, helps increase fire protection capacity, increases residential connections, helps increase tariff revenues from incremental water production, increases agricultural yield, results in industrial and employment spinoff, creates jobs, increases property value, and improves health and sanitation standards. The costs include the innundation of the valley slopes, changed downstream water quality, changed pattern of water quality, exposure of the dam site to erosion from rainfall runoff, the deterioration of the rain forest, the diversion of banana land, the risks of dam malfunctioning, and long-tem income loss for small farmers.

International

Hirschman (1967) studied eleven World Bank-financed projects in Ecuador, El Salvador, Ethiopia, India, Nigeria, Pakistan, Thailand, Uganda and Uruguay, covering such sectors as agriculture, energy, industry, infrastructure, resource development, and telecommunications. He examined the ways in which decision-making was activated or hampered by the specific nature of the project undertaken, and dealt with such traits as action, uncertainty, latitude, discipline, design, and side-effects. Some of the findings are revealing, e.g. all projects are more or less problem-ridden; the principle of 'hiding hand' beneficially conceals the difficulties from one which facilitates embarking on development activities; if project-makers had known in advance the difficulties that were lying in store for the project, they probably would never have touched it; and implementation may be the most *critical* phase in determining project success or failure.

In a study of nineteen highway projects in five Central American countries funded by four international agencies, Wynia (1972) found common patterns of problems and behavior in implementation. Despite differing conditions, the behavior of all the projects was similar. They experienced similar patterns of delay and unexpected cost increases. Wynia identified two types of conditions permeating the projects: process factors, i.e. delays resulting from ministerial decision-making, legislative process and consultancy process, and project-specific factors, i.e. interparty disputes, design/quality problems, climatic factors and contractual hitches.

Birgegard (1975) probed nineteen projects in the agricultural sector in Kenya, Zambia and Tanzania in such fields as livestock, credit, irrigation, processing, crop production, grain storage, and research and training. Some of the findings are: the search for alternatives/designs and the comparison between alternatives was very limited; the early phase in the project cycle was the most significant; funding agencies were brought into the selection process at an early stage; and the skill level in project appraisal was found to be rather low and uneven.

The research by Lele (1975) draws on evidence from seventeen rural development projects in sub-Saharan Africa, e.g. Cameroon, Ethiopia, Kenya, Malawi, Mali, Nigeria, and Tanzania. While looking at ways of designing projects that could be accomplished despite limited resources, one fact which emerged was that interactions among policies, institutions, trained human resources, physical resources and technology were complex and diverse and that no single project package was universally applicable. The Project exercises were less than fully effective in making the process of development of the low-income sector self-sustaining and were not sensitive enough to the sociocultural and institutional setting in which they were carried out. Considerably more planning was necessary if goals were to be managed more effectively.

The work by Roemer and Stern (1975) is devoted to four projects of the early 1970s in Ghana. The transport project dealt with the timing of an investment project, while the industrial project used project appraisal to determine whether the investor required certain subsidies. While the mining project sought approval and funds to expand mining operations in the western region, the agricultural project was designed to coordinate and sustain the spontaneous rice development taking place in the northern region.

The next study (Dupriez, 1979) is concerned with ten rural development projects undertaken in nine African countries during the 1960s and the 1970s, namely, Benin, Central African Republic, Chad, Ivory Coast, Niger, Rwanda, Togo, Upper Volta, and Zaire. The ventures - concerning cotton, coffee, rice and food crops production, cooperatives, export promotion, farm viability, and nutrition - related to small-size farms characterized by low productivity and minimal integration into trading activity. Some of the payoffs included the continuity of technical backstopping, improvement of the output-input ratio, and farmer awareness. The unfavorable factors pointed to farmer resistance, low-level management skill, deficiency of supervisory staff, and insufficient coordination.

The five projects probed by Goodman and Love (1979) - extending to livestock, land tenure, rural development, water development, health and migration, and covering the South Pacific, the Philippines, Thailand, Indonesia, and the United States - underlined that project management must be integrative and flexible. The problems common to planning and management were pointed out, viz. development assistance alone could not overcome the critical internal obstacles to development, the demanding nature of feasibility conditions was underestimated, paucity of positive attitudes and social competencies, and insufficiency of organizational reforms.

Nine projects from Brazil, Colombia, India, Kenya, Peru and Zambia illuminate the general process of implementation and the more specific parameters of political activity (Grindle, 1980). Highlighting agricultural, cooperative, health, housing, urban renewal and rural development sectors, the projects bring up the issue of resource allocation and target community. The study addresses the link between formulation and implementation, the incidence of nondecisions, and the choice of implementation strategies.

In yet another study (Cracknell, 1984) concerned with livestock projects in Bolivia, Colombia, Kenya, Lesotho and Malawi, research results showed that the ventures failed to achieve objectives, there was no evidence of increased production, the rates of return were slow and low, the projects were too dependent on expatriates, and marketing lacked effectiveness. Some successes came along by being able to control animal diseases and increase carcass weight. Conyers and Kaul (1990) report on the management of successful projects. The projects deal with rural development, community development, education, health, housing, credit, cooperatives, family planning, population control and human settlement. The countries covered are Bangladesh, Botswana, Gambia, India, Kenya, Malawi, Nigeria, Sri Lanka, Tanzania, Zambia, and Zimbabwe. The factors contributing to the success of the projects included the project environment, the basic character of the project, the mode of project initiative, and project organization and management.

Notwithstanding accomplishments, achievements, performance and results, a common finding is that projects continue to reveal recurrent lapses and shortfalls, viz. underutilization of existing resources, limited regard for sustainability in the posthandover period, overestimation of project output price, poor project design, objective and design change, lack of well-designed and rapidly-implementable projects, lengthy project process, lack of target-group participation, paternalistic attitude of project personnel, limited collection of initial baseline data, fuzzy and implicit objective-setting, lack of specific goals and targets, unspecified success conditions for target groups, ignorance of local and on-site conditions, unavailable target-group cooperation, inability to change unhelpful institutional practices for small-scale target groups, inability to impose costs on misbehaviors, political skulduggery, and unhelpful funding-agency conditionalities.

Summary

We have looked at some development decisions, scanned project performance and examined project behavior across countries and cultures in terms of success, strengths, mistakes, and limitations. Diverse conditions influenced the reported projects. They were financed in part by different international agencies, their costs and size differed, and they were implemented by different executing agencies. Costs revealed departures from scheduled performance. Actual costs exceeded estimated costs. Some projects shared a common experience of unexpected cost increase.

Differing conditions notwithstanding, the behavior of the reported cases is in several respects comparable. This is to stress that the behavior of projects funded by any one international agency differed little from projects funded by others. Large and expensive projects implemented by one executing agency differed little from small ones carried out by other agencies. Just so, economic-sector projects did not differ significantly from social-sector ones in respect of implementation. The projects sustained several common constraining forces, too, e.g. external dependence, design changes, time overruns, cost overruns, intergroup conflicts, and insufficient organization and management development. Likewise, the projects uniformly displayed a few driving forces, e.g. high-level policy inputs, environmental interaction, social interventions, and resource-group participation. In spite of dissimilarities and peculiarities, we identify these forces permeating the projects as being fairly generic and systemic.

Measurement Dimension

Notwithstanding such formulations as 'what gets measured gets done', 'measurement affects every employee one way or another', 'if something cannot be measured, it cannot be improved', 'measurement makes productivity and quality performance visible', 'an organization without measurement does not have control' and 'one cannot manage what one cannot measure', organizational and managerial indifference to measurement is more widespread than one cares to admit. By not getting measurement as much as necessary, the Projects are missing out on systematic and continual improvement in their capability, reliability, and efficiency.

The reasons why organizational measurement is not widely accepted and practiced are multiple. Measurement is a difficult task and provokes resentment and defensiveness. It sometimes appears to be esoteric and may be considered an academic exercise. Measurement is usually presented to management in isolation, separate from other facets. Measurement must compete with a full array of concerns and issues shared by management. There is a lack of a clear understanding of how measurement has an impact on the overall organizational quality. Besides, measurement's difficulty stems from outputs tending to be somewhat fuzzy and hard to quantify, employees continue to be suspicious of it, people are nervous about the issue of measurement, it often feels like extra work from which there are few possible payoffs, and the right data are not collected.

Organizational measurement is an important dimension. Measurement is a key indicator of how efficiently resources are transformed into goods and services. The impact of measurement is considerable. When data on individuals, groups and organizations are collected, this activity triggers a chain of perceptual, cognitive, motivational, and behavioral events. Measurement is the assignment of numerals to objectives, events or persons, and the symbolic connection of these numerals with these aspects. It is noteworthy that unless one keeps score, it is difficult to know whether organizational activities aimed at specific services and products are succeeding or failing. Measurement is crucial to management's information and planning needs, objective-setting, and performance monitoring. If we want to build and maintain highly effective organization, we need adequate measurement of the various aspects of the organization.

The intention here is to attempt to specify and quantify part of the realities and activities of the Projects through a process of approximation. We go for discrete measurement with the recognition that continuous measurement is unattainable within the scope of the study. We use various types of quantitative indicators: output measures, percentage-type indicators, physical measures, effectiveness indicators, utilization-availability measures, and workload indicators. We are concerned here with only a facet of organizational measurement - some productivity, some capacity, and some output. We envisage measurement as a developmental rather than as a punitive tool. Measurement assumes crossproject comparisons and is carried out in relation to two reference points: comparison over time to provide information on trends and progress and comparisons made among project organizations.

We underscore measurement because it is inextricably interwoven with the management process and because it is a key step in strategic management. The purpose of measurement is to steer performance improvement. We recognize the usefulness of measurement for analysis, projection, goal-setting and goal management, competitiveness, and capability development. Its usefulness further extends to demonstrating efficiency, identifying opportunities for improvement, making resource allocation decisions, supporting budget planning, tracking organizational accountability, providing necessary information, exerting cost and waste control, improving the quality of service, focusing attention on output, facilitating the allocation of incentives, and keeping employees informed of snags as well as gains.

Organizational measurement makes for a number of beneficial results, e.g. assessing progress, adjusting to ongoing changes, addressing motivation, improving accountability, transparency and capability, providing a basis for change of attitude among personnel, identifying problem or workable areas, helping set priorities and goals, identifying and correcting mismanagement, facilitating comparison, helping achieve and stimulate gains, helping improve operation and monitor situations, achieving standardization, and dealing with wasteful, dilatory and counterproductive factors. At this stage, we look specifically at some of the sample Projects.

Greenland

Such measurement activities as determining the effect on output of the Greenland Project and estimating its proportion of output increase have not been carried out. The lapse is almost exclusively owing to the persistence of traditional operating culture of the Station in particular and the larger public sector in general. One is not sure, for example, if the output increases at the Station have led to or are associated with significant reduction in output in other areas/organizations. It is obvious that any drop in the output of sheep-raising farms would have to be set off against any increase at the Station.

Handicraft

The Handicraft Project, whose turnover exceeds BDS$1m., has made an impact on Barbados' economy and society in terms of home-based employment, resource ownership and control, entrepreneurship, income generation, diversification, and indigenization. To be sure, any inclination to use sales as the almost sole criterion for measuring the success of the Project is partial as well as misleading.

Polytechnic

There are three main approaches to the measurement of the returns on the Polytechnic investment. First, the macroeconomic approach relates increases in aggregate production to increases in labor and capital. Second, it calculates the lifetime excess earnings of people who have undergone various lengths of education/training over those who have not. Third, it attempts to relate all social benefits with all social costs of spending on education/training. Some quantifications are available, viz. numbers trained, placements secured, and projected excess earnings of trained students over the untrained ones.

The direct output is often not easily measurable, the existing measurement tools are not broadly known, the effects are widely diffused and spread over a long time, and no determinate functional relation exists between inputs and outputs. A difficult task is the determination of what revenues should be assigned to the Institute. Some output categories of the Polytechnic Investment seem to be overlooked. The measurement of the Polytechnic's achievement and capacity has not been effected, viz. the use to which the vocational training experience has been put, whether the roles of the Polytechnic graduates or those of their parents have been effected, whether vocationally-trained people are prepared to live in rural areas, whether they are willing to become self-employed, the appropriateness of the Polytechnic training, whether the Institute can create new programs, and so on. Measures such as freshness ratio, student job placement success rate, student attendance rate, faculty recruitment rate and computer utilization rate are not on stream.

Sewerage

Attention has been paid to measuring output increases, viz. the amount of sewage disposed, the size of the target area served, etc. As yet, measuring the Plant's technical and managerial competence to carry out a greater volume of sewage disposal has not generated sustained interest. The Project's different outputs - sanitary, preventive, training and development, environment - do not seem to be equally recognized and assessed.

Ferneihurst

Measurement cannot be applied to a social investment, such as Ferneihurst, entirely satisfactorily. First, the quality of housing cannot be measured easily. Housing has many features - floor area, building materials, location, etc. - which are valued in different ways by different households. Linked to this is the problem of discreteness. Second, there may not be reliable market data for housing. The housing market may be imperfect, segmented, and slow to adjust. As a result, it may be difficult to establish any kind of demand function for housing. Finally, housing generates externalities in relation to health, education, behavior and urban amenities, which may be significant but difficult to establish with reasonable accuracy.

At this point, we provide tabular data on the observable, identifiable and measurable aspects of the organizations. We are aware that several indicators presented here are not measurement per se and give an incomplete picture of project development, yet they are partly useful, serving an exploratory and cumulative purpose. We are cognizant that nearly any measurement may be objected to on the ground of bias, self-selection, low precision, restricted generality, and other factors. Further, quantification does not equal correctness, accuracy or scientific standing, quantification does not equate with analysis, a quantitative approach is not *a priori* better than a qualitative one, quantitative data are not seen as more compelling than qualitative data, and there is no presumption of value neutrality. Still further, measurement cannot take the place of having a solid core service or product, and measurement is not a substitute for strategy, leadership, motivation, and visioning. Some of the data presented here are factual, while others are conceptual. Some are statistical data, still others are descriptive materials. The tabular data relate to in-project as well as postproject time-periods.

The coding system, comprising a number of descriptors used uniformly in the tables, is as follows: aprox. (approximate), avg. (average), est. (estimated), I/D (incomplete data), m.(million), N/A (not applicable, not available), N/K (not known), no. (number), and yr. (year).

Instead of ignoring or omitting columns which do not have reliable information, we put out a few tables in which certain columns report such status as 'not known', 'not applicable', or 'not available' with a view to underlining the extent of data gaps and the usefulness of data collection.

Table 1
Basic Features

Projects	Sectors	Goals	Cost (BDS$)	Duration (lead/ implementation time)	Target groups
Greenland	Agriculture	Producing sheep toward self-sufficiency	1.6m.	1978-82; 1978-82	Sheep farmers/ consumers
Handicraft	Industry	Intensifying handicraft production/ marketing	2.2m.	1974-79; 1975-79	Craft producers/ consumers
Cave	Tourism	Developing cave as tourist attraction	4.8m.	1973-81; 1978-81	Visitors/ residents
Pulverization	Infrastructure	Establishing cost effective waste disposal	4.2m.	1967-80; 1979-80	Householders/ workplaces
Polytechnic	Education	Advancing technical/ vocational education	20.6m.	1974-82; 1979-82	Students/ faculty
Sewerage	Health	Developing sewerage system to relieve sewage problems	42.0m.[1]	1970-82; 1978-82	Residents/ commuters
Ferneihurst	Housing	Accommodating low-income/ low middle-income consumers	4.7m.	1978-81; 1979-81	Households/ families

Table 2
Organizational Specifics

Projects	Ministries	Predecessors/ year	Structure/ number	Managing agencies/ year
Greenland	Ministry of Agriculture	Peasant Agricultural Service/1936	Chief Agricultural Officer; Deputy Chief Agricultural Officer (Extension & Development); Senior Agricultural Officer (Animal Husbandry)	Animal Husbandry Unit/1966
Handicraft	Ministry of Industry	Barbados Development Board/1956	Board/7	Barbados Industrial Development Corporation/ 1962
Cave	Ministry of Housing	Parks and Beaches Commission/1970; Barbados Caves Authority /1975	Board/11	National Conservation Commission/ 1982
Pulverization	Ministry of Health	Scavenging Department/1945; Sanitation and Cemeteries Board/1969	Board/12	Sanitation Service Authority /1974
Polytechnic	Ministry of Education	Barbados Technical Institute/1956	Board of Management/7	Samuel Jackman Prescod Polytechnic/ 1969
Sewerage	Ministry of Health	Waterworks Department/1895	Board of Directors/11	Barbados Water Authority/ 1981
Femeihurst	Ministry of Housing	Housing Board/1939; Housing Authority/1956; Urban Development Corporation/1965	Board/11	National Housing Corporation/ 1973

Table 3
Project Participants

Projects	Monitoring agencies	Funding agencies	Consulting/technical assistance agencies	Executing agencies
Greenland	Planning and Priorities Committee; Public Investment Unit; Ministry of Finance and Planning	GOB USAID	Caribbeana Council (USA); State University of New York, Farmingdale (USA)	Implementation Team; Project Advisory Group
Handicraft	Idem	GOB	Commonwealth Fund for Technical Cooperation (UK); David Key and Partners	Implementation Team
Cave	Idem	GOB	National Speleological Foundation (USA); Dames and Moore (Canada); Barbados Cave Project, Inc. (USA); American Explorers Association (USA); Consulting Engineers Partnership Ltd.	Project Execution Unit
Pulverization	Idem	GOB	Millbank Technical Services Ltd. (UK); Consulting Engineers Partnership Ltd. ; Sir William Halcrow & Partners (UK); Gillespie & Steel Associates Ltd.; Stanley Associates (Canada)	Implementation Team
Polytechnic	Idem	GOB IDB CDB	Gillespie & Steel Associates Ltd.	Project Execution Unit
Sewerage	Idem	GOB IDB USAID	Lawler, Matusky & Skelly, Engineers (USA); David Lashley & Partners Inc.; Commonwealth Fund for Technical Cooperation; Pan American Health Organization	Project Execution Unit
Femeihurst	Idem	GOB	Richard Gill Associates Ltd.; Gillespie & Steel Associates Ltd.; Tyrone Mapp Architect	Implementation Team

Table 4
Human Resources

Projects	Project managers	Consultants/ advisors	Other personnel	In-project personnel (est.; peak period)
Greenland	Harold C. Patterson	Robert Erikson	N/K	19
Handicraft	Anthony D. Browne	Shyamadas Sengupta; Trevor Hardlees; Clement Devonish; Pat Holton; Ruth Dayan	N/K	40
Cave	Ole Sorenson; Otto D. St. Hill; Harold D. Bannister	Ole Sorenson; Russel H. Gurnee	David A. Gooding; Frederick A. Cozier	52
Pulverization	Peter Foye	Michael Abrahams; Robert L. Anderson; Arthur B. Archer; David K. Todd; J.M.N. Zikusoka; William P. Aspinall	Brian Lewis; Wycliff Leacock; Avril Gollop	60
Polytechnic	Edward Layne; Rudolph Spencer; Gladstone Pollard	Michael Chiapetta; John Moldstad; John J. Hanitchak; Delbert E. Lewis; Herman Urrejola; Hector Correa	E. I. Munasinha; R.D.S. Goodridge; Brian Meade	400
Sewerage	Arthur B. Archer	James E. Foxworthy; Ron Layton; C.K. Abraham; Leonard Penner; Peter J. Meynell; Paul Toretta; Wayne Hunte; Clinton Davis	R.D. Ebersale; Andrew Hutchinson; Wilton Conliffe; Lawrence A. Greene	250
Fernehurst	Louis B. Redman; Edward A. Corbin	Richard C. Gill; Richard P. Shepherd; Andrew F. Steel; Tyrone Mapp	Abdulhai A. Pandor; George Greaves; Andrew Bannister	150

Table 5
Process Features

Projects	Project inputs (sample)	Projects outputs (sample)	Focal elements	Process features
Greenland	Technical assistance; operative training; livestock; equipment	Breeding stations; trained capacity; farmer identification; sheep registration; marketing outlets	Livestock development	Breeding; crossbreeding; marketing
Handicraft	Technical assistance; operative training; raw materials; equipment	Production plant; training centers; marketing outlets; trained capacity; producer identification	Craft entrepreneurship	Production; training; marketing
Cave	Technical assistance; operative training; promotional activity	Showcave; visitor identification; skill acquisition	Visitor attendance	Tour operation; maintenance
Pulverization	Technical assistance; operative training	Processing plant; disposal site; environmental/ infrastructural viability	Infrastructural support	Refuse collection; processing; disposal
Polytechnic	Technical assistance; program review	Campus complex; skill acquisition; skill utilization	Skill development	Technical skill acquisition; human resource development
Sewerage	Research findings; technical assistance; community resettlement	Sewage plant; sewage network; pumping station; marine outfall	Disease control	Sewage collection; treatment; disposal
Ferneihurst	Policy initiative; construction materials	Housing units; landscaped areas; access roads; ancillary constructions	Housing provision	Accommodation; tenancy; maintenance

Table 6
Contracting Organizations

Projects	Contracting organizations/ parties
Greenland	N/K
Handicraft	A. Barnes & Co. (1971) Ltd. ; Dennis Belle; Jeffrey Wotton; Lawson Hooper; Macdonald Walcott; Margarita Martijam; Parris Electrical Services; Phoenix Building Services (Barbados) Ltd.; Rentokil Barbados Ltd.
Cave	Arthur Chase; Athelston King Partnership Ltd.; Boyertown Battronic Corporation (USA); Courtney Rice; C.O. Williams Construction Ltd.; Cumberland Caverns, Inc. (USA); Farmer Jack Ltd.; Grantley Small; Julian Hunte; Roy Davis
Pulverization	Brown Lenox & Co. Ltd. (UK); Caribbean Industrial Research Institute (Trinidad); Caribbean Painting Services Ltd.; Central Foundry Ltd.; Coles Engineering Ltd.; C.O. Williams Construction Ltd.; Crawford & Massiah Associates Ltd.; Durahome Construction Ltd.; Phoenix Building Services (Barbados) Ltd.; Plantrac Industries Ltd.; Seismic Research Unit/University of the West Indies, Trinidad; Structural Systems Ltd.; Subsurface Exploration (Barbados) Ltd.; W.A. Kaufman & Associates Ltd.
Polytechnic	Adams Construction Ltd.; A.D. Bursford International; AdeB Consultants Ltd.; A. S. Bryden and Sons Ltd.; Barbados Mastic Asphalt Ltd.; Brian F. Griffith and Co. ; Canadex Distributions Ltd. (Canada); Caribbean Painting Services Ltd.; Caribbean Pest Control Ltd.; Carrington Engineering Consultants Ltd.; Concrete Products Ltd.; C.O. Williams Construction Ltd.; Electric Sales and Services Ltd.; Electrical Systems Ltd.; Emtage & Sons Ltd.; Gas Products Ltd.; Gittens and Co. Ltd.; Gulf Stream Industries (Caribbean) Ltd.; Husbands Wrought Iron and Engineering Works Ltd.; Hydro Flow Systems Barbados Ltd.; John Hampden Furniture Ltd.; Mahy Chadderton and Ridley Ltd.; Richard Coghlan; Sargeant-Welch Ltd. (UK); Solar Dynamics Ltd.; Structural Systems Ltd.;Tecaids Ltd. (UK); Ven-rez Products Ltd. (Canada); Visual Arts Ltd.; W. A. Kaufman & Associates Ltd.; Wilmac Construction Co. Ltd. (Canada)
Sewerage	Allen Industrial Rubber Products Ltd. (Canada); Ashbrook-Simon-Hartley (USA); Associated Shippers and Packers (Canada); Calorific Construction Ltd. (Canada); Canadian Blower/Canadian Pump Ltd. (Canada); Canron Inc. (Canada); Canval Supply Ltd. (Canada); Concrete Mix Ltd.; Crawford Metal Corporation (Canada); Degremont Infilco Ltd. (Canada); Dezurik of Canada Ltd. (Canada); Duman Ltd. (Canada); Durahome Construction Ltd.; Environtech Canada Ltd. (Canada); Feb Caribbean Ltd.; Fitzpatrick Construction Ltd. (Canada); Forbes International Moving & Storage Co. Ltd.; Floral Equipment Ltd. (Canada); Flygt Canada (Canada); Haufman Air & Filtration Systems (USA); Imperial Electrical Co. Ltd. (Canada); ITT Grinell Sales Ltd. (Canada); Kennedy Valve Manufacturing Co. (USA); Kuehne and Nagel International Ltd. (Canada); Millar Industrial Equipment Ltd. (Canada); Misener Marine Construction, Inc. (USA); Napier-Reid Ltd. (Canada); Power Plant Supply Co. (Canada); Rayside Asphalt Paving Co.; Rayside Concrete Works Ltd.; S. B. Simpson Ltd. (Canada); Scepter Manufacturing Co. (Canada); Sintra Inc. (Canada); Teff-Line Ltd. (Canada); Thibadeau-Finch Express Ltd. (Canada); Trane Company of Canada Ltd. (Canada); Try Service Equipment Ltd. (Canada); Waste-Tech (USA); Westburne Central Supply Ltd. (Canada); Worthington Canada Ltd. (Canada); Whipps Inc. (USA); Vallance Brown & Company Ltd. (Canada)
Fernihurst	A.S. Brydens & Sons (Barbados) Ltd.; Decorex Ltd.; Early Bird Exterminating Co. Ltd.; Everson R. Elcock & Co. Ltd.; Rudolph C. Walcott; Rayside Asphalt Paving Co. ; Trowel Plastics Barbados Ltd.

Table 7
Participating Organizations

Projects	Contracting organizations/ parties
Greenland	Agricultural Stations; Animal Control Center; Animal Nutrition Unit; Artificial Insemination Unit; Barbados Agricultural Development Corporation; Barbados Agricultural Society; Barbados Marketing Corporation; Barbados Sheep Farmers Association; Caribbean Agricultural Research and Development Institute; Central Livestock Station; Grassland Research Station; Inter-American Foundation (USA); Lincoln University (USA); Ministry of Agriculture; Soil Conservation Section; State University of New York at Farmingdale (USA); United States Peace Corps (USA); Veterinary Laboratory
Handicraft	Barbados Board of Tourism; Barbados Development Bank; Barbados Hotel Association; Barbados Marketing Corporation; Barbados National Bank; Barbados National Standards Institution; Barbados Port Authority; Barbados Small Business Association; Barbados Workers Union; Central Purchasing Department; Commonwealth Fund for Technical Cooperation (UK); Community Development Division; Customs and Excise Department; Government Information Service; Grantley Adams International Airport; Ministry of Agriculture; Ministry of Labor; Ministry of Industry; Soil Conservation Section; United States Peace Corps; Young Women's Christian Association
Cave	Barbados Board of Tourism; Barbados Light & Power Co. Ltd.; Barbados National Trust; Barbados Water Authority; Civil Aviation and Tourism Division; Environmental Engineering Division; Ministry of Housing and Lands; Ministry of Transport and Works; National Conservation Commission; National Speleological Foundation (USA); Organization of American States (USA); Town Planning Department; Travel agencies
Pulverization	Accountant-General's Department; Barbados Light & Power co. Ltd.; Barbados Telephone Co. Ltd.; Barbados Water Authority; Barbados Youth Council; Crown Agent for Overseas Governments and Administrations (UK); Environmental Engineering Division; Government Information Service; Ministry of Agriculture; Ministry of Communication and Works; Ministry of Health; Pan American Health Organization; Sanitation Service Authority; Town Planning Department; Valuation Division
Polytechnic	Barbados Community College; Barbados Institute of Management and Productivity; Barbados Light & Power Co. Ltd.; Barbados Telephone Co. Ltd.; Barbados Transport Board; Barbados Water Authority; Caribbean Conservation Association; Caribbean Institute of Meteorology and Hydrology; Central Purchasing Department; Environmental Engineering Division; Labor Department; Ministry of Education; National Petroleum Corporation; National Training Board; Office of the Solicitor General; Statistical Services Department; Town Planning Department
Sewerage	Barbados Chamber of Commerce; Bridgetown Harbor; Barbados Light & Power Co. Ltd.; Barbados Telephone Co. Ltd.; Barbados Transport Board; Barbados Water Authority; Bellairs Research Institute; Central Purchasing Department; Child Care Board; Community Development Division; Environmental Engineering Division; Fisheries Department; Government Information Service; Lands and Surveys Department; Labor Department; Ministry of Education; Ministry of Finance and Planning; Ministry of Health; Ministry of Housing and Lands; Ministry of Labor; Ministry of Transport and Works; National Sports Council; National Petroleum Corporation; Office of the Solicitor General; Pan American Health Organization; Police Department; Project Division/Ministry of Health; Town Planning Department; Welfare Department; University of the West Indies
Fereihurst	Barbados Light & Power Co. Ltd.; Barbados Telephone Co. Ltd.; Barbados Water Authority; Community Development Division; Environmental Engineering Division; Government Information Service; Lands and Surveys Department; Ministry of Education; Ministry of Health; Ministry of Housing and Lands; Ministry of Labor; Ministry of Transport and Works; National Assistance Board; National Conservation Commission; National Petroleum Corporation; Post Office Department; Sanitation Service Authority; Town Planning Department; Welfare Department

Table 8
Project Finance

Projects	Funding type	Interest rate	Payback period/ frequency	Grace period	Conditionalities	Credit commission	Inspection/supervision fee
Greenland	Capital financing, grant	NA	NA	NA	NA	NA	NA
Handicraft	Capital financing	NA	NA	NA	NA	NA	NA
Cave	Capital financing	NA	NA	NA	NA	NA	NA
Pulverization	Capital financing, supplier credit	NA	NA	NA	NA	NA	NA
Polytechnic	Capital financing, loan financing	2%/yr.	35yrs/ semiannual payment	8yrs.	Financial charges; competitive public bidding; organization and management study	NA	NA
Sewerage	Capital financing, loan financing	2%/yr.	35yrs/ semiannual payment	8yrs.	Financial charges; competitive public bidding; organization and management study; operational/ maintenance manual	0.5%/yr.	1% on loan capital
Ferreihurst	Capital financing	NA	20yrs.	NA	NA	NA	NA

Table 9
Technical Specifics

Projects	Appraisal techniques	Implementation techniques
Greenland	Technical appraisal; budgetary appraisal; organizational appraisal	Gantt chart; logical framework analysis; progress-status report
Handicraft	Cost-benefit analysis; budgetary appraisal; organizational analysis	Time and motion study; systems planning and analysis; work breakdown structure; bar chart; progress-status report
Cave	Technical appraisal; budgetary appraisal; breakeven analysis; organizational analysis	Gantt chart; workflow chart; bar chart; progress-status report
Pulverization	Technical appraisal; budgetary appraisal	Bar chart; Gantt chart; site meeting; progress-status report
Polytechnic	Technical appraisal; budgetary appraisal; organizational appraisal; social appraisal; economic appraisal	Gantt chart; critical path analysis; progress-status report
Sewerage	Technical appraisal; budgetary appraisal; organizational appraisal; economic appraisal; breakeven analysis	Work breakdown structure; Gantt chart; progress-status report; critical path analysis
Femeihurst	Technical appraisal; budgetary appraisal	Time schedule; site meeting; progress-status report

Table 10
Target Groups

Projects	Group size (est.)	Group specifications	Beneficiary impact	Beneficiary participation
Greenland	200 [1]	Sheep farmers; exporters; butchers; supermarkets; retailers; minimarts	Low	Low
Handicraft	911[2]	Craft producers; trainees; retailers; suppliers; exporters	High	Moderate
Cave	10, 300[3]	Visitors; hotels; travel agencies; tour operators; transport operators; activities directors; transport agencies	High	Low
Pulverization	142, 162[4]	Householders; workplaces; open-area users	Moderate	Low
Polytechnic	3, 000[5]	Students; faculty; staff	High	Low
Sewerage	32, 500[6]	Householders; visitors; commuters; workplaces	Moderate	Moderate
Femeihurst	750[7]	Families; individuals	Moderate	Low

1.Excludes consumers; 2. Excludes consumers; 3. Excludes residents; indicates an average of 10, 000 visitors/month and other participants; 4. Embraces the population of the catchment area - St. George, St. John, St. Joseph, St. Michael and St. Thomas; 5. Excludes employers and parents; 6. Includes 7, 500 residential population and 25, 000 nonresident transient population; and 7. Excludes ancillary beneficiaries.

Table 11
Budget Size

Projects	Cost size (BDS$)	Pari passu (BDS$)	Ranking
Greenland	1.6m.	GOB : .4m.; 25.0% USAID: 1.2m; 75.0%	7
Handicraft	2.2m.	GOB : 2.2m.; 100.0%	6
Cave	4.8m.	GOB : 4.8m.; 100.0%	3
Pulverization	4.2m.	GOB : 4.2m.; 100.0%	5
Polytechnic	20.6m.	GOB : 7.8m.; 37.8%	2
Sewerage	42.0m.	GOB : 7.3m.; 17.4% IDB : 29.4m.; 70.0%	1
Femeihurst	4.7m.	GOB : 4.7m.; 100.0%	4

Table 12
Cost Overrun

Projects	Scheduled cost (BDS$)	Actual cost (BDS$)	Revised cost (BDS$)	Overrun rate
Greenland	1.4m.	1.6m.	1.4m. 1.6m.	14.3%
Handicraft	N/K	2.2m.	N/K	I/D
Cave	3.1m.	4.8m.	1.5m. 1.7m. 3.1m. 3.3m. 4.8m.	54.8%
Pulverization	1.2m.	4.2m.	.3m. 1.2m. 2.1m. 4.2m.	250.0%
Polytechnic	11.6m.	20.6m.	10.6m. 11.6m. 20.6m.	77.5%
Sewerage	27.2m.	42.0m.	27.2m. 27.5m. 28.0m. 29.0m. 39.5m. 39.8m. 39.9m. 42.0m.	54.4%
Femeihurst	N/K	4.7m.	N/K	I/D

Table 13
Lead Time

Projects	Time period	Lead time (months)	Ranking
Greenland	February 1978-June 1982	53	6
Handicraft	September 1974-September 1979	61	5
Cave	March 1973-November 1981	105	3
Pulverization	March 1967-April 1980	158	1
Polytechnic	April 1974-May 1982	99	4
Sewerage	September 1970-June 1982	142	2
Femeihurst	January 1978-March 1981	39	7

Table 14
Implementation Time

Projects	Time period	Implementation time (months)	Ranking
Greenland	May 1978-June 1982	50	3
Handicraft	November 1975-September 1979	47	4
Cave	October 1975-November 1981	74	1
Pulverization	March 1979-April 1980	14	7
Polytechnic	May 1979-May 1982	37	5
Sewerage	April 1978-June 1982	51	2
Ferneihurst	January 1979-March 1981	27	6

Table 15
Time Overrun

Projects	Implementation time (scheduled; months)	Implementation time (actual; months)	Overrun rate
Greenland	N/K	50	I/D
Handicraft	N/K	47	I/D
Cave	15	74	393.3%
Pulverization	10	14	40.0%
Polytechnic	23	37	60.8%
Sewerage	21	51	142.8%
Ferneihurst	N/K	27	I/D

Table 16
Schedule Slippage

Projects	Scheduled completion	Organizational downtime	Actual completion
Greenland	N/K	N/K	June 1982
Handicraft	N/K	N/K	September 1979
Cave	December 1976; May 1977; September 1978; October 1980; December 1980; June 1981; October 1981	January 1978-January 1979	November 1981
Pulverization	December 1979; March 1980; April 1980	Multiyear lapse	May 1980
Polytechnic	March 1981; May 1981; August 1981; September 1981; December 1981; February 1982	N/K	May 1982
Sewerage	December 1979; September 1981; December 1981; March 1982	N/K	June 1982
Ferneihurst	N/K	January 1979-November 1979	March 1981

Table 17
Performance Indices

Projects	Status index[1]	Implementation ratio[2]	Performance index[3]
Greenland	I/D	I/D	I/D
Handicraft	I/D	I/D	I/D
Cave	3.14%	64.5%	0.65%
Pulverization	0.39%	28.5%	0.29%
Polytechnic	I/D	I/D	I/D
Sewerage	1.58%	64.7%	0.65%
Femeihurst	I/D	I/D	I/D

1. Status index is a means of relating actual progress and cost to the scheduled progress and cost. An index of 1.0 is par, while an index above that indicates better than expected progress for the money spent, and anything below 1.0 indicates less than expected progress. The status index of a project is derived as follows:

$$\frac{\text{progress}}{\text{scheduled progress}} \times \frac{\text{budgeted cost}}{\text{actual cost}} = \text{status index};$$

2. Implementation ratio indicates actual cost as ratios of scheduled cost, comparing scheduled cost and actual spending. The measure, as it is used here, gives an incomplete picture of implementation, yet it represents a beginning; and 3. Performance index is obtained from: $\frac{\text{original budgeted cost}}{\text{actual cumulative cost}}$

Table 18
Structural Conditions

Projects	Policy level	Super visory level	Agency heads/ operating agency	Support staff	Personnel number/ core skill	Organizational link	Technology type	Systemic rigidities	Decision cycle
Greenland	Minister/ Ministry of Agriculture; Deputy Chief Agricultural Officer/ Livestock Development	Senior Agricultural Officer/ Animal Husbandry Unit, Ministry of Agriculture	Manager/ Greenland Agricultural Station	Trainee manager, foreman, general workers	14; technical	Crosswalk	Diverse	High	Long
Handicraft	Minister/ Ministry of Trade; Chairman/ Board of Directors, BIDC	Deputy General Manager/ Commercial Operations Divisions, BIDC	Manager/ Handicraft Department	Assistant manager, workshop supervisor, general workers	92; artisinal	Direct	Standard	Idem	Idem
Cave	Minister/ Ministry of Housing Chairman, Board of Directors, NCC	Manager/ NCC	Officer-in-Charge/ Harrison's Cave	Maintenance supervisor, assistant officer, tour guides, office workers, support staff, general workers	40; commercial	Crosswalk	Diverse	Idem	Idem

Table 18
(continued)

Pulverization	Minister/ Ministry of Health; Chairman/ Board of Directors, SSA	Manager/ SSA	Superintendent/ Workmans Plant	Assistant plant superintendent, support staff	16; technical	Direct	Diverse	Idem	Idem
Polytechnic	Minister/ Ministry of Education; Chairman/ Board of Management, Samuel Jackman Prescod Polytechnic	Permanent Secretary/ Ministry of Education	Principal/ Samuel Jackman Prescod Polytechnic	Deputy principals, faculty members, support staff	107; pedagogical	Crosswalk	Diverse	Idem	Idem
Sewerage	Minister/ Ministry of Transport; Chairman/ Board of Directors, BWA	General Manager/ BWA	Superintendent/ Bridgetown Sewage Treatment Plant	Technical staff, support staff	21; technical	Crosswalk	Diverse	Idem	Idem
Ferneihurst	Minister/ Ministry of Housing, Chairman/ Board of Directors, NHC	Manager/ NHC	Senior Housing Officer/Housing Management Division	Housing officer, assistant housing officer, support staff	10; supervisory	Direct	Standard	Idem	Idem

Table 19
Operational Specifics

Projects	Operating cost (avg; BDS$)	Operating revenue	Service/ production cycle	Program/ activity cycle	Capacity utilization
Greenland	80, 000/yr. (partial)	32, 000/yr.	Long	Mating; lambing; husbandry; selling; slaughtering; marketing; exporting	Low
Handicraft	1.0m.-2.5m./yr.	1.2m.-1.3m./yr.	Short	Production; research; design; training/development; quality control; purchasing	Low
Cave	180, 000/yr.	1.8m./yr.	Short	Promotion; marketing; exporting; tours; promotion; maintenance	Moderate
Pulverization	455, 000/yr.	N/A	Short	Storage; collection; unloading; shredding; collection; disposal; levelling	Moderate
Polytechnic	2.0m./yr.	N/A	Long	Admission; operation; teaching/learning; evaluation; employment	Moderate
Sewerage	900, 000/yr.	500, 000/yr.	Short	User influent; collection; treatment; reuse; disposal	Low
Ferneihurst	100, 000/yr.	212, 000/yr.	Long	Tenancy agreement; rent collection; complaint service; property maintenance	High

Table 20
Marketing Specifics

Projects	Customer/ user base	Sales ratio	Market size/ value (est.; BDS$)	Market share (est.)	Import value (BDS$)	Export revenue (BDS$)	Export targets
Greenland	Sheep farmers; exporters; butchers; supermarkets; minimarts; public markets; hotels; restaurants; individuals/ households; abattoir	N/K	2.5m/yr.	12.0%	7.8m/yr.	<1.0% of sheep stock	2,000 sheep/yr.
Handicraft	Craft producers/ entrepreneurs; trainees; wholesalers; retailers; suppliers; exporters; visitors; souvenir collectors; householders; building contractors	Tourist to indigenous sales/ 9 to 1	12-20m/yr	20-30%	7.0m/yr.	100,000/yr	N/K
Cave	Visitors; hotels; travel agents; tour operators; activity directors; transport operators/ agencies	N/K	400,000 visitor arrivals/yr.	25.0%	N/A	N/A	N/A
Pulverization	Households; workplaces; streets; open areas	N/K	72.0m kilos of refuse/yr.	60.0%	N/A	N/A	N/A
Polytechnic	Students; faculty; educational institutions; public sector organizations; private sector organizations	N/A	44,000 employees working in technical fields/yr.	8.0%	N/A	N/A	N/A
Sewerage	Households; visitors; commuters; workplaces	N/K	200,000 gallons of effluent disposal/ day	16.0%	N/A	N/A	N/A
Ferneihurst	Tenants; families; suppliers	N/A	63,250 house-holds; 69,400 units	N/K	N/A	N/A	N/A

Table 21
Productivity Indices

Projects	Service/ production process	Service/ production usage rate	Productivity index/ ratio [1 2 3]	Return yield/ rate
Greenland	Constant processing	N/K	1.4 (240 sheep pounds produced / 100 working hrs.)	N/K
Handicraft	Random/batch processing	N/K	16 (1600 units produced / 100 working hrs.)	N/K
Cave	Batch processing	N/K	1 (100 cave tours completed / 100 working hrs.)	N/K
Pulverization	Batch processing	N/K	45 (4500 refuse tons collected / 100 working hrs.)	N/K
Polytechnic	Batch processing	N/K	1.3 (130 contact hours logged / 100 working hrs.)	N/K
Sewerage	Constant processing	N/K	N/K	N/K
Femeihurst	Constant processing	N/K	0.25 (25 tenant-service calls attended / 100 working hrs.)	N/K

1. Productivity ratio is the ratio of input to output. The higher the numeral value of this ratio, the greater the productivity. However, the quality of output is not factored into the productivity ratio. The ratios in the table are partial and simplified; 2. Again, project services/products are not strictly comparable, e.g. sheep poundage gained in 100 working hours is not strictly comparable to sewage gallon disposed in the same hours; and 3. An approach to developing a productivity index involves determining an input-output relation. If it takes 100 working hours to produce 100 handicraft products, for example, the productivity index is 1. The productivity index 1 can be used as a base point on which to measure increases or decreases in productivity. If in a 100-hour work period 105 handicraft units are produced, the productivity index is 1.05. If 95 units are produced, the productivity index/rate is 0.95.

Table 22
Output Level

Projects	Service/ production targets (est.)	Employment share (est.; production number)	Per unit cost (BDS$)	Output level/ capacity (est.)
Greenland	25,000 lambs/yr.	500-2,000	N/K	740 sheep sold & slaughtered/yr.; growth rate/0.25-0.40 lb/day
Handicraft	N/K	1600-1800	N/K	169 product types produced/yr.; 300 trainees trained/yr.
Cave	200,000 visitors/yr.	N/A	N/K	162,680 visits generated/yr.; 16-22 tours/day
Pulverization	N/K	N/A	44/tonne	16,705 tons of refuse disposed/yr.; landfill capacity/20 yrs.
Polytechnic	N/K	N/A	851/student yr.	3,000 student intake/yr.; success rate 60%
Sewerage	N/K	N/A	N/K	73.0m sewage disposed/yr.; plant capacity/2.4m gallons/day
Ferneihurst	N/K	N/A	N/K	750 tenants housed/yr.; room occupancy rate 1.1

Table 23
Success Rating

Projects	Driving forces	Constraining forces	Overall success rating
Greenland	High breeding rate	Low-key marketing	Low
Handicraft	Growing market demand	Deficient marketing	Moderate
Cave	Growing attendance rate	Proceduralism	High
Pulverization	Developing infrastructural/support services	Limited disposal space	Moderate
Polytechnic	Technical/vocational skill delivery/acquisition	Limited skill absorption	Moderate
Sewerage	Environmental protection	Slow sewage connection rate	Moderate
Ferneihurst	Growing tenant population	Low rent payment rate	Moderate

23 tables have been produced here, dealing with a range and variety of aspects of the sample Projects in terms of orientation, features, time, cost, approaches, schedules, performance, process, personnel, resources, support, capacity, operation, outcome, and so forth.[1]

We also find that the target Projects can be approached in terms of some quantitative formalisms (Correa, 1981; Bryant and White, 1982) which help illuminate, inter alia, three specific aspects of the project process. The formalisms are set out succinctly. First, a formalism can be used to determine the utility of project performance and quantify the monetary value of project intervention.

$\Delta U = (N)\ (T)\ (d_t)\ (Sdy) - (C)$

where

ΔU = the expected increase in utility resulting from successful project intervention;

N = number of project activities successfully completed;

T = expected duration of effects of the completed project activities;

d_t = the difference in average project performance between the completed project activities in standard deviation units;

Sdy = the standard deviation of dollar value on project among the completed project activities; and

C=cost of successfully completing project activities.

The second formalism relates to the degree of implementation success which is defined as the similarity between intended consequences and actual achievement in project implementation.

$I = (A - P)^2 / P$

where

I = the value of implementation success;

A = achieved rate of success; and

P = planned rate of success.

Implementation success is measured by the mean square of the deviation of the achieved rate of success minus the planned rate of success, expressed as a proportion of the planned rate of success. Noteworthy too is that the value of implementation success increases, while the degree of project implementation decreases. A zero value means perfect achievement of the planned rate of success, while large values denote lack of implementation.

Thirdly and finally, we refer to the target-group participation.

$P = [(B \times Pr) - (DC + OC)] R$

where

P = target-group participation;

B = target-group benefits;

Pr = probability;

DC = direct cost;

OC = opportunity cost; and

R = risk.

Project participation is a function of the benefits to be gained by the target group times the probability of gaining them, minus direct costs and opportunity costs, all times the amount of risk the target group can afford to take. It is readily apparent that the low-income target group is much less likely to participate in the project process than those with more resources, access, and influence.

Problems

There are practical as well as conceptual problems in organizational measurement relating to the Projects. One of the lapses has been the absence of coherent and clear measurement. Nearly any measurement which has been done by the Project managements appears to be random responses to particular situations rather than part of an organized and directed strategy. The organizations have been slow, and in some instances reluctant, to introduce and enforce usable criteria, standards, and performance measures. The tendency to approach measurement as a temporary add-on to regular activities is entrenched.

Managers, supervisors and employees are typically wary of measurement because the resultant data and information may be used against them and their activities. Some managers tend to view measurement even as a fad that encroaches on the already strained time, resources, and capacity. Resisting and overlooking measurement is widespread. A drop in output, a lapse in responsiveness, an insensitivity to waste and loss, or a gap in work readiness is not noticed or acted on, and is either explained away or not bothered about.

Measurement remains unattempted or is done perfunctorily because personnel operate in a system of indifferent work culture, adversarial tradition, partisan behavior, selective rewards, and shifting criteria. The casual assumption that measurement cannot be done in the public sector runs deep and wide in Barbados and the region. Lack of integration of output measurement into other management functions and lack of incentives for output gains continue. An underlying issue is the inability of the existing reward system to get the personnel to cooperate in the measurement effort and process. Besides, the analytical capabilities, including data collection and analysis, of the organizations under review are sparse and unused.

At the time this study was undertaken in Barbados, statistical materials and specific data that were available had many gaps which added to the difficulties of measurement and specification. The outputs of the sample organizations are difficult to define in some instances and, even when defined, are difficult to measure. Those output measures that are available often do not adequately reflect the real purposes of the activities they purport to measure. The output indicators seldom consider the quality of those outputs or the level of services provided. Measuring activities in these organizations has been weak and sporadic. The focus is often exclusively on cost savings. Little or no concern is shown for organizationwide measurement or how the various functions affect and interact with one another. Most efforts have short time horizons and are geared toward quick fixes. The involvement of top management in these efforts tends to waver. Efforts to put in place and facilitate organizational measurement by means of service/product development, process improvement, work-system development, employee motivation and organizational changes are nearly nonexistent.

Problems occur while measuring benefits. The value placed on, for instance, pollution control, inconvenience alleviation or amenity creation can be uncertain or contentious. The designing and compiling of unit costs has not been done much, e.g. cost per mutton pound, cost per souvenir, cost per cave visit, cost per household waste disposal, cost per student place, cost per sewage user premise, and cost per housing unit. Downtime is not infrequent in these organizations, caused by scheduling conflicts, work breakdowns, and material shortages. Work standards are neither in place nor followed up comprehensively and uniformly in the sample organizations, with the upshot that individual work activities are not examined systematically to determine the amount of time that an activity should require, i.e. the standards. Few comparative output and performance data exist. The lack of such data constrains the progress in measurement. Effectiveness measurement has not made much discernible headway either. Obtaining effectiveness data by analyzing organizational records, using employee surveys, employing expert ratings, using observer ratings and conducting client surveys is as yet rare. At present, neither managers nor policy-makers have indicated much willingness or ability to use, institutionalize, and reinforce measurement.

Conclusion

Measurement is complex, frustrating, difficult, challenging, abused, and misused. The importance of measurement cannot be overstated. If one cannot measure it, one cannot understand it. If one cannot understand it, one cannot control it. If one cannot control it, one cannot improve it. Lack of measurable or identifiable output and reluctance to quantify such output and disseminate findings hurt the Projects. Measurement should not be made in terms of finance and output alone. It needs to be concerned with other aspects, such as human resources, behavior, interpersonal and intergroup relations, and goal management.

Measurement initiative should track work activities that produce significant public value rather than areas that are easy to count. Further, measurement cannot take the place of having a solid core service or product. Nor is measurement a substitute for strategy, leadership, visioning, motivation, and design. Without strong support from the top, dedication to zero defects and some form of quality circles, the best measures will have minuscule impact.

The generalization that investments in the social sectors do not generate productive activity and that the output categories from these sectors are not quantifiable represents orthodoxy. A recurring oversight was that the sample Projects failed to design and utilize measurement systems during early phases of the project cycle when baseline collectible data were available. The lapse undermined the measurement process.

The Projects have not integrated the output measurement process into the organizations' procedural system, goal-setting practices, budget process, management information systems and human resource systems, with the result that traditional behavior and culture remain largely unchanged. There appears to be scanty realization that output indicators mean little on their own, unless they are generally used to demonstrate relationships, show trends, and make comparisons. The Projects have been missing these exciting possibilities. Part of the problem stems from weak marketing approaches to service provisions, i.e. what is missing is a more rigorous scrutiny of what consumers want and a greater determination to promote services to consumers by demonstrating both what the organizations can offer and what they have achieved. Also, measurement could be easier and improved if more outputs were sold at reasonable prices rather than provided at little or no charge, as it occurs to the Pulverization and Sewerage Projects.

There is no tradition of vigorous and thrusting measurement either in the sample Projects or in the larger public sector, with some exceptions in central banking, data processing, and statistical services. Systemic and continuous measurement is neither in existence nor in sight. Seldom does a single measure capture enough information to provide a satisfactory overview. Few public sector organizations, including the ones under study, collect organizational data or measure outputs regularly and methodically. Even when they do, each uses somewhat different standards and procedures without sharing findings with each other. Determining the appropriate, relevant and workable output measures is not easy. Aspects easiest to quantify often are not the most significant measures, but they tend to become significant because of the ease of management. Managements in the sample Projects continue to perceive measurement as a control measure: setting objectives, appraising progress, and evaluating performance. Management, however, should not threaten employees with measurement, rather help, support, guide, and counsel them. When measurements are used for self-guidance and self-development rather than downright policing, the motivation to revile and distrust measurement is largely removed.

Successful and results-oriented measurement in the Projects and the larger public sector is possible, desirable, and long overdue. In addition to learning all that can be gleaned from private sector experience, a manager who deliberately selects a few strategically significant outputs to monitor, who communicates a clear and reasonable purpose for measuring work, who involves the people whose work is to be measured, who uses existing sources of data and who takes a realistic and nonpunitive approach to changing the organizational framework for measuring work will find success and credibility.

NOTE

1. A series of other indicators/measures are not known or in existence because supporting data are not collected and, in some instances, available data are not released to researchers. We originally intended to present a large series of data, but, eventually even a limited cache of data could not be put together because of paucity of data. The measures, for instance, are: per capita project investment, project generation rate/year, project completion rate/year, method study, work measurement, flowcharting, work standards, work/activity sampling, work simplification, Pareto analysis, value analysis, output mapping, service/production rejection rate, customer return rate, turnover rate, performance benchmarking, waste reporting/reduction, supervisory index, maintenance schedule, safety measure, quality control, materials supply/control, records/forms management, and satisfaction quotient. Also, a number of temporal measures could not be captured, viz. basic time, response time, down time, runout time, setup time, waiting time, throughput time, and cycle time.

REFERENCES

Ahmad, Yusuf J. (1977) "Project Identification, Analysis, and Preparation in Developing Countries", in Dennis A. Rondinelli (ed.) *Planning Development Projects*. Stroudsburg, Penn.: Dowden, Hutchinson & Ross.

Archer, Arthur B. (1985) "The Bridgetown Sewerage Project: Its Environmental Impact", in Tighe Geoghegan (ed.) *The Caribbean Seminar on Environmental Impact Assessment*. St. Michael, Barbados: Center for Resource Management and Environmental Studies, University of the West Indies.

Benjamin, Colin D. (1987) "A Heuristic Algorithm for Scheduling Capital Investment Projects", *Project Management Journal* 18 (September).

Birgegard, Lars-Erik (1975) *The Project Selection Process in Developing Countries*. Stockholm: Economic Research Institute.

Browne, Anthony D. (1980) "The Economic Potential of the Local Handicraft Industry", *Speech delivered at the Handicraft Seminar*, Industry Week, Hilton Hotel, Barbados.

Bryant, Coralie and Louise White (1982) *Managing Development in the Third World*. Boulder: Westview Press.

Chambers, Robert (1987) *Sustainable Livelihoods, Environment and Development: Putting Poor Rural People First*. Sussex: Institute of Development Studies,

University of Sussex.

Chase, Winston B. (1983) *A Study of the Spring Garden/St. Barnabas Road Development Projects*. St. Michael, Barbados: Unpublished undergraduate paper, University of the West Indies.

Conyers, Diana and Mohan Kaul (1990) "Strategic Issues in Development Management: Learning from Successful Experiences", *Public Administration and Development* 10(April-June).

Correa, Héctor (1981) "Quantitative Analysis of the Implementation of Economic Plans in Latin America", *Planning Bulletin* 7 (June).

Coverdale, A.G. and J.M. Healey (1987) "Project Appraisal and Project Aid: A Decade of Experience in Rural Development", *Journal of Agricultural Economics* 38(1).

Cracknell, B.E. (ed.) (1984) *The Evaluation of Aid Projects and Programs*. London: Her Majesty's Stationery Office.

Dupriez, Hughes (ed.) (1979) *Integrated Rural Development Projects in Africa: Evaluation and Outlook for the Future*. Brussels: Commission of the European Community.

Esman, Milton J. and John D. Montgomery (1969) "Systems Approach to Technical Cooperation: The Role of Development Administration", *Public Administration Review* 29(September-October).

Evans, Colin (1986) *The Oistins Fisheries Complex*. St. Michael, Barbados: Unpublished undergraduate paper, University of the West Indies.

Frederick, Richard (1991) *Cost-Benefit Study of the Roseau Dam Development Project in St. Lucia*. St. Michael, Barbados: Unpublished undergraduate paper, University of the West Indies.

Gayle, Dennis J. and Israel D. Drori (1984) "Project Oasis: A Case Study in Jamaican Development Administration", *International Journal of Public Administration* 6(1).

Gittinger, P. (1972) *Economic Analysis of Agricultural Projects*. Baltimore: John Hopkins University Press.

Goodman, Louis J. and Ralph N. Love (eds.) (1979) *Management of Development Projects: An International Case Study Approach*. New York: Pergamon Press.

Grindle, Merilee S. (ed.) (1980) *Politics and Policies Implementation in the Third World*. Princeton: Princeton University Press.

Gurnee, Russell and Jeanne Gurnee (1980) *Gurnee Guide to American Caves*. Teaneck, New Jersey: Zephyrus Press.

Gurnee, Jeanne (1981) "Rediscovered After 200 Years: The Development of Harrison's", *The Bajan and South Caribbean* (May).

Harvey, Charles (1983) *Analysis of Project Finance in Developing Countries*. London: Heinemann.

Herschman, Albert (1967) *Development Projects Observed*. Washington, D.C. Brookings Institution.

Interview (1983) *Official, Ministry of Agriculture*. Christ Church, Barbados: Ministry of Agriculture (May 27).

Jones, Edwin (1970) *Pressure Group Politics in the West Indies.* Manchester: Ph.D. dissertation, University of Manchester.

Joseph, Michael B. (1984) *An Ex Post Benefit-Cost Study of the Demerara Harbor Bridge Project.* St. Michael, Barbados: Unpublished undergraduate paper, University of the West Indies.

Kahn Kaen University (1987) *Proceedings of the 1985 International Conference on Rapid Rural Appraisal.* Kahn Kaen, Thailand.

Korten, D.C. (1980) "Community Organizations and Rural Development: A Learning Process Approach", *Public Administration Review* 40(5).

Kottak, C.P. (1985) "When People Don't Come First: Some Sociological Lessons from Completed Projects", in M.M. Cernec (ed.) *Putting People First: Sociological Variables in Rural Development.* New York: Oxford University Press.

Lele, Uma (1975) *The Design of Rural Development: Lessons from Africa.* Baltimore: John Hopkins University Press.

Lecombe, B.J. (1986) *Project Aid: Limitations and Alternatives.* Paris: Organization for Economic Cooperation and Development.

Little, I.M.D. and J.A. Mirrlees (1974) *Project Appraisal and Planning for Developing Countries.* London: Heinemann.

Mara, Duncan (1982) *Appropriate Technology for Water Supply and Sanitation: Sanitation Alternatives for Low-Income Communities.* Washington, D.C. International Bank for Reconstruction and Development.

Norgaard, R.B. (1988) "Sustainable Development: A Coevolutionary View", *Futures* (December).

Oakley, P. et al. (1991) *Projects with People: The Practice of Participation in Rural Development.* Geneva: International Labor Organization.

Pandor, Abdulhai Ahmed (1980) *A Low-Cost Housing System for Barbados.* Clemson, North Carolina: Unpublished graduate thesis, Clemson University.

Patterson, Harold C. and James J. Nurse (1974) *A Survey on Sheep Production in Barbados 1972.* Christ Church, Barbados: Ministry of Agriculture.

Paul, Samuel (1989) "Poverty Alleviation and Participation", *Economic and Political Weeklies* 24(2).

Phillips, Walter D. (1979) *A Study of the Livestock Industry in Barbados between 1968-75.* St. Michael, Barbados: Unpublished undergraduate paper, University of the West Indies.

Reid, George L. (1974) "Planning and Small State Development", *Paper presented at the Conference on the Independence of Very Small States with Special Reference to the Caribbean*, Institute of Social and Economic Research, University of the West Indies, Barbados (March 25-28).

Roe, E.M. (1991) "Making the Best of Blueprint Development", *World Development* 19(4).

Roemer, Michael and Joseph J. Stern (1975) *The Appraisal of Development Projects: A Practical Guide to Project Analysis with Case Studies and Solutions.* New York: Praeger.

Rondinelli, Dennis A. and Kenneth Ruddle (1977) "Local Organization for Integrated Rural Development: Implementing Equity Planning in Developing Countries", *International Review of Administrative Sciences* (63).

Sabatier, P.A. (1986) "Top-down and Bottom-up Approaches to Implementation Research: A Critical Analysis and Suggested Synthesis", *Journal of Public Policy* (6).

Samuel Jackman Prescod Polytechnic (1980-83) *Report Files 1980-83*. St. Michael, Barbados; Samuel Jackman Prescod Polytechnic.

Seale, Patricia (1983) *A Critical Examination of the Barbados Drug Service Project*. St. Michael, Barbados: Unpublished undergraduate paper, University of the West Indies.

Sealy, Andrew V. (1983) *The Arawak Cement Plant Project: A Social Cost-Benefit Analysis*. St. Michael, Barbados: Unpublished undergraduate paper, University of the West Indies.

Simmons, Zedna (1980) *Caribbean Examinations Council Secondary Education Certificate: The Implementation Process of a Development Project*. St. Michael, Barbados: Unpublished undergraduate paper, University of the West Indies.

Stanley Associates Engineering Ltd. (1986) *Feasibility Analysis of the Roseau Dam Development Project*. Castries, St. Lucia: Ministry of Finance and Planning.

St. John, Andrew (1981) A Cost-Benefit Study of the Heywoods Holiday Village Project. St. Michael, Barbados: Unpublished undergraduate paper, University of the West Indies.

Stone, Carl (1983) *Democracy and Clientelism in Jamaica*. New Brunswick: Transaction Books.

The Barbados Advocate (1983,1985) *News Reports*. St. Michael, Barbados: The Barbados Advocate.

The Nation (1984) *News Report*. St. Michael, Barbados: The Nation (January 17).

Wynia, Gary W. (1972) *Politics and Planners: Economic Development Policy in Central America*. Madison: University of Wisconsin Press.

7
SURVEY DATA

Mention was made earlier in chapter 2 of one questionnaire survey and three interview schedules conducted in an attempt to generate some primary data directly and obtain information that was not available from other sources. First, the project-maker survey sought to identify the roles of development projects and to underscore respondent perceptions of the project process. Secondly, the general-beneficiary survey was an attempt to capture beneficiary reactions to development projects and related matters. While the operating-agency survey was concerned with the personnel of the postproject agencies, the target-group survey related to specific target groups. The specifications of the surveys, e.g. preparatory research, pretesting, sampling type, sampling frame, follow-up measures, response rate and interview process were provided earlier in chapter 2 and are not repeated here. The study questionnaire and the interview schedules are produced in their entirety in the appendix. The basic survey data and the sociodemographic data are furnished in tables 24 and 25.

Table 24
Survey Data

Study	Survey	Measure	Population[1]	Sampling	Sampling[2] frame specification	Population[3] N	Sample N	Sampling[6] fraction	Response rate
Project-maker survey	Questionnaire survey	Mail questionnaire	Policy-makers, resource actors	Random sampling	8 specialty areas	120	60	50.0%	75%
General-beneficiary survey	Interview survey	Interview schedule	Non-institutional civilian population	Quota sampling	11 parishes	161,741	220	0.1%	100%
Operating-agency survey	Interview survey	Interview schedule	Postproject operating agency personnel	Quota sampling	7 operating agencies	285	35[4]	12.2%	100%
Target-group survey	Interview survey	Interview schedule	Target group beneficiaries	Quota sampling	7 target groups	179,823	35[5]	0.01%	100%

1. Project-makers, i.e. policy-makers, project analysts, project managers, civil servants, funding-agency personnel, consulting-agency personnel, contracting-agency personnel, and trade unionists; general beneficiaries, i.e. noninstitutional, civilian, resident, adult, male-female population; the operating-agency personnel represent the Greenland Agricultural Station, Handicraft Center, Harrison's Cave, Pulverization Plant, Samuel Jackman Prescod Polytechnic, Bridgetown Sewage Treatment Plant, and Housing Maintenance Division; and the target-group beneficiaries represent farmers, producers, visitors, householders, students, users and tenants; 2. The 8 speciality areas (from policy-makers to trade unionists), the 11 parishes (Christ Church, St. Andrew, St. George, St. James, St. John, St. Joseph, St. Lucy, St. Michael, St. Peter, St. Philip and St. Thomas), the 7 operating agencies (from the Greenland Agricultural Station to the Housing Maintenance Division), and the 7 target groups (from the sheep farmers to the housing tenants) comprise the sampling frame; 3. 120 policy-makers and varied resource actors; 161,741 general beneficiaries according to the 1980 population census; 285 operating-agency personnel; and 179, 823 target-group beneficiaries; 4,5. One widely-used convention of statistical sampling requires a satisfactory sample to consist of at least 30 units (Freund, 1973; Daniel and Terrell, 1975: 132; Welch and Comer, 1983: 168; Clover and Balsley, 1984:219); and 6. It is the ratio of the size of the sample to the size of the population.

Table 25
Sociodemographic Data
(Project-maker Survey)

	Characteristics	N	%
a.	Sex		
	Male	55	91.7
	Female	1	1.6
	Nonresponse	4	6.7
	Total	60	100.0
b.	Age		
	<40	19	31.6
	>40	37	61.7
	Nonresponse	4	6.7
	Total	60	100.0
c.	Education		
	Secondary	9	15.0
	Postsecondary	47	78.3
	Nonresponse	4	6.7
	Total	60	100.0
d.	Work status		
	Senior-level	41	68.3
	Middle-level	15	25.0
	Nonresponse	4	6.7
	Total	60	100.0
e.	Work specialization		
	Managerial	22	36.6
	Professional	34	56.7
	Nonresponse	4	6.7
	Total	60	100.0

Table 25
(continued)
(General-beneficiary Survey)

Characteristics	N	%
a. Residence		
Rural	125	56.8
Urban	95	43.2
Total	220	100.0
b. Sex		
Male	135	61.4
Female	83	37.7
Nonresponse	2	0.9
Total	220	100.0
c. Age		
<30	97	44.1
>30	115	52.3
Nonresponse	8	3.6
Total	220	100.0
d. Education		
Secondary	114	51.8
Postsecondary	93	42.3
Nonresponse	13	5.9
Total	220	100.0
e. Employment		
Support-level	87	39.6
Managerial/ professional/ technical	82	37.3
Self-employed	9	4.1
Unemployed	4	1.8
Nonresponse	26	11.8
Others, e.g. students, homemakers & retirees	12	5.4
Total	220	100.0

Table 25
(continued)
(Operating-agency Survey)

Characteristics	N	%
a. Sex		
Male	26	74.3
Female	9	25.7
Total	35	100.0
b. Age		
<35	18	51.4
>35	17	48.6
Total	35	100.0
c. Work specialization		
Management, supervisory, professional, technical & functional	24	68.6
Support-level	11	31.4
Total	35	100.0

Table 25
(continued)
(Target-group Survey)

Characteristics	N	%
a. Residence		
Rural	14	40.0
Urban	21	60.0
Total	35	100.0
b. Sex		
Male	23	65.7
Female	12	34.3
Total	35	100.0
c. Age		
<40	20	57.1
>40	15	42.9
Total	35	100.0

With open-ended studies and interviews being involved, the survey respondents gave multiple answers, as can be seen in tables from 26 to 58. This resulted in the number of observations exceeding the number of respondents. There were altogether 37 questions in the four surveys, which involved a total of 350 respondents and elicited a total of 6,098 separate responses. The distribution of responses was 908,4650,260 and 280 for the project-maker survey, general-beneficiary survey, operating-agency survey and target-group survey respectively. Of the 6,098 responses, there occurred 5 (unclear responses), 16 (not sure), 51 (don't know), 5 (irrelevant responses), 1 (not clear), 33 (incomplete responses), 45 (incorrect responses), and 133 (nonresponses). In these surveys, we approached the analysis of the tables by focusing largely on the modal categories. Multiple responses from the study population and nonresponses have given rise to variation of the total of the frequencies from one table to another.

Many observations received low values ranging from 0.1% to 1.9% due to open-endedness and response-multiplicity. Virtually, all the tables have their share of small and very small values. This is true especially of tables 27,37,38,39,41, and 45. Even though several observations reported in the tables are rather low in value, the relatively high range of diversity, thoroughness, variety, coverage and depth of participant responses may have some compensatory effects. The range of responses, for instance, points to relatively less known, less obvious and less recognized areas of project management, which merit attention and action. A large number of observations occurred in respect of several tables, especially tables 27, 28,29,31,34,37,39,41,44, and 45. Some of the questions in the survey have produced a spectrum of responses which are not only wide-ranging and far-reaching but also enrich the primary and indigenous information-base of development activities in developing countries. It is doubtful if such a cache of information would have been generated by means of closed questionnaires.

Outright negative responses numbered 346, i.e. 5.7% of a total of 6,098 responses. These responses occurred to tables 27,29, 30, 31, 32, 36, 39, 40, 41, 42,43,44,50, 51,53,54,55,56, and 58. Such responses, for instance, intimated 'no impact', 'not satisfied' , 'no differences', 'no evaluation', 'no benefits', 'no costs', 'no problems', 'no complaints', 'no weaknesses', and so forth. The values went as high as 47.6%, 34.1%, 23.5%, 20.0%, 19.8%, 17.0%, 12.8%, 10.6% and 9.7%, while the moderate values were 12.8%, 10.6%, 9.7%, 7.9%, 6.8%, 5.7%, 5.4%,4.6%,4.3%, 4.0%, 3.5% and the low values ranged from 0.5% to 1.9%.

While we used random sampling for the first survey, i.e. project-maker survey, quota sampling was employed for the other three surveys, i.e. general beneficiaries, operating agencies and target groups. We do not generalize the findings reported here to the population, nor do we estimate some population values. Our goal, instead, was to obtain reactions, views, motives, attitudes , beliefs and evaluations from the sample population, and to get some idea of the variety of elements available in the population.

There are certain nonresponses among the respective samples, and by the respondents to particular questions on the schedules. Our survey material was not, nor ever could be, entirely under our control, and we never got information about more than a part of it. We have dealt with nonresponse by including in the tables a category 'nonresponse' for the missing observations, especially because some analysts are interested in the spread of nonresponse and, therefore, this is necessary for analysis. Altogether, there occurred 135 nonresponses in the four surveys. The high number of nonresponses - 5,6,5,16,17,10,7,27 and 9 - occurred to tables 34,35,39,40,41,42,43,44,45, and 48. We see that the four surveys intimated certain characteristics of survey research in Barbados, which partly accounts for the large number of nonresponses. There appears to be a tendency for many people to be somewhat reluctant to express their views in public or before strangers on projects and similar concerns. Some of them are hesitant and watchful, and, in some cases, visibly uncomfortable and unwilling. Some do not seem to like to articulate clearly their choices or interests. There are, however, atypical cases. When anonymity was repeatedly assured, some of them opened up.

Some analyses of the survey material are now in order. We analyze the masses of numerical data so as to present the essential features and relationships of the data in order to generalize from the analysis to determine patterns of behavior, particular outcomes or future trends and to infer information about the population from the samples. The information may help discern the general trends as well as capture the experience.

Project-maker Survey

The findings of the survey are reported in tables 26 through 34. Table 26 discloses that, of the 127 responses tabulated, 26.8% considered 'socioeconomic development' to be a project role, followed by 15.8% ('infrastructural support'), 13.4% ('employment generation'), 7.1% ('resource and strategy development'; 'income generation') and 6.3%

'product-base expansion'; favorable climate-setting'). Curiously, risk-taking was cited only once by the respondents. It is not surprising that 'socioeconomic development', 'infrastructural support' and 'employment generation' obtained high response rate because these roles of development projects are much discussed and shared among project professionals generally.

Table 26
Project Roles

Response	Frequency	%
Risk -taking	1	0.8
Overall community benefit	7	5.5
Infrastructural support	20	15.8
Employment generation	17	13.4
Productive-base expansion	8	6.3
Socioeconomic development	34	26.8
Skill acquisition & development	6	4.7
Favorable climate-setting	8	6.3
Resource & strategy development	9	7.1
Educational, cultural & attitudinal development	3	2.3
Income generation	9	7.1
Welfare maximization	3	2.3
Unclear response	2	1.6
Total	127	100.0

Table 27
Appraisal Deficiencies

Response	Frequency	%
Not regarded as a dynamic process	1	0.9
Inability to use quantitative measures	4	3.7
Failure to identify & anticipate problems	2	1.9
Inaccurate costing	4	3.7
Technical criteria overridden	3	2.8
Overriding political criteria	7	6.6
Shortage of skills	15	14.0
Lacks local-level relevance	16	15.0
Choice of projects/options limited	3	2.8
Weak database & forecasting techniques	10	9.4
Lacks sequencing, updating, monitoring, comprehensiveness & objectivity	10	9.4
Insufficient attention to market analysis	2	1.9
High cost	1	0.9
Commitment lacking	1	0.9
Low in-house programming capacity	3	2.8
Long lead time	8	7.5
Insufficient statement of objectives & targets	3	2.8
Funding agency strings & standard-setting	3	2.8
Avoids asking tough questions	1	0.9
Managerial inadequacy	1	0.9
Beneficiary impact underappraised	1	0.9
Overelaborate procedures	2	1.9
Lack of understanding of basic principles determining success or failure	1	0.9
Negative externalities disregarded	2	1.9
Nonresponse	3	2.8
Total	107	100.0

Table 28
Implementation Inadequacies

Response	Frequency	%
Shortage of skilled project management personnel	32	23.2
Insufficient interfacing	2	1.5
Restrictive public sector practices	7	5.1
Poor time management	26	18.8
Limited managerial & operational planning	9	6.5
Faulty costing	3	2.2
Industrial unrest	5	3.6
Financing constraints	6	4.4
Scheduling problems	5	3.6
Cost overruns	9	6.5
Poor control & management	16	11.6
Wrong attitudes	2	1.5
Insufficient measurement	5	3.6
Lack of policy support	1	0.7
Funding agency stringency & incapacity	4	2.9
Low productivity	1	0.7
Ad hoc routine orientation	2	1.5
Stop-go problems	1	0.7
Data obsolescence	1	0.7
Nonresponse	1	0.7
Total	138	100.0

Table 29
Public Service Impact

Response	Frequency	%
Limited & uneven impact	27	25.5
Noticeable impact & recognition	8	7.6
Better time management	4	3.8
Greater efficiency, effectiveness, productivity & accountability	10	9.4
Project management often misunderstood & unrecognized	5	4.7
Public service loss of skilled personnel	4	3.8
Formation of project implementation teams	3	2.8
Public service's professionalism, capability, quality & skill not much improved	8	7.6
Gap between generalists & technical staff widened	2	1.9
Project management civil service's extension	4	3.8
Project management skills not permeated public service	3	2.8
General service not much influenced by project management	5	4.7
Rise of interorganizational tension	1	0.9
Widen career management	1	0.9
Project management not well integrated into general public service	3	2.8
Impact rising	2	1.9
No clear impact	6	5.7
No impact	1	0.9
Not sure	4	3.8
Don't know	2	1.9
Nonresponse	3	2.8
Total	106	100.0

Table 30
Project Management Training

Response	Frequency	%
Not satisfied	39	47.6
Satisfied	12	14.7
Difficulties exist	6	7.3
Improvability	18	22.0
Mixed reaction	1	1.2
Not sure	2	2.4
Don't know	2	2.4
Irrelevant response	2	2.4
Total	82	100.0

Table 31
Civil Service Agencies/Project Authorities

Response	Frequency	%
No differences	11	9.7
Little differences	6	5.3
Civil service rigidity; project authority flexibility	12	10.6
Project authority operates within civil service limitations	5	4.4
Civil service in routine operations; project authority for value-adding activities	4	3.6
Greater autonomy in project authority than civil service	12	10.6
Greater goal orientation & sharper accountability in project authority than civil service	5	4.4
Orientation & motivation vary from project authority to civil service	8	7.1
Project authority more professional & task-oriented than civil service	7	6.2
Project authority better staffed & funded than civil service	5	4.4

Table 31
(continued)

More budgeting & costing in project authority than civil service	4	3.6
Project personnel often seconded from civil service; bring in civil service norms and orientations	5	4.4
Project authority extension of civil service	11	9.7
More need in civil service than project authority for multiple clearance resulting in increased costs	1	0.9
High compensation in project authority than civil service	1	0.9
Quicker action & greater sense of urgency in project authority than civil service	13	11.5
Don't know	1	0.9
Irrelevant response	1	0.9
Nonresponse	1	0.9
Total	113	100.0

Table 32
Postcompletion Evaluation

Response	Frequency	%
Little evaluation	16	24.2
Some evaluation	13	19.7
Selective cases	7	10.6
No evaluation	12	18.2
Not sure	4	6.1
Don't know	10	15.2
Irrelevant response	2	3.0
Nonresponse	2	3.0
Total	66	100.0

Table 33
Regional/International Agency Participation

Response	Frequency	%
Extensive participation	35	56.5
Selective/moderate participation	24	38.7
Intrusive & conditional participation	2	3.2
Nonresponse	1	1.6
Total	62	100.0

Table 34
Financial Problems

Response	Frequency	%
Funding agency bias & conditionality	16	15.0
Deficiency in setting financial priority	1	0.9
Difficulty in funding projects dealing with fundamental problems	3	2.8
Difficulty in extending locally-funded projects	2	1.9
Cashflow problems	4	3.7
Local counterpart funding difficulty	10	9.4
Scarcity of investible funds	9	8.4
Inflationary pressure on finance	4	3.7
Time-consuming & complicated process of financing	23	21.5
Scarcity of concessionary finance	3	2.8
Difficulty in meeting recurrent & maintenance costs	2	1.9
Inadequacy of supplementary finance	3	2.8
Frequent cost overruns	4	3.7
Difficulty in meeting cost overruns	8	7.5
Unrealistic pari passu	1	0.9
Foreign exchange depletion	2	1.9
Debt servicing problem	3	2.8
Limited absorptive capacity	1	0.9
Don't know	3	2.8
Nonresponse	5	4.7
Total	107	100.0

15.0% of the total sample, as can be seen in table 27, stated that one of the major deficiencies of project appraisal lay in the 'lack of local-level relevance'. This was followed by 14.0% ('shortage of skills'), 9.4% ('weak database, techniques and forecasting'; 'lacks sequencing, updating, monitoring, comprehensiveness and objectivity'), and 7.5% ('insufficient statement of objectives and targets'). Quite a few responses had low percentage points from 0.9 to 1.9. The first four responses - accounting for almost 50.0% of the sample - are in keeping with generally-held views of project appraisal in Barbados.

Insofar as the implementation inadequacies are concerned, as can be seen in table 28, 'shortage of skilled project management personnel' scored a 23.2%, with 'poor time management' and 'poor control and management' netting 18.8% and 11.6% respectively. Several responses netted between 3.6% and 6.5%.

Table 29 reveals that 25% of the target population responses pointed to project management's limited and uneven impact on Barbados' public service. Rallying behind this value in the data set are 9.4% ('greater efficiency, effectiveness, productivity and accountability') and 7.6% ('noticeable impact and recognition'; 'public service's professionalism, capacity, quality and skill not much improved'). It is noticeable that 6.6 % of the observations showed that there was no clear impact or none at all.

With respondents making more than a single choice, as can be seen in table 30, there were as many as 82 responses. The responses were widely distributed in the data set, ranging from 47.6% at the upper extreme of distribution to 1.2% at the lower extreme. While 14.7% showed satisfaction, 22.0% thought there was scope for further improvement. It is remarkable that the largest bloc of the sample - nearly 50% of the observations - expressed lack of satisfaction with the type and level of project management training in Barbados.

The next table furnishes as many as 19 separate responses in relation to the real as well as perceived differences between regular civil services agencies and project authorities of the recent vintage. Of the sample as a whole, over 20% pointed out 'rigidity constraint and autonomy need in relation to civil service' in table 31. These were followed by 11.5% ('quicker action and greater sense of urgency in project authority than civil service'), 9.7% ('project authority an extension of civil service'), 7.1% ('orientation and motivation vary from project authority to civil service'), and 6.2% ('project authority more professional and task-oriented than civil service'). It is remarkable that as high as 15.0% considered that there was 'no or little difference between civil service agencies and project authorities'.

In table 32, 'little evaluation', 'some evaluation', 'no evaluation' and 'selective cases' were cited, each counting 24.2%, 19.7%, 18.2% and 10.6% respectively of the total number of observations recorded. Interestingly, 'don't know' counted for a noticeable 15.2%. This information is in keeping with the reality of ex post facto evaluation in many parts of the developing world, including Barbados, in that it is one of the most neglected and perfunctory phases of the project cycle. It is not surprising that over 63.0% of the sample population observed that there was little or no evaluation and that they did not know much about project evaluation.

In the next table, while 56.5% pointed to 'extensive participation', 38.7% chose 'selective and moderate participation'. Some, i.e. 3.2% considered that the regional/international agency participation in project development was 'intrusive and conditional'. This low morale is somewhat contrary to the widespread articulation of popular concern that international funding institutions tend to have considerable control over development finance.

Table 34 indicates that 'time-consuming and complicated process of financing' (21.5%), 'funding-agency bias and conditionalities' (15.0%), 'local counterpart' 'funding difficulty' (9.4%), 'scarcity of investible funds' (8.4%) and 'difficulty in meeting cost overruns' (7.5%) were picked as the five most specific problems facing project finance. Several answers obtained smaller values, e.g.3.7%, 2.8%, 1.9%, and 0.9%. 'Don't know' and 'nonresponse' together accounted for 7.5%.

General-beneficiary Survey

We turn to the general-beneficiary survey the findings of which are presented in tables 35 through 45. Table 35 shows that of the 341 responses recorded, 55 or 16% viewed 'development projects as creating and improving facilities', while 53 or 15.5% chose 'improving overall conditions'. Reasonably noticeable values went to 'facilitating socioeconomic development' (14.7%), 'advancing infrastructure' (11.1%), 'improving people's living standards'(10.0%), 'boosting popular welfare' (7.6%), 'generating employment' (5.6%) and 'generating income'(4.7%).

Table 36 reveals that of the total 221 responses registered, 210 responses or 95.0% had knowledge of ongoing projects at the time the survey was conducted. This finding is significant in that it demonstrates a high level of awareness on the part of the general beneficiary population in Barbados. It is also striking to note that only 9 responses (4.0%) were in the negative.

Table 37 highlights a wide distribution of responses ranging from 10.0% to 0.1%. Numerous answers were received, pointing to beneficiaries' awareness of project development in the country. As many as 94 of the total 939 responses tabulated named 'Spring Garden Highway Project' as one of the completed projects. Other responses recorded 6.3% ('Central Bank of Barbados Project'; 'General Post Office Project'), 9.2% ('Arawak Cement Plant Project'), 8.2% ('Heywoods Holiday Village Project'), 4.9% ('St. Barnabas Highway Project'), 4.3% (Bridge Road Project'), and 3.9% ('Industrial Access Road Project'). Remarkable is the fact that while 41 answers (4.4%) were incorrect, 22 (2.3%) were incomplete. The spread of responses was so wide that as many as nine projects received one citation each and seven projects obtained 14 citations. Five projects were mentioned three or four times.

Table 35
Project Nature

Response	Frequency	%
Improving people's living standards	34	10.0
Generating income	16	4.7
Advancing infrastructure	38	11.1
Boosting popular welfare	26	7.6
Generating employment	19	5.6
Promoting autonomy, self-reliance & belongingness	3	0.9
Creating & improving facilities	55	16.1
Facilitating socioeconomic development	50	14.7
Human resource development	12	3.5
Improving overall conditions	53	15.5
Improving quality of life	9	2.6
Environmental protection	4	1.2
Raising production capacity	12	3.5
Getting votes	1	0.3
Linking sectors	1	0.3
Spending resources	2	0.6
Nonresponse	6	1.8
Total	341	100.0

Table 36
Ongoing Projects

Response	Frequency	%
Yes	210	95.0
No	9	4.0
Not clear	1	0.5
Nonresponse	1	0.5
Total	221	100.0

Table 37
Completed Projects

Response	Frequency	%
Central Bank of Barbados Project	59	6.3
General Post Office Project	59	6.3
Airport Ring Road Project	16	1.7
Bridge Road Project	40	4.3
Arawak Cement Plant Project	86	9.2
Spring Garden Highway Project	94	10.0
St. Barnabas Highway Project	46	4.9
Oistins Fisheries Terminal Project	28	3.0
West Terrace Housing Project	9	1.0

Table 37
(continued)

Heywoods Holiday Village Project	77	8.2
Grantley Adams International Airport Project	24	2.6
Bridgetown Harbor Development Project	9	1.0
Harrison's Cave Development Project	7	0.8
World Bank Education Project	23	2.4
St. Cecilia Housing Project	22	2.3
Spring Hall Land Lease Project	11	1.2
Industrial Access Road Project	37	3.9
Ladymeade Polyclinic Project	14	1.5
Samuel Jackman Prescod Polytechnic Project	14	1.5
Glebe Polyclinic Project	15	1.6
Oistins Development Project	20	2.1
Speightstown Development Project	1	0.1
Pine East West Road Project	4	0.4
Fairchild Street Bus Terminal Project	14	1.5
Clapham Housing Project	4	0.4
Wildey Road Project	4	0.4
Barbados Flour Mills Project	7	0.8
Children's Development Center Project	2	0.2
St. Philip Irrigation Project	1	0.1
National Health Service Project*	11	1.2
Fruit Orchard Project	2	0.2
Broiler Breeder Project	1	0.1
Wildey Polyclinic Project	9	1.0
Bridgetown Sewerage Project	20	2.1
East Coast Road Project	14	1.5
Deacon's Farm Housing Project	2	0.2
Woodbourne Oil Drilling Project	7	0.8
Halls Road Project	13	1.4
Industrial Park Project	18	1.9
Handicraft Development Project	1	0.1

Table 37
(continued)

Wildey Housing Project	5	0.5
Scotland District Soil Conservation Project*	2	0.2
Barbados Community College Project	2	0.2
Queen Elizabeth Hospital Project	1	0.1
Kensington Court Housing Project	3	0.3
Wind Energy Project*	3	0.3
Furniture Development Project	1	0.1
Pine Hill Dairy Project	1	0.1
Maynard Housing Project	2	0.2
Lammings Housing Project	1	0.1
Integrated Rural Development Project*	2	0.2
Beach Conservation Project*	1	0.1
Don't know	5	0.5
Incomplete response	22	2.3
Incorrect response	41	4.4
Nonresponse	2	0.2
Total	939	100.0

*These projects were either scrapped or were underway in one form or another.

Table 38
Project Awareness

Response	Frequency	%
Radio programs	56	12.4
Television programs	55	12.1
Interpersonal communication	19	4.2
News media	148	32.7
Personal contact	28	6.2
Newspaper reports	64	14.1
Personal observations & site visits	42	9.3
Personal interest & research	5	1.1
Information Service releases	7	1.5
Parliamentary reports & budget speeches	4	0.9

Table 38
(continued)

Billboards & poster displays	5	1.1
Classroom discussions	1	0.2
Ministerial & politician disclosures	4	0.9
Organization news releases	1	0.2
Political party releases	1	0.2
Policy statements	1	0.2
Development plan documents	4	0.9
Press conferences	3	0.7
Periodicals	1	0.2
Budget documents	1	0.2
Nonresponse	3	0.7
Total	453	100.0

Table 39
Project Benefits

Response	Frequency	%
Increased employment	124	25.7
Improved living standards	39	8.1
Increased income	30	6.2
Investment return	11	2.3
Foreign exchange savings & earnings	27	5.6
Social & economic benefits	36	7.4
Export trade facilitation	10	2.1
Net output & value addition	9	1.9
Facilities & amenities improvement	82	17.0
Improved working conditions	3	0.6
Modernization	3	0.6
Greater self-reliance	7	1.5
Greater production & productive investment	14	2.9
Improved infrastructure	15	3.1

Project 39
(continued)

Better image & acceptance	3	0.6
Greater capacity & learning experience	13	2.7
Environmental benefits	12	2.5
Improved quality of life	5	1.0
Increased access to business	7	1.5
Money circulation	1	0.2
Financial benefits	1	0.2
Knowledge & skill acquisition	5	1.0
Technology transfer	2	0.4
Overall development	10	2.1
People upliftment	1	0.2
Improved services	1	0.2
No benefits	6	1.2
Incorrect response	1	0.2
Nonresponse	5	1.0
Total	483	100.0

Table 40
Beneficiary Gains

Response	Frequency	%
Indirect benefits	46	16.0
No benefits	49	17.0
Employment benefits	14	4.9
Income benefits	10	3.5
Consumer convenience, safety & satisfaction	80	27.8
Raised living standards & life quality	40	13.9
Awareness & training benefits	10	3.5
Career development	1	0.3
Increased services & products	12	4.2

Project 40
(continued)

Social benefits	1	0.3
Not sure	4	1.4
Don't know	2	0.7
Incomplete response	2	0.7
Incorrect response	1	0.3
Nonresponse	16	5.5
Total	288	100.0

Project 41
Project Costs

Response	Frequency	%
No cost	2	0.5
High spending	2	0.5
High financial costs	115	31.2
Environmental disamenities	27	7.3
Increased taxation	28	7.6
Cost overruns	5	1.4
Skill training neglect	1	0.3
Time overruns	2	0.5
Inconvenience generation	16	4.4
Social sector neglect	3	0.8
Social, cultural & environmental costs	26	7.1
Disrupted families & communities	34	9.2
High debt & debt servicing stress	8	2.2
Opportunity cost	9	2.5
Costly maintenance	7	1.9
Foreign exchange stress	5	1.4
Land loss & distortion	6	1.6
Excessive foreign domination	7	1.9
Negative externalities	13	3.5
Morality neglect	2	0.5
Litigation increase	1	0.3
High & conditional loan commitments	6	1.6
Consumption deferment	1	0.3
High import intensity	6	1.6

Table 41
(continued)

Declining human values	1	0.3
Resource misallocation	2	0.5
Priority mixup	2	0.5
Not sure	2	0.5
Don't know	8	2.2
Incomplete response	3	0.8
Unclear response	2	0.5
Nonresponse	17	4.6
Total	369	100.0

Table 42
Beneficiary Costs

Response	Frequency	%
Tax payments	170	66.1
Increased user fees & service charges	25	9.7
Increased stress, fatigue, inconvenience, delay, disruptions & disamenity	19	7.4
No direct cost	9	3.5
Foregoing alternative consumption benefits	4	1.6
No cost	14	5.4
Declining human values	1	0.4
Not sure	1	0.4
Don't know	1	0.4
Incomplete response	1	0.4
Incorrect response	2	0.8
Nonresponse	10	3.9
Total	257	100.0

Table 43
Public Information

Response	Frequency	%
Yes	116	26.0
No	105	23.5
Reasons for sufficiency, e.g. extensive & varied media coverage; public reaction; job advertisements; political communication; press conferences; parliamentary reports; call-in programs; general discussion; general observation; published documents; billboards & poster displays; adequate feedback	107	24.0
Reasons for insufficiency, e.g. media consumer disinterest & preoccupation; factual, relevant & prompt reporting lacking; low level of awareness & understanding; incomplete, inadequate, inaccurate & misleading information; people involvement lacking; progress reporting lacking; lack of trust in media reports; lack of public consultations; conflicting reporting; lack of honest, open, objective & effective reporting; constituency reporting lacking; early reporting lacking; indepth & sustained reporting lacking; lack of follow-up; short attention span of media consumers; critical & investigative reporting lacking; uninformed & confused consumer; high level of hearsay; communication policy lacking	107	24.0
Don't know	4	0.9
Nonresponse	7	1.6
Total	446	100.0

Table 44
Improvement Measures

Response	Frequency	%
Increased & varied media coverage	67	19.7
Reporting & updating at greater frequency	24	7.1
Proper, realistic & long-term planning	4	1.2
Less partisan involvement	1	0.3
Greater, systematic & early media utilization	19	5.6
Greater people/community interest & involvement	43	12.7
Greater & direct interpersonal communication	31	9.1
Greater media display	5	1.5
Opinion polls & attitude surveys	3	0.9
High constituency reporting	3	0.9
Improved & simple reporting	28	8.2
Honest, open & participatory communication	14	4.1
School-based communication	4	1.2
Public rallies	8	2.3
Public/parliamentary debates	4	1.2
Media interviews/discussions	5	1.5
Greater use of poster displays	2	0.6
No improvement needed	12	3.5
Cannot be improved	23	6.8
Don't know	7	2.1
Incomplete response	5	1.5
Nonresponse	27	8.0
Total	339	100.0

Table 45
Project Problems

Response	Frequency	%
Time mismanagement	26	5.0
Inadequate control & management	28	5.4
Cost overruns	28	5.4
Poor industrial relations	39	7.6
High overall costs	27	5.2
Project bunching	4	0.8
Managerial & technical skill inadequacy	50	9.7
Inadequate financing	109	21.2
Heavy spending	3	0.6
Paucity of sound research & planning	29	5.6
Foreign exchange stress & leakage	4	0.8
Local resource & expertise underutilization	11	2.1
Public apathy	6	1.2
Community disruption & dislocation	5	1.0
Unfavorable funding conditions	3	0.6
Imported expertise, materials & technology	20	3.9
Employee dissatisfaction	7	1.3
High borrowing & debt servicing	6	1.2
Conflict, powerplay & resistance	11	2.1
Low workforce productivity	6	1.2
Poor communication	3	0.6
Political party pressure	5	1.0
Trade union pressure	4	0.8
Negative work attitude	9	1.7
Poor postproject operation & maintenance	5	1.0
Low public acceptance	2	1.0
Resource shortage & pilferage	16	3.1
Low level of compensation	4	0.8

Table 45
(continued)

Shortage of concessionary finance	6	1.2
Inadequate & substandard work	2	0.4
Lack of multiparty support	3	0.6
Poor location	6	1.2
Weak intersectoral linkages	2	0.4
Unresponsive market	1	0.2
Environmental disamenity	5	1.0
Social & emotional cost	1	0.2
Poor relation between expatriates & counterpart personnel	2	0.4
Declining morality & ethics	3	0.6
Don't know	2	0.4
Unclear response	2	0.4
Nonresponse	9	1.7
Total	514	100.0

Table 38 shows that 32.7% of the sample population obtained project information by means of the news media. The two electronic media - radio and television - together accounted for almost 25%. 'Newspaper reports', 'personal observations and site visits', 'personal contacts' and 'interpersonal communication' each scored 14.1%, 9.3%, 6.2%, and 4.2%. Answers were many and varied, with the result that some of the values became smaller. What is interesting and striking about responses like these is that respondents get to know about projects in so many different ways.

Table 39 records the respondents' views of project benefits. 25.7% and 17.0% of the respondents indicated 'increased employment' and 'facilities/amenities improvement' as benefits derived from projects. The high values were followed by 8.1% ('improved living standards'), 7.4% ('social and economic benefits'), 6.2% ('increased income') , and 5.6% ('foreign exchange saving and earning'). The table records several smaller values.

Likewise, 'consumer convenience, safety and satisfaction' (27.8%), 'indirect benefits' (16.0%) and 'raised living standards and life quality' (13.9%) were tagged as the high-rated beneficiary gains, as shown in table 40. Significantly, a high percentage of the beneficiary population thought that it had derived no benefits from the projects.

An analysis of the answers on project costs is presented in table 41. As shown in the table, 'high financial costs' came at the top with 31.2%, while 'disrupted families and communities' (9.2%), 'increased taxation' (7.6%), 'environmental disamenities' (7.3%), and 'social, cultural and environmental costs' (7.1%) clustered closely. 4.4% was captured by 'inconvenience generation' and 3.5% went to 'negative externalities'. As many as 24 responses - 75% of the total responses tabulated in this table - scored low and did not exceed three percentages points.

A further analysis of the costs paid by the beneficiary population was undertaken by the use of table 42, which reveals that 170 out of 257 responses tabulated pointed to 'tax payments' as the most frequent beneficiary cost with 66.1%. This was followed by 9.7% ('increased user fees and service charges', 7.4% ('increased stress, fatigue, inconvenience, delay, disruption and disamenity'), 5.4% ('no cost') 3.9% ('nonresponse'), and 3.5% ('no direct cost').

While 26.0% of the sample registered 'sufficiency of information' concerning projects as shown in table 43, 23.5% did not believe that the general public was sufficiently informed. The respondents, answering in the affirmative as well as in the negative, offered over 200 reasons why the general public was or was not sufficiently informed of the project in Barbados.

Table 44 displays the gamut of responses concerning the measures of improving project-related public information. The answers varied from a high of 19.7% ('increased and varied media coverage') to a low of 0.3% ('less partisan involvement'). This particular question elicited as many as 26 separate responses.

A large number of observations occurred in respect of table 45. Of the 514 responses received, 'inadequate financing' (21.2%), 'managerial and technical skill inadequacy' (9.7%) and 'poor industrial relations' (7.6%) obtained the highest frequency. Tagging along these values were 'paucity of sound research and planning' (5.6%), 'inadequate control and management' (5.4%), 'cost overruns' (5.4%), 'high overall costs' (5.2%), and 'time mismanagement' (5.0%).

Operating-agency Survey

During the survey, 35 sample respondents answered in a particular way, and of this number 24 (68.5%) indicated that they became happy with 'regularity, reasonableness and progress of operations' as shown in table 46. ‘Goal achievement’ tailed far behind with 8.5%. Five other responses copped 2.9% each. It is important to note that nearly 70% of the sample population place a premium on the dependability and continuity of the projects’ operation and services.

As shown in table 47, the unhappiness level presented three responses each with 11.4% frequency, i.e. ‘smooth functioning lacking’, ‘shortage of money, equipment and accessory’, and ‘staff problems’. Other answers unfolded the span of unhappiness, e.g. ‘insufficiency of in-house training and staff development’ (8.6%), ‘delay problems’ (5.7%), and ‘cooperation lacking’ (2.9%). It is noticeable that ‘nonresponse’ cleared 28.5% of the observations. When asked to identify something about the project organizations which made the respondents unhappy, one wonders why so many respondents chose not to answer.

Table 46
Happiness Level

Response	Frequency	%
Program continuity	1	2.9
Product/service demand continuity	1	2.9
Regularity, reasonableness & progress of operations	24	68.5
Employee competence & reliability	1	2.9
Good management-employee relations	1	2.9
Goal achievement	3	8.5
Learning experience & opportunity	1	2.9
Nonresponse	3	8.5
Total	35	100.0

Table 47
Unhappiness Level

Response	Frequency	%
Smooth functioning lacking	4	11.4
Insufficiency of in-house training & staff development	3	8.6
Shortage of money, equipment & accessories	4	11.4
Staff problems	4	11.4
Delay problems	2	5.7
Cooperation lacking	1	2.9
Operational problems	2	5.7
Lack of infrastructural support	2	5.7
Poor design & layout	1	2.9
Unreliable clientele	1	2.9
Prompt maintenance lacking	1	2.9
Nonresponse	10	28.5
Total	35	100.0

Table 48
Service Adequacy

Response	Frequency	%
Adequate & reasonable service	27	56.2
Inadequate & improvable service	12	25.0
Reasons for service inadequacy, e.g. varied resource & initiative limitations, means-end mismatch, time mismanagement, relational constraints	9	18.8
Total	48	100.0

Table 49
Main Achievements

Response	Frequency	%
Not as expected	3	4.3
Program development & control	15	21.4
Indigenous resource use	2	2.9
Opportunity generation & motivation sustenance	4	5.7
Facilities/services creation & maintenance	6	8.6
Employee training & advancement	4	5.7
Employment & income generation	7	10.0
Product/service promotion	9	12.9
Operational efficiency	5	7.1
Environmental protection	8	11.4
Skill development	6	8.6
Not sure	1	1.4
Total	70	100.0

Table 50
Major Problems

Response	Frequency	%
Design & formulation problems	6	4.9
Growth constraints	11	9.0
Operational problems	21	17.2
Time mismanagement	11	9.0
Inadequate financial & material resources	24	19.7
Human resource & managerial limitations	18	14.8
Marketing problems	4	3.3
Relational & behavioral problems	15	12.3
High partisanship	1	0.8
Policy constraints	1	0.8
Low compensation level	6	4.9
High cost	2	1.7
No problems	1	0.8
Nonresponse	1	0.8
Total	122	100.0

Table 51
Oranizational Prospects

Response	Frequency	%
Program updating & resource redesign/renewal	12	24.0
Program development & diversification	27	54.0
Potential	9	18.0
Not sure	1	2.0
Don't know	1	2.0
Total	50	100.0

Table 48 displays information on the adequacy of service. 'Adequate and reasonable service' had the highest percentage of answers with 56.2%. 'Inadequate and improvable service' trailed as a distant second with 25.0%. Multiple reasons were advanced which the respondents stated had caused the inadequacy of service.

The operating agencies' main achievements are reported in table 49. While 'program development and control' cleared 21.4%, 'production/ service promotion' scored 12.9% and 'environmental protection' got 11.4%. These values gradually slipped to 10.0% ('employment and income generation'), 8.6% ('facilities/services creation and maintenance'; 'skill development'), 7.1% ('operational efficiency'), 5.7% ('opportunity generation and motivation'; 'employment training and advancement'), 4.3% ('not as expected') and 2.9% ('indigenous resource use').

The major problems faced by the operating agencies, as summarized in table 50, embody 19.7% ('inadequate financial and material resources'), 17.2% ('operational problems'), and 14.8% ('human resource and managerial limitations'). Next in the lineup were 'relational and behavioral problems'(12.3%), 'growth constraints' and 'time mismanagement' (9.0%), and 'design/formulation problems' and 'low compensation level' (4.9%).

54.0% of the total sample, as can be seen in table 51, assessed 'program development and diversification' as being the operating agencies' desirable and long-term outlook. 'Program updating and resource redesign/renewal' and 'potential' scored 24% and 18% respectively.

Target-group Survey

The tables 52 through 57 illustrate responses assembled for the target-group survey. The respondents' expectation level has been tabulated in table 52. Of the 35 people interviewed, 45.7% stated that the projects met their expectation and 34.1% stated that the former did not meet their expectation. 15.9% of the answers specificd rcasons for not meeting the target group's expectation. It is important to note that over one-third of the sample target-group population clearly stated that the projects under review did not meet their expectations.

Table 52
Expectation Level

Response	Frequency	%
Meet expectation	20	45.4
Did not meet expectation	15	34.1
Reasons for not meeting expectation, e.g. poor management, unusual design, low productivity, little effectiveness, unreliability	7	15.9
No particular expectation	2	4.6
Total	44	100.0

Table 53
Need Level

Response	Frequency	%
Satisfy needs, e.g. basic, educational, environmental, occupational, recreational	28	71.8
Did not satisfy needs	5	12.8
Reasons for not satisfying needs, e.g. different individual need, unmet need, poor location	6	15.4
Total	39	100.0

Table 54
Project Benefits

Response	Frequency	%
Certain benefits, e.g. basic, civic, social, economic, occupational, educational, environmental, infrastructural	26	74.3
Some assistance	2	5.7
No benefits	7	20.0
Total	35	100.0

Table 55
Main Complaints

Response	Frequency	%
Management inadequacies	12	15.8
Poor interfacing	12	15.8
Insufficient results	6	7.9
Negative competition	3	3.9
Marketing constraints	3	3.9
Growth constraints	2	2.6
Import control lacking	4	5.3
Environmental pollution & disamenity	5	6.6
Resource shortage & waste	8	10.5
High user charge	6	7.9
No complaints	15	19.8
Total	76	100.0

Table 56
Main Strengths

Response	Frequency	%
Good idea	4	8.3
Indigenous resource development	6	12.5
High potential & improvability	7	14.6
Diversification	2	4.2
Manifold contributions, e.g. civic, social, economic, educational, environmental, occupational, infrastructural	22	45.8
Some operational facilitators	5	10.4
Nonresponse	2	4.2
Total	48	100.0

Table 57
Main Weaknesses

Response	Frequency	%
Poor execution	1	2.6
Design & formulation deficiencies	6	15.8
Little impact	1	2.6
Inadequate planning	2	5.3
Excessive political control	1	2.6
Low acceptance & image	1	2.6
Operational inadequacies, e.g. materials, logistics, time, quality, externalities, capacity, resources, workflow, personnel, renewal	22	58.0
No weaknesses	3	7.9
Don't know	1	2.6
Total	38	100.0

Likewise, the target population's need level was shown in table 53. While 71.8% of the responses signalled the satisfaction of needs, the same needs remained unsatisfied for 12.8%. However, 15.4% offered reasons for not having their needs satisfied.

Insofar as project benefits are concerned, as can be seen in table 54, 'certain benefits' gained a high 74.3%. The value dropped to 20.0% for 'no benefits' and 5.7% for 'some assistance'. It is remarkable that a high 20.0% of the sample population stated that they had not derived any benefits from the projects under review.

Table 55 highlights the main complaints reported by the target population. The answers varied from 'no complaints' (19.8%) through 'management inadequacies' (15.8%), 'resource shortage and waste' (10.5%), 'high user charge' (7.9%) to 'negative competition' (3.9%) and 'import control lacking' (2.6%). Interestingly enough, as high as 19.8% did have complaints about the projects under review.

Table 56 reveals that, of the 48 responses tabulated, a high 45.8% took time to consider the projects' main strengths. The principal contributions intimated by the respondents were by nature civic, social, economic, environmental, educational, occupational, and infrastructural. Some interesting data emerged, such as 'high potential and improvability' (14.6%), 'indigenous resource development'(12.5%), 'some operational facilitators' (10.4%), 'good idea' (8.3%), and 'diversification' (4.2%).

Finally, in table 57, varied 'operational inadequacies' were labeled the projects' main weaknesses (58.0%). Curiously, a mere 2.6% identified 'poor execution' and 'excessive political control' as weaknesses, while 'inadequate planning' netted 5.3%. However, higher values went to 'design and formulation deficiencies' (15.8%). The target group's finger-pointing of 'operational inadequacies' in large numbers as the projects' main weaknesses is indicative of its disappointment with unsatisfactory project operation and of the pressing need for its improved performance.

Summary

Checking different tables in terms of comparable question categories from across the four surveys yields the following information.

Table 58
Data Summary

Tables	Questions	Responses	Frequency %
26	what are project roles	socioeconomic development	26.8
35	what is project nature	creating & improving facilities	16.1
36	name ongoing projects	affirmative	95.0
37	name completed projects	affirmative	92.6
40	how beneficiaries gain from projects	consumer convenience safety & satisfaction	27.8
54	how target groups gain from projects	certain basic socioeconomic & environmental benefits	74.3
38	how beneficiaries know about projects	news releases	32.7
43	are people infomed of projects	affirmative	26.0
42	how beneficiaries pay costs	tax payments	66.1
55	what are target-group complaints	management inadequacies	15.8
46	what makes agency personnel happy	regularity, reasonableness & progress of operations	68.5
56	what are project strengths	civic, socioeconomic, environmental & infrastructural contributions	45.8
47	what makes agency personnel unhappy	smooth functioning lacking	11.4
55	what are target-group complaints	management inadequacies	15.8
48	is clientele receiving service	adequate & reasonable service	56.2
53	has project satisfied need	basic, environmental & recreational need satisfaction	71.8
49	what are project achievements	program development & control	21.4

Table 58
(continued)

51	what are project problems	inadequate financial & material resources	19.7
58	what are project weaknesses	operational inadequacies	58.0
53	has project met expectations	meets expectations	45.4
56	what are project strengths	civic, socioeconomic, environmental & infrastructural contributions	45.8

The survey research produces evidence that lends support to a number of findings and conclusions. The latter may also be regarded as dominant and underlying themes and trends. These findings seem in line with the results obtained elsewhere.

First, the project-makers place a great deal of emphasis on socioeconomic development, infrastructural support and employment generation while conceiving and planning projects. Appraisal seems to be undermined by lack of local relevance, shortage of skills, unreliable information base, and weak process orientation. Implementation is thwarted by the shortage of trained personnel, time mismanagement, and undynamic management and control. For policy-makers and practitioners, certain information seems relevant, e.g. project management has so far made a limited and uneven impact on the public service, project management training is not satisfactory, there needs to be greater operational autonomy and action orientation in public sector management, there is little ex post facto project evaluation, and the international funding agencies extensively participate in Barbados' project development. Of the financial problems, the three stand out prominently, i.e. time-consuming and complicated process of financing, funding-agency conditionality, and local counterpart financing insufficiency.

Second, the general beneficiaries point out creating facilities, improving overall conditions and socioeconomic development as being resultant of development projects. Their interest in a host of ongoing and completed projects - especially infrastructural, tourism and industrial projects - suggests their level and type of general awareness. Related to this are the news media, providing periodic information on projects. While employment generation, new facilities and improved living standards were regarded as project benefits, high financial costs, disrupted families, increased taxation and sociocultural decay were put as project costs. The respondents named consumer satisfaction and high living standards as beneficiary gains, and tax payments, service charges and stress as beneficiary costs. In terms of whether or not the public clientele was sufficiently informed of projects, attention was drawn to gaps in media coverage, development communication, and reporting. The important measures included increased and varied media coverage, people and community involvement, and open and objective reporting. The problems projects faced involved inadequate financing, skill shortage, and poor industrial relations.

Third, the operational-agency personnel pointed to, inter alia, the importance of regularity and reasonableness in operations, the lack of smooth functioning, the adequacy and improvability of service, the development of programs, the availability of products and services, the generation of employment and income, resource insufficiency, behavioral flaws, managerial limitations, and program updating. Fourth, for the target-group members, expectation was met and need was satisfied in some instances, and in others the outcome was in the negative. While project benefits and strengths clustered around indigenous resource development and payoffs of basic, socioeconomic, infrastructural and environmental nature, constraints and weaknesses pointed to design flaw, management incapacity, operational insufficiency, poor interfacing, resource shortage, high user cost and perfunctory planning.

Overall, the underlying meaning of the available data suggests that the project-makers in Barbados look for greater effectiveness and purposefulness in project management. This was certainly true of the project-makers interviewed for this study, most of whom implied that project-making in the island left much to be desired. The beneficiaries appear to maintain an even approach to projects; they seem to appreciate those aspects of projects which are eufunctional, and remain critical when the outcome gets dysfunctional. While the operating-agency personnel like to see dynamism and progress in organization management, the target-group members seem critical as well as appreciative of the sample Projects.

REFERENCES

Freund, J.E. (1973) *Modern Elementary Statistics*. London: Prentice-Hall International.

Daniel, Wayne W. and James C. Terrell (1975) *Business Statistics: Basic Concepts and Methodology*. Boston: Houghton Mifflin.

Clover, Vernon T. and Howard L. Balsley (1984) *Business Research Methods*. New York: John Wiley.

Welch, Susan and John C. Comer (1983) *Quantitative Methods for Public Administration*. Homewood, Illinois: Dorsey Press.

8
FINDINGS

We do not mean to be exhaustive in our discussion on findings. The findings are cited - some major and others minor - which in our judgement produce the realities of the sample Projects. The issues, neither handful nor uniform, were and still are internally as well as externally located. Some of the findings are empirically grounded, while others are based on inferences. We distinguish between two forms of project development, making impact on Barbados: the first process tending to produce development *in* Barbados, and the second advancing the development *of* Barbados.

The very complexity and multifacetedness of the Projects mean that the findings shown here need to be considered as working hypotheses. It is not possible, on the basis of the current research, to set out definitive judgements on the conditions and facts which make for success or failure and cause delays in projects. We have not searched in this work for absolute laws. The research results fill some crucial gaps in the empirical analysis of development projects in Barbados as well as the Caribbean. Worthy of note is that sweeping generalizations and superficial judgements about project success and failure can be inaccurate and misleading, and that the failure or shortfall of a project tends to have negative consequences for the particular sector in which it is located. We live in a world in which stochastic processes are important, and our studies and findings must take account of this feature.

What follows here is linking, i.e. the connection between our theoretical model and empirical data is examined. Some aspects of the connection are confirmed, while the others are disclaimed. We are concerned here with the research need to link our Project model and Project behavior. We want to demonstrate an appreciation of such a need between theory or research and practice or behavior. We marshal substantive and corroborative evidence in keeping with our research objectives and attempt to do a measure of genetic, contextual, dispositional, and functional explanations. Similarity or unity as well as dissimilarity or diversity are here together and at the same time. The extent to which we make the link among the project-setting model, institutional matrix, project behavior, analysis, survey data and project operation, the more indepth, far-reaching and wide-ranging our understanding is likely to be of the issues, tasks and problems involved in sound and successful project management.

Introduction

Development projects tend to receive only modest attention from social science research. While emphasis has been placed on economic/technical appraisal and project planning/control, the multifaceted project process is overlooked. Project research reveals several strands, e.g. institutional experience-building, project behavior and misbehavior, systems-analytical appraisal, appraisal studies, planning and control focus, project cycle studies, project implementation, and project management environment.

Development projects need thorough study for several reasons. Projects help accentuate the pace of economic and social progress, put resources in place and set dynamics in motion, represent tangible expansion of large-scale activities, exemplify human achievement, and provide socioeconomic leadership.

The study, with an interest in project behavior, pursues the premise that development projects in Barbados - embedded in the social setting - proceed in an evolutionary, incremental, and collaborative mode. This has been done by pressing on with laying out a model, examining projects as a tool of development activity, examining appraisal, implementation and management capability functions, highlighting project institutionalization, illustrating the project cycle of a sample of projects, and presenting sample survey data.

Based on research on a small sample of projects in one country, it is untenable to set out precise judgements on the conditions and facts which make for successes or setbacks in development activities. The findings reported in this volume are more in the nature of working hypotheses. Given the complexity and enormity of the fieldwork situation, the findings shown here may perhaps be considered initiatory. This and similar research, serving as a basis for further research, should be extended and verified by additional studies.

Methodology

Methodologically, the study, opting for a strategy of multioperationalism, uses secondary analysis, comparative analysis, observational method, and survey method. Secondary analysis made possible use of information, data and evidence from previous studies and documents. Comparative analysis involved putting together a sample of projects, representing the sectors of agriculture, industry, tourism, infrastructure, education, health, and housing. Comparison, entailed single-country but intersectoral and interproject comparison, crossnational comparison and synchronic as well as diachronic comparison. Observational method related to pursuing published data, finding facts from respondents and informants, and observing directly sample organizations, processes and behaviors. Structured, direct and nonparticipant observation was employed, observational repertoires were compiled, and fieldnotes were taken.

Involving four sets of survey, the survey method used mail questionnaire, interview schedules, crosssectional approach, probability as well as nonprobability sampling, and standardized as well as scheduled approach incorporating open-ended questions. The project-maker survey sought to identify the roles of development projects and to underscore respondent perception of the project process. The general beneficiary survey was an attempt to capture beneficiary reactions to development projects and related concerns. While the operating-agency survey was concerned with personnel of the project-operating agencies, the target-group survey related to specific target groups associated with the sample projects.

To address problems and meet needs, several supplementary research strategies were used, including routine correspondence, telephone calls, field checks, site visits, occasional meetings, extended discussions, technical briefings, direct contacts, brief queries, and focused interviews. The research questions dealt with were derived from a general theoretical context, the data were collected with the strategy of multioperationalism, and sampling was utilized to obtain data. Many and varied challenges, difficulties and uncertainties were encountered in the fieldwork process in relation to accessing, collecting and generating data and information via secondary analysis, comparative analysis, observational method, and survey method. We confirm that compromise, adjustment and modification are inherent in the research process, that research studies tend to generate a dynamic of their own which can rarely be foreseen in the planning process, and that the research process is much more muddled, disjointed and dialectic than textbooks typically reflect. To minimize varied and unsettling uncertainties and costs, to exert effective control over the fluid, and at times runaway, fieldwork process and to achieve research goals, an operational accommodation between the ideal and the practical must be made.

Project-setting Model

Past research, not grappling with the entire project process, tended to discuss development projects in a theoretical vacuum, as though projects were autonomous organizational responses unrelated to the ongoing social, political, economic, technological, and moral realities. We have attempted to place, as far as possible, the Projects in the context of the entire project process.

In this volume, projects are approached with the aid of a theoretical context and a model. Regardless of whether causes and effects are ever determinable in nature or in human affairs, we proceed with our model. An eight-element schematic model of development projects - a project-setting model comprising elements, processes and interactions - is laid out. The model, in our judgement, holds together. We returned repeatedly to fieldnotes and ancillary material to check, test and extend the model. The model provides a conceptual analytical framework around which a set of relationships are developed. The model, laid out theoretically and empirically, is designed to be an adaptive model - attempting to adjust to contingencies - and a learning model - having flexibility and capacity to react to emerging conditions and demonstrating synergy and interdependence inherent in the Projects.

Development projects, as the first element, introduce ideas, innovations, goals or intentions into a setting. The project cycle, secondly, transfer ideas or assumptions into reality. Third, the appraisal process ensures the examination of alternatives and their soundness. The implementation process manages the actual delivery of intentions. Management capability undergirds the delivery system's capacity. Output is what is actually delivered to clients as goods and services. Feedback provides the flow of information and ensures adjustment and remedial or corrective action. Environment, in which projects operate, represents a milieu, an interaction of interests, and a mix of resources.

We find functional relationships between and among the model elements. We produce evidence like concomitant variation and sequence of occurrence to make inferences from the assembled data. We also find

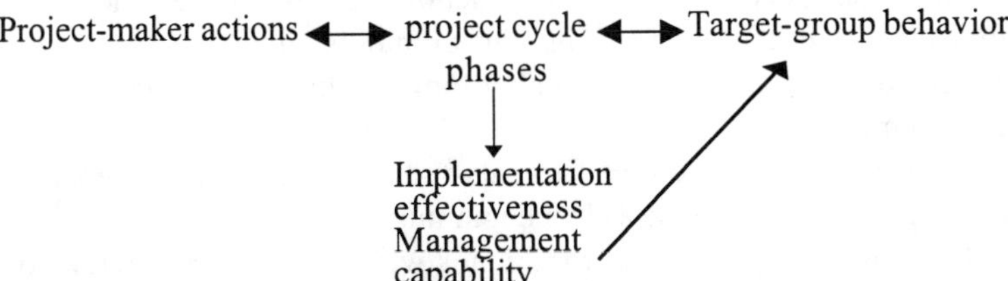

that the actions, links, effectiveness and capabilities produce a sequence of events and a sequence of occurrences which have a cascading effect on the target-group behavior. With the recognition that the effects are probably caused by multiple factors, we infer a relationship. The Projects go through a flow of events. Some of these events occur before other events, some after. We find active connections between and among the events and elements. We come across temporal precedence, constant conjunction and directionality in parts of the data.

Among other things, the Projects show receptivity and adaptation to political will, government change, policy directives and shifts, donor preferences, management initiatives, resource constraints, organizational culture, and interorganizational relations. Adaption has been painful as well as rewarding, slow, uncertain and hesitant as well as prompt and self-assured. Learning has been fruitful when decisions and initiatives converged; it diverged when tension and friction prevailed. The sample Projects, in their journey from conception to evaluation, confirm an element in our project-setting model, i.e. virtually all aspects of the real world, development projects included, are subject to various degrees of instability and uncertainty. We found all along that the Projects showed varied and daunting stresses, and had to live through and cope with ever-changing, shifting, and uncertain reality.

Development Project

Development projects, having been influenced by rapid sociotechnical changes and critical lead times, have come into greater use and acceptance in recent times because the traditional forms of organization and management do not ordinarily carry out operations promptly, effectively and efficiently. Few activities are more crucial to accelerating the pace of economic and social progress in low-income countries than effective planning and implementation of projects. Certain major activities, and even routine operations at times, are put on a project basis to achieve greater impact, better results, quicker action, and faster pace. The project approach is useful in meeting the demands of complexity, size, independence, target group, technological change, regulation, and development.

To be able to achieve specific goals and respond to special demands, a project - an entity having a clear beginning, a finite task and a specified end, and producing outputs from inputs within a time limit and a cost schedule - requires lateral coordination, procedural latitude, and a central technical and managerial interface.

We have marshalled evidence in our study by pointing out that the use of project concept and successful project-building have helped to advance innovation within organizations. Innovation comes about because an idea is born in which the relevant resource groups have faith and are committed to it. The openness, the dynamism, the advocacy, the autonomy, the teamwork and the demonstrativeness seem to spawn exploratory drive, achievement orientation and creativity in the Projects. The Projects succeeded in acting as vehicles for social change, creating the capacity for ameliorating problems that obstruct growth and delay progress. The output of all the seven Projects has resulted in expanded productive capacity, increased problem-solving and management capability, and added to the stock of management talent.

Moving in an evolutionary and collaborative mode, the Projects, their evolution, behavior, operation and overall ethos clearly underpin the fact that building a project is never a self-executing or self-fulfilling process. In fact, uncertainties, contingencies, unintended reactions and consequences, human and technological inadequacies, financial and resource limitations, donor dependency and competing interests characterize, and even dominate, projects. Some negative and nonoutput payoffs of the Projects stem, among other things, from clear deficiencies in sustained cooperation and collaboration at all levels between regular public sector organizations and Project entities, and adoption of priorities or practices which differ strikingly from those of the general public sector environment. Despite all the novelty, intensity and dynamism, projects are, in the final analysis, work systems and our sample Projects show that amply. In each phase of the Project process, a group of people collaborated to form a work organization which - like any other - had characteristic problems of planning, structure, leadership, motivation and control in the pursuit of goal management.

Project Cycle

The project cycle is common to all projects. A project involves a continuous and self-sustaining cycle of activity, which runs through several phases. Projects follow a process which can be construed a cycle because one phase normally leads to the next, the terminal point of one phase is often the initial part of a new one, and feedback to an earlier phase is not only possible but necessary. This is considered a cycle because each phase not only grows out of the preceding ones, but leads to the subsequent ones. Also, a project is considered cyclical because its phases, elements and processes constitute a feedback loop that makes reiteration and refinement possible.

The cycle has a number of features, e.g. interdependence, continuity, orderliness, self-sustenance, and repeatability. The phases are overlapping and interdependent rather than discrete. Phasing in and phasing out occurs throughout the cycle. Several parallel activities can take place within each phase and overlap into the succeeding phase. The strength and integrity of the earlier phase largely determines the ultimate performance of the subsequent phases. The cycle as a reiterative, learning tool is undergirded by aggregation, cumulativeness, consistence, regularity, transferabiliy, maintainability, and correctibility. The cycle is, to all intents and purposes, a work system, and that was underlined by the Projects. The Project as a work system had put together wide-ranging human, organizational, technical, material, physical and financial resources, employed and extended management functions like planning, organizing, staffing, budgeting, scheduling, reporting, controlling, coordinating, leading and motivating, designed and executed work in such a way as to satisfy performance, time and cost criteria, intensified workflow, carried out work streamlining and simplification, and established and maintained task-oriented work relations.

As an ordering and organizing framework, the cycle is useful in that it presents a structure within which the project may be viewed, it presents a clear picture of the varied phases of a project, it indicates how the various phases and tasks are carried out, it provides an overview of tasks performed by participating organizations, it works as a conversion process turning intentions into reality, it enables one to see the complexity of the entire process in its totality, it helps visualize the phases as links in a chain, and it helps one to identify and remedy problems at each phase of the cycle.

Although several accounts of the project cycle are available, current project management practices lay stress on a multiple-phase sequential project cycle. To start with, conception is the phase where a need has been identified and as idea has been recognized. The impetus for project ideas may come from varied sources. Formulation means developing a plan, spelling it out in greater deal and in specific terms. The activities in this phase are research, review, projection, and solution-oriented. Appraisal - an ex ante analysis of the effects of a determined course of action - is concerned with the allocation of resources to achieve the best, the maximum, or the most effective production of goods and services. A project - which may be accepted, rejected, delayed, changed, modified, or scaled down - has an approval phase which entails securing endorsement from competent authorities. The purpose of implementation is to ensure that a project is executed as planned, or modified in the light of changing conditions. It may be viewed as a process of interaction between goal-setting and goal-achieving actions. Reporting embraces information-gathering, documentation, review, and status-reporting. The purposes are to ensure control, take necessary action and communicate relevant information to contact points. Termination, a brief but technically critical transitional span, links the preceding phases and the succeeding sage. The transition from the project status to that of normal operation cannot take place spontaneously, and has to be planned early and related activities must be carried out carefully. Evaluation relates to postcompletion assessment and provides information which allows the project cycle to close.

Behavior of the sample Projects shows linearity - movement beginning at the first phase and developing to the last. Each task within the phases was more or less distinct, proceeded more or less in an orderly time sequence, and embodied more or less a logical sequence - all these features reflected linearity. Second, the movement through the phases was also circular or cyclical. The relations between the phases were cyclical as well as iterative. The Projects' progress was like a series of circular loops. Straddling various phases, the Projects moved consecutively as well as progressively from conception to completion.

We find that the development of the Projects can be viewed as an exploratory and creative exercise, although once the Projects are completed, they must be long-term operations. In developing countries, such as Barbados, the project cycle imparts certain spatial and temporal discipline, as demonstrated by the subject Projects, without which projects cannot achieve goals, retain viability, and sustain purposefulness. The cycle has helped develop and maintain certain systems, plans, schedules, operations, procedures, practices, and targets. By means of all these, the Projects started, moved, progressed, accelerated, and ended. Had it not been for an enabling mechanism like the cycle, ad hocism - so widespread in Barbados' public sector environment - long gestation period, inertia, long decision cycle, system rigidity, unresponsive behavior and slow operating culture might have turned the Projects into loss-incurring, time-wasting nonstarters. This is not to say that the Projects had no problems, such as time loss and cost escalation. Indeed, the Projects had their share of problems and even the cycle as a firm orderly framework could not stave off these problems because the environment is not always or entirely controllable. But in the absence or laxity of urgency, focusing, tenacity, deadlines, pressures and sanctions, the Projects might have succumbed to customary behavior in the public sector. The cycle, moreover, laid stress on team-building, group dynamics, integrated management, productivity, and results-orientation. The cycle - whose propriety, behavior and dynamics are watched by all the concerned parties, including the funding agencies - can also discourage, though not always succeed in curbing, conventional politics from using such projects as a power base for patronage, partisanship, influence-peddling, pork-barrel operations, job offers, contract-awarding, and electoral largesse.

The cycle, in addition, has influenced Barbados' public sector management in two ways: transiently and permanently. It was transient in terms of positive and ameliorative impact a Project made on the wider public service while it was under way. It was permanent because the cycle convincingly showed that a group of people - against heavy odds, traditional habitual forces, and varied constraints in the public sector - could conceive a worthwhile idea, pursue it persistently and give it a tangible and durable shape, and that the group was capable of creating, achieving, performing, mobilizing, competing and winning, provided the group was endowed with mission, technology, autonomy, and competence.

The project cycles, it is notable, were not uniform in frequency, dimension, or duration either. The Project processes seldom took place within a single institution. In fact, a host of organizations - policy-making units, ministries, financial/technical assistance organizations, departments, private sector organizations and other participating organizations - were involved throughout the input and output phases. The cycles, as we have seen, were anything but mechanical and rigid. A great deal of creativity, innovativeness, judgement, heuristics, selection and flexibility played continuing roles throughout the process. It is further notable that strict linearity is not essential, and may at times even run counter to the needs of the situation. The ultimate success of the Projects rested on each of the phases. There was, of course, a clear need to mobilize all the phases that were required to producc thc final project action. Lapse or showdown at any phase - for example the initial input phases of the Pulverization Project - caused the entire effort to suffer. The cycle, cyclical logic, continuity and transition were monitored by Project personnel more or less, and any major deviations, fomented by any group of Project participants, from the cycle would not have gone unnoticed or unchallenged and would most likely have aroused disagreement or conflict.

The examined Projects have shown us that the cycle did not always run in strict sequential order, the activities were phased through time, two or more phases were collapsed and executed, the tasks were carried out at different times during the cycle, and the phases behaved not so much sequentially as cyclically. Smooth sequence was not always observed, and the phases did not always terminate in the same order. The Projects, to be sure, could not keep to a neat, tidy and one-way timeframe, nor did activities and events move tidily or predictably at all times. The actual Project process did not follow the neat and tidy logic of the project cycle model, it was not always possible to clearly distinguish between one phase and the nest, the phases were not completely self-contained, and some phases had relevance to and impact on more than one phase. Nor were the phases exclusionary one way or the other, the phases nearly always tended to represent mix and blend, and there was considerable interplay among the phases.

Some of the Project organizations - for example Greenland - were not fully geared to process, if not generate, project ideas rapidly and efficiently. There is a clear danger that projects, which are initiated hastily or without much careful analysis and implementation support, tend to result in the misappropriation of efforts and resources. What is more disheartening is the weak conceptual and operational links between overall planning and project identification and ineffective communication of planning goals to various resource groups. In some cases, projects appear to serve interests of particular pressure groups. In Greenland, for example, allegations were made by small sheep farmers that the Venture was dominated by and the benefits gravitated toward big-time farmers and that the Project catered more to the business interests of the latter. Also mentionable are deficiency in conducting a satisfactory design, differences in the perception of project objectives among project participants, and inappropriate or ineffective adaptation to local conditions. Greenland, for instance, was subject to criticisms in all these respects, viz. design was less than realistic and thorough, considerable perceptual differences existed between funding agency personnel and counterpart staff, and concerted attention should have been paid to local conditions to ensure compatibility and success.

The subject Projects presented indepth economic, financial and technical appraisals, but tended to marginalize social, cultural, political and organizational appraisals. The absorptive capacity and management capability of a country to execute and operate projects was sometimes insufficiently approached. The oversight occurred to, for instance, the Cave Project. Approval of the Projects not only took in some instances a long time but also, in the case of the Pulverization Project, an unpredictably long time. When not properly monitored, implementation can endanger the potential worth or merit of a project. The Cave and the Pulverization Projects languished at different times, raising anxiety and heightening concerns. Of the subject Projects, the Polytechnic and Sewerage Projects tended to ask for multiple reports and separate periodic reports at frequent intervals. The reports and report-making overlapped in some instances, produced superfluous and repetitive information and took considerable staff time away from other needed activities. Advance planning and proactive drive for a smooth changeover, despite receiving a great deal of rhetoric, tended to be neglected in practice. All the Projects under review slowed down when it came to timely termination planning and orderly execution. All the Ventures, except Polytechnic and Sewerage, chafed under low-priority evaluation, caused by the lack of appreciation for timely and thorough evaluation and follow-up and the tendency to overlook accountability and transparency in public sector projects.

Appraisal Process

Project appraisal is critical to the project cycle because it seeks to ensure investment viability and worth, provide a comprehensive review of all aspects of the project, and lay the foundation for implementing the project and evaluating it when completed. The essential purpose of appraisal is that of allocating inherently limited resources rationally to a variety of different uses in such a way that the net benefit to society is as large as possible. Appraisal involves examining objectives and alternative means of achieving them, clarifying the nature of alternatives, examining viability and efficiency, identifying the quality, quantity and timing of physical inputs and outputs, determining effective demand for the output, and establishing costs and benefits. The rationale for appraisal lies in finding out what differences a project would make if it were not chosen. Several objectives are upheld in appraisal, e.g. investment, aggregate consumption increase, income distribution, net contribution to equity, employment effect, net foreign-exchange effect, international competitiveness, and net-value addition.

Of the several selection criteria based on a comparison of cost incurred and benefit to be derived in the future, cost-effectiveness analysis is concerned with an assessment of the least cost per unit of physical output. Net present value appraises present net benefits by comparing different time steams of benefits and costs. Under benefit-cost ratio, the present value of both cost and benefit is stated as a ratio. Internal rate of return is a measure of the earning capacity, value, or profitability of a project. Other criteria in use include payback period method, simple rate of return method, output-capital ratio, accounting rate of return method, annual value method, and terminal value method. On the whole, there is no one best criterion for estimating project worth, although net present value, benefit-cost ratio and internal rate of return are better-known, discounted , precise, dynamic and time-adjusted criteria, taking into consideration the entire life of a project and discounting the future inflows and outflows to their present values.

There are a number of types of project appraisal, e.g. technical, economic, financial, social, political, and organizational. Technical appraisal relates, for instance, to topographical data, hydrological data, demographic data, site planning, and equipment planning and installation. While economic appraisal ascertains whether a project makes economic sense and identifies ways of making projects less risky and more cost-effective, financial appraisal finds out if a project can secure finance, repay loans and remain viable. Social appraisal addresses the issue of productivity and development, income distribution, and self-reliant growth. Political appraisal points to the degree of acceptance of a project idea by the various resource and interest groups. Last but not least, organizational appraisal is concerned with staffing, manageability, implementability, structuring, and organization.

The sample Projects in the study show that careful project appraisal can do considerably better and secure greater gains than ad hoc rules of thumb or policy-maker preferences. By using well-established selection criteria, unrealistic or questionable assumptions have been largely avoided, ruinous partisan and personalist preferences have been eschewed, rationality in public sector decision-making has been given a chance, and improving income-producing capacity or increasing net organizational worth has been put on the agenda. As a result, several incremental income flows and effects have occurred, e.g. project surplus, incremental labor income, domestic price change, incremental effects, net benefit accrual, and welfare increment. The Projects, thus tested by sound criteria and nothwithstanding constraints, had a much improved chance of being implemented within reasonable time and cost schedules and of yielding reasonable benefits. Although the common impression is that the goal of appraisal is to produce a set of numbers that tells whether a project is good or bad, in reality, and insofaras the sample Projects are concerned, it is not the numbers themselves that are important, but rather the appreciation of the Projects' relative strengths and weaknesses that is gained in the course of analytical work. Undue reliance should not be placed on these criteria, one must point out, given what we have seen in respect of the sample Projects, because the appraisal techniques, eventually, are approaches, the many calculations, approximations and estimates used in appraisals are subject to a range of error and variance, conflict and uncertainty cannot be ruled out, and appraisal tools are hardly value-neutral. Evidence shows that the depth, breadth and coverage of appraisal varied from Project to Project. Notwithstanding theory stressing technical, economic and financial rationality, social, cultural, political, organizational and environmental aspects had cast a fundamental influence on the Projects in terms of morale, momentum, motivation, and team-building.

Implementation Process

The criticality of implementation is undeniable because it bridges the gap between what is envisaged and what actually occurs and it may be the most decisive phase in determining project success or failure. Project experience shows chasm between intention and achievement, promise and performance and plan and reality, thus underscoring the importance of implementation.

Implementation seeks to ascertain whether an organization can bring together people and material in a cohesive organizational form and motivate them in such a way as to carry out the organization's stated objectives. The time factor being critical in the implementation phase, it involves developing and pursuing a strategy of organization and management to ensure that a project not only starts but reaches completion with the minimum of delays, overruns, deviations, and problems. Implementation involves a capacity to forge links in the causal chain, connecting activities to objectives. The longer the chain of causality, the more numerous the reciprocal relations among the links and the more complex implementation gets. The logic of implementation is not unilinear but multilinear, requiring divergences and convergences at strategic points and coordination of activities at multiple levels.

The degree and quality of implementational success rests on the executing agency. As a delivery system, as an instrument of implementation, as a catalyst of modification and adaptation and as an intermediary of constantly varying complex of human forces and emotions, an executing agency succeeds or fails to the extent it is strategically located in the entire action network, it is supported by cooperation, collaboration, and synergy, it is staffed by competent and committed personnel, it is reinforced by political resources and achievement need, it is facilitated by participatory culture and open communication, it is strengthened by proactive and fair leadership, it is buttressed by the reciprocity and support of intended beneficiaries, it is assisted by the continuity and persistence of organized efforts, and it is able to maximize driving forces and minimize restraining forces. To reiterate, the availability of suitable personnel and the presence of management capability often decide a project's success or failure. The attitude of management, real as different from cosmetic, is an important factor in improving implementation. As a matter of fact, wanting better implementation goes a long way towards achieving it. Effective and successful implementation requires that implementators know, actually do and follow through what they are supposed to do.

Implicit in the sample Projects is the fact that implementation is not self-executing and that projects do not implement themselves. It is not a process that follows automatically or spontaneously once a project has been formulated. Projects neither get implemented as planned and expected nor do they take place as quickly or easily as desired. Sometimes, in fact, they never occur. Some projects, in fact, slow down, bog down, peter out, run into snags, and never produce the expected results. Implementation, even under the best of conditions, is exceedingly difficult because of a smaller degree of control and higher number of variables over a given situation. Those ventures which do manage to get through the tortuous process of implementation often look or turn out somewhat or considerably different from what was originally intended or planned. To be sure, naive assumptions abound in that once a project has been approved, it will be executed and the desired results will be near those expected, that once a decision is made or a project formulated, the results that subsequently follow are those originally intended, and that what has been decided would be achieved or what happens is what was intended.

The sample Projects embrace the reactive process of converting resources into goods and services (Honadle, 1979), the assembly process of strategic interaction among various interests (Bardach, 1977), and the unitary process of goal-setting and plan-enforcing (Majone and Wildavsky, 1979). The Projects were neither entirely predictable nor always manageable (Grindle, 1980), moved among decisions, compliance and impacts (Mazmanian and Sabatier, 1981), guided by interactive and dynamic elements (Jones, 1977), and forged links in a causal chain (Pressman and Wildavsky, 1973).

The Projects exhibited various implementation features, e.g. interaction patterns, target-group reactions, executing-agency activities and environmental factors (Smith, 1973), the developmental model stressing that the original decision or idea builds the blueprint, the aggregative model focusing on getting project activities done (Dunshire, 1978), the control/planning model positing that implementation is logically implied by planning, the interaction model stating that implementation builds consensus on goals, and the evolution model changing or modifying intentions, learning from experience and correcting errors (Majone and Wildavsky, 1979). In a similar vein, the Projects are in keeping with the structural approach (different structures being appropriate to different tasks), the managerial approach (employing management techniques and procedures), the behavioral approach (recognizing resistance to, fear of and resentment toward change), and the political approach (taking into account realities of power to ensure project success) (Hogwood and Gunn, 1984).

All too often, implementation was swamped, as we have seen in the Projects under review, by constant pressures of problems, crises, delays, setbacks, and frustrations. Many, if not all, implementation problems were not only unexpected, unforeseen, protracted and downplayed, but lacked prompt attention, deft handling, tenacious monitoring, and cooperative ethos. Implementation faced constraints, with the plans going wrong, anomaly and entropy persisting, the assumptions breaking down in real life and the delivery of intentions to the target groups getting delayed. The domino effect was at work in some instances in that when one or two initial phases were in trouble, the trouble was transmitted to the later phases. The Project showed signs of vulnerability to such forms as drift or mutation, which tended to put the Ventures somewhat away from their original designs. Penetration as another force occurred with respect to almost all the Projects whereby external actors and organizations were able to influence project behavior. Penetration was especially visible in respect of funding practices, budgetary measures, procurement practices, and technological entry. Encapsulation as yet another force - whereby a more powerful entity surrounds and dominates a less powerful one - characterized the Projects varyingly. Difficulty followed and tension surfaced when a packaged external solution was attempted to be hoisted on an implementation team, as it occurred to Greenland.

A weak area in the Projects relates to overlooked and underutilized follow-up activities. Such enforcement and control forms as reporting, accounting control, audit control, on-site visit, in-situ assessment, management review, parliamentary review, sample survey, customer survey and other feedback forms tend to languish and are not in use as much as necessary. The sample Projects' experience firmly recognizes that specific approaches and techniques must be utilized if projects are to move from the realm of intention to the ambit of reality. Experience suggested that the fewer and clearer the steps included in carrying out a project, the fewer the chances for setback to overtake it, and that the more directly a project aimed at the project and the fewer the detours involved in its ultimate realization, the greater the likelihood that it would be implemented. Sometimes, what had paid off and worked out in the Projects, for instance Ferneihurst, involved trying to do less, doing it right and better the first time, and staying focused.

In spite of theory prescribing that certain conditions foster a climate that facilitates and nourishes implementation, they were not always observed in practice, with the upshot that the pooled evidence points to the undermining of synergy, goal management, equifinality, cohesiveness, and deliverability. Theory appears to overlook that the analytic techniques may be less useful at times than careful attention to implementation and implementability. The Project participants tended to function in an adversarial and oppositional setting at times, zealously guarding their prerogatives and perquisites, and operating under the delusion that each subsystem could be managed independently of the others. The differences that arose, which hurt the Projects, were not so much over policy, ideology, values, ideals, or analytical/operating procedures as they were personal, dispositional, perceptual, affective, and relational.

Management Capability

Successful project development requires high levels of management capability. The enhancement and expansion of management capability is needed to achieve project goals. In almost any project, the delivery of goals and the actual outcome depend on management capacity. Raising management capacity is critical because an increase in workload, escalation in complexity and involvement in new activities without a corresponding change in personnel competence tends to lead to underperformance. The need for capacity growth is high. A country must invest in it, plan and carry forward such investments like any other. Management capability requires strong political, legislative and executive support and widespread institutionalization. It requires a sense of direction, a resolve to overcome many snags, a high standard of leadership, a high level of communication, sustained and cautions attention, and a regular allocation of resources.

Management capacity is a specific function necessary for the successful implementation of a project as well as its effective postcompletion operation. Its purpose is to develop competencies and attitudes essential to effective performance. Management capacity is the ability to mobilize and use physical, human and financial inputs, establish and manage organizations for goal achievement, collect and process information, analyze and develop measures and options, formulate responses and set directions, design and maintain systems and procedures, implement programmatic goals and values, and control and evaluate results.

Management capacity is a resource, a resource which has to be consistently allocated to yield a return on the investment. But it is not a mobile resource capable of flowing spontaneously to the point where it is needed most or where it can yield the highest return. Management capacity is also complementary rather than substitutable. The more interdependent a project is, the more management capacity it needs. It is not only concerned with what is to be done but also with how it is to be done. Substantively, it consists of decision-making ability, competence-boosting, skill-raising, responsiveness, organization-building, human resource development, morale maintenance, capacity-building, performance and output consciousness, and adaptiveness. Management capacity is susceptible to conscious improvement as well as the improvement that comes indirectly from related changes.

Management capability is significant, especially in project development. The quality of capability and skill can affect projects in several ways. A project may take longer to complete than is planned initially. The period between a project's completion and its operation may be prolonged. The project's related capacity may not be attained. Even if it is attained, it may be done only with the use of more costly inputs. Frequent changes in designs, schedules or budgets, extension or curtailment of completed schedules, reordering of priority, heavy reliance on external assistance and indefinite postponement and stretchout counteract against projects.

The Projects confirm that management capacity is a scare and valuable resource, with its attribute of making a difference between success and failure. The quality of management can be seen often as a major factor which makes nearly everything go right or makes nearly everything go wrong. The Barbados public sector's involvement in the socioeconomic domain places and continues to put a heavy demand on management capability, political support and direction, policy effectiveness, resource mobilization, interorganizational synergy and technological interface. The Projects under review - conceived, completed and operational - show that management capability played a contributory role in the project process, touching on all phases the Projects, i.e. generation, study, formulation, execution, and operation. In spite of numerous snags and setbacks, it influenced the quality and outcome of Project activities. It was helpful not only to the Projects' implementation progress but also their postcompletion operational continuity and success. In the project cycle management, certain competencies in management capability were demonstrated, albeit varyingly, e.g. Project personnel operating within the functional and personnel subsystems, communicating at Project sites, in committees and in crossfunctional groups, working with diverse people, coordinating group effort, providing leadership and direction, providing continuity, stability, cohesiveness and momentum, settling conflicts and disputes, accelerating efforts, minimizing constraints, flushing out obstacles, and integrating efforts.

Yet, implicit in the Project behavior is the observation that actual systemwide capability is more uneven and selective than one expects and that potential capability is not being traced and pursued as vigorously as necessary in order to turn potential into reality. Management capability remains insulated and limited, and proactive leadership inducing capability growth is low-key. One should constantly keep in mind, given Barbados' context, that imported or externally-driven initiatives are no real and effective substitutes for local initiative, direction, commitment, and participation. Grounding problem-solving in the local setting, using local capacity more frequently and intensively and drawing resources and support from the local environment - rather than unduly and uncritically depending on foreign expertise - do not seem to have wider top-level currency. Despite theory prescribing the development and sustenance of indigenous in-house competence in project development, accumulated evidence reveals as yet remarkable dependence on overseas finance, technology, marketing, consultancy, contracting and, even, subcontracting. The mobilization, deployment and intensification of management capability in Barbados continues to be slow-moving and sporadic, lacking in sequential continuity, strategic focus, systemic depth, and bipartisan support. Regardless of several reform initiatives and numerous exhortations, management capability is uneven and sparse and constraints are myriad and daunting, but corrective measures are not effective as yet. It is desirable, in our judgement, to treat management as a sector in Barbados' development planning, susceptible to programmed development in its own right, a field with its own identity - a compelling move not in sight yet.

The needs in building, expanding and improving management capability are pressing, but they are not being pushed methodically. Barbados needs to invest more in it and plan such investment like any other more rigorously and continuously. Planning for and executing management capability deserves the same degree of proactive attention as that given to other activities, such as finance, trade, investment, business development, technology transfer, commercial orientation, market promotion, and human resource development. As a matter of fact, capability planning needs to be geared to the main shaft of management decision-making so that management effectiveness, promptness and fairness can increase readily. Sustained efforts are required, more than ever before, to expand and improve existing management capability and generate recognition throughout the public sector system at all levels that continuous capacity growth is necessary. Noteworthy too is that building a capable management is not an easy, glamorous and quick-fix task, and that one should not expect dramatic results or give up too easily.

Outputs

The Projects have produced a number of outputs which are being delivered to customers and clients. The goods and services would not have been produced in the absence of the Projects. The outputs create impact on the country as a whole, including groups and individuals. The outputs extend to a breeding station, a production workshop, a showcase, a processing plant, a campus, a sewage plant, a housing complex, and ancillary activities.

The outputs of the Projects which are varied and diverse - goods and services to the beneficiary and client groups and to personnel in other segments of the public and private sectors - reflect the interaction of many different decisions, concerns and issues, carry the results of Project action to the environment, signify the interplay of the social, economic and political features in the environment, provide legitimacy and continuity, promote visibility, and forge interfunctional/interorganizational linkages. The outputs, representing certain transactions that emanate from Project action, include specific services, tangible goods, decisions, regulations, standards, sanctions, gestures, statements, symbolic messages, information, technical advice, and future-specific proposals. Also, negative outputs - failure to provide desired services and deliver desired results in a timely and equitable fashion - emanated from the Projects, carrying short-term as well as long-term deprivations for both the target groups and the management system. The impact of the outputs on the actions of the recipients is made at various levels, ranging from stimulative to additive and substitutive. Some Project impacts, however, are not altogether clear, varying with intervention type and frequency, time periods, beneficiary capability and status, and measurement usage.

Feedback

Feedback is integral to our project-setting model. It provides the principal justification for many decisions taken within the Project about the outputs that should be produced. The feedback process - comprising a whole array of interactions, nonlinear effects and feedback - is seen in operation, which is indicated by client reactions and responses, media reports, consultant reports, official reactions, and evaluation studies. Feedback is evident in the flow and continuity of varied, diverse and frequent interactions among the Project organizations/personnel and the many sources of their inputs and the recipients of their outputs.

Feedback provides the flow of information between and among subsystems, tends to influence inputs, makes for adjustment in work systems to accomplish organizational objectives, and, in some instances, promotes remedial action. Feedback, often in less formal ways in the Projects under review, has helped modify and improve existing services, helped expand the size of services to provide for increased and diverse target population, and helped expand the scope of the Projects to provide for certain unmet needs.

Even so, the tendency to pay little, and occasionally grudging, attention to feedback is widespread, aside from noting its importance. Worse yet, the operating culture relating to the Projects' feedback seemed to be marked by defensiveness, delay, hesitancy, and oversimplification. Beneficiary/client groups, policy-makers, decision-makers and participating organizations tend to be less remedy and task-oriented, prompt and persistent and more reactive and verbal.

Environment

The model shows us via Project behavior that the Projects operate in an environment. While the effect of the environment on project development is discernible, it is often overlooked. In fact, what happens to a project is conditioned by both the task and contextual environments. The Projects had to interact varyingly with a changing, complex, varied, and evolving environment. The Projects survive in an environment, having been adapted and altered. The Projects that started out to accomplish one set of objectives evolved into retaining some initial goals and putting on some other additions, changes, or modifications. Adaptation to the environment did take place, or else the sample Projects would not have culminated and remained operational.

Project research is emphatic about the target-group involvement. In fact, the question of how to involve the target communities in project planning and implementation commands a great deal of attention. In our study, the Sewerage Project presents disquieting evidence. It appears that there is a tension between the need for prompt implementation - ensuring quick cost recovery and revenue generation - and the need to facilitate beneficiary participation by seizing the net opportunities offered by projects.

The Projects have introduced not only innovations but also unintended consequences. Far from the Ventures operating in vacuum or isolation, these represent tangible entities which draw resources from and put back services/products into a milieu. Environment influences the quality and quantity of both inputs and outputs. The Project process tends to be swayed by some of the dominant ideas and practices at play in Barbados, viz. value, perception and belief system, cultural norms and practices, authority type, institutional orientation, interpersonal relations, resource-allocation type, leadership orientation, achievement orientation, conflict-resolution mode, and consensus-building capacity.

Institutional Matrix

Project development in Barbados, with its inception in planning, had its origin in the Colonial Development and Welfare Act of 1940 and the Moyne Commission Report of 1945. The first plan 'A Ten Year Development Plan for Barbados: Sketch Plan of Development 1946-56' has been followed by a series of medium-term plans. Since independence in 1966, planning has been recognized as a tool to ensure efficiency in the implementation of a development strategy, as a strategy designed to promote change, as a means to select the best available alternatives to achieve specific goals, and as an attempt to allocate resources in a rational manner and with optimum results.

The Development Plan 1946-56 sought to provide a framework for Barbados' welfare and indicated the broad lines of development. The Development Plan 1952-57 mounted projects in agriculture and infrastructure. While during 1955-60 the construction of the Bridgetown Harbor was taken up, the Development Plan 1960-65 looked at unemployment reduction, poverty alleviation, etc. Resources were committed to social and economic sectors in the Development Plan 1962-65. Tourism received a boost in the Development Plan 1965-68. Agriculture, health and community development featured prominently in the Development Plan 1969-72. The Development Plan 1973-77 put stress on consolidation. Industrialization marked the Development Plan 1979-83. The Development Plans 1983-88, 1988-93 and 1993-2000 unfolded initiatives in resource allocation and management, including housing and transportation.

Project institutionalization in Barbados comprises a high-level political and policy-making body (Planning and Priorities Committee), a central planning agency (Ministry of Finance and Economic Affairs), and a planning and coordinating unit (Public Investment Unit). In 1962 the Central Planning Committee was created to coordinate investment activity. The Committee was replaced in 1978 by a similar body called the Planning and Priorities Committee (PPC). The PPC monitors the project cycle and plan/project implementation. Likewise, the Ministry of Finance and Planning, becoming operational in 1973, is an agency responsible for formulating, coordinating, supervising, negotiating and financing development plans and projects. The Public Investment Unit, created in 1978, identifies, plans, coordinates, monitors, reports and pursues planning/project activities with a view to increasing the efficiency and effectiveness of decision-making in public sector capital resource allocation. Project institutionalization at the operating or departmental level was carried out with a view to strengthening management capability and accelerating implementation. The Ministry of Agriculture, for instance, established Special Assignments Division in 1978, the Ministry of Education put Project Execution Unit in place during 1978-79, the Ministry of Health's Project Design and Implementation Unit became operational in 1978, and the Ministry of Transport's Project Division came on board in 1979.

There are many factors and forces which influence sectoral activities in Barbados. Efficient and dynamic agriculture - considered important in Barbados' overall development strategy - aims at raising income and productivity, reducing dependence on food imports and increasing export revenue. The industrial sector plays a leading role in contributing towards growth, employment, output generation, income generation, and export expansion. The country's beaches, climate, landscape, including overall stability, general amiability and locational advantage represent the tourism sector's key resources. It has a relatively high labor content, is a generator of foreign exchange and domestic revenue, contributes to GDP, provides employment, and stimulates infrastructural spread. The existence of an adequate infrastructural base being essential to development, Barbados' infrastructure is a booster for continued improvement and expansion, development acceleration, and production/service expansion. High priority is attached to the continuous modernization and expansion of the educational sector. Education is considered an important vehicle for self-development, social progress, cultural vibrancy, attitudinal change, and productive development. For the health sector in Barbados, organized delivery of health services is held to be basic to socioeconomic achievement, health is a fundamental human right, a healthy population is essential to a productive nation, improved human health adds to goal attainment, and attaining high level of health is an important social goal. Housing, one of the basic human needs, is recognized as being essential to satisfying the needs of welfare, security, safety, freedom, and identity.

We recognize, such being the case, that development projects in Barbados, moved in an evolutionary, incremental and collaborative mode. The projects, rooted as these were in Barbados' socioeconomic setting, evolved over time, emerging from the colonial period in the 1940s, unfolding as an instrument of long-term development planning, and embracing a range of social and economic sectors. The successive plans gradually incorporated and instituted the project structure in the country. This is seen in institution-building, involving the Planning and Priorities Committee, Ministry of Finance and Economic Affairs, Public Investment Unit, and the operating agencies and developments over time of such functions and skills as collaboration, pooling, sharing, negotiation, coordination, monitoring, linking, analysis, evaluation, and follow-up.

Project Behavior

Historically, the Projects from Greenland to Ferneihurst reveal certain patterns of evolution. The Blackbelly sheep, in existence in Barbados for over three hundred years, has been raised by private farmers and the Ministry of Agriculture, its agricultural stations, and its extension services. Sheep-breeding has come a long way from haphazard selection and culling practices, unsystematic breeding, low selection pressure, few sheep pastures, casual pasture rotation and parasitic control, and few outlets for marketable sheep. Handicraft has a tradition in Barbados extending back to the times of the Arawaks, the emancipation period, the 1930s, the 1940s, the Handicraft Development Center in 1955, retail outlets such as Women's Self Help in the 1960s, the Barbados Industrial Development Corporation-initiated Handicraft Division in the 1970s, and subsequent development in the 1980s and 1990s. Harrisons' Cave, whose existence has been known for hundreds of years, lay buried under the ground near the geographical center of Barbados for many years until 1970 when it was rediscovered by speleologist Ole Sorensen.

During the preemancipation period, refuse disposal in Barbados was neglected, resulted in outbreaks of diseases and high mortality. Waste management has moved from parish-based activity, contract service, tipping method to reorganization until it came under the ambit of the Sanitation Service Authority in 1974. Technical-vocational education straddles the 1920s when the Board of Technical Training came into being and the Barbados Technical Institute, set up in 1953, out of which the Polytechnic was established in 1969. Unsatisfactory in Barbados' urban areas, sewage disposal witnessed parish-based service organization and fragmentation, pit closets, poor sanitation, health hazards, disease spread, and environmental pollution. Housing conditions during the 1920s, 1930s and 1970s were deplorable, with 70% of land being held in rented sites in the 1950s. The National Housing Corporation, established in 1973, represents a long succession of institutional evolution, starting with the Bridgetown Housing Board of 1939.

The Projects were conceived internally within the public sector agencies, including some stimuli originating in organizations outside the public sector. Greenland was initiated following a mandate given in 1975 by the Heads of Government to CARICOM. It was consistent with the agreement of the CARICOM ministers of agriculture known as the

Caribbean Food Plan. Handicraft was pushed as a project in 1974 by the BIDC because of its importance to the economy and its output containing a high local content. The Cave Project idea was born in 1973 after it was thoroughly surveyed, its significance realized, and its potential identified. Several specialist assessments influenced the Pulverization Project's conception throughout the 1960s and the 1970s until the Ministry of Health indicated in 1977 GOB's plan to build a pulverization plant. The Polytechnic Project's conceptual phase was informed by several studies undertaken and reports put out in the 1960s and the 1970s, especially those establishing the demand for Polytechnic trainees and estimating the annual trainee output required to meet skilled personnel needs.

Several years of consulting and reporting in the 1960s and the 1970s took place before it was decided by the Ministry of Health in 1974 to sewer parts of Bridgetown. After plan for land acquired in 1972 at Ferneihurst by another ministry got changed, the Ministry of Housing decided in 1978 to utilize the site for a housing project. In the conception phase, problem analysis did not always proceed in an orderly or serial fashion.

The Projects' formulation facilitated the movement and progress of the successive phases. Greenland's formulation stressed that the Project's success rested on the cooperation of the sheep farmers, collaboration between and among several organizations, thoroughness of the initial proposal, and planning, coordination and execution of a set of activities. Handicraft's formulation hinged on identifying certain strategies, e.g. producing local raw material-utilizing crafts, facilitating private craft entrepreneurship, diversifying production, effecting design improvement, providing training, and promoting markets. The Cave Project's formulation embraced various moves to improve the tourism product and to expand the range and number of attractions and services. As to the Pulverization Project, several refuse disposal methods were examined in relation to feasibility, storage, collection, disposal, finance, environmental soundness, reusability, location, and support services. Formulation pointed out that the Polytechnic should be sited at a permanent central location, expanded to provide accommodation for a high full-time and part-time intake, provided with academic program development and diversification, and reinforced by support services.

For the Sewerage Project, site selection consumed considerable work. Several treatment processes were examined in relation to energy conservation, operational simplicity, low sludge generation, environmental soundness, and maintainability. It was formulated that 120 medium-density two-storey terrace units and other ancillary facilities would be built at Ferneihurst as a low-income housing development to help meet the country's pressing demand for housing. It is remarkable that theory makes a distinction between conception and formulation. Evidence, however, points to considerable and frequent overlapping between the two phases. In fact, the two phases were collapsed in some cases. In this phase, the Projects' organizational-managerial aspects were generally omitted.

The Projects' appraisal along technical and economic lines provided the basis for the allocation of resources. Appraisal showed that Barbados' climatic conditions allowed for the production of the Blackbelly sheep, that a net resource outflow could be turned into a self-sufficing position, that income for the economy could be generated, and that a project coordinator needed to be appointed. As for Handicraft, appraisal was informed by cost-benefit analysis, budgetary analysis, and implementation assessment. The Cave's appraisal concerned testing, engineering, civil works, transportation, visitor tours, maintenance, safety, environmental soundness, financial viability, and implementation assessment. As regards the Pulverization Project, appraisal underscored alleviating waste management problems, protecting the island's water-supply, containing pollution, and allowing for reasonable waste control capability. The Polytechnic's appraisal dealt with site selection, ground condition tests, design analysis, architectural planning, material specification, cost-benefit analysis, forecasting, budgetary analysis, educational access creation, and institutional strengthening.

For the Sewerage Project, appraisal went into analyzing target area conditions, design criteria, sewage disposal effects, treatment methods, sludge disposal, material specifications, environmental and urban renewal, tourism and business growth, financial viability and cost impact, budgetary analysis, general-beneficiary social payoffs, time scheduling, and institutional development. For Ferneihurst, appraisal involved work in topographic survey, cartographic analysis, site planning, design objectives, architectural consultancy, data collection, environment-friendliness, material specifications, utilities, sanitation, low-income tenancy assessment and financial affordability, budgetary estimates, and implementation team-building. Project research affirms the need for consistent political support for investments. Evidence shows that such support for and commitment to investments tends to waver, especially when governments change and policies shift. More effort went into technical and financial appraisal, with social, organizational and environmental appraisal being treated cursorily.

Each Project was approved by the concerned authority at the highest policy and decisional level. Project funding for Greenland was authorized in 1978, especially when the Cabinet rendered approval and agreement was reached among the Ministry of Agriculture, USAID, the Caribbeana Council and the Barbados Blackbelly Sheep Association. Handicraft's approval was secured in 1975 from the Ministry of Trade and the Cabinet via the Planning and Priorities Committee. A high-level steering committee's sanction was followed by the Cabinet approval for the Cave Project in May 1975 and supportive legislation to provide for organization-building. Following initial deliberations on consultant inputs and technical measures, in September 1973 the Cabinet mandated the installation of the Pulverization Project, with complete approval being granted in August 1974. The Polytechnic in its entirety was approved by the Cabinet-level Planning and Priorities Committee in July 1977 when the loan agreement between GOB and IDB was signed.

While approval for the Sewerage Project was granted by the Cabinet initially on condition that the prefeasibility studies showed promise, the signing of the loan agreement in April 1976 with IDB was an affirmation of approval. With full endorsement by NHC and the Ministry of Housing, a Cabinet decision was reached in April 1978 to proceed with Ferneihurst. The Project did not always emerge from the process of choice among alternatives as offering the best claim on scarce resources. The comparative merits of projects in competition with other possible alternatives or variants were not spelled out. Sometimes, approval was undermined by delay and enough time was not available to approving authorities to undertake a thorough scrutiny.

The Projects were implemented by a mix of piloting organizations, specialist staff, project personnel, and other participating agencies. Greenland, implemented in two stages through the Ministry of Agriculture and covering the period 1978-82, benefitted from an interorganizational implementation team. Located within BIDC, an in-house implementation team, having appointed a project manager and trained other personnel, bore the responsibility for executing the Handicraft Project. As to Harrison's Cave, a project execution unit came into being with the project manager being appointed in October 1975, other executive and support staff being hired, and a technical committee coming on stream to oversee work. An implementation team within the Ministry of Health directed the overall execution of the Pulverization Project, including equipment and vehicle acquisition, site clearance, property relocation, tendering, public relations, utilities installation, and construction. As a part of the Ministry of Education, a project execution unit, with responsibility for the Polytechnic, and a project manager, as its head, came on stream in 1978. Headed by a project manager and assisted by management, engineering, technical, accounting and support services, a project execution unit for Sewerage was established in 1977 within the Ministry of Health. A few committees were set up which functioned in advisory capacity. To realize the Ferneihurst Project, an implementation team was put together from the staff of the NHC's Technical Division. The Project's special management needs were met by NHC's financial, supplies, legal, and housing staff.

Although planned and scheduled, speedy implementation was not realized. Myriad constraining forces surfaced, delaying and prolonging the delivery of intentions to the target population. Efficient implementation seemed to be obstructed by tensions between foreign and local project personnel. Implementation suffered from inadequate leadership, hesitant direction, unfocused supervision, lack of realistic activity breakdown, absence of realistic lead time, insufficient monitoring, interrupted workflow, and infrequent progress-tracking. The Projects' time and cost management, i.e. uncontrolled lead time, frequent schedule slippages, lengthy implementation time, cost escalation, frequent shutdowns and unscheduled delays left a trail of lapses.

Reporting ensured some measure of corrective action, generated information, enforced accountability, and assisted decision-making. Greenland gained from record-keeping in respect of the sheep's date of birth, parent history, genetic traits, etc., and quarterly reports on the Project's progress. Handicraft's reporting, dealing with production, sales and personnel information, was done weekly, monthly and quarterly, with weekly meetings generating oral reports on the Project's movement. The Cave Project took on board daily, weekly and quarterly reports. Periodically, progress schedules were turned in by the implementation team to the Barbados Caves Authority. As for the Pulverization Project, reporting involved site meetings and progress/status reports being written and circulated. Reports were periodically sent to PIU, including the consulting firm submitting progress reports to the Ministry of Health. For Polytechnic, the executing agency was answerable to the Ministry of Education, reporting through the Education Planning Unit. The agency transmitted status reports periodically to PIU and PPC.

As regards Sewerage, the executing agency, responding to PPC through PIU and externally to IDB, reported on the Project's status on a monthly, quarterly, and biannual basis. Reports were prepared and transmitted periodically by the implementation team to NHC's directorial board, the Ministry of Health, PIU, and the participating organizations. Besides, site meetings, oral interactions, completion notices, interim payment applications, payment certificates, pay vouchers and local purchasing orders were used as tools of communication. Reporting, in some instances, were sketchy, tardy and vague, failed to establish timely and proper accountability, and faltered to provide a basis for management decisions. The reporting formats were not satisfactory in some cases. Useful information was not collected and transmitted in time.

Termination entailed wrapping up, winding down, closing out and scaling down activities, including dismantling the implementing units, absorbing the Projects into the regular management systems, transferring/reallocating/reassigning/separating personnel, releasing machinery/equipment/assets/resources, preparing for maintenance and follow-up, and diffusing Project results. Greenland's project status ended in 1982, with project functions being absorbed into the Ministry of Agriculture's Central Livestock Station and the Greenland Agricultural Station. With the ending of the project status in 1979, Handicraft was placed under the ambit of BIDC. The Cave was completed in 1981, though some more work continued until 1982, and its management under the Barbados Caves Authority. The Pulverization Plant's commissioning took place in 1980, the project status was ended around the same time and the Ministry of Health's Sanitation Service Authority was charged with operation. Although the Polytechnic was mostly completed by May 1982, it was not until January 1983 that completion was formally certified. While the executing agency was merged with an ongoing World Bank education project, the Polytechnic itself became a unit of the Ministry of Education.

The Sewerage Project was completed, commissioned and opened in 1982 and was placed under the authority of the Barbados Water Authority. With the completion of Ferneihurst, the implementation team was not disbanded but was reorganized within the NHC's technical division and the completed Estate was handed over to NHC's housing management division. The transition from the project stage to normal operation was not planned thoroughly in all the cases under review, thereby compromising, to some extent, investment worth, maintenance and operation. Yet, the Handicraft, Cave, Polytechnic and Sewerage Projects proved exceptional in that such work as planning, user training, remedial work, test runs and additional consultancy were in place to ensure smooth changeover.

The evaluation phase involved performing some on-site checks, obtaining feedback from output users and beneficiaries and making in-house assessment of strengths and deficiencies. Nor formal in-house or external review or ex post facto in situ evaluation was conducted for Greenland. Nor any feedback from beneficiaries and users was obtained. However, available information disclosed that basically the Project had met its objectives, viz. breeding was generally successful, a flock of purebred Blackbelly sheep had been established, and demand for lamb and mutton had been generated. A system for the review and evaluation of Handicraft was put in place, including periodic in situ reviews. Reviews revealed that the Project had realized some objectives, that production was adequate, that on-schedule performance was achieved in each phase, and that there were no significant errors of estimation. The Cave gave no indication of any evaluation or review being initiated with its completion. Yet, available information pointed to initial goal-setting and subsequent achievement. The Pulverization Project did not hire evaluators, and no formal review was done to examine whether the goals were attained and impact was made on overall development. In October 1980, however, external evaluators ran vibrational tests on the shredders and reported on the suitability of the support structure system.

The Polytechnic went through several postcompletion reviews, touching on Project background, implementation, scheduling, financing, performance, tendering, institutional capacity-building, and internal operating procedures. Although a formal review mandated by the loan agreement failed to materialize, several other evaluations were run in relation to Sewerage. The marine surveys found that water quality and the health of marine communities had been deteriorating in the greater Bridgetown area since 1972. Another study found that the equipment was in satisfactory condition, process control occasionally resulted in an unstable flow condition, the Plant met all its discharge parameters and did not pollute the sea, the effluent was in satisfactory condition, operation was not entirely risk-free, sludge was treated at an uneconomical low rate, the Plant personnel needed to be fully familiar with the operation of the Plant, and there was a need for training in performance sampling, testing, record-keeping, and laboratory procedures. As regards Ferneihurst, an in situ evaluation was made to ensure that the construction was in keeping with the approved plans, the target dates were being met, the cost was within the budget and the scheduled activities were properly coordinated. Secondly, an in-house postcompletion evaluation looked at cost overruns, site performance, equipment efficiency, problem areas, and benefit stream. Despite emphasis being placed on evaluation in theory, the evidence points to diminished inclination to learn through evaluations about the Projects' actual and potential worth. Evaluation proved to be the weakest link in the chain, with the problems manifesting variously, viz. unwillingness to produce self-analysis and to learn from errors, lack of follow-up, inadequate preparation and unrealistic target-setting, expected results failing to materialize, obscuring of performance, blaming and counterblaming, little evaluation of results achieved, little analysis of continuing or unmet needs, delayed and missing completion reports, secretiveness, and unwillingness to make evaluation reports available publicly. To illustrate, when parts of the expected results of the Greenland Project failed to materialize, blaming and counterblaming among the participating groups occurred.

Operation and maintenance are on stream to help sustain and maintain the Projects, extend the useful life of the assets, get return on investment, ensure operational readiness and ensure the safety of personnel. Greenland covers a wide-ranging area, viz. introducing, selecting, lambing, mating, mothering, nutrition, weaning, health, sanitation, grazing, selling, slaughtering, and job rotation. Handicraft extends from raw materials, procurement, storing, processing and production to maintenance, health, safety and training. As to the Cave Project, operation spans from ticketing, slide presentation, tram-boarding, touring, exiting to maintenance and safety provision. The Pulverization Plant's operation spans from refuse collection, unloading, conveyor feeding, pulverization, ejection, refuse loading, disposal, maintenance, and safety provision. The wide-ranging operation of the Polytechnic runs the entire gamut of admission, classroom activities, guidance counseling, placement service, industrial attachment, testing, evaluation, certification, and maintenance. At the Sewerage Project, the principal operations consist of sewage collection, multilevel treatment processes, disposal, and maintenance. For Ferneihurst, the operational areas contain tenancy agreement, rent collection, complaint service, and property maintenance.

Evidence points to a multiplicity of problems, viz. low status and acceptance of maintenance function, suboptimality, negligence and indifference to maintenance, lack of timely maintenance, poor maintenance costing, unsuitable format for presentation of maintenance data, revenue loss, systemic delays, work stoppages and interruptions, eroding credibility, diminished equipment life, low facility utilization, general waste, decreased product and productivity, cost inefficiency, and escalation. Evidence also shows that it takes time and effort to learn to operate new and completed projects efficiently, produce goods and services of right standards and reliable quality and establish sound clientele relations.

It is noteworthy that the project approach does not necessarily promote development. Some of the nonoutput effects, for example, include a variation between the estimated cost and the actual cost, the originally-estimated construction time stretching with considerable time and cost overruns, certain unusable equipment and materials, certain structural defects, design flaws and equipment defects, the expected revenues not materializing, and so forth.

As regards some negative results, examples include schedule slippages, inconvenience, and hardship caused by disruption in traffic and utilities, anxiety and stress, disamenity and disbenefit, loss of life, serious injury, accident at the Project sites, dust pollution, noise emanation, hazardous work conditions resulting in industrial action and work stoppage, and so forth.

We come across more negative evidence via 'project orthodoxy' (Morgan, 1983: 329-339). Projects - being discrete activities and aiming at specific objectives with earmarked budgets, mission-driven work process, and limited timeframes - tend to be donor-dominated and short-lived development experiences, with limited, and sometimes negligible, local initiative and institution-building. The project approach has been reinforced by the desire for quick and visible results shared by policy-makers in donor as well as recipient countries. This desire has led to an overemphasis on infrastructural and physical projects that do not address many important and significant issues and nuances of development and transformation. Such projects, even though well-known, have often failed to benefit the poor - indeed the poor and the powerless have often suffered from a particular mode of development effort, viz. marginalization, exclusion, and benign neglect. There has been, hence, a call for a reassessment of the limitations of the project approach.

Analysis

All the dimensions analyzed in chapter 6 stem from, arise out of and are related to development projects. The dimensions, relating to our model's input and output phases, have helped bring out the Investments' core and secondary features. The dimensions are the various facets or aspects of our Projects. As a tangible investment in growth , development and entrepreneurship, a project is not a monolith. It is a multifaceted, complex, interactive, and interdependent entity. The sample Projects were processed by project cycle throughout the eight phases. Of particular significance were the appraisal process, implementation process and management capability, which singly as well as collectively scrutinized and tested the Projects' investment worth, feasibility, implementability, and operational capacity.

The outputs - such as mutton, handicrafts, cave tour, shredded waste, technical/vocational graduates, effluent, and housing units - form part of, add to and draw resources from the general environment. More to the point, some of the Projects are doing a good or fair job, subject to varied constraints of the public sector environment, in terms of meeting social and economic objectives, but get rapped on the knuckles from time to time about making losses, not breaking even, or producing outputs without having ready financial value. Feedback from the environment and the general beneficiary population provided legitimacy, imparted discipline, prevented the Projects from making great mistakes, discouraged significant deviation from original goals, and make remediation and correction possible and kept them on the track.

The Projects, hardly working in a theoretical vacuum and cognitive isolation, are infused with several mutually-inclusive theoretical strands, viz. the hiding hand principle, comprehensive planning approach, quantitative analysis approach, blueprint approach, design approach, adaptive approach, and participatory approach. As interventions in Barbados' social and economic processes, the Projects relate to and arise out of theoretical clusters in myriad ways, e.g. import, design, resource, support, intention, instrumentality, action, direction, movement, relationship, reinforcement, resolution, evaluation, continuity, cause, effect, consistency, and implication.

The Projects succeeded in transforming inputs into outputs - a stream of goods and services, a group of services and production - involving a transition from theoretical realm to empirical reality. The Projects, because of traditional persistence, topheaviness and directiveness, did not make as much use of feedback from the wider environment and the target communities as desirable and possible.

From what we have seen in the Project model and the Project behavior, there appears a clear difference in how a project is ideally planned and how it is actually implemented. We recognize the difference between the ideal and the actual and the model-based idealization and implementation-level realities, and this recognition adds realism to our model and analysis. The differences between the initial activities - development project initiative, project cycle, appraisal process, implementation process, management capability - and the subsequent activities - outcome, feedback, operation, and corrective action - make us aware of the limitations of our model and the complexities of reality. Moving back and forth purposefully between project planning and plan implementation is likely to help us design more achievable projects and exert greater control over the implementation process.

A recurrent task of the Project had been interface management - the coordination of the various elements of the Investments so that they had met their goals of performance, schedule, and budget. Managing consisted - and this permeated all the Projects under review - largely in the management of differences in roles, perceptions, goals, and skills. All the phases of the project cycle involved the concerted work of people in a variety of subsystems, with a range of skills, orientations, abilities, interests, and work practices. The actual Project developments were not always consistent with the project cycle and planned schedules. The project cycle had to adapt to the needs and exigencies of the Projects because sometimes phases, and even activities and processes, overlapped. The Projects did not always go through all the phases fully either. In some cases, the project cycle was shortened to save time and accelerate competition.

From inception to termination, the law pervaded the Project activities. The observed Projects were established by organizations that were set up under the law and operated under the rule of law. It was expected that the Projects would abide by the law and pay penalties for any infringement or violation of law. Legal provisions like propriety, accountability and the due process restricted options and consumed time in building the Projects through a tangle of real-life situations. Although the contract documents had set up target time and delivery schedule, the contracting firms, more often than not, could not adhere to the scheduled time.

Moral and ethical values are at the core of organization management, including the sample Investments. A set of moral-ethical values lay implicitly in the unfolding of the Projects, viz. development drive, achievement orientation, accountability, responsiveness, equity, and compassion. However, a high and abiding commitment to ethical behavior appears to be exceptional and low-key.

In the entire project management process, policy occupies a central position in that projects succeed or fail only as they draw life from the policy environment. The Projects are only as good as the policies that guided, and still steer, their identification, selection, approval, implementation, and operation. The cyclical relationships within and between the Projects are linked together by policy. In the Investments, inadequate policies - for instance, in the areas of planning, funding, monitoring, or operation - have caused unsatisfactory procedures and follow-up, which have resulted not only in routine avoidable delays but also costly delays and damaging setbacks, for example the Cave and Pulverization Projects.

Institutional aspects, an essential part of our model, entail a process of exploration, initiative, leadership, entrepreneurship, experiment and adaptation. Building and managing institutions in relation to our Projects - the Ministry of Finance and Economic Affairs, the Planning and Priorities Committee, the Public Investment Unit, and the operating agencies - has ensured institutional responsiveness and performance, project development and resource management. As and when cost-effectiveness analysis, cost-benefit analysis, Gantt chart, logical framework analysis and critical path analysis were used during the Projects' implementation, it was the institutional process that helped determine whether and to what degree particular analytical or operational techniques could be employed. The Projects, however, have tended to suffer, for instance in the area of feedback, dialog and idea-sharing, because Barbados has not fully integrated project planning and overall development planning. Institutional development has been held back by a shortage of qualified, skilled, experienced and dedicated personnel, dependence on external resources, resistance to planning and analysis, uneven project planning capability, low degree of institutionalization of planning capacity, lack of frequent open communication, and lack of nurturing-type monitoring.

Looking at our model and examining the Projects' behavior, we note that no sector functions in isolation from the rest of the country, analysis helps make choice and set priority, the sectoral milieu helps determine the impact of a sector on the development of other sectors and ensure a degree of consistency in policy and investment measures from one sector to another, sectoral monitoring helps assess development potential of different programs and projects, and planning analysis furnishes information for formulating a broad-based investment program and for advancing projects that respond favorably to the pressing needs of the sector.

Some Projects provide collective benefits and stimulate categorical demands in that goods and services are equally available to all, viz. the Pulverization and Polytechnic Projects. Others provide divisible benefits and mobilize more particularistic kinds of demands, viz. the Cave,

Sewerage, and Ferneihurst Projects. In meeting the objectives of the concerned sectors, the Projects satisfied reasonable priority needs. Having varied costs and consequences, the Investments suffered because of shortage in Barbados of general sector surveys and special sector studies, somewhat unfocused sector studies, fluctuating guidelines for conducting sector studies, inadequate communication between central planners and operating-agency project planners, the sector policy framework not being entirely satisfactory and sectoral investment not functioning efficiently, and the need for adaptation in Project development not being sufficiently recognized and acted on. Not as much close attention as necessary was paid to the interconnections between the Projects and the relevant sectors, between one sector and another, and between sectors and Barbados as a whole. The process of translating more aggregate objectives into specific sectoral programs as well as more specific individual Projects was not done as competently as desirable.

The social dimension speaks to the Projects' social significance and soundness, points to experiments in social change, highlights achievements in social adaptiveness, signals changing social values and priorities, and underlines social issues and objectives. Each of the Projects has an impact on people. New opportunities for work, leisure, income, or training - which affect behavior - have been created. The Projects represent attempts at improving condition of various income groups by distributing income and benefits, increasing customer access to collective goods, increasing the efficiency of human productive capacities, promoting indigenous resources, pushing human resource development, and serving clientele. In spite of varied benefits, the Investments tend to make for social tension and income inequality. The Projects also inflict pain, perhaps unintentionally and unavoidably. The cleavages, chasms, distinctions and anxieties in the social environment appear repeatedly. Project design tends to stress technical solutions to the neglect or exclusion of social issues. As yet, the Projects have not enabled the target groups to acquire greater control over their situation, greater autonomy in their behavior and greater vigor into their initiatives.

Project development is certainly not apolitical. The process of organizing and mobilizing resources and improving target communities and beneficiary groups is a political function. The Investments succeeded in securing a variety of political gains - attracting resources, securing status, initiating and sustaining relations, maintaining legitimacy, enlisting support, generating consciousness, and broadening participation. The evidence of development and redistribution via the sample Projects in terms of significant empowerment and enabling of low-income and low-status target communities is not strong. Even the Greenland, Handicraft and Ferneihurst Projects could do more and respond differently to enable the target groups to pursue self-development and self-transformation . Clientelism and cronyism, in such forms as patronage, favor and influence, are not rare.

The economic dimension informs that the Projects represent the desired level of investment and expansion in the productive sector, involving resource allocation, efficiency, and income distribution. From what we see in our Project model and Project behavior, we confirm the contributions of the Investments as accruing to the entire economy, both costs and benefits being distributed within the population, and the signal the Investments send that the Ventures would not sacrifice or undermine future consumption and well-being in favor of immediate consumption.

We look at the sample Ventures not as ends in themselves but as creating economic infrastructure, creating externalities, spurring growth, securing intersectoral linkage, creating present as well as future streams of consumption, expanding the net national value added, raising the population's standard of living, utilizing skills, securing diversification, inducing scale economies, creating and sustaining market, and increasing capital assets. The Projects' negative results, nonoutput effects and disamenity effects are evident, i.e. noise nuisance, inconvenience, discomfort, pain, disruption, dislocation, relocation, delays, stench, site injury, accidental death, home and neighbor loss, and property depreciation. Some disutilities occurred, i.e. some dissatisfaction, unhappiness, risks, losses and uncertainties were generated. In terms of costs, the Projects confronted direct outlays, operation/maintenance/repair costs, indirect and external costs, opportunity costs, transfer payments, transaction costs, life cycle costs, and dilatory costs.

The Projects point to the need for protecting investible resources and ensuring financial soundness and credibility. As a result of the Projects, the net worth of the public sector, which uses its fund both for investment, consumption and stream of goods and services, has augmented. All the investments, however, are not performing equally well in breaking even, recovering cost, or generating revenue.

The organizational dimension is critical in unlocking potential, unleashing verve, releasing synergy, advancing implementation, and ensuring performance sustainability. The Projects produce goods and services with the management and workforce carrying out the mission and mandate, making decisions, allocating resources, doing plans and strategies, exerting control, running operations, and carrying out maintenance. The inability, unwillingness, hesitancy or indecisiveness to resolve existing, or sometimes potential, organizational problems tends to push the Projects and their management into suboptimal and indifferent performance. The Projects certainly leave room for higher efficiency, cost containment and recovery, investment return, greater capacity utilization, and greater accountability and transparency.

Technology is one of the prime movers in the development of observed Projects. Technology, for instance, has helped achieve objectives, accelerated action, saved and utilized scarce resources, adapted Project ideas to make them workable under local conditions, and has helped upgrade and learn skills. The Projects show technological dependence, such as relatively low utilization of installed capacity, wider use of foreign and imported technology, limited linkage with the local economy, etc. The technological base remains weak, in some cases tenuous, and lacks the mobilizational capacity to assimilate foreign technology creatively.

The environment with its wide range of resources and services supports and enhances the Projects. As a result of the Projects, the enjoyment and quality of life - in terms of environmental choices, security, viability, and diversity - for many people in the target group has risen. Large as well as small communities have become more viable and more serviced, for instance, with outputs from the Pulverization, Sewerage and Ferneihurst Projects. Nearly all the discharges from the Projects have more or less adverse effects on the environment. Environmental degradation is poorly understood by the community, considered marginal or remote, is of the slowly-accruing type, they are frequently overlooked, and its effects underestimated because they are almost always public goods, not priced in the marketplace.

The various transactions, interactions, linkages and relationships via the Projects mean increased incorporation into the global structure. By participating in international capital markets and international transactions, Barbados has used its resources and development potential more effectively, grown faster in certain respects, raised its rates of capital formation, increased its revenue base, diversified service and production network, expanded consumer choice, and built assets. Despite success in increasing such aggregates as financial flows, the Projects reflect dependent and nonreciprocal linkages, dependency on foreign capital, technology, trade, market, expertise, skill and institutional rationality, conformity to conditionalities and strings of external assistance, asymmetrical interdependence, and slow-moving social institutions and human attitudes.

Making comparison and learning from comparison are integral parts of project development. The Projects uniformly displayed a few driving forces, e.g. high-level policy inputs, environmental interactions, social interventions, and resource-group participation. Several common constraining forces were sustained, e.g. external dependence, design changes, time overruns, cost overruns, intergroup conflicts, and insufficient organization and management development.

Measurement is a salient dimension and a key indicator of how efficiently and effectively resources are turned into goods and services. Measurement has benefitted the reviewed Projects in collecting and analyzing data, keeping records, monitoring situation, tracking operation, making comparison, identifying problem areas, establishing accountability, and providing a basis for planning and control. Even so, the Projects, in general, suffer from lapses in consistent, clear and coherent measurement, have been slow in introducing usable performance measures, and resistance to measurement is widespread.

Survey Data

One questionnaire survey and three interview surveys were conducted in an attempt to generate some primary data directly and to obtain information that was not available from other sources. The project-maker survey sought to identify the role of development projects and to underscore respondent perceptions of the project process. The general-beneficiary survey was an attempt to capture beneficiary reactions to development projects and related concerns. While the operating-agency survey was involved with the personnel of the postproject organizations, the target-group survey related to specific target groups.

The study population provided multiple answers in response to open-ended studies and interviews. We analyzed the survey data with a view to identifying their defining characteristics and pointing out their patterns, trends, and directions. We soon discovered that in the real world of sample surveys, we had to be flexible and adaptable, and that there was no room for a doctrinaire approach unless we cared less about our efforts and outcomes.

There were many nonresponses in the four surveys, i.e. nonresponses by the respondents to particular questions in the study questionnaire and interview schedules. It perhaps shows that, contrary to careful, or even meticulous, planning, survey material and empirical situation are hardly under complete researcher control and that there are gaps between research planning and research reality. In some instances, we did not receive adequate information, but we decided to settle for what we got and move on with what we had. It perhaps also shows that incrementalism and satisficing reflect realities of life more than comprehensiveness and optimization.

Somewhat contrary to prevailing social science research practices and trends, the four surveys evinced certain characteristics of survey research in Barbados. There was a clear tendency - and it did not take us long to discern it - for many respondents to be somewhat reluctant to express their views on projects and similar concerns. Some were hesitant and guarded, while others appeared uncomfortable with questions, responses, probing, pause, and documentation Some did not like to articulate in public before interviewers their choices, preferences, views, reactions, feelings, and judgements. Curiously enough, even the repeated assurance of anonymity in a few instances proved to be unconvincing. A few factors seemed to emerge: in a small-size, tightly-knit community like Barbados confidentiality was given a high premium by respondents; surveying seemed to be perceived as intrusive, an invasion of the respondents' privacy and security; some respondents did not seem to have much faith in a research process where they were asked to participate; they did not seem to like exposure even though they were assured of total confidentiality and anonymity; and some respondents' overt behavior belied their perceived anxiety of running the risk of being identified with certain 'views' or 'positions' and jeopardizing their standing in the community.

First, the project-maker survey population highlighted 'socioeconomic development' as a pivotal project role, 'lack of local-level relevance' as a major deficiency of project appraisal, and 'shortage of skilled project management personnel' as a serious implementation inadequacy. High citation went to 'project management's limited and uneven impact on Barbados' public service', 'public sector's rigidity characteristics', 'public sector's autonomy need', 'neglect of ex post facto project evaluation', 'extensive participation by regional/international agencies in Barbados' project development', and 'time-consuming and complicated process of financing as a serious impediment in project finance'. These responses are informative and helpful in terms of not only project planning and implementation but also project design and general sectorwide reform. Barbados' traditional conception and use of time as a resource and organizational factor and topheavy management style were buffeted by such citations as 'poor time management' and 'poor control and management'. Postcompletion evaluation continued to be a neglected and perfunctory phase of the project cycle. This certainly is a reminder of customary inattention that the phase receives in numerous parts of the developing region. Respondents' perception that regional/international organizations tended to be 'intrusive' in Barbados' project development touched a common chord, too. One would have thought that risk-taking and accompanying entrepreneurship would be cited frequently as a role of development project. But the latter, in fact, did not score high. As regards the general-beneficiary survey, responses were indicative, among other things, of the current civic thinking in Barbados. Respondents viewed 'development projects as creating and improving facilities' as an important aspect of development project. The survey reveals that in general majority of the sample population knew about various projects going on around the time the survey was conducted. This finding is significant, especially because it demonstrated a fair level of awareness on the part of the general-beneficiary population in Barbados. It points to a connection among Barbados' high literacy rate, widespread education infrastructure, and high incidence of media penetration in civic life and general awareness of development projects and similar public/private initiatives of significance to the country as a whole. Remarkable too is the fact that a part of the beneficiary population thought that it had derived no *particular* benefits from the Projects appearing around Barbados. Significant is the fact that many respondents thought the general public was not as sufficiently informed of projects, their developments/contributions and related aspects as to make a difference between apathy and activism.

As to the operating-agency survey, a remarkable aspect to note is that nearly 70% of the sample population attaches importance to the Projects' dependable and continuous operation, service provision and viability. It implies that the operating personnel look forward to investment success, good management, reliable operation, customer service, and effective linkage with other sectors and activities. The operating personnel are citizens, taxpayers and customers, are knowledgeable about the functioning and overall performance of these projects, feel concerned about inadequacies hurting these investments, and do not want to see recurring losses, causing haemorrhage to public finance and scarce investible resources. Nonresponse, silence and vagueness came up once again. For instance, some respondents, when asked to identify what caused unhappiness to them concerning development projects in

Barbados, were not or chose not to be responsive. The question that appears is why this tendency is there in the first place, why it persists, what the sociopolitical forces are which sustain it, what the prognosis is and what can be done about it. There is no short or easy answer to this question except to point out the desirability of consciousness-raising, civic training, media information and awareness-building in the Barbadian community.

Concerning the target-group survey, our judgement informs us that when over one-third of the sample population unambiguously states that the reviewed Projects did not meet their expectations, decision-makers need to pause and take stock. But, then again, it need not be surprising. General social science theories and management models have been emphatic for some time about a considerable gap between generally well-informed, articulate, self-assured, cosmopolitan, strategically-located decision-makers on the one hand and the amorphous, loosely-knit, unfocused and isolated target groups on the other. The gap - which tends in some instances to increase - relates to education, training, experience, lifeview, worldview, attitudes, perceptions, value systems, belief system, and power relations. What project-makers plan, do or attempt to achieve in and via projects are not necessarily shared, regardless of how much one may desire it, by the target groups. Gaps tend to widen when consultation between project designers and target groups is desultory, tokenist, or nonexistent. Gaps may exist even when consultation does occur. There are, it is hardly surprising, differences in perception, purpose, method, and expectation.

Likewise, a sizable proportion of the sample population stated that they had not derived any or much benefits from the sample Projects. It is possible that benefits did not reach them or got diverted and part of the target population was not quite aware of the benefit stream, or the benefits were paltry, did not meet their expectation, caused resentment and produced rejection. Interestingly enough, another large part of the survey population did not voice complaints about the reviewed Projects. One wonders whether they did not genuinely have specific complaints, or did not wish to register complaints in public before interviewers, or wanted to appear nice and acceptable, or demonstrated the well-known courtesy bias, or did not wish to be branded as grouse, malcontent or 'ungrateful'.

Last but not least, the target group's finger-pointing of 'operational inadequacies' as the sample Projects' main weaknesses sharply underscore general disappointment with project performance. This finding should not be taken glibly or casually. For some time past, and increasingly so nowadays, the target group, like any other part of the larger consumer population, is keen on receiving prompt service, value for money and customer satisfaction, is concerned with and about operational efficiency, generic inefficiencies and ineffectiveness, service-provider discourtesy, resources loss, investment waste, revenue squandering, and goal deflection. Equally notable is the underlying need for improved, more conscious and results-oriented performance of the sample Projects. The target population does not approve of their tax dollars being wasted, their hopes being dashed, and organizations being undercut by partisanship and politicization. The client groups clearly call for and like to see accountability, transparency, cost containment and goal achievement as part of improved performance of the sample Projects.

Observations

Management, like life, is never simple. Management is seldom simple. Projects do not just happen nor do they suddenly appear - they are planned, laid out, processed, and finally develop to maturity. A project is an entity with its own momentum which must be sustained so that it moves on and materializes. The old conception that the project is an initiative - stated in time and space, localized into various functions and restricted its flexibility - is untenable. The Project is much like a process than a fixity, and this process is continually evolving. Unlike an entity which is fixed, frozen, motionless, rigid and constant, a project is flowing, moving, mobile, flexible, and changing. Successful projects mobilize people around their goals and motivate them to act with greater enthusiasm, purposefulness, and self-reliance.

Since we cannot wish the constraints away, we must learn to minimize and cope with them, work with and through them, take advantage of them, and enhance our ability to change course at short notice. We agree with Hirschman (1967) that a country's development experience is importantly influenced by the kind of projects it places, and that what a country becomes is a result of what it does. Everything important in a society ultimately rests on the values and ideals that the society holds. There are tradeoffs in the allocation process. The use of resources in some other sectors or projects reduces the resources available for use in some other sectors or projects. Pursuing some objectives in each projects involves a sacrifice in other objectives. As a result, Barbados has more of some things and less of others, but cannot have more of everything at once.

Project management is an organizational form of the future that could integrate complex efforts and diminish *bureaucratism*. The search goes on to 'projectize' traditional organizations or normal operations. The move towards the increasing use of project approaches is spurred by managers facing great pressure to manage change, change occurring at an ever increasing pace, the complexity of tasks growing, more effective control systems being required to monitor progress, and time pressure for completing tasks increasing.

As the concept of development advances, Barbados undertakes large and more complex projects that present serious technical, logistical and coordinative challenges and, therefore, demand more management capability and organizational leadership.

The initial stage of any project is important. If mistakes are made at the outset, it may be difficult, or even impossible, to regain the community/ target group's support and trust.

The Projects could be done better. With more research, coordination, management, leadership and visioning, the driving as well as the constraining forces could be better appreciated and controlled. With more partnering, networking, leveraging, strategizing and synergizing, the Projects would have turned out better.

Political power as a variable directly influences project implementation because the amount of resources that can be mobilized in favor of or in opposition to a specific project is vital to assessing its likelihood of speedy implementation. To be effective, project-makers must have a general and clear idea of how power is distributed in the society, must be skilled in the political process and must understand well the environment in which they seek to realize Projects.

The implementation process, embodying collective and concerted action, is a transition process, which is dominated by many organizations and participants, all moving and contending with each other for end results as well as strategic gains. It is also a complex and open system where there are considerable interdependencies among interacting elements.

The performance and potential of the Projects are related to the process of synergy in that the whole being greater than the sum of its parts and people working together and fully utilizing relevant expertise can produce something significant and organization members acquiring a state in the output which they have jointly produced. Likewise, the best predictor of success is the extent of local action in a project, such as local-level commitment, involvement, identification, and enthusiasm. Success can be specified as the capacity to deliver projects as defined and articulated.

Project development is much less predictable than it sounds. The project dynamics itself is hardly entirely controllable. Project development is an evolutionary rather than a mechanistic process. It is also an organic process. Factors evolve new questions, and relationships change in unforeseeable ways. Many factors interact and affect the whole.

Decisions in project development, especially major ones, are characterized by a number of attributes, e.g. interconnectedness, complicatedness, uncertainty, ambiguity, conflict, and social constraints. The problems have to be dealt with in an analytical as well as in a holistic way - determining the nature of the linkages, i.e. analysis, and understanding the problem as a whole, i.e. holism. The fundamental problems of organized complexity must ultimately be dealt with in their totality.

To achieve greater understanding of project development, one must examine under what constraints, pressures and tensions projects and project personnel operate in Barbados. It is helpful to appreciate how progress can at times meander strangely through many peripheral areas before it is able to subdue real-life muddle.

By means of the target Projects, Barbados has secured more of some gains and payoffs and less of others, but, as expected, not more of everything at once. In the quest to expand socioeconomic horizons and bring about better living standards for its people, Barbados' public sector authority has found itself as the principal initiator, designer and implementor of projects. Barbados' experience shows that a project is nothing if not a collection of relationships among participants, organizations, and tasks.

The target Projects tend to show a single-loop learning capacity, i.e. learning from incremental as well as cumulative experience as to how to operate and, where necessary, design activities so that they can produce or hope to produce better results in the future. There are as yet few signs that the Projects have a double-loop learning capacity, i.e. learning how to improve the way one learns and sustaining the way. Put another way, there does not seem to be much motivation to learn from past experience and even less to admit, analyze, and actively learn from past lapses. Raking over past setbacks or inadequacies is generally considered poor form, and seldom brings any organizational reward. Hulme (1989) observes that if project evaluation is to contribute effectively, it will be necessary to move on from the cosy ground of formal structures and procedures to the more unstructured area of analyzing learning processes within and between organizations involved in development initiatives, and that one has to recognize that the lessons of experience are not neutral or decorative data, but a strategy resource.

Caution

The project approach - if not carefully planned and monitored - may result in the frittering away of scarce and competing investment resources on too many unrelated projects, overinvestment and overloading in some sectors, stagnation or starvation in other fields, cause serious imbalances and disruptions, create fiscal stress and result in enclavement and inflexibility. The project approach does not *necessarily* and adequately result in improving development because it can and does lead, albeit unintentionally, to negative results, unequal conditions, and nonoutput effects. There are risks and uncertainties and one should not assume that things will *spontaneously* turn out for the best. A project, as evidence shows nearly everywhere, could be an unruly horse and dangerous to ride. Since the real-life constraints cannot be wished away, we must learn to minimize, simplify and cope with them, work with and through them, and try to turn them into functionality.

One should be cautioned that despite a project being a tool of development activity, injection of resources via a project *alone* is insufficient and unpredictable in its ultimate development impact. Few truly appreciate a project as an interrelated set of purposeful activities, and few plan and implement projects within an integrated management framework. Most organizations, including projects, are imprisoned in the present and often cannot change, even when the future threatens them. Should something go wrong with a project after its completion, there is apparently none to deal with it. A project is specially prone to this problem of discontinuity when it is small and of short duration. Among the negative effects and unintended consequences are the incidence of the unknown, uncertain and hazardous, the 'ignorance of ignorance', uncertainties and difficulties, new or heightened social tension, fresh opportunities for spread of corruption, loss of resources, unsolved socioeconomic problems, dissipation of opportunities for accelerated development, dashing of beneficiary hopes, the nonrepetitive short-term nature of projects presenting special difficulties in decision-making, and rise of intergroup and interpersonal problems and conflicts.

Then again, the larger the size of project and the greater its complexity, problems and attendant costs tend to be more and worse. The duplication of effort and staffing may occur, personnel may be maintained on the project longer than needed, corner-cutting may be common, a strong 'we-they' divisiveness may grow, and 'projectitis' may develop. Projects may have less strength in creative innovation and in functioning as a mission-driven group and evince general inability to resolve conflict. Various kinds of costs tend to come up: the cost of delay, the cost of assembling and dispersing the project workforce, the cost of organizational change and accommodation, and the cost of failure.

Project planning should not become an exercise in 'economism' or 'technicism' and lose sight of the holistic and integrative forces. For example, window-dressing is sometimes noticeable. One seems to perceive that the more technical and complex the appraisal, the more the use of shadow prices, discounting, tradeoffs, coefficients, weights, investment criteria, statistical prediction, the greater the recognition of intellectual attainment and the better the chance of finding a donor.

Project research, too, has sometimes generated a great deal of false and facile optimism. One of the common errors is expecting events to work out as planned. The only instance where this is likely to occur is in the short term, or where there is simple sequence of events with known resource needs. Even with the best of planning, very few projects are completed to their original plan. This is because there is never sufficient information available at the start of a project to plan accurately. Besides, new obstacles appear faster than the old ones have been cleared. Somehow, 'organized complexity' seems to prevent the project-makers from doing their job right.

Perfecting appraisal techniques is no substitute for establishing the necessary structure and securing the desirable behavior to ensure efficient and effective implementation. An error relating to implementation is the belief that it is not worth bothering about and that implementation issues seem to be more operational than theoretical or analytical. The implementation issues tend to come up toward the end of an analytical process. Those who insist on raising these issues at the early stages of the project cycle risk being called small-minded. The erroneous belief that implementation problems are usually minor persists.

Project development is much less predictable than it sounds. The project dynamics itself is hardly entirely controllable. Problems come in flocks, solutions as rare strays. The fractionalization of power in the decision-making process, the working of powerful special interests that influence or control decisions, and the complex multifacetedness of planning function render project-making a difficult task. Project development, further, entails change and changes involves unsettlement of the status quo. The power community is not prepared to tolerate a drastic unsettlement of the status quo. It is prepared to go along with change and renewal insofar as its does not impinge much on its power, authority, control, influence, status, preeminence, and well-being. In some instances, formal as well as informal forces combine to nullify, negate or reduce the effectiveness of projects.

Further, the Projects are not such that it makes sense to think in terms of a standardized, routinized, uniquely correct, and permanently valid set of management responses. We, in point of fact, confirm Hirschman's findings (1967) that if project planners are able to anticipate all of the problems, few projects would be found feasible and actually undertaken, that implementation is affected by a high degree of complexity, initial ignorance and uncertainty and that implementation may often mean a long voyage of discovery in the most varied and challenging domains from technology to politics.

Special care in the form of highlighting and packaging the outcome is missing from the Projects. Unless this is done, results may diminish, the impact decreased and the focus diluted. It is shortsighted and wasteful to permit cost and time overruns, as these have occurred to the Projects. Every project, which exceeds budgeted costs or overruns the targeted completion time, presents problems, increases the strains and hardships, and creates inconvenience and frustrations. Aside from the intended output and outcome, the full effects of the Projects tend to be somewhat diffuse, usually complex, frequently unanticipated, and sometimes disagreeable.

The findings do not support the widespread belief that management is omniscient. No management system, as our Projects indicate, can be so finely designed that it can anticipate all exigencies or solve all problems that may arise. Project management, besides, has never been the simple and unitary command system once assumed wrongly. The assertion that a single correct answer to a management problem or task exists is unreal or untenable. Much to the contrary, the level of complexity and interaction, as seen in the Investments, has been increasing steadily. In fact, managing public sector projects is a challenging task. The very nature of projects, their difficult goals, broad-ranging benefits, diverse reactions from the environment in which the projects remain operational and the increasing degree of fusion between the public and private sectors make project development and management more difficult. Nor should project management be regarded as a miraculous and instant panacea, given the historical and cultural constraints that exist in Barbados. Perhaps the most obvious are operating culture and traditions, the ubiquity of hierarchies, lack of initiatives, civil service practices which stymie proactive efforts, cultural practices that may condition the interaction between superiors and subordinates, the extent of the delegation of authority, and the type and effectiveness of oversight and control tools. Organizational problems are sometimes identified in superficial terms, which may misdirect the search for solution. Many of the organizational and institutional problems, commonly encountered in implementing projects, have deeper causes. Many of these problems are likely to take decades to overcome, since they reflect part of systemic lag as well as sociocultural constraints. Organizations and their practices have to take root in their societies and adapt their specific responses to the greater cultural milieu, thus making for gradual acquisition of organizational competence.

There may be high, if not immediately visible, human costs to project management. Project participants suffer more stresses and anxieties than those working in functional organizations. Some of them may fear loss of employment more, experience instability, are more frustrated by delay and uncertainty, can be more fatigued by pressures and varieties of assignment, are more worried about being set back in their careers, feel less loyal to their organization, and are more frustrated by conflict with other organizations and with multiple levels of management. A mistaken notion lingers for many that the problems of social entropy - incompetence, variability, poor coordination, and disagreeableness - can be *effectively* solved by designing better management tools and procedures and by giving more power to management organizations. The result, unfortunately, is an expanded set of tools and procedures against the entropic forces played out in the hope of achieving better control. Complete rationality can seldom be achieved in human and social affairs. The managing of the Projects, as we have seen, often involved 'bounded' rationality. The decisions reflected at times 'satisficing', picking a course of action that was satisfactory or good enough under the circumstances.

The larger the amount of investment, the more important it is to avoid inappropriate decisions. The larger the size of investment and the greater the need for interfunctional control and coordination, the more important it is to eschew questionable decisions. The price the community pays for errors resulting from poor project decisions tends to be proportional to the size of the investment. The temptation of management in terms of abusing power, evading accountability and transparency, indulging in self-serving behavior and becoming wrapped up in arrogance and corruption must be watched. Postcompletion management capability is essential to preserve the value of investment. Unless management capability is nurtured, the investment may losc its worth as a result of indifferent management.

As development problems and strategies become more complex and interdependent, the success of projects becomes less certain.

Planning is hardly, perhaps never, achieved once and for all. To expect error-free planning and perfect performance is illusory.

It is important that our Projects break even, recover cost, make a return on investment, make profit, and achieve some nonprofit community goals. It is equally important, however, to note and recognize that a *balance* should be struck and the Projects should not be *overwhelmed* by the rhetoric of market forces. Market forces are, contrary to widespread perception, embedded in concrete social situations with profound sociopolitical impact, rather than being invisible mechanisms or value-neutral tools that allocate resources on the basis of abstract efficiencies.

Conflict or disagreement among participants involved in project development, which reflect their positions and interests, is inevitable. No amount of analysis can resolve these role-based or dispositional conflicts.

Appraisal techniques have limited value because the characteristics of factors and relationships evolve in unpredictable ways over time. The techniques can be easily discredited and their usefulness negated if there is not the *will* to apply these properly. The techniques neither solve problems spontaneously or easily nor there is theoretical guarantee that project decisions based on sound appraisal tools will lead a project in the right direction.

Dysfunctions, social pathologies and costly delays can crush implementation. Much effort has to be expended in keeping implementation simple, functional, cost-effective, and goal-specific.

We understand only imperfectly the theoretical limits of organizations and processes concerned with implementation. We can limit the number of constraining forces or contain the damage they inflict, but in the end we are nearly always faced with certain irreducible risks posed by implementation.

The failure or success of a project has something to do with its management, among other things. Looking at project failure or inadequatcy enhances learning, relearning, and unlearning. No failure occurs in isolation. All failures are system failures in that they are actually the upshot of an inadequate system and that failure is spawned by ignoring the systemic nature of projects.

A great deal depends on the quality of the theory within which project ideas and assumptions are determined. If the theory is complete and accurate, including setting realistic goals, it should effectively generate project ideas and facilitate execution. If it is incomplete or inaccurate, it may generate poor or unimplementable projects. If the analysis and subsequent activities are based on faulty theory and dubious assumptions, it can lead to project failure, setback, and disappointment.

Experience with projects has shown them to be something of a mixed blessing, in a sense, for Barbados and, for that matter, myriad developing countries. While individual projects can effectively achieve specific targets if well-designed and managed, the cumulative and long-term effect of promoting development in a project mode has led to some troubling side-effects (Honadle and Klauss, 1979; Gray and Martens, 1983; Morgan, 1983; Rondinelli, 1983; Morss, 1984; Brinkerhoff, 1992), such as excessive and uncritical dependence on donor funding and external NGOs, short-term implementation perspective, duplication of effort, personnel attrition from the public sector, proliferation of semiautonomous organizational units loosely attached to public sector entities, multiplication of managerial and financial systems and procedures, ballooning recurrent cost burdens once external funding ends, and inability to continue on a full-scale basis the provision of goods and services following project completion.

Findings

An overall policy context and support network are vital to the success of projects. Projects tend to succeed or fail only as they draw life from the policy environment. It is not only the intrinsic merit of a project that influences its success, but also the overall environment that inspires its achievement.

There is an important link between sound policies and successful projects. Project development occurs in communities that pursue sound and consistent policies, but in communities with unsound or fickle policies project has no discernible or lasting impact. A project to expand vocational education, for example, is more likely to be successful if overall policies are good. In addition, projects are more likely to succeed if local communities are involved in design, implementation, and decision-making. Our research results suggest that communities that succeed in putting good policies and management structure in place can make effective use of project intervention to accelerate overall productive growth. Where these preconditions are not in place, project intervention does not seem to achieve much. Where domestic social and political forces induce reform of policies and institutions, project intervention can provide effective support by bringing technical expertise and lessons from other countries into a receptive environment. When there is little domestic movement toward reforms, institution-building and management-capability growth, project intervention has had minor impact.

The Projects were more in line with the blueprint approach than the learning process approach. The interacting elements in our Project model have connection with each other - they are related to each other and the behavior or outcome in one affects another. While the blueprint approach emphasizes detail, specification and contingency of a plan before the project starts, the learning approach is one in which people and human institutions develop new capabilities and learn through enough problem-solving action, projects evolve and change in response to beneficiary needs, priorities and experiential lessons, and involved actors demonstrate mutual respect and willingness to learn from each other and from experience. The Projects represent modest, but fairly clear, shifts from a focus on inputs - how much and where resources were spent - to outputs - action and activities produced and outcome - the consequences, effects, and impacts produced.

The Projects relate to and satisfy certain development objectives, i.e. output growth, employment creation, import substitution, export promotion, income generation and distribution, capital ownership, foreign exchange earning, market integration, infrastructural growth, social development, and customer need satisfaction.

The Project can be seen as tools of development management. They cut down energy-sapping and time-consuming procedures, enhanced programming capacity, delivered goods and services faster, achieved prompt action and impact, secured greater consistency between stated goals and final results, exerted greater control over concerted action, showed sensitivity to time management in a general way, used indigenous personnel as and when possible, promoted indigenous management capability in ways more than one, made some impact on the larger public service system, was fairly responsive to target population, caused beneficial linkages and externalities, and generated tangible and identifiable output. The Projects' success made for increased incomes, opportunities, and benefits. Project development can be seen as wrestling with decision-making structures, redistributing income, opportunities and power, and transforming institutions.

We come across two overriding phases: input phases - conception, formulation, appraisal, approval - and output phases - implementation, reporting, termination, and evaluation. While the unfolding of the Projects can be viewed initially as creative phases, with the completion they must be viewed as long-term operation. With the Projects evolving through a life cycle, management efforts require adaptation to each of the phases. A finding in relation to the life cycle is that each phase called for a specific managerial approach. Project managers knew, sometimes intuitively and sometimes through experience, how to shift gears from one phase to the next, starting off conceptually, moving into resource planning, then to the managing of actual implementation, and finally putting on pressure to bring the venture to a close.

In actual practice, few projects move tidily and neatly through the sequential process of the project cycle. The documentation of the Projects does not bear full resemblance to the actual events as they occurred. Fast-moving project dynamics is not only cyclical but also concurrent, thus sometimes disregarding the tidy cyclical construct, neat phasic symmetry, and precise sequential order. The project cycle is really less a series of discrete phases leading from one to another than a matrix of steady interaction between project participants and actors, with multiple feedback loops.

Project planning, in terms of control and form, is a major key to successful project development and management. We see ongoing reciprocal relationship between overall planning and projects. This relationship underpins the cooperative nature of planning and project development. We see the Projects as creating link in the process of development planning, including plan formulation and implementation.

The Projects' impetus originated internally within public sector agencies as well as in organizations outside the public sector. The Projects began as ideas, ideas that became movement via concrete actions. Project ideas arose in response to problems and opportunities. The Projects received more specification and greater detailing during formulation. Technical, economic and financial appraisals were prominent in nearly all the Projects under review. Each Project was approved by the authority at the highest policy level before implementation started or some implementation got underway.

Implemented by a network of organizations and a pool of skills, the Projects identified and handled critical aspects, maintained the flow of information and liaised with participating organizations. Executing agencies and the Project settings were influential in shaping project outcomes. Reporting, used as a management tool, related to communication on the Projects' status, progress and problems, thus increasing accountability and transparency. Termination entailed scaling down, wrapping up, winding down and closing out Project activities, involving the transfer of resources, the dismantling of implementation units and the takeover of operation. Evaluation succeeded in carrying out on-site checks, obtaining feedback, doing in-house assessment and, in a limited way, contributed toward postcompletion review, performance assessment, and future planning. It takes time and effort to learn to operate new and completed Projects efficiently, produce goods and services of acceptable standards and reliable quality, and establish customer relations. Seen in the Project process, feedback provided the flow of information among the subsystems, made for adjustments in the work processes, and set in remedial action.

Projects survive and develop in an environment, underlying adaptation, modification, or expansion. It is at the grassroots level that decisions and programs have effect, influence the project-group behavior, and adapt to the environment. Adaptation to the environment has been achieved, or else the Projects would not exist. People's understanding of their situation and their willingness and efforts to improve it are essential conditions for the Projects' success.

Certain universals are identifiable in the Projects, i.e. policy, decision, action, value, hierarchy, ideology, power, institution, culture, interest, role, interaction, structure, function, and interdependency. The public sector generally sets the priorities of policy and secures the necessary finance to implement its objectives. Besides employing general policy instruments, Barbados uses projects as a tool to obtain the desired level of investment in the country, and generates and uses resources through social and economic investments.

The Projects did not evolve or produce results as expected. Building a project was and still is not a self-executing task or a self-fulfilling process. Nor did it suddenly appear - the process started, unfolded, developed, matured, and continued. The amount of resources, efforts, time and care that were put into an idea before it became a reality was considerable. The Projects moved in an evolutionary, incremental, collaborative, synergistic, and multilateral mode. The Projects did not spring up in vacuo. They, far from being self-generating, were planned and executed laboriously.

It was the project-makers' collaboration and creative resources which were brought into play in tackling Project-specific problems. Institutional development takes times. Correcting mistakes, learning from experience and building up from limited success are slow and time-consuming. Through the Projects, Barbados' striving toward institution-building continues. The Projects have added to the increasing importance and significance that project management enjoys today in Barbados and around the globe. Relying on reasonably developed infrastructure and absorptive capacity, Barbados carried out, working within familiar constraints of developing countries, the Projects and made increased use of development assistance from funding agencies relative to other Caribbean countries.

The conception of project management identifying that something has a beginning and an end is a motivation and the process lends itself to measurement. The realization that project management is goal-oriented has taken roots. It gears up, meets goals and winds down activities to completion in a complex interdependent environment. The setting is not only complex and time-critical but also involves different groups and various technologies. The Projects, representing visible achievements, have pushed and diversified socioeconomic development, functioned as reliable tools of goal management and development management, and improved planning/implementing capability. The Projects have been instruments of loan finance and technical backstopping and have contributed to output expansion and opportunity generation. Put in place by a pool of project personnel and professionals, the Projects, made possible tangible output generation and service delivery and caused beneficial externalities and linkages, i.e. mutton production, handicraft production, showcave operation, refuse disposal, technical-vocational training, sewage disposal, and family accommodation.

The Projects have made contributions in several areas: identifying and involving participant groups, experiencing teamwork, discharging accountability, organizing and integrating workforce, mobilizing and harnessing resources, highlighting decision-making and priority-setting, utilizing management skills and operational competencies, improving project design and implementation, recognizing local situation and culture, sharpening management techniques and work systems, cutting down time-consuming procedures and questionable practices, enhancing programming skills and capacities, delivering development goals faster, achieving faster results and greater impact, targeting goal management, controlling organized human action, achieving sequence, synchronization and acceleration, promoting indigenous management capability, doing indigenous research and documentation, highlighting output, outcome and impact, responding to target-group needs, concentrating on interfacing, retaining personnel to manage postproject organizations, showing leadership during the interactive phase of the project cycle, and developing and using rules, benchmarks, indicators, criteria, procedures and mechanisms to facilitate project development and management. The Projects also show that despite the limited resource base, restricted technology capacity and diffuse management capability, development gains can be achieved.

Aside from public organizations being normally concerned with regulation, justice, infrastructure, social sector development and welfare attainment, an enclave within the public sector - joint ventures, some project entities, some public enterprises, some state companies - is increasingly becoming more concerned about revenue acquisition, i.e. return on investment, cost control and containment, cost recovery, self-financing, revenue generation, and performance and output consciousness. In Barbados, where the economy is getting increasingly diversified, the Projects' multiplier effects and knock-on results throughout the economy are likely to be moderate.

The Projects showed some willingness and ability to learn from mistakes, identify and remedy weaknesses, learn from diverse experiences and difficult or challenging situations, build up from small and modest successes, develop capacity, meet some expectations, expect the unexpected, listen to intuition and respect instinct, scale down unsustainable aspiration and focus on more attainable targets, and feed findings back into the Projects. The Project offered some useful lessons: recognizing the need for tradeoffs and concessions, reducing risk by advance planning, making a tradeoff between efficiency and equity, making allocation decisions on the basis of more, rather than less, information concerning feasibility, and stressing research, information, analysis, training and planning. Implied in the Projects is the finding that those investments which persist in convincing the target population that it is to its advantage to do things differently can expect to survive or thrive long. The investments which reward, not merely accept, changed ways of doing things tend to persist. The Project experience and evidence showed that negotiation, communication, persuasion, tradeoff and bargaining proved to be more efficient than unilateralism, hierarchical control and management by fiat. There was no way - and this is not sui generis to Barbados - that the target Projects could ignore inconvenient features of the world, like the sparse supply of managerial, supervisory, behavioral and technical competence, the considerable variety and exigency of field-level and implementational conditions, the high incidence of dispositional conflict, and the perennial difficulty of coordinating large-scale activities.

Results

In terms of project planning, problems, pressures, and tensions occurred. Planning frequently failed to be a 'real time' activity, remained unable to react quickly to unexpected crises and events, was not used adaptively and as a dynamic model, was looked on as a peripheral or staff activity, and was an exercise in 'economism' and overlooked the Projects' multivariate nature. Plans did not seem to be used integrally and quickly by project management, and the speed of the planning activity lagged behind the pace of project execution. In the process, managers took decisions on a judgmental basis without waiting for planning analysis. Disappointments were caused by inadequate work in design, analysis, target-setting , or management feasibility. There were lapses in environmental planning, integrating project planning and overall planning, and dovetailing strategic planning and contingency planning. Planning was more conspicuously technical and far less strategic and holistic.

The capacity to realize specific objectives successfully as well as speedily varied. Evidence shows that the policy, political, institutional and managerial behavior exert a decisive influence on a country's objective-setting and goal management capability. The Projects' objectives and operations are not reviewed as rigorously and periodically as necessary, and, as a consequence, some of the Projects are not run so as to yield as high a social return in each year as possible. Some of the lapses included frequent and unplanned changes in objectives, high incidence of ad hocism, vague initial objectives being couched more in global terms than in operational specificity, deflection from the stated objectives, and lack of clarity, consistency and attainability of objectives.

The project process revealed limited search for alternatives and limited comparison between alternatives. It is doubtful that comprehensive attempt was made at the early phases in the project cycle to look for an optimal solution except for the Polytechnic and Sewerage Projects. If an alternative that appeared acceptable was found, search was possibly halted. The kinds of special problems that needed working out before the Projects got into an active mode were underestimated. The time and effort needed to identify and establish the preparatory process was underrated. The institutionalized analytical/management capability to adapt the Project's design and needs to local conditions varied considerably from Venture to Venture.

The current project development modality in Barbados has succeeded more in providing physical facilities - for example, livestock station, plant, showcave, educational institution, and housing complex - than in influencing behavior, attitudes, responses, and values underlying these Projects. Notable is that the Projects exemplify selective attention and enclave-type management and are not a mirror image of the country's public sector. The rest of the public sector is only selectively influenced and, in numerous cases, little affected or left almost entirely untouched.

One of the key realities of project development is that a project has to contend with a number of situations that unfold in the uncertain contingent future, that analysis is subject to a high degree of uncertainty about what is likely to happen, and that action is limited by lack of knowledge about what might happen or relative uncertainty about how to cope with what has already happened. The current process of project development tends to lead to a growing economic, political, social, cultural and ideological penetration of Barbados - albeit a hardly unique situation - by metropolitan capital, organization and culture, spawning an increasing dependence on the external network and being incorporated into the international system. Even though the number of completely implemented projects is yet relatively small, external penetration and dependence is evidenced by Barbados having one of the highest ratios of externally-funded projects per head of population in the world.

The funding agencies provided funding, but the domination they enjoyed and the number and range of conditionalities they attached often ended up, perhaps unintentionally in many instances, spending a sizable part of these funds in elaborate proceduralism which rendered the Projects somewhat topheavy. Part of the problems with financing were that the lending institutions tended to push some of their ideas and conditionalities rather than using the indigenous expertise of Barbados to determine what was the most useful for the country.

Implementation faced setbacks recurrently because of general and specific factors as well as exogenous developments. The relevant human behavior underlying implementation was too subtle and variable, the policy texture too rich and interactive, and the chances for organizational actors to err too numerous. Entropic forces were strong in that despite being implemented by a network of organizations, professionals and personnel, the level of competence and commitment varied from Project to Project, with delays occurring, costs escalating, tensions mounting, confusion spreading, and leadership faltering. Noticeable, too, is that the Projects did not succeed as well as they should have, given the type and amount of inputs that went into those, in controlling downtime, waiting time, idle time, turnaround time, set-up time and process time, cutting down losses, waste, leakage and defects, designing special office forms to ensure speedy implementation, and exerting cost control and containing costs.

Traditional management with all its nuances and limitations persists in Barbados' public sector. When the Projects were underway, the executing agencies were subjected to varied pressures and restrictions. Weaknesses in internal controls to secure compliance, raise performance and protect investments from inefficiency held out. Communication problems existed between executing agencies and funding agencies, viz. resentment, touchiness, and avoidance. Overdependence on the part of the executing agencies on the standard schedule of the lending institutions gave rise to a lack of flexibility. The executing agencies tended to get blamed when expected results failed to materialize.

The Projects' initial costs and operating costs were underestimated. The tendency to introduce and put the Projects in place with insufficient regard for downstream cost was detectible. The rigor and quality of analysis in project appraisal and its underlying theory as well as in investment analysis was uneven. Appraisal was not regarded as a dynamic process with the Projects not being reappraised on an ongoing basis in the light of changes in the environment, which sometimes resulted in the Projects not achieving all the initial objectives. There had been insufficient use of shadow pricing for the estimation of relevant costs and benefits of the Projects. By increased use of shadow prices it would have been possible to correct imbalances in the market, anticipate major contingencies and assign a greater value to these effects. Greater creativity and efforts should have been utilized in measuring and monetizing social benefits and costs as well as factors of time, congestion and stress. Less attention was given to the institutional, organizational, behavioral, social and cultural aspects, political realities and vicissitudes, implementation dynamics, and institutional orientation and capacity.

Evaluation proved to be the weakest link in the chain, somewhat obscuring the performance of several of the Projects, perpetuating the practice of little or not systematic postcompletion evaluation of projects in general in Barbados and undercutting the value of evaluation as a useful managerial tool. The possibilities of learning and unlearning by experience, learning the significant lessons and feeding findings back into everyday organizational reality are being either diminished or lost. Few completed Projects bothered to work out and submit completion or termination reports and performance audit rcports. All too often, research or evaluation findings are not applied because they seem to challenge set assumptions, arouse apprehension, and produce resentment. After the Projects became operational, there was a tendency to turn away from critical but nonpunitive reviews that are essential for organizational vitality and renewal. The practice of viewing a project as a self-contained limited activity, rather than as a set of related functions designed to achieve development goals, causes reluctance to pursue evaluation and follow-up. Sustained attention is not given to maintenance in order to ensure that the Projects' physical components do not deteriorate beyond repair.

The Projects' record of managing human relations was not outstanding, viz. managing across functional lines of command and organizational lines of command to bring together the required activities and securing individual and group performance in achieving the preset objectives. The ineffective group syndrome - showing occasional apathy, conflict, bickering, and disjointed efforts - was manifest. Especially, the management of conflict was a weak area. Intergroup and interfunctional dissension appear frequently, i.e. differences of approach, views, values, objectives, and so forth. Conflict weakened commitment, identification and affiliation, undermined human relations, led to lack of trust, harmony and cooperation between groups and brought about lapses in communication with information being distorted, censored, or held back.

Project development not merely took a long time but also, in some respects, an unpredictably long time. Unexpected and prolonged delays were more common than generally assumed. The Projects started at various times with certain gestation period, some experiencing delay which are costly, uncertain, and diversionary. A long lead time was involved, several years elapsing between inception and operation, for instance, the Pulverization Project. Delay was palpably longer in those Projects where procedural formality and interorganizational friction was protracted. This was compounded by inertia, negative operating culture, negotiation delay, and long turnaround time. Inability to eliminate or reduce lengthy time overruns, and consequential cost overruns, almost always led to fixing the blame and finding a scapegoat. Long uncertain delays tended to undermine stability and cohesiveness, introduce questionable changes, and cause changed expectations and demands from participants and less acceptance of the Projects once developed.

Inadequate marketing, especially in relation to pricing, promotion, distribution channels and research permeated the Projects. Besides, the financing of the Projects was overshadowed by inadequate financial base, insufficient cost estimates, irregular counterpart funding, preeminence of external financing, ineffective resource allocation, and sparse cost accounting-based analyses and slow-moving financial management.

Management capability was highly insulated, varied from Project to Project and impacted unfavorably on the Projects' implementation. Managerial and organizational costs delayed project completion, raised management costs, delayed Project outputs, and lessened the development impact, thrust and return. After Project completion, the same constraints, by and large, continue to hamper the attainment of full development benefits.

Contrary to habitual assumptions, the target population is not homogeneous, and is almost always diverse and stratified with respect to income, occupation, ethnicity, educational attainment, family background, and mobility. Even if project payoffs available to low-income target groups are noticeable, it is, nearly always, the high and middle-income groups which seem to derive greater benefits and higher visibility more frequently from the Projects. While there is a growing consensus that the poor in Barbados, as elsewhere, can best improve his condition by his direct participation in the development process, an effective methodology for such a people-based forum remains somewhat elusive. In reality, it is the topheavy model, and not the bottomup variant, which continues to persist.

The problems of analysis and measurement appeared with regular frequency, viz. lack of a consistent system of discount rate and shadow price, inattention to measure the Projects' physical assets, failure to measure the opportunity cost of capital in the Investments, failure to appraise second-round income flows and distribution effects of the Investments, failure to quantify the social costs to determine the Investments' impact on the net social product, insufficient attention to the Projects' social and environmental aspects, scanty work on establishing a workable boundary between traded and nontraded goods and services, insufficient attention to risk and uncertainty issues, shortage of consideration of alternative solutions to stated problems, making assumptions about benefit diffusion or project outcome on scanty evidence or untested premises, and overplaying the efficiency criteria and downplaying the equity criteria.

Once the Projects became operational on completion and were absorbed into the regular mainstream system, traditional management reasserted itself - time mismanagement, compartmentalized behavior, excessive rule and regulation orientation, operational rigidity and inflexibility, insufficient output measurement, inadequate customer orientation, infrequent social communication, indifferent revenue generation, and uncreative operating culture. Though clear responsibility rests with the operating agencies for running and maintaining the completed Projects, a culture that tends to permeate the Project organizations 'officializes' perception and responses and creates resistance to or slows down change by sanctifying the status quo.

The recognition of project management as a specialty area requiring certain skills, competencies, values and attitudes is not yet clear. Overall management underlying the Projects revealed that the concern was more with 'control' and 'containment' than with 'management' and 'visioning'. Interface management - the process and timing of the coordination of the various elements of the Projects - was a soft belly. So was multilateral management - the willingness and ability to involve and partner a variety and range of societal organizations. Three distinct management processes - strategic planning, management control, and operational control - were shallow. Strategic planning was nearly perfunctory. Management control was uneven and unfocused. Operational control had many kinks. It is perhaps the organizational resource - team-building, organization development, capacity-building, mobility, and momentum maintenance - that is truly scarce in Barbados, perhaps more so than investment resources. The management of the Projects succeeded less in integrating and coordinating diverse activities, meeting schedule, cost and performance objectives, defining responsibilities and assignments soundly, distributing workload carefully or equitably, providing adequate and supportive supervision, effecting interorganizational coordination, and using persuasive and participative strategies. The management of the Projects was beset with a host of kindred problems, viz. unsupportive policies, late and unreliable delivery of materials and equipment, wrong or rash decisions, contractual changes, information-flow deficiencies, variable internal controls, centralized and paternalistic action, imprecise problem definition and formulation, lack of thoroughness and tenacity, persistent delays, dispositional conflicts, cost escalation, unrealistic expectations, resource constraints, unforeseen impediments, uneven management skills, disparate programming capacity in operating organizations, authoritarian management style, shortage of trained, skilled, spunky and experienced personnel, lengthy and time-consuming personnel management, and unreal overoptimistic timetable.

Operational in an environment characterized by fragmentation, partisanship, technological and financial dependence and occasional unreceptivity, the Projects underline limited ability to respond to a changing environment with clear gaps between intention and performance.

Part of the pattern of organizational behavior, as seen in the Projects, can be explained by the past pattern of acculturation in Barbados' colonial past and inherited management system. The internal operating culture, for instance, is characterized, more often than not, by authoritarianism, nonparticipation, tardiness, and proceduralism. Culturally, the Projects failed to move from a person and power culture to a role and task culture. The cultural values underlying the Projects have been largely hierarchy and control and failed to make a shift to a culture that values collaboration and community.

Certain orientation, inimical to fast-track management, persists, e.g. following a single 'master' strategy, following a fixed path, blend of authoritarianism and personalism, frequent and numerous checks and balances, and project management continuing to be more process-oriented and less results-conscious.

The importance attached to the learning process was more verbal than real. Some of the gaps in the learning process comprised inability to recognize mistakes and learn from errors, failure to change course at short notice and correct errors, unwillingness to intensify learning and adaptation, inclination to expect quick results, inability to follow up and take remedial action doggedly, and incapacity to enhance the quality and richness of life by collective action.

Various lapses cluttered the Project process, i.e. not paying enough attention to social impact, cultural shocks and environmental adversities, not stepping up systematic research in respect of modernizing, updating, renewing and accelerating work system, flaws in material control, snags in tendering procedures, traditionality in personnel management, outdatedness in standard operating procedures, fluffs in planning priorities, tardiness in reporting, tracking and follow-up, not enough attention to counterparting, time and cost overruns, performance variation and schedule slippages, and occasionally unhelpful attitudes and questionable behavior of some expatriate consultants and contractors.

The Projects have not been able, as much as possible or necessary, to generate backward and forward linkages, technological infrastructure, management capability, local value-added, job creation, foreign exchange earnings, and skill diffusion. The extent to which the Projects established and continue to create backward linkages - raw materials, supplies, components, services - and forward linkages - products, services, sales - have not been as large as one hopes. The extent to which the Projects develop linkages with other organizations and enterprises and pressure them to move over time into higher value-added operations - with a view to maximizing overall benefits - have not been as thrustful as one desires. The Ventures did not generate high-value added within Barbados and did not retain foreign earnings as much as necessary - both directly by its own efforts and indirectly by their linkages with other organizations and enterprises. The continuous development and steady upgrading of skills of managers, supervisors and support personnel employed by the Projects was not as achieved as necessary. As a result, high potential for technological and managerial learning and varied spin-off effects were not realized as much as possible. The transfer of technology by the Projects was not as diffused and indigenized in the wider environment as possible. The Projects' technology-learning capabilities and innovation-driven services, essential to dynamic and prosperous societies, are, consequentially, circumscribed. The working conditions of the Projects' workforce - compensation, benefits, overtime, working hours, supervisory control, health hazards, safety provisions - remained and continue to remain traditional in ways more than one. The distribution of income generated by the Projects was not as widely-based as anticipated initially during the earlier phases of the project cycle. Noteworthy too is that the Projects suffer some degree of leakage, i.e. spending that leaves Barbados as profits, dividends, salaries, wages, benefits, and goods-services imports.

Understanding the true nature of the project cycle, and the task orientation inherent in it, has not yet suffused. A tradition of creativity, innovation, entrepreneurship and quantification has not been fully developed within the Projects. Nor do the organizations show much equifinality. There may be, and often are, different ways to achieve success and realize goals. The organizations are yet to be fully multiaxial, i.e. structured around work, results, performance, relationships, and decisions.

Project development does not fit well with the realities of conventional politics. While project development requires stability, predictability and leadership, politics operates in the background of varied social divisions, conflicting and competing interest groups, large-scale uncertainties, and shifting priorities. Conventional party politics tends to lead to a partisan, sectarian and short-term approach to projects and related tasks, thus impairing the project ethos. Even when and where managers/supervisors are competent and dedicated, they must acquiesce in the occasionally questionable ministerial decisions and stances as a matter of course. Political actors are sometimes known to divert limited project resources to new, and at times fleeting, purposes, delay key decisions, inadequately define organizational mission, and show faltering support. Policy leadership is not averse to impose serious constraints on project development and management, despite the political imperative of development. Project development is shaped by the complex process of policy decision, political interaction, and social learning. But the Projects' control-oriented management systems have not adequately reflected the underlying concerns of proactive entrepreneurship. Considerable funds are spent on project development based, curiously enough, on untested or dubious premises without much investment in supporting research. There seems to be indifference among practitioners toward research that is not immediately 'relevant' or 'applied'. Organization/management research continues to be infrequent, investment in independent research remains low, and research activity has not been accorded high visibility, access or acceptance that it deserves.

Several limiting factors curb the attainment of the Project objectives, even though the factors are not always clearly recognized by the management, thus resulting in an inability to select the most favorable alternative. The limiting factors comprise, for example, securing commitment and cohesiveness, maintaining continuity and tenacity, providing sanction, rewarding achievement, measuring work, upholding fairness, and maintaining accountability and transparency. Moreover, combinations of dependency, traditionalism and vulnerability persist. A project, for instance, which does not or cannot persuade the target population that it is to its own advantage to do things differently cannot expect to perform creditably. Limitation in the Projects stems not only from long-held and ingrained attitudes against change but also from an incapacity of the management system to persuade personnel as well as beneficiaries to modify behavior and convince them of the rewards emanating from changed behavior. Further, the presence of the Official Secrets Act, the absence of the Freedom of Information Act, the deficiency in productivity measurement/performance appraisal and the absence of client/consumer pressure continue to vitiate public sector management, including project planning and management. Especially, it is wasteful that the public management system, because of its tradition and legality, does not let public personnel - experienced and trained as some of them are - take part publicly in community-level open discussions on organization/management problems, issues, and concerns. Part of such oversight, or perhaps failure, has been in the continuing unwillingness to learn from practice, experience, and reality.

The managements in all the target Projects met resistance, particularly during the formative stages. The bottomline is that project management is a clear departure from Barbados' traditional, functional, and hierarchical management. Many tended to resist the Project-inducing change because they found it uncomfortable, unsettling, disruptive, risky, uncertain and threatening, and many did not apparently knew how to deal with those phenomena.

The target Projects used a number of project planning and control tools under variable and uneven conditions, such as work breakdown structure, precedence diagramming method, responsibility matrix, logical framework analysis, Gantt charts, milestone charts, critical path analysis, program evaluation and review technique, cost estimating, budgeting, variance analysis, and earned value technique. But it was at the level of project control - the process of keeping the Projects on targets and as close to plan as possible - that project managements showed their weakness. Project control - initiating action, guiding work toward goals, ensuring resource utilization, correcting problems, and consolidating goals achieved - showed weakness. The control process - setting performance standards, comparing the standards with actual performance, taking necessary corrective action - showed weakness. Project monitoring - involving tracking, observing, data collection and information reporting, and facilitating timely and effectively control - was weak. Data for monitoring the Projects - plans, outputs, schedules, budgets, and studies - were not used purposefully and vigorously. Internal as well as external control lacked sustained continuity and thrust. Although variance analysis as a cost control tool was employed to see if the actual costs were more or less than planned costs, the tool was by itself inadequate because it indicated neither how much work was completed nor what the future expenses were likely to be. The earned value technique was not used consistently, thereby management missing an opportunity to track work progress and actual costs. It could not be ascertained if project managements used any variant of performance analysis to assess work progress, schedules, cost performance, and technical performance.

Despite some control systems in existence, project control kinks occurred. Far too often, only one factor, such as cost, was employed, while others, such as schedule and technical performance, were subdued. Control measures were resisted and did not receive as much compliance as expected. Information was inaccurately or partially reported. Project personnel acted defensively and failed to provide unprejudiced information. Bias was an obstacle to achieving accurate control. Managers were diffident on controversial or contentious issues, apparently believing that with time problems resolved themselves. The belief that poor performance in one was offset by good performance in others militated against the control process. Information reporting, accountability and intervention mechanisms were delay-prone and feeble, giving the impression that management did not care much about the control process, an attitude likely to spread to other phases throughout the Projects.

Specifications

Our study comes up with specific findings in respect of each Project in terms of analytical dimensions, driving forces, and constraining forces. The evidence of a Project's success is measured by the goods and services it delivers and their use by the customers.

Theoretical dimension

Each theoretical approach and strand - the blueprint approach, the design approach, the adaptive or participative approach, the hiding hand principle, the comprehensive planning mode, and the quantitative analysis mode - is reflected varyingly in the Projects and in the various phases of the project cycle.

Formative dimension

Driving forces

Greenland: The Project established a Blackbelly sheep breeding station, completed sheep feeding trials, facilitated sheep breeding, carried out pasture management, conducted sheep registration, and used logical framework analysis.

Handicraft: The Project was reorganized and expanded, people were trained in different craft areas, marketing outlets were opened, production was intensified, research and design capacity were improved, raw-material base was expanded, product quality was improved, and promotional strategies were developed.

Cave: The entrance area was reshaped to give a natural appearance and contour, the Cave walls were roughened to simulate naturalness, interior trails were paved, special lighting effects were put in place, a Visitor's Center was built, and progress schedules were used.

Pulverization: Various methods of refuse disposal and types of equipment were compared, an implementation team was put in place promptly, the Plant's commissioning or startup was successful, and the Plant personnel received timely training.

Polytechnic: Feasibility studies were informative, appraisal was advised in part by cost-effectiveness analysis, extensive reporting was carried out, engineering was of acceptable standard, and contract performance was fair.

Sewerage: The Project site was chosen promptly, the target area was cleared, appraisal was informed by cost-effectiveness analysis, several components were completed on schedule, reporting and feedback was regularly used, and the system was put on multitype process.

Ferneihurst: The Project was executed reasonably efficiently, appraisal was done in part by cost-effectiveness analysis, wastage was pushed back, and construction economies were effected.

Constraining forces

Greenland: The Project could not meet its commitments under the Caribbean Food Plan, the specialist services were provided perfunctorily, and work on the Venture's genetic, productive, management, promotional, commercial and ethical aspects slowed down and ran into problems.

Handicraft: Among the constraints were delay in personnel placement, paucity of training and purchasing centers, and failure to form craft cooperatives.

Cave: The Venture faced engineering and planning setbacks, unstable management structure, personnel setbacks, cost escalation, appraisal lapses, time losses and overruns, equipment breakdown, and unfavorable weather.

Pulverization: The relocation of the residents in the Plant area, electrical and mechanical problems, structural and equipment problems and frequent delays and schedule slippages caused concern. The cost of long gestation showed up with the Plant not yielding benefits readily.

Polytechnic: The cost of tying to external sources and prolonged delay was high. Getting the workforce to produce reasonable output was hard.

Sewerage: The Project cost was underestimated, the Plant capacity to serve the target area was underestimated, schedules slipped, delay and time-loss were incurred, design errors occurred, and infrastructural services were disrupted.

Ferneihurst: A review of postcompletion status was lacking. Inadequate site supervision, centralized and delayed purchasing and delivery, incomplete budgeting, material shortage, and indifferent scheduling affected the Project process.

Legal dimension

From inception to termination of the project cycle, the law pervaded. The Projects were established by organizations that were set up under the law and operated, and continue to operate, under the rules of law. A host of legal and quasilegal inputs went into the loan agreement.

Legal provisions like propriety, accountability and the due process restricted options and consumed time in building the Projects through a tangle of real-life situations. Although the contract documents had set up target time and delivery schedule, the contracts neither adhered to the scheduled time nor performed exactly as planned.

Ethical dimension

Moral and ethical values influence the actions and intentions that create the Projects' social impact of performance. The Project decisions point to the accountability of decision-makers to the people's will, the discretion and prudence displayed in making choices among competing values and the ethical principles in relation to consultancy, contracting, subcontracting, procurement, and collaboration.

Yet, unethical practices and behavior, the abuse of power, expediency and opportunism persist partly because control measures are weak and selective, partly because power criteria push out organizational ethics, and partly because of the belief that ethics and economic do not mix.

Policy dimension

An overall policy context is vital to the success or failure of projects. Projects succeed or fail *only* as they draw life from the policy environment. The sample Projects are as good as the existing policies that guided their identification, selection, approval, and implementation. The cyclical relationships within and between the Projects are linked together by policy.

Overall policy was rigid in that the lack of flexibility and ease delayed the Projects' implementation. Financial planning was weak, e.g. budgeting of an adequate flow of funds on a multiyear basis was on shaky ground. Human resource planning did not benefit from promptness in placement or incisiveness in problem-solving capability. Evaluation was not a prioritized part of the project framework.

Institutional dimension

Institutional capacity continues to be variable and difficult. While colonial planning was mainly indicative and short-term, postindependence planning focused on allocating resources and pushing growth. More recently, planning has shown keenness on assessing resources and ordering priorities to assume attainable growth. Although the Planning and Priorities Committee plays a policy-making and decision-making role, yet it tends to get bogged down in minutiae. The Public Investment Unit's facilitative role in project development is recognized, but the Unit's activities may succeed more in attracting external finance than in improving internal project management . The operating agencies play their role in project development, but project planning capacity has not yet permeated throughout the public sector.

Sectoral dimension

Driving forces

Greenland: The Venture has registered modest success in improved selection, breeding and crossbreeding, retaining breed homogeneity, pasture management, livestock research, disease resistance, useful experimental data, trying difficult production system, and upgrading stock by artificial insemination.

Handicraft: Sectorally, the industry has allowed for developed and expanded industrial base, indigenous craft entrepreneurship, creativity and cultural awareness, small-scale employment and cash income, retail marketing, decentralized production, diversified materials, designs, training and marketing, and standardized exportable products.

Cave: The Project, featuring a scenic limestone cave of unusual and unique beauty and high amenity value with sightseeing and educational experience, has enhanced Barbados as a major, attractive and popular tourist destination and provides an experience unlike anything else in nature.

Pulverization: The Project manages waste stream, maintains sanitation standards and ensures safe and reliable infrastructure. It serves households, workplaces, open space, leisure areas, streets, sidewalks, and neighborhoods.

Sewerage: The sewering of Bridgetown promotes health and well-being, reduces health risks and hazards, improves personal hygiene, alleviates insanitary conditions, contains communicable diseases, and decreases infection rate.

Ferneihurst: Ferneihurst represents a relatively new housing concept in Barbados - terrace housing - which links together under one roof independent family units and is accepted as a desirable option for comparatively dense development in urban areas. It has a visual character and a coherent architectural feature, expressing naturally the close-knit community life of the country.

Constraining forces

Greenland: The drawbacks include occasional indiscriminate crossbreeding, inadequate flesh on legs and loin, difficult pasture management, lean carcasses, high lamb mortality, limited meat yield, lower conformation, and growth rate. Greater success in achieving high weight gains relative to feed intake is missing.

Handicraft: The industry is featured by low productivity and low gross revenue per product. The link between handicraft and other sectors is not robust.

Cave: The Venture operates in a foreign-dominated tourism sector with restricted local entrepreneurship and limited linkages with the rest of the sectors.

Pulverization: Inadequate disposal of hazardous and industrial waste, weak enforcement and regulation, improper collection and handling, and roadside dumping pose social disbenefits.

Polytechnic: The Polytechnic has not as yet blossomed into a locally-oriented, adaptive, innovative, educationally-assertive, and decentralized institution.

Sewerage: The delay in service connection exacerbates the health risks.

Ferneihurst: The prejudice against terrace housing continues, with multiple-type housing associated with the fear of loss of privacy. The concern is real that Fernihurst does not decline into residualization, which certainly lowers the status and increases the stigma attached to public housing.

Social dimension

Driving forces

Greenland: The Project, based on sheep-raising skills, is shared by many farmers with varying degrees of land resources and financial ability.

Handicraft: The Project underscores indigenous entrepreneurship, boosts small business, promotes cultural heritage, creates public awareness, and expands handicraft production.

Cave: The Cave offers a high amenity value, provides a joy of unique underground experience, produces a thrilling experience of sound and light effects, generates interest in people, lifestyle, contacts, understandings and goodwill, and informs visitors of local history, culture and cuisine.

Pulverization: The social value of the Project exceeds the social value of consumption. The user role in placing refuse at the right place and time for proper collection and disposal is a recognized fact.

Polytechnic: The Polytechnic underlines technical-vocational training, skill acquisition, greater employability, social access and mobility, and opportunity diversification.

Sewerage: The Project's social quality, significance and soundness increase by eliminating downtown slums, cleaning pollution, and discouraging human waste and household wastewater.

Ferneihurst: The Complex at Ferneihurst - providing housing for low-income households, the elderly segment, and other disadvantaged groups - represents a fundamental human and social need.

Constraining forces

Greenland: Livestock production is a demanding occupation with long working hours and constant vigilance.

Handicraft: Social rejection, stereotyping of trainees and producers, poor image and low social acceptance of the industry endure.

Cave: The Cave may suffer at the hands of careless visitors, metropolitan tourism interests are strong, and contacts between visitors and residents remain superficial.

Pulverization: The poor image of waste management of the past and the unwholesome practice of improper, casual and ad hoc waste disposal linger.

Polytechnic: The Polytechnic suffers low status, slender acceptance, and uncharitable social image.

Sewerage: The problems include the users disposing improper objectives into the system, residents complaining of strong stench coming from the Plant occasionally, and low-income users remaining reluctant to make in-house connection due to high connection cost.

Ferneihurst: Prejudice against terrace housing continues, the image of public housing as poverty enclaves persist, and stereotyping and uncharitable labeling in respect of low-income tenants linger.

Political dimension

Project development is certainly not apolitical. In fact, fundamental political values are at the core of project development and the relation between project and politics is abiding. Policy-maker disposition toward a project can be strategic to its success. A redistributive strategy via the Projects can be seen at work. The Project's political feasibility - sufficient political push and support - was reasonably clear. The Project points to egalitarianism and developmentalism.

Implicit, and sometimes explicit, in the funding and technical assistance process is the recipient Barbados' dependence on the donor community for capital and technology, her sensitivity to donors and her need to avoid outguessing the donors for ensuring a continuing flow of assistance.

Economic dimension

Driving forces

Greenland: The Project has links with agriculture, rural economy, rural development, small-farm promotion, nutrition, employment, import substitution, and export promotion.

Handicraft: The Venture concerns an indigenous, labor-absorbing, local value-added and small-scale industrial activity, presenting relatively low entry costs and making a reasonably successful transition from a noncommercial welfare-oriented initiative to a commercial operation.

Cave: The Project raises the value of output, creates backward linkages, produces externalities, promotes exports, utilizes indigenous resources, substitutes imports, serves decentralization, enlarges tourist by-products, raises recreation values, and creates multiplier effects.

Pulverization: The Venture's impact includes increasing and diversifying employment, spurring infrastructural and traffic growth, encouraging movement, facilitating service and production, and enhancing the safety and reliability of resources.

Polytechnic: The Project services productive and service functions, produces trained workforce, responds to labor market needs, stimulates entrepreneurship, and creates forward linkages.

Sewerage: The Venture helps facilitate urban renewal, business development, tourist arrival, environmental protection and revenue generation, and is economically consequential with the outputs benefitting users directly and widely.

Ferneihurst: The payoffs include curbing the cost of shelter to low-income households, creating steady and long-term tenancy, low rent protecting low-income tenants from high-market rents and housing shortages, generating multiplier effects, saving or curbing external costs, and offering substitution and complementarity.

Constraining forces

Greenland: The Project's vulnerabilities are that sheep-farming for mutton alone is not profitable, mutton production requires much land for pasturing, the externalities of sheep-farming have not been explored much, limited mutton production because of imported mutton, slow commercialization, and inadequate marketing.

Handicraft: Handicraft's share in the industrial sector is modest in terms of value added, output, investment, and employment.

Cave: The Venture faces some weaknesses with respect to limited local participation, limited investment capital, tourism seasonality, and restricted penetration of tourist market.

Pulverization: Some externalities have been overlooked, some diseconomies prevail, replacement cost has been difficult, resource recovery and revenue generation has been slow, and measuring reduction in user cost is difficult.

Polytechnic: It is difficult to establish pricing for nontraded outputs, employment has been slow and uneven, self-employment is limited, job market is small, and job openings are limited.

Sewerage: Significant costs incurred include acquiring factor services, absorbing labor costs, acquiring equipment, unscheduled transportation costs, replacement costs, property relocation costs, water costs, and operating costs.

Ferneihurst: The market system points to low return on investment in rental housing, low buying power of low-income tenants, reduced supply of such housing, and decreased replacement of substandard housing.

Financial dimension

Driving forces

Greenland: Sheep farmers, the beneficiaries of export and local marketing provide lambs for sale to individual and institutional consumers.

Handicraft: The Venture produces goods and services for which demand is reasonably high, considering other consumer options.

Cave: The rate of growth of net income is considerable.

Pulverization: The discounted value of gains from managing the disposal site is noteworthy.

Polytechnic: A maximum of quality results at lowest possible unit-cost is stressed.

Sewerage: Property value is raised in the sewered area.

Ferneihurst: The Estate is a capital asset with a regular income.

Constraining forces

Greenland: Reliable data on production cost at the Station cannot be produced because information is dispersed throughout the Ministry of Agriculture. The Project has not yet succeeded in making the country self-sufficient in mutton.

Handicraft: The accounting system is not operating at its best in many enterprises, especially the smaller ones.

Cave: The Cave's operating revenue is not high enough relative to its attractiveness and resourcefulness.

Pulverization: Narrow financial base cannot ensure Plant modernization and maintenance.

Polytechnic: The average cost per student per year has risen over the years.

Sewerage: The rate of return on high capital investment has been low so far.

Ferneihurst: The cost of maintaining Ferneihurst is high partly because possible cost savings are not effected.

Organizational dimension

Driving forces

Greenland: The Station, which pays attention to equipment maintenance, working area, slaughtering time and capacity, sanitary conditions and after-hour services, is manageable with comparatively low labor content and low capital outlay. The management system is intensive and commercial in that the sheep are managed in confinement with little or no grazing.

Handicraft: Job-order and batch production systems are in existence, the process layout is in operation, and production planning and control are in force.

Cave: A comprehensive operational schedule is in force, embracing underground plants, lighting, refuse disposal, trail maintenance, speleothems, vehicle maintenance, safety measures, access roads, carpark, and so forth..

Pulverization: The collection service and equipment/vehicle maintenance follow an established process and a regular sequence to ensure clean, competent and professional waste management.

Polytechnic: The Polytechnic has helped mobilize greater institutional capability to service the country's technical-vocational training needs.

Sewerage: The collection system functions satisfactorily, with a minimum of blockages, effluent treatment continues in keeping with the set standard, septage is accepted and treated daily and physical emissions are reduced to tolerable levels.

Ferneihurst: The Estate enjoys steady and long-term tenancy, resident wardens identify and communicate tenant concerns, and rent collection has improved.

Constraining forces

Greenland: Work on animal selection, homogeneity retention and export production have been scaled down, interpersonal and interunit communication continue to be insufficient, and sound livestock management practices are not always observed. The inability to attain cost reduction - the cost of lamb production and the feed cost - persists.

Handicraft: Marketing decisions remain somewhat uninformed by strategic criteria. Small producers do not have access to export subsidies. The current practices are stacked in favor of large producers. Unsteady supply of raw materials and short production runs persist.

Cave: Tight schedule reduces equipment lifespan, lapses occur in preventive maintenance, and multifaceted professional marketing is not a strong forte.

Pulverization: There are slips in collection, the waste management process is not fully integrated, the Plant suffers occasional downturn, there are inefficiencies in regular enforcement, and there is a shortage of roadworthy collection vehicles. The disposable waste has not yet been used in agriculture, and illegal dumping and indiscriminate littering continue.

Polytechnic: High dropout rate, tight budget, small revenue base, limited training and skill development programs and restricted work-study programs linger.

Sewerage: Oily substance and industrial waste cannot be treated, sludge disposal is odorous, the cost of treatment is high, and the number of user connections is still low.

Ferneihurst: Maintenance is not regular, material control is tardy, tenancy agreement is breached occasionally, rent payment is not always regular, and advance or indicative planning is lacking.

Technological dimension

Driving forces

Greenland: Marked most particularly by technological challenge, the

Project provides on a limited scale a flock of purebred Blackbelly sheep.

Handicraft: It is hand tool-oriented, semimechanical, craft-based production activity, with tools being hand-powered, simple, reliable, and inexpensive.

Cave: The Cave required the application of science and technology and their careful integration in the development effort.

Pulverization: Technical support services made possible the proper location of the Plant and the prevention of leaching into underground water supplies.

Polytechnic: The Venture responds to, enhances and retains technological capability in the local environment.

Sewerage: Technological soundness and safety is built into the system, with the Plant's operation embracing mechanical, physical, biological, and chemical processes.

Ferneihurst: Work in physical planning and development design was conducted professionally.

Constraining forces

Greenland: Research and development work at the Station is carried on at a slow pace.

Handicraft: Technological support for work relating to the improvement, treatment and discovery of suitable local materials is not strong.

Cave: Technological support for maintenance of the Cave and expansion of the facilities is not steadfast.

Pulverization: Training for the Plant personnel in the technological aspects of waste management lacks continuity and updating.

Polytechnic: Personnel training in wastewater control and management is inadequate as well as infrequent.

Ferneihurst: Technological synergy, which is required in maintaining premises, buildings, families, drainage and sewage and ensuring health and safety, is absent.

Environmental dimension

Driving forces

Greenland: The Station makes use of and builds on natural resources.

Handicraft: The Venture draws on the local environment.

Cave: The Cave is linked closely with the environment.

Pulverization: The Plant ensures a hazard-free environment.

Polytechnic: The landscape provides comfort to the user of the Campus.

Sewerage: The Plant operates with minimum adverse environmental impact.

Ferneihurst: The Estate is landscaped, providing natural vegetation and foliage.

Constraining forces

Greenland: The Station has occasional herbage contamination.

Handicraft: The raw materials, derived from the local plant population, and the accessories, obtained from the local plant population, and the accessories, obtained from industrial by-products, are in shortage seasonally.

Cave: The Cave's interior survives in a fragile and delicate environment.

Pulverization: The Pulverized refuse tends to leach impurities in Barbados' fissured soil, causing groundwater pollution.

Polytechnic: Managing Barbados' renewable resources, such as human capital and skill pool, without reducing environment's carrying capacity, leaves room for improvement.

Sewerage: The impact of chlorine and chloramine on the ecology of the marine environment tends to be harmful.

Ferneihurst: Paint drift from the Estate's eastern boundary affects trees, undergrowth, and housing units.

International dimension

The domestic and international subsystems are intertwined and the Projects underpin interaction and interdependence. The Projects' externalization and internationalism came through via several routes in nearly all the phases, including financing feasibility studies, conducting complex negotiations, organizing technical assistance provisions, finalizing loan agreements, doing consultancies, arranging procurements, supplying equipment and doing installation, undertaking training, and executing marketing. International transaction has functioned as an instrument for a wider availability and allocation of resources through international specialization and differentiation. The Ventures, through their activities and effects, show greater affinity with the international community, notwithstanding a welter of downsides.

The Projects reflect dependent development and mirror some disbenefits. Donor control and influence tends to increase at both covert and overt levels. The donor-recipient relations can be and are, periodically, strained in relation to finance, personnel, technology, and resource access.

Comparative dimension

Comparing project traits, performance and behavior across countries and cultures reveals that diverse, and sometimes counteracting, conditions influenced the reported Projects - their objectives , costs and size differed, they were funded by different international and regional agencies, they were implemented by different executing agencies and they started from different initial conditions.

Despite differing conditions, the Projects were comparable - costs departed from scheduled performance, actual costs exceeded estimated costs, unexpected cost increases occurred, behavior of Projects financed by any one international agency differed little from Projects funded by others, large and expensive Projects implemented by one executing agency differed little from small ones carried out by other units, and economic-sector Projects did not differ significantly in implementation from social-sector Projects.

While the Projects uniformly displayed a few punches, e.g. high-level policy inputs, environmental sensitivity and social participation, several common constraints were suffered, e.g. external dependence, repetitive time and cost overruns, and intergroup conflict/tension. The question was raised why projects intended to benefit certain target groups in a certain way do not often do so, and how choices made, far too often by a select group of key participants, during implementation affect the output and credibility of particular projects.

Measurement dimension

Organizational measurement for the Projects is designed to provide a basis for planning and control, improve accountability and transparency, alleviate mismanagement and malperformance, improve operation and monitoring, stimulate organization and management development, and assist standardization. But, in reality, the Projects' lapses point to the absence of and gaps in coherent and clear measurement, employee wariness of measurement, resistance to measurement, perfunctory and unintegrated measurement, casual and uninformed attitude toward management, measurement-indifferent work culture and environment, lack of incentives for measurement, gaps in existing data and information, irregularity in collecting data, and unwillingness and inability to use measurement. There is, as yet, no inclination for vigorous and thrusting measurement within the Projects.

Summary

It is time for closure, wrapping up much of the material covered in this volume. We kicked off by initiating a study of development projects in Barbados. Throughout the research, the Projects' multifaceted holistic processes were examined. The Projects, going through the various phases of the project life cycle and many other activity modes or decisional factors which were part of the project management process, show their varied, engaging, defining, chequered, and interactive facets. The essence of project development and management, so also, lies in actual behavior - the factors, variables, events, forces, dynamics, and issues - that exist in and cast influence on the life of an organization. Central to our analysis is that the Projects, having served as tools of development activity, have helped transform Barbados, in part and in a certain way, in her quest for fulfilment. Even so, there were, as always, prices to pay, challenges to face, setbacks to overcome, problems to disentangle, adversities to contain, conflicts to resolve, gaps to fill, bridges to cross, hurdles to jump, resources to mobilize, strategies to plan, and goals to chase. For sometime now, the Projects have become fully operational, serving the community, responding to people , providing benefits, and gaining experience. The Projects and similar initiatives continue to enrich life in Barbados.

REFERENCES

Bardach, Eugene (1977) *The Implementation Game*. Cambridge: MIT Press.

Brinkerhoff, D.W. (1992) "Looking Out, Looking In, Looking Ahead", *International Review of Administrative Sciences* 58 (4).

Dunsire, Andrew (1978) *Implementation In A Bureaucracy*. Oxford: Martin Robinson.

Gray, Clive and Andre Martens (1983) "The Political Economy of the Recurrent Cost Problems in theWest African Sahel", *World Development* 11 (2).

Grindle, Merilee S. (ed.) *Politics And Policy Implementation in the Third World*. Princeton: University Press.

Hirschman, Albert O. (1967) *Development Projects Observed*. Washington, D.C.: Brookings Institution.

Hogwood, Brian W. and Lewis A. Gunn (1984) *Policy Analysis for the Real World*. London: Oxford University Press.

Honadle, George and Rudi Klauss (eds.) (1979) *International Developemnt Administration*. New York: Praeger.

Hulme, D. (1989) "Learning And Not Learning From Experience in Rural Project Planning", *Public Administration and Development* (9).

Jones, Charles O. (1977) *An Introduction to the Study of Public Policy*. North Scituate, Mass. : Duxbury Press.

Majone, Giandomenico and Aaron Wildavsky (1979) "Implementation As Evolution", in Jeffrey L. Pressman and Aaron Wildavsky (eds.) *Implementation*. Berkeley: University of California Press.

Mazmanian, Daniel A. and Paul A. Sabatier (1981) *Effective Policy Implementation*. Lexinton: Lexinton Books.

Morgan, E. P. (1983) "The Project Orthodoxy In Development", *Public Administration And Development* (3).

Morss, E. R. (1984) "Institutional Destruction Resulting from Donor and Project Proliferation in Sub-Saharan African Countries", *World Development* 12 (4).

Pressman, Jeffrey L. and Aaron Wildavsky (1973) *Implementation*. Berkeley: University of California Press.

Rondinelli, Dennis A. (1983) "Project As Instrument of Development Administration", *Public Administration and Development* 3 (4).

Smith, Thomas B. (1973) "The Policy Implementation Process", *Policy Sciences* 4 (June).

APPENDICES

Project Location Map

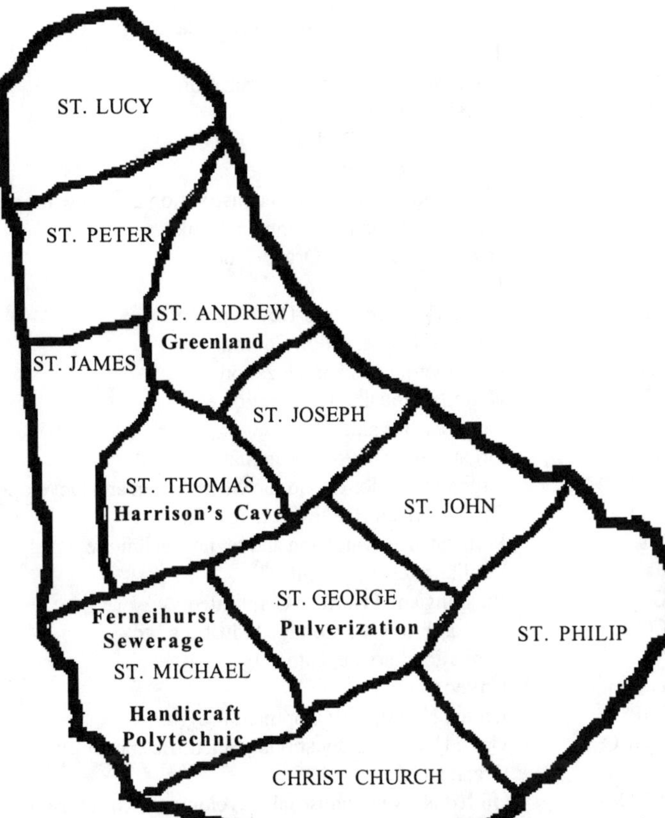

Acronyms/Abbreviations

BADC	Barbados Agricultural Development Corporation
BCA	Barbados Caves Authority
BCR	Benefit-cost ratio
BDS$	Barbados dollars
BIDC	Barbados Industrial Development Corporation
BIMAP	Barbados Institute of Management and Productivity
BWA	Barbados Water Authority
CARICOM	Caribbean Community and Common Market
CARIFESTA	Caribbean Festival
CDB	Caribbean Development Bank
CFTC	Commonwealth Fund for Technical Cooperation
EC$	Eastern Caribbean dollars
FAO	Food and Agriculture Organization
GDP	Gross domestic product
GOB	Government of Barbados
GUY$	Guyanese dollars
IBRD	International Bank for Reconstruction and Development
IDB	Inter-American Development Bank
ILO	International Labor Organization
IRR	Internal rate of return
MOD	Ministry of Overseas Development
NCC	National Conservation Commission
NGO	Nongovernmental organization
NHC	National Housing Corporation
NPV	Net present value
OAS	Organization of American States
OECD	Organization for Economic Cooperation and Development
PAHO	Pan American Health Organization
PERT	Performance evaluation and review technique
PIU	Public Investment Unit
PPC	Planning and Priorities Committee
PPCCIL	Pelican Pride and Cottage Industries Ltd.
SSA	Sanitation Service Authority
UN	United Nations
UNDP	United Nations Development Program
UNESCO	United Nations Educational, Scientific and Cultural Organization
UNIDO	United Nations Industrial Development Organization
UNITAR	United Nations Institute of Training And Research
USAID	United States Agency for International Development
WHO	World Health Organization

STUDY QUESTIONNAIRE

PROJECT-MAKER SURVEY

The questionnaire is concerned with a survey of problem-orientation and problem-identification of project-makers in relation to the nature of development projects in Barbados. The study is an independent research exercise being undertaken at the University of the West Indies, Barbados.

The answers you give to our questions will in no way be identified with you personally. Since we are interested in aggregates rather than in the responses of any one individual, you will remain completely anonymous. Our only request is that you be as frank as you can in your responses.

a.	Date..........................	b.	Sex......................................
c.	Age...........................	d.	Education.............................
e.	Post..........................	f.	Work specialization...............

1. What in your view are the roles of development projects in Barbados?
2. Speaking specifically about project appraisal, what in your view are the major deficiencies of project appraisal in Barbados?
3. What about project implementation? What would you say are the major inadequacies of project implementation in the country?
4. There are different views on project management. What, if any, has so far been the impact of project management on the public service of Barbados?
5. Are you satisfied with the type and level of management training in Barbados as far as it relates to project management?
6. In your view, are there any differences between civil service agencies and project authorities?
7. If yes, what are those differences?
8. Is there any postcompletion evaluation of development projects in Barbados?
9. What, if any, has been the extent of participation by regional/international agencies in Barbados' project development?
10. What specific problems, if any, would you say exist in the area of project finance?

We are grateful for your help. Please return the completed questionnaire.

INTERVIEW SCHEDULE

GENERAL-BENEFICIARY SURVEY

The questionnaire is concerned with an examination of how people feel about development projects in Barbados. The study is an independent research exercise being undertaken at the University of the West Indies, Barbados.

The answers you give to our questions will in no way be identified with you personally. Since we are interested in general feelings and not in any particular individual answer, you can be certain that your replies will be treated confidentially. So, we would like you to be as frank as possible in your answers.

a.	Date....................................	b.	Residence..............................
c.	Sex.....................................	d.	Age ....
e.	Education............................	f.	Employment.........................

1. From time to time, there are discussions in Barbados these days on development projects. What in your view are development projects?
2. Do you know of any ongoing development project in Barbados?
3. Can you name some completed development projects in the country?
4. How did you come to know about such development projects?
5. What in your view are the benefits of development projects in Barbados?
6. How, if at all, have you gained from these benefits?
7. What, if any, are the types of costs of development projects?
8. How, if at all, have you paid any costs?
9. Would you say that the general public is sufficiently informed of development projects in Barbados?
10. Why do you say so?
11. Is there in your view any way in which this can be improved?
12. What would you say are the major problems of development projects in Barbados?

The interview is over. Thank you.

INTERVIEW SCHEDULE
OPERATING-AGENCY SURVEY

The questionnaire is concerned with a survey of how the staff feel about the organizations in which they work (whichever is applicable: Greenland Agricultural Station; Handicraft Center; Harrison's Cave; Pulverization Plant; Samuel Jackman Prescod Polytechnic; Bridgetown Sewerage Treatment Plant; National Housing Corporation). The study is an independent research exercise being undertaken at the University of the West Indies, Barbados.

The answers you give to our questions will in no way be identified with you personally. Since we are interested in general feelings and not in any particular answer, you can be certain that your replies will be treated confidentially. So, we would like you to be as frank as possible in your answers.

a.	Date............................	b. Sex..
c.	Age.............................	d. Work specialization................

1. Can you tell us anything about the organization which makes you happy?

2. Can you tell us anything about the organization which makes you unhappy?
3. Are you satisfied that the clientele is receiving adequate service?
4. If not, why not?
5. What would you say have been the main achievements of the organization?
6. What would you say are the major problems faced by the organization?
7. In your assessment, what are the prospects for the organization?

The interview is over. Thank you.

INTERVIEW SCHEDULE

TARGET-GROUP SURVEY

The questionnaire is concerned with an examination of how people feel about some specific development projects in Barbados (whichever is applicable: Greenland Sheep Development Project; Handicraft Development Project; Harrison's Cave Development Project; Pulverization Plant Project; Samuel Jackman Prescod Polytechnic Project; Bridgetown Sewerage Project; Ferneihurst Housing Project).

The answers you give to our questions will in no way be identified with you personally. Since we are interested in general feelings and not in any particular answer, you can be certain that your replies will be treated confidentially. So, we would like you to be as frank as possible in your answers.

a.	Date..........................	b.	Residence..............................
c.	Sex............................	d.	Age......................................

1. Has the project lived up to your expectation?
2. If no, why not?
3. Has the project satisfied your need?
4. If no, why not?
5. What benefits, if any, have you derived from the project?
6. What, if any, are your main complaints about the project?
7. What in your view are the main strengths of the project?
8. What in your view are the main weaknesses of the project?

The interview is over. Thank you.

DATABASE

Data on the Project's overall status and aggregate features are provided in this section. Data are presented for each of the seven Projects in the following order: physicality, output, volume, operation/capacity, marketing, and legislation. Under these six divisions are placed 421 separate indicators. The data have been assembled, organized and presented around a general framework, rather than through a series of more or less unrelated efforts.

The data are principally of informational and comparative value. It is notable that while the data set out in this section are wide-ranging in terms of scope and content, they are by no means complete.[1] Some pertinent data and information were neither available or known nor were they gathered by the Project organizations themselves. The content, scope and sources of the data evolved intermittently over a one-year period. A special effort was made to compile, from a variety of published sources and oral communication, a basic working set of Project information. The outcome is that a volume of numerical and descriptive materials appears in this section, thus making a cache of data available to practitioners, researchers, and users. Data updates have not been possible in all cases since, unfortunately, data are not always released, shared or become available as soon as changes occur.

Numerical data or descriptive materials do not refer to any particular calendar or fiscal year, unless specifically noted. In a number of indicators, the reported data represent aggregate numbers, which take into account the available statistics for a number of comparable years.

The coding system, comprising a number of descriptors used uniformly in the database, is as follows: approx. (approximately), avg. (average), BDS$ (Barbados dollars), est. (estimated), ^{0}F (Fahrenheit), ft. (feet), ft.^{2} (square feet), hrs. (hours), in. (inches), lbs. (pounds), m. (million), max. (maximum), min. (minimum), mi^2 (square miles), N/K (not known), ≈(approximately equal to), < (less than), > (more than), ton/tonne (imperial; metric), and yr. (year).

GREENLAND

Location	Greenland, St. Andrew; 17.2 miles northeast from Bridgetown; located off Highway 2 & linked with Highway 1 & East Coast Road; communication/ transportation available
Zoning factor	Farm situated in agricultural area
Physical size	Farm building: 6,500 ft.^{2}; farmyard: 16,000 ft.^{2}; offices: 1,200 ft.^{2}; pasture: 30 acres of fenced paddocks used for sheep-farming out of a total of 240 acres
Farm layout	5 farm buildings housing sheep, portable water-tank & pasture; office-block about 210 ft. from farm; farm buildings split into 12 sections; farm buildings oriented northsouth, office-block eastwest

Structure type	Farm buildings made of galvanized sheets, mesh, wire & wood
Space allocation	Access roads; farm buildings; farmyard; offices; pastures; storage area
Enclosure type	Pasture fenced in with mesh wire
Sheep farms	Est. 500-2,000
Sheep population	Est. 25,000-30,000 islandwide; avg. 2,000 sheep/ yr. at Station; 57% owned by landless producers/ small farms; 35% owned by landholding producers
Sheep type	Castrated Blackbelly rams; crossbred castrated rams; crossbred ewes; crossbred rams; hair sheep; polled Dorset rams; pure Blackbelly ewes; pure Blackbelly rams; Suffolk rams
Breed traits	Reddish brown to dark brown in color; conspicuous black undersides; distinct black points on face & legs; deep black color of entire ventral parts; leggy but deep bodies & well-sprung ribs; wide back & loin but deficient rump; steep rump from hip to tail head; tail not fatty & set low; well-set legs; both sexes normally hornless; typically on-hair breed; lack of woolliness; resembles goat; well-developed mane in male; well-developed udder in female
Ewe features	Good milk producers; can raise four lambs without supplemental feeding; high feed & water intake
Concentration areas	Christ Church; St. Andrew; St. Lucy; St. Peter; St. Philip
Usage pattern	Domestic consumption; export marketing
Breeding type	Inbreeding; outbreeding; crossbreeding
Genetic traits	Appearance; body capacity; disease resistance; fertility; growth rate; meat quality; size
Conception rate	90%

Breeding cycle	September-December; May-June; when grass plentiful
Breeding practices	Ewes kept on increasing level of nutrition around breeding time as this intensifies ovulation rate
Mating behavior	Similar to other sheep; greater heat in ewes; ewes come on heat every 16-17 days lasting for 30-36 hrs.; tupping done during last part of heat period
Mating age	Rams: approx. 12 months; ewes: approx. 9-10 months
Stud service	Ministry of Agriculture's subsidized stud services available at several animal improvement centers throughout country
Fecundity index	550%, e.g. number of lambs born/yr. per hundred ewes mated
Gestation period	150 days/5 months
Lambing techniques	Various practices operational at Station
Lambing interval	>200 days
Lambing rate	220%
Birth weight	Avg. 5-10 lbs.
Prolificacy rate	5.5 lambs/ewe/yr. (best conditions); 3 lambs/yr. (avg.); 8 lambs/yr. (record)
Lambing frequency	2 litters/yr.; lambing in any month of yr.
Growth rate	Est. 0.25-0.40 lb./day; 85-90 lbs./6-7 months
Growth factors	Breed; lactation length; milk yield
Lactation peak	2-4 weeks
Milk supply	Good
Maternal behavior	Generally high mothering ability; poor mothering

	common among young nervous mothers with first lambings
Weaning time	2-3 months
Weaning weight	Avg. 26 lbs.
Adult height	Est. 2-2.2 ft.
Adult weight	Ram: approx. 150 - 200 lbs; ewe: approx. 90 - 130 lbs.
Longevity span	5-6 yrs. avg. productive life in organized flocks
Husbandry practices	Introduction; selection; breeding; castration; small flock mating method; lambing; lactation; weaning; culling; foot trimming; deworming; drenching; docking; shearing; pasture control; feed control; disease/parasite control
Flock size	5-10 sheep/flock; avg. 250 ewes at Station
Pasture type	Covers 9% of land area; rough grazing with native tropical grass
Pasture features	Pangola/elephant grass & legumes grown; paddocks & rotational grazing in use to control parasite, prevent soil erosion & maintain soil fertility; avoiding overgrazing & undergrazing; shade trees on pasture provide relief from heat stress; nursing mothers & lambs graze separately; younger sheep graze ahead of old ones
Foraging rate	7 sheep/acre
Grazing practice	Tethering; pasturing; grazing on edges of cultivated land & scrub land
Grazing cycle	6-8 weeks
Grazing time	Sheep on ground for approx. 6 hrs. from 0700 hrs. to approx. 1300 hrs.
Culling rate	15%

Replacement rate	20%
Quality control	Introduction; selection; breeding
Feeding regimen	Elephant grass; feed supplements; forage concentrates; high-fibre roughages; legumes; molasses; pangola grass; salt; silage; supplying primary nutrients like carbohydrates, proteins, fats, minerals, supplements & trace elements; water
Sanitation measures	(Sample): treating footrot; controlling & treating parasites; cleaning & disinfecting pens; draining pastures; isolating infected animals; safekeeping watering & feeding tools; rotating pastures; consulting veterinarian; running diagnostic tests
Deworming	Ewes dewormed prior to mating & lambs dewormed at weaning; lambs dewormed at 6-8 week intervals following weaning
Disease patterns	Diarrhoea; foot-rot; internal & external parasites; mange; mastitis; metritis; pneumonia; relatively free from major diseases & low incidence of illness
Mortality patterns	Most lamb mortality between birth & weaning; postweaning mortality not major; lambs vulnerable during first two weeks of life
Mortality rate	5-10%; avg. 12% in organized flocks
Production run	Long
Production lifespan	5-6 yrs.
Mutton production	40 tons/yr.; 34.3% increase in 1990
Seasonality pattern	Year-round activity
Customer/user base	Abattoirs; butchers; exporters; hotels; individuals/ households; minimarts; public markets; restaurants; sheep farmers; supermarkets
Business hours	0700 hrs. -1600 hrs.; emergency afterhour services available; security provided during nights

Labor practice	Full-time/part-time labor; family labor
Activity cycle	Sheep raising; stud service; selling; slaughtering; marketing; exporting
Program type	Lamb production; mutton production; sheep export
Program cycle	Exporting; husbandry; lambing; mating; marketing; selling; slaughtering
Purchase price	Avg. BDS$75.00/head
Sale price	BDS$4.50/lb.
Turnover rate	High
Market weight	85-95 lbs.
Slaughtering time	A reasonable size before slaughtering; takes at least 1 yr. to have flavor to meat
Slaughtering fee	BDS$ 10.00/head
Cut type	Chops; legs; necks; shanks; shoulder; stew
Preservation practice	Meat hung up at 4^0 Celsius
Meat quality	Flavor; high quality; widespread appreciation
Dressing percentage	Lamb: 50%; sheep: 50-55%
Tendering cycle	5-8 days of ageing
Cyclical trends	Sheep production & meat marketing year-round activities; no particular seasonality
Usage trends	Lambs sold at weaning; sheep sold at 8-10 months; lamb/sheep kept as replacement stock; lambs periodically moved to Animal Nutrition Center for feeding trials
Output measures	Exporting; fresh meat; frozen meat; processed meat; tanning

Operating cost	Avg. BDS$300,000/yr.
Operating revenue	Avg. est. revenue BDS$32,000/yr.; revenue sources include sales & slaughters
Maintenance schedule	Preventive maintenance; routine maintenance
Odor factor	Negative
Noise factor	Negative
Resource reuse	Farmstead manure in compost form
Market size	Est. BDS$ 2-5m./yr.
Sales outlet	Barbados Agricultural Society; Barbados Agricultural Development and Marketing Corporation; Greenland Agricultural Station
Marketing patterns	2-months old lambs sold to local farmers; 8-10 months old sheep slaughtered
Output level	Est. 15-20 lambs slaughtered/month; est. 500 lambs sold/yr.
Meat import level	35% of total food imports
Mutton import	2, 500 tons/yr.
Export target	Est. 2, 000 sheep/yr.; est. 1% of island's sheep stock
Export price	Est. BDS$ 5.00/lb. live weight
Legislative measures	(Sample): Animals (Diseases and Importation) Act 1949, 1973, 1995; Soil Conservation Act 1958, 1967, 1973, 1991; Dogs Act 1975; Export Promotion Act 1979, 1981; Animals Act 1980; Dogs (Licensing and Control) Act 1983 ; Livestock (Control of Strays) Act 1990; Barbados Investment and Development Corporation Act 1992; Livestock (Control of Strays) Regulations 1992

HANDICRAFT[2]

Location	Pelican Industrial Park, St. Michael; 0.8 miles northeast from Bridgetown; located off Prescod Boulevard &linked with Fontabelle Road, Princess Alice Highway & President Kennedy Drive; communication/transportation available
Zoning factor	Situated in industrial park
Physical size	Total area: approx. 1 acre; floor space: approx. 22,000 ft.^{2}; offices: approx. 1,100 ft.^{2}; sales area: 3,839 ft.^{2}; store area: 1,800 ft.^{2}; workshops, training areas, toilet blocks, including St. Bernards: 18,800 ft.^{2}
Plant layout patterns	Workshop oriented in easterly direction
Divisionalization	Embroidery; handbag; miscellaneous crafts (leathercraft, screen-printing, shellwork, woodwork); pottery; strawwork; tannery; weaving
Structure type	Concrete structure with wooden walls & arborite roof
Space allocation	Lunch room; offices; rest area; sales area; store area; training areas/workshops
Training centers	Heywoods Holiday Village; St. Bernards; St. Joseph; St. Peter
Product group/type	(Sample) accessory; bag; basket; batik; bedspread; braid; card; ceramics; costume jewelry; curio; doll; drape; figurines; glasswork; hammock; handbag; hat; household ware; jewelry; leatherwork; mat; needlework; plaque; pottery; print; rug; screen-printing; shellwork; souvenir; stonework; strawwork; toy; upholstery; wall hanging; weaving; woodwork
Usage patterns	Domestic consumption; export marketing; import substitution; tourist demand
Trademark	'Pride Craft'

Specialty areas	Bag-making; ceramics; glasswork; hat-making; leatherwork; marblework; needlework; screen-printing; shellwork; strawwork; stonework; tannery; taxidermy; toy-making; weaving; woodwork
Skill type	A variety & range of skills & motion; dexterity; creativity; proportionality; culture-consciousness
Early/contemporary developers	Officials/trainers (sample): Betty Arne; Clyde Gollop; Dean Spencer; Edna Harrison; Ernesta Branker; Glenroy Straughan; Gordon Walters; Jean Blondel; Lomar Alleyne; Louis Gordon; Marjorie Blackman; Marjorie Edwards; Marjorie Manning; Maurice Cave; Thelma Vaughan; Tom Phillips Producers/marketers (sample): Adolphus Cummins; Alfred Weekes; Alphonzo Sealy, Arthur Clarke; Basil Weatherhead; Cecil Marshall; Charles Barrow; Clayton Thompson; Clement Devonish; Clifford Goodman; Darrel Boyce; Denzil Francis; Elizabeth Toppin; Eric Watson; Frank Watson; George Herbert; Goldie Spieler; Hazel Yearwood; Herbert Beckles; Hilda Goring; Hilda Ince; Ira Dangleben; Ira Phillips; James Pigott; John Flavius; John Lewis; John Springer; Jospeh Kellman; Kenrick Williams; Larry von de Husen; Leroy Green; Loretta Yearwood; Lydia Campbell; Manning Marshall; Mark Alexander; Mildred Archer; Monica Hoyle; Muriel Kellman; Patricia Rouse; Pauline D'Hayle; Percy Edwards; Radcliffe Harewood; Ralph Clarke; Reginald Medford; Reynold Rudder; Roslyn Watson; Undine Sealy; Veronica Edwards; Violet Howell; Wibert Harding; William Bertalan; Winston Harris
Employment type	Approx. 33% of producers devote full-time to handicraft production; rest part-time with another occupation
Raw/basic materials	(Sample): acrylic; balsam; bamboo; bead; black sage; bow string; cabbage bark; cabbage palm; cane lily; clay; cloth; coconut leaf; coconut shell; cotton; fibre; grass; hemp; industrial scrap; iron; jute; khus;

	leather; loofah; maypole; metal; nylon; palm; palm leaf; pandanus; plastic; raffia; rag; river rush; root; sanseveria; screw pine; seed; shakshak; seashell; sisal; stone; strainer; straw; turtle shell; wild cane; wild cucumber; wood; wool
Production run	Short
Production volume	Est. 420-515 types of products; avg. 169 products/ yr.
Production cost	Est. BDS$675,000+/yr.
Seasonality pattern	Lean: June, October, November; peak: January, February, March
Customer/user base	Building contractors; craft producers/entrepreneurs; exporters; householders; retailers; souvenir collectors; suppliers; tourists; trainees; wholesalers
Business hours	0800 hrs. - 1600 hrs.; Monday-Friday; emergency afterhour services occasionally available; night-time security provided
Program cycle	Design; exporting; marketing; production; promotion; purchasing; quality control; research; training/development
Producer number	Est. 1,000+countrywide; est. 200-550 registered with Workshop
Trainee number	Avg. 300 trainees /yr.
Process type	(Sample): handbag-making: lining, decorating, assembling; leather-tanning: shaving, staking, scudding, buffing; pottery: throwing, glazing, trampling, wedging/kneading, firing, tempering, trimming; weaving: soumak, tapestry, turkish knots
Operating cost	Avg. BDS$1m. - 2.5m./yr.
Operating revenue	Avg. BDS$1.2m.-1.5m./yr.
Maintenance schedule	Periodic maintenance; routine maintenance

Health measures	Compensation for work-related injury; gloves; medical attention; respirators
Odor factor	Negative
Noise factor	Low noise level
Market size	Est. BDS$12m.-20m./yr.
Market value	Total local market accounts for approx. BDS$12m. of which indigenous product market records BDS$1.4m.
Market share	Local product accounts for 20% or less of total handicraft market
Market segment	Export: regional, extraregional; local: indigenous, tourist
Marketing missions	(Sample): Bahamas; Europe; Miami; St. Lucia; St. Maarten; Trinidad-Tobago; United States Virgin Islands
Sales outlets/BIDC	Carlisle Bay Center/St. Michael; Fairchild Street/ St. Michael; Grantley Adams International Airport/ St. Philip; Harbor Road/St. Michael; Harrison's Cave/St. Thomas; Heywood Holiday Village/St. Peter; Pelican Industrial Park/St. Michael; Sam Lords Castle/St. Philip
Private sector outlets	Approx. 30-40 outlets
Sales techniques	Cash; consignment; discount; retailing; wholesaling
Sales ratio	Ratio of tourist to indigenous sales 9:1
Purchase statistics	Est. BDS$458,562+
Promotional tools	Annual handicraft competition/exhibition; annual industry week; craft fair; marketing/sales mission; media campaign; wayside craft market
Export marketing	(Sample): Botswana; Canada; St. Lucia; Sweden; Trinidad; UK; USA; Venezuela

Legislative measures	(Sample): Barbados Industrial Development Corporation Act 1965, 1973; Industrial Development (Export Industries) Act 1969, 1971, 1978; Fiscal Incentives Act 1974, 1982; Customs Tariff Order 1979, 1982, 1989, 1991, 1993, 1995, 1998; Export Promotion Act 1979, 1981; Barbados Investment and Development Act 1992, 1996

CAVE

Location	Welchman Hall, St. Thomas; near center of island & above 800-ft. contour zone; 8 miles northeast of Bridgetown; sited off Allen View Road & linked with Highway 2; communication/transportation available
Zoning factor	Situated in agricultural area encircled by residential communities
Physical size	Total area: approx. 3 acres; approx. 1 acre taken up by built-up area; offices: 4,033 ft.^{2} ; scenic walk: 37,500 ft.^{2}; service area: 2,800 ft.^{2}
Cave size	.375 mile in length; 55 station points indicating places & location in Cave
Tunnel size	Approx. 3,000 ft. in length; at its deepest point approx. 150-200 ft. below surface; 12 ft. in height & width
Cave formation	Cascades; cataracts; cavefills; chambers; draperies; flowstones; fossils; lakes; passages; pools; stalactites; stalagmites; streams; vegetation; waterfalls
Cave layout	Starting from tunnel entrance Cave dips southeast, shifts northeast & spiralls and bifurcates in 2 polar directions - downstream passage advancing northwest, upper passage heading southeast taking eventually northeasterly course; 2 areas; developed & undeveloped; some sections not developed & expected to stay as restricted areas for many years to come

Ceiling height	Ranges from 10.5-55 ft.
Cave depth	Ranges from 6.9-157.9 ft.
Elevation	Land surface: > 830 ft.; natural entrance: ≈980 ft.; tunnel entrance: ≈820 ft.
Soil type/depth	Shallow & permeable in surface area above Cave; depth of 1-3 ft. over limestone bedrock
Cave temperature	Ranges from ^{0}F75-^{0}F78
Relative humidity	Ranges from 97.5%-100%
Ventilation type	Cave with multiple entrances; enjoys natural airflow; provision for artificial ventilation at 2 points
Structure type	Visitors Center Building built in natural contour in limestone bedrock; conical-shaped roof made of greenheart & cedar shingles
Space allocation	Access road; boutique; carpark; office; presentation/exhibition room; rest area; restaurant; scenic walk; service area; surface drainage; waiting area; workshop
Physical features	Scenic limestone Cave; est. to be 500, 000 yrs. old; considerable dimensions; slightly inclined; numerous slopes & drops; absence of flooding; almost total subterranean drainage; 27 large/small pools/lakes; deposition occurs because water entering Cave saturated with dissolved calcium carbonate; water loses some carbon dioxide gas to cave atmosphere; water can no longer hold much calcium carbonate in solution; excess calcium carbonate deposited in calcite as cave formations: Cave gradually enlarged by erosive actions of subterranean streams; shapes of natural passages derived from solution process; presents an environment where temperature almost constant; took many years to create formations from small mineral-laden drops of water; seemingly static condition sustains unusual biological lifeforms; formations alive, crystalline, growing & integral part of total underground landscape; capped by coral-

	rock formation; presence of reef & other limestones, stalactites & draperies attached to ceilings & walls; Cave formations actively growing, e.g. calcite deposition substantial & speleothem deposition rapid; stream course runs northsouth, eastwest & southnorth at various points; two main streams come from upper passage & natural entrance, follow west-southeast direction toward sea; upstream/ downstream passages; natural/tunnel entrances; Cave formations; ornamental plants & trees; lush tropical vegetation; open-air flowery scenic walk; factors that make Cave - solution & erosion - are also factors that destroy it
Service run	Short
Seasonality patterns	Brisk: February; good: September-May; lean: June-August
Customer/user base	Activity directors; hotels; tour operators; transport operators/agencies; travel agencies; visitors
Business hours	0900 hrs.- 1630 hrs. day tours 7 days/week except some public holidays; 1800 hrs.-2230 hrs. night tours
Program cycle	Maintenance; promotion; tours
Booking category	Advance; current; group; individual; group tours arranged by reservation
Rate schedule	BDS$17.25/adult; $8.63/child; $12.65/adult in organized tour; $5.75/child in organized tour; 2 counsellors admitted free of cost in organized tour of children; concessionary rate available June-August/yr.
Arrival sources	Apartels; apartments; beach houses; cruiseships; houses; hotels; guest houses; schools; service clubs; workplaces
Transport	5 battery-operated tram-trailers transport visitors through cavern; battery-operated trams charged every night

Guide service	Commentary in English; provision for commentary in French, German & Spanish
Visitor number	Est. 190,000-206,000 visitors/yr.
Tour number	Avg. 30-40 tours/day (when cruisehips visit Barbados); avg. 20 tours/day (on non-cruiseship days); avg. 10 tours/day (weekends)
Tour time	Avg. 40 minutes/tour
Intertour time	Avg. 15 minutes
Tour capacity	Avg. 32 visitors/tour
Tour length	A mile-long tour
Visitor route	Upper level/Great Hall; Explorer Pool; Twin Falls; lower level/Great Hall; unusual formation 1; unusual formation 2; complete vehicle & light turnoff; Cascade Pool; Rotunda Room
Tour regulations	Drinking, eating or smoking prohibited; littering, polluting or vandalizing punishable offence
Operating cost	Avg. BDS$2.5m./yr.
Operating revenue	Avg. BDS$475,000+/yr.
Maintenance schedule	Periodic/regular maintenance covering access road, carpark, directional signs, guide/operator training, lighting, refuse trail, safety, speleothems, underground plants, vehicles & visitor reception
Health measures	Cave ventilation adequate; falling stalactites & draperies from ceilings & walls unlikely; groundwater pollution controlled; power-driven vehicles in Cave reduce Cave temperature, eliminate haze & fogging & prevent moisture loss; rockfall & ceiling collapse not likely; stable & fireproof Cave
Odor factor	Power-driven vehicles reduce subterranean pollution; natural airflow

Noise level	Low noise level
Pollution control	Power-driven vehicles reduce subterranean pollution; groundwater pollution controlled; tram tires leave residue which is considered an element of pollution
Market size	Est. 400,000 visitor arrivals/yr.
Legislative measures	(Sample): Land Acquisition Act 1967, 1994; National Conservation Commission Act 1982, 1990, 1996

PULVERIZATION

Location	Workmans, St. George; 6.5 miles northeast from Bridgetown; located near Free Hill on Workmans Road & linked with Highway 4; communication/transportation available
Zoning factor	Plant located in mixed agricultural & residential community
Physical size	Total area: 9.4 acres; built-up area: N/K; landfill: N/K; office: 630 ft. ^{2}; plant area: 16,480 ft.^{2}
Plant layout	Plant oriented in easterly direction
Structure type	Plant made of steel & reinforced concrete
Space allocation	Access roads; carpark; control room; guard/scale room; landfill; office; oil room; plant; rest area; store area; tool area; transformer room; workshop
Enclosure type	Built-up area fenced in with chainlink fencing
Plant capacity	Each shredder 25 tons of refuse/hr.; 400 tons of refuse/8-hr. shift; can operate in 2 alternating sections; pulverizing, grinding, shredding; can take 4 truckloads of refuse simultaneously; can load 4 vehicles with pulverized refuse
Equipment/parts	Reception hopper (equipped with a 6-foot wide chainlink-plate conveyor); plate feeder (equipped

	with a 4-foot wide chainlink-plate conveyor); conveyors (driven by 5-hp motor with a slip-in clutch system); shredder (driven by 400-hp motor & spinning 1,000 rpm); a slip-in clutch system (placed between motor & rotor within the shredder); a 5-foot wide refuse-carrying rubber-belt conveyor; a 5-foot wide reversing rubber-belt conveyor; a large transformer; small back-up transformers; control panels; chutes; guards; maintenance platforms; welding unit; industry-size weighing scale; open-type trucks; tractor; support structures
Plant features	Takes only domestic refuse to minimize damage to shredders & other components
Design factors	Domestic/household waste; excludes industrial & other wastes; involves no heat or chemicals
Disposal methods	Pulverization, sanitary landfilling
Catchment areas	St. George; St. John; St. Joseph; St. Michael: St. Thomas
Disposal sites	(Sample): Bannantyne, Christ Church; Black Bess, St. Peter; Hannays, St. Lucy; Lonesome Hills, St. Peter; Mangrove, St. Thomas; Oldbury, St. Philip; Workmans, St. George
Collection areas	Northern area; southern area; St. Michael areas
Collection service	Collection vehicles on prescribed routes making necessary stops; loading; returning; unloading
Collection service type	Bulk refuse collection; communal receptacle collection; domestic refuse collection
Collection vehicle type	Dust-reducing, enclosed, full load-carrying, rear-loading vehicles
Refuse composition	Cloth; glass; grass; leaves; metal; paper; plastic; putrescible; wood
User delivery facilities	Concrete bins; garbage cans; oil drums; paper bags; plastic bags

Emission type	Heat; noise; smell; vibration
Production run	Short
Customer/user base	Households; open areas; streets; workplaces
Business hours	0800 hrs.-1600 hrs./5-day week; open public holidays
Activity cycle	Storage; collection; unloading; shredding; collection; disposal; levelling
Refuse shredding cost	Est. BDS$37-44/tonne
Refuse generation rate	Est. 1.7- 2.2 lbs. of refuse/capita/day
Refuse breakdown	Municipal waste (58%); bulky waste (31%); yard waste (11%)
Target population size	Est. 142,162 users/5-parish catchment area
Collection points	> 100
Collections trips	Est. 11,661+/yr.
Disposal process	Conveyor feed; pulverization sequence; ejection; refuse loading
Disposal volume	Est. 22, 465 tons+/yr.
Collection/shredding dispoasl relation	Plant provides shredding/disposal for approx. 60% of total waste collection
Downtime	1st type: no disposable refuse, est. 20%; 2nd type: repair or servicing, est. 10%
Landfill operation	Shredded refuse dropping into waiting vehicles; vehicles unloading refuse at landfill; vehicles levelling off refuse on surface; only shredded waste deposited; dumping of raw refuse prohibited
Landfill capacity	11-20 yrs. to fill

Operating cost	Avg. BDS$600,000/yr.
Operating revenue	No revenue generated currently; mandated to function as nonrevenue service organization
Maintenance schedule	Equipment maintenance; landfill maintenance; preventive maintenance; routine maintenance; vehicle maintenance
Health measures	4 fire extinguishers; machines equipped with safety stops; medical checkup every 6 months; protective devices - boots, gloves, head gears, protective suits, respirators, uniforms - worn; 3 power hoses
Odor factor	Intermittent stench
Noise factor	In-plant noise muffled with Plant built in low-lying quarry
Pollution control	Monitored; no threat in neighborhood
Reuse type	Compost; landfill; recycling
Market size	Est. 72m. kilos of refuse/yr.
Output measures	Est. 16,705 tons of refuse disposal/yr.
Legislative measures	(Sample): Health Services Act 1969, 1972, 1973, 1974, 1975, 1978, 1983, 1984, 1985, 1992, 1995; Sanitation Service Authority Act 1974, 1975, 1984, 1996; Health Services (Collection and Disposal of Refuse) Regulations 1975, 1978; Factories Act 1981, 1982, 1983, 1986

POLYTECHNIC

Location	Wildey, St. Michael; 3 miles east from Bridgetown; located on ABC Highway; Division of Agriculture located at Eckstein Village, St. Michael; communication/transportation available
Zoning factor	Located in industrial area
Physical size	Eckstein Campus/total area: 4.5 acres; Wildey

	Campus/total area: 11.5 acres; access areas: 22,000 ft.^{2}; covered walkways: 15, 000 ft. ^{2}; gross internal area: 128,000 ft.^{2}
Campus layout	Buildings oriented northsouth
Structure type	Concrete natural-finish structure; naturally-cooled buildings using passive energy techniques; physical structure supported by absorption wells, drainage, electrical installation, internal plumbing, rainwater drains & septic tanks
Space allocation	Access roads; administration center; assembly hall; audiovisual aids room; cafeteria; carpark; classrooms; conference room; laboratories; library; locker area; museum; offices; playground; rest areas; staff rooms; staircases; store area; workshops
Enclosure type	Part of campus fenced in with chainlink fencing
Building layout	Block A: Commerce; Block Al: Administration, Library; Block B: Assembly Hall; Block C: Garment Design; Block D: Housekeeping; Block E: Electronics; Block F: Plumbing, Welding; Block G: Automechanics, Masonry; Block H: Painting, Machine Shop; Block I: Refrigeration; Block J: Photography, Printing, Hairdressing; Block K: Mechanical Engineering; Block L: Carpentry, Joinery; Block M: Central Stores
Facilities breakdown	20 ½-level building blocks: 6 2-level; 14 1-level; 4 classroom blocks: 22 classrooms; 6 workshop blocks: 34 workshops/laboratories; 1 assembly hall/ examination block; 1 administration block: administration offices, ancillary accommodation, bath area, central stores, faculty office, toilet blocks; a museum comprising relics of past technology
Institution type	Technical-vocational training
Curriculum type	A mix of British & local technical-vocational educational theory & practice

Majors	Agriculture; Automechanics & Welding; Building; Business Studies; Distance & Continuing Education; Electrical Engineering; General Studies; Human Ecology; Mechanical Engineering & Printing
Catchment area	Local; overseas
Academic year	September-December; January-March; April-July
Age range	16-34 yrs. full-time students; avg. age 17.7 yrs.; mode 18 yrs.
Entry criteria	16 yrs. +; school-leaving certificates in 4 subjects including English & Mathematics; interview; for unqualified applicants entrance examination & interview; evening students selected by interviews & recommendations
Residency factor	Nonresidential institution; no provision for student/staff housing; assists with student accommodation where possible
Scholarship provision	Available; Student Revolving Loan Fund
Program type	Full-time; part-time day; part-time evening
Program duration	Full-time 2-yr.; full-time accelerated; part-time 1-yr. advanced-crafts; part-time 2-yr. secondary-technical; evening; short-duration special
Program details	Full-time: class attendance 5 days/week for 2 academic yrs.; part-time: 1 day/week of classwork & 4 days/week of industrial practice; evening programs
Program phasing	General basic training: during first half yr.; special basic training: during second half yr.; specialized-skill training: during second yr.
Program rationale	Existing skill upgrading; skill acquisition; theoretical understanding
Program base	Day/evening courses in 30 disciplines

Training level	Ordinary craft: advanced craft
Training mode/focus	Pre-service; in-service; retraining
Training-area type	Theoretical; practical; apprenticeship; attachment; familiarity with principles, tools & materials of skill-area
Training duration	3 months; 6 months; 1 yr.; 2 yrs.; 2 yrs.+
Training orientation	Understanding/application of principles, tools & materials
Course type	Full-time courses; diploma courses; day-release courses; evening courses; short-term courses
Course description	Accounting; agriculture; airconditioning; architectural drawing; arithmetic; autobody repairs; automechanics; basic metal work, building drawing, business studies; carpentry & joinery; clothing craft; cosmetology; economics; electrical installation; electronics; engineering drawing; English; general studies; home economics; human ecology; machine & fitting; masonry & tiling; mechanical engineering; mechanical drawing; office practice; painting; plumbing; printing; radio & television work; refrigeration; sewing machine operation; sheetmetal work; shoemaking; shorthand; tailoring; typing; welding
Course timing	Most courses full-time & evening over 1-2 yrs.; engineering & geometric drawing available only evenings
Course balancing	Formerly: 50% theoretical, 50% practical; currently: 30% theoretical, 70% practical
Overseas examinations	Associated Examining Board; City & Guilds of London Institute; London Chamber of Commerce; Pitmans Examination Institute
Qualification type	Certificate; diploma
Placement type	Communication service; engineering; financial

	service; manufacturing; private sector; public service; processing; transportation; utilities
Foreign studentship	Overseas students, especially from Eastern Caribbean, admitted
Faculty development	Overseas training; refresher training; short-course participation; trainee-faculty continuing supervised studies/observing teaching methods, receiving overseas training; workshop experience
Special services	Apprenticeship; audiovisual service; career showcase participation; guidance counselling; industrial attachment; library service; occupational development; placement service; recreation program; student council; tracer studies
Service run	Long
Customer/user base	Educational institutions; faculty; private sector organizations; public sector organizations; students
Business hours	Management: 0815 hrs. -1630 hrs.; faculty: 0900 hrs.-1545 hrs.; evenings: 1700 hrs.-1900 hrs.; 2 evenings/week
Faculty size	Est. 91 permanent & part-time faculty members
Staff size	60 nonteaching/support personnel (management, executive, library, maintenance)
Faculty-student ratio	1:22
Intake capacity	2,000+ students/yr.; additional 184 secondary school students; max. capacity 3,000 students
Student enrollment	2,065
Application process	Forms available from April 1; submission by April 30; nonnationals apply through Ministry of Education
Entrance rate	Est. 18.2% in some subject-areas; 274 students applied to do electronics in recent years, 15 accepted

Fee schedule	Nationals: free tuition; overseas students: tuition fee BDS$1,500.00/yr.; registration fee: $154.00-$300.00; tools & equipment: $300.00/yr.; student affairs fee: $10.00/yr.
Contact time	4 periods of varying duration/day
Course number	89; full-time: 35; day-release: 6; part-time/evening: 48
Class duration	Avg. 45 minutes
Class size	Avg. 17 students/class
Classroom practice	Audiovisual aids; handouts; periodic visits; student involvement; teaching tools
Workshop practice	Demonstration method; group projects; individual assignments; practicals; problem-solving exercises
Attachment practice	Faculty member-supervised 8-week attachment in industries, plants, workshops & offices
Grading system	A (90%+) - E (<40%)
Success rate	Est. 60% in internal examinations; 78% in external examinations
Apprenticeship	An integral part; a collaboration between Barbados Vocational Training Board & Polytechnic
Faculty recruitment	Full-time & part-time faculty; qualifications: advanced-level crafts certificate, technical equivalent of college degree, teacher/technical teacher training certificate, other certificates/ diplomas; industrial training
Disciplinary measures	Reprimand; suspension; expulsion
Evaluation practices	Terminal tests; final examinations; terminal/annual progress reports transmitted; examination time: May-June; examination duration: 1-3 hrs.;

	supplementals for overseas examinations
Dropout rate	Avg. 27%/yr.
Operating cost	Avg. BDS$7.3m./yr.
Operating revenue	Avg. BDS$340,000/yr.
Maintenance schedule	Preventive maintenance; routine maintenance
Odor factor	Negative
Noise factor	Noisiest workshops downwind to extreme west; quiet sections upwind; away from residential areas
Market size	Est. 44,000 employees working in technical fields/yr.
Output measures	Est. 1,800 graduates/yr.
Legislative measures	(Sample): Occupational Training Act 1979, 1980, 1982, 1985, 1985, 1987, 1993, 1993, 1996; Education Act 1981, 1983, 1984, 1990, 1995, 1996; Education Regulations 1982, 1995; Occupational Training Regulations 1982; Technical and Vocational Education and Training Act 1983
SEWERAGE	
Location	Lakes Folly, St. Michael; 0.7miles northwest from Bridgetown; linked with Emmerton Lane, Fontabelle Road & Mason Hall Street; communication/transportation available
Zoning factor	Plant located in mixed semiindustrial/semiresidential area
Physical size	Building area: 11,000 ft.^{2}; lift stations: N/K; River Road pumping station: 3,000 ft.^{2}; treatment plant area: 5 acres
System components	1 pumping station; 5 lift stations; sewer network; treatment plant; marine outfall; user connection

System layout	Contact stabilization tanks to north of treatment plant building; marine outfall starts eastwest and advances northsouth; sewer network in all directions; treatment plant oriented in easterly direction
Structure type	Marine outfall: polyethylene pipes; sewer system: ductile iron, epoxy-lined asbestos cement, polyvinyl chloride pipes; treatment plant/pumping stations: reinforced concrete
Space allocation	Access roads; carpark; guard room; laboratory; laundry room; locker area; lunch room; office; plant (blower room, dry well, wet well); rest area; store area; tanks; workshop
Enclosure type	Fenced in with chainlink fencing
Sewer area	Approx. 1mile^2
Sewer size	Approx. 13 miles of sewers ranging from 6-36 in. in diameter
Catchment area	504 acres in central area of Bridgetown; 5 areas covering Bay Street, Jemmotts Lane, Martindale Road, Halls Road, Roebuck Street, Country Road, White Park Road, Light Foot Lane, Mason Hall Street, Lakes Folly, Fontabelle & Harbor Industrial Park
Station location	Bay Street; Bridgetown Port; Harbor Road; Prescod Boulevard; River Road; White Park Road
Outfall type	Marine outfall 984 ft. long; discharging in 39ft. of water
Sewage type	Permissible: faecal waste, wastewater; impermissible: detergents, industrial waste, toxic chemicals; 98% water: flowing from baths, water closets, wash basins, laundry sinks, kitchen sinks, industrial processes; 2% solids: human excreta, other solid waste
Sewage flow	Raw waste pump station; communitor; wet well; flow distribution chamber; contact stabilization

	tanks/units (contact zone, sedimentation tank/ clarifier, reaeration zone; sludge digester)
Influent composition	Biological oxygen demand; chromium; copper; iron; lead; mercury; nickel; nitrate; suspended solids
Effluent composition	Biological oxygen demand; suspended solids
Effluent quality	Biological oxygen demand: 84.04% removal efficiency; suspended solids: 87.00% efficiency
Treatment type	Chemical treatment aided by aerobic digestion; effluent treated by hypochlorides derived from electrolysis of seawater
Treatment process	Influent collected; primary/physical treatment (communitor) shreds solids; secondary/biological treatment (return sludge, contact tank, reaeration tank, digester) adds dissolved oxygen to sewage; tertiary/chemical treatment (cholorinator) disinfects effluent; disposal by outfall into sea; sludge treatment aerobic digestion; sludge spread into farmlands
Disposal type	Effluent discharge to sea by outfall; sludge spread into farmlands
Emission type	Effluent; heat; noise; slurry; smell; vibration
Connection type	Mandatory
Production run	Short
Design period	Max.: 50 yrs.; min.: 30 yrs.
Customer/user base	Commuters; households; visitors; workplaces
Plant capacity	Avg. expected capacity: 2.4m. gallons of sewage/ day; maximum/designed capacity: 3.6m. gallons of sewage/day; emergency: 5m. gallons/short period
Plant utilization	Current utilization: 0.61m. gallons of sewage/day; 30,000 gallons of septage/day

Business hours	24-hr. rotational shift; 0700 hrs.-1500 hrs.; 1500 hrs.-2300 hrs.; 2300 hrs.-0700 hrs.
Activity cycle	User influent; collection; treatment; reuse; disposal
Sewage flow	1.7m. gallons of sewage/day
Discharge rate	Avg. 228,566 US gallons/day
Effluent volume	200,000 gallons/day; target: 1.5m. gallons/day
Sludge volume	4,000 gallons of sludge/day (designed); 5,000 gallons of septage/day (designed)
Septage capacity	25 truckloads of septage/day; 5,000 gallons of septage/day
User number	3,000 user premises
Target population	Initial: 37,000 users; subsequent: 50,800 users
Connection charge	One-time payment; domestic users: BDS$120; institutional users: BDS$300
Rate schedule	Periodic payment; sewage charge: domestic users/ 33% of water consumed; institutional users/66% of water consumed; septage charge: BDS$50/ truckload
Revenue measures	Public sector budgetary support; septage charges; sewer charges to domestic/institutional users
Operating cost	Avg. BDS$ 1.8m./yr.
Operating revenue	Est. BDS$ 500, 000/yr.
Maintenance schedule	Operational & maintenance manuals for preventive & routine maintenance on stream
Health measures	Certain gas generated in wet well; gloves & boots worn when handling sewage or equipment; masks worn & other devices used for protection; plant with laundry service; uniforms worn & not to be taken off plant premises

Odor factor	Occasional stench
Noise factor	Intermittent low-level noise
Pollution control	Extensive control measures in use; effluent meets aesthetic & sanitary standards; prevents beach & marine pollution; underwater effluent dilution prevents pollution
Resource reuse	Cooling water; crop irrigation; fertilization; reclamation
Market size	Est. 73m.sewage/yr.
Output measures	Est. 200, 000 gallons of effluent disposal/day
Legislative measures	(Sample): Health Services Act 1969, 1972, 1973, 1974; Barbados Water Authority Act 1980, 1982, 1988; Barbados Water Authority (Sewerage Regulations) 1982, 1983

FERNEIHURST

Location	Black Rock, St. Michael; 2 miles north from Bridgetown; located off Deacons Road, linked with Highway 1 & Westbury Road; communication/ transportation available
Zoning factor	Housing area
Physical size	Total area: 10.2 acres; house curtilage: 4.20 acres; total floor space: 104,000 ft.^{2}
Estate layout	Buildings oriented in all directions
Structure type	Multiple concrete blocks, roofed with asbestos
Space allocation	Access roads; carparks; church area; drainage; houses; open space; playing field; refuse disposal areas; sidewalks
Enclosure type	Estate not fenced in, but each block of units provided with a walled enclosure at its back
Building/unit type	2-storey terrace houses; 2-bedroom & 3-bedroom

	units; a row of similar houses built end-to-end; each unit provided with waterborne toilet & patio
Building materials	Basically aluminium, concrete, glass, steel & wood
Access road	Off Black Rock Main Road; off Deacons Main Road
Housing type	High-density; low-income; multiple; rental; terrace; urban
Option type	Rented; subletting disallowed; unfurnished
Tenant type	Family; low-income; low middle-income
Plot ratio	1:4.2 (104,000 $ft.^2$ building to 444,312 $ft.^2$ land)
Residential density	Net density: 22 houses/acre; gross density: 16 houses/acre
Housing mix	1:2.3 (46 3-bedroom to 108 2-bedroom units)
Lot size	2BR: 864 $ft.^2$; 3BR: 952 $ft.^2$
Unit schedule	Backyard; bathroom; 2/3 bedrooms; kitchen; living room; patio
Foundation type	Concrete strip footing suitably reinforced
Floor area	2BR: 635 $ft.^2$; 3 BR: 770 $ft.^2$
Floor length/width	2BR: 22ft. 6in. front-back length, 12ft. side-side width; 3BR: 24ft. 9in. front-back length, 14ft. side-side width
Floor covering	Ground floor: reinforced concrete slab on compacted marl fill; first floor: suspended concrete floor using precast concrete planks & infill blocks with in situ concrete topping
Wall type	External walls & cross walls: 8in. concrete blocks; other walls: 4in. concrete blocks; partitions: timber frames & hardboard
Door number	2 BR: 6 doors; 3BR: 7 doors

Window number	2 BR: 4 windows; 3BR: 5 windows
Ceiling type	Negative
Ceiling height	7ft. 4in.
Roof type	Corrugated asbestos sheets supported on timber purlins; purlins exposed internally with no false ceiling being used
Toilet type	Water closet
Tap number	2 taps
Power outlet number	2BR: 4 outlets; 3BR: 5 outlets
Other provisions	Fittings; fixtures
Ventilation type	Natural
Insulation type	Negative; however, use of concrete blocks, containing voids & consequently trapping air, facilitates insulation; air being a poor conductor of heat prevents excessive heat transfer through walls
Vertical circulation	Staircase
Utility services	Common septic tanks & absorption wells for each block; electricity, gas, sewage disposal, telephone, waste disposal & water available; individual units linked with tanks & wells; no provision for solar heating; tanks driven by tank pumping; wells run by well pumping
Drainage system	Overground stormwater drainage system operational
Waste disposal	Refuse disposal: collection vehicle pickup; sewage disposal: septic tanks & absorption wells
Sewage disposal type	Chokes for individual units & common tanks/wells
Recreational service	A playing field; indoor games
Average unit cost	Approx. BDS$30,519

Average sq.ft. cost	BDS$45.93
Building/housing code	No code as such; guidelines from Town Planning Department & Ministry of Health
Insurance coverage	Estate houses in estate covered by comprehensive insurance
Subsidization rate	Est. 30-40%
Service run	Short
Customer/user base	Friends; relations; tenants; suppliers
Business hours	Management: 0815hrs.-1630hrs.; maintenance: 0700hrs.-1600hrs.: emergency & urgent weekend services available
Activity cycle	Tenancy agreement; rent collection; complaint service; property maintenance
Building/block number	24
Unit number	Total: 154 units; 2BR: 108 units; 3BR: 46 units
Tenant number	Approx. 750
Household size	4.0
Tenancy agreement	Conditions: arrears disallowed; premise maintenance; proper notification; regulation observance; subletting disallowed
Room occupancy rate	1.1
Rent schedule	2BR: BDS$40/week; 3BR: BDS$45/week
Rent payment frequency	Weekly
Operating cost	Avg. BDS$146,000/yr.
Operating revenue	Est. BDS$212,160/yr.(Ferneihurst); avg. BDS$5.7m./yr. (39 estates)

Maintenance schedule	Preventive maintenance; routine maintenance; emergency & urgent weekend services in existence
Maintenance areas/depots	5
Odor factor	Negative; infrequent; complaints if blockages occur
Noise factor	Low-level noise; traffic on main road
Market size	Est. 63,250 households/countrywide
Output measures	Est. 750 tenants housed
Legislative measures	(Sample): Mortgage Insurance Act 1962, 1965, 1971, 1981, 1988; Landlord and Tenant Act 1969, 1977, 1978, 1979, 1980, 1982, 1997; Housing Act 1973, 1973, 1976, 1978, 1980, 1983; Property Act 1979, 1979, 1981, 1990, Tenantries Development Act 1980; Tenantries Freehold Purchase Act 1980, 1981, 1981, 1981, 1982, 1984, 1984, 1985, 1986, 1989, 1989, 1991, 1992, 1996

The data presented here show the Projects' existing conditions and ground-level realities. The presented data are expected to provide a basis for general information and crossproject comparison in relation to certain variables. While some indicators provide useful information in terms of location, size, volume, operation and capacity, certain data deficiencies and gaps, especially in the area of marketing and output diffusion, have impeded the presentation of the Project data. Even when and where sound data are available for some or all the Projects, they are not always comparable because of variation in definition and coverage. Taken as a whole, the Project data present both achievements and limitations.

NOTES

1. We sought to collect and put together as much information on the target Projects as possible. We provide a small sample of indicators for which information, despite putting in effort, was not available.

Greenland: Bred/crossbred sheep number, carcass weight, export rate, feed/weight ratio, marketed sheep number, meat conversion ratio, muscle/bone ratio, mutton consumption rate, production volume, registered sheep number, slaughter rate.

Handicraft: Production volume, sales volume.

Pulverization: Collection routes, routing vehicles.

Polytechnic: Average student hours, computer power, cost per faculty, cost per student, graduation rate, library stock size, placement rate, retention rate, staff workload, technical-vocational applicant market share, unit cost, vocational enrollment ratio.

Ferneihurst: Default rate, housing lifespan, vacancy rate.

2. The Barbados Investment and Development Corporation - formerly Barbados Industrial Development Corporation - has divested the Handicraft Workshop and all the ancillary activities and, subsequently, the entire Handicraft Project has been privatized, with Barbados' handicraft producers playing their roles in the Project's current operations. The Project's data are presented here in the interest of historical record and continuity.

INDEX

Doing Projects is a study of development projects in Barbados, representing such sectors as agriculture, industry, tourism, infrastructure, education, health, and housing. Using secondary analysis, observational method, comparative analysis and survey method to collect, sift and analyze data and placing the reviewed projects against comparable projects from other parts of the world, the study highlights projects as a tool of development activity and examines projects as multifaceted interventions in Barbados' social and economic development. The volume fills a gap in project research in the Caribbean.

Jamal Khan, a faculty member in the Department of Management Studies at the University of the West Indies, Barbados, teaches and researches on public sector management. Dr. Khan has published extensively in the Caribbean and internationally. He has published in many journals, including Caribbean Quarterly, Caribbean Labor Journal, Project Management Quarterly, International Review of Administrative Sciences, International Journal of Public Sector Management, Bangladesh Journal of Public Administration, Pakistan Administration, Borneo Review, Middle East Studies in Development, Public Administration Review, and International Journal of Educational Management. His teaching and research interests include public sector management, development management, policy analysis, and project management. He is the author of *Development Administration: Field Research in Barbados* (1976), *Managing Development: Theory and Practice* (1978), and *Public Management: The Eastern Caribbean Experience* (1982, 1987).

Wayne Soverall, besides being a civil servant in Barbados with work experience in the Government Training Center, the Ministry of Tourism and the Office of Public Sector Reform, teaches and publishes in organization behavior and public sector management. As a practitioner, his work embraces management training, social impact analysis, public sector reform, and organization/management reform. He has published in the International Journal of Public Sector Management and the Broad Street Journal, and has recently completed research on the *Plantation Economy Model* and the *Dialectics of Poverty and Human Development in Trinidad and Tobago*.